Lecture Notes of the Institute
for Computer Sciences, Social Informatics
and Telecommunications Engineering 127

Tanveer Zia   Albert Zomaya
Vijay Varadharajan   Morley Mao (Eds.)

Security and Privacy in Communication Networks

9th International ICST Conference, SecureComm 2013
Sydney, NSW Australia, September 25-28, 2013
Revised Selected Papers

 Springer

Volume Editors

Tanveer Zia
Charles Sturt University
School of Computing and Mathematics
Wagga Wagga, NSW, Australia
E-mail: tzia@csu.edu.au

Albert Zomaya
The University of Sydney
School of Information Technologies
Darlington, NSW, Australia
E-mail: albert.zomaya@sydney.edu.au

Vijay Varadharajan
Macquarie University, Department of Computing
North Ryde, NSW, Australia
E-mail: vijay.varadharajan@mq.edu.au

Morley Mao
University of Michigan, Department of EECS
Ann Arbor, MI, USA
E-mail: zmao@umich.edu

ISSN 1867-8211   e-ISSN 1867-822X
ISBN 978-3-319-04282-4   e-ISBN 978-3-319-04283-1
DOI 10.1007/978-3-319-04283-1
Springer Cham Heidelberg New York Dordrecht London

Library of Congress Control Number: 2013956812

CR Subject Classification (1998): K.6.5, C.2, E.3, K.4.4, H.4, H.3

Typesetting: Camera-ready by author, data conversion by Scientific Publishing Services, Chennai, India

Printed on acid-free paper

Springer is part of Springer Science+Business Media (www.springer.com)

Preface

Owing to the increase in the scale and sophistication of cyber crimes conducted through the communication networks, it is imperative for the research community to ensure the protection of data disseminated through these networks. Online information assets are further threatened because of the increasing trend toward adoption of cloud computing and virtualization. Stakeholders need to be aware of the potential threats to the information assets and critical infrastructure and how to mitigate and eliminate these threats.

In past nine years, SecureComm has emerged as a leading international forum that covers all aspects of information and communications security with particular emphasis on security in communication and networking. SecureComm also serves as a venue for learning about the emerging trends in security and privacy research, giving participants the opportunity to network with experts in the field. The strategic objectives of SecureComm are to provide a common platform for security and privacy experts in academia, industry, and government as well as practitioners, standards developers, and policy makers to engage in discussions on the common goals in order to explore important research directions in the field. This year SecureComm was held in Australia for the first time. This coincided with one of the 15 recently announced Australian government Strategic Research Priorities in Cyber Security, securing Australia's place in a changing world.

For SecureComm 2013, 70 high-quality papers were submitted from over 15 countries. Unfortunately, the acceptance rate set for this conference did not allow us to accept all papers with relevant merits. In this respect, special thanks to the Technical Program Committee members for handling of the challenging task and selecting 21 outstanding papers with a significant contribution to the field to be included in the proceedings. The 21 accepted papers can be broadly classified under the following themes:

- Security and privacy in mobile, sensor, and ad hoc networks
- Malware, botnets, and distributed denial of service
- Security for emerging technologies: VoIP, peer-to-peer, and cloud computing
- Encryption and key management
- Security in software and machine learning
- Network and system security model
- Security and privacy in pervasive and ubiquitous computing

In addition to the papers presented at the conference, we also had following four exciting keynote speakers:

- Mike Holm, Operations Manager, AusCERT (Computer Emergency Response Team in Australia)

- James Turner, Chair, AISA (Australian Information Security Association) Advocacy Group
- Mark Goudie, Regional Manager – Investigations, Dell SecureWorks
- Jiankun Hu, Professor and Research Director Cyber Security Lab, Australian Defence Force Academy

Finally, we are very grateful to the NSW government for their sponsorship, as well as the European Alliance for Innovation (EAI) and the Institute for Computer Sciences, Social Informatics and Telecommunications Engineering (ICST) for allowing SecureComm 2013 to be held in Australia. We also thank the local Organizing Committee and its many members and volunteers for their support. A special thank goes to Erica Polini, EAI Conference Manager, and Elisa Mendini, EAI Venue Manager and Conference Coordinator, for their utmost professionalism in managing the administrative aspects of the conference. Last but not least, our gratitude goes to the Steering Committee members, in particular to Peng Liu, for his continuous supervision to make SecureComm a very successful event.

September 2013

Tanveer Zia
Albert Zomaya
Vijay Varadharajan
Morley Mao

Organization

General Chair

Tanveer A. Zia   Charles Sturt University, Australia
Albert Y. Zomaya   University of Sydney, Australia

Technical Program Committee Chairs

Vijay Varadharajan   Macquarie University, Australia
Morley Mao   University of Michigan, USA

Local Chairs

Junbin Gao   Charles Sturt University, Australia
Adel Al-Jumaily   University of Technology Sydney, Australia
Maumita Bhattacharya   Charles Sturt University, Australia

Publicity Chairs

Salil Kanhere   University of New South Wales, Australia
Jianming Yong   University of Southern Queensland, Australia
Weili Han   Fudan University, China

Publication Chairs

Aldar Chan Chun Fai   Institute for Infocomm Research (I2R),
                            Singapore
Quazi Mamun   Charles Sturt University, Australia

Workshop Chairs

Javed Taheri   University of Sydney, Australia
Md Rafiqul Islam   Charles Sturt University, Australia

Sponsorship Chair

Sabih-ur Rehman   Charles Sturt University, Australia

Web Chair

Saman Shafigh   Charles Sturt University, Australia

Conference Manager

Erica Polini   EAI, Italy

Steering Committee

Peng Liu   Pennsylvania State University, USA
Imrich Chlamtac   CREATE-NET, Italy

Table of Contents

Session IV: Encryption and Key Management

Session V: Security in Software and Machine Learning

Session VI: Network and System Security Model

Session VII: Security and Privacy in Pervasive and Ubiquitous Computing

ATIS 2013: 4th International Workshop on Applications and Techniques in Information Security

Anomaly Detection in Beacon-Enabled IEEE 802.15.4 Wireless Sensor Networks

Eirini Karapistoli and Anastasios A. Economides

Department of Information Systems,
University of Macedonia
Egnatia 156, Thessaloniki, Greece
{ikarapis,economid}@uom.gr

Abstract. During the past decade, wireless sensor networks (WSNs) have evolved as an important wireless networking technology attracting the attention of the scientific community. With WSNs being envisioned to support applications requiring little to no human attendance, however, these networks also lured the attention of various sophisticated attackers. Today, the number of attacks to which WSNs are susceptible is constantly increasing. Although many anomaly detection algorithms have been developed since then to defend against them, not all of them are tailored to the IEEE 802.15.4 standard, a dominant communication standard for low power and low data rate WSNs. This paper proposes a novel anomaly detection algorithm aimed at securing the beacon-enabled mode of the IEEE 802.15.4 MAC protocol. The performance of the proposed algorithm in identifying intrusions using a rule-based detection technique is studied via simulations.

Keywords: Wireless Sensor Networks, Beacon-enabled IEEE 802.15.4 MAC, Rule-based Anomaly Detection.

1 Introduction

WSNs raise the interest of different business domains, including that of security [1]. Their ability to monitor and control physical environments and large scale critical infrastructures make them a promising candidate. WSNs can be relatively easily deployed in a large geographical span, and can provide with fault diagnosis, intrusion detection and monitoring services in a cost-efficient manner since they do not require additional infrastructure. While the distributed nature of a WSN increases the survivability of the network in critical situations (it is much less likely that the network will be affected in its entirety by failures or attacks), defensive mechanisms that could protect and guarantee the normal operation of the WSN in the presence of adversaries are still needed.

Currently, research on providing security solutions for WSNs has mainly focused in key management [2], [3], secure authentication and routing [4], secure localization and data aggregation [5], [6], and recently, in intrusion detection [7].

T. Zia et al. (Eds.): SecureComm 2013, LNICST 127, pp. 1–18, 2013.

Within the limited scope of this paper, we restrain our focus on the latter approach in an attempt to defend against strong inside attackers that have penetrated the first perimeter of defense. An Intrusion Detection System (IDS) monitors the events occurring in the network and analyzes them to detect signs of intrusion [8]. Various signature-based and anomaly-based IDS architectures have been proposed for flat and hierarchical WSNs [9], [10], [11]. However, to the best of our knowledge, none of them is applicable to IEEE 802.15.4-compliant WSNs.

The IEEE 802.15.4-2011 standard [12] is a dominant communication standard developed to provide low-power and highly reliable wireless connectivity among inexpensive, battery-powered devices. While emphasis has been given on improving the performance of the 802.15.4 MAC protocol [13], limited work has been contacted on securing its *beacon-enabled* mode. As identified in [14], [15], this mode is vulnerable to a number of attacks. Some of the attacks (i.e., radio jamming and link layer jamming) are common to all MAC layer definitions. Others like the back-off manipulation and the attacks against the acknowledgement mechanism may also occur in IEEE 802.11 wireless networks due to some common properties in the MAC layer implementations [16]. However, several attacks including the Personal Area Network (PAN) identifier conflict attack, and the Guaranteed Time Slot (GTS) attack are only applicable to the 802.15.4 MAC layer mechanisms defined by the standard. Therefore, the latter category of attacks requires novel, anomaly-based intrusion detection algorithms to defend against them.

Accordingly, this work contributes to the area of anomaly detection for IEEE 802.15.4-compliant wireless sensor networks. We propose a distributed anomaly detection algorithm for securing the beacon-enabled mode of the IEEE 802.15.4 MAC protocol. Vulnerabilities of the underlying MAC are exposed and dealt with using a rule-based detection approach. Our algorithm differentiates from existing works in that it does not rely on the existence of special types of nodes, i.e. monitor nodes or watchdogs, to perform the anomaly detection task. Finally, the proposed algorithm does not require expensive communication between the sensor nodes, since anomaly detection and revocation are performed distributively.

The remainder of the paper is organized as follows: in Section 2, existing work on securing the beacon-enabled mode of the 802.15.4 MAC is outlined. In Section 3, we review several features of the underlying MAC protocol and analyze its vulnerabilities in order to provide a better understanding of the proposed algorithm. In Section 4, we provide a detailed description of our anomaly detection algorithm. Section 5 illustrates the obtained simulation results, followed by detailed reports. Finally, conclusions are given in Section 6.

2   Related Work

Several defensive methods have been proposed for securing the beacon-enabled mode of the IEEE 802.15.4 MAC protocol. The standard itself encompasses built-in security features to provide data secrecy and data authenticity. However, as Sastry *et al.* [17] pointed out, these security features have vulnerabilities related to the initial vector (IV) management, key management, and integrity protection. To address these issues, Alim *et al.* introduced EAP-Sens [18], a link layer secure protocol implementation for 802.15.4 sensor networks in beacon-enabled mode. While effective in its design, as with any authentication protocol, EAP-Sens is vulnerable to insider attacks launched by compromised (malicious) nodes.

Sokullu *et al.* [14], [19] were the first to analyze insider attacks targeting the beacon-enabled mode of the IEEE 802.15.4 MAC protocol. The authors used ns2 simulations to demonstrate DoS-like GTS attacks whose main goal was to create collisions at the GTS slots and deny the guaranteed communication. While effective, the major drawback of their work is that it lacks a clear description of how to defend against such attacks. Amini *et al.* [20] proposed a Received Signal Strength Indicator (RSSI)-based solution to detect Sybil attacks in IEEE 802.15.4 beacon-enabled clusters. The coordinator is tasked with detecting anomalies inside its cluster based on deviations in the tuple (disc number, device ID) it assigned to its cluster members. However, this method does not consider the case of compromised coordinators. Moreover, if a malicious node is close enough to a legitimate node, its RSSI may be confused with the RSSI of the legitimate node, thus enabling the malicious node to escape detection. Recently, Jung *et al.* [15] performed an in-depth study of the vulnerable properties of the beacon-enabled mode of the IEEE 802.15.4 standard. The authors implemented on real devices four potential insider attacks associated with those vulnerabilities, and presented mechanisms to defend against them. While the authors provide a good framework to analyzing IEEE 802.15.4 MAC layer attacks, no implementation or testing exists relative to the defensive mechanisms they propose in their paper.

Overall, a concrete framework for securing IEEE 802.15.4-compliant sensor networks against insider attacks is still missing. Our approach to the problem is to use rule-based anomaly detection. As analyzed in [11], rule-based anomaly detection is attractive because its methodology is flexible and resource-friendly and benefits from the absence of an explicit training procedure. In rule-based detection, the anomaly detector uses predefined rules to classify data points as anomalies or normalities. While monitoring the network, these rules are selected appropriately and applied to the monitored data. If the rules defining an anomalous condition are satisfied, an anomaly is declared. Da Silva *et al.* [21] where among the first to propose a rule-based distributed ADS for WSNs. While the authors provide a good framework to rule-based detection, the defined rules are not applicable to attacks targeting beacon-enabled WSNs. This is also the case for other similar rule-based anomaly detection systems (ADS) proposed for WSNs [22], [23].

Therefore, in this paper, we attempt to move towards that direction proposing a specific modular rule-based ADS architecture tailored to IEEE 802.15.4-compliant wireless sensor networks operating under the beacon-enabled mode.

3   Preliminaries

3.1   The IEEE 802.15.4 MAC

The MAC sublayer of the standard provides services such as beacon generation and synchronization, PAN association and disassociation, GTS management, and channel access among others [12]. It also provides support for star and peer-to-peer network topologies. Peer-to-peer topologies allow more complex network formations to be implemented, such as mesh and cluster tree topologies that are better suited for security-oriented applications. When lines of communication exceed the implementation-specific personal operating space (POS), an 802.15.4 network can be a self-configuring, multi-hop network. Two different device types can participate in an IEEE 802.15.4 network; a full-function device (FFD) and a reduced-function device (RFD). An FFD device can operate in three modes serving as a PAN coordinator, a coordinator, or a device. An RFD device instead, only connects to a cluster tree network as a leaf device at the end of a branch (see Fig.1).

The IEEE 802.15.4 MAC operates in two modes, the *beacon-enabled* mode and the *nonbeacon-enabled* mode. In the beaconless mode, coordinators do not emit regular beacons. Moreover, channel access is managed through the unslotted version of the CSMA-CA algorithm. In beacon-enabled PANs, which can assume only a star or tree topology, all non-leaf nodes periodically transmit beacon frames. In this mode, a PAN coordinator relies on a superframe (SF) structure to enable transmission and reception of message that consists of a beacon, an active period, and an inactive period. While starting a PAN, coordinator sets its *macPANId* and the length of both active and inactive periods, defined by the *macBeaconOrder*, BO=[0,15), and the *macSuperframeOrder*, SO=[0,BO), respectively. The active period consists of 16 equal sized time slots and contains a contention access period (CAP), which uses slotted CSMA/CA for channel access, and a contention free period (CFP), which consists of guaranteed time slots (GTS) that are allocated on demand to nodes for a contention-free access to the channel. Member nodes can switch over to sleep mode during the inactive period to save battery.

3.2   Attacking the IEEE 802.15.4 MAC

The beacon-enabled mode of the IEEE 802.15.4 MAC protocol is vulnerable to a number of internal and external attacks several of which are common to all wireless MAC layer definitions. Therefore, in this paper we concentrate on attacks that target peculiar mechanisms of the underlying MAC, namely its PANID conflict resolution procedure, the GTS allocation and deallocation mechanisms and the data transmissions during the CAP and CFP portions of the superframe.

PANId Conflict Attack. According to the IEEE 802.15.4 standard [12], the PAN identifier conflict resolution procedure is executed when more than one PAN coordinators with the same PANId operate in the same POS. If such a conflict

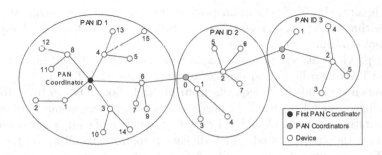

Fig. 1. An IEEE 802.15.4 cluster tree network. (Source: [12]).

occurs, a member device that receives beacons from both PAN coordinators, can notify its PAN coordinator to perform the conflict resolution procedure. An adversary device can take advantage of this vulnerability and frequently send fake PANId conflict notification commands to the coordinator and oblige the latter to perform the conflict resolution procedure. Such an attack may prevent or greatly delay communication between devices and the PAN coordinator.

GTS Attack. According to [12], a GTS slot is the portion of the superframe that provides contention free communication between a device that reserved the slot and a coordinator. The GTS allocation mechanism is executed as follows. First, the device has to receive the beacon frame to identify the superframe boundaries. A GTS allocation request is sent in the CAP portion of the super-frame to the coordinator. The request includes the required length and direction (uplink or downlink) of the GTS slot. The coordinator may send an ACK packet to confirm the successful reception of the GTS request. If GTS slots are available, the coordinator assigns them to the requesting device using the beacon frame. Once assigned, the data transmission takes place in the GTS slots of the following superframes. Similarly, a deallocation request results to the deallocation of a GST slot.

As it can be seen, the GTS management scheme does not verify the ID of each device that requests GTS allocation or deallocation. Therefore, an inside attacker can easily compromise this procedure by either impersonating existing legitimate nodes' IDs or creating new IDs for devices that do not exist (i.e., implement a Sybil attack at the MAC layer [24]). Let us examine the possible attack scenarios separately. In the first attack scenario, a malicious node that is in the POS of the PAN coordinator first obtains the IDs of existing legitimate nodes in the PAN by either overhearing the list of pending addresses in the beacon frame or the GTS allocation requests that are sent during the CAP. Accordingly, when a legitimate node requests GTS allocation to transmit data in the CFP portion of the next superframes, the malicious node can cancel this transmission by sending a GTS deallocation request using the spoofed ID immediately after the GTS allocation request as shown in Fig 2. Since the PAN coordinator receives the deallocation request while processing the GTS allocation from the legitimate node, it ignores the GTS allocation coming first and does not assign any GTS to the legitimate node. As a result, the legitimate node is not assigned any GTS and cannot transmit its sensed data.

In the previous attack, a malicious node impersonates a legitimate node to cause the PAN coordinator to deallocate the requested GTSs. In this attack, a malicious node sends GTS requests from multiple fake IDs (up to 7) to completely allocate the CFP period. To perform this attack, a malicious node continuously monitors the available GTS slots with the intent of completely occupying them. Then, the attacker sends GTS allocation requests to fill up all the available GTSs in the superframe (see Fig. 3 for an explanation). By occupying the available GTSs and not allowing legitimate nodes to reserve GTSs the malicious node performs an exhaustion and unfairness type of attack. The malicious node does not necessarily need to send data at the assigned time slots. However, occasionally it may need to do so in order to prevent the PAN coordinator from dropping the assigned GTSs.

False Data Injection. In this attack, the malicious node first identifies which legitimate node has not requested GTS allocation by looking at the GTS descriptors of the beacon frames. Then, it chooses the legitimate node's ID that does not have any GTS allocation request and sends a GTS allocation request using that ID. After it confirms that a GTS is allocated by the PAN coordinator, the malicious node uses the spoofed ID and sends false data to the PAN coordinator during the CFP. The legitimate node at the same time sends its sensed data during the CAP. After checking the node's ID, the PAN coordinator regards the false data as time-sensitive ones and ignores the data sent from the legitimate node during the CAP.

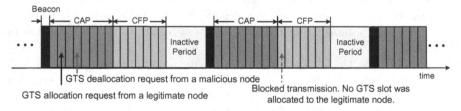

Fig. 2. A malicious node launching a GTS deallocation attack

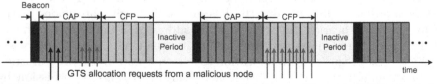

Fig. 3. A malicious node stealing all 7 GTSs of the CFP period

DoS-like Attacks. In this attack, the attacker has the ability to create collisions by jamming the beacons or specific GTS slots, which are broadcast in nature. In order to jam the beacons the malicious node must align to the superframe boundary and produce a collision by sending data at the start of the beacon. In the second case, it may intercept the beacons and learn in which GTS slots legitimate nodes send data. Then, it can corrupt the guaranteed communication between this device and the coordinator by jamming one or multiple GTSs.

Selective Forwarding and Black Hole Attacks. The communication flow in IEEE 802.15.4 beacon-enabled PANs, allows a captured (compromised) coordinator to perform a selective forwarding attack. In this attack, the malicious nodes refuses to forward all or a subset of the messages it receives from its child devices and simply drops them. If the attacker drops all the packets, the attack is then called black hole.

4   Anomaly Detection in 802.15.4-Based WSNs

This section highlights our anomaly detection framework, stating assumptions, and describing the proposed algorithm.

4.1   Assumptions of the Model

A number of assumptions are made concerning the framework in which the wireless sensor nodes operate. First, we consider a cluster tree 802.15.4 network in which most devices are FFDs. We assume that there is no pre-existing distributed trust model or peer-to-peer trust model, and hence no node can be fully trusted. Sensor nodes comprising the WSN remain stationary all the time. Once the clusters are formed and nodes are assigned short addresses, they maintain the same members, except for cases where nodes are blacklisted, die, or when new nodes join the network. Each node shall maintain a data structure that facilitates the storage of direct observations of all its *parent-child* nodes. Moreover, since sensor nodes are "weak" devices, we assume that an adversary can completely take over nodes and extract their cryptographic keys or load malicious software to launch an insider attack. Accordingly, and in order to limit the complexity of our model, we do not implement any cryptographic security mechanism, even though the MAC sublayer of the standard provides hooks that can be harnessed by upper layers to achieve authentication, message integrity, confidentiality and replay protection [17]. Next, we describe our anomaly detection algorithm in detail.

4.2   Detailed Algorithm Description

The core of the proposed algorithm relies on the periodic normal/guarding operation of the nodes comprising the WSN. To implement the aforementioned dual behavior, nodes inside the network adopt a *periodic operation*. Each node establishes the periods of normal/guarding operation during the *cluster formation* and *guarding initialization* phases. After the clusters are formed and guards are assigned, the monitor node collects statistics for its peers, which are used during the *anomaly detection and node revocation* phase to detect signs of intrusion. The different phases of our algorithm are analyzed below.

Phase 1: Cluster Formation. In the proposed algorithm, sensor nodes follow the association procedure defined by the standard in order to gradually connect and form a multicluster network structure. Before starting a PAN, the first action a device needs to perform is to initiate an active or passive scan in order to locate other PANs within its POS. Once a new PAN is established, the PAN coordinator is ready to accept requests from other devices to join the PAN. In the process of joining a PAN, the device requesting association will perform a passive scan to determine which PANs in its POS are allowing association. A device should attempt to associate only with a PAN through a coordinator that is currently allowing association (i.e., a coordinator whose *macAssociationPermit* is set to TRUE). In order to impose topological restrictions on the formation of the network, the *macAssociationPermit* is set to FALSE when the number of nodes joining a particular PAN exceeds the parameter N_u. If the original candidate device is not able to join the network at that coordinator, it will search for another parent device or it will become the PAN coordinator of a new PAN adjacent to the first one by selecting a suitable PAN identifier (see Fig. 1). Every device follows this association procedure and gradually connects to a PAN.

After the clusters are formed, each node starts operating in one of the available two modes; the *normal mode* in which it collects and forwards application-specific sensor measurements to the base station (BS), and the *guarding mode* in which it promiscuously listens to its peers' transmissions in order to detect signs of intrusion. During the normal mode, nodes may exchange data in the active portion of the superframe. Three types of data transfer transactions are allowed in the IEEE 802.15.4 MAC. The first one is the *direct transmission* in which a device sends data to a coordinator. The second data transfer model is the *indirect transmission* in which a coordinator sends data to a device, and the third transaction is the *peer-to-peer* data transfer (see Fig. 4 for an explanation). Within our algorithm, nodes are allowed to perform direct transmissions in both the CAP and CFP portions of the superframe resembling a sink-based reporting scheme that is typical in WSNs. Each device shall transmit a data frame following the successful application of the slotted version of the CSMA-CA algorithm. The transmission procedure, which includes the acknowledgement mechanism, begins with a randomly selected back-off time. Any transmission procedure can be repeated (attempted), if it can be completed within the same portion of the superframe. The remaining data, if any, will be deferred to the next active portion of the superframe.

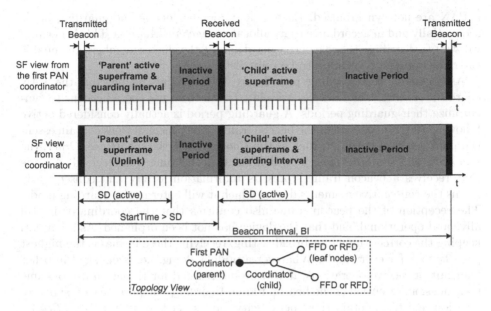

Fig. 4. Periodic normal/guarding operation of the nodes inside a PAN

Phase 2: Guarding Initialization. After completion of phase I, nodes periodically enter the guarding phase by enabling the *macPromiscuousMode* of the standard for a time equal to a *superframe duration*, SD. Time SD determines the active portion of the superframe in symbols, and relates to the *macSuperframeOrder*, $0 \leq SO \leq BO \leq 14$, as follows:

$$SD = aBaseSuperframeDuration * 2^{SO} symbols \qquad (1)$$

where *aBaseSuperframeDuration*=960, and BO is the interval at which the coordinator shall transmit its beacon frames. During this time, also called the guarding interval, each node gathers traffic-related attributes for all its parent and child nodes (if any) by promiscuously listening to the packets transmitted over the shared communication channel (see Fig. 4). As it can be seen, a functional difference between the first PAN coordinator and the rest PAN coordinators is that the latter alternatively acts as an associated device (during the active period of the superframe of the first PAN coordinator) and as the coordinator (guard) of a set of surrounding FFDs or RFDs.

So, a node in the guarding mode is in charge of monitoring its parent-child nodes by turning the promiscuous listening mode on or equivalently by setting the *macPromiscuousMode* to TRUE. When in promiscuous mode, the MAC sublayer shall pass all frames correctly received to the next higher layer for further processing. Note that each guarding period is a unique guarding round for collecting traffic-related attributes. These attributes may then be used by the ADS system running on each sensor node to detect signs of intrusions. At this point we should also state that the guarding periods of the nodes inside a PAN are not synchronized. Each cluster member enters the guarding mode sequentially and in accordance to its allocated *macShortAddress*. This is because we want to distribute the role of the guard among the cluster members and enable the detection and revocation to be fully distributed.

As apparent, the guarding periods are bounded by the beacons the PAN coordinators sent. Child devices associated with them use these beacons to synchronize their guarding periods. A guarding period is actually considered active following the transmission of the beacon frame. The beacon frames contain essential parameters of the PAN, such as the *CoordPANId*, the *macBeaconOrder*, the *macBSN*, and the *StartTime* at which the beacon frame was received. A node that receives a beacon frame stores its information locally and consequently learns the consecutive moments during which it will enter in the guarding mode. The reception of the beacon frame also confirms that the coordinator is still alive and operational, and that the device has not been orphaned. As apparent, keeping the correct timing for broadcasting/receiving these frames is the highest priority task for every node. Whatever a node is doing, i.e. is engaged in other transmit or receive operations, it will be interrupted for the accurate, on-time transmission/reception of the beacon frame. In order to acquire beacon synchronization and to maintain their periodicity, nodes need to set the *TrackBeacon* parameter to TRUE. This will enable a node to switch on its radio slightly before the expected broadcast of the beacon in order to receive it.

Phase 3: Anomaly Detection and Node Revocation. Our network-based ADS detects anomalies based on the packets that it monitors. Hence, following the data acquisition, anomaly detection and revocation come next. As already revealed, each node activates its ADS functionality when the MAC sublayer is in the so-called *promiscuous* (receive all) mode. During this guarding mode, each node keeps track of the transactions of all its parent-child nodes and stores the collected packet in a data structure. Since we follow a rule-based approach to anomaly detection, each data structure is evaluated according to the sequence of rules defined in Table 1. A packet is discarded after being tested against all rules without failing any of them. On the opposite case, an alarm will be raised if a violation of these rules occurs.

Indeed, an alarm indicates that a node is an intruder and needs to be revoked. Revocation is initiated following a process similar to the disassociation mechanism defined by the standard. Since nodes enter the guarding mode periodically, every node can independently verify intrusion instances and take revocation on the intruder. Note that revocation can be lazy, in that a node does not need to verify the intruder unless the latter is its parent or its child. In this way, attacks are detected and revoked in a fully distributed manner.

The MAC sublayer of the 802.15.4 standard allows us to implement the node revocation functionality easily since it defines procedures on how a device can disassociate from a PAN. The disassociation procedure may be initiated either from the PAN coordinator or from an associated device. Following the completion of a guarding period and the declaration of an anomaly, the coordinator

Table 1. Rules definition for detecting IEEE 802.15.4 MAC attacks

Rule Description	Attack Detected	Malicious actor
When a PANId conflict notification command is received at the coordinator, increase a counter. If after SD symbols, less than half of the associated devices report this conflict, raise an alarm.	PANId conflict attack	Associated device
If both GTS allocation & deallocation requests arrive from the same device in the CAP, raise an alarm. If an associated device does not send data during its allocated GTS slots for two consecutive CFP periods, raise an alarm.	GTS deallocation attack, GTS allocation attack	Associated device, Associated device
If data arrives in both the CAP and CFP portions of the same superframe, and originates from the same device, raise an alarm.	False data injection	Associated device
When half of the associated devices send an orphan notification request following the transmission of a beacon, raise an alarm.	DoS-like beacon attack	Associated device
If after two consecutive CFP periods, no packets are received during allocated GTS slots, raise an alarm.	DoS-like GTS attack	Associated device
When a packet is not forwarded as it should, increase a counter. When this counter reaches a threshold, t, after SD symbols, raise an alarm.	Selective Forwarding & Black hole attacks	Coordinator

may send a disassociate notification command to instruct a device to leave the PAN (*malicious associated device case*) or an associated device may request disassociation from the coordinator (*malicious coordinator case*). Let us examine these two cases separately.

When a coordinator wants one of its associated devices to leave the PAN, it sends a disassociation notification command to the malicious device. Because the disassociation command contains an acknowledgment request, the associated device shall confirm its receipt by sending an ACK frame. Even if the ACK is not received, the coordinator should consider the device disassociated. The next higher layer of a coordinator should disassociate a device by removing all references to that device. The device will soon conclude that it has been orphaned and will attempt to join other PANs within its POS. If no PANs exist in its POS, the revocation of the node would be global. In the opposite case, a similar procedure will be followed to revoke this node from the rest of the PANs it will attempt to associate with in the future.

In the second case, an associated device may send a disassociate notification command to notify the malicious coordinator of its intent to leave the PAN. Again, this command contains an ACK request. However, even if the ACK is not received, the device should consider itself disassociated. The orphaned device will in turn have to perform an active or passive scan in order to join other PANs that exist in its POS, or initiate a new PAN in case the active or passive scans fail. Since gradually all nodes associated with the malicious coordinator will independently verify the intrusion and leave its PAN, new clusters will be formed and the malicious coordinator will be completely revoked.

5   Performance Evaluation

5.1   Simulation Environment

In order to implement the proposed algorithm, we extended the capabilities of the existing IEEE 802.15.4 model developed in the OMNeT++ simulator [25]. This model was adapted from a version for ns-2 by Chen and Dressler. The model, which is described in more details in [26], implements the IEEE 802.15.4-2006 protocol stack. It also consists of two protocol-independent modules supporting energy measurement and mobility in the simulations. Our extension to the model targeted only the MAC sublayer (the PHY layer remained intact). Besides adding C++ code for the anomaly detection engine, modifications were made to the beacon-enabled mode of the model in order to support 802.15.4 cluster-tree topologies similar to [27]. In order to prevent overlapping, the emission of beacons is governed by an offset time. The offset for each PAN coordinator is set in a special *StartTime* parameter in the *omnetpp.ini* file. The particular value of the offset, which is null for the first PAN coordinator, for any other PAN coordinator is proportional to its *CoordPANId*.

We simulated a 802.15.4 cluster-tree network configured with our ADS. 20 nodes were placed uniformly at random in a rectangular playground of 100 x $100m^2$ (the first PAN coordinator (host[0]) was placed on the upper-left corner of the network). Each node has a communication range (POS) of $20m$ and operates under the 2.4 GHz PHY. We set the maximum number of octets added by the MAC sublayer to the PSDU without security equal to *aMaxMPDUUnsecuredOverhead*, 25 octets. This leads to a DATA PPDU length of 31 bytes, a beacon PPDU length of 17 bytes and an ACK PPDU length of 11 bytes. Regarding the transceiver characteristics, we use those of the IEEE 802.15.4-compliant CC2420 Chipcon radio [28], where each sensor consumes as high as 19.7 mA, 17.4 mA and 20 μA, in receive, transmit and sleep modes respectively.

We simulated a security-oriented application supporting sink-based reporting, that is to say, traffic flowing from the devices to the BS (typical case of a sensor network). Since nodes perform upstream transmissions this fact guarantees that the packet will reach the BS. In this scenario, only leaf node were generating traffic. The traffic load was set equal to 2 packets per second. During the simulation, randomly selected intelligent adversaries include themselves in the network by replicating legitimate (captured) nodes. The malicious nodes selectively launch one of the attacks identified in Section 3.2. All the presented results were averaged over 10 simulation runs. Each run lasts for 20 minutes, which gives as an overall simulation time of 10 hours.

5.2 Simulation Results

In this section, we evaluate the performance of the proposed anomaly detection algorithm through simulations. Comparison of our algorithm with existing rule-based anomaly detection schemes would not be appropriate, as they are not tailored to the IEEE 802.15.4 standard. Two metrics were used to evaluate the effectiveness of our algorithm. These are the *percentage reduction in network lifetime*, which is used to examine the extent by which our ADS degrades the network lifetime when being implemented in common sensor nodes, and the *detection accuracy* defined as the ratio of the detected attacks to the total number of detected and undetected attacks.

Energy Consumption. Fig. 5a illustrates the percentage reduction in network lifetime as a function of the percentage increase in the number of compromised nodes. To simulate the described scenario, we chose at random a number of network nodes and we programmed them to selectively launch one of the attacks depicted in Table 1. With regard to selective forwarding attacks (launched only by non-leaf nodes), the attacker was dropping packets with a probability $p_d = 30\%$. When $p_d = 100\%$, the attacker was executing a black hole attack. We set the threshold value for the percentage of packets being dropped over the guarding interval, SD, to be $t = 20\%$. Above this threshold, an alarm was generated and node revocation was initiated. For all other types of attack, the counter-criterion rules of Table 1 are evaluated in succession and, if violated, an alarm is raised.

As the three curves show in Fig. 5a, the percentage reduction in network lifetime increases smoothly as the percentage of malicious nodes increases. This is because more energy-consuming intrusion detection functions are being executed

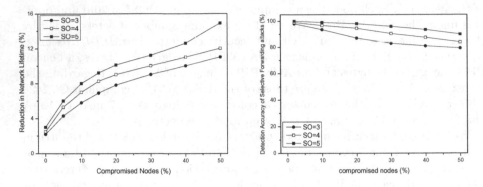

Fig. 5. a) Percentage reduction in network lifetime, and b) Detection accuracy of Selective forwarding attacks

following the introduction, identification and revocation of an increasing number of adversaries. Overall, the network lifetime decreases by as high as 14.8%. The relatively small decrease in network lifetime is achieved because the energy-consuming role of the guard is rotated among the network nodes, a fact that uniformly distributes the energy dissipation among the nodes. As expected, the percentage reduction in network lifetime is low when the network contains no malicious nodes. The obtained curves also indicate the trade off between the value of the *macSuperframeOrder*, SO={3,4,5} and the energy cost. According to Eq. (1), bigger SO values extend the guarding interval, SD, or equivalently the time window the monitor node is hearing in the promiscuous mode. As such, the longer a monitor node stays in the 'receive all' mode, the higher is the associated energy cost.

Detection Accuracy. The rest of the figures evaluate the effectiveness of our algorithm against the attacks depicted in Table 1. In each attack scenario, there was always one single type of attacker, which was varied in each simulation.

One interesting aspect these figures present is that the variation of the value of the SO does not impact the detection efficiency of our algorithm. Only the selective forwarding attacks and PANId conflict attacks, which are assessed over a time window SD, are affected by the value of SO. Indeed, as shown in Fig. 5b, smaller SO values result in lower detection levels. This happens because small SO values, result in small guarding intervals SD. Recall that the interval SD relates to the time window that a monitor node has in order to gather packets and analyze them for signs of intrusion. Since less packets are being collected as a result of the smaller SD interval, this affects the decision making process of anomaly detection and produces less accurate intrusion detection results. One aspect that is common in all types of attack is that if there is a high fraction of compromised nodes inside the network (50 percent or more), the detection levels achieved by our anomaly detection algorithm tend to drop below 90 percent,

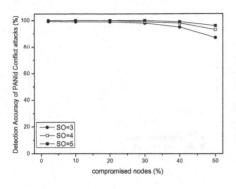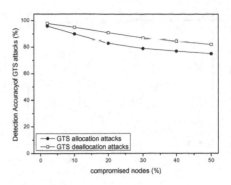

Fig. 6. Detection accuracy of a) PANId conflict attacks, and b) GTS attacks

which is considered low for an effective ADS. We can thus say that our ADS works acceptable when having 45% or less of compromised nodes inside the WSN.

As already revealed, Fig. 5b shows results on the detection accuracy of selective forwarding attacks. In this type of attack, since packets are dropped probabilistically, there might be the case that during the guarding interval of some nodes, the dropped packets are less than $t = 20\%$, and no alert is produced by those nodes. Then, the detection rule over that time window will not be satisfied, and would produce no alarm. This is less probable to happen if the value of SO gets bigger or if the nodes launch black hole attacks (the results on black hole attacks are not presented here due to space restrictions). In this case, the probability that during an SD interval the dropped packets are less than t, resulting in a false negative, is close to zero, and hence the accuracy in detecting that kind of attack is close to 100%.

Fig. 6a illustrates the detection accuracy of PANId conflict attacks. In PANId conflict attacks, detection was always close to 100% due to the rule being applied to detect this kind of attack. Another factor that keeps the detection levels high is that these attacks are not mistaken with any other kind of attack or with occasional network failures, and as such, a small number of false negatives is only generated. However, an increase in the number of misdetections is obtained when half, or more, of the nodes behave maliciously. In this case, the minority vote rule being applied does not prevail any more.

According to Fig. 6b, the detection of GTS attacks ranges between 99% and 80%. In this scenario, since the SO does not impact the detection levels, only results for SO=4 are depicted. The two curves indicate that the detection of GTS allocation attacks is less successful. This happens because this type of attack may be confused with the DoS-like GTS attacks, and as such, it may generate a higher number of false negatives.

Fig. 7a on the other hand, shows that false data injection attacks, similar to PANId conflict attacks, are detected with very high accuracy. Again, this attack is not mistaken with any other kind of attack or network failure, generating few false negatives.

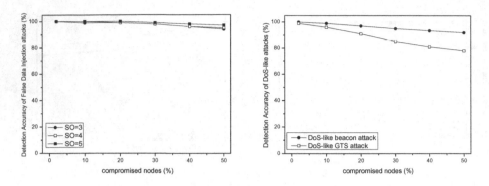

Fig. 7. Detection accuracy of a) False data injection attacks, and b) DoS-like attacks

Fig. 7b illustrates the obtained results on the detection accuracy of DoS-like attacks. While the DoS-like beacon attacks are detected with an accuracy always above 95%, the detection effectiveness drops in the case of DoS-like GTS attacks. This happens because in this type of attack there is no internal mechanism (similar to the lost synchronization) to notify the coordinator and assist the decision making process of anomaly detection. Moreover, these type of attacks may be confused with the GTS allocation attacks when jamming occurs in multiple GTS slots, a fact that may further increase the number of false negatives.

6   Conclusions and Future Work

In this paper, we presented a distributed anomaly detection algorithm for securing IEEE 802.15.4-compliant WSNs operating in the beacon-enabled mode. The proposed algorithm exploits the peculiar characteristics of the standard in order to incarnate the concept of periodic guarding for anomaly detection purposes. The OMNeT++ simulator has been used to implement our algorithm and to collect various results aiming at assessing its performance. The results showed that our approach maintains the energy consumption overhead at very low levels, while at the same time, it achieves high detection accuracy for all types of identified attacks. In the future, we intend to examine the proposed algorithm in larger networks operating under more hostile conditions.

Acknowledgments. This work is implemented within the framework of the Action "Supporting Postdoctoral Researchers" of the Operational Program "Education and Lifelong Learning" (Actions Beneficiary: General Secretariat for Research and Technology), and is co-financed by the European Social Fund (ESF) and the Greek State.

References

1. Akyildiz, I.F., Su, W., Sankarasubramaniam, Y., Cayirci, E.: Wireless sensor networks: a survey. Computer Networks 38(4), 393–422 (2002)
2. Karlof, C., Wagner, D.: Secure routing in wireless sensor networks: Attacks and countermeasures. In: First IEEE International Workshop on Sensor Network Protocols and Applications, pp. 113–127 (2002)
3. Camtepe, S.A., Yener, B.: Key distribution mechanisms for wireless sensor networks: a survey. Rensselaer Polytechnic Institute, Tech. Rep. (2005)
4. Shi, E., Perrig, A.: Designing secure sensor networks. IEEE Wireless Communications 11(6), 38–43 (2004)
5. Lazos, L., Poovendran, R.: Serloc: Robust localization for wireless sensor networks. ACM Transactions on Sensor Networks (TOSN), 73–100 (2005)
6. Dimitriou, T., Krontiris, I.: Secure In-network Processing in Sensor Networks. In: Security in Sensor Networks, pp. 275–290. CRC Press (August 2006)
7. Farooqi, A.H., Khan, F.A.: Intrusion detection systems for wireless sensor networks: A survey. In: Ślęzak, D., Kim, T.-H., Chang, A.C.-C., Vasilakos, T., Li, M., Sakurai, K. (eds.) FGCN/ACN 2009. CCIS, vol. 56, pp. 234–241. Springer, Heidelberg (2009)
8. Scarfone, K.A., Mell, P.M.: Sp 800-94. Guide to intrusion detection and prevention systems (idps). National Institute of Standards & Technology, Gaithersburg, MD, United States, Tech. Rep. (2007)
9. Rajasegarar, S., Leckie, C., Palaniswami, M.: Anomaly detection in wireless sensor networks. IEEE Wireless Communications 15(4), 34–40 (2008)
10. Hu, J.: Host-based anomaly intrusion detection. In: Handbook of Information and Communication Security, pp. 235–255 (2010)
11. Xie, M., Han, S., Tian, B., Parvin, S.: Anomaly detection in wireless sensor networks: A survey. J. Netw. Comput. Appl. 34(4), 1302–1325 (2011)
12. IEEE 802.15.4^{TM} -2011: IEEE Stadard for Local and metropolitan area networks– Part 15.4: Low-Rate Wireless Personal Area Networks (LR-WPANs) (2011)
13. Koubaa, A., Alves, M., Nefzi, B., Song, Y.-Q.: Improving the IEEE 802.15.4 Slotted CSMA/CA MAC for Time-Critical Events in Wireless Sensor Networks. In: Proceedings of the Workshop of Real-Time Networks (RTN 2006), Dresden, Germany (July 2006)
14. Sokullu, R., Korkmaz, I., Dagdeviren, O., Mitseva, A., Prasad, N.: An Investigation on IEEE 802.15.4 MAC Layer Attacks. In: Proceedings of the 10th International Symposium on Wireless Personal Multimedia Communications (WPMC 2007), pp. 1019–1023 (2007)
15. Jung, S.S., Valero, M., Bourgeois, A., Beyah, R.: Attacking beacon-enabled 802.15.4 networks. In: Jajodia, S., Zhou, J. (eds.) SecureComm 2010. LNICST, vol. 50, pp. 253–271. Springer, Heidelberg (2010)
16. Radosavac, S., Baras, J.S., Koutsopoulos, I.: A framework for MAC protocol misbehavior detection in wireless networks. In: Workshop on Wireless Security, pp. 33–42 (2005)
17. Sastry, N., Wagner, D.: Security considerations for IEEE 802.15.4 networks. In: Proceedings of the 3rd ACM Workshop on Wireless Security, WiSe 2004, pp. 32–42. ACM, New York (2004)
18. Alim, M.A., Sarikaya, B.: EAP-Sens: a security architecture for wireless sensor networks. In: Proceedings of the 4th Annual International Conference on Wireless Internet, WICON, pp. 1–9 (2008)

19. Sokullu, R., Dagdeviren, O., Korkmaz, I.: On the IEEE 802.15.4 MAC Layer Attacks: GTS Attack. In: Second International Conference on Sensor Technologies and Applications, SENSORCOMM 2008, pp. 673–678 (2008)
20. Amini, F., Misic, J., Pourreza, H.: Detection of sybil attack in beacon enabled IEEE 802.15.4 networks. In: International Wireless Communications and Mobile Computing Conference, IWCMC 2008, pp. 1058–1063 (2008)
21. da Silva, A.P.R., et al.: Decentralized intrusion detection in wireless sensor networks. In: Proceedings of 1st ACM International Workshop on Quality of Service and Security in Wireless and Mobile Networks (Q2SWINET 2005), pp. 16–23. ACM Press (2005)
22. Onat, I., Miri, A.: An intrusion detection system for wireless sensor networks. In: IEEE International Conference on Wireless and Mobile Computing, Networking and Communications (WiMob 2005), vol. 3, pp. 253–259 (August 2005)
23. Yu, B., Xiao, B.: Detecting selective forwarding attacks in wireless sensor networks. In: Proceedings of the 20th International Conference on Parallel and Distributed Processing, IPDPS 2006, p. 351. IEEE Computer Society (2006)
24. Douceur, J.R.: The Sybil Attack. In: Druschel, P., Kaashoek, M.F., Rowstron, A. (eds.) IPTPS 2002. LNCS, vol. 2429, pp. 251–260. Springer, Heidelberg (2002)
25. Varga, A., Hornig, R.: An overview of the omnet++ simulation environment. In: Simutools 2008: Proceedings of the 1st International Conference on Simulation Tools and Techniques for Communications, Networks and Systems & Workshops, pp. 1–10, ICST (2008)
26. Chen, F., Dressler, F.: A Simulation Model of IEEE 802.15.4 in OMNeT++. In: 6. GI/ITG KuVS Fachgesprach Drahtlose Sensornetze, Poster Session, pp. 35–38 (2007)
27. Hurtado-López, J., Casilari, E., Ariza, A.: Enabling IEEE 802.15.4 Cluster-Tree Topologies in OMNeT++. ICST, Brussels (2009)
28. Chipcon AS SmartRF© CC2420, preliminary datasheet, rev. 1.2 (2004), http://www.chipcon.com/files/cc2420_data_sheet_1_3.pdf

Secure and Verifiable Top-k Query in Two-Tiered Sensor Networks

Ting Zhou, Yaping Lin, Wei Zhang, Sheng Xiao, and Jinguo Li

Dept. of Information Science and Engineering, Hunan University,
Changshang 410082, China
{zhouting,yplin,zhangweidoc,xiaosheng,lijg1985}@hnu.edu.cn

Abstract. Two-tiered sensor networks have been widely adopted since they offer good scalability, efficient power usage and storage saving. Storage nodes, responsible for storing data from nearby sensors and answering queries from the sink, however, are attractive to attackers. A compromised storage node would leak sensitive data to attackers and return forged or incomplete query results to the sink. In this paper, we propose SVTQ, a Secure and Verifiable Top-k Query protocol that preserves both data confidentiality and integrity of query results. *To preserve data confidentiality*, we propose prime aggregation whereby storage nodes can process *top-k* queries precisely without knowing actual data values. *To preserve integrity of query results*, we further propose a novel scheme called differential chain that allows the sink to verify any forged or incomplete result. Both theoretical analysis and experimental results on the real-world data set confirm the effectiveness and efficiency of SVTQ protocol.

Keywords: Two-tiered sensor networks, Data confidentiality, Prime aggregation, Integrity, Differential chain.

1 Introduction

1.1 Motivation

Two-tiered sensor networks have been widely adopted since they offer good scalability, efficient power usage and storage saving. In this paper, we focus on a two-tiered sensor network as illustrated in Fig. 1, where resource-rich storage nodes act as an intermediate tier between sensor nodes and the sink. The storage nodes store data from their nearby sensors and process queries from the sink.

Compared with traditional sensor networks, two-tiered sensor networks have three major advantages. First, sensors periodically submit their collected data to their nearby storage node in one hop instead of sending them to the sink via multiple hops, which saves power for energy-limited sensors. Second, storage nodes store sensor collected data for future retrieval and data analysis, which saves storage space for memory-constrained sensors. Third, when issuing a query, instead of flushing the whole sensor network, the sink only needs to communicate with storage nodes, and storage nodes only need to process queries over the data stored on them locally, which makes the query more efficient. Two-tiered sensor networks were first introduced by

T. Zia et al. (Eds.): SecureComm 2013, LNICST 127, pp. 19–34, 2013.

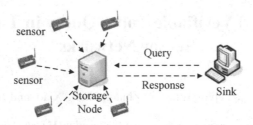

Fig. 1. Architecture of two-tiered sensor networks

Sylvia Ratnasamy [13], and then have been widely adopted for various applications [5], [15], [17], [20]. Several commercial products of storage nodes, such as RISE [14] and StarGate [19], have been available and widely used.

However, the central role of storage nodes in this tiered framework makes them attractive to attackers when the network is deployed in a hostile environment. A compromised storage node poses great threats to the network. First, a compromised storage node would leak sensitive information collected from sensors to attackers. Second, a compromised storage node would also return forged or incomplete query results to the sink. It is especially dangerous when the query results are used to make critical decision such as military actions. Therefore, a secure and verifiable query protocol for two-tiered sensor networks is imperative.

As a typical query type in two-tiered sensor networks, *top-k* query asks for data items whose numerical attributes are among the k highest of all data items [21], which is important for monitoring extreme conditions. Therefore, this paper aims to design a secure and verifiable *top-k* query protocol for two-tiered sensor networks. For data confidentiality, the proposed query protocol should enable storage nodes to process queries correctly without knowing actual data values, so that compromising a storage node will not lead to the leakage of sensitive data. For integrity of query results, the query protocol should allow the sink to verify whether the storage nodes has injected forged data into or omitted some qualified data items from query results.

1.2   Technical Challenges

There are two key challenges in designing a secure and verifiable *top-k* query protocol for two-tiered sensor networks. First, to prevent a compromised storage node from disclosing sensitive data to attackers, each sensed data should be encrypted before being sent to storage nodes, hence, the storage nodes need to process queries over encrypted data items without knowing their actual data values. Second, upon receiving a query result from a storage node, the sink needs to verify whether the query results indeed contain the *top-k* data items and do not contain any forged data.

1.3   Limitations of Prior Arts

Although important, only in recent years has secure *top-k* query in two-tiered sensor networks become a focus of research. Zhang & Shi firstly propose schemes for verifiable *top-k* query in their recently seminal work [21]. By exploiting crosscheck approach, the integrity of query results can be well preserved. Nevertheless, data confidentiality is not taken into consideration. A subsequent solution to secure *top-k* query was presented by Liao and Li [11], which covers both data confidentiality and integrity of query results. All the schemes proposed in [11] are based on the system model where each sensor submits only one sensed data to storage node each time. However, it is a more general case in real-world applications where each sensor has multiple sensed data per submission, as adopted in prior arts [3], [16], [18], [21]. Liao's scheme for data confidentiality preservation would be unworkable when performed on this general system model. In addition, Liao's scheme does not enable storage nodes to obtain precise query results while ensuring data confidentiality. Up to now, no research effort was conducted on both confidentiality and integrity preserving *top-k* query in the general system model of two-tiered sensor networks.

1.4 Our Approach and Major Contributions

In this paper, we propose SVTQ, a secure and verifiable *top-k* query protocol for two-tiered sensor networks. To preserve data confidentiality, we propose a novel scheme called prime aggregation whereby storage nodes can process queries correctly without knowing actual data values. To preserve integrity of query results, we propose a differential chain, a novel scheme which enables the sink to verify the authenticity and completeness of query results. The major contributions of this paper are listed as follows:

(1) To the best of our knowledge, this paper is the first that considers both data confidentiality and integrity issues when processing *top-k* queries in the general system model of two-tiered sensor networks.

(2) We propose a novel data confidentiality preserving scheme which can precisely obtain *top-k* query results without disclosing any sensitive information to storage nodes.

(3) We introduce a data storage scheme which allows the sink to verify any forged or incomplete query result.

(4) We evaluate our solutions on a real-world data set, and the results show that SVTQ achieves confidentiality and integrity goals efficiently.

The rest of this paper is organized as follows. In Section 2, we give a brief review of the related work. Section 3 describes the system model and the threat model. In section 4 and 5, we give a detailed description of our data confidentiality and integrity preserving scheme respectively. In Section 6, we discuss the security and performance of our proposed schemes. We present our performance evaluation and experimental results in section 7 and conclude this paper in section 8.

2   Related Work

2.1   Secure Range Query in Two-Tiered Sensor Networks

Secure range query in two-tiered sensor networks has attracted much attention in recent years [3], [16], [18]. To preserve data confidentiality, Sheng & Li [16] and Shi *et al.* [18] adopt the bucket partitioning scheme first introduced by Hacigumus *et al.* [8]. The basic idea of bucket partitioning is to divide the domain of data value into multiple buckets, after collecting data items from environment, each sensor firstly distributes the collected data into a corresponding bucket, encrypts data items in each bucket, and then sends each encrypted data along with its bucket ID to the closest storage node. When the sink wants to execute a range query, it first converts the query into a smallest set of bucket IDs and then sends the set to the storage node. Once receiving the queried set of bucket IDs, the storage node first finds all the encrypted data items that fall into these buckets, and then reports them to the sink as the query result. However, as pointed out in [9], the bucket partitioning scheme allows a compromised storage node to make a reasonable estimation on both sensed data and queries. To address this problem, Chen & Liu proposed SafeQ [3], a prefix based scheme to encode both data and queries such that the aforementioned estimation can be avoided. In SafeQ, after collecting n data items from the environment, each sensor firstly converts the n data items into $n + 1$ ranges, and then employs prefixes to represent these ranges before sending them to storage node. However, suffering from the inherent drawback of prefix membership verification technique, SafeQ usually needs a series of prefixes to represent a range, which is unfavourable for resource-limited sensors.

To preserve integrity of query results, Sheng & Li [16] proposed an encoding technique where each sensor generates a distinct encoding number for the bucket that has no data item, these encoding numbers are used by the sink to verify the integrity of query results. However, this technique will introduce extra communication overheads by sending the encoding number for these empty buckets. To address this problem, Shi *et al.* [18] proposed a spatiotemporal crosscheck approach. In their scheme, each sensor uses a bit map to represent which buckets have data, and then broadcasts its bit map to nearby sensors. Each sensor attaches the bit maps received from others to its own data and then encrypts them together. The sink verifies the integrity of query result from a sensor by examining the bit maps from its nearby sensors. However, this scheme would be efficient only in the event detection scenarios since data broadcast would introduce considerable communication overheads. With respect to this problem, Chen & Liu [3] proposed a technique called neighborhood chain, by concatenating the neighboring data items, the sink can detect the integrity of query results efficiently.

2.2   Secure Top-k Query in Two-Tiered Sensor Networks

Secure *top-k* query in two-tiered sensor networks has been recently studied [11], [21]. Zhang & Shi firstly proposed three schemes for verifiable *top-k* query in their recent work [21]. All their schemes share the same basic idea that each data item is attached with a Message Authentic Code (MAC) such that injecting forged data can be easily detected. Specially, in their later two schemes, sensors exchange data information by broadcasting their highest data score to others. Each sensor embeds the received information into its own data and then sends these new data items along with MACs to its closest storage node. The sink then verifies the authenticity and completeness of query results by examining the MACs and the information extracted from each data. By using this crosscheck approach, the integrity of query results can be well preserved. However, as we aforementioned, the broadcast mechanism would introduce considerable communication overheads for energy-constrained sensors. Furthermore, data confidentiality is not taken into consideration in [21].

A subsequent solution to secure *top-k* query in two-tiered sensor network was proposed by Liao and Li [11], which covers both data confidentiality and integrity of query results. By using the revised order-preserving symmetric encryption (*OPSE*) proposed by Boldyreva *et al.* [1], the storage nodes can process *top-k* query as efficient as for the unencrypted data items. However, the simply use of *OPSE* would incur order-relation and distance-relation privacy leakage. To overcome this problem, Liao *et al.* further propose a secret perturbation scheme. The basic idea of secret perturbation is to randomly select some sensors, and then perturb the data of these sensors by adding a secret data to the original one before encrypting them with *OPSE*. However, this scheme would lead to imprecise query results, which means the query results would contain data items that do not satisfy the query. What's more, all the schemes proposed in [11] are based on the system model where each sensor submits one sensed data to storage node each time. This means that the *top-k* queries would be performed on the data set where each sensor only has one data. However, it is a more general case in real-world applications where each sensor has multiple data items per submission, as assumed in [3], [16], [18], [21]. The data confidentiality preserving scheme proposed in [11] would be unworkable when performed on this general system model. In contrast, this paper aims at designing a *top-k* query protocol in the general system model as adopted in prior arts [3], [16], [18], [21], which preserves both data confidentiality and integrity of query results.

3   Models and Problem Statement

3.1   System Model

We assume a similar system model as in [3], [16], [18], [21]. The architecture of this two-tiered sensor network is shown in Fig. 1. Specifically, each storage node is in charge of a cell composed of many sensors, storage nodes are often resource-rich in the aspects of energy, storage and computation while sensors are usually resource-constrained in every regard. Sensors collect data from the environment and periodically submit their collected data to storage nodes. Storage nodes store data received from their nearby sensors and process queries from the sink. Without loss of generality, we assume that all sensors and storage nodes are loosely synchronized. We divide time into fixed time intervals, and every n intervals form an epoch. Each sensor sends its data to the storage node at the end of each epoch as follows.

$$S_i \rightarrow \text{Storage Node}: \quad i, t, \{d_{i,1}, \ldots, d_{i,n}\}$$

where i is the sensor ID and t is the sequence number of the epoch during which n data items $\{d_{i,1}, \ldots, d_{i,n}\}$ are collected. Similarly, we consider the following query mode.

$$\text{Sink} \rightarrow \text{Storage Node}: \quad Q = (A, t, k)$$

where A denotes the ID set of queried sensors, t is the queried time epoch and k denotes the number of data items the sink asks the storage node to return. To sum up, $Q = (A, t, k)$ denotes that the sink asks for the k highest data items generated in a queried set A during epoch t.

3.2 Threat Model and Security Goals

Similar with prior arts, we assume that storage nodes are vulnerable to be compromised while sensors and the sink are always trustworthy. Due to the important role of storage nodes in two-tiered sensor networks, compromising a storage node will lead to great damage to the system. First, once a storage node is compromised, the large quantity of confidential data stored on the storage node will be leaked to the attackers. Second, after receiving a query from the sink, the compromised storage node can also be manipulated to return forged or incomplete query results to the sink. Therefore, this paper aims to achieve the following security goals.

Data Confidentiality preservation: To enable storage nodes to process queries correctly over encrypted data without knowing actual data values, so that compromising a storage node will not lead to the leakage of any sensitive data.

Integrity preservation: To enable the sink to verify the authenticity and completeness of query results. The authenticity check is to detect forged data items in query results while the completeness check is to make sure that no qualifying data items are maliciously omitted by compromised storage nodes. Thus, any misbehavior of a compromised storage node can be detected by the sink.

4   Confidentiality Preservation for Sensed Data

In order to preserve data confidentiality, it seems that the simplest way is to encrypt data before sending them to the storage node. But a subsequent challenge is how to process a query over encrypted data without revealing plaintext data.

4.1   Prefix Membership Verification

Prefix membership verification was first introduced in [4] and later formalized in [12]. The basic idea of this technique is to convert the question of whether a number is in a range to another question of whether two sets share a prefix. Given a number x whose binary format is $b_1 b_2 \ldots b_w$, where w is the bit length of number x. The prefix family of number x is defined as $F(x) = \{b_1 b_2 \ldots b_w, b_1 b_2 \ldots b_{w-1}*, \ldots, b_1 * \ldots *, * \ldots *\}$.

For example, the prefix family of number 11 is $F(11) = \{1011, 101*, 10**, 1***,$ $****\}$. Similarly, a range can be converted into a minimum set of prefixes which we call the range prefix of this range. We use $R[d_1, d_2]$ to denote the range prefix of range $[d_1, d_2]$. For example, $R[10, 15] = \{101*, 11**\}$. Given a number x and a range $[d_1,$ $d_2]$, if $F(x) \cap R[d_1, d_2] \neq \emptyset$, we can draw the conclusion that $x \in [d_1, d_2]$ according to the theory proposed in [12].

Inspired by works [4] and [12], we propose to make use of the prefix membership verification technique to meet the data confidentiality preserving goal. However, there are still two challenges need to be overcome before we can apply this technique to our problem. First, the aforementioned method is just used to determine whether a number belongs to a range, how to make comparison between two encrypted data is still a difficult question. Second, given a number d_1 and a range $[d_2, d_3]$, where $d_1, d_2,$ and d_3 are numbers with w bits. We need $w + 1$ prefixes to denote the prefix family of d_1 and $2w-2$ prefixes to denote the range prefix of this range in the worst case [7]. This is heavy-laden for resource-constrained sensors if so many prefixes need to be submitted for each sensing data for the sake of data comparison. Thus, how to reduce these massive overheads remains another question.

4.2 Prime Aggregation

To meet aforementioned challenges, we propose prime aggregation, a novel scheme which enables the comparison between two encrypted data items while fewer additional overheads are introduced. The basic idea of prime aggregation is to aggregate multiple prefixes in a prefix set into a single number with the aid of primes, which can be done in two steps. First, map each prefix in prefix set to a unique prime. Second, perform multiplication on the primes obtained from each prefix set.

For simplicity, the *Prime* aggregation result from prefix *Family* will be denoted by *PF*, while the *Prime* aggregation result from *Range* prefix will be denoted by *PR*. Then we have the following theorem.

Theorem 4.1: Given a number x and a range $[y, z]$, $x \in [y, z]$ if and only if the following inequality holds:

$$gcd\,(PF(x), PR([y, z])) \neq 1 . \tag{1}$$

Proof: Let f_i and r_j be the prefix in the prefix family and range prefix respectively, while the total number of prefixes in the prefix family and range prefix are denoted by V and M respectively. Then we have

$$F(x) = \bigcup_{i=1}^{V} f_i , \quad R([y, z]) = \bigcup_{j=1}^{M} r_j .$$

Similarly, let pf_i and pr_j be the corresponding prime of f_i and r_j respectively, then

$$PF(x) = \prod_{i=1}^{V} pf_i , \quad PR([y, z]) = \prod_{j=1}^{M} pr_j .$$

If $x \in [y, z]$, we have

$$F(x) \cap R([y, z]) = f_h = r_l \neq \emptyset, \quad h \in [1, V], \quad l \in [1, M] .$$

Then $pf_{h} = pr_{l}$

i.e. $x \in [y, z] \Rightarrow gcd(PF(x), PR([y, z])) = pf_{h} = pr_{l} \neq 1$.

The inversion of this expression can be proved similarly, thus

$$x \in [y, z] \Leftrightarrow gcd(PF(x), PR([y, z])) \neq 1.$$

Next, we introduce the detailed process for applying prime aggregation to our scheme.

Before distributing all sensors to their working sites, a sequence of prime numbers will be pre-generated and stored in all sensors. For convenience of mapping, each prefix in prefix set would be firstly numericalized before mapped to a corresponding prime.

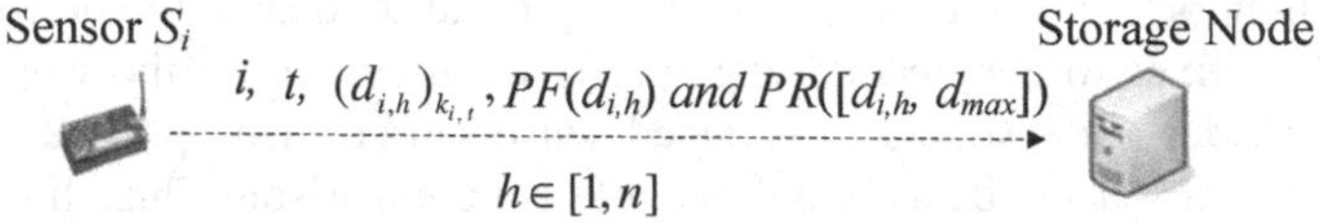

Sensor S_i Storage Node

$i, t, (d_{i,h})_{k_{i,t}}, PF(d_{i,h})$ and $PR([d_{i,h}, d_{max}])$

$h \in [1, n]$

Fig. 2. Data submission for a sensor node

The basic idea of prefix numericalization is to convert a prefix into a corresponding number. Given a prefix $b_1 b_2 \cdots b_h * \cdots *$ of w bits, we first insert 1 between b_h and the symbol * to separate $b_1 b_2 \cdots b_h$ and $* \cdots *$, and then replace each * with 0. Note that if there is no symbol * in the prefix, we will add 1 at the end of this prefix. For example, prefix {1***} will be converted into {11000} = 24 while {1110} will be converted into {11101} = 29 after numeralization. The detailed process of prefix numeralization falls out of scope of this paper. A formal definition of this process can be found in [2].

For mapping each prefix to a unique prime, we introduce a pseudorandom function in our scheme. The pseudorandom number generated by the pseudorandom function acts as a medium for mapping each prefix to a unique prime. Specifically, at the beginning of each epoch, a list of pseudorandom numbers will be generated using a pseudorandom function shared by all sensors. Note that the seed for this pseudorandom function varies with epoch changing, i.e., $seed_t = hash(seed_{t-1})$. When mapping each prefix to a prime, each sensor firstly finds the corresponding pseudorandom number according to the value of each numericalized prefix, e.g., if the value of a numericalized prefix is 12, the sensor finds the $12th$ pseudorandom number in the pseudorandom number list. Then the value of this pseudorandom number will be used as the address for indexing the prime stored on each sensor.

For the second step of prime aggregation, we perform multiplication to the obtained primes. Note that each large number is regarded as a string in our scheme, and we adopt the large number multiplication algorithms proposed in [6] to perform multiplication. Thus, the product of primes can be any length and the overflow can be avoided.

4.3   Data Submission

Let $d_{i,1}, \ldots, d_{i,n}$ be the data items collected by sensor S_i during epoch t, where each data item belongs to range (d_{min}, d_{max}). Here d_{min} and d_{max}, known to both sensors and the sink, denote the public lower and upper bounds of sensor collected data. Fig. 2 illustrates the information sent to storage node by sensor S_i at the end of epoch t.

Upon collecting n data items, sensor node S_i performs the following steps:

(1) Sort the n data items in descending order, *i.e.*, $d_{i,1} > d_{i,2} > \ldots > d_{i,n}$. For simplicity, we assume that all data items are different from each other.

(2) Compute the prefix family $F(d_{i,h})$ and the range prefix $R([d_{i,h}, d_{max}])$ for each data item, where $h \in [1, n]$, and then numericalize them.

(3) Perform prime aggregation to the numericalized prefixes. We use $PF_{i,h}$ to represent the aggregation result of $d_{i,h}$ while $PR_{i,h}$ to denote that of range $[d_{i,h}, d_{max}]$.

(4) Encrypt each data with the secret key $k_{i,t}$, shared between each sensor and the sink, *i.e.*, compute $(d_{i,1})_{k_{i,t}}, \ldots, (d_{i,n})_{k_{i,t}}$, where $k_{i,t}$ is generated using an embedded hash function, *i.e.*, $k_{i,t} = hash\,(k_{i,t-1})$.

(5) Send the encrypted data items along with the prime aggregation results to storage node, *i.e.*, send $\{[(d_{i,1})_{k_{i,t}}, PF_{i,1}, PR_{i,1}], \cdots, [(d_{i,n})_{k_{i,t}}, PF_{i,n}, PR_{i,n}]\}$ to its closest storage node.

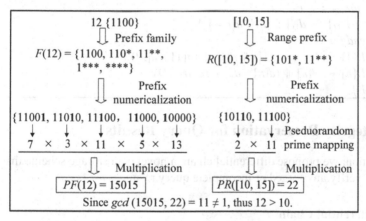

Fig. 3. An example of data comparison using prime aggregation

4.4   Query Processing

After receiving a query $Q = (A, t, k)$ from the sink, the storage node finds the largest k data items of queried set A based on theorem 4.1.

Given two encrypted data items $(d_{i,h})_{k_{i,t}}$ of sensor S_i and $(d_{j,l})_{k_{j,t}}$ of sensor S_j, where $i, j \in A$ and $h, l \in [1, n]$. Storage nodes compare these two encrypted data items by checking whether the following expression holds.

$$gcd\,(PF_{i,h}, PR_{j,l}) \neq 1$$

If the above expression holds, then

$$d_{i,h} \in [d_{j,l}, d_{max}]$$

Namely

$$d_{i,h} > d_{j,l}.$$

By doing this, storage nodes can make comparison between two numbers without knowing their actual values. Thus the *top-k* results can be precisely obtained.

As an illustrative example, shown in Fig. 3, when given two encrypted data $(12)_{k_{i,t}}$ and $(10)_{k_{j,t}}$, storage nodes compare these two data items by verifying whether $gcd\ (PF(12), PR([10, 15])) \neq 1$. Here, we assume the public upper bound of data is 15.

Algorithm 1. $diff\_C\ (d[], d_{max}, d_{min})$

1. $sort\ (d)\ by\ descending\ order;\ n = d.size$
2. $if\ \ n = 1\ then$
3. $D[1] \leftarrow (d_{max} - d[1]) \parallel d[1] \parallel (d[1] - d_{min});\ return(D)$
4. $else\ if\ \ n = 2\ then$
5. $D[1] \leftarrow (d_{max} - d[1]) \parallel d[1] \parallel (d[1] - d[2])$
6. $D[2] \leftarrow d[2] \parallel (d[2] - d_{min});\ return(D)$
7. $else$
8. $for\ \ i = 2: n\text{-}1$
9. $D[i] \leftarrow d[i] \parallel (d[i]\text{-}d[i + 1])$
10. $end\ for$
11. $D[1] \leftarrow (d_{max} - d[1]) \parallel d[1] \parallel (d[1] - d[2])$
12. $D[n] \leftarrow d[n] \parallel (d[n] - d_{min});\ return\ (D)$
13. $end\ if$

---

5   Integrity Preservation for Query Results

In this section, we propose differential chain, a novel data storage scheme that enables the sink to verify any forged or incomplete query result.

5.1   Differential Chain

The basic idea of differential chain is to embed the difference of two adjacent data items into the prior one, hence, data items are linked with each other just like a chain. The procedure for transforming the list of sensed data to a differential chain is shown in Algorithm 1. Here, " $\parallel$ " denotes the concatenation of data items.

After collecting n data items at the end of each epoch, sensor S_i firstly converts these sensed data into a corresponding differential chain, and then sends the encrypted differential chain of $(D_{i,1})_{k_{i,t}}$, $(D_{i,2})_{k_{i,t}}$, ..., $(D_{i,n})_{k_{i,t}}$, instead of $(d_{i,1})_{k_{i,t}}$, $(d_{i,2})_{k_{i,t}}$, ..., $(d_{i,n})_{k_{i,t}}$, to its closest storage node.

For simplicity, we assume that all data items are different from each other. In fact, when come to the case in which some sensed data are the same, we can adjust our scheme by further embedding the sequence number of the sensed data into its predecessor. Hence, the embedded information for each data item will be unique.

5.2   Query Response

Note that if sensor S_i has β_i data items satisfying a *top-k* query, they must be the first β_i data items since data items are ordered before being sent to storage node. Then:

If $\beta_i = 0$, the storage node need to respond a *VI* (*Verification Information*) for sensor S_i for the final verification.

Storage $\rightarrow$ Sink : $VI_i = \{\ i,\ (D_{i,1})_{k_{i,t}}\}$

If $\beta_i \neq 0$, we call sensor S_i a qualified sensor, thus the satisfied *QR* (*Query Result*) of sensor S_i would be:

Storage $\rightarrow$ Sink : $QR_i = \{\ i,\ (D_{i,1})_{k_{i,t}},\ \dots,\ (D_{i,\beta_i})_{k_{i,t}}\}$.

After receiving a query result from storage node, the sink first decrypts QR_i for each qualified sensor using the secret key shared between each sensor and the sink, then obtains the final *top-k* result by extracting the embedded information from each data item. Finally, the sink verifies the authenticity and completeness of the query result by checking whether the differential chain of each sensor is complete or not. Only when the query result has passed the verification, will the result be received.

6   Analysis

6.1   Data Confidentiality Analysis

If a storage node is compromised, it wouldn't disclose any sensed data to attackers since each data is encrypted using a secret key only known by sensor itself and the sink. The only choice left for an attacker to obtain data information is the two aggregation results attached to each data item. However, by mapping each prefix to a unique prime randomly, attackers can only obtain the exact mapping relationship between prefixes and primes with probability $\frac{1}{(2^{w+1})!}$, where w is the bit length of each sensed data. Furthermore, the seed for the pseudorandom function varies with epoch changing, this means the mapping relationship between prefixes and primes will also change with epoch changing, which makes the inference even more difficult. Therefore, even if storage nodes are compromised, confidentiality of the collected data would be preserved.

6.2   Integrity Analysis

Theorem 6.1: Our scheme can enable the sink to detect any forged or incomplete top-k query result.

Proof: Consider a sensor S_i who has β_i data items satisfying the query, *i.e.*, $QR_i = \{(i)_{k_t},\ (D_{i,1})_{k_{i,t}},\ \dots,\ (D_{i,\beta_i})_{k_{i,t}}\}$. Since data items in QR_i are constructed into a chain, inserting forged data into or omitting qualified data from QR_i can be easily detected. An alternative way for a compromised storage node is to replace some qualified data of one sensor, say D_{i,β_i} of S_i, with some unqualified data of another sensor, say D_{j,β_j+1} of S_j, i.e., $QR_i = \{ (i)_{k_t}, (D_{i,1})_{k_{i,t}}, \ldots, (D_{i,\beta_i-1})_{k_{i,t}} \}$ and $QR_j = \{ (j)_{k_t}, (D_{j,1})_{k_{j,t}}, \ldots, (D_{j,\beta_j})_{k_{j,t}}, (D_{j,\beta_j+1})_{k_{j,t}} \}$. However, after extracting the embedded information from each data, the sink will know the existence of d_{i,β_i} with the difference extracted from D_{i,β_i-1}. Since there is still a data larger than one of the data in query result, i.e., $d_{i,\beta_i} > d_{j,\beta_j+1}$, the query result will be deemed as untrustworthy and discarded. Thus, any forged or incomplete query result can be detected.

6.3   Performance Analysis

In this paper, we use the following performance metrics to analyze and evaluate our proposed schemes.

C_{tra}-*Transmission Consumption*: the extra communication costs during a data submission for each sensor. The cost for transmitting actual data items, sensor ID and the epoch number will not be considered since it is inevitable for any scheme.

C_{spa}-*Space Consumption*: the space costs for a storage node to store the extra information received from the whole cell within an epoch.

C_q-*Query Consumption*: the extra communication costs for a storage node to respond a query. The cost for sending the satisfied k data items and the qualified node IDs will not be considered similarly.

We assume that each cell contains N sensors and each sensor S_i collects n data items during an epoch as we aforementioned, where $i \in [1, N]$. Recall that in our scheme, each data item is accompanied with two prime aggregation results when being submitted to storage node. These prime aggregation results contribute to the extra transmission consumption of our scheme. Specifically, let $lf_{i,h}$ and $lr_{i,h}$ be the bit length of the aggregation results of $PF_{i,h}$ and $PR_{i,h}$ respectively, then we can derive the extra transmission consumption C_{tra} for sensor S_i.

$$C_{tra} = \sum_{h=1}^{n} \left(lf_{i,h} + lr_{i,h} \right). \tag{1}$$

Similarly, we can derive the extra space consumption C_{spa} for a storage node.

$$C_{spa} = \sum_{i=1}^{N} \sum_{h=1}^{n} \left(lf_{i,h} + lr_{i,h} \right). \tag{2}$$

Note that in our scheme, except for the satisfied *top-k* query result, the storage node is asked to return the largest data item of each unqualified sensors for the sake of final integrity verification, which contributes to the additional query consumption of our scheme. Let l_{id} and l_d be the bit length of the encrypted node ID and the encrypted data respectively, and δu be the number of unqualified sensors, then we have

$$C_q = \delta_u \left(l_{id} + l_d \right). \tag{3}$$

7   Performance Evaluation

7.1   Evaluation Methodology

To compare SVTQ with the state-of-the-art presented by Zhang & Shi [21] which we call Z&S scheme, we implemented both schemes and performed side-by-side comparison on a large real data set from Intel Lab [10], which is collected from 54 sensors during one month. For easy division, we selected data from 45 sensors in our experiments and evenly divided these 45 sensors into 3 cells. Specially, for Z&S scheme, each cell is further divided into 3 subcells.

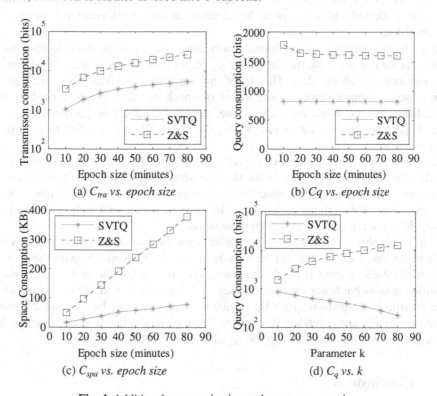

(a) C_{tra} vs. epoch size

(b) C_q vs. epoch size

(c) C_{spa} vs. epoch size

(d) C_q vs. k

Fig. 4. Additional communication and space consumption

7.2   Evaluation Setup

We adopted DES cipher in SVTQ as the encryption algorithm to encrypt sensor collected data. Since each block size in DES is 64 bits, there is enough space to embed the difference between two adjacent sensed data before we encrypted each data item. For the implementation of Z&S scheme, we adopted MD5 with 16-bit keys for massage authentication code (MAC) as mentioned in their scheme. We experimented on different size of epochs ranging from 10 minutes to 80 minutes. We also generated 8 different queries ranging from *top-10* to *top-80* to verify the impact of parameter k

on the communication cost of both schemes. We performed 1,000 times for each *top-k* query and took the average value as our final experimental results.

7.3   Result Analysis and Summary

Through our side-by-side comparison, we can see that SVTQ outperforms Z&S scheme in terms of power and space consumption while preserving the data confidentiality.

Fig. 4. (a) shows that as epoch size increases, both the transmission consumption of SVTQ and Z&S scheme grow up. This is clear since larger epoch means more data items are collected within an epoch, hence more additional information is needed to be submitted.

Fig. 4. (b) illustrates the additional query costs for a storage node to respond a query. As we can see from the figure, the C_q of our scheme remains unchanged with the variation of epoch size. This is of no surprise since the additional query consumption of our scheme is independent of epoch size and mainly caused by the unqualified sensors. While for Z&S scheme, the C_q is inversely proportional to epoch size. This is because the larger epoch size, the fewer IDs are attached to each data item as mentioned in [21].

Fig. 4. (c) demonstrates the extra space consumption on a storage node during an epoch. We can learn from the figure that the space consumption in both schemes grows up with the increase of epoch size. The reason is obvious since larger epoch size means more data items are collected by sensors within an epoch, and therefore more additional information is needed to be stored.

Fig. 4. (d) shows the impact of parameter k on the additional costs for a storage node to respond a query. We can see that the C_q of SVTQ decreases with the growth of k while Z&S scheme is on the contrary. This is because larger k implies more qualified sensors but fewer unqualified ones, and therefore less additional information is needed to be responded in SVTQ. While for Z&S scheme, larger k means more additional MACs and redundant IDs returned with each qualified data item, hence, the extra query costs of Z&S scheme grow up when parameter k increases.

8   Conclusions

In this paper, we propose SVTQ, a novel and efficient query protocol for processing *top-k* query in two-tiered sensor networks. SVTQ can precisely process *top-k* queries while preserving data confidentiality. SVTQ also enables the sink to detect any forged or incomplete query result efficiently. Experiments on the real-world data set show that SVTQ significantly outperforms the state-of-the-art in terms of both communication and storage consumption while preserving data confidentiality.

Acknowledgements. This work is supported in part by the National Natural Science Foundation of China (Project No. 61173038) and Important National Science & Technology Support Projects of China (Project No. 2012BAH09B02).

References

1. Boldyreva, A., Chenette, N., O'Neill, A.: Order-Preserving Encryption Revisited: Improved Security Analysis and Alternative Solutions. In: Rogaway, P. (ed.) CRYPTO 2011. LNCS, vol. 6841, pp. 578–595. Springer, Heidelberg (2011)
2. Chang, Y.K.: Fast binary and multiway prefix searches for packet forwarding. Computer Networks 51(3), 588–605 (2007)
3. Chen, F., Liu, A.X.: SafeQ: Secure and Efficient Query Processing in Sensor Networks. In: Proceedings of the 29th IEEE International Conference on Computer Communications, INFOCOM 2010, pp. 1–9. IEEE, California (2010)
4. Cheng, J., Yang, H., Wong, S.H.Y., Zerfos, P., Lu, S.: Design and Implementation of Cross-Domain Cooperative Firewall. In: Proceedings of the IEEE International Conference on Network Protocols, ICNP 2007, pp. 284–293. IEEE, Beijing (2007)
5. Desnoyers, P., Ganesan, D., Li, H., Shenoy, P.: Presto: A predictive storage architecture for sensor networks. In: 10th Workshop on Hot Topics in Operating Systems, HotOS 2005, pp. 23–28. USENIX, New Mexico (2005)
6. Fürer, M.: Faster integer multiplication. In: Proceedings of the 39th ACM Symposium on Theory of Computing, STOC 2007, pp. 57–66. ACM, New York (2007)
7. Gupta, P., McKeown, N.: Algorithms for packet classification. IEEE Network 15(2), 24–32 (2001)
8. Hacigümüs, H., Iyer, B., Li, C., Mehrotra, S.: Executing SQL over encrypted data in the database-service-provider model. In: Proceedings of the ACM Conference on Management of Data, SIGMOD 2002, pp. 216–227. ACM, New York (2002)
9. Hore, B., Mehrotra, S., Tsudik, G.: A privacy-preserving index for range queries. In: Proceedings of the 30th International Conference on Very Large Data Bases, VLDB 2004, pp. 720–731. ACM, Toronto (2004)
10. Intel lab data, http://db.csail.mit.edu/labdata/labdata.html
11. Liao, X., Li, J.: Privacy-preserving and secure top-k query in two-tier wireless sensor network. In: Proceedings of the IEEE Global Communications Conference, GLOBECOM 2012, pp. 335–341. IEEE, California (2012)
12. Liu, A.X., Chen, F.: Collaborative enforcement of firewall policies in virtual private networks. In: Proceedings of the 27th ACM Symposium on Principles of Distributed Computing, PODC 2008, pp. 95–104. ACM, New York (2008)
13. Ratnasamy, S., Karp, B., Shenker, S., Estrin, D., Govindan, R., Yin, L., Yu, F.: Data-Centric Storage in Sensornets with GHT, a Geographic Hash Table. Mobile Networks and Applications 8(4), 427–442 (2003)
14. Rise project, http://www.cs.ucr.edu/rise
15. Sheng, B., Li, Q., Mao, W.: Data storage placement in sensor networks. In: Proceedings of the 7th ACM International Symposium on Mobile Ad hoc Networking and Computing, MobiHoc 2006, pp. 344–355. ACM, New York (2006)
16. Sheng, B., Li, Q.: Verifiable Privacy-Preserving Range Query in Two-Tiered Sensor Networks. In: Proceedings of the 27th IEEE International Conference on Computer Communications, INFOCOM 2008, pp. 46–50. IEEE, Phoenix (2008)
17. Sheng, B., Tan, C.C., Li, Q., Mao, W.: An Approximation Algorithm for Data Storage Placement in Sensor Networks. In: Proceedings of the International Conference on Wireless Algorithms, Systems and Applications, pp. 71–78. IEEE, Chicago (2007)

18. Shi, J., Zhang, Y., Zhang, Y.: Secure Range Queries in Tiered Sensor Networks. In: Proceedings of the 28th IEEE International Conference on Computer Communications, INFOCOM 2009, pp. 945–953. IEEE, Rio de Janeiro (2009)
19. Stargate gateway (spb400), http://www.xbow.com
20. Zeinalipour-yazti, D., Lin, S., Kalogeraki, V., Gunopulos, D., Najjar, W.A.: Microhash: An efficient index structure for flash-based sensor devices. In: Proceedings of the 4th Conference on File and Storage Technologies, FAST 2005, pp. 31–44. USENIX, Newcastle upon Tyne (2005)
21. Zhang, Y., Shi, J., Liu, Y., Zhang, Y.: Verifiable Fine-Grained Top-k Queries in Tiered Sensor Networks. In: Proceedings of the 29th IEEE International Conference on Computer Communications, INFOCOM 2010, pp. 1–9. IEEE, California (2010)

CamTalk: A Bidirectional Light Communications Framework for Secure Communications on Smartphones

Mengjun Xie[1], Liang Hao[1], Kenji Yoshigoe[1], and Jiang Bian[2]

[1] University of Arkansas at Little Rock, Little Rock, AR 72204, USA
{mxxie,lxhao,kxyoshigoe}@ualr.edu
[2] University of Arkansas for Medical Sciences, Little Rock, AR 72205, USA
jbian@uams.edu

Abstract. In this paper we present CamTalk, a novel bidirectional communications framework using front-facing cameras and displays of smartphones. In the CamTalk framework, two smartphones exchange information via barcodes: information is encoded into barcodes that are displayed on the screen of the origin device, and those barcodes are captured by the front-facing camera of the destination device and decoded; Both devices can send and receive barcodes at the same time. The general design of data transmission enables CamTalk to support a wide range of applications. More importantly, CamTalk's communications channels are short-range, highly directional, fully observational, and immune to electromagnetic interference, which makes CamTalk very appealing for secure communications and bootstrapping security applications. We have implemented CamTalk on the Android platform and conducted extensive experiments to evaluate its performance on both Android smartphones and tablets. Our experimental results demonstrate the efficacy of CamTalk in short-range wireless communications.

Keywords: bidirectional light communications, mobile application, secure communication, key exchange.

1 Introduction

With the popularity of camera equipped smartphones, a nonconventional communications channel through display and camera becomes more accessible to smartphone users. It is already common for a smartphone user to obtain information through the phone's camera. For example, we can use a smartphone to easily scan a barcode (e.g., a UPC code [8] or QR code [7]) printed on an item sold in a grocery store or on an ad wallpaper and then read the information encoded by the barcode. The visual data channel for this type of uses has been leveraged to create new schemes of data streaming from a screen (e.g., LCD) to a smartphone [10,9,5] and to design new mechanisms of authentication [11,18]. However, information flows through the visual channels in those schemes and mechanisms are all unidirectional, which seriously limits the functions of

T. Zia et al. (Eds.): SecureComm 2013, LNICST 127, pp. 35–52, 2013.

those applications. For example, the mutual authentication protocol proposed in [18] has to introduce a second channel due to the visual channel being one way.

In this paper, we present CamTalk, a novel bidirectional communications framework using front-facing cameras and displays of smartphones. Similar to previous camera phone based schemes, CamTalk also employs barcode for information transmission. Information is encoded into barcodes that are displayed on the screen of the sending smartphone, and those barcodes are captured by the front-facing camera of the receiving smartphone and then decoded. However, by using front-facing cameras and displays, in the CamTalk framework, the smartphone that is receiving information can simultaneously send its data by rendering the corresponding barcodes on its display, and those barcodes can also be captured by the other party that is doing sending at the same time. To our best knowledge, CamTalk is the first bidirectional camera-based communications scheme for smartphones (and tablets).

Thanks to the communications medium, i.e., visible light, communications through CamTalk are short-range, highly directional, fully observational, and immune to electromagnetic interference. These properties make CamTalk an appealing choice for secure communications and mutual authentication between two smartphones in close proximity. CamTalk can further bootstrap other security applications. Diffie-Hellman key exchange, a basic building block for secure communications, can be easily implemented based on CamTalk to securely share a secret between two smartphones without prior knowledge of each other. The shared secret can be used not only for the CamTalk communications, but also for other communications such as those through Bluetooth and Wi-Fi.

We have implemented a fully functional prototype of CamTalk on the Android platform. Our prototype adopts ZXing library [20], a popular open source barcode processing library, for handling low-level barcode encoding and decoding. We choose QR code as the underlying barcode technique as a recent study shows that QR code has the best decoding performance among the barcodes supported by ZXing library [19]. We have conducted extensive experiments to evaluate the impacts of different factors on communications of CamTalk and measure its performance on both Android smartphones and tablets. Our experimental results demonstrate the efficacy of CamTalk in short-range wireless communications.

The rest of this paper is organized as follows: Section 2 briefly describes the background and related work. Section 3 presents the structure of CamTalk framework and the design of communications mechanisms, especially the two transport modes. Sections 4 and 5 detail the implementation of the prototype and its evaluation using Android smartphones and tablets, respectively. Section 6 discusses the applications of CamTalk in security. Section 7 concludes this paper and discusses future work.

2 Background and Related Work

2.1 Visible Light Communication

Recently, visible light communication (VLC) has received strong interest as an alternative wireless communication channel. Generally speaking, VLC refers to wireless information transmission (usually in a short range) using visible light through free space. A number of studies on VLC have been conducted, e.g., high-speed (gigabit rate) VLC using light emitting diodes (LEDs) [16] and VLC based indoor positioning [17]. Compared to radio frequency (RF) based wireless communications technologies, VLC has the following advantages: using unlicensed spectrum, being immune to electromagnetic interference, and having no interference with RF systems. More importantly, the communications medium, visible light, can also be used for illumination, display, decoration, etc. Besides using LEDs and photodiodes, researchers have also leveraged liquid crystal displays (LCDs) and digital cameras for visible light communications [15,6]. Existing systems based on the LCD-camera pair require high-end digital cameras and large and high resolution LCD screens and involve high computational overhead, which is relatively difficult for smartphones.

2.2 Barcode Techniques

A barcode is an optical machine-readable representation of information. There are two types of barcodes: one-dimensional (1D) barcodes and two-dimensional (2D) barcodes. 1D barcodes are usually made up of parallel lines (bars) with various widths and spacings representing specific patterns. Universal Product Code (UPC) [8] is a very popular 1D barcode. 2D barcodes encode data in rectangles, dots, hexagons and other geometric patterns in two dimensions. Popular 2D barcodes include QR code [7], Data Matrix code, MaxiCode, etc. The main differences between 1D and 2D barcodes lie in the amount of encoded data and the error correction they provide. In the past, reading of barcodes required special optical scanners called barcode readers. Nowadays, more devices including camera equipped mobile phones support barcode scanning and information interpretation [13].

Quick Response code (QR code) [7] is a popular 2D barcode. All major smartphone platforms including Android, iOS, Blackberry, and Windows Phone support QR code scanning either natively or through third-party applications. ZXing project [20] provides an open source cross-platform barcode scanning library, which fully supports QR code encoding and decoding. Compared to other 2D barcodes, QR code has more features including large capacity, small printout size, and high speed scan. Scheuermann *et al.* evaluated barcode decoding performance using ZXing library and reported that QR code delivers the best results [19]. The amount of data that can be stored in a QR code symbol depends on the data type (mode), version (indicating the overall dimensions of the symbol), and error correction level.

Traditionally, barcodes use only black and white for information encoding. With the popularity of the camera based barcode scanning techniques that are capable of detecting colors, more colors are used to develop new types of barcodes with higher information capacity. High Capacity Color Barcode (HCCB) [14] is such a colored 2D barcode that employs clusters of colored triangles for encoding data. Langlotz and Bimber proposed another type of colored 2D barcode called 4D barcodes, which essentially are time-multiplexing colored 2D barcodes. Liu *et al.* proposed a video barcode scheme called VCode in [10] and analyzed its data transmission capacity in [9]. Hao *et al.* presented another 2D barcode scheme for data streaming on smartphones, called COBRA, in [5]. Both VCode and COBRA rely on specially designed colored 2D barcodes and use those barcodes to achieve high-speed data streaming between a screen and a smartphone. CamTalk is distinct from VCode and COBRA schemes in that data communications in CamTalk are bidirectional while in those schemes are unidirectional. In addition, CamTalk can adopt VCode and COBRA barcode techniques as its communications building block.

2.3   Mobile Visual Channel

Mobile visual channel has been applied to security applications. McCure *et al.* proposed an authentication scheme called Seeing-is-Believing (SiB) [11], which leverages the visual channel between a 2D barcode and a camera phone for authentication and demonstrative identification of devices. The visual channel of SiB is unidirectional. Therefore, operations requiring bidirectional communications such as Diffie-Hellman key exchange have to be decomposed into multiple unidirectional operations and direction switches must be coordinated manually.

Sexena *et al.* proposed a secure device pairing protocol, VIC (Visual authentication based on Integrity Checking), based on a visual channel [18]. Similar to SiB, the visual channel in [18] is also unidirectional. To achieve mutual authentication in secure device pairing, another insecure channel, e.g., Bluetooth, is introduced in VIC.

SiB and VIC are two special authentication schemes built on top of a unidirectional mobile visual channel. Compared to them, the bidirectional communications capability makes CamTalk support Diffie-Hellman key exchange and mutual authentication in an easier and automatic manner. Moreover, CamTalk supports more general communications such as file transfer.

3   System Design

CamTalk is designed as a wireless communication framework for smart mobile devices (e.g., smartphones and smart tablets) that enables bidirectional communications between two devices solely through display-camera links. As an analogy of face-to-face talk between two persons, CamTalk aims to achieve a face-to-face "talk" between two mobile devices. Thus, CamTalk merely requires mobile devices with a front-facing camera and a display of reasonable resolution, which are ubiquitous for today's smartphones and smart tablets. CamTalk is designed for short-range communications. Depending upon the display size and camera

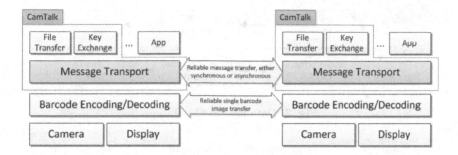

Fig. 1. The architecture of CamTalk framework

capability, the distance between two communicating devices can vary, e.g., from around ten centimeters to fifty centimeters in our experiments. Given the strong directional communication medium, fully observational communication process, and being entirely free from radio frequency interference, CamTalk provides a unique and advantageous channel for secure communications between two mobile devices.

Figure 1 depicts the architecture of CamTalk. The CamTalk framework relies on reliable single barcode image transfer provided by the underlying barcode encoding/decoding service, which is further supported by barcode scanning through front-facing camera and barcode rendering through device display. Making an analogy between CamTalk and a normal networking stack, CamTalk comprises the transport layer and part of the application layer. Based on the service of single barcode image transfer, the message transport layer of CamTalk realizes bidirectional reliable message transfer between two mobile devices, in either synchronous or asynchronous mode, and provides it as a service to the upper application layer. To demonstrate the efficacy and facilitate application development of CamTalk, two directly applicable applications, file transfer and Diffie-Hellman key exchange, are also incorporated into CamTalk. The design of CamTalk eases the development of other applications based on visible light communications, e.g., achieving secure file transfer through an encrypted channel by leveraging the existing file transfer and key exchange applications or building it directly on top of the message transport layer.

CamTalk framework is orthogonal to the underlying barcode technique, as illustrated in Figure 1. In other words, the design of CamTalk is generic, applicable to a variety of barcodes, and different implementations of CamTalk may use different barcodes that best suit the application requirements and given conditions (e.g., hardware capabilities, environment constraints, etc) for information transmission. In our prototype, we adopt QR code as the barcode encoding/decoding mechanism given its popularity and ubiquitous support on smart mobile devices.

For bidirectional communications, each CamTalk device is capable of both sending and receiving information, that is, encoding and rendering a barcode and scanning and decoding a barcode image. Figure 2 shows the data flow in CamTalk and those modules involved in data sending and receiving. The message to be

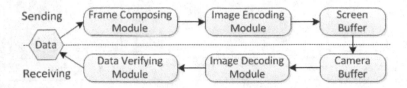

Fig. 2. Data flow in CamTalk

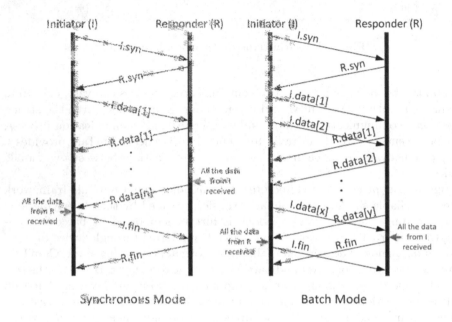

Fig. 3. Two message transport modes of CamTalk

transferred may be too large to be conveyed by a barcode image. Therefore, a large message will be split by the frame composing module into multiple smaller segments that can fit into a barcode image (also called frame). Then, each segment is encoded into a barcode by the image encoding module and copied into the screen buffer for rendering. When a picture is taken by the camera, the content in the camera buffer will be examined by the image decoding module. If the content contains a recognizable barcode and that barcode image can be successfully decoded, the decoded data will be validated and merged if necessary by the data verifying module. In practice, data sending and receiving can be carried out simultaneously by CamTalk.

A message can be transported in different fashions. To explore the display-camera channel capacity and provide flexibility, CamTalk incorporates two transport modes: synchronous mode and batch mode, which are illustrated in Figure 3. Alternation between sending and receiving is enforced for communications in the synchronous mode, in other words, frame $i+1$ cannot be sent out before the frame i from the other party is successfully received. On the other hand, multiple frames can be sent out in a batch without waiting for the reception of the corresponding frames from the other party. For better presentation, we only show ideal scenarios of communications in the two modes in Figure 3. For example, duplicate or out-of-order frame transmissions that are possible in the Batch mode are not shown in the diagrams. In the diagrams, the party initiating the communication is called initiator and the other party is called responder. The initiator and responder are no difference in functionality and their roles are solely dependent on which initiates the communication.

There are two types of frames–control frame and data frame–in the communication. Control frames include (1) `syn` (for synchronization) and `fin` (for finish) frames sent at the beginning and ending of communications in either mode, respectively, and (2) status frames, which are used to notify the other party what frames are missing in the current batch, in the batch mode (not shown in the Batch Mode diagram in Figure 3). Each frame has a header and payload. To reduce overhead, a frame header has a sequence number and an acknowledgment number, each taking two bytes. The choice of small sequence number space is based on that CamTalk is intended for transferring a relatively small amount of data as an alternative to RF channels. The payload for `syn` frames contains the size of the whole message (in bytes), the capacity in a data frame (in bytes), and some other meta information. The payload for `fin` frames contains the SHA-256 hash value of the message for verifying data integrity. The exchange of `syn` frames before actual data transmission also has a practical consideration–to ensure the establishment of communication channels. If the display-camera links are not set up appropriately, `syn` frames will not be exchanged, i.e., the content in the screen will not change. A user usually needs to adjust the distance and positions of two CamTalk devices before communications and the visual changes of barcodes notify her of the establishment of the links.

4 Implementation

We have implemented a prototype system of CamTalk that runs on the Android platforms (API level $\geq$ 15) and works for both smartphones and tablets. Our implementation uses ZXing [20] (version 2.1) for underlying barcode encoding and decoding. The cross-platform compatibility of ZXing will ease the porting of our prototype to other mobile platforms such as iOS for iPhone. The prototype consists of around 2,300 lines of Java code (excluding ZXing library).

Our prototype is implemented as a standalone application (refer to as "CamTalk" in the remaining of the section for simplicity), supporting general information exchanges and also providing file transfer and Diffie-Hellmen key exchange functions. Thanks to the Android framework, CamTalk can also be invoked by other applications for information exchange through camera-display links, similar to how a barcode scanner application is invoked by another application such as Amazon mobile app on an Android smartphone.

Figure 4 (in Section 5.1) shows the communication interface of CamTalk on a Motorola Atrix 4G smartphone. The phone screen is split into two parts: The top half (in portrait/vertical orientation) is for communication by displaying the barcode in an ImageView instance. The bottom half shows the view captured by the front-facing camera using a SurfaceView instance. The rationale for displaying a barcode at the top half (or the half closer to the front-facing camera) is that most of smartphones and smart tables place their front-facing cameras at the top. Thus, it is relatively easier to capture a barcode at the top than at the bottom of the display when two phones are placed face to face for communication. The bottom camera view is primarily to help a user adjust the distance between and/or positions of the two devices for better communication quality.

The prototype of CamTalk follows modular and layered implementation practice. The display and capture of single barcode forms the basic building block of communication, similar to the transfer of an Ethernet frame between two LAN nodes. We implement the single barcade transfer function based on ZXing. Two transport modes–synchronous mode and batch transfer mode–are implemented as two modules in parallel on top of single barcode transfer service. The upper level application can decide which transport mode to use for a specific information transfer task.

The CamTalk prototype is a multi-threaded application, which employs multiple threads to speed up data processing and offload computation from the main thread (also called UI thread), following Android programming guide. The communications between threads are through messages (and handlers) and each module (encoding, decoding, transport) is developed in an event (or message) driven manner. The main thread is responsible for UI rendering and message dispatch. Two work threads are used by ZXing for encoding and decoding respectively. Transport module itself is implemented as a separate thread, handling message segmentation/assembly.

5   Evaluation

In this section, we describe how we evaluate the CamTalk prototype. We use three types of mobile devices all with both front-facing camera and display, and their hardware parameters related to our evaluation are listed in Table 1. From the table, we can see that the front-facing cameras have rather low resolutions and their positions vary. The Android platform versions on Atrix 4G, Nexus S, and Nexus 7 are 4.1.2, 4.1.1, and 4.2.2, respectively. As Android 2.3.6 is the latest version officially supported for Atrix 4G, we install a customized cyanogenmod version on our Atrix 4G phones for meeting the API level requirement of our prototype. Most of our experiments are carried out between two devices of the same type, that is, Atrix phones or Nexus 7 tablets. We also test the CamTalk between two different phones and between one phone and one tablet, and those devices are held in hand. Our experiments confirm that CamTalk can be used between two different devices in practice.

Since bidirectional communications through visible light between smart mobile devices have not been reported yet, our evaluation mainly focuses on the communication performance of CamTalk. We categorize the factors that can affect the communication performance into two categories: external and internal.

Table 1. The smart mobile devices used in the experiments

Device (type)	Motorola Atrix 4G (phone)	Google Nexus 7 (tablet)	Google Nexus S (phone)
Release Time (in the U.S.)	Feb. 2011	July 2012	Dec. 2010
CPU	1 GHz ARM A9 (dual-core)	1.2 GHz ARM A9 (quad-core)	1 GHz ARM A8 (single-core)
Front-facing Camera	0.3 Megapixels (top left)	1.2 Megapixels (top middle)	0.3 Megapixels (top right)
Display Size	4.0 inch	7.0 inch	4.0 inch
Display Resolution	540 × 960	1280 × 800	480 × 800

(a)   (b)

Fig. 4. The experiment testbed. These two pictures are for demonstration purpose, therefore not taken in a real experiment. The light was turned off for better display of phone screen in Figure (a). The phone in Figure (b) was rotated around both Y-axis and Z-axis.

The external category consists of those factors that are not CamTalk specific, including distance, rotations, lighting, etc. The factors in the internal category are related to the CamTalk design, including barcode image size, barcode capacity (i.e., number of bytes encoded in a barcode), barcode error correction level, etc. Note that we only study those factors that are not implementation specific. In the following, we first describe how CamTalk is affected by the external factors and then detail the impact made by the internal factors. After that, we present the experiment results of CamTalk's throughput with the two transport modes described in Section 3.

To conduct the experiments in CamTalk evaluation, we make a simple testbed as shown in Figure 4. Figure 4 (a) shows the scenario of CamTalk communication between two Atrix phones when they are aligned face to face, and Figure 4 (b) illustrates the rotation of device. Without further notice, all the experiments in the following are conducted on the testbed.

5.1   Impact of External Factors

As CamTalk employs visible light as its communication medium, many external factors can affect CamTalk, including ambient light, screen brightness, screen reflection, distance, rotations, etc. Among them, we have quantitatively studied the impact of distance and rotations on the communication, as those two factors can be easily controlled by a user and their effects can be instantly observed.

We use the decoding rate, the percentage of successfully decoded barcodes, as the metric to measure the impact of distance and rotations. As the barcode image size can affect decoding, we measure the decoding rate with two different sizes of barcode image: medium size and large size. The medium and large sizes are relative to the device display dimension; therefore, the dimension of a medium-sized or large barcode may vary on different devices. The length of a medium-sized QR code is 65% of the half of the longer side of the display and that of a large QR code is 90%. Both medium-sized and large barcodes contain the same amount of payload (32 bytes) in the experiments.

Ambient Light and Screen Brightness We observe that dark or very bright ambient lighting conditions can significantly degrade and even disable the CamTalk communications. When the ambient light is too bright, e.g., the phone screen under direct light of a fluorescent tube, the screen reflection will become very strong and therefore sharply worsen the quality of images taken by a front-facing camera. We conduct all the experiments in an indoor environment with illuminance of 400 to 500 *lux*, measured by Mastech Light Meter LX1010B.

With this ambient lighting, we find that it is easier to successfully decode a barcode image when the screen brightness is relatively low (e.g., half full brightness or less). The better decoding rate with lower brightness is attributed to the reduced screen reflection. When two phones or tablets are placed face to face in close proximity (tens of centimeters), high screen brightness will cause strong screen reflection. The impact of screen brightness on the communication performance is negligible when the brightness is relatively low (between 30 *lux* and 160 *lux*). The device screen brightness in the following experiments is between 40 *lux* and 80 *lux*, measured by the same light meter.

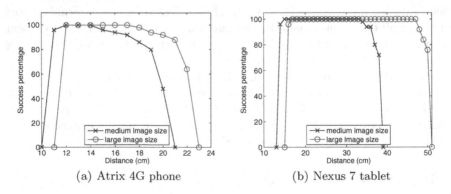

(a) Atrix 4G phone   (b) Nexus 7 tablet

Fig. 5. The impact of distance

Distance. We measure the impact of distance on both smartphones and tablets. The two devices, one as sender and the other as receiver, are aligned face to face without shifting or rotation in the experiments, as illustrated in Figure 4 (a). We measure the decoding rate with different distances and show them in Figure 5. Apparently, the larger the barcode image, the longer the distance allowed for communication. The practical communication distance for Atrix smartphone ranges approximately from 11cm to 22cm, while that for Nexus 7 tablet is from 15cm up to 50cm. The ideal distances for Atrix and Nexus 7 are 12-14cm and 17cm-33cm respectively, where a barcode image (either medium-sized or large) can always be decoded successfully.

The effective communication distance of CamTalk can vary in practical use but should not significantly deviate from the measured range under similar conditions. The short-range and observational communication properties of CamTalk offer high security assurance.

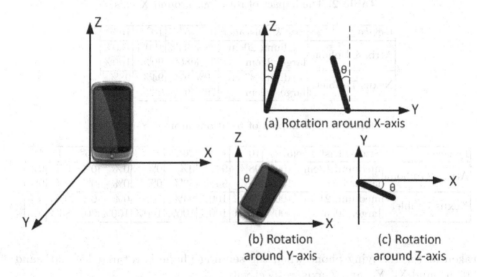

Fig. 6. Illustration of rotations around X-, Y-, and Z-axis. θ represents the rotation degree.

Rotations. Devices may be rotated in different manners and those rotations have different impacts on the decoding rate. We measure the impact of rotation around X-, Y-, and Z-axis respectively. Figure 6 illustrates how a device is rotated around X-, Y-, and Z-axis with a certain degree. Note that both the sending device and receiving device are rotated with the same degree in the experiments for rotations around X-axis, as depicted in Figure 6 (a), while in the experiments for rotations around Y- and Z-axis, only the sending device is rotated and the receiving device stays fixed. Without further notice, both devices in the following experiments are aligned initially. Figure 7 shows the pictures

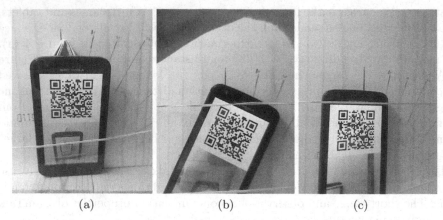

(a)   (b)   (c)

Fig. 7. The snapshots of rotations around (a) X-axis, (b) Y-axis, and Z-axis

Table 2. The impact of rotations around X-axis

Device	Size & Distance	0°	5°	10°	15°
Atrix 4G phone	medium, 20cm	48%	94%	100%	100%
	large, 22cm	64%	86%	90%	100%
Nexus 7 tablet	medium, 37cm	80%	92%	94%	98%
	large, 50cm	76%	90%	92%	100%

Table 3. The impact of rotations around Y-axis

Device	Size & Distance	5°	10°	15°	20°	25°	30°	35°	40°	45°
Atrix 4G phone	medium, 13cm	100%	98%	94%	0%	0%	0%	0%	0%	0%
	large, 15cm	100%	95%	94%	80%	0%	0%	0%	0%	0%
Nexus 7 tablet	medium, 21cm	100%	100%	100%	94%	90%	0%	0%	0%	0%
	large, 30cm	100%	100%	100%	100%	100%	100%	90%	84%	0%

taken at the receiving phone when the sending phone is rotated 15°, 20°, and 20° around X-, Y-, and Z-axis, respectively.

Because the front-facing camera is at the top of the device in the portrait orientation, when Atrix phones or Nexus 7 tablets are tilted forward (device bottom fixed) towards each other in a small degree, the distance between the barcode and the camera is shortened. Thanks to the tolerance of QR code to the perspective distortion brought by the rotation, shortened distance increases the possibility of barcode image being successfully decoded. Table 2 shows the impact of X rotation on the decoding rate when two devices are placed in such a distance that only partial barcodes can be decoded without rotation. Clearly, small scale rotations around X-axis help decoding.

Tables 3 and 4 show the average decoding rates when the sending device is rotated a certain degree around Y- and Z-axis, respectively. We can see that those rotations affect the decoding rate negatively. Due to this reason, the devices are placed in an ideal distance for each experiment. When the sending device is

Table 4. The impact of rotations around Z-axis

Device	Size & Distance	5°	10°	15°	20°	25°	30°
Atrix 4G phone	medium, 13cm	100%	100%	96%	90%	0%	0%
	large, 15cm	100%	98%	94%	94%	0%	0%
Nexus 7 tablet	medium, 21cm	100%	100%	96%	94%	82%	0%
	large, 30cm	100%	100%	98%	94%	74%	0%

rotated beyond a certain degree, the barcode image is either moved out of the camera view partially or entirely or distorted too much so that image decoding will fail.

5.2 Impact of Internal Factors

The internal factors we mainly consider include QR code error correction level, QR code data capacity, and QR code image size. We use encoding time and decoding time as the metrics for measuring the impact of each of those factors on CamTalk performance.

We first consider the QR code error correction level and its impact on encoding and decoding. QR code uses Reed-Solomon error correction algorithm with four levels: low (L), medium (M), quartile (Q), and high (Q). The higher the level, the more errors can be corrected. We measure the times of encoding and decoding at each of these four levels and find no significant difference among them. Therefore, we use error correction level M in the rest of experiments.

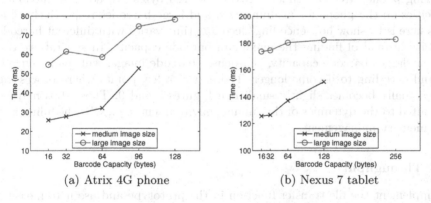

(a) Atrix 4G phone   (b) Nexus 7 tablet

Fig. 8. Average encoding time

Barcode data capacity and image size are two major internal factors that affect the encoding and decoding performance. Barcode capacity refers to the amount of data, including both header and payload, carried by each data frame (excluding the error correction bits). Figures 8 and 9 display how the average encoding time and decoding time vary with different capacity and image size,

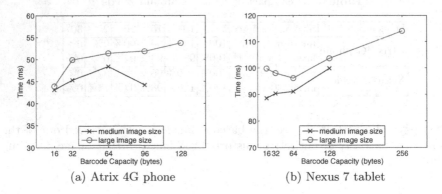

(a) Atrix 4G phone   (b) Nexus 7 tablet

Fig. 9. Average decoding time

respectively. In those experiments, two devices are well aligned and in an appropriate distance. Intuitively, larger image size with more pixels will take more time for encoding and decoding, which is confirmed by our experiment results. The increase of encoding time is more evident than that of decoding time, which is true for both phone and tablet.

To study the impact of barcode capacity, we measure the average encoding and decoding times with different capacity but same image size. Constrained by the camera capability (e.g., resolution), the maximum capacity for different barcode image size varies. For example, a medium-sized QR code on the Atrix phone cannot contain 128-byte data, which simply cannot be decoded at the receiving phone. We note that 96 bytes and 128 bytes are not the maximum capacities on the phone for medium-sized and large barcodes respectively. The focus here is to show how encoding/decoding time varies with different barcode capacity instead of finding the maximum barcode capacity. In general, we can see that larger barcode capacity, i.e., denser barcode image, will render encoding and decoding to become longer. There exist a few points where processing time actually becomes slightly smaller in Figures 8 and 9. Those dips may be attributed to the dynamics of the running environment, e.g., OS scheduling and Java memory management.

5.3   Throughput

We implement the file transfer function in the prototype and use it to measure the throughput in each of the two transport modes. The throughput is obtained by dividing the size of file over the duration from sending the first data frame to sending the `fin` frame (indicating that all data frames have been received). Note that we only measure unidirectional file transfers to simplify the experiments, while CamTalk supports bidirectional information transmission. Thus, the effective throughputs should be the double of those results.

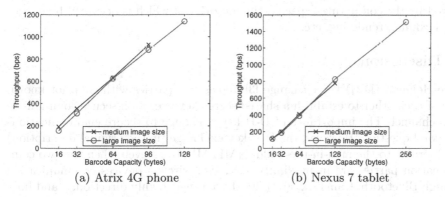

(a) Atrix 4G phone   (b) Nexus 7 tablet

Fig. 10. Average throughput in the synchronous mode

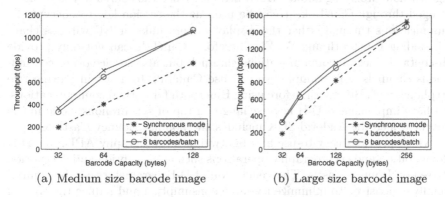

(a) Medium size barcode image   (b) Large size barcode image

Fig. 11. Average throughput in the batch mode on Nexus 7 tablet

Figure 10 presents the relationship between throughput and barcode capacity (size) in the synchronous mode. Interestingly, a linear relation between throughput and barcode capacity exhibits, and appears insensitive to the size of barcode, which applies to both the phone and the tablet. As doubling the barcode capacity halves the number of barcodes to be sent, that is, reducing the overall transmission time approximately to the half of the original, throughput is mainly affected by barcode capacity in the synchronous mode.

As multiple barcodes are sent in a batch in the batch mode, intuitively, the throughput in the batch mode should be higher than that in the synchronous mode. We compare the throughputs of 4 barcodes/batch and 8 barcodes/batch in the batch mode and the corresponding throughput in the synchronous mode on the tablet and show them in Figure 11. We can see that sending multiple barcodes in a batch does improve the throughput. However, the improvement becomes very small when doubling the number of barcodes from 4 to 8. There is even a slight performance degradation when doubling the number for large barcode capacities. The limitation of improvement can be attributed to the hardware capacity. When too many barcodes are sent consecutively, the throughput is limited by the computing capacity, the majority of which is occupied by encoding, decoding, rendering, etc.

6 Discussions

Diffie-Hellman (D-H) key exchange [3] allows two parties without prior knowledge of each other to establish a shared secret key over an insecure communications channel. The importance of D-H key exchange to secure communications is beyond question. However, the D-H key exchange (in the original description) is vulnerable to the man-in-the-middle (MITM) attack even when the two communication parties are in proximity, e.g., two wireless devices communicating through Bluetooth. CamTalk, given its short-range, highly directional, and fully observational communications characteristics, can use D-H protocol for key exchange without worrying about MITM attacks. Once the shared key is securely exchanged through CamTalk, it can be used as the session key to encrypt the communications through either the display-camera links or RF wireless channels including Bluetooth and Wi-Fi. Therefore, CamTalk can not only provide a self-contained secure communications channel, but also service other communications channels. For example, we can use CamTalk to assist in pairing two smartphones with Bluetooth before using Bluetooth for normal communications.

We have implemented D-H key exchange on top of synchronous mode in the prototype. Since the Andorid SDK includes the popular Bouncy Castle Crypto suite, which provides easy-to-use and lightweight cryptography APIs, our D-H implementation and cryptographic operations such as encryption and decryption are based on Bouncy Castle. The generation of D-H parameters can be computationally expensive. To minimize resource consumption and reduce the time of key pair generation, we use the pre-generated safe 1024-bit prime modulus for D-H as suggested in [1] on the devices of CamTalk. Each device independently generates a large random number as its private key and then exchange the public key. Combining the other party's public key and its private key, a shared secret key can be derived. Thanks to the layered implementation of CamTalk, the public keys can be easily transferred as normal messages in both directions. The overhead of D-H key exchange mainly lies in computing the public keys and shared secret key. However, compared to the communication latency, computational overhead of D-H key exchange is minor. A D-H key exchange can be completed within 10 seconds using Atrix phones with barcode capacity being 64 bytes in the synchronous mode.

Offering a unique bidirectional communications channel, CamTalk can be extended beyond communications between mobile devices. For example, we envision that CamTalk may be applied to the communications between a smartphone and a PC or laptop equipped with a camera. Such extensions can catalyze new applications that leverage CamTalk for secure communications and authentication. Today, smartphones have become a popular choice of the second factor in a two-factor authentication (TFA) system. In conventional phone-based TFA systems, e.g., Mobile-OTP [12] and Google 2-step verification [4], the authentication process requires a user to manually enter a one-time password (OTP) received by the smartphone on a PC to authenticate her identity. However, this manual input process may create usability issues and the OTP is usually short for easy type. Using CamTalk, we can replace manual typing by putting the smartphone in front of the PC camera and complete the authentication in an automatic manner. Without typing, longer OTPs can be employed to enhance the security. Bluetooth is a popular choice for the communications between a PC and a smartphone in many phone-based TFA systems, e.g., PhoneAuth proposed by Czeskis *et al.* [2]. However, Bluetooth is vulnerable to the RF interference and subjected to MITM and jamming attacks. CamTalk is free of those concerns and can replace Bluetooth as the communications channel. We note that this replacement cannot be achieved by previous visual channel based approaches (e.g., [11,18]) as those channels are unidirectional.

7 Conclusion

We have presented CamTalk, a novel bidirectional communications framework leveraging display-camera links on smart mobile devices, and discussed its application to secure communications in this paper. We have described the design and implementation of CamTalk in detail and conducted extensive experiments to evaluate its performance and understand the factors affecting its performance. Our experiments show the throughput of CamTalk can reach 3Kbps using a Nexus 7 tablet, which provides a reasonable user experience for transferring a small amount of sensitive data in a fairly secure manner.

The relatively low throughput is mainly attributed to the low capacity of front-facing cameras (less than 2 megapixels and no auto focus) and the underlying barcode technique, i.e., QR code, which is not designed for high-throughput data transfer. We plan to replace the QR code with other barcodes designed for data streaming such as COBRA [5] and assess the performance change of CamTalk.

Our future work also includes a usability study of CamTalk. We have tested practical uses such as file transfer using CamTalk on both smartphones and tablets by holding those devices in close proximity, in which placing two devices in an appropriate position takes several seconds. We want to know the experience of an average user in using CamTalk and improve CamTalk based on the feedback in the future.

References

1. Aziz, A., Markson, T., Prafullchandra, H.: IETF internet-draft: Simple key-management for internet protocols, skip (1995),
   http://tools.ietf.org/html/draft-ietf-ipsec-skip-06
2. Czeskis, A., Dietz, M., Kohno, T., Wallach, D., Balfanz, D.: Strengthening user authentication through opportunistic cryptographic identity assertions. In: Proceedings of the 2012 ACM CCS, pp. 404–414 (2012)
3. Diffie, W., Hellman, M.: New directions in cryptography. IEEE Trans. Inf. Theor. 22(6), 644–654 (2006)

4. Google. Google 2-step verification, http://www.google.com/landing/2step/
5. Hao, T., Zhou, R., Xing, G.: COBRA: color barcode streaming for smartphone systems. In: Proceedings of MobiSys 2012, pp. 85–98 (2012)
6. Hranilovic, S., Kschischang, F.: A pixelated mimo wireless optical communication system. IEEE Journal of Selected Topics in Quantum Electronics 12(4), 859–874 (2006)
7. International Organization for Standardization. ISO/IEC 18004:2006: Information technology – automatic identification and data capture techniques – QR code 2005 bar code symbology specification (2006)
8. International Organization for Standardization. ISO/IEC 15420:2009: Information technology – automatic identification and data capture techniques – EAN/UPC bar code symbology specification (2009)
9. Liu, X., Doermann, D., Li, H.: A camera-based mobile data channel: capacity and analysis. In: Proceedings of the 16th ACM International Conference on Multimedia, pp. 359–368 (2008)
10. Liu, X., Doermann, D., Li, H.: Vcode - pervasive data transfer using video barcode. IEEE Trans. Multi. 10(3), 361–371 (2008)
11. McCune, J.M., Perrig, A., Reiter, M.K.: Seeing-is-believing: Using camera phones for human-verifiable authentication. In: Proceedings of the 2005 IEEE Symposium on Security and Privacy, pp. 110–124 (2005)
12. Mobile-OTP Project. Mobile one time passwords, http://motp.sourceforge.net/
13. Ohbuchi, E., Hanaizumi, H., Hock, L.A.: Barcode readers using the camera device in mobile phones. In: Proceedings of the 2004 International Conference on Cyberworlds, pp. 260–265 (2004)
14. Parikh, D., Jancke, G.: Localization and segmentation of a 2d high capacity color barcode. In: Proceedings of the 2008 IEEE Workshop on Applications of Computer Vision, WACV 2008, pp. 1–6 (2008)
15. Perli, S.D., Ahmed, N., Katabi, D.: Pixnet: Interference-free wireless links using lcd-camera pairs. In: Proceedings of MOBICOM, pp. 137–148 (2010)
16. Pisek, E., Rajagopal, S., Abu-Surra, S.: Gigabit rate mobile connectivity through visible light communication. In: Proceedings of IEEE International Conference on Communications, pp. 3122–3127 (2012)
17. Rahman, M.S., Kim, K.-D.: Indoor location estimation using visible light communication and image sensors. International Journal of Smart Home 7(1), 99–114 (2013)
18. Saxena, N., Ekberg, J.E., Kostiainen, K., Asokan, N.: Secure device pairing based on a visual channel: Design and usability study. IEEE Trans. Info. For. Sec. 6(1), 28–38 (2011)
19. Scheuermann, C., Werner, M., Kessel, M., Linnhoff-Popien, C., Verclas, S.A.W.: Evaluation of barcode decoding performance using zxing library. In: Proceedings of the Second Workshop on Smart Mobile Applications, SmartApps 2012 (2012)
20. ZXing Project. ZXing–Multi-format 1D/2D barcode image processing library with clients for Android, Java (2013), https://code.google.com/p/zxing/

Botnet Triple-Channel Model: Towards Resilient and Efficient Bidirectional Communication Botnets

Cui Xiang[1], Fang Binxing[1,2], Shi Jinqiao[3], and Liu Chaoge[1]

[1] Institute of Computing Technology, Chinese Academy of Sciences, P.R. China
[2] Beijing University of Posts and Telecommunications, P.R. China
[3] Institute of Information Engineering, Chinese Academy of Sciences, P.R. China
cuixiang@ict.ac.cn

Abstract. Current research on future botnets mainly focuses on how to design a resilient *downlink* command and control (C&C) channel. However, the *uplink* data channel, which is generally vulnerable, inefficient even absent, has attracted little attention. In fact, most of current botnets (even large-scale and well-known) contain either a resilient (maybe also efficient) unidirectional downlink C&C channel or a vulnerable bidirectional communication channel, making the botnets either hard to monitor or easy to be taken down. To address the above problem and equip a botnet with resilient and efficient bidirectional communication capability, in this paper, we propose a communication channel division scheme and then establish a Botnet Triple-Channel Model (BTM). In a nutshell, BTM divides a traditional communication channel into three independent sub-channels, denoting as *Command Download Channel (CDC)*, *Registration Channel (RC) and Data Upload Channel (DUC)*, respectively. To illuminate the feasibility, we implement a BTM based botnet prototype named *RoemBot*, which exploits URL Flux for CDC, Domain Flux for RC and Cloud Flux for DUC. We also evaluate the resilience and efficiency of RoemBot. In the end, we attempt to make a conclusion that resilient and efficient bidirectional communication design represents a main direction of future botnets.

Keywords: Botnet, C&C, BTM, URL Flux, Domain Flux, Cloud Flux.

1 Introduction

A botnet refers to a group of compromised computers that are remotely controlled by botmasters via C&C channels. Botnets are the main cause of many Internet attacks such as DDoS, Email spam, seeding malware, and the recent BitCoin Mining [1, 2, 28] etc. As botnet-based attacks become popular and dangerous, researchers have studied how to detect, track, measure and mitigate them. Besides, some researchers focus on possible design of future botnets in order to fight against them [3-9]. However, current research on future botnets **only** focuses on how to design a resilient and efficient *downlink* (from botmasters to bots, generally used to deliver commands and new executables) C&C channel. However, the *uplink* (from bots to botmasters,

T. Zia et al. (Eds.): SecureComm 2013, LNICST 127, pp. 53–68, 2013.

generally used to monitor botnets and collect data) data channel, which is generally vulnerable, inefficient even absent in most of current botnets, has attracted little attention. In this paper, we mainly focus on the problem and discuss the model, feasibility and methodology of designing a resilient and efficient bidirectional communication botnet which supports both a resilient downlink C&C channel and an efficient uplink data channel. This kind of advanced botnet will no doubt be very attractive for botmasters, thus we should promote the development of more efficient countermeasures in advance.

1.1   Weaknesses of Current Botnets

The first generation botnets have a static centralized topology. The earliest well-known botnets, such as SDbot, Rbot and Agobot, mainly use the IRC protocol. In order to be stealthier, botmasters begin to adopt HTTP protocol, such as Bobax, Rustock, Clickbot and Coreflood. Due to the static centralized topology and the hardcoded C&C servers, both IRC and HTTP based botnets surfer from the single-point-of-failure problem. That is, once the domain name and IP address are located by defenders, the whole botnet could be shut down easily. For example, the well-known Rustock and Coreflood botnets have been taken down on Mar. 2011 and Apr. 2011, respectively [19].

The second generation botnets turn to adopt a decentralized topology, such as Slapper, Nugache, Storm [22], Waledac [20], Kelihos [16], Zeus [15] and ZeroAccess [21]. It's generally admitted that the essential driving force of the botnet evolution from centralized to decentralized structure is to eliminate the single-point-of-failure problem. At first glance, P2P botnets seem to be more resilient to takedown attempts than centralized botnets, because they have no single-point-of-failure. However, previous work has shown that P2P-based botnets are not really secure [10, 11, 22]. For structured P2P botnets which employ distributed hash table (DHT), such as Storm, are vulnerable to Index Poisoning and Sybil attack [11] inevitably; for unstructured P2P botnets which use custom P2P protocols, such as Waledac, Miner [1, 2], Zeus and ZeroAccess, are vulnerable to crawling and sensor injecting inescapably [10]. For example, the well-known Waledac and Kelihos botnets have been taken down on Feb. 2010 and Sep. 2011, respectively [19]. Another significant problem is that P2P botnets have no uplink data channel, so it is difficult for a P2P botnet to monitor the botnet and collect information from bots. To build a temporal uplink data channel, temporal central servers are indispensible.

Based on the above analysis, we can see that a resilient and efficient bidirectional communication botnet is more desirable than a P2P botnet. Therefore, the third generation botnets, such as Conficker [23] and Torpig, begin to adopt a dynamic centralized topology named Domain Flux. However, Domain Flux is significantly limited by the performance of C&C servers, making uploading massive files by large-scale botnets very hard. Furthermore, if the authentication mechanism is not strong enough, the botnet will suffer from sinkhole attack. For example, the well-known Torpig [24] and Kraken [27] botnets have been sinkholed by defenders on Jan. 2009 and Apr. 2008, respectively.

To the best of our knowledge, most of current botnets (even large-scale and well-known) contains either a resilient (perhaps also efficient) unidirectional downlink C&C channel or a vulnerable bidirectional communication channel, making the botnets either hard to monitor or easy to be taken down. How to construct a resilient and efficient bidirectional communication botnet poses a great challenge to this day.

1.2   Intrinsic Cause Analysis

The internal cause of the above problems can partly explained by the fact that current botnets always rely on only one C&C protocol to accomplish all tasks, however, it is impossible for any existing C&C protocol to satisfy all requirements solely. For example, the relatively resilient P2P and URL Flux [5] protocols are limited by monitorability; the recoverable Domain Flux protocol is limited by robustness and efficiency. In a word, each C&C protocol has its particular advantages as well as corresponding limitations. Although Conficker employs both Domain Flux and P2P protocols, it only use its P2P components as backup channels in case the Domain Flux being ineffective. The proposed Botnet Triple-Channel Model aims at solving the problem to some degree.

1.3   Proposed Bidirectional Communication Botnet

Considering the above problems encountered by current botnets, the design of an advanced botnet, from our understanding, should satisfy four basic security properties denoting as *Resilience, Openness, Efficiency* and *Monitorability*, respectively. We believe that the four basic security properties are indispensible for constructing a practical advanced botnet.

Definition 1. *Resilience* denotes the **robustness** of a botnet when the crucial nodes of its infrastructure are attacked; and the **recoverability** of a botnet in case of being "shut down" temporally.

Definition 2. *Openness* is the **risk level** of a botnet faced in case the DNS/IP of C&C servers, the hard-coded symmetric/public keys and the hard-coded algorithms are exposed. If the risk level is low, we say the botnet has openness.

Definition 3. *Efficiency* is the **performance** of a botnet when managing large-scale botnets (Downlink Performance), accepting massive files in parallel and continuously (Uplink Performance), and storing massive files uploaded by large-scale botnets (Storage Performance).

Definition 4. *Monitorability* is the **capability** of a botnet to accept the initial *One-time Registration* (see definition 7) and the subsequent *Persistent Status Report* (see definition 8).

From the perspective of security properties requirement, the proposed bidirectional communication botnet should satisfy all the security properties shown in Table.1 (in Section 2).

In summary, our contributions are:

● We analyze the weaknesses of current botnets and the possible intrinsic cause, and then propose a Botnet Triple-Channel Model.
● We implement a BTM based botnet prototype, which is proved to satisfy the four basic security properties – *Resilience, Openness, Efficiency* and *Monitorability*.
● We propose an **open and efficient** Data Upload Channel design named *Cloud Flux*, which is generally absent in most of current botnets.
● We find that BTM based botnets make takedown efforts more challenging, which should be given more consideration in advance.

1.4   Paper Organization

The remainder of this paper is structured as follows. Section 2 gives an overview of BTM. In Section 3, we introduce the implementation of RoemBot based on BTM. Section 4 provides an analysis of the resilience and efficiency of RoemBot. In Section 5, we discuss how to defend against RoemBot. Finally, we outline related work in Section 6 and summarize our work in Section 7.

2   Botnet Triple-Channel Model

To construct an "Ideal Botnet" which could satisfy all the four basic security properties, we proposed a *Botnet Triple-Channel Model (BTM)*.

Architecture. BTM (shown in Fig.1) divides a traditional C&C channel into three independent sub-channels, denoting as *Command Download Channel (CDC), Registration Channel (RC)* and *Data Upload Channel (DUC)*, respectively. That is, BTM includes three independent but cooperative C&C sub-channels.

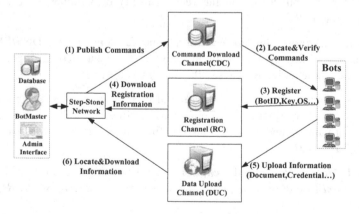

Fig. 1. Botnet Triple-Channel Model

Security Properties Requirement. Each sub-channel, determined by its functionality and characteristic, requires particular properties (summarized in Table.1) and is only responsible for particular tasks.

Command Download Channel (CDC). CDC is **only** responsible for commands distribution. CDC must be resilient and open to defend against coordinated countermeasures, and must have excellent downlink performance to support large-scale management. However, the uplink channel could be absent. Thus, a resilient, open and efficient unidirectional C&C protocol is suitable for CDC.

Definition 5. *RI* denotes Registration Information. RI=<BotID, SymmetricKey, HostInfo>, where *BotID* is used to identify a bot uniquely and is generated randomly based on host information when a bot compromises a new victim; *SymmetricKey* is used to encrypt all kinds of uploading data such as SI (see definition 6) and stolen files. Since the hardcoded key can in all cases be found through reverse engineering, each bot should generate an individualized and different symmetric key. In this way, investigating one or more bots will not impact the confidentiality of the whole botnet; *HostInfo* includes basic information describing a victim such as internal IP address, operation system and version, CPU/Memory, installed Antivirus software, and system language etc. Note that BotID and SymmetricKey must keep unchanged in the whole lifespan of a bot, and RI must be encrypted by the **hardcoded public key** of bots.

Definition 6. *SI* denotes Status Information. General SI includes *command received, command execution finished, download finished, upload finished, victim environment changed* etc. Note that SI must be encrypted by the individualized *SymmetricKey* (see Definition 5) to ensure confidentiality; thus detecting and then investigating one or more bots will not impact other bots.

Definition 7. *One-time Registration (a.k.a. Call-Home)* means a bot must report its individualized RI after initial execution. One-time Registration makes a botmaster could monitor the membership, population size, and geographical distribution of a botnet.

Definition 8. *Persistent Status Report* means a bot should report its SI persistently or on-demand according to the received commands. Persistent Status Report makes a botmaster could monitor the active size and activities of botnets in time.

Registration Channel (RC). RC is **only** responsible for RI and SI collection. RC must be recoverable and open to defend against the physical control and sinkhole attack, and must have uplink channel to accept the incoming RI and SI during one-time registration and persistent status report, respectively. Since the registration servers must be lightweight and easy to deploy, the robustness and efficiency is not necessary. Since the RI and SI could be downloaded and removed by botmasters in time, the excellent storage performance is not indispensable. Thus, a recoverable, open and monitoring bidirectional communication protocol is suitable for RC.

Table 1. The Security Properties Requirement of the Divided Sub-Channels

RO=Robustness, RE=Recoverability, D/I=DNS/IP, K=Key, AL= Algorithm, DP=Downlink Performance, UP=Uplink Performance, SP=Storage Performance, OR= One-time Registration, PSR= Persistent Status Report

Sub-channel\ Property	Resilience		Openness			Efficiency			Monitorability	
	RO	RE	D/I	K	AL	DP	UP	SP	OR	PSR
CDC	√	√	√	√	√	√				
RC		√	√	√	√				√	√
DUC			√	√	√	√	√	√		

Data Upload Channel (DUC). DUC is **only** responsible for transferring stolen data to botmasters. DUC must have excellent uplink performance to enable massive data uploading in parallel by large-scale botnets, have excellent downlink performance for botmasters to download the massive files, have huge storage performance to store the uploaded data for some time. However, DUC itself is not necessary to be very resilient because the DUC related resources (i.e., the address of the given cloud services) could be dynamically delivered to bots via CDC, hence providing a recoverable capability indirectly; DUC need not Monitorability, because the uploading status could be sent to botmasters using SI via RC. Another important thing we have to considerate is that DUC must ensure the uploaded data can and can only be located and decrypted by botmasters who own the RI of each bot. Thus, an open and efficient bidirectional communication protocol is suitable for DUC.

3   RoemBot: A BTM-Based Botnet

To explain the proposed BTM in more detail, we implement a prototype named *RoemBot* (a *R*esilient, *O*pen, *E*fficient and *M*onitoring *b*ot). We analyze and evaluate the resilience and efficiency of RoemBot emphatically in section 4.

3.1   Overview of RoemBot

The architecture of RoemBot is shown in Fig.2. RoemBot exploits URL Flux [5] for CDC, Domain Flux for RC and a new protocol (named *Cloud Flux* for convenience) for DUC. The C&C procedures of RoemBot are explained as below.

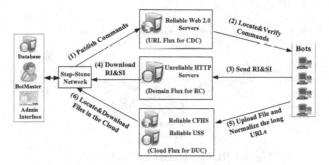

Fig. 2. Architecture and Implementation of RoemBot

Phase 1: A botmaster encrypts and signs the commands, and then publishes them to reliable Web 2.0 servers (i.e., Twitter).

Phase 2: The bots try to locate the authentic commands using URL Flux protocol.

Phase 3: The bots begin to locate the authentic registration servers using Domain Generation Algorithm (DGA) [14], depending on the *Seed* value such as current date/time and Twitter trends obtained from commands. Note that the *Seed* value must be distributed via commands to defend against sinkhole attack (see Section 4.3).

Phase 4: The botmaster downloads the encrypted RI and SI, and then decrypt them using the corresponding private key and *SymmetricKey*, respectively.

Phase 5: Based on the URL of *Cloud-based File Hosting Services* (*CFHS*) obtained from commands, the bots begin to upload the collected data to CFHS. And then normalizes the long URL to shorten URL which could be predicted by the botmaster who owns the RI of each bot.

Phase 6: The botmaster locates each file uploaded by each bot and then downloads the files one by one. Note that the files can and can only be identified and decrypted by the botmaster who owns the RI of each bot.

3.2   URL Flux Protocol for CDC

Protocol Selection. According to the requirement of CDC (Table.1) and the security properties of each C&C protocol (Table.2), we can see that URL Flux is suitable for CDC. The architecture of URL Flux is described in Fig.3. More detail about URL Flux is introduced in [5].

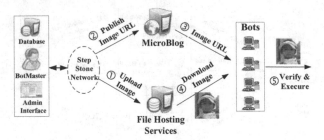

Fig. 3. URL Flux based CDC of RoemBot

3.3   Domain Flux Protocol for RC

This registration procedure is very crucial for botmasters to monitor the botnet and locate the uploaded stolen files.

Protocol Selection. According to the requirement of RC (Table.1) and the security properties of each C&C protocol (Table.2), we can see that Domain Flux is suitable for RC. The registration procedure is described in Fig.4.

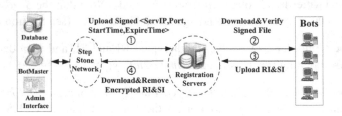

Fig. 4. Registration Procedure of RoemBot

Phase 1: Botmasters upload a certification to the registration server. The certification must include but not limited to Server IP Address, Server Port, Start Time and Expire Time. In this way, it is impossible for defenders to forge registration servers. After this, botmasters publish the randomly generated DGA *seed,* making bots could locate the registration servers using Domain Flux protocol.

Phase 2: Bots retrieve commands via CDC, subtract the seed and then calculate the domain names of registration servers using the hard-coded DGA which is shared with botmaster.

Phase 3: Bots upload RI and SI to the authentic registration servers, encrypted by the hard-coded public key and the generated *SymmetricKey*, respectively.

Phase 4: Botmasters download and decrypt the RI and SI, and then remove them, eliminating the risk of computer forensics or other kinds of data leakage.

3.4   Cloud Flux for DUC

Motivation. Although it seems a simple task to construct a DUC which could satisfy all of the requirements of DUC listed in Table.1, it is not the case. In fact, even well-known botnets such as Conficker, Mariposa, Torpig, Coreflood, Waledac, and Kelihos botnets are all ineffective in the aspect of retrieving the collected data from bots. Let us take Torpig as an example, which is mainly designed to harvest sensitive information from its victims. Stone-Gross took control of the Torpig botnet and observed more than 180 thousand infections and recorded almost 70 GB of data that the bots collected [24]. How to construct an **open** DUC with good downlink performance, uplink performance, and storage performance poses a great challenge to this day.

Cloud Flux Designing. To address the above difficulties, we propose a new protocol named *Cloud Flux* for convenience. We attempt to employ *Cloud-based File Hosting Services (CFHS)* and *URL Shortening Services (USS)* to build a qualified DUC. More specifically, CFHS provide an efficient way to upload and store files anonymously, which could also be exploited by bots. However, the cloud servers usually return a random URL pointing to the uploaded file. It happens that USS could solve the problem by mapping a given URL to a customized shorten URL. In a word, we could combine the two services together to establish an open and effective DUC. To describe the idea in detail, we outline the complete working procedure in Fig.5.

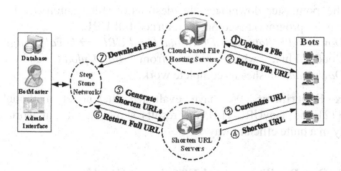

Fig. 5. Cloud Flux based DUC of RoemBot

Phase 1: A bot collects interesting contents such as credentials and sensitive files on the victim, encrypts (RC4) them using its *SymmetricKey* and stores the ciphertext into a file. After that, the bot uploads the file to a randomly selected CFHS which is obtained from the received commands. This phase can be described more formally as below:
Bot_Upload = Bot.Encrypt (File, Key) → CFHS

Phase 2: The cloud server returns a random URL representing the downloading URL of the uploaded file (i.e., http://www.sendspace.com/file/rz3ivc) to the bot.
CFHS_Response = CFHS.Response (Full URL) → bots

Phase 3: The bot visits a randomly selected shorten URL server which is obtained from the received commands, submits the above full URL and a desired customized shorten URL based on its *BotID* (already generated in the procedure of registration and reported to botmasters via RC) and current date. For example, if the BotID is abcd1234, the current date is 20130508, then the desired shorten URL is "http://tinyurl.com/abcd123420130508".
Bot_Request = Bot.Request (Full URL, Desired Shorten URL)→ USS

Phase 4: If successful, the desired shorten URL will be returned; otherwise, if the desired shorten URL is occupied (a low probability event), the bot has to queue the file to the next day.
USS_Response = USS.Response (Desired Customized Shorten URL, RetCode)→ bots

Phase 5: The botmaster owns all BotID thanks to the registration procedure, so he can enumerate each BotID one by one (we prefer to wait for an *"upload finished"* SI report for efficiency consideration, otherwise, enumerating the whole botnet population is very inefficient) and then generates the possible destination URL by combing the BotID with current date.
Botmaster_Request =   Botmaster. Request (http:// USS Domain /
BotID#CurrentDate)→ USS, where '#' denotes conjunction of two strings.

Phase 6: If the shorten URL does exist, the corresponding full URL will be returned.
USS_Response = USS.Response (Full URL) → Botmaster

Phase 7: The botmaster downloads the destination files automatically (using an automated crawler program) based on the returned full URL.
Botmaster_Download = Botmaster.Download (Full URL) → LocalStorage
   Here, Cloud Flux, which starts from *Bot_Upload* and ends with *Botmaster_Download*, finishes its complete work.

Cloud Flux Experiment. We have evaluated the novel methodology using SendSpace [12] and TinyURL [13], the results show that it can work completely automatically in a quite efficient way.

4   RoemBot Resilience and Efficiency Study

4.1   Security Properties of Current C&C Protocols

Although the C&C protocols of botnets have evolved from centralized to decentralized topology and from static to dynamic addressing, to the best of our knowledge, there is no publicly reported botnets that could satisfy all of the four basic security properties. The summary of current C&C protocols as well as the proposed Cloud Flux is shown in Tab.2. In comparison, we also exhibit the security properties of BTM.
   For an IRC botnet, it has a group of IRC servers which could link together in a P2P topology, so its CDC is robust. However, in case the DNS/IP addresses of IRC servers, the hard-coded login password in bots are exposed, the botnet will suffer

from a single-point-of-failure or hijacking. The bot can only push some limited text messages to botmasters, so the uplink performance is low.

For a HTTP protocol, it has only limited HTTP servers, more badly, all kinds of resources, such as Domain Name, publicly accessible IP address, and the physical computers, must be considered by botmasters. In case the DNS/IP addresses of HTTP servers are exposed, the botnet will also suffer from a single-point-of-failure. Although the efficiency can be enhanced by increasing the number and performance of HTTP servers, it is generally very limited and cost sensitive.

For structured P2P protocol, it is vulnerable to Index Poisoning and Sybil attack inevitably; for unstructured P2P protocol, it is vulnerable to crawling and sensor injecting inescapably. In case the hardcoded keys are exposed, the commands broadcasted among the P2P botnet could be monitored in time by defenders who employ Sybil nodes.

IP Flux (a.k.a. Fast Flux) protocol evolves from HTTP protocol. When the Domain Name of its mothership [17] is exposed, it still has a single-point-of-failure risk. Although there are multi step-stones, the efficiency of mothership is not enhanced at all. The main objective of IP Flux is to conceal the real IP address of motherships.

Domain Flux protocol evolves from HTTP protocol, it introduces a DGA to make the Domain Name of C&C servers predictable so as to equip with recoverability [23]. Although the DGA could be easily reverse analyzed, the botmasters will not lose control due to certification mechanism.

URL Flux protocol also involves from HTTP protocol, it introduces a UGA (Username Generation Algorithm) to make the URL of C&C servers predictable so as to equip with recoverability [5]. Same to DGA, UGA is also resilient to reverse engineering. The downside of URL Flux lies in its absence of uplink capability.

Table 2. The Security Properties of Common C&C Protocol

RO=Robustness, RE=Recoverability, D/I=DNS/IP, K=Key, AL= Algorithm, DP=Downlink Performance, UP=Uplink Performance, SP=Storage Performance, OR= One-time Registration, PSR= Persistent Status Report, H=High, L=Low, S=Support, O=On-demand, Y=Yes, N=No

Protocol\	Resilience		Openness			Efficiency			Monitorability	
Property	RO	RE	D/I	K	AL	DP	UP	SP	OR	PSR
IRC	H		N	N		H	L	L	S	O
HTTP	L		N	Y		L	L	L	S	S
IP Flux	L		N			L	L	L	S	S
Domain Flux	L	H	Y	Y	Y	L	L	L	S	O
URL Flux	H	H	Y	Y	Y	H				
P2P	L-H	L-H		N		L				
Cloud Flux			Y	Y	Y	H	H	H		
BTM	H	H	Y	Y	Y	H	H	H	S	O

4.2   URL Flux Resilience and Efficiency Study

URL Flux Attack Model. Security defenders such as CERT, ISP and the most important Web 2.0 providers, could reverse analyze the UGA and monitor the behavior of particular usernames which could be generated by UGA. In addition, defenders may try to *replay* the commands.

Resilience and Efficiency Analysis. For username monitoring attack, URL Flux exploits a large number of public Web 2.0 services as downlink C&C servers; thus, its robustness depends on the Web 2.0 services. Only when all the hard-coded Web 2.0 services become unavailable, URL-Flux fails. Obviously, the extreme situation is an extremely low-probability event. In case the usernames generated by UGA on one Web 2.0 service is blocked by the service provider, botmasters could switch to other Web 2.0 services. Therefore, RoemBot is very resilient. The C&C servers are high-performance websites which could serve millions of communications concurrently. Therefore, RoemBot is very efficient. The published commands always   include *"StartDate"* and *"ExpireDate"* [5], making replay attack impossible. Furthermore, because the private key is owned only by botmasters, injecting malicious commands is impossible.

4.3   Domain Flux Resilience and Efficiency Study

Domain Flux Attack Model. Security defenders could identify the active authentic registration servers in time using the same DGA with bots. After that, they could either setup a **sinkhole** to measure the botnet or **physically control** the active registration servers.

Resilience and Efficiency Analysis. Since the *Seed* used by DGA is distributed via commands dynamically, so the defenders could not predict the future domain names used by bots until they monitor the issued commands, so they can't register the domain names in advance, making sinkhole attack difficult. For botmasters, they should always setup the servers in advance, and then publish the *Seed*. In this way, bots will always firstly locate the authentic servers rather than the fake sinkhole servers. Since bots encrypt the RI using the hard-coded public key, even if the registration servers are completely controlled by defenders, the RI is also secure. Anyhow, the RI and SI will never be accessed by unauthorized people.

4.4   Cloud Flux Resilience and Efficiency Study

Cloud Flux Attack Model. The desired shortened URL (i.e., BotID+Date) makes it easy for the USS providers to enumerate potential bots by searching (and disabling) short URLs that have such a date suffix. Also, once a BotID is discovered, those URLs can be banned going forward.

Resilience and Efficiency Analysis. CFHS and USS could ensure sufficient performance even for large-scale botnets (i.e., more than ten millions) to store numerous files and request shortening services in parallel. So DUC is very efficient. Since the files uploaded by bots are encrypted and have random filenames, CFHS providers are hard to find them out. Since the combination of BotID and current date is not unusual, there is a relatively high collision probability with normal URLs, it is impossible for USS providers to block all malicious requests. Furthermore, the Cloud Flux technique could also use some simple enhancements. For example, it is more useful to use keyed hashes. Hence, a better shortened URL could be HMAC (BotID+Date, SymmetricKey), where SymmetricKey is reported in RI via RC. This would defeat such enumeration efforts.

5 Defense against RoemBot

We introduce possible defense strategies in three ways. First, a coordinated cooperation channel should be set up to identify and defend against this technology; second, we should infiltrate botnets to monitor their activities in time; third, we should pay more attention to the relatively vulnerable step-stones used by botmasters.

Building International Coordinated Mechanism: RoemBot relies on Web 2.0, CFHS and USS heavily. For this reason, defenders should focus their defense effort on security enhancement for publicly available services. This effort can prevent these services from being abused to some degree. In the case that abnormalities are detected, there should be a coordinated channel such as CERT and ISP to stop the corresponding services.

Infiltration: Since all bots must find commands in an active way, all of them are inescapably vulnerable to an infiltrator [18, 25]. After reverse engineering of RoemBot, an infiltrator can be written using the same protocol and algorithm to simulate RoemBot. In this way, defenders are able to track the botnet activities in time.

Step-stone Penetration and Forensics: Botmasters always use step-stones to conceal their origination; however, step-stones are generally vulnerable and relatively easy to penetrate. Once compromising one or more step-stones, defenders could monitor the incoming traffic, making tracing back to the active botmasters possible. In addition, defenders could also infer the characteristic of botmasters based on their habits such as the keyboard layout, language preference and time-zone [26].

Although the above defense mechanisms cannot shut down or decrease the C&C capability significantly, they still could increase the cost of botmasters to some degree.

6 Related Works

Wang et al. [3] presented the design of an advanced hybrid peer-to-peer botnet. Vogt et al. [4] presented a "super-botnet" - that works by inter-connecting many small botnets together in a peer-to-peer fashion. Ralf Hund et al. [6] introduced the design of an advanced bot called Rambot, developed from the weaknesses they found when tracking a diverse set of botnets. Starnberger et al. [9] presented Overbot, which uses an existing P2P protocol, Kademlia, to provide a stealth C&C channel. Singh et al. [8] evaluated the feasibility of exploiting email communication for botnet C&C. Cui et al. [5] proposed URL-Flux for botnets C&C which has proved to be robust and efficient. Kui et al. [29] conducted a systematic study on the feasibility of solely using DNS queries for massive-scale stealthy communications among entities on the Internet. Their work shows that DNS can be used as an effective stealthy C&C channel for botnets.

Nevertheless, none of existing research works has studied how botmasters might design a **resilient and efficient bidirectional** communication channel. Specially, all of the above proposed P2P and URL-Flux based botnets are unidirectional although they are resilient. Although the DNS-based C&C channel is bidirectional, its authoritative domain name servers suffer from single-point-of-failure problem, making massive-scale uploading stolen data in parallel very hard; furthermore, the botmasters must create and register the new domain names continuously. Thus, our study compliments the existing research works to some degree.

7   Conclusion and Future Works

In this paper, we present a Botnet Triple-Channel Model and implement a corresponding prototype named RoemBot. RoemBot exploits URL Flux for CDC, Domain Flux for RC and a new proposed protocol named *Cloud Flux* for DUC. Compared with traditional botnets, RoemBot has a more resilient commands distribution channel, a recoverable information registration channel, and a more efficient data uploading channel, which could satisfy all of the four security properties of botnets, thus promising to be very attractive for botmasters. We believe our findings demonstrate that research on alternative advanced botnets mitigation methods is urgently needed.

We also believe that BTM-based botnet design represents a main direction of future botnets. Therefore, we plan to prove that any botnet must accomplish a BTM-style architecture in order to construct an "ideal" botnet. The ultimate goal of our work is to increase the understanding of advanced botnets; we will invest more research on how to fight against this kind of advanced botnet in the future.

Acknowledgment. The authors would like to thank the anonymous reviewers for their helpful comments for improving this paper. This work is supported by the National Natural Science Foundation of China under grant (No. 61202409) and the National High Technology Research and Development Program (863 Program) of China under grant (No. 2012AA012902 and 2011AA01A103).

References

1. Plohmann, D., Gerhards-Padilla, E.: Case Study of the Miner Botnet. In: Proceedings of the 4th International Conference on Cyber Conflict (2012)
2. Werner, T.: The Miner Botnet: Bitcoin Mining Goes Peer-To-Peer, Blog article by Kaspersky Lab (2011), http://www.securelist.com/en/blog/208193084/
3. Wang, P., Sparks, S., Zou, C.C.: An advanced hybrid peer to peer botnet. In: Proceedings of the First Workshop on Hot Topics in Understanding Botnets, HotBots 2007 (2007)
4. Vogt, R., Aycock, J., Jacobson, M.: Army of botnets. In: Proceedings of 14th Annual Network and Distributed System Security Symposium, NDSS 2007 (2007)

5. Cui, X., Fang, B.X., Yin, L.H., Liu, X.Y.: Andbot: Towards Advanced Mobile Botnets. In: Proceedings of the 4th Usenix Workshop on Large-scale Exploits and Emergent Threats, LEET 2011 (2011)
6. Hund, R., Hamann, M., Holz, T.: Towards Next-Generation Botnets. In: Proceedings of the 2008 European Conference on Computer Network Defense (2008)
7. Yan, G., Chen, S., Eidenbenz, S.: RatBot: Anti-enumeration Peer-to-Peer Botnets. In: Lai, X., Zhou, J., Li, H. (eds.) ISC 2011. LNCS, vol. 7001, pp. 135–151. Springer, Heidelberg (2011)
8. Kapil, S., Abhinav, S., et al.: Evaluating Email's Feasibility for Botnet Command and Control. In: Proc. of the 38th Annual IEEE/IFIP International Conference on Dependable Systems and Networks, pp. 376–385. IEEE Computer Society, Washington, DC (2008)
9. Starnberger, G., Kruegel, C., Kirda, E.: Overbot: A Botnet Protocol Based on Kademlia. In: Proceedings of the 4th International Conference on Security and Privacy in Communication Networks (2008)
10. Rossow, C., Andriesse, D., Werner, T., Stone-Gross, B., Plohmann, D., Dietrich, C.J., Bos, H.: P2PWNED: Modeling and Evaluating the Resilience of Peer-to-Peer Botnets. In: 34th IEEE Symposium on Security and Privacy, S&P 2013, San Francisco, CA (2013)
11. Wang, P., Wu, L., Aslam, B., Zou, C.C.: A Systematic Study on Peer-to-Peer Botnets. In: Proc. of International Conference on Computer Communications and Networks (ICCCN), pp. 1–8. IEEE Computer Society, Washington, DC (2009)
12. Roland, D.P.: Malware Uses Sendspace to Store Stolen Documents (2012), doi: http://tinyurl.com/use-Cloud-but-no-ShortenURL
13. Neumann, A., Barnickel, J., Meyer, U.: Security and privacy implications of url shortening services. In: Proceedings of the Workshop on Web 2.0 Security and Privacy (2010)
14. Antonakakis, M., Perdisci, R., Nadji, Y., Vasiloglou, N., Abu-Nimeh, S., Lee, W., Dagon, D.: From Throw-Away Traffic to Bots: Detecting the Rise of DGA-Based Malware. In: Proceedings of the 21st USENIX Security Symposium (2012)
15. Bukowski, T.: ZeuS v3 P2P Network Monitoring, Technical Report by CERT.pl (2012)
16. Bureau, P.-M.: Same Botnet, Same Guys, New Code: Win32/Kelihos. In: VirusBulletin (2011)
17. Holz, T., Gorecki, C., Rieck, C., Freiling, F.C.: Detection and mitigation of fast-flux service networks. In: Proc. of the 15th Annual Network and Distributed System Security Symposium. USENIX Association, Berkeley (2008)
18. Cho, C.Y., Caballero, J., Grier, C., Paxson, V., Song, D.: Insights from the Inside: A View of Botnet Management from Infiltration. In: Proc. of the 3th USENIX Conference on Large-Scale Exploits and Emergent Threats: Botnets, Spyware, Worms and More, p. 2. USENIX Association, Berkeley (2010)
19. Dittrich, D.: So You Want to Take Over a Botnet. In: Proceedings of the 5th USENIX Conference on Large-Scale Exploits and Emergent Threats (2012)
20. Stock, B., Engelberth, M., Freiling, F.C., Holz, T.: Walowdac Analysis of a Peer-to-Peer Botnet. In: Proc. of the 2009 European Conference on Computer Network Defense, pp. 13–20. IEEE Computer Society, Washington, DC (2009)
21. McNamee, K.: Malware Analysis Report: ZeroAccess/Sirefef, Technical Report by Kindsight Security Labs (2012)
22. Holz, T., Steiner, M., Dahl, F., Biersack, E., Freiling, F.: Measurements and Mitigation of Peer-to-Peer-based Botnets. A Case Study on Storm Worm. In: Proceedings of the 1st USENIX Workshop on Large-Scale Exploits and Emergent Threats (2008)
23. Porras, P., Saidi, H., Yegneswaran, V.: A Foray into Conficker's Logic and Rendezvous Points. In: USENIX Workshop on Large-Scale Exploits and Emergent Threats (2009)

24. Stone-Gross, B., Cova, M., Cavallaro, L., Gilbert, B., Szydlowski, M., Kemmerer, R., Kruegel, C., Vigna, G.: Your Botnet is My Botnet: Analysis of a Botnet Takeover. In: Proc. of the 16th ACM Conference on Computer and Communications Security, pp. 635–647. ACM, New York (2009)
25. Jonell, B., Joey, C., Ryan, F.: Infiltrating waledac botnet's convert operation[EB]. Trend Micro (2009), http://us.trendmicro.com/imperia/md/content/us/pdf/threats/securitylibrary/infiltrating_the_waledac_botnet_v2.pdf (June 10, 2011)
26. APT1: Exposing One of China's Cyber Espionage Units, http://intelreport.mandiant.com/Mandiant_APT1_Report.pdf
27. Amini, P., Pierce, C.: Kraken Botnet Infiltration [EB]. Blog on DVLabs (2008), http://dvlabs.tippingpoint.com (June 10, 2011)
28. Barrett, B.: http://gizmodo.com/gaming-network-employee-turns-14-000-users-into-bitcoin-487054354
29. Xu, K., Butler, P., Saha, S., Yao, D.: DNS for Massive-scale Command and Control. IEEE Transactions of Dependable and Secure Computing (TDSC) 10(3), 143–153 (2013)

Contrasting Permission Patterns between Clean and Malicious Android Applications

Veelasha Moonsamy, Jia Rong, Shaowu Liu, Gang Li, and Lynn Batten

School of Information Technology, Deakin University
221 Burwood Highway, VIC 3125, Australia
v.moonsamy@research.deakin.edu.au, jiarong@acm.org,
{swliu,gang.li,lynn.batten}@deakin.edu.au

Abstract. The *Android* platform uses a permission system model to allow users and developers to regulate access to private information and system resources required by applications. Permissions have been proved to be useful for inferring behaviors and characteristics of an application. In this paper, a novel method to extract contrasting permission patterns for clean and malicious applications is proposed. Contrary to existing work, both *required* and *used* permissions were considered when discovering the patterns. We evaluated our methodology on a clean and a malware dataset, each comprising of 1227 applications. Our empirical results suggest that our permission patterns can capture key differences between clean and malicious applications, which can assist in characterizing these two types of applications.

Keywords: Android Permission, Malware Detection, Contrast Mining, Permission Pattern.

1 Introduction

The increase in *Android* smartphone sales has led to a surge in the number of applications available on application markets. Additionally, the freedom of installing applications from third-party markets, rather than being constrained to only the official market, has boosted the number of *Android* applications. This, in turn, has incentivized application developers to churn out applications and upload them on different third-party markets [1]. As no application review process is in place for third-party markets, the cleanliness of these applications cannot be guaranteed [2]. Users can only rely on the description and permissions listed on the application market to decide whether or not they should install an application.

Android platform employs a permission system to restrict application privileges in order to secure a user's private information [3]. However, its effectiveness highly depends on the user's comprehension of permission approval [4]. The permissions requested during application installation are referred to as *required permissions*. Unfortunately, as noted by Felt et al. [4], not all the users read or understand the warnings of *required* permissions shown during installation. In

T. Zia et al. (Eds.): SecureComm 2013, LNICST 127, pp. 69–85, 2013.

order to have a better understanding of permission requests, Frank et al. [3] proposed a probability model to identify the common *required* permission patterns for all *Android* applications. Zhou and Jiang [5] listed the top *required* permissions for both clean and malicious applications, but only individual permissions were considered by frequency counting.

We observed that the following issues have been overlooked in the area of *Android* permissions analysis:

- *Contrasting Permissions Patterns.* Despite the numerous research endeavors [4,6,7] aimed at interpreting *Android* permissions and their combinations, there is no existing work that aims at identifying the permission differences between clean and malicious *Android* applications.
- *Used Permission.* No work has considered incorporating *used* permissions, which can be extracted from static analysis by the *Andrubis* system [8], into the permission patterns. Compared to *required* permissions, *used* permissions provide a better understanding of the permissions that are needed by an application in order to function properly. Whenever an API call is invoked during the execution of an application, the *Android* platform will verify if the API call is permission-protected before proceeding to execute the call; such permissions are referred to as *used* permissions.

With the availability of the *Andrubis* framework and the advances in data mining, it is now possible to consider both *required* and *used* permissions, together with the use of our new pattern mining algorithm to generate contrasting permission patterns for clean and malicious applications. While most of the existing work is based on *required* permissions, *used* permissions are equally important and should be considered to better differentiate between permission patterns for clean and malicious applications. Therefore, our aim is *to identify a set of unique and common permission patterns that can contrast clean applications from malicious ones.*

In order to apply our pattern mining technique to identify the desired contrast permission patterns, a clean and a malware dataset are considered. In 2012, Zhou and Jiang [5] published the first benchmark dataset of malicious applications, which comprises of 49 malware families. The applications were collected from third-party markets between August 2010 and October 2011. As there was no clean dataset publicly available, we proceeded to collect our own clean applications that were released during the same time period as the malware dataset. The clean applications were downloaded from two popular third-party application markets: *SlideME* (http://slideme.org) and *Pandaapp* (http://android.pandaapp.com). The applications were sorted based on the number of downloads and the ratings given by the users, and only the top ones were selected.

To our knowledge, this work reports one of the first pattern mining methods that can generate unique and common permission patterns, which include both *required* and *used* permissions, for clean and malicious applications. The novelty and contributions of this work can be summarized as follows:

- To find the permission combinations, a new contrast permission pattern mining algorithm (CPPM) is proposed to identify the permission patterns that can significantly differentiate between clean and malicious applications.
- To our knowledge, this is the first work to incorporate both *required* and *used* permissions to generate permission patterns. Based on our empirical results, it can be deduced that such patterns can help to contrast clean applications from malicious ones.

The rest of the paper is organized as follows: Section 2 briefly reviews the *Android* platform, the permission system and the current research work in malware detection. In Section 3, we present our initial analysis on the collected datasets using statistical methods followed by the proposed contrast pattern mining algorithm. The experiments and the obtained results are then reported in Section 4 together with a discussion of our findings. Finally, Section 5 concludes the paper together with our future work.

2   Background and Related Work

2.1   Android and Its Permission System

Android is a Linux-based Operating System (OS) which was designed and developed by the *Open Handset Alliance* in 2007 [9]. The *Android* platform is made up of multiple layers consisting of the Linux-kernel, libraries and an application framework with built-in applications [10]. Additional applications can be downloaded and installed from either official market, *Google Play* [11], or third-party markets.

Google applies the permission system as a measure to restrict access to privileged system resources. Developers have to explicitly mention the permissions, that require user's approval, in the **AndroidManifest.xml** file. *Android* adopts an 'all-or-nothing' permission granting policy. Hence, the application is installed successfully only when the user chooses to grant access to all of the *required* permissions.

There are currently 130 official *Android* permissions and they are classified into four categories: *Normal, Dangerous, Signature* and *SignatureOrSystem* [12].

- *Normal* permissions do not require the user's approval but they can be viewed after the application has been installed.
- *Dangerous* permissions require the user's confirmation before the installation process starts; these permissions have access to restricted resources and can have a negative impact if used incorrectly.
- A permission in *Signature* category is granted without the user's knowledge only if the application is signed with the device manufacturer's certificate.
- The *SignatureOrSystem* permissions are granted only to the applications that are in the *Android* system image or are signed with the device manufacturer's certificate. Such permissions are used for special situations where the applications, built by multiple vendors, are stored in one system image and share specific features.

After an application is installed, a set of Application Programming Interfaces (APIs) are called during the runtime. Each API call is associated with a particular permission. When an API call is made, the *Android* OS checks whether or not its associated permission has been approved by the user. Only a matching result will lead to the execution of the API call. In this way, the *required* permissions are able to protect the user's privacy-relevant resources from any unauthorized operations. However, it cannot deter malware developers from declaring additional *required* permissions for their applications. From the above observation, several studies [3, 6, 7] have tried to identify the common *required* permissions that are frequently declared by *Android* application developers.

2.2   Android Permissions and Related Work

Understanding Android Permissions. Frank et al. [3] selected 188, 389 applications from the official market and analyzed the combinations of permission requests by these applications using a probabilistic model. Bartel et al. [13] proposed an automated tool that can statistically analyze the methods defined in an application and subsequently, generate the permissions required by the application. This, in turn, ensured that the user did not grant access to unnecessary permissions when installing the application. A model designed by Sanz et al. [14] was based on features that comprised solely of *Android* permissions, which helped to understand the *Android* permission system and the patterns for *normal* permission requests.

Permission-Based Malware Detection. Malware detection is an emerging topic in the study of the *Android* platform with many successful achievements; however, not much attention has been paid on detection using permission patterns. Chia et al. [7] argued that the current user-rating system is not a reliable source of measurement to predict whether or not an application is malicious. Their dataset consisted of 650 applications from the official market and 1, 210 applications from a third-party market. The *required* permissions were extracted from the dataset, together with other application-related information to develop a risk signal mechanism for detecting malware.

Sahs and Khan [15] focused on feature representation as one of the challenges to malware detection. The features included: (i) permissions extracted from manifest files and (ii) control flow graphs for each method in an application. Each feature was processed independently using multiple kernels and the authors applied a one-class *Support Vector Machine* to train the classifiers. However, the evaluation results showed that the common features existing in both the clean and malware datasets affected the detection error rate.

Wu et al. [16] put forward a static feature-based technique that can aid towards malware detection. First, they applied *K-means* algorithm to generate the clusters and used *Singular Value Decomposition* to determine the number of clusters. In the second step, they classified clean and malicious applications using the *k-Nearest Neighbor* (kNN) algorithm.

Zhou et al. [17] proposed a two-layered system, known as *DroidRanger* and used "permission-based behavioral foot-printing and heuristics-based filtering". The authors observed that the permissions extracted from the malicious applications gave an insight into uncommon permission requests by some malware families.

In [14], Sanz et al. proposed to extract the permissions and the hardware features to build the feature set. As a result, they observed that clean applications required two to three permissions on average, but some of malicious applications only had one permission and were still able to carry out the attack.

2.3 Summary and Problem Identification

Malware proliferation is rising exponentially and the attack vectors used by malware authors are getting more sophisticated. Current solutions proposed to thwart attacks by malicious applications will struggle to keep up with the increase of malware. The *Android* platform relies heavily on its permission system to control access to restricted system resources and private information stored on the smartphone. However, there is no evidence providing a clear understanding on the key differences for permissions in clean and malicious applications.

Thus, we identify the following research questions:

- How can we measure the similarities and differences between permission requests for clean and malicious applications?
- What method can be used to incorporate *used* permissions in the permission patterns?

To answer these questions, we have extended the current statistical method used for identifying both *required* and *used* permission patterns in *Android* applications. A contrast pattern mining technique has been proposed to identify the most useful permission combinations that can distinguish between clean and malicious applications.

3 Mining Contrast Permission Patterns

3.1 Experimental Dataset

For our malware dataset, we used Zhou and Jiang's [5] collection of 1227 malicious applications, which comprises of 49 malware families. These were collected from third-party markets between August 2010 and October 2011. In order to maintain the same timeline as the malware dataset, we proceeded to collect our set of 1227 clean applications that were released during the same period as the malicious ones. The clean applications were downloaded from two popular third-party application markets: *SlideME* (http://slideme.org) and *Pandaapp* (http://android.pandaapp.com). The applications were sorted based on the number of downloads and the ratings given by the users, and only the top ones were selected.

3.2   Statistical Analysis on Android Permissions

Statistical analysis has been widely used to analyze *Android* permissions. Accordingly, we started our work with an initial analysis on the clean and malware datasets using frequency counting and extended Zhou and Jiang's work [5] to explore *used* permissions. A novel contrast pattern mining algorithm is then presented to identify specific permission patterns that differentiate clean applications from malicious ones.

We employed statistical analysis to study both *required* and *used* permissions for clean applications as well as malicious ones. Based on the aforementioned two types of permissions for clean and malicious applications, we further generated the following four sub-datasets: (1) *Required* permissions for *clean* applications; (2) *Required* permissions for *malicious* applications; (3) *Used* permissions for *clean* applications; and (4) *Used* permissions for *malicious* applications. Direct frequency counting was employed on all four sub-datasets to find out the most popular permissions required or used.

By comparing the top 20 *required* permissions for clean and malicious applications listed in Table 1, we found that malicious applications requested a total of 14, 758 permissions, in contrast to the 4, 470 permissions requested by clean applications. Among these permissions, we found some of them only appeared in one dataset, in other words, those permissions were only *required* or *used* by clean applications but not malicious ones, and vice versa. We refer to these permissions as the *'unique permissions'*. Similarly, we name those permissions that appear in both clean and malware datasets the *'common permissions'*. In total, there are 33 unique *required* permissions for clean applications and 20 for malicious ones; and also 70 common *required* permissions. Another 5 permissions were never requested by any application. For *used* permissions, there are 9 unique ones for clean applications and only 4 for malicious ones. The number of common *used* permissions dropped to 28, and a large number of 87 permissions was never used by any application. The four most frequently requested common permissions by both clean and malicious applications are: INTERNET, ACCESS_COARSE_LOCATION, WRITE_EXTERNAL_STORAGE and VIBRATE.

In contrast, among the top 20 *required* permissions, 9 of them appeared frequently in the malware dataset. Moreover, when comparing the top 20 *used* permissions in clean and malicious applications in Table 2, we observed that 16 out of 20 popular *used* permissions were common in both datasets.

Statistical analysis such as direct frequency counting is suitable for identifying single permissions that are popular in each sub-dataset. However, it still requires further manual checking to confirm the obtained permission lists for clean and malicious applications. This, in turn, further complicates the counting process if permission combinations are to be considered instead of individual permissions. Therefore, we extended the analysis of *Android* permissions by proposing a contrast pattern mining algorithm.

Table 1. Top 20 Required Permissions by Clean and Malicious Applications

| Clean Applications | | Malicious Applications | |
Required Permission	Frequency	Required Permission	Frequency
INTERNET	1121	INTERNET	1199
ACCESS_NETWORK_STATE	663	ACCESS_COARSE_LOCATION	1146
READ_PHONE_STATE	391	VIBRATE	994
WRITE_EXTERNAL_STORAGE	362	WRITE_EXTERNAL_STORAGE	823
ACCESS_COARSE_LOCATION	236	READ_SMS	779
VIBRATE	210	WRITE_SMS	762
WAKE_LOCK	188	READ_CONTACTS	680
ACCESS_FINE_LOCATION	162	BLUETOOTH	633
GET_TASKS	125	WRITE_CONTACTS	542
SET_WALLPAPER	102	DISABLE_KEYGUARD	491
ACCESS_WIFI_STATE	64	WAKE_LOCK	471
RECEIVE_BOOT_COMPLETED	60	RECORD_AUDIO	461
READ_CONTACTS	58	ACCESS_FINE_LOCATION	446
WRITE_SETTINGS	45	ACCESS_NETWORK_STATE	416
CAMERA	43	READ_PHONE_STATE	414
CALL_PHONE	42	SET_ORIENTATION	413
SEND_SMS	34	CHANGE_WIFI_STATE	384
RESTART_PACKAGES	32	READ_LOGS	361
RECEIVE_SMS	31	BLUETOOTH_ADMIN	342
RECORD_AUDIO	27	RECEIVE_BOOT_COMPLETED	325

3.3   Contrast Permission Pattern Mining

In order to discover a set of permission patterns that can visibly show contrast between clean and malicious applications, we propose the *Contrast Permission Pattern Mining* (CPPM) method. The output permission patterns were expected to have the ability to indicate the difference between the clean and malicious applications. *CPPM* was designed to process more than one dataset and take both individual and combined permissions and their combinations into consideration. Two major processes were involved in *CPPM*: (1) candidate permission itemset generation, and (2) contrast permission pattern selection, as illustrated in Fig. 1.

1. **Candidate Permission Itemset Generation**
   The purpose of this process is to obtain a number of candidate permission combinations that are likely to be the expected contrast patterns. *CPPM* takes at least two datasets as input. In our case two datasets were loaded, each of which contained either clean or malicious applications. We generated the candidate permission itemsets from every dataset using the same procedure, which included the following two steps:
   Apriori-Based Itemset Enumeration. Given Dx is one of the input datasets with either *required* or *used* permissions, which contains n applications. Let $I = \{A, B, C \dots\}$ be the set of possible items in Dx. Each item can be considered as a permission required or used by an application and an itemset is formed by a set of items (permissions required or used). The *Apriori-based* approach [18] enumerates candidate itemset from the simplest structure with only a single item. Based on this single item, a more complex itemset is then obtained by adding new items. This joining operation is repeated continuously to increase the number of the items in the itemsets. In

Table 2. Top 20 Used Permissions by Clean and Malicious Applications

Clean Applications Used Permission	Frequency	Malicious Applications Used Permission	Frequency
INTERNET	1029	INTERNET	1161
WAKE_LOCK	816	ACCESS_COARSE_LOCATION	1125
ACCESS_NETWORK_STATE	738	VIBRATE	954
VIBRATE	608	WAKE_LOCK	826
READ_PHONE_STATE	457	ACCESS_WIFI_STATE	584
ACCESS_COARSE_LOCATION	372	ACCESS_NETWORK_STATE	519
SET_WALLPAPER	126	READ_SMS	473
ACCESS_FINE_LOCATION	116	WRITE_CONTACTS	426
GET_ACCOUNTS	98	READ_PHONE_STATE	354
ACCESS_WIFI_STATE	85	RECORD_AUDIO	319
READ_SMS	82	SET_WALLPAPER	297
RESTART_PACKAGES	65	ACCESS_FINE_LOCATION	199
GET_TASKS	61	GET_ACCOUNTS	178
CHANGE_CONFIGURATION	55	GET_TASKS	124
RECEIVE_SMS	37	RECEIVE_BOOT_COMPLETED	111
FLASHLIGHT	37	ACCESS_CACHE_FILESYSTEM	101
WRITE_CONTACTS	34	WRTIE_OWNER_DATA	59
RECEIVE_BOOT_COMPLETED	23	CHANGE_CONFIGURATION	52
WRTIE_OWNER_DATA	12	READ_HISTORY_BOOKMARKS	49
WRITE_SETTINGS	10	EXPAND_STATUS_BAR	41

each iteration, one new item is tentatively added into the existing candidate itemset. However, the *Apriori-based* approach can generate a large number of candidate itemsets with high computational cost. To alleviate this problem, a support-based pruning technique is employed to reduce the number of candidate itemsets and consequently, the experimental time.

Support-Based Candidate Pruning. *Support* is usually used to measure the occurrence frequency of a certain item or itemset in a dataset. Let A, $B \subseteq I$ be two items, and $\{A, B\}$ forms a candidate itemset. The support of the candidate itemset $\{A, B\}$ can be calculated by:

$$supp(A, B) = \frac{number\ of\ applications\ that\ contain\ A\ and\ B\ in\ Dx}{total\ number\ of\ applications\ in\ Dx} \qquad (1)$$

The candidate itemset $\{A, B\}$ is considered as *frequent* only if $supp(A, B) \geq \delta_{supp}$, where δ_{supp} is user-specified minimum *support* threshold. In classic pattern mining methods, only the frequent itemset is considered. Any itemset with a lower support than the pre-determined threshold is treated as *infrequent* and discarded. However, in our case, the statistical analysis results showed most of the unique permissions were requested or used by few applications. This indicated that they have low support value. In order to inadvertently miss any valuable patterns, we decided to take both frequent and infrequent candidate itemsets, but only used frequent ones to generate new candidate itemsets to cut down the computational cost.

2. **Contrast Permission Pattern Selection**

The permission itemsets obtained from the previous steps need to be reduced according to the pre-defined selection criteria. This process guarantees that the output itemsets are highly contrasted between clean and malicious applications. The contrasts are shown by the different occurrence behaviors

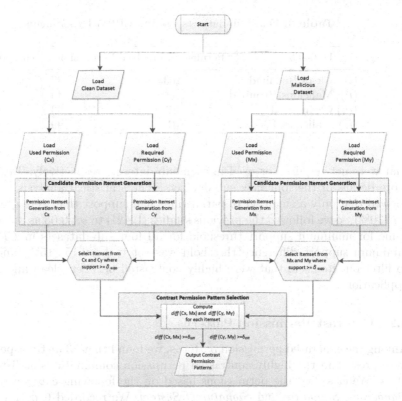

Fig. 1. CPPM-based Framework

in two datasets. If one permission itemset is frequent in one dataset, it is often considered to carry more common features than the infrequent ones. Therefore, the selection of specific contrast permission pattern is based on comparison of its supports between two datasets. The bigger the difference is in support values, the greater the contrast a permission pattern has.

Given one candidate permission itemset $\{A, B\}$ and its *supports* in clean and malware datasets, $supp(A, B)_{clean}$ and $supp(A, B)_{malicious}$, calculate the difference by $diff(A, B) = supp(A, B)_{clean} - supp(A, B)_{malicious}$. Then, $\{A, B\}$ is identified as a contrasted permission pattern only if $diff(A, B) \geq \delta_{diff}$, where δ_{diff} is a user-specified *minimum support difference*. All the candidate permission itemsets need to be tested using this approach, and the ones with big support difference will be selected as the final output contrast permission patterns.

4 Experiments and Results

4.1 Experiment Settings

According to the statistical analysis not all the permissions were required or used. Hence, to evaluate the proposed CPPM algorithm, we ignored the permissions

Table 3. Four Sub-datasets Used in CPPM Experiments

Dataset	Permission involved	Permission Discarded
(*i*) Clean_Required	103	27
(*ii*) Malicious_Required	90	40
(*iii*) Clean_Used	37	93
(*iv*) Malicious_Used	31	99

that were not required or used in each sub-datasets respectively. Table 3 gives more details of the four new sub-datasets. The statistical analysis results also showed that only a small set of permissions had support that were greater than 0.1 (10%), so we followed the previous studies [19–21] to set 0.05 as an acceptable value for minimum support threshold for all four sub-datasets in *CPPM*. The minimum support difference threshold was set to be 0.15 (15%) and applied to filter out itemsets that were highly contrasted between clean and malicious applications.

4.2   Contrast Permission Patterns

Among the generated permission patterns, we found that 23 distinct permissions were present in the highly contrasted permission combinations as listed in Table 4. We classified the permissions based on the following categories: *normal, Dangerous, Signature* and *SignatureOrSystem*. We recorded 6 permissions belonging to the *Normal* category, 15 permissions for the *Dangerous* category and 1 permission each for the *Signature* and *SignatureOrSystem* category.

We found that the generated permission combinations were correlated and differed between clean and malicious applications. Based on the experimental results, we recorded 56 *required* permission patterns that were unique to the malware dataset, 31 *used* permission patterns that only appeared amongst malware, 17 *required* permission patterns and 9 *used* permission patterns that were present in both clean and malware dataset. These findings are presented as permission patterns (described in Table 5) which are listed in Tables 6-10, and summarized below.

Unique Required Permission (URP) Patterns. In Table 6 and 7, we presented the permission patterns that were frequently required by the applications in our dataset. It should be noted that these *required* permission patterns were unique to the malware dataset only; hence the support value for the clean applications was 0.

In Table 6, the top 15 permission combinations, where the first permission in the listed patterns belonged to the *normal* permissions category, are presented. The permission combinations from $URPSet_1$ and $URPSet_2$ were both required by more than 60% of the malware. In fact, we found that the INTERNET permission ($pms0001$) is frequently requested along with other permissions and their

Table 4. Permission Index

Permission Category	Permission ID	Permission Name
Normal	$pms0001$	INTERNET
Normal	$pms0006$	ACCESS_NETWORK_STATE
Normal	$pms0007$	VIBRATE
Normal	$pms0012$	RESTART_PACKAGES
Normal	$pms0013$	RECEIVE_BOOT_COMPLETED
Normal	$pms0023$	ACCESS_WIFI_STATE
Dangerous	$pms0002$	ACCESS_FINE_LOCATION
Dangerous	$pms0003$	WAKE_LOCK
Dangerous	$pms0004$	WRITE_EXTERNAL_STORAGE
Dangerous	$pms0005$	READ_PHONE_STATE
Dangerous	$pms0008$	READ_CONTACTS
Dangerous	$pms0011$	READ_LOGS
Dangerous	$pms0020$	ACCESS_COARSE_LOCATION
Dangerous	$pms0021$	SEND_SMS
Dangerous	$pms0022$	GET_TASKS
Dangerous	$pms0024$	CHANGE_WIFI_STATE
Dangerous	$pms0028$	WRITE_CONTACTS
Dangerous	$pms0029$	RECEIVE_SMS
Dangerous	$pms0030$	READ_SMS
Dangerous	$pms0031$	WRITE_SMS
Dangerous	$pms0036$	CALL_PHONE
Signature	$pms0010$	FACTORY_TEST
SignatureOrSystem	$pms0052$	INSTALL_PACKAGES

Table 5. Types of Permission Patterns

Permission Patterns	Description
Unique Required Permission (URP)	*Required* permission patterns present only in malware dataset
Unique Used Permission (UUP)	*Used* permission patterns present only in malware dataset
Common Required Permission (CRP)	*Required* permission patterns present in both clean and malware datasets
Common Used Permission (CUP)	*Used* permission patterns present in both clean and malware datasets

support values are relatively high. The permission combination, INTERNET and RECEIVE_BOOT_COMPLETED were present in 55% of the malware dataset. Other such patterns involving the INTERNET permission are listed in Table 6.

In Table 7, we listed the patterns that can have an impact on the following actions: access location information, read/write/send and receive SMS, access to contact list, write to external storage and access to phone state.

Unique Used Permission (UUP) Patterns. In Table 8, the combinations of the *used* permissions that are unique to the malware dataset only are reported. It can be noted that the INTERNET permission is included in the top 3 permission combinations, $UUPSet_1$ to $UUPSet_3$ and appears in over 40% of the malware samples.

Table 6. Unique Required Permission Sets in Malware Dataset (*Normal Permissions*)

Permission Set	Support		Permission Set ID
	Clean	Malware	
$pms0001, pms0005, pms0023$	0	0.6309	$URPSet_1$
$pms0001, pms0006, pms0023$	0	0.6031	$URPSet_2$
$pms0001, pms0013$	0	0.5542	$URPSet_3$
$pms0006, pms0013$	0	0.5168	$URPSet_4$
$pms0006, pms0031$	0	0.4964	$URPSet_5$
$pms0001, pms0021$	0	0.4312	$URPSet_6$
$pms0013, pms0023$	0	0.4263	$URPSet_7$
$pms0021, pms0029$	0	0.3701	$URPSet_8$
$pms0004, pms0013$	0	0.3660	$URPSet_9$
$pms0001, pms0005, pms0020$	0	0.3562	$URPSet_{10}$
$pms0001, pms0005, pms0006, pms0007$	0	0.3497	$URPSet_{11}$
$pms0001, pms0004, pms0020$	0	0.3122	$URPSet_{12}$
$pms0023, pms0024$	0	0.3097	$URPSet_{13}$
$pms0006, pms0008$	0	0.2975	$URPSet_{14}$
$pms0013, pms0031$	0	0.2943	$URPSet_{15}$

Table 7. Unique *Required* Permission Sets in Malware Dataset (*Dangerous/Signature/SignatureOrSystem Permissions*)

Permission Set	Support		Permission Set ID
	Clean	Malware	
$pms0002, pms0005, pms0020$	0	0.2690	$URPSet_{16}$
$pms0002, pms0004, pms0020$	0	0.2576	$URPSet_{17}$
$pms0002, pms0005, pms0023$	0	0.2307	$URPSet_{18}$
$pms0002, pms0004, pms0023$	0	0.2234	$URPSet_{19}$
$pms0030, pms0036$	0	0.3228	$URPSet_{20}$
$pms0021, pms0036$	0	0.3163	$URPSet_{21}$
$pms0031, pms0036$	0	0.2690	$URPSet_{22}$
$pms0029, pms0036$	0	0.2674	$URPSet_{23}$
$pms0021, pms0028$	0	0.2519	$URPSet_{24}$
$pms0008, pms0030$	0	0.3269	$URPSet_{25}$
$pms0008, pms0021$	0	0.2894	$URPSet_{26}$
$pms0008, pms0031$	0	0.2649	$URPSet_{27}$
$pms0008, pms0029$	0	0.2429	$URPSet_{28}$
$pms0028, pms0036$	0	0.2413	$URPSet_{29}$
$pms0004, pms0006, pms0023$	0	0.4475	$URPSet_{30}$
$pms0004, pms0030$	0	0.3896	$URPSet_{31}$
$pms0004, pms0005, pms0020$	0	0.3106	$URPSet_{32}$
$pms0004, pms0021$	0	0.2462	$URPSet_{33}$
$pms0005, pms0013$	0	0.5453	$URPSet_{34}$
$pms0005, pms0031$	0	0.5094	$URPSet_{35}$
$pms0005, pms0021$	0	0.4190	$URPSet_{36}$

Another interesting observation is the presence of the READ_LOGS ($pms0011$) permission in over half of the permission patterns presented in Table 8. It is often combined with the INTERNET ($pms0001$) and ACCESS_FINE_LOCATION ($pms0002$) permissions. The remaining patterns include combinations of network-related and SMS-related permissions.

Common Required Permission (CRP) Patterns. Previously, we presented the permission patterns that were unique to malicious applications only. In Table 9, we listed the permission combinations that appeared in both clean and

Table 8. Unique *Used* Permission Sets in Malware Dataset

Permission Set	Support Clean	Support Malware	Permission Set ID
$pms0001, pms0005, pms0006, pms0007$	0	0.5542	$UUPSet_1$
$pms0001, pms0005, pms0011$	0	0.4687	$UUPSet_2$
$pms0001, pms0006, pms0011$	0	0.4320	$UUPSet_3$
$pms0005, pms0006, pms0011$	0	0.4312	$UUPSet_4$
$pms0001, pms0007, pms0011$	0	0.4149	$UUPSet_5$
$pms0005, pms0007, pms0011$	0	0.4133	$UUPSet_6$
$pms0006, pms0007, pms0011$	0	0.3855	$UUPSet_7$
$pms0001, pms0002, pms0005, pms0007$	0	0.3423	$UUPSet_8$
$pms0001, pms0021$	0	0.3358	$UUPSet_9$
$pms0001, pms0002, pms0011$	0	0.2845	$UUPSet_{10}$
$pms0002, pms0005, pms0011$	0	0.2845	$UUPSet_{11}$
$pms0001, pms0002, pms0006, pms0007$	0	0.2829	$UUPSet_{12}$
$pms0002, pms0005, pms0006, pms0007$	0	0.2829	$UUPSet_{13}$
$pms0002, pms0006, pms0011$	0	0.2755	$UUPSet_{14}$
$pms0001, pms0020$	0	0.2600	$UUPSet_{15}$

Table 9. Common *Required* Permission Sets in Both Clean and Malware Datasets

Permission Set	Support Clean	Support Malware	Difference	Permission Set ID
$pms0001, pms0005$	0.3121	0.9307	−0.6186	$CRPSet_1$
$pms0005$	0.3187	0.9340	−0.6153	$CRPSet_2$
$pms0005, pms0023$	0.0236	0.6308	−0.6072	$CRPSet_3$
$pms0001, pms0023$	0.0505	0.6349	−0.5844	$CRPSet_4$
$pms0023$	0.0522	0.6349	−0.5827	$CRPSet_5$
$pms0006, pms0023$	0.0399	0.6031	−0.5632	$CRPSet_6$
$pms0005, pms0006$	0.2421	0.7905	−0.5485	$CRPSet_7$
$pms0001, pms0005, pms0006$	0.2421	0.7897	−0.5477	$CRPSet_8$
$pms0001, pms0004, pms0005$	0.1328	0.6544	−0.5216	$CRPSet_9$
$pms0004, pms0005$	0.1337	0.6553	−0.5216	$CRPSet_{10}$
$pms0004, pms0005, pms0006$	0.1149	0.5623	−0.4474	$CRPSet_{11}$
$pms0004, pms0023$	0.0293	0.4637	−0.4344	$CRPSet_{12}$

malware datasets. However, it can be observed based on the support value difference that the permission patterns are more prevalent in the malware dataset, as shown by the negative support difference values. We identified four permissions: INTERNET ($pms0001$), READ_PHONE_STATE ($pms0005$), ACCESS_NETWORK_STATE ($pms0006$) and ACCESS_WIFI_STATE ($pms0023$) that were present in different permission combinations and appeared in more than 40% of the malware dataset.

Common Used Permission (CUP) Patterns. In Table 10, we presented the *used* permission combinations that appeared in both the clean and malware datasets. Although both datasets had the same permission patterns, the ones in the malware dataset have higher support values. The patterns include the following permissions: INTERNET ($pms0001$), READ_PHONE_STATE ($pms0005$), ACCESS_NETWORK_STATE ($pms0006$), VIBRATE ($pms0007$) and lastly, READ_LOGS ($pms0011$). The same support difference for $CUPSet_1$ and $CUPSet_2$ indicated that the occurrence of these permission combinations are highly relevant. Moreover, we observed that even though READ_LOGS ($pms0011$) permission did not

Table 10. Common *Used* Permission Sets in Both Clean and Malware Datasets

| Permission Set | Support | | Difference | Permission Set |
	Clean	Malware		ID
$pms0001$, $pms0005$	0.2991	0.9152	−0.6161	$CUPSet_1$
$pms0005$	0.3032	0.9169	−0.6137	$CUPSet_2$
$pms0001$, $pms0005$, $pms0006$	0.2363	0.7718	−0.5355	$CUPSet_3$
$pms0005$, $pms0006$	0.2363	0.7718	−0.5355	$CUPSet_4$
$pms0001$, $pms0005$, $pms0007$	0.2168	0.6512	−0.4344	$CUPSet_5$
$pms0005$, $pms0007$	0.2192	0.6528	−0.4336	$CUPSet_6$
$pms0005$, $pms0011$	0.0538	0.4686	−0.4148	$CUPSet_7$
$pms0011$	0.0693	0.4760	−0.4067	$CUPSet_8$
$pms0001$, $pms0011$	0.0685	0.4711	−0.4026	$CUPSet_9$

appear in the common *required* permission patterns, but it appeared in three common *used* permission patterns READ_LOGS, $CUPSet_7$ - $CUPSet_9$.

4.3   Discussion

Observations from Statistical Analysis. From our statistical analysis in Section 3.2, we observed that the INTERNET permission remained the most required (97.72%) and used (94.62%) permission in our experimental dataset. We also found, from Tables 1 and 2, that there was a significant difference in the frequencies of required and used permissions for the clean and the malware datasets. This further confirmed the observation made by Felt et al. in [22] that both clean and malicious applications can be over-privileged. Till date, most of the proposed solutions have only considered *required* permissions extracted from the AndroidManifest.xml files. From our statistical results, we argue that *used* permissions should also be considered as part of the feature set and as such, can aid towards malware detection.

Observations from Contrast Permission Patterns. In Section 4.2, we present the most significant permission sets generated by contrast mining. We found that a large number of *required* and *used* permission sets were unique in malicious applications only. The same permission sets were non-existent in clean applications, as shown by the 0 support value. This is a good indication that the contrast permission sets can be further applied during the malware detection phase to identify malicious applications. For *normal* required permissions, we observed from Table 6 that the permission set IDs, $URPSet_1$ and $URPSet_2$ were required by 63% and 60% of the malicious applications in our dataset, respectively. We deduced that this might be the case due to the fact that 25% of our experimental malware samples (malicious applications) belong to the *Droid-KungFu3* malware family. As demonstrated in [23], malware samples classified under *DroidKungFu3* attempt to extract device ID, network-related information and send all information back to the attacker's server.

As for the *Dangerous* required permissions sets included in Tables 7, we noticed several interesting permission sets on which we provide further explanation. For permission set IDs $URPSet_{16}$ and $URPSet_{17}$, we found that 25%

of malicious applications required both ACCESS_FINE_LOCATION ($pms0002$) and ACCESS_COARSE_LOCATION ($pms0020$) permissions. While $pms0002$ is used to access to GPS location sources, $pms0020$ is used for location information related to network sources. However, the documentation [24] provided by *Google* specifies that if a developer requires network and GPS location information, they do not need to include both permissions in the application; only requesting ACCESS_FINE_LOCATION should suffice. The presence of unused permission can be exploited via permission inheritance during inter-component communications, as explained in [25].

For the *used* permission sets that were unique in our malware dataset (Table 8), we observed that the permission set: INTERNET ($pms0001$), READ_PHONE_STATE ($pms0005$), ACCESS_NETWORK_STATE ($pms0006$), VIBRATE ($pms0007$) with permission set ID $UUPSet_1$ was used by 55% of the malware samples. Interestingly, the same permission set can be found in Table 6 under the permission set ID $URPSet_{11}$, with the exception that it was required by only 35% of the malware samples.

Moreover, it can be noted from Table 8 that the READ_LOGS ($pms0011$) permission was frequently associated with the permission sets and appeared in 25% to 50% of the malware dataset. There was previously no indication that the READ_LOGS ($pms0011$) permission was a highly used permission among malicious applications as the permission did not appear in the Top 20 most *Used* permission, in Table 2. This further consolidates our argument that permission patterns cannot be generated by only considering the number of frequencies for that particular permission.

Furthermore, we also noted that there are several permission sets which appeared in both clean and malware datasets, shown in Tables 9 and 10. The negative support difference given in the table shows that the permission sets were more prevalent in malicious applications than in clean ones. We observed that the top two permission sets, $CRPSet_1$ and $CRPSet_2$ in Table 9 and $CUPSet_1$ and $CUPSet_{11}$ in Table 10 are the same.

5   Conclusion

Android uses a permission system to control access to restricted resources on smartphones. The permissions are indicative of the characteristics of an applications and as such, can be used to differentiate clean applications from malicious ones. However, most of the existing work only focused on *required* permissions and there is no extensive work on understanding key similarities and differences in permission patterns between clean and malicious applications.

To address these aforementioned issues, in this paper we combined both *required* and *used* permissions to identify a set of unique and common contrast permission patterns. Additionally, an efficient pattern mining method that can identify contrasting permission patterns for our clean and malware datasets was proposed. We observed that some permission sets were common in both datasets, while others were unique to only the clean or the malicious dataset.

By applying support value to the set of permission patterns, we filtered out the permission combinations that are less significant. Compared to Frank et al.'s work [3] where the authors had to simulate permission request data to test their generated patterns, we applied our proposed methodology to combine the *required* and *used* permissions and retained those which can be used to contrast clean and malicious applications. Last but not least, since obfuscation methods cannot be applied to *Android* permissions, the generated permission sets can be used to contrast clean and malicious applications. In the future, we would like to work on finding contrasting patterns that can differentiate between an original application and a repackaged one.

References

1. Orozco, A.: Is Google Acknowledging Android is not Secure? Malwarebytes (June 2013), http://blog.malwarebytes.org/intelligence/2013/06/is-google-acknowledging-android-is-not-secure-hmm/
2. Gilbert, P., Byung-Gon, C., Landon, P.C., Jaeyeon, J.: Vision: automated security validation of mobile apps at app markets. In: Proceedings of the 2nd International Workshop on Mobile Cloud Computing and Services (MCS 2011), Washington, USA, pp. 21–26 (June 2011)
3. Frank, M., Dong, B., Felt, A.P., Song, D.: Mining permission request patterns from Android and Facebook applications. In: Proceedings of the IEEE International Conference on Data Mining, Brussels, Belgium (ICDM 2012), pp. 1–16 (December 2012), http://arxiv.org/abs/1210.2429
4. Felt, A.P., Ha, E., Egelman, S., Haney, A., Chin, E., Wagner, D.: Android permissions: User attention, comprehension and behavior. In: Proceedings of the Symposium on Usable Privacy and Security (SOUPS 2012), Washington, D.C., vol. 3, pp. 1–14 (July 2012)
5. Zhou, Y., Jiang, X.: Dissecting Android malware: Characterization and evolution. In: Proceedings of the IEEE Symposium on Security and Privacy (SP 2012), San Francisco, CA, pp. 95–109 (May 2012)
6. Felt, A.P., Greenwood, K., Wagner, D.: The effectiveness of application permissions. In: Proceedings of the USENIX Conference on Web Application Development (WebApps 2011), Portland, Oregon, pp. 1–12 (June 2011)
7. Chia, P.H., Yamamoto, Y., Asokan, N.: Is this app safe? a large scale study on application permissions and risk signals. In: Proceedings of the 21st International Conference on World Wide Web (WWW 2012), Lyon, France, pp. 311–320 (April 2012)
8. International Secure Systems Lab. Andrubis: Analyzing Android binaries, http://anubis.iseclab.org (accessed in May 2012)
9. Open Handset Alliance. Android, http://www.openhandsetalliance.com/android_overview.html (accessed in November 2007)
10. Ableson, F.: Introduction to Android development, http://www.ibm.com/developerworks/library/os-android-devel (accessed in May 2009)
11. Google. Google play, https://play.google.com (accessed in December 2012)
12. Google. Android permissions, http://developer.android.com/guide/topics/manifest/permission-element.html (accessed in December 2012)
13. Bartel, A., Klein, J., Monperrus, M., Traon, Y.L.: Automatically securing permission-based software by reducing theattack surface - an application to Android. In: Proceedings of the 27th IEEE/ACM International Conference on Automated Software Engineering (ASE 2012), Essen, Germany, pp. 274–277 (September 2012)

14. Sanz, B., Santos, I., Laorden, C., Ugarte-Pedrero, X., Bringas, P.G., Álvarez, G.: PUMA: Permission usage to detect malware in android. In: Herrero, Á., et al. (eds.) Int. Joint Conf. CISIS'12-ICEUTE'12-SOCO'12. AISC, vol. 189, pp. 289–298. Springer, Heidelberg (2013)

15. Sahs, J., Khan, L.: A machine learning approach to Android malware detection. In: Proceedings of the European Intelligence and Security Informatics Conference (EISIC 2012), Odense, Denmark, pp. 141–147 (August 2012)

16. Wu, D.J., Mao, C.H., Wei, T.E., Lee, H.M., Wu, K.P.: DroidMat: Android malware detection through manifest and API calls tracing. In: Proceedings of the 2012 Seventh Asia Joint Conference on InformationSecurity (Asia JCIS 2012), Tokyo, Japan, pp. 62–69 (August 2012)

17. Zhou, Y., Wang, Z., Zhou, W., Jiang, X.: Hey, You, Get Off of My Market: Detecting Malicious Appsin Official and Alternative Android Markets. In: Proceedings of the 19th Annual Network and Distributed System Security Symposium (NDSS 2012), San Diego, California, pp. 1–13 (February 2012)

18. Agrawal, R., Imieinski, T., Swami, A.: Mining association rules between sets of items in large databases. In: Buneman, P., Jajodia, S. (eds.) Proceedings of the ACM SIGMOD International Conference on the Managementof Data, Washington, D.C., pp. 207–216. ACM Press (1993)

19. Liu, S., Law, R., Rong, J., Li, G., Hall, J.: Analyzing changes in hotel customers' expectations by trip mode. International Journal of Hospitality Management (2012) (in press)

20. Rong, J., Vu, H.Q., Law, R., Li, G.: A behavioral analysis of web sharers and browsers inhong kong using targeted association rule mining. Tourism Management 33(4), 731–740 (2012), http://dx.doi.org/10.1016/j.tourman.2011.08.006

21. Law, R., Rong, R., Vu, H.Q., Li, G., Lee, H.A.: Identifying changes and trends in hong kong outbound tourism. Tourism Management 32(5), 1106–1114 (2011)

22. Felt, A.P., Chin, E., Hanna, S., Song, D., Wagner, D.: Android permissions demystified. In: Proceedings of the ACM Conference and Communications Security (CCS 2011), Chicago, USA, pp. 627–638 (October 2011)

23. F-Secure. Trojan:android/droidkungfu.c, http://www.f-secure.com/v-descs/trojan_android_droidkungfu_c.shtml (accessed in January 2013)

24. Android Developer. Location strategies, http://developer.android.com/guide/topics/location/strategies.html (accessed in January 2013)

25. Chin, E., Felt, A.P., Greenwood, K., Wagner, D.: Analyzing inter-application communication in Android. In: Proceedings of the 9th Annual International Conference on Mobile Systems, Applications, and Services (MobiSys 2011), Washington, USA, pp. 239–252 (June 2011)

DroidAPIMiner: Mining API-Level Features for Robust Malware Detection in Android

Yousra Aafer, Wenliang Du, and Heng Yin

Dept. of Electrical Engineering & Computer Science
Syracuse University, New York, USA
{yaafer,wedu,heyin}@syr.edu

Abstract. The increasing popularity of Android apps makes them the target of malware authors. To defend against this severe increase of Android malwares and help users make a better evaluation of apps at install time, several approaches have been proposed. However, most of these solutions suffer from some shortcomings; computationally expensive, not general or not robust enough. In this paper, we aim to mitigate Android malware installation through providing *robust* and *lightweight* classifiers. We have conducted a thorough analysis to extract relevant features to malware behavior captured at API level, and evaluated different classifiers using the generated feature set. Our results show that we are able to achieve an accuracy as high as 99% and a false positive rate as low as 2.2% using KNN classifier.

Keywords: Android, malware, static detection, classification.

1 Introduction

As Android mobile devices are becoming increasingly popular, they are becoming a target of malware authors. To protect mobile users from the severe threats of Android malwares, different solutions have been proposed. Several systems have been proposed based on Android permission system. In [12], if an app requests a specific or a combination of critical permissions, a risk signal will be raised. In [22], several risk signals have been proposed depending on an app's requested permissions, its category, as well as the requested permissions from apps belonging to the same category. In [17], different risk scoring schemes have been designed using probabilistic generative models. However, the permission-based warning mechanisms fall short for several reasons:

- The existence of a certain permission in the app manifest file does not necessarily mean that it is actually used within the code. According to [13, 14, 26], a large percentage of Android apps are over-privileged.
- A large number of requested permissions, specially the critical ones, are actually not used within the application's code itself, but rather are required by the advertisement packages.
- Malware can perform malicious behavior without any permission [15].

Another direction to detect malicious activities in Android apps relies on the semantic information within the application bytecode. CHEX [16] statically

T. Zia et al. (Eds.): SecureComm 2013, LNICST 127, pp. 86–103, 2013.

vets Android apps for component hijacking vulnerabilities through performing data flow analysis and conducting reachability tests on the generated system dependency graphs to detect potential hijack enabling flows. Similarly, Woodpecker [15] exposes capability leaks through using data flow analysis and exploring the reachability of a dangerous permission from a non-protected interface. While these approaches are effective in detecting the particular vulnerabilities that they target, they cannot be generalized to detect other malicious activities. DroidRanger [29], on the other hand, combines permission-based behavioral footprints and a heuristic based filtering scheme to detect malicious apps.

In this paper, we aim to overcome the shortcomings of the permission-based warning mechanisms and build a robust and lightweight classifier for Android apps that could be used for malware detection. To select the best features that distinguish between malware from benign apps, we rely on API level information within the bytecode since it conveys substantial semantics about the apps behavior. More specifically, we focus on critical API calls, their package level information, as well as their parameters.

Instead of following a heuristic based approach for identifying critical features for malware functioning, we have analyzed a large corpus of benign and malware samples, generated the set of APIs used within each app, and conducted a frequency analysis to list out the ones which are more frequent in the malware than in the benign set. Furthermore, for certain critical APIs which were frequent in both sample sets, we have conducted a simple data flow analysis on the malware APK samples to identify potentially dangerous inputs. We generated a list of frequently used parameters, thoroughly examined them to filter out the dangerous ones and flagged all apps that request them. To perform API level feature extraction and data flow analysis, we have developed a tool called DroidAPIMiner built upon Androguard [2] reverse engineering tool. We use RapidMiner [7] to build the classification models.

In summary, the contributions of this paper are as follows:

- We introduce a robust and efficient approach for describing Android malware that relies on the API, package, and parameter level information.
- Based on the identified feature set of Android malware, we provide valuable insights about malware behavior at API-level.
- We produce and evaluate different classifiers for Android apps. Our testing shows that some of them achieve a high accuracy and low false positive rate compared to the permission-based classifiers. In fact, KNN achieves a 99% accuracy and 2.2% false positive rate.

2   Approach Overview

In our work, we follow a generic data mining approach that aims to build a classifier for Android apps. The classifier should be able to automatically learn to identify complex malware patterns and make smart decisions based on that. The classifier should also be able to generalize from the input set to correctly predict an accurate class of given new apps. As depicted in Fig. 1, our approach

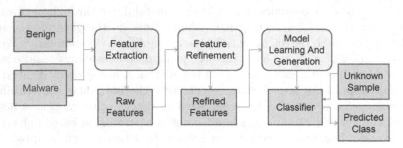

Fig. 1. Our Approach

is divided into three phases: feature extraction, feature refinement, and models learning and generation.

During the feature extraction phase, we statically examine the collected benign and malware APK samples to determine and extract the necessary features for malware to function. In selecting the feature set, we focus on some semantic information encapsulated within the bytecode of apps. More specifically, we extract API calls and their package level information. Besides, we extract the requested permissions of the apps for the generation of the baseline model.

During the feature refinement phase, we remove the API calls that are exclusively invoked by third-party packages such as advertisement packages. We reduce our feature set further to include only those APIs whose support in the malware set is significantly higher than in the benign set. For those APIs which were frequent in the two sets, we perform data flow analysis to recover their parameter values and select only the APIs that invoke dangerous values. Subsequently, for each APK file, we generate a set of feature vectors along with associated class labels, i.e. malware or benign. For the last two steps, we have implemented DroidAPIMiner, a python program that import libraries from Androguard static analysis tool for Android apps [2]. Section 3 will be dedicated to discuss in more details how we conduct feature extraction and refinement. We discuss in Section 4 some of the insights that we have gained based on the identified features.

During the model learning and generation phase, we feed the representative vectors to standard classification algorithms that build the models by learning from them. We have generated 4 different classifiers: ID5 DT [20], C4.5 DT [21], KNN [8] and SVM [25]. We test the generated classifiers to estimate the accuracy using split validation. Two thirds of the data set are randomly selected for training and the rest one third is dedicated for testing. For this step, we use RapidMiner [7] to generate the classification models and evaluate them. In Section 5, we perform the classification and evaluate the models.

3   Feature Extraction and Refinement

In this section, we aim to systematically determine and extract necessary features for malware functioning. Android app's bytecode contains information that could be used to describe its behavior. From the bytecode, we can retrieve information ranging from coarse-grained levels as packages to fine-grained levels as instructions. We do not perform sophisticated program analysis because it is computationally expensive. Rather, we focus on extracting package and API level information since they clearly capture the app's behavior. More specifically, we consider class name, method name, and some parameters of the callee and the package name of the caller, which we will describe in the next subsections.

3.1 Extraction of Dangerous APIs

Contrary to previous work, we do not follow a heuristic-based approach to identify dangerous APIs for malware functioning. Instead, we aim to reliably identify the major APIs that malwares invoke by statically analyzing our samples.

Effectively, we have statically analyzed a large set of malware and benign apps and generated a list of distinct API calls within each set. A distinct API refers to a distinct combination of Class Name, Method Name, and Descriptor. We then conduct a frequency analysis to select those APIs which are more used in the malware than in the benign set. We further refine the API list to include only those with a usage difference higher or equal to a certain threshold.

3.2 Extraction of Package Level Information

Most of Android apps contain one or more third-party packages (according to our analysis, 71 % of the benign apps contain at least one advertisement package). These packages often exhibit some suspicious behavior. For instance, many ads use encryption to hinder their removal. Also, `getCellLocation()` and `getDeviceId()` methods are often called by ad kits for users' identification and tracking purposes. We aim to identify at what package level a certain API is invoked. To achieve this goal, we have performed the following tasks:

– **Extract advertisement and similar packages:** Using Androguard, we generate all distinct packages invoked within each APK in our collected sample. We remove from the generated packages names all common packages such as Android specific packages, Java packages, etc. We inspect the remaining items and compile a list of advertisement, web tracking, web analysis and application ranking packages. In total, we have identified around 412 distinct advertisement and similar packages. Some commonly used advertisement packages are: Admob, Flurry, Millennialmedia, Inmobi, Adwhirl, Adfonic, Adcenix, etc.
– **Identify calling packages:** We check at what package a certain API is called. In other words, we distinguish if an API is invoked only by a third-party package, only by the application specific packages, or by both. We white-list any APIs that are exclusively invoked by third-party packages.

3.3 Extraction of APIs Parameters

Certain frequent APIs in the malware set did not yield to a high support difference between the malware and the benign sample as they were also common in the benign sample. For example, some methods within string manipulation and IO classes are almost as frequent in the malicious set as in the benign sample. To

Table 1. Categorization of Parameters to Frequently Used Malware APIs

Classes	Methods	Parameter Category
Intent IntentFilters	setFlags, addFlags, setDataAndType, putExtra, init	Flag is either: CALL, CONNECTIVITY, SEND, SENDTO, or BLUETOOTH
ContentResolver	query, insert, update..	URI is either: Content://sms-mms, Content://telephony, Content://calendar, Content://browser/bookmarks, Content://calllog, Content://mail, or Content://downlaods
DataInputStream BufferedReader DataOutputStream DataOutputStream	init, writeBytes...	Reads from process Reads from connection Uses SU command
InetSocketAddress	init	parameter IP is explicit or port is 80
File Stream StringBuilder String StringBuffer	init, write, append, indexOf, Substring	Dangerous Command such as: su, ls, loadjar, grep, /sh, /bin, pm install, /dev/net, insmod, rm, mount, root, /system, stdout, reboot, killall, chmod, stderr Accesses external storage or cache Contains either: An identifier (e.g. Imei), an executable file(e.g. .exe, .sh), a compressed file (e.g. jar, zip), a unicode string, an sql query, a reflection string, or a url

increase this difference, we have performed data flow analysis on these specific APIs in order to recover the parameters values that have been passed to them through inspecting the registers invoked.

Based on our initial investigation, these APIs generated distinct parameters which resulted in a big number of features. To reduce the parameter feature set, we have categorized the parameters based on different criteria. Table 1 includes the APIs on which we have performed the data flow analysis along with the criteria that we have adopted to categorize their input parameters.

4   Insights in API-Level Malware Behavior

Based on the API level analysis, we have identified the top APIs that Android malwares invoke. Fig.2 shows the top 20 APIs that produce the highest difference of usage between malware and benign apps. As illustrated, we get a better difference after filtering out third-party packages. For example, the method `init` in `Java.Util.TimerTask` initially produced 14% usage difference between the two sets. This difference increased to 28% after whitelisting this API in third-party packages since it is mainly invoked by them in the benign sample.

We discuss here some of the top commonly used malware features that our study generated after refining the initial feature set. To help understand malware behavior and gain more insight into what resources are accessed and what actions are performed, we classify the APIs by the type of requested resources and utilities. At the end of the section, we present the data flow analysis results.

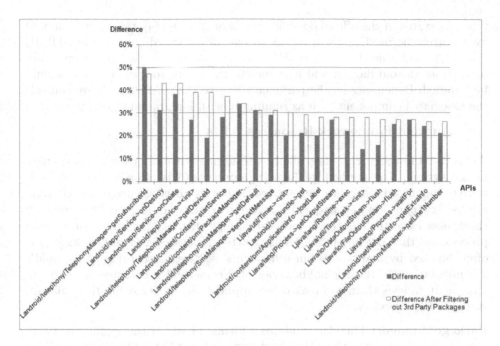

Fig. 2. Top 20 APIs with the Highest Difference Between Malware and Benign Apps

4.1   Application-Specific Resources APIs

Content Resolver: This class provides access to content providers. It processes requests (CRUD operations) by directing them to the appropriate content provider. The most frequent methods used in this class by malware are insert(), delete() and query(). This latter can be invoked to grab sensitive information from content providers of other apps if they are not protected by permissions. As stated in [5], some vendor pre-installed apps have implicitly exported content providers which allowed other apps to successfully obtain sensitive information from them without acquiring the necessary permissions.

Context: Context class provides global application information such as its specific assets, classes, and resources. startService() is very frequently used methods within this class with a support of more than 70% in malware and less than 34% in benign ones. This API can be invoked to start a given service in the background without interacting with the user. getFilesDir() and openFileOuput() are other frequent APIs in this class that malwares call to create files and get their absolute paths. getApplicationInfo() is often used by malwares for obtaining various information about the app such as whether it's debuggable, installed on external storage, holds factory test flag, etc.

Intents: Intents allow launching other activities and services and interacting with the phone's hardware. The most frequent APIs used by malwares within Intents are setDataAndType(), setFlags() and addFlags(). setDataAndType() allows setting the URI path for the intent data with an explicit MIME data type. As stated in the official documentation of Android [4], this method should "very rarely be used" since it allows to override the ordinary inferred MIME type of data of a newly specified MIME type. `setFlags()` and `addFlags()` are used to set the old flags or add new ones to the intent to specify how it should be handled. Depending on the parameter flag to these APIs, malware controls the associated component such as running it with foreground priority.

4.2   Android Framework Resources APIs

ActivityManager: This class allows interacting with other activities running in the system. The method `getRunningServices()` is often invoked by malware to inquire whether a certain service (like Anti-virus) is currently executing. `getMemoryInfo()` is also frequently invoked by malware and might be used to check how close the system to have no enough memory for other background process and thus needing to start killing other processes. `restartPackage()` is often invoked by malware to kill other apps' services. According to Android's documentation [1], the original behavior of this method is no longer available to apps as it "allows them to break other applications by removing their alarms, stopping their services, etc".

PackageManager: This class contains information about the application packages installed on the device. Malicious apps call `getInstalledPackages()` to scan the system against a list of known anti-virus and take an appropriate action based on that (e.g. remain dormant, kill the anti-virus process, etc.) .

Telephony/ SmsManager and telephony/ gsm/ SmsManager: These classes allows managing various SMS operations. Malware authors invoke many methods within theses classes. `sendTextMessage()` is very frequently used by malwares authors to send sms messages to premium rate numbers without the user's consent and thus incur financial losses. Examples of SMS Trojans include malware belonging to the following families: SpyEye, OpFake, Gemini, etc.

TelephonyManager: This class retrieves various information about telephony services on the device. The most frequently used APIs by malwares are: `getSubscriberId()`, `getDeviceId()`, `getLine1Number()`, `getSimSerialNumber ()`, `getNetworkOperator()`, and `getCellLocation()`. Malware authors collect these private data and send it to remote servers to build users profiles and track them. As illustrated in Fig. 2, `getSubsriberId()` is the mostly used API by our malware sample.

4.3   DVM Related Resources APIs

DexClassLoader: This class allows loading classes from external .jar and .apk files containing a classes.dex. `loadClass()` is one of the most frequently invoked APIs by malware and is used to execute code not installed as part of the app and consequently evade malware detection techniques that rely on static analysis.

Runtime and System: Runtime class allows apps to interact with the environment in which they are running. Malware invokes `Runtime.getRuntime.exec`

() method to execute dangerous Linux commands along with the supplied arguments in a newly spawned native process and thus avoid the normal execution lifecycle of the program. System class provides system related facilities such as standard input, output and error output streams. loadLibrary()dynamically loads native libraries and can be used maliciously through running native code exploiting some known system vulnerabilities.

4.4   System Resources APIs

ConnectivityManager, NetworkInfo, and WifiManage: These classes provide network related functionalities such as answering queries about different connections (Wifi, GPRS, UMTS) and network interfaces. Android malware calls APIs within ConnectivityManager class (getNetworkInfo()), NetworkInfo (getExtraInfo(), getTypeName(), isConnected(), getState()), and within WifiManager(setWifiEnabled() and getWifiState()) to establish a network connection and interact with malicious remote servers.

HttpURLConnection and Sockets: APIs within these classes are used to send and receive data over the web and establish communication with remote servers. The most frequent APIs used by malwares in HttpURLConnection are setRequestMethod(), getInputStream(), and getOutputStream() which manage transferring data between the malware apps and the malicious servers. Similarly, malware applications often invoke getInputStream() and getOutputStream() in Socket class for the same purpose. We have also noted a heavy use of InetSocketAddress which implements an IP socket address given an IP address and a port number.

OS Package: A lot of frequently used APIs in malware belong to OS package which allows message passing, ipc services, process and threads management. sendMessage() method in os.Handler class inserts messages into message queues of different executing threads, while obtainMessage() retrieves messages from the message queues. Malware authors often invoke myPid() and killProcess() in Process class to request killing processes based on a given pid. However, the kernel will impose restrictions on which processes an application can actually kill [6]; only apps and packages sharing common UIDs can actually kill each other. Unfortunately, these restrictions will not prevent Android malware from killing processes beyond their scope once they can root the device.

IO Package: IO package provides IO processing services such as reading and writing to streams, files, internal memory buffers, etc. Malwares invoke APIs within IO.DataOutputStream (such as writeBytes()) to write data and upload files through a URL connection. Similarly, they call APIs in IO.DataInputStream (such as readLines(), available()) to read and download malicious payloads from a certain URL connection. Methods within IO.FileOutputStream (such as writo()) are used to write the malicious content downloaded from a remote server to local files. mkdir(), delete(), exists() and ListFiles() are other used APIs in IO.File by malware for file management.

4.5   Utilities APIs

String, StringBuilder and StringBuffer: These classes provide an interface for creating and manipulating strings. Malware heavily call `substring()`, `indexOf()`, `getBytes()`, `valueOf()`, `replaceAll()`, and `Append()`. These methods can be used for code obfuscation, construction of payloads to be sent to servers, and evasion of static malware detection techniques through dynamically creating URLs, parameters to reflection APIs, and dangerous Linux commands.

Timer: Timers facilitate scheduling one-shot or recurring tasks for future execution. Malware can invoke APIs within this class (such as `schedule()` and `cancel()`) to avoid dynamic analysis by remaining dormant until a fixed date is reached, or until a specific event has been fired.

ZipInputStream: This class allows decompressing data from an InputStream ZIP archive. Malwares rely on methods in this class to decompress and read data from compressed files (.jar, .apk, .zip) downloaded during execution or originally attached to the app. Commonly used APIs by malware in this class are `read()`, `close()`, `getNextEntry()` and `closeEntry()`.

Crypto: This package serves as an interface for implementing cryptographic operations such as encryption, decryption, and key agreement. Methods within Crypto.Cipher such as `getInstance()` and `doFinal()` transform a given input to an encrypted or decrypted format while `Crypto.spec.DESKeySpec()` allows specifying a DES key. These methods can be used for code obfuscation and avoiding static detection through encrypting root exploits, SMS payloads, targeted premium SMS numbers, and URLs to remote malicious servers.

w3c.dom: This package provides the official w3c Java interfaces for the Document Object Model (DOM), which is used in apps for XML document processing. Malwares use several APIs in w3c.dom such as `getDocumentElement ()`, `getElementByTagName()`, and `getAttribute()` to parse XML files. XML can be used by malwares to establish bot communication, encode data, and process local configuration files.

4.6   Parameters Features

Based on the data flow analysis that we have conducted, we obtained the frequent parameters (categorized as discussed in Table 1) that are used by malwares applications more often than the benign ones in certain API invocations. Table 2 depicts some of the top invoked parameters types that yield to the highest support difference between the malware and benign sample.

From the data flow analysis results depicted in Table 2, we can gain more insight on Android malware behavior. A large percentage of String manipulation operations are performed on dangerous Linux commands (such as SU, mount, sh, bin, pm install, killall, chmod). These commands are mainly used by malware authors to root the phone and exploit some well known vulnerabilities. After getting superuser privilege, malwares perform various dangerous Linux operations through

Table 2. Some Frequent API Parameters in Malware

Class	Method	Parameter type	Difference (%)
StringBuilder	append	Dangerous command	35.95
ContentResolver	query	SMS or MMS	23.65
StringBuilder	append	Unicode string	23.6
StringBuilder	init	Dangerous command	23.07
DataOutputSream	writebytes	Reads from process	21.80
DataOutputSream	init	Reads from process	21.62
runTime	exec	Dangerous command	21.27
InetSocketAddress	init	Port 80	19.91
StringBuilder	append	Compressed file	19.58
DataInputStream	init	Reads from connection	19.27
String	valueOf	Unicode string	18.05
StringBuilder	append	File manipulation	17.79
File	init	Accesses external storage	16.92
InetSocketAddress	init	Explicit IP	14.87
String	getBytes	URL manupilation	14.05
Intent	setFlags	SendTo	12.94
Intent	setFlags	Call	11.67
ContentResolver	query	Telephony	10.88
Intent	setFlags	Send	10.47
ContentResolver	query	Call_log	10.12

invoking runtime.exec(). Most of the ContentResolver operations are performed on SMS, MMS, telephony or call log content providers.

5   Classification and Evaluation

5.1   Data Set

To extract malware and benign apps' features, generate and evaluate the classification models, we have collected and analyzed around 20,000 apps. Our malware sample consists of 3987 malware apps that we collected from different sources (McAfee and Android Malware Genome Project [3]). The malware sample belongs to different Android malware families. Our benign sample consists of the top 500 free apps in each category in Google Play (around 16000 apps) that we collected in July 2012.

5.2   Classification Models

As discussed earlier, our objective is to build a model that classifies unknown apps as either benign or malware. For that, we have employed four different algorithms for the classification: ID3 DT [20], C4.5 DT [20], KNN [8], and linear SVM [25]. These inducers belong to different family of classifiers. C4.5 and ID3 are related to decision trees and KNN belong to Lazy classifiers. SVM is a supervised learning method that proceeds through dividing the training data by an optimal separating hyperplane. We have decided to employ algorithms from different classifiers because we hope that they will produce different classification models for Android apps. Our analysis shows that KNN and ID3 DT models lead to a better accuracy compared to the other models.

To test our generated classification models, we use split validation. That is, we randomly split our dataset into training (2/3) and testing set (1/3). We build the classification models based on the training set and feed the testing instances to evaluate the models. To evaluate each classifier's performance, we measured the True Positive Ratio (TPR), i.e., the proportion of malware instances that were correctly classified:

$$TPR = \frac{TP}{TP + FN}$$

where TP is the number of malware apps correctly identified and FN is the number of malware apps classified as benign apps. Similarly, we measure the True Negative Ratio (TNR), i.e., the proportion of benign instances that were correctly classified:

$$TNR = \frac{TN}{TN + FP}$$

where TN is the number of benign apps correctly identified and FP is the number of benign apps identified as malware apps. To capture the overall performance, we measure the models' accuracy, i.e., the total number of benign and malware instances correctly classified divided by the total number of the dataset instances:

$$Accuracy = \frac{TP + TN}{TP + TN + FP + FN}$$

By means of our collected dataset, we conducted different experiments to find the optimum feature set that will produce the best cut between the malware and benign sample.

5.3   Permission-Based Feature Set

In the first experiment, we extract the permissions requested by malware and benign apps and obtain their perspective percentage usage in the two sets. We then rank the permissions based on the difference usage and took the top k permissions that are more frequently requested in malware than in benign apps. To determine the optimum k permissions, we evaluate the performance of the models for k = 10, 20, 30..., up to 124.

Fig. 3 depicts the results obtained for the permission-based feature set in terms of accuracy, TPR, and TNR. As illustrated, the models' accuracy increases as the feature set includes more permissions. It should be noted that only 64 permissions were more frequent in the malware set than in the benign set, which means that after the top 64 permissions, the classifiers start to learn also from the permissions that are frequent in the benign set. This makes the classifiers not solid enough since they can fail to detect malicious apps in the following two scenarios. First, malware authors can easily defeat the permission-based classifiers through merely declaring "benign" permissions in the manifest file.

Second, the classifiers will not be able to correctly classify repackaged android malware; which is based on legitimate apps but embeds extra payload to achieve a malicious goal. The manifests of the repackaged apps include both the original permissions of the benign app and the permissions needed for the malicious behavior and thus confuse the classifiers.

To demonstrate that the permission model is not robust enough, we designed an experiment in which we modify our malware set and feed it to the classifiers. In each malware manifest, we declare 10 new permissions (the top 10 in the benign set) and keep everything else unchanged. As shown in Fig. 3(d), when the feature set contains the permissions used in the benign set, the classifiers are not able to correctly classify the malware set. In fact, using the top 80 permissions, the classification rate of KNN drops to 67% and of ID3 to 43%.

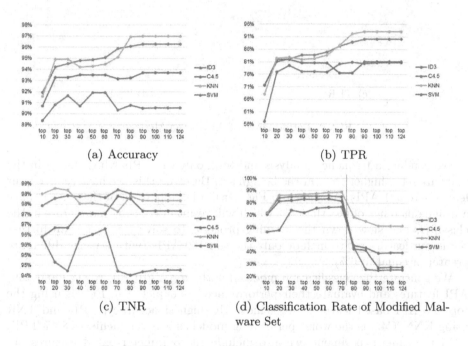

(a) Accuracy

(b) TPR

(c) TNR

(d) Classification Rate of Modified Malware Set

Fig. 3. Performance of Permission-based Models

5.4 API-Based Feature Set with Package Level and Parameter Information

In the second experiment, our feature vector includes the generated APIs within each set, which make up in total 8375 distinct APIs. We also embed package level information. That is, we white-list the APIs that are exclusively called by third-party packages. We specifically filter out these APIs to avoid the case where a benign app might be classified as malicious if a third-party package invokes a possibly "malicious" API. Consequently, the support of white-listed APIs drops in the benign set.

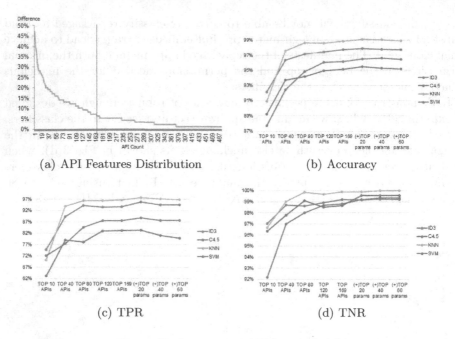

(a) API Features Distribution

(b) Accuracy

(c) TPR

(d) TNR

Fig. 4. Performance of API-based Models

We conduct a frequency analysis and took only the APIs whose usage in the malware set is higher than in the benign set. Based on this, we have reduced our features to 491 APIs. As shown in Fig. 4(a), a large portion of these APIs have a usage difference of less than 6% which will result in creating more noise in the classifiers and slow down the learning process. To solve this issue, we further refine our feature set to include only the top 169 APIs (with a usage difference greater or equal to 6%).

We generate the classification models for the top k (10, 40, 80, 120 and 169) API features and evaluate their performance. As depicted in Fig. 4, using the top 169 API based features, we achieve the highest accuracy, TPR and TNR using KNN. C4.5 is the worst performing model as it barely achieves 83% TPR.

In the same experiment, we also include the parameter-based features obtained using data flow analysis on the original set. We re-generate the models and evaluate them after adding 20, 40, and 60 parameters to the 169 filtered APIs. As shown in Fig. 4, by adding the top 20 used parameters, we are able to achieve the highest accuracy (99%) and TPR (97.8%) using KNN algorithm. The other algorithms also perform better with the newly added parameter-based feature set.

Unlike permission-based classifiers, it is not possible to trick API-based classifiers through declaring benign APIs, because the models do not rely on benign features to classify a given app. Rather, they only rely on the APIs (along with parameters) that are more frequently used in malware than in benign apps.

5.5   Models Comparison

To show the improvement achieved over the experiments performed, we plot the accuracy, TPR, and TNR of the classification models together as depicted in Fig. 5. We consider two permission models. The first one is trained on the top 60 frequent permissions in malware and the second one on all the permissions. For the API filtered model, the feature vector includes all the top 169 features. The last model that we consider is trained on the top 169 filtered APIs along with the top 20 frequent parameters in certain APIs within malware.

As shown in Fig. 5, our API based features performs better than the permission-based one. We were able to improve the accuracy, TPR and TNR of the models by embedding package and some parameter features to our original features. KNN is the best performing model, followed by ID3, SVM then C4.5.

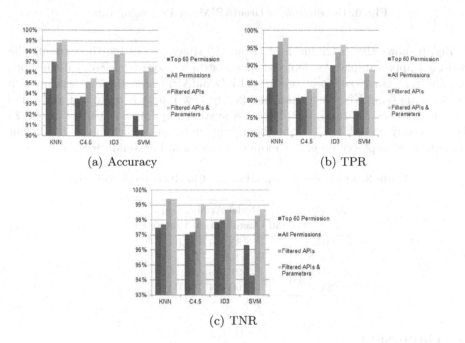

(a) Accuracy   (b) TPR

(c) TNR

Fig. 5. Models Comparison

5.6   Processing Time

It is evident that the processing time is a crucial metric for a scalable detection system. In this section, we report the execution time of DroidAPIMiner which consists of the time required to de-assemble an apk file and to extract the API and parameter feature set. We also report the time that RapidMiner requires for applying different classification models to classify a new instance. We perform the analysis an Intel Core i5-2430M machine with 6GB of memory.

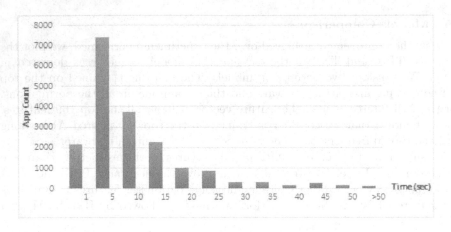

Fig. 6. Distribution of DroidAPIMiner Processing time

Fig. 6 shows the distribution of DroidAPIMiner processing time among the collected apps sample. As depicted in the graph, more than 80% of the apps require less than 15 sec to be analyzed by DroidAPIMiner. Besides, as shown in Table. 3 applying KNN algorithm to classify new inputs is quite fast and takes less than 10 sec. In total, our detection system requires on average about 25 sec to classify an apk file as either benign or malicious, which makes it efficient enough to be deployed on either mobile devices and back-end servers.

Table 3. Processing Overhead of the Classification Algorithms

Algorithm	Model Application and Classification time (sec)
ID3	185.0 +- 32.0
KNN	9.0 +- 1.0
C4.5	21.0 +- 4.0
SVM	160.2 +- 40.0

6   Discussion

In this section, we discuss some potential evasion techniques that malware authors may adopt in order to thwart our classifiers. Furthermore, we discuss how our tool handles these cases.

– Reflection: Malware authors may use reflection to easily obfuscate any dangerous API call and thus evade the static detection of the occurrence of that API by our analysis tool. However, it should be noted that our study has shown that reflection APIs are more frequently used by our malware set than in the benign set, which makes them part of the feature vector for the classification.
– Native Code: To avoid static detectors at the bytecode level, malwares sometimes embed malicious payload within native content. Since our detection tool

only works at bytecode level, it will not be able to detect any dangerous methods invoked. However, the use of JNI calls such as System.loadLibrary() is also used as a classification feature by our tool.

- Bytecode Encryption: To prevent reverse engineering of Java code, malware authors may encrypt their code and allow the decryption at runtime. Our tool considers decryption APIs as a classification feature.
- Dynamic Loading: As discussed earlier, DexClassLoader allows loading classes from .jar and .apk files at runtime and executing code not installed as part of an app. loadClass() in DexClassLoader also belongs to our feature set.
- More Benign Calls: Since our classifiers rely on the frequency of API calls, malware authors might think of introducing more benign API calls into their code. However, our tool is not susceptible to this problem, because we do not rely on the occurrence of benign API calls as a feature for the classification. Rather, we only consider the occurrence of malicious call as a feature.

7   Related Work

Several studies have been conducted in the field of Android malware detection. One much-studied direction focuses on the permission system. Kirin [12] blocks apps that declare risky permission combinations or contain any suspicious action strings used by activities, services or broadcast receivers. Zhou et al. [29] detect Android malware based on the similarities of the requested permissions and the behavioral footprints to different known malware families. Sarma et al. [22] propose different risk signals based on the requested permissions, category as well as requested permissions of apps belonging to the same category. In another work, Sarma et al. [17] employ probabilistic generative models to compute a real risk score of Android apps based on the permissions that they request.

Another direction of related work relies on system level events to detect possible malicious behavior. Schmidt et al. [23] extract library and system function calls from Android executables and compare them to malware executables to classify apps. Crowdroid [10] collects system call traces of running apps on different Android devices and applies clustering algorithms to detect malwares.

More similar research to our study rely on semantics within the bytecode to detect specific vulnerabilties in Android applications. Potharaju et al. [19] aim to detect plagiarized apps through different detection schemes relying on symbol tables and method-level Abstract Syntactic Tree fingerprints. In [28], Zhou et al. aim to systematically detect and analyze repackaged apps on third party Android markets based on fuzzy hashing techniques.

Other related work for detecting malware through bytecode level information have been proposed by Blasing et al. [9] and Zhou et al. [29]. However, the first one (AASandbox) relies on a trial and error approach to identify suspicious patterns in the source code, while DroidRanger performs the detection with regards to a heuristic based filtering. In our work, we conduct a thorough frequency analysis of API calls within benign and malware apps to extract malware features and employ machine learning to get the most relevant ones.

A different direction for detecting Android malware relies on dynamic analysis. Andromaly [24] continuously monitors various system metrics to detect suspicious activities through applying supervised anomaly detection techniques. In [11], Enck et al. perform dynamic taint analysis to track the flow of private and sensitive data through third party apps, and detect any leakage to remote servers. Portokalidis et al. [18] propose a security model for protecting mobile devices which performs multiple attack detection techniques simultaneously on remote servers hosting an exact replica of the devices. Lok and Yin [27] present DroidScope, a virtualization based platform for Android malware analysis. It rebuilds both the operating system and Java level semantics, and enables instrumentation of the Dalvik and native instructions. Consequently, Droidscope can be used to understand the behavior of malware both at the native code level as well as at the interaction with the system.

8   Conclusion and Future Work

We have presented a robust and lightweight approach for detecting Android malware based on different classifiers. To predict whether an app is benign or malicious, the classifiers rely on the semantic information within the bytecode of the applications ranging from critical API calls, package level information and some dangerous parameters invoked. Rather than following a heuristic based approach for determining the feature vector of the classifiers, we have statically analyzed a large corpus of Android malwares belonging to different families and a large benign set belonging to different categories. We have conducted a frequency analysis to capture the most relevant API calls that malware invoke, and refined the feature set to exclude API calls made by third-party packages. We performed a simple data flow analysis to get dangerous input to some API calls.

Our classification results indicate that we are able to achieve a better accuracy, TPR and TNR using a combination of API, package, and parameter level information in comparison to the permissions-based feature set. As future work, we plan to further reduce the false positives and negatives through analyzing the samples that were not correctly classified and finding out the reasons behind the misclassification.

Acknowledgment. We would like to thank anonymous reviewers for their comments. This research was supported in part by NSF grants #1017771, #1018217, #1054605, and #1116932, Google research grant, and McAfee research grant. Any opinion, findings, conclusions, or recommendations are those of the authors and not necessarily of the funding agencies.

References

1. ActivityManager, http://developer.android.com/reference/android/app/ActivityManager.html
2. Androguard, http://code.google.com/p/androguard/
3. Android Malware Genome Project, http://www.malgenomeproject.org/
4. Intent, http://developer.android.com/reference/android/content/Intent.html

5. Malware that Takes Without Asking, http://labs.mwrinfosecurity.com/tools/2012/03/16/mercury/documentation/white-paper/malware-that-takes-without-asking/
6. Process, http://developer.android.com/reference/android/os/Process.html
7. RapidMiner, http://rapid-i.com/content/view/181/190/
8. Aha, D.W., Kibler, D., Albert, M.K.: Instance-Based Learning Algorithms. Machine Learning 6, 37–66 (1991)
9. Blasing, T., Batyuk, L., Schmidt, A.-D., Camtepe, S.A., Albayrak, S.: An Android Application Sandbox System for Suspicious Software Detection. In: MALWARE (2010)
10. Burguera, I., Zurutuza, U., Nadijm-Tehrani, S.: Crowdroid: Behavior-Based Malware Detection System for Android. In: SPSM (2011)
11. Enck, W., Gilbert, P., Chun, B.-G., Cox, L.P., Jung, J., McDaniel, P., Sheth, A.N.: TaintDroid: An Information-Flow Tracking System for Realtime Privacy Monitoring on Smartphones. In: USENIX, OSDI (2011)
12. Enck, W., Ongtang, M., McDaniel, P.: On Lightweight Mobile Phone Application Certication. In: CCS (2009)
13. Felt, A.P., Chin, E., Hanna, S., Song, D., Wagner, D.: Android Permissions Demystied. In: CCS (2011)
14. Felt, A.P., Greenwood, K., Wagner, D.: The Effectiveness of Application Permissions. In: USENIX, WebApps (2011)
15. Grace, M., Zhou, Y., Wang, Z., Jiang, X.: Systematic Detection of Capability Leaks in Stock Android Smartphones. In: NDSS (2012)
16. Lu, L., Li, Z., Wu, Z., Lee, W., Jiang, G.I.: CHEX: Statically Vetting Android Apps for Component Hijacking Vulnerabilities. In: CCS (2012)
17. Peng, H., Gates, C., Sarma, B., Li, N., Qi, Y., Potharaju, R.: Using Probabilistic Generative Models for Ranking Risks of Android Apps. In: CCS (2012)
18. Portokalidis, G., Homburg, P., Anagnostakis, K., Bos, H.: Paranoid Android: Versatile Protection for Smartphones. In: ACSAC (2010)
19. Potharaju, R., Newell, A., Nita-Rotaru, C., Zhang, X.: Plagiarizing Smartphone Applications: Attack Strategies and Defense. In: Barthe, G., Livshits, B., Scandariato, R. (eds.) ESSoS 2012. LNCS, vol. 7159, pp. 106–120. Springer, Heidelberg (2012)
20. Quinlan, J.R.: Induction of Decision Tree. Machine Learning 1(1), 81–106 (1986)
21. Quinlan, J.R.: C4.5: Programs for Machine Learning. Morgan Kaufmann (1993)
22. Sarma, B., Li, N., Gates, C., Potharaju, R., Nita-Rotaru, C., Molloy, I.: Android Permissions: A Perspective Combining Risks and Benets. In: SACMAT (2012)
23. Schmidt, A.-D., Bye, R., Schmidt, H.-G., Clausen, J., Kiraz, O., Yuksel, K.A., Camtepe, S.A., Albayrak, S.: Static Analysis of Executables for Collaborative Malware Detection on Android. In: ICC (2009)
24. Shabtai, A., Kanonov, U., Elovici, Y., Glezer, C., Weiss, Y.: Andromaly: a Behavioral Malware Detection Framework for Android Devices. Journal of Intelligent Information Systems Archive 38(1) (2012)
25. Vapnik, V.: The Nature of Statistical Learning Theory. Springer, NY (1995)
26. Wei, X., Gomez, L., Neamtiu, I., Faloutsos, M.: Permission Evolution in the Android Ecosystem. In: ACSAC (2012)
27. Yan, L.K., Yin, H.: DroidScope: Seamlessly Reconstructing the OS and Dalvik Semantic Views for Dynamic Android Malware Analysis. In: USENIX, Security (2012)
28. Zhou, W., Zhou, Y., Jiang, X., Ning, P.: Detecting Repackaged Smartphone Applications in Third-Party Android Marketplaces. In: CODASPY (2012)
29. Zhou, Y., Wang, Z., Zhou, W., Jiang, X.: Hey, You, Get off of My Market: Detecting Malicious Apps in Official and Alternative Android Markets. In: NDSS (2012)

Disabling a Computer by Exploiting Softphone Vulnerabilities: Threat and Mitigation

Ryan Farley and Xinyuan Wang

Department of Computer Science
George Mason University
Fairfax, VA 22030, USA
{rfarley3,xwangc}@gmu.edu

Abstract. As more and more people are using VoIP softphones in their laptop and smart phones, vulnerabilities in VoIP protocols and systems could introduce new threats to the computer that runs the VoIP softphone. In this paper, we investigate the security ramifications that VoIP softphones expose their host to and ways to mitigate such threats.

We show that crafted SIP traffic (noisy attack) can disable a Windows XP host that runs the official Vonage VoIP softphone within several minutes. While such a noisy attack can be effectively mitigated by threshold based filtering, we show that a stealthy attack could defeat the threshold based filtering and disable the targeted computer silently without ever ringing the targeted softphone.

To mitigate the stealthy attack, we have developed a limited context aware (LCA) filtering that leverages the context and SIP protocol information to ascertain the intentions of a SIP message on behalf of the client. Our experiments show that LCA filtering can effectively defeat the stealthy attack while allowing legitimate VoIP calls to go through.

Keywords: VoIP, Softphone, Security, Attack on Host, Host Defense.

1 Introduction

As VoIP is getting increasingly popular, it becomes an attractive target to attackers [8]. Many known VoIP exploits stem from vulnerabilities of the de facto signaling protocol in use, Session Initiation Protocol (SIP) [16]. Previous works [27,12,8,23] have shown that SIP weaknesses make it possible for the attackers to do such things as remotely monitor a call, modify billing control signals, and even implement voice pharming attacks. As with any device on the Internet, if a VoIP phone is vulnerable and unprotected, then an attacker can exploit it from anywhere in the world.

In this paper we take an alternative point of view by focusing on the stability and security of the systems that host VoIP softphones. As with most network based applications softphones enlarge a device's attack surface, which increases the chance that an attacker can find a point of leverage and pivot to compromise the host machine. In this paper we case study the softphone provided by Vonage,

T. Zia et al. (Eds.): SecureComm 2013, LNICST 127, pp. 104–121, 2013.

which at one point had the largest US residential VoIP market share [13,14], in order to investigate stability and security threats that a VoIP softphone can introduce to the host running it and how we can mitigate such threats.

Specifically, we present two attacks against a Windows XP host running the official Vonage softphone. These attacks use crafted SIP messages and can make the Windows XP Host completely unusable until reboot. Indirectly, these attacks also prevent the victims from receiving incoming and making outgoing calls within seconds. The first attack (the noisy attack) can remotely disable a machine running the Vonage softphone by occupying all available physical and virtual memory within minutes. The second attack (the stealthy attack) takes longer to achieve the same effect, but it never rings the softphone. These attacks illustrate that weaknesses in a VoIP softphone can introduce fatal vulnerabilities to the host system. Few people may realize that, indeed, a vulnerable application can enable a remote attacker to completely disable the computer that runs the vulnerable application.

We have investigated ways to mitigate the identified attacks from the network. We have first used threshold based filtering to detect the spikes in arrival rates of Invite messages, and we have found that it can effectively diminish the effects of the noisy attack by as much as 99.8%. However, threshold based filtering is not effective against the stealthy attack, which neither rings the softphone nor use abnormally high rate of SIP messages. We have designed the *limited context aware (LCA)* approach, which buffers all incoming packets in a waiting queue to determine whether they are attack related or safe legitimate traffic. Our experimental results show that our LCA method can eliminate 100% of the stealthy attack's packets without interfering with standard SIP operation.

The rest of the paper is organized as follows. In section 2 we illustrate the basis of our two attacks by presenting signal flooding techniques to disable the operation of the softphone itself. We then present our two attacks for the softphone host in section 3, and two defense mechanisms against the identified attacks in section 4. In section 5, we empirically evaluate the two attacks and the effectiveness of our proposed defenses against them. We discuss the existing related work in section 7 and the implications of the identified attacks on a softphone host in section 6. Finally we conclude in section 8.

2   Background

Session Initiation Protocol (SIP) [16], is a general purpose application layer signaling protocol used for creating, modifying, and terminating multimedia sessions, such as VoIP calls, among Internet endpoints known as User Agents (UAs). To facilitate locating UAs, all users in a SIP network are identified by a SIP Uniform Resource Identifier (URI), which typically includes an username and hostname in a format much like an email address.

Signaling between UAs is based on the request-response paradigm. A User Agent Client (UAC) sends requests to a User Agent Server (UAS) which then replies with both the appropriate response and a corresponding status code. An endpoint can function as both UAC and UAS at the same time.

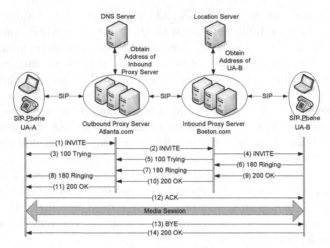

Fig. 1. An example SIP message flow for a VoIP call

```
INVITE sip:17031234567@129.174.130.175:5060 SIP/2.0 Via:
SIP/2.0/UDP 216.115.20.41:5061 Via: SIP/2.0/UDP 216.115.20.29:5060
Via: SIP/2.0/UDP 216.115.27.11:5060;branch=z9hG4bK8AE8A3914F0
From: "GMU" <sip:17032345678@216.115.27.11>;tag=455412559 To:
<sip:17031234567@voncp.com> Call-ID:
58A8C0B-8D6F11DC-B8E18C7A-2083704C@216.115.27.11 CSeq: 101 INVITE
Contact: <sip:17032345678@216.115.20.41:5061> Max-Forwards: 13
X-Von-Relay: 216.115.27.30 Content-Type: application/sdp
Content-Length:    361

v=0 o=CiscoSystemsSIP-GW-UserAgent 5330 7344 IN IP4 216.115.27.30
s=SIP Call c=IN IP4 216.115.27.30 t=0 0 m=audio 13598 RTP/AVP 0 18
2 100 101 c=IN IP4 216.115.27.30 a=rtpmap:0 PCMU/8000 a=rtpmap:18
G729/8000 a=fmtp:18 annexb=no a=rtpmap:2 G726-32/8000 a=rtpmap:100
X-NSE/8000 a=fmtp:100 192-194 a=rtpmap:101 telephone-event/8000
a=fmtp:101 0-16
```

Fig. 2. An example SIP Invite message with SDP information

Figure 1 illustrates the message flow of a normal SIP VoIP session between UA-A and UA-B without authentication. Initially, A only knows the URI of B. Since this does not provide the specific location information needed to complete a call, A must send the Invite to its outbound proxy server, atlanta.com. Once atlanta.com resolves the URI, it forwards the Invite to the appropriate next hop, boston.com. Next, boston.com relays the Invite to B and sends a Trying back to atlanta.com, which is relayed to A. Once B receives the Invite, it sends a Ringing to A. When B finally answers the call, it sends a 200 Ok to A, to which A responds with an Ack.

During this exchange, the packets also contain a session description protocol, or SDP. This establishes the voice data parameters each client will use, such as media codec and port numbers. Figure 2 shows an example of an Invite message with SDP information.

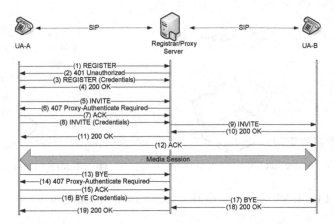

Fig. 3. Typical registration, as well as call setup and termination

At the end of the call, the UAC that first hangs up sends a BYE to the other UAC. The other UAC then responds with a 200 Ok and terminates its RTP stream. Upon receiving the 200 Ok, the first UAC terminates its RTP stream as well.

Based on HTTP digest authentication [3], SIP provides authentication of Invite, Register and Bye messages from UAC to UAS. Figure 3 illustrates the message flows of typical authenticated registration, call setup and termination. Because SIP does not require the UAC to authenticate the Invite message from UAS, most VoIP service providers (e.g., Vonage, AT&T) do not have authentication protection of the Invite message sent from the SIP server to SIP phone. This enables attackers to freely spoof Invite message and ring any targeted SIP phone with the spoofed Invite message.

Once the Vonage softphone receives a spoofed Invite, it will keep ringing for 3 minutes unless the user picks up the softphone or a corresponding Cancel message is received. The SIP softphone will not ring for duplicate Call-IDs repeated within a certain period (60 seconds for the Vonage softphone). The Vonage softphone has two ports allocated for incoming RTP audio streams, creating a limit of two simultaneous phone "lines." Therefore, attackers only need to send two spoofed Invite messages to occupy the two lines of the targeted Vonage softphone.

In our experiments we have found that two things will happen when both lines of the Vonage softphone are ringing. First, all additional incoming call requests are given a Busy response. For legitimate calls routed through the client's proxy, this means that the caller is sent to voicemail. Second, since no line is free, the target can not make an outgoing call. If the target answers and hangs up on a fake Invite, then that line would become free until the next Invite arrives. For the Vonage softphone, lines become available again when audible ringing stops at three minutes. In other words, only two spoofed Invite messages are needed every three minutes to occupy both lines and prevent the softphone from receiving incoming calls. In the rest of this paper, we investigate how attackers can exploit the vulnerabilities of the SIP protocol and SIP softphones to disable a Windows XP host that runs the official Vonage SIP softphone.

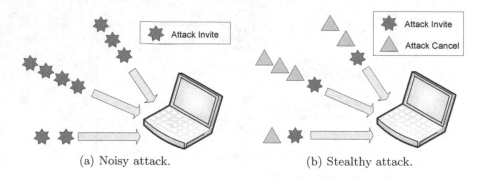

(a) Noisy attack.   (b) Stealthy attack.

Fig. 4. Visualization of the Attack from Multiple Sources

3   Disabling the Softphone Host

Most previous attacks on VoIP have targeted either the VoIP infrastructure (such as the proxy servers, billing systems, network usability, and fundamentals of SIP signaling) or the physical VoIP devices. It is not clear precisely how weaknesses in the softphone open the host up for attack. In the following sections we show how attackers can disable Windows XP machines running the official Vonage softphone. In section 3.1, we describe a host DoS attack that can consume a target machine's memory resources in minutes. In section 3.2, the attack is significantly refined into a slower but much stealthier form.

3.1   Noisy Attack on Softphone Host

According to the SIP specification [16], the signaling processing at the the caller's and callee's sides are inherently stateful. In other words, the end UAC needs to allocate memory for keeping the state information for every Call-ID seen in any received `Invite` so that the UAC can respond to all requests that require repeated responses. For example, if all incoming lines are busy, up to three `Busy` responses over ten seconds are sent for every `Invite` request received. This enables attackers to deplete the memory of the host running SIP softphone.

To launch such a noisy attack, the attacker only needs to make sure that each crafted `Invite` message has an unique Call-ID. The attacker can easily spoof the source IP address and launch the attack from distributed places as visualized in figure 4(a).

Specifically, the attacker can send a large number of crafted `Invite` messages at a high rate (e.g., hundreds per second) to the targeted softphone. The recipient will only hear as many simultaneous rings as they have lines (e.g., Vonage softphone has two lines). The high rate of crafted `Invite` messages will disable the softphone even if the user keeps hanging up the fake calls.

Because the softphone will allocate memory for each incoming `Invite` message even if the phone lines are busy, a high rate (e.g., hundreds messages per second) of `Invite` messages can occupy almost all free physical memory on the host

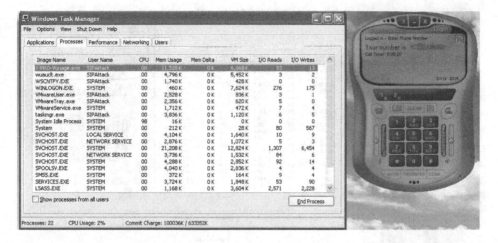

Fig. 5. Screenshot of the memory usage of the Windows XP host before the attack

within a few minutes. As the attack continues and memory usage grows, if the system does not have enough RAM to handle the allocations, then the user will receive out of memory errors and excessive virtual memory page swaps will make the host completely unresponsive.

The fundamental vulnerabilities here are: 1) the softphone needs to keep the state of every incoming Invite message as specified in the SIP RFC; 2) the deallocation of the memory can not keep up with the high rate of memory allocation triggered by the high rate of Invite messages. Therefore, even if the softphone can hang up (the fake calls) faster that the incoming Invite messages, the memory consumption would continue to increase and eventually lead to occupying all free memory of the host. We found these vulnerabilities are specific to the Invite message. Other SIP messages, such as Cancel and Bye do not have a similar effect on memory allocation.

We implemented this attack and were able to deplete almost all available free memory of a Windows XP host running a Vonage softphone in just several minutes. The host begins thrashing indefinitely and is unusable until reboot.

3.2   Stealthy Attack on Softphone Host

The noisy attack will cause the target softphone to ring if it is not used. From the attacker's point of view, it is desirable to attack the softphone host without ever ringing the softphone so that the softphone users will not be alerted.

In SIP, the call initiator is allowed to send Cancel messages after sending out the Invite message. This essentially tells the receiver to ignore any Invite message that has the matching Call-ID. As a result, the receiver SIP phone will not ring.

As indicated in figure 4(b), the stealthy attack exploits this feature of SIP by sending a number of Cancel messages with the matching Call-ID immediately

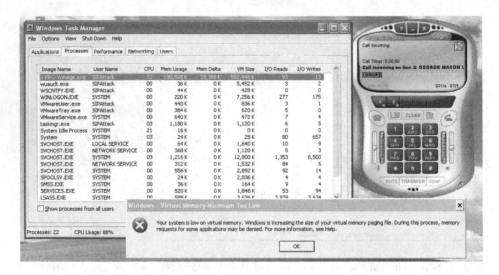

Fig. 6. Screenshot of the memory usage of the Windows host after the attack. The error message notes that the virtual memory is filled and the the swap file size needs to be increased.

after every `Invite` message is sent. While only one `Cancel` message is needed to silence the receiver SIP phone, multiple `Cancel` messages are used here to make sure any sent `Invite` message will not ring the receiver SIP phone even if some `Cancel` messages are lost in the network.

Because of the n extra `Cancel` messages per `Invite` message, the rate of `Invite` messages needs to be reduced to $\frac{1}{n+1}$ of that of noisy attack to avoid network congestion and packet loss. This slows down the memory consumption due to the attack and it takes longer to disable the softphone host. However, since the stealthy attack will never ring the softphone, it can remain undetected over a significantly longer time period. The end result is the same, almost all memory is occupied and the machine will need to be rebooted in order to be usable again.

We have implemented this stealthy attack. The empirical results show significant effects on a target system within the first half-hour. It takes about two hours depending on the rate of `Invite` messages for the stealthy attack to deplete the host memory and disable the host completely.

Figure 5 shows the memory usage and CPU utilization of the Windows XP host before the attack. The official Vonage softphone used less than 12MB memory and less than 7MB virtual memory file. The CPU utilization of the Windows XP host is only 2%.

As shown in Figure 6, memory usage and CPU utilization of the Windows XP host went up significantly after an attack. Specifically, the attack has not only increased the memory usage of the Vonage softphone from 11MB to 190MB, but also increased its virtual memory usage from 6MB to 552MB. This effectively depleted the available free memory of the entire Windows XP host and caused it to hang.

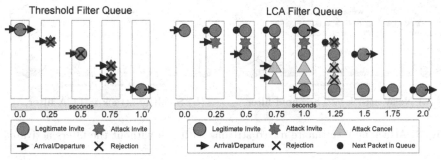

(a) Packets are processed im- (b) Packets are held for one second, then processed.
mediately.

Fig. 7. Visualizations of the filter queueing systems

4   Defense Mechanisms

Proper defense against SIP spoofing attacks is not an easy solution without authentication or encryption. As discussed in section 2, the softphone is programmed to respond to even vaguely authentic looking signals, which makes it very difficult to distinguish between real and fake on a packet to packet basis. In order to make a decision, a grouping or series of packets must be analyzed.

Of course, analyzing too many packets per grouping in the defense may introduce unacceptably high latency for SIP to remain operational. On the other hand, too few packets would make it hard for the defense to reliably determine whether the traffic is an attack or not. Analyzing only previous packets, such as with state machines, prevents the mechanism from blocking the beginning of attacks. This is a serious disadvantage if the attack only consists of unrelated single packets, such as our noisy DoS attack.

There are some external factors that can guide the defense mechanism though. For instance, the average person should not expect to receive more than one or two calls a second. Anything more than that is probably due to network error or a flooding attack. For another example, if a call is cancelled by the caller before the callee would have a reasonable chance to answer, then it is unnecessary to ring the callee at all. There heuristics allow us to simplify the defense by excluding the those SIP messages that would not set up meaningful calls.

Given previous work and noted limitations, we present two defense mechanisms for SIP flooding attacks. The threshold (TH) filter, in section 4.1, considers only one factor: the rate at which `Invite` messages are arriving. The limited context aware (LCA) filter, in section 4.2, queues `Invite` messages long enough to determine if there is any associated cancelling signals. If state machine based filtering can be thought of as using the past to guide decisions, then the threshold filter uses the present, and the LCA filter uses a slice of the relative future.

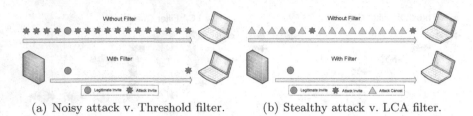

(a) Noisy attack v. Threshold filter.   (b) Stealthy attack v. LCA filter.

Fig. 8. Attack and legitimate mixed streams with and without the filters activated

4.1   Defending against Noisy Attack with the Threshold Filter

As detailed in section 3.1, the noisy attack consists of large number crafted Invite messages. To protected the softphone and its host, we want to filter out attack Invite messages while allowing legitimate Invite messages to pass.

Ideally the filter should be able to definitively distinguish attack packets from legitimate traffic. Given that the whole attack Invite message can be crafted and spoofed by the attacker, there is no meaningful content "pattern" or "signature" in the Invite message we can use to distinguish attack Invite messages from legitimate Invite messages. In addition, the attack Invite messages can spoof the source IP address of legitimate SIP servers. Therefore, we can not filter the noisy attack based on source IP either.

This leaves the arrival rate as the only usable detection factor—anything above a certain arrival rate indicates that an attack is more than likely occurring. How do we decide on that threshold level? While it can change from user to user, we can safely assume that even a heavy telephone user should not expect more than one to two legitimate phone calls per second. Any higher rate of incoming calls can not be manually handled by a human.

Figure 7(a) illustrates the filtering with threshold of one Invite message per second. For high rate (e.g., hundreds of attack Invite messages per second) noisy attack, threshold based filtering can be a very effective mitigation as it can filter out most, if not all attack Invite messages. However, threshold based filtering can still let very few attack Invite messages to reach the protected machine at the rate of no more than one attack Invite message per second as shown in figure 8(a). In addition, threshold based filtering has a very small chance to block legitimate Invite message while the high rate noisy attack is going on. This, however, is not a concern as the high rate noisy attack would have made the softphone unusable anyway.

If the noisy attack uses a rate of Invite messages less than one per second, it will not be effectively blocked by the threshold based filtering. However, it would take much longer time for such a low rate noisy attack to deplete the memory of the softphone host. In addition, keeping ringing the softphone during such extended period of time (e.g., several hours) would most likely alert the softphone user. Therefore, low rate noisy attack is likely to be stopped before it causes real problem to the softphone and its host.

The stealthy attack, on the other hand, would never ring the target softphone. This makes it unlikely to be noticed by the user of the targeted softphone. Since the stealthy attack has a much lower rate of Invite messages than the noisy attack, it can not be effectively filtered by the threshold based filter. Therefore, it is necessary to develop other defense against the stealthy attack.

4.2 Defending against Stealthy Attack with the LCA Filter

As detailed in section 3.2, the stealthy attack sends a low rate of cancelled Invite messages, consuming memory slowly while preventing the target softphone from ringing.

To filter such a stealthy attack with low rate Invite messages, we need to find some characteristics that can distinguish such stealthy attack from legitimate traffic. One unique characteristics of the stealthy attack is that every Invite message is followed by at least one Cancel message with matching Call-ID. This enables us to filter out the stealthy attack while allowing legitimate calls to go through.

Specifically, we introduce a queue to temporarily hold every incoming SIP message for a fixed period of time T. Such a queue of incoming SIP messages gives us a *limited context* from which we can ascertain the intentions of the incoming SIP messages by looking for any Cancels associated with any Invite in the queue. As shown in figure 7(b), the queue consumer periodically checks the front packets in the queue. If the packet is an Invite, then the rest of the queue is searched for any Cancel message with a matching Call-ID). If any are found, then the Invite and the associated Cancels are dropped. If any packet in the queue has waited for at least the required time of T, we pull it off the queue and forward it along the incoming path.

Note such a *limited context aware* filtering could indeed block legitimate Invite followed by legitimate Cancel caused by immediate hanging up after dialing the number. This is fine as the legitimate call has been cancelled by the caller already.

The period of time T for the queue needs to be long enough to catch all the associated Cancel that can prevent the previous Invite from ringing the callee's SIP phone. On the other hand, it can not be too long to interfere with legitimate SIP signaling. For Vonage, if an Invite from a proxy server is held for more than 1.5 seconds, then the proxy automatically sends a Cancel. Thus 1.5 seconds is the upper limit of T. For the lower time limit, we must consider that it is advantageous for the attacker to send Cancels as soon as possible; the fewer they send and longer they wait, then the more likely that the softphone might ring. In our limited context aware (LCA) filter, we use a one second wait time.

By searching for an associated Cancel, the LCA filter has a way to distinguish calls that should be allowed from those that shouldn't. This eliminates any dependency of the effectiveness on the arrival rate. As seen in figure 8(b), the LCA filter can effectively filter all the stealthy attack traffic while virtually never blocking legitimate traffic. The only theoretical false positive is when the (31 hexadecimal digits) Call-ID of a Cancel message from a stealthy attack happens to match that of a legitimate Invite message.

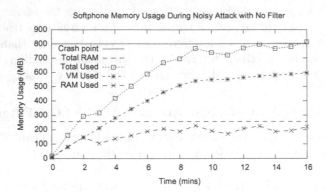

Fig. 9. Details of the escalating memory usage during the Noisy DoS attack without the Threshold filter

5   Experiments

To prove the concept of the attack and defense, we have implemented both the noisy and the stealthy attacks in Linux, the threshold based and LCA filters within the transparent network bridge in FreeBSD using divert sockets.

We have conducted two sets of experiments. In section 5.1 we demonstrate the effect of both noisy and stealthy attacks on the softphone host by measuring the memory usage caused by the attacks. In section 5.2 we analyze the effectiveness of the defense mechanisms, and present the overhead required to implement both filtering systems.

The target for these experiments is a virtual machine of 256 MB RAM running Windows XP and the X-PRO Vonage 2.0 softphone, release 1105x build stamp 17305. To avoid sending unnecessary outbound traffic, we have filtered out any replies related to our attack traffic.

5.1   Attacks

We created the initial `Invite` template from a PCAP trace of a legitimate call captured at the target's gateway. While this is the easiest solution given our setup, it is possible for the attacker to gather enough information through other means and create a template from scratch without a man-in-the-middle, or MITM. For instance, the proxy server IP addresses are relatively static if the target's geographical location is known and the attacker could scan the target's open ports to see which the softphone is using. This means that an attacker can execute this threat from anywhere in the world as long as they know the target's IP address.

The memory usage over the course of the noisy DoS attack is detailed in figure 9. Note that in the first minute there was a dramatic climb in the softphone's memory usage from 17MB to 161MB. Also, the processor utilization rose to 80–100% as soon as the flooding began. In nine minutes, the Vonage softphone

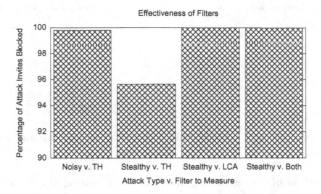

Fig. 10. Effectiveness of the filters against the various attacks measured by percent of attack INVITE messages blocked

has occupied over 500MB virtual memory and almost all 256MB RAM. By the sixteenth minute, as in shown in figure 6, the system has been resizing the swap file, the processor has become still swamped, and the UI has become completely unresponsive. The system did not return to usable state, even after several days, until rebooted.

Figure 11(b) shows the the memory usage of the Vonage softphone under the stealthy DoS attack. The memory usage growth under stealthy attack is much slower than the noisy DoS attack, and the processor utilization does not spike as soon as flooding begins. The end result is the same though, after roughly two hours, the Windows XP host will have no free memory and an UI that remains unresponsive until the system is rebooted.

For these attacks, the average memory allocated per `Invite` was 13KB. This is slightly higher, 49KB, during the first minute of the noisy attack. Considering that only the Call-ID had to be changed, and it has 31 hexadecimal digits, then this could theoretically consume even large memory systems.

5.2   Defense Mechanisms

In this section we analyze the effectiveness of the defense mechanisms against their associated attacks. Additionally, we present the maximum packet handling rate and the overhead of the filters. We have conducted experiments with various combinations of attacks and the filters: 1) threshold filter against noisy attack; 2) threshold filter against stealthy attack; 3) LCA filter against stealthy attack; and 4) combination of LCA filter and threshold filter (LCA filter first and threshold filter second) against stealthy attack. Since the LCA filter is only effective against stealthy attack, we do not test LCA filter against noisy attack.

Figure 10 shows the measured effectiveness, in term of attack packets blocked, of various filters against various attacks. Specifically, the threshold filter is able to block 99.8% of the noisy DoS attack and 95.6% of the stealthy attack at their maximum rate of `Invite`. This illustrates that the threshold filter's effectiveness

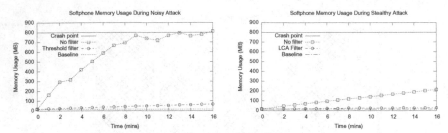

(a) Noisy attack with and without the Threshold filter.

(b) Stealthy attack with and without the LCA filter.

Fig. 11. Comparison of the escalating memory usage during the attacks with and without a filter

decreases if the `Invite` arrival rate decreases. Note that the threshold filter can not block `Cancel`s, so only 15.2% of all attack traffic was blocked. In addition, the threshold filter has a slight chance to block legitimate `Invite` messages since it does not distinguish legitimate and illegitimate `Invite` messages. The LCA filter, on the other hand, is able to block 100% the stealthy DoS attack at any capacity. In the LCA filter experiments, we mixed the legitimate `Invite` messages (from legitimate calls) with stealthy attack `Invite` messages. The LCA filter has never blocked any legitimate `Invite` messages mixed within the stealthy attack traffic. In summary, the threshold filter and LCA filter are complementing each other, and the combination of them are effective against both noisy and stealthy attacks.

We have measured the memory consumption caused by the noisy and stealthy attacks as well as the impact of the threshold based filtering and the LCA filtering. As seen in figure 11(a), the threshold filter effectively slows down the memory growth during a noisy attack. Without any filtering, noisy attack has consumed 813 MB of memory of the softphone host in 16 minutes. With threshold filtering, noisy attack has only occupied 67.7 MB in 16 minutes. Figure 11(b) compares the memory consumptions of the stealthy attack with and without the LCA filtering. The LCA filtering has successfully prevented the stealthy attack from occupying additional memory from the softphone host.

We have measured the maximum throughput (i.e., fastest packet rate without packet loss due to congestion) of both the noisy and stealthy attacks with and without threshold and LCA filtering. As shown in figure 12, noisy attack can achieve rate of about 300 `Invite` per second. Threshold filtering can handle rate close to 600 `Invite` per second. While maximum rate of stealthy attack is less than 250 `Invite` per second, LCA filtering can handle rate close to 500 `Invite` per second.

Per RFC 2544, we have measured the processing latency of our filters at the maximum throughput. As shown in figure 13, the threshold filter introduces no more than one millisecond processing delay when running against either the noisy or stealthy attack. The LCA filter adds less than five milliseconds processing

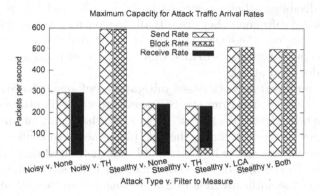

Fig. 12. An approximation of throughput for the filters under the DoS attacks

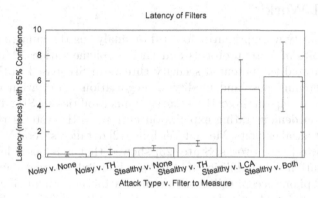

Fig. 13. Latency caused by the filters' packet processing under the DoS attacks with confidence intervals

delay in addition to one second queueing delay. Neither the one second queueing delay nor the processing delay has shown any noticeable impact on the normal VoIP signaling functionality in our experiments.

6   Discussion

The host disabling attacks we present in this paper are relatively straight forward to implement. In fact, since the softphone chooses a predictable port number, the attacker only needs to know the target's IP address. Our experience shows that when the Vonage softphone is behind a NAT enabled router, often the external mapping retains the internal port number. Therefore, to disable a targeted softphone behind NAT, the attacker only needs the public IP address of the targeted softphone, which can be easily obtained by observing any SIP traffic from the targeted softphone anywhere along its path. Since the process of spoofing SIP messages implies changing the source IP address, and optionally the caller ID information, there is an innate layer of stealth in the attack.

While host disabling attacks described in sections 3.1 and 3.2 are conducted against the Vonage softphone, they are actually exploiting features defined in the SIP protocol. Therefore, these attacks could be applicable to other softphones as well. It is one of our future works to investigate if other softphones are vulnerable to the newly identified attacks.

Besides our proposed network based mitigation, enforcing the SIP authentication on `Invite` messages from the SIP server to the SIP phone could help mitigate the newly identified attacks. To prevent the replay of authenticated `Invite` messages to the SIP phone, the SIP phone needs to challenge each authenticated `Invite` message to it. This would introduce substantial overhead to the SIP phone. To the best of our knowledge, no US residential VoIP service provider enforces the authentication of SIP messages from the SIP server to the SIP phone.

7   Related Work

Early VoIP security work primarily focused on analyzing the vulnerabilities and potential exploits of VoIP protocols and their implementations. McGann and Sicker [11] analyzed the potential security threats in SIP-based VoIP, creating an invisible listening post and modifying negotiation information on the fly. Geneiatakis et al. [4] surveyed the security vulnerabilities in SIP. Later work focused more on demonstrating exploits on current VoIP systems rather than illustrating potential exploits. Me and Verdone [12] detailed several VoIP attacks over insecure wireless networks. State [23] showed that it is possible to exploit the implementation vulnerabilities of a SIP stack in order to make any targeted GXV-3000 SIP phone accept calls from a remote attacker without ringing or user interaction. Zhang et al. [27] demonstrated that vulnerabilities in SIP can be used to launch billing attacks on currently deployed commercial VoIP services. Wang et al. [24] investigated the trust of several leading VoIP services (e.g., Vonage, AT&T) and showed that their VoIP calls can be transparently diverted and redirected—leading to voice pharming attacks on the VoIP users. It has been further detailed [26] that these call diversion attacks can be launched by a remote attacker who is not initially in the path of VoIP traffic of the target. Lee et al. [10] showed how flooding attacks can cause constant ringing on the target UAC but did not discuss the effects on host resources. Herculea et al. [7] surveyed eight VoIP flooding attacks and arrival rates, but did not address host resource effects. Seedorf et al. [17] demonstrated single message attacks for eight SIP UAC implementations, but did not discuss remotely disabling the host. Kapravelos et al. [9] detailed arrival rates and cancelling a pending call, but did not claim that their attack is silent nor discussed its effects on the host. To the best of our knowledge, no previous work discusses how crafted SIP messages can be used to remotely disable a host that executes VoIP applications.

On the other side of the line significant work exists in securing VoIP. Geneiatakis et al. [5] surveyed SIP security mechanisms. In a later paper, Geneiatakis et al. [6] detailed memory usage of a SIP proxy under a flooding attack but did not discuss effects of such an attack on the UAC host. Additionally, they presented a bloom filter system to track call state in order to detect Invite floods. However, unlike our LCA filter, once a flood is detected their system can not distinguish legitimate packets. Reynolds and Ghosal [15] proposed a multi-protocol scheme to defend against flooding attacks on VoIP networks. Wu et al. [25] and Sengar et al. [18] presented using state information and cross-protocol correlation to detect denial-of-service attacks on VoIP. Sengar et al. [19] detailed a VoIP intrusion detection based interactive protocol state machine. Deng and Shore [2] proposed using nonces to protect the SIP servers from flooding attacks. Kapravelos et al. [9] presented a flow state based filter mechanism for preventing nuisance dialing but did not address false positive rates. Soupionis et al. [22] detailed an audio based anti-bot verification method and more formal methods later [20,21]. In general, most existing VoIP defense mechanisms are designed to protect the VoIP servers, and be deployed close to them, rather than end hosts such as SIP softphones. Additionally, most existing detection methods are somewhat post-mortem and do not provide real-time flood protection while guaranteeing to keep legitimate VoIP calls alive against the attacks that we have described. To the best of our knowledge there is no existing work focused on securing against SIP messages that can remotely disable a host executing VoIP applications.

8   Conclusion

VoIP is a quickly growing dependence for modern communication needs. Unfortunately, its benefits come with an increased risk of attacks from the Internet. Most current exploits (e.g., billing attacks and remote eavesdropping attempts), however, have focused on the VoIP devices (e.g., servers, clients) or users. To the best of our knowledge, we are the first to demonstrate that an attacker can completely disable the very host that runs vulnerable VoIP applications.

We have developed two attacks that can disable a Windows XP computer running the official Vonage softphone. The noisy attack, which rings the targeted softphone, can disable the targeted Windows XP host within a few minutes. The stealthy attack, which never rings the targeted softphone, can completely disable the targeted Windows XP host within a couple of hours. Both versions can be launched from anywhere in the world as long as the target's IP address is known. Given the large subscriber base of VoIP and the ease of implementing such attacks, this is a viable threat to systems stability and security.

To mitigate the host disabling attacks, we have designed and evaluated two network based defense mechanisms. The threshold based filtering has very low overhead and can block 99.8% of the attack traffic at its maximum rate. However, threshold based filtering is not effective against slow and stealthy attacks and can block critical portions of legitimate VoIP traffic. Limited context aware (LCA) filtering can reliably filter all stealthy attack traffic while allowing virtually all legitimate traffic to pass in real-time. Therefore, the combination of threshold and LCA filters are effective against both the noisy attack and stealthy attack.

References

1. Arkko, J., Torvinen, V., Camarillo, G., Niemi, Λ., Haukka, T.: Security Mechanism Agreement for the SIP. RFC 3329 (January 2003)
2. Deng, X., Shore, M.: Advanced Flooding Attack on a SIP Server. In: Proc. of the Intl. Conf. on Availability, Reliability and Security (ARES), pp. 647–651. IEEE Computer Society (March 2009)
3. Franks, J., Hallam-Baker, P., Hostetler, J., Lawrence, S., Leach, P., Luotonen, A., Stewart, L.: HTTP Authentication: Basic and Digest Access Authentication. RFC 2617 (June 1999)
4. Geneiatakis, D., Dagiouklas, A., Kambourakis, G., Lambrinoudakis, C., Gritzalis, S., Ehlert, S., Sisalem, D.: Survey of Security Vulnerabilities in Session Initiation Protocol. IEEE Commun. Surveys and Tutorials 8(3), 68–81 (2006)
5. Geneiatakis, D., Kambourakis, G., Dagiuklas, T., Lambrinoudakis, C., Gritzalis, S.: SIP Security Mechanisms: A State-of-the-Art Review. In: Proc. of the 5th Intl. Netw. Conf. (INC), pp. 147–155. ACM (2005)
6. Geneiatakis, D., Vrakas, N., Lambrinoudakis, C.: Utilizing Bloom Filters for Detecting Flooding Attacks against SIP based Services. Computers & Security 28(7), 578–591 (2009)
7. Herculea, M., Blaga, T., Dobrota, V.: Evaluation of Security and Countermeasures for SIP-Based VoIP Architecture, pp. 30–34 (August 2008)
8. Jaques, R.: Cyber-Criminals Switch to VoIP 'Vishing', http://www.vnunet.com/vnunet/news/2160004/cyber-criminals-talk-voip
9. Kapravelos, A., Polakis, I., Athanasopoulos, E., Ioannidis, S., Markatos, E.P.: D(e|i)aling with VoIP: Robust Prevention of DIAL Attacks. In: Gritzalis, D., Preneel, B., Theoharidou, M. (eds.) ESORICS 2010. LNCS, vol. 6345, pp. 663–678. Springer, Heidelberg (2010)
10. Lee, C., Kim, H., Ko, K., Kim, J., Jeong, H.: A VoIP Traffic Monitoring System based on NetFlow v9. Intl. Journal of Advanced Science and Technology 4 (2009)
11. McGann, S., Sicker, D.C.: An Analysis of Security Threats and Tools in SIP-Based VoIP Systems. In: Proc. of the 2nd Workshop on Securing VoIP (June 2005)
12. Me, G., Verdone, D.: An Overview of Some Techniques to Exploit VoIP over WLAN. In: Proc. of 2006 Intl. Conf. on Digital Telecommun. (August 2006)
13. Moskalyuk, A.: US VoIP Market Shares (August 2006), http://blogs.zdnet.com/ITFacts/?p=11425
14. Now, V.: Vonage Is Still # In VoIP Market Share (July 2006), http://www.voipnow.org/2006/07/vonage_is_still.html
15. Reynolds, B., Ghosal, D.: Secure IP Telephony using Multi-layered Protection. In: Proc. of the 10th Netw. and Distrib. Syst. Security Symp. (NDSS) (February 2003)
16. Rosenberg, J., Schulzrinne, H., Camarillo, G., Johnston, A., Peterson, J., Sparks, R., Handley, M., Schooler, E.: SIP: Session Initiation Protocol. RFC 3261
17. Seedorf, J., Beckers, K., Huici, F.: Single-Message Denial-of-Service Attacks Against Voice-over-Internet Protocol Terminals. Intl. Journal of Electronic Security and Digital Forensics 2, 29–34 (2009)
18. Sengar, H., Wijesekera, D., Wang, H., Jajodia, S.: Denial of Service Attacks on IP Telephony. In: Proc. of the 14th IEEE Intl. Workshop on Quality of Service (IWQoS). IEEE Computer Society (June 2006)
19. Sengar, H., Wijesekera, D., Wang, H., Jajodia, S.: VoIP Intrusion Detection Through Interacting Protocol State Machines. In: Proc. of the Intl. Conf. on Dependable Syst. and Netw. (DSN), pp. 393–402. IEEE Computer Society (2006)

20. Soupionis, Y., Basagiannis, S., Katsaros, P., Gritzalis, D.: A Formally Verified Mechanism for Countering SPIT. In: Xenakis, C., Wolthusen, S. (eds.) CRITIS 2010. LNCS, vol. 6712, pp. 128–139. Springer, Heidelberg (2011)
21. Soupionis, Y., Gritzalis, D.: ASPF: Adaptive anti-SPIT Policy-based Framework. In: Proc. of the Intl. Conf. on Availability, Reliability and Security (ARES), pp. 153–160 (2011)
22. Soupionis, Y., Tountas, G., Gritzalis, D.: Audio CAPTCHA for SIP-based VoIP. In: Gritzalis, D., Lopez, J. (eds.) SEC 2009. IFIP AICT, vol. 297, pp. 25–38. Springer, Heidelberg (2009)
23. State, R.: Remote eavesdropping with SIP Phone GXV-3000 (August 2007), http://www.voipsa.org/pipermail/voipsec_voipsa.org/2007-August/002424. html
24. Wang, X., Zhang, R., Yang, X., Jiang, X., Wijesekera, D.: Voice Pharming Attack and the Trust of VoIP. In: Proc. of the 4th Intl. Conf. on Security and Privacy in Commun. Netw., pp. 1–11. ACM (2008)
25. Wu, Y.S., Bagchi, S., Garg, S., Singh, N., Tsai, T.: SCIDIVE: A Stateful and Cross Protocol Intrusion Detection Architecture for Voice-over-IP Environments. In: Proc. of the Intl. Conf. on Dependable Syst. and Netw. (DSN), pp. 433–442. IEEE Computer Society (July 2004)
26. Zhang, R., Wang, X., Farley, R., Yang, X., Jiang, X.: On the Feasibility of Launching the Man-in-the-Middle Attacks on VoIP from Remote Attackers. In: Proc. of the 4th Intl. Symp. on Information, Computer, and Commun. Security (ASIACCS), pp. 61–69. ACM (March 2009)
27. Zhang, R., Wang, X., Yang, X., Jiang, X.: Billing Attacks on SIP-Based VoIP Systems. In: Proc. of the 1st USENIX WOOT (August 2007)

VCCBox: Practical Confinement of Untrusted Software in Virtual Cloud Computing*

Jun Jiang, Meining Nie, Purui Su, and Dengguo Feng

Trusted Computing and Information Assurance Laboratory,
Institute of Software, Chinese Academy of Sciences,
Beijing 100190, China
{jiangjun,niemeining,supurui,feng}@tca.iscas.ac.cn

Abstract. Recent maturity of virtualization has enabled its wide adoption in cloud environment. However, legacy security issues still exist in the cloud and are further enlarged. For instance, the execution of untrusted software may cause more harm to system security. Though conventional *sandboxes* can be used to constrain the destructive program behaviors, they suffer from various deficiencies. In this paper, we propose *VCCBox*, a practical sandbox that confines untrusted applications in cloud environment. Leveraging the state-of-the-art hardware assisted virtualization technology and novel design, it is able to work effectively and efficiently. VCCBox implements its system call interception and access control policy enforcement inside the hypervisor and create an interface to dynamically load policies. The in-VMM design renders our system hard to bypass and easy to deploy in cloud environment, and dynamic policy loading provides high efficiency. We have implemented a proof-of-concept system based on Xen and the evaluation exhibits that our system achieves the design goal of effectiveness and efficiency.

Keywords: Sandbox, Hypervisor based security, Hardware assisted virtualization, Cloud computing.

1 Introduction

In recent years, cloud computing has become a heated topic in both industry and academia. Virtualization, as an underlying technology of cloud computing, plays a key role in utility computing and private cloud. Among all virtualization techniques, hardware assisted virtualization has been widely adopted since it is compatible with existing OS kernels and is supported by various commodity and open-source hypervisors.

Cloud computing is a double-edged sword from the perspective of security. It provides better environment for solving security problems but also enlarges the

---

* This work is supported in part by National Natural Science Foundation of China (NSFC) under Grant No. 61073179, National Basic Research Program of China (973 Program) under Grant No. 2012CB315804, and Natural Science Foundation of Beijing under Grant No. 4122086.

T. Zia et al. (Eds.): SecureComm 2013, LNICST 127, pp. 122–139, 2013.

harm of legacy security issues. For example, some programs may behave maliciously while providing desired features, and this could be either intentional or not. How to securely execute untrusted applications and confine their destructive behaviors has been an everlasting issue in system security. Generally, this problem can be resolved by *sandbox*, a mechanism that controls the runtime environment of a program and mediates its interactions with the outside. Hence, the program behavior can be limited to what the user allows. Unfortunately, most currently available sandboxes possess various deficiencies, such as liability to be bypassed, and requirement of modified or dedicated kernel. More importantly, as we step into the cloud computing era, it becomes difficult and even impossible to deploy them in real production environment. We present a detailed examination of representative sandbox mechanisms in Section 6.2.

To overcome such shortcomings, we present *VCCBox*, a sandbox architecture constructed on top of the hypervisor, which embraces contemporary hardware assisted virtualization technology for robustness and ease-of-deployment. We observe that the system call is the only entry for an application to perform sensitive operations and access system resources. Hence, we intercept system calls from the hypervisor level and check whether they violate access control policies that are compiled from policy scripts written by the user in a C-like language and loaded into the hypervisor dynamically at runtime. The decision made to a system call can be either *permitted*, *disallowed* or *deceived*.

In summary, we make the following contributions:

- We *first* propose a sandbox architecture based on hardware assisted virtualization technology, which overcomes several defects of existing solutions.
- We have implemented a mechanism to dynamically load code into the hypervisor at runtime. To the best of our knowledge, we are the *first* to use this technique in hypervisor-based security mechanisms.
- We have devised a special variant of C programming language as the policy description language, which enables fast development of effective, flexible and powerful policies.
- We have implemented a Xen-based prototype system named VCCBox and performed detailed evaluation showing that our system is effective and efficient for adoption in production cloud environment.

The remainder of this paper is organized as follows. Section 2 presents not only the application scenario and technical background of our system, but also the design of the system, while Section 3 details the implementation. Then we present the results of evaluation in Section 4 and analyze possible limitations of our system and some future work in Section 5. Finally, we discuss several related work in Section 6 and conclude our paper in Section 7.

2   System Overview and Design

In this work, we utilize the contemporary hardware assisted virtualization technology to design a sandbox mechanism named VCCBox. We take advantage of the higher privilege of the hypervisor to achieve non-circumventable protection. Moreover, hardware assisted virtualization is prevalent in cloud computing nowadays, rendering our system suitable for real production environment.

2.1 Application Scenario

To demonstrate the usefulness of our VCCBox system, we provide the following two scenarios:

- Peter is an administrator of several virtual servers running a few services such as HTTP and FTP in a company. However, he is not sure whether these server programs contain malicious parts. It is possible for a web server to possess a backdoor that sends out sensitive files when triggered by a special URL.
- James is a manager of a few virtual private servers, and he rents his virtual machines to individuals. Unfortunately, some tenants use the VMs to perform malicious activities such as sending spams or launching DDoS attacks. It can be trivial and time-consuming to manually stop these behaviors.

In above scenarios, sandboxes can be used to confine the vicious behaviors of untrusted or malicious programs. However, traditional in-OS sandboxes may not fulfill this need. In the first scenario, it could be a tedious and non-trivial task to install and configure sandboxes for respective virtual servers considering the large amount of VMs on a physical machine. Furthermore, in-OS sandboxes are not applicable to the second scenario at all, since the end user has full control on the virtual machine and can easily disable the sandbox. Under such circumstances, our VCCBox system is useful, since it runs at the hypervisor level, and thus is easy to be deployed in cloud environment and hard to bypass.

2.2 Technical Background

Since our approach involves hardware assisted virtualization, specifically, Intel VT, we give a brief introduction of it. The traditional x86 architecture has four privilege levels, ring 0 (highest) for kernels to ring 3 (lowest) for applications. In Intel VT, these four rings are categorized into *VMX non-root mode*, and a new *VMX root mode* with even higher privilege is introduced. Since the legacy four rings still exist, the operating system can run without modification. When virtualization is enabled, several sensitive instructions change their semantics and trap into the hypervisor for the whole system to run correctly. Namely, the virtual machine and the hypervisor alternately obtain the CPU time slice. When the operating system tries to execute a sensitive instruction or an external interrupt occurs, an event called *VMexit* is triggered. Therefore, the processor switches its privilege level to VMX root mode and a previously registered *VMexit handler* is called to enable the hypervisor to deal with the event appropriately for correct virtualization. After that, *VMentry* gives the control back to the operating system and reverts to the previous status. Therefore, the hypervisor naturally provides security applications with an opportunity due to its higher privilege and its capability to intervene in the execution of the virtual machine systems. Currently, modern processors equipped with this technology are widely used in production environment.

Assumption. Since our method involves virtualization, we assume that the hypervisor and the management domain are trusted. We believe that this assumption is reasonable since it is a fundamental assumption shared by many other hypervisor-based security mechanisms [8,14,16,24] and can be consolidated by existing hypervisor protection techniques [1,21,23]. Though attacks to the VMM exist, they are out of the scope of our work.

2.3 System Architecture

VCCBox is constructed on an existing hypervisor in order to be compatible with the production environment. As is illustrated in Fig. 1, our system resides in both the hypervisor and the management domain and is composed of four parts: policy manager, policy library, system call interception and system call feedback. The asterisks indicate that the corresponding parts can be multiple.

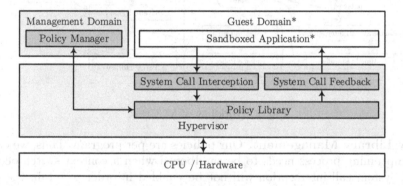

Fig. 1. Architecture of VCCBox

VCCBox works in a straightforward way. It intercepts system calls since they are essential for an application to access system resources, and then consults the policy library to find out applicable measures. Leveraging the higher privilege of the hypervisor and proper design, our system call interception mechanism cannot be bypassed. Moreover, the policies in the library can be added, removed and updated dynamically at runtime, eliminating domain-hypervisor context switches and making our system highly efficient. The policies are compiled from flexible policy scripts written by the user of our system (usually an administrator) using a C-like policy description language. Fig. 2 depicts the entire system workflow.

System Call Interception and Feedback. System call interception is the first step towards sandboxing. Currently, two approaches can be used by an application to request system services, i.e., software interrupt and fast system call mechanism. However, the hypervisor cannot intercept them directly since neither of them triggers *VMexit* events. Fortunately, there are multiple approaches which allow the system calls to be intercepted *indirectly*. Once a system call is intercepted, we look for the corresponding policy and enforce it. The policy uses virtual machine introspection [8] to obtain necessary information and makes a decision out of the following three: *permitted*, *disallowed* and *deceived*. To feed back the result, we take the following approach: nothing additional is required for *permitted*; for *disallowed* and *deceived*, we "skip" the system call and provide appropriate return value to the application by modifying relevant registers; one extra thing is needed for *deceived*, i.e., filling the "output" parameters of the system call with specific value.

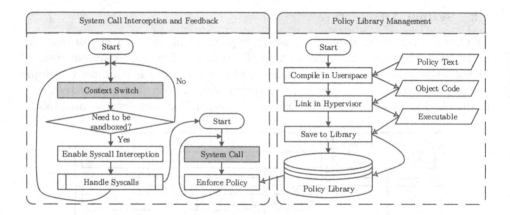

Fig. 2. Workflow of VCCBox

Policy Library Management. Our policies are per program. Thus, we check if the upcoming process needs to be sandboxed when a context switch occurs. If not, system call interception will not be enabled in order to retain the performance. Otherwise, each interesting system call of the sandboxed process is associated with a policy routine. The policies can be added, removed and updated dynamically at runtime. Thus, we need to modify the hypervisor to provide an interface for management of policies. This interface is not complicated since we only need to load executable code into the hypervisor space. Our policy is written by the administrator using a C-like policy language. We do not adopt existing policy languages [9,12,17,18] since they are not sufficiently flexible and powerful. We use a customized compiling tool chain to compile the policy into executable code. Finally, the code is transferred to the hypervisor.

2.4   Policy Description Language

Our policy description language is designed to be a real "programming language" that is powerful and flexible and can be easily compiled to native code. Previous sandboxing policy languages do not fulfill this need so we do not adopt them in our system. To better illustrate our policy language, we first show a policy example written in this language in Lst. 1.

```
/* notepad.exe NtOpenFile */
sandbox_t policy(unsigned int params)
{
    sandbox_t result = permit;
    wchar_t filename1[] = L"password.txt";
    wchar_t filename2[] = L"secret.txt"
    wchar_t *filename;
    unsigned int pos, len;
    guest_read_int_at(params + 12, &pos);
    guest_read_int_at(pos + 8, &pos);
    guest_read_int_at(pos, &len);
    filename = (wchar_t *)malloc(len); /* assume malloc succeeds */
    guest_read_string_at(pos + 4, len, filename);
    if (!wstrcmp(filename, filename1))
    {
        result = disallow;
    }
    else if (!wstrcmp(filename, filename2))
    {
        guest_write_int_at(params + 4, -1);
        result = deceive;
    }
    free(filename);
    return result;
}
```

Listing 1. Policy Example

We can see from the above sample that our policy language is C-like. It can be considered as a subset of C programming language since not all features are necessary and a few limitations are imposed:

- The first line is a *directive*, i.e. a comment indicating the target program and system call name, which is similar to the #!/bin/bash in a shell script.
- The code cannot #include files since it will run in hypervisor kernel.
- Float types and computations are not supported, which are also unnecessary.
- Global variables are not allowed, and literal strings must be initialized with a char/wchar_t array, since the final binary does not have a constant section.
- The code must have the policy function and be self-contained. User-defined functions are allowed (though not shown here), and built-in functions can be used such as memory management (e.g., malloc), string operation (e.g., strcpy), and guest memory reading/writing functions.

3   Implementation Details

In this section, we detail our implementation with a focus on how to modify the existing VMM (hypervisor and management domain) in order to satisfy our needs. Our prototype system uses Xen hypervisor (version 4.1.2), while the dom0 (management domain) and the domU (guest domain) are CentOS 5.5 (64bit) with a patched kernel (version 2.6.34.4) and Windows XP SP3 (32bit), respectively. The development machine has an Intel Core i5 processor with the latest hardware assisted virtualization support. In the following, we present some implementation details for the key techniques in our approach.

3.1   Data Structures and Definitions

We first briefly introduce some key data structures used in our system. As is shown in Fig. 3, our policy library is implemented as a single list and its each node is a `policy_entry` corresponding to a process. Another important data structure is `policy_item`, which is used for loading the executable policy code to the hypervisor. It pertains to one process and one system call. The meanings of most fields are evident, so we do not explain them here. The following sections will explain how these data structures are made use of.

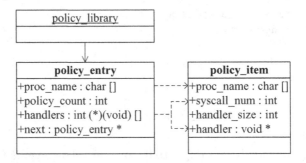

Fig. 3. Data Structures

3.2   Additional VMexit Handler

In order to capture necessary events, we need to modify some existing *VMexit handlers*. Moreover, several events must be intentionally processed to trigger *VMexit* events. We detail how these events are intercepted and handled.

Process Switch Interception. Since our policy is per process, we need to intercept process switches in order to correctly sandbox target applications. The task state segment (TSS) mechanism provided by the x86 architecture is not used by modern operating systems for task switching. In contrast, paging mechanism is widely adopted by operating systems to isolate process spaces. Hence, process switch involves the alteration of page table base address register (cr3 under x86). Moreover, though Windows uses a thread-based scheduling method, the context switch routine will not overwrite the cr3 register if the upcoming thread and current thread belong to the same process. Therefore, we consider VMexit events caused by cr3 write to be process switches.

When such an event occurs, we read the process name from the kernel data structure, and then look it up in the policy library. We traverse the single list and compare the current process name with the proc_name field. If a match is found, the handlers field is copied to a per-domain variable active_handlers, and system call interception is enabled. Otherwise, system call interception is disabled in order to retain performance.

System Call Interception. Intercepting the system call is a pivotal step in our system. Unfortunately, neither software interrupt nor fast system call (sysenter) can be directly intercepted. Hence, we must deliberately trigger some events that can trap into the hypervisor. Multiple ways can be used to achieve this. After comparing their pros and cons, we take the method similar to that in Ether [4], i.e., deliberately modifying the SYSENTER_EIP model specific register (MSR) to generate a page fault. We observe that no program actually uses the conventional software interrupt mechanism to perform system calls, and thus do not intercept such interrupts. Existing approaches are available if necessary[4].

To implement this, we first need to intercept access to the SYSENTER_EIP MSR. For write operations, we store the value at a safe place for future use, while for read operations, we always return the real value for transparency. When system call interception is enabled, a carefully chosen magic value is written to that MSR. Thus, we consider a page fault to be a system call if 1) the page fault linear address (cr2 under x86) is equal to the magic value and 2) the page fault error code indicates an instruction fetch.

When a system call is intercepted, we look up the corresponding handler in the per-domain variable active_handlers using system call number (eax under x86). The handler is executed if it exists. Otherwise, the system call is *permitted* by default. The handler returns a value that is either *permitted, disallowed* or *deceived*. For *permitted* system calls, we simply assign the saved real SYSENTER_EIP value to the eip register. For *disallowed* and *deceived*, we skip the system call, and return error and success, respectively. Note that when sysenter is executed, the current privilege level (CPL) will be ring 0. Thus, to skip the system call, we must get back to ring 3. This is implemented by preparing several sysexit related registers (e.g., ecx, edx) and pointing eip to a sysexit instruction.

3.3   Management of Policies

We load policies into the hypervisor dynamically at runtime to avoid performance penalty caused by context switches between the hypervisor and the management domain. We use a technique called *runtime hypervisor manipulation*, i.e., we create a hypervisor interface and employ the *hypercall* mechanism for implementation.

Hypercall is a domain-hypervisor communication mechanism that is similar to system calls in the operating system. To make use of it, we first register a new hypercall in Xen named do_vccbox_op, which has only one argument, a pointer to the structure struct policy_item, and then implement its handler routine. If the policy with the same process name and system call number exists, we consider it to be a *policy update*, otherwise it is treated as a *policy add*. Specially, if the value of the handler_size field is 0, we consider it as a *policy removal*. Upon policy removal, if the policy count decreases to 0, the whole policy entry is removed from the library. A policy manager in the management domain fills the structure struct policy_item with necessary information and then issues a hypercall to tell the hypervisor what to do.

We observe that policy code execution and policy management are concurrent, so a race condition that the currently executing policy is being updated or removed may occur and must be eliminated. To this end, we use a *spinlock* to synchronize these two actions. We also point it out here that, though our mechanism is similar to *loadable kernel modules* under Linux, we do not consider this to be an insecure factor because, 1) the whole VMM is considered as our trusted computing based by assumption, 2) this mechanism is not designed to accommodate all loadable modules but only our policies, i.e., it is a dedicated channel for policy management, not a generic interface.

3.4   Policy Code Generation

Generating the policy code is an essential part in our system. Since our policy code ultimately runs in the hypervisor, we must keep the application binary interface compatible. Thus, we use the same arguments as Xen is compiled. Moreover, we need a preprocessing step to add necessary dependencies (e.g., declarations of guest memory reading/writing functions) to the policy file in order to make the policy compilable by *gcc*. Thus, we devise the following code generation procedure shown in Fig. 4.

The first step is to validate whether the policy text conforms to our limitations. It is performed by canonical tokenizing and parsing tools (i.e., *flex* and *bison*)[1]. Once the policy is validated, we use a preprocessing part to add some necessary declarations and definitions to the policy text. Then, the completed compilable policy is fed to *gcc* to generate an object file in ELF format using arguments obtained from Xen's *makefile*. Next, we obtain the addresses of the functions in the hypervisor that is called by our policy. For example, our guest memory reading functions are implemented via hvm_copy_from_guest_virt_nofault. We look up relevant information in the object file (e.g., symbol table) and then fill the corresponding locations with real addresses. This process can be considered as a simplified "linking". After that, the policy function binary can be loaded into the hypervisor using the hypercall mechanism mentioned above.

---

[1] This part is not yet fully implemented in our current prototype system.

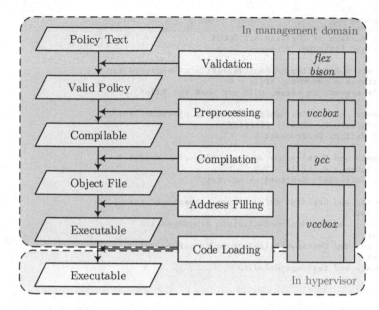

Fig. 4. Procedures of Policy Code Generation

4   Evaluation

In this section, we present the analytical and experimental evaluation of our VCCBox prototype. The two goals of our evaluation are to demonstrate that VCCBox can sandbox real applications, and to measure the performance degradation introduced by our system. The following experiments were all conducted on a machine with Intel Core i5-760 processor and 8GB memory. The version of Xen used in our experiment is the latest 4.1.2 and the dom0 is 64 bit CentOS 5.5 with kernel version 2.6.34.4. The guest OS is Windows XP SP3 allocated with one processor core and 2 GB memory.

4.1   Effectiveness Evaluation

In order to evaluate the effectiveness of our system, we write three different policies targeting the same system call. We choose NtOpenFile here since it is representative. (Note that not all system calls can be deceived). In fact, the policy example in Lst. 1 is for this system call. We give a brief explanation of the policy here. NtOpenFile has 6 parameters. The first one is an output parameter used to return the handle of the opened file, and is our deception target. The third parameter is a structure, which designate the path of the file to be opened. Thus, the sample policy means: if the program tries to open "password.txt", it will get an error; if it tries to open "secret.txt", it will be provided with an invalid handle; otherwise, the open operation is successful.[2]

---

[2] Note that the sample policy is only for demonstration and still needs to be improved for practical use.

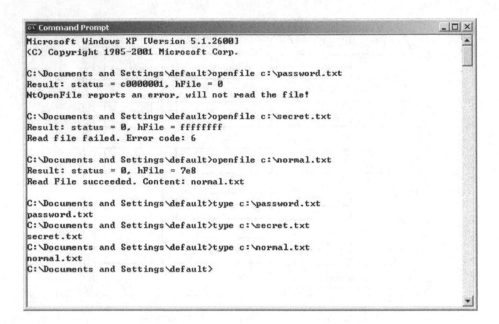

Fig. 5. Effectiveness Evaluation Result

We devise a test program to open the file designated in its argument. The program is sandboxed by our system, and we provide different arguments to this program and observe its output. We call `NtOpenFile` directly from `ntdll.dll` for accuracy, and print the return value and the first parameter containing the opened file handle. To verify the correctness of the handle, we use it as the parameter of `ReadFileEx`, a user space function that reads file content from a handle. Moreover, we use `type` command (similar to `cat` under Linux) to show the real file content for comparison. The result is shown in Fig. 5, from which we can see that our policy is successfully enforced. For `password.txt`, the system call is disallowed, so the return value is set to `0xC0000001`, indicating a failure. Our program checks this failure and reports it. For `secret.txt`, the system call is deceived. We set the return value to 0, meaning a successful system call, but set the output parameter of `NtOpenFile` to `0xFFFFFFFF`, which indicates `INVALID_HANDLE`. Our program reports an error code 6, which exactly means `ERROR_INVALID_HANDLE`, proving that our method has successfully *deceived* the system call[3]. Our test program is not designed to be malicious. However, due to the higher privilege and ability to intercept events of the virtual machine, our method can not be circumvented.

4.2   Performance Evaluation

The runtime overhead of our system comes from the additional VMexit handler routines and hypercalls. However, policy management is not a periodical event,

---

[3] A real `NtOpenFile` does not necessarily returns 0 when it provides an invalid handle. Here we only use this sample to indicate that our *deceived* policy works correctly.

and it does not often happen in practice since system administrators do not frequently change the policies once they are successfully loaded. Moreover, context switches occur much less frequently than system calls, and thus contribute little to the performance degradation according to our experiences. Therefore, we focus on the performance penalty caused by intercepting and handling system calls.

We look into the difference between normal system call execution and sandboxed execution. We denote the time for normal system call as τ_x. If an application is not sandboxed, we do not enable system call interception, hence incurring no performance overhead. If an application is sandboxed, all of its system calls will be trapped into the hypervisor. Thus, unhandled system calls will go through the process of interception *without* policy execution. This time is denoted as τ_e. While handled system calls are intercepted with policy execution, so we denote the time of policy execution as τ_p. Note that since only one policy for a program can lead to system call interception, and the per system call policies will not run together for one system call, the number of policies does not influence the overall performance. Tab. 1 shows the time of execution for different situations.

Table 1. Time Comparison for Different Situations

Situation	Time
Normal	τ_x
Intercept + No handler	$\tau_e + \tau_x$
Intercept + Handler + *permitted*	$\tau_e + \tau_p + \tau_x$
Intercept + Handler + *disallowed/deceived*	$\tau_e + \tau_p$

However, the magnitude of τ_e, τ_p and τ_x is indeterminate, since τ_p and τ_x are respectively per policy and per system call, and the time of execution depends on which path is taken. Thus, we cannot theoretically calculate the performance impact, and micro-benchmark is rendered difficult. So we perform macro-benchmark to measure the performance impact caused by our system. Thus, we enable system call interception for all processes and *permit* all system calls.

Results from Benchmark Tools. We use Super PI, DAMN Hash Calculator, Everest, Crystal DiskMark to benchmark the performance overhead of the processor, memory access and I/O introduced by our system. The results are summarized in Fig. 6, which exhibit that our system is highly efficient.

Results with Real Workload Experiment. To evaluation the efficiency of VCCBox under real workloads, we employ kernel building, a comprehensive task that represents a typical workload and is used widely for profiling. Specifically, we record the time of building the Windows Research Kernel (WRK) under different circumstances. Through scrutinizing possible policies, we observe that the most time-consuming part of a policy is read memory access operations, since the

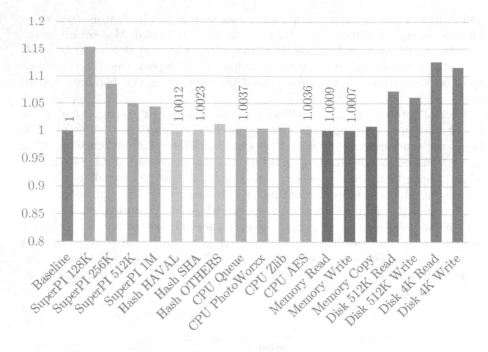

Fig. 6. Benchmark results (Lower is better)

kernel data structures are complicated and frequently point to other structures, leading to multiple memory accesses in retrieving a single piece of information. For example, to obtain the filename from the handle, a parameter of `NtReadFile`, around 7 memory reads are performed. Such read access to memory content is implemented by `hvm_copy_from_guest_virt_nofault` function (HVMCOPY for short). Thus, we add different numbers of synthetic `HVMCOPY` function calls in the system call handler and record the kernel building time. The result of the experiment is shown in Tab. 2.

Table 2. Time for Kernel Building

Situation	Time (ms)	Overhead
Normal	99734	N/A
Intercept + No HVMCOPY	102750	3.0%
Intercept + 10 HVMCOPYs	106617	6.9%
Intercept + 20 HVMCOPYs	110595	10.9%
Intercept + 30 HVMCOPYs	114094	14.4%
Intercept + 40 HVMCOPYs	119922	20.2%

We can see the system call interception itself causes only 3.0% runtime overhead. Moreover, the performance degradation is gradually aggravated as the number of HVMCOPYs (representing the policy complexity) increases. Ordinary policies such as preventing a file with specific name from being read will never use more than 40 HVMCOPYs, and two decisions (*disallowed* and *deceived*) will cause the system calls to be skipped. Thus, we may safely consider the overhead of 20.2% as the worst case, which is acceptable.

5   Discussion and Future Work

The above evaluation exhibits that our current prototype can work effectively and efficiently. In this section, we discuss several limitations of our VCCBox prototype and some future work.

5.1   Extensibility Related Issues

VMM and OS Support. Our current implementation targets Xen and Windows only. However, other hypervisors and operating systems can also be supported. KVM [13] is a rising star among VMMs and wins high favor from both academia and industry, while Linux is the dominating operating system in production environment. We would like to integrate support for them into future versions of VCCBox.

Heterogeneous VM Situation. We currently assume that all virtual machines run the same operating system and/or software. The server environment for load balancing usually satisfies this requirement. However, virtual machines in multi-tenant cloud environment can be *heterogeneous*. Fortunately, our architecture can support such situation. Preliminarily, we can add VMID and OS-Type entry to the policy to distinguish virtual machines and guest operating systems, Further, we can automatically identify the running operating system using oracles [14] or fingerprinting methods [10].

5.2   Insufficiencies and Improvement of Policy

Policy Complexity. Our policy description language is flexible and powerful, which sacrifices its simplicity. It is more complex than other current policy languages and requires the writer (usually a system administrator) to be familiar with operating system data structures. We intend to reduce the policy complexity by integrating recent advances in automatically narrowing the semantic gap such as Virtuoso [5] and VMST [6].

Policy Robustness. Since we need to retrieve the data inside the virtual machine, our policies depend heavily on virtual machine introspection [8]. However, this mechanism can be subverted by direct kernel structure manipulation (DKSM), a technique that directly modified the kernel data structures to mislead security applications [2]. This issue is considered as an open problem by state-of-the-art tools on bridging the semantic gap [5,6] and is not solved to date. Fortunately, DKSM can be prevented by our sandbox mechanism by disallowing untrusted drivers to be loaded, since DKSM requires the kernel privilege to work. In the future, we plan to investigate reliable virtual machine introspection method so as to thoroughly address this issue.

Policy Debugging. Since our policies are ultimately running as code inside the hypervisor, a bug such as access violation can cause more severe results such as crashing the whole physical machine. Hence, we need a mechanism to debug the policy binary. To this end, we can add a *debug* option in our preprocessing module. When this option is enabled, we insert several validations into the generated compilable C code and use dedicated secure versions of necessary functions. The debug version of C code is not designed for daily use since the additional security examination will degrade the performance. The primary purpose of policy debugging is to prevent the policy writer from making careless mistakes.

6   Related Work

6.1   Hypervisor Based Security

With the advent of the cloud computing era, virtualization technology has been widely adopted in research of system security. Hardware assisted virtualization provides powerful processor-level support for privilege separation, memory isolation and access control, which are all desirable features for security applications. Currently, security research efforts based on hardware assisted virtualization can be categorized in malware analysis [4,15,25], kernel protection [19,22,24] and execution monitoring [11,16,20].

Malware analysis platforms use hardware assisted virtualization chiefly for the purpose of transparency. In essence, malware analysis tools have different goals with sandboxes. They *passively observe* the behavior of potentially harmful programs, while sandboxes *actively interfere* with the execution process of untrusted applications. Some techniques of malware analysis can be naturally used for sandboxing. For example, the system call interception method adopted by our system is first proposed in Ether [4].

Kernel protection mechanisms do not address the issue of application behavior confinement. Instead, they are concerned about how to secure the operating system kernel. Thus, most of them fall into the category of anti-rootkit mechanism. In contrast, VCCBox confines the user-level behaviors of an application, and does not care about kernel execution. Interestingly, VCCBox can defeat kernel-level rootkit in a trivial way, i.e.,enforcing a policy to prevent untrusted applications from loading malicious kernel extensions via system calls.

Execution monitoring is a fundamental underlying technique for malware analysis and other security tasks. A significant challenge to correctly monitoring the process inside the virtual machine is *semantic gap* [3], which can be chiefly addressed by virtual machine introspection. However, some execution monitoring tools employs a *hybrid* approach, i.e., using an in-guest component to actually monitor the execution process, while the hypervisor protects this component from being detected or tampered. Though this hybrid approach better solves semantic gap and improves efficiency, VCCBox insists the conventional *out-of-the-box* approach in order not to lose the ease-of-deployment.

6.2   Application Sandbox

Application sandboxing is not new in security area. Many approaches have been used to construct sandboxes. Here we introduce a few representative relevant research efforts in sandbox and compare them with our VCCBox.

Janus [9] is an early and simple sandbox system. It runs entirely in user space and takes advantage of the */proc* interface under Linux for system call interposition. Hence, it is subject to race condition attacks such as "Time of Check to Time of Use" (TOCTTOU), and is liable to be bypassed [7]. Moreover, this interface is not available under such operating systems as Microsoft Windows.

Systrace [17] takes a hybrid approach that involve both user-space and kernel-space to address the TOCTTOU race condition. Systrace however uses an interactive policy generator, which makes it not suitable for production environment where nobody can always stay before the screen. Systrace also assumes the sandboxed application is *intrinsically benign* and only behaves viciously under external attacks, which limits it usage to defend *intrinsically malicious* applications.

Authenticated system calls [18] is a cryptographic approach towards securing the system calls. To initialize, the to-be-sandboxed application is processed by a *trusted installer*, which statically analyzes the program to locate system calls and mine their legal usages to generate policies. Then, it replaces each conventional system call with an authenticated one containing the policy and a message authentication code (MAC). The kernel verifies the MAC and enforces the policy when executing the system call. A main shortcoming of the sandbox is that when the program is obfuscated, the static analysis can hardly get useful system call information.

TxBox [12] introduces the concept of transaction from database for sandboxing. It allows a program to run as a transaction, hence is able to roll back any devastating impact caused by the program. The transaction mechanism has several inherent advantages when used to construct a sandbox. For example, it allows the concurrent execution of sandboxed application and damage detection process, and is able to recover from a multi-staged attack. However, TxBox relies on a dedicated Linux kernel with transaction features, limiting its practicality.

7   Conclusion

In this paper, we have presented the motivation, design, implementation and evaluation of VCCBox, a hypervisor-based sandbox which eliminates various deficiencies of previous work and is a practical sandbox solution for cloud environment. In particular, by leveraging the state-of-the-art hardware assisted virtualization and implementing the sandbox routine totally inside the VMM, VCCBox can not be bypassed and is easy to deploy in virtual cloud infrastructure. Moreover, *runtime hypervisor manipulation* is adopted to dynamically load policies into the hypervisor, which ensures the high performance of VCCBox.

References

1. Azab, A.M., Ning, P., Wang, Z., Jiang, X., Zhang, X., Skalsky, N.C.: HyperSentry: enabling stealthy in-context measurement of hypervisor integrity. In: Proceedings of the 17th ACM Conference on Computer and Communications Security, CCS 2010, pp. 38–49. ACM, New York (2010)
2. Bahram, S., Jiang, X., Wang, Z., Grace, M., Li, J., Srinivasan, D., Rhee, J., Xu, D.: DKSM: subverting virtual machine introspection for fun and profit. In: Proceedings of the 29th IEEE Symposium on Reliable Distributed Systems, SRDS 2010, pp. 82–91. IEEE Computer Society, Washington, DC (2010)
3. Chen, P.M., Noble, B.D.: When virtual is better than real. In: Proceedings of the 8th USENIX Workshop on Hot Topics in Operating Systems, HotOS 2001, pp. 133–138. IEEE Computer Society, Washington, DC (2001)
4. Dinaburg, A., Royal, P., Sharif, M., Lee, W.: Ether: malware analysis via hardware virtualization extensions. In: Proceedings of the 15th ACM Conference on Computer and Communications Security, CCS 2008, pp. 51–62. ACM, New York (2008)
5. Dolan-Gavitt, B., Leek, T., Zhivich, M., Giffin, J., Lee, W.: Virtuoso: narrowing the semantic gap in virtual machine introspection. In: Proceedings of the 32nd IEEE Symposium on Security and Privacy, S&P 2011, pp. 297–312. IEEE Computer Society, Washington, DC (2011)
6. Fu, Y., Lin, Z.: Space traveling across VM: automatically bridging the semantic-gap in virtual machine introspection via online kernel data redirection. In: Proceedings of the 33rd IEEE Symposium on Security and Privacy, S&P 2012, San Francisco, CA (May 2012)
7. Garfinkel, T.: Traps and pitfalls: practical problems in system call interposition based security tools. In: Proceedings of the 10th Annual Network and Distributed Systems Security Symposium, NDSS 2003 (2003)
8. Garfinkel, T., Rosenblum, M.: A virtual machine introspection based architecture for intrusion detection. In: Proceedings of the 10th Annual Network and Distributed Systems Security Symposium, NDSS 2003 (2003)
9. Goldberg, I., Wagner, D., Thomas, R., Brewer, E.A.: A secure environment for untrusted helper applications. In: Proceedings of the 6th USENIX Security Symposium, Security 1996. USENIX Association, Berkeley (1996)
10. Gu, Y., Fu, Y., Prakash, A., Lin, Z., Yin, H.: OS-Sommelier: memory-only operating system fingerprinting in the cloud. In: Proceedings of the Third ACM Symposium on Cloud Computing, SoCC 2012, pp. 5:1–5:13. ACM, New York (2012)
11. Gu, Z., Deng, Z., Xu, D., Jiang, X.: Process implanting: a new active introspection framework for virtualization. In: Proceedings of the 30th IEEE International Symposium on Reliable Distributed Systems, SRDS 2011, pp. 147–156. IEEE Computer Society, Washington, DC (2011)
12. Jana, S., Porter, D.E., Shmatikov, V.: TxBox: building secure, efficient sandboxes with system transactions. In: Proceedings of the 32nd IEEE Symposium on Security and Privacy, S&P 2011, pp. 329–344. IEEE Computer Society, Washington, DC (2011)
13. Kivity, A., Kamay, Y., Laor, D., Lublin, U., Liguori, A.: KVM: the Linux virtual machine monitor. In: Proceedings of the 9th Ottawa Linux Symposium, vol. 1, pp. 225–230 (2007)
14. Litty, L., Lagar-Cavilla, H.A., Lie, D.: Hypervisor support for identifying covertly executing binaries. In: Proceedings of the 17th USENIX Security Symposium, Security 2008, pp. 243–258. USENIX Association, Berkeley (2008)

15. Nguyen, A.M., Schear, N., Jung, H., Godiyal, A., King, S.T., Nguyen, H.D.: MAVMM: lightweight and purpose built VMM for malware analysis. In: Proceedings of the 25th Annual Computer Security Applications Conference, ACSAC 2009, pp. 441–450. IEEE Computer Society, Washington, DC (2009)
16. Payne, B.D., Carbone, M., Sharif, M., Lee, W.: Lares: an architecture for secure active monitoring using virtualization. In: Proceedings of the 29th IEEE Symposium on Security and Privacy, S&P 2008, pp. 233–247. IEEE Computer Society, Washington, DC (2008)
17. Provos, N.: Improving host security with system call policies. In: Proceedings of the 12th USENIX Security Symposium, Security 2003. USENIX Association, Berkeley (2003)
18. Rajagopalan, M., Hiltunen, M., Jim, T., Schlichting, R.: System call monitoring using authenticated system calls. IEEE Transactions on Dependable and Secure Computing 3(3), 216–229 (2006)
19. Seshadri, A., Luk, M., Qu, N., Perrig, A.: SecVisor: a tiny hypervisor to provide lifetime kernel code integrity for commodity OSes. In: Proceedings of 21st ACM SIGOPS Symposium on Operating Systems Principles, SOSP 2007, pp. 335–350. ACM, New York (2007)
20. Sharif, M.I., Lee, W., Cui, W., Lanzi, A.: Secure in-VM monitoring using hardware virtualization. In: Proceedings of the 16th ACM Conference on Computer and Communications Security, CCS 2009, pp. 477–487. ACM, New York (2009)
21. Wang, Z., Jiang, X.: HyperSafe: a lightweight approach to provide lifetime hypervisor control-flow integrity. In: Proceedings of 31st IEEE Symposium on Security and Privacy, S&P 2010, pp. 380–395. IEEE Computer Society, Washington, DC (2010)
22. Wang, Z., Jiang, X., Cui, W., Ning, P.: Countering kernel rootkits with lightweight hook protection. In: Proceedings of the 16th ACM Conference on Computer and Communications Security, CCS 2009, pp. 545–554. ACM, New York (2009)
23. Wang, Z., Wu, C., Grace, M., Jiang, X.: Isolating commodity hosted hypervisors with HyperLock. In: Proceedings of the 7th ACM European Conference on Computer Systems, EuroSys 2012, pp. 127–140. ACM, New York (2012)
24. Xiong, X., Tian, D., Liu, P.: Practical protection of kernel integrity for commodity OS from untrusted extensions. In: Proceedings of the 18th Annual Network and Distributed System Security Symposium, NDSS 2011 (2011)
25. Yan, L.-K., Jayachandra, M., Zhang, M., Yin, H.: V2E: combining hardware virtualization and software emulation for transparent and extensible malware analysis. In: Proceedings of the 8th ACM SIGPLAN/SIGOPS Conference on Virtual Execution Environments, VEE 2012, pp. 227–238. ACM, New York (2012)

Integrated Security Architecture for Virtual Machines

Vijay Varadharajan and Udaya Tupakula

Information and Networked Systems Security Research
Faculty of Science, Macquarie University, Sydney, Australia
{vijay.varadharajan,udaya.tupakula}mq.edu.au

Abstract. Currently virtualisation technology is being deployed widely and there is an increasing interest on virtualisation based security techniques. There is a need for securing the life cycle of the virtual machine based systems. In this paper, we propose an integrated security architecture that combines access control, intrusion detection and trust management. We demonstrate how this integrated security architecture can be used to secure the life cycle of virtual machines including dynamic hosting and allocation of resources as well as migration of virtual machines across different physical servers. We discuss the implementation aspects of the proposed architecture and show how the architecture can counteract attack scenarios involving malicious users exploiting vulnerabilities to achieve privilege escalation and then using the compromised machines to generate further attacks.

Keywords: Virtualisation, Trusted computing, Access Control, Intrusion detection, Security attacks.

1   Introduction

Security issues play a vital role in every organisation, as greater availability and access to information in turn imply that there is a greater need to protect them. To address this issue, several access control mechanisms, languages and systems [1-6] have been proposed in the past. Many of these systems make certain basic assumptions about the state of the platform that is hosting and running the applications and systems software. There is an inherent trust that is placed on the underlying platform when a user or an upper level application is authenticated or authorised to perform actions. In the current networked world with heterogeneous platforms and numerous software applications and system software running on these platforms, it is important such underlying trust assumption about the system state be properly examined. There are several reasons for this. Firstly, computing platforms have become very powerful and can run many applications simultaneously. In particular, as the number of software applications increases, greater is the possibility for security vulnerabilities. These vulnerabilities in turn make the platform more vulnerable to attacks. Secondly, attacks themselves are becoming more and more sophisticated. Furthermore, attackers also have easier access to ready-made tools that enable exploitation of platform vulnerabilities more effective. Thirdly, platforms are

T. Zia et al. (Eds.): SecureComm 2013, LNICST 127, pp. 140–153, 2013.

being shared by multiple users and applications (belonging to different users) both simultaneously as well as at different times. Therefore there is a great chance of the platform being left in a vulnerable state as different users and applications run. Finally, because platforms have become much more complex today, users themselves are unaware of their platform vulnerabilities. Hence there is need for techniques for integrated security techniques for enhancing the security of the systems.

In this paper, we propose an integrated security architecture which combines policy based access control intrusion detection techniques and trusted computing for securing the lifecycle of distributed applications running on virtual machines. The paper is organized as follows. Section 2 presents an application scenario which highlights the need for such integrated security techniques in the current environment. In Section 3, we propose novel integrated security architecture for securing the life cycle of virtual machine based distributed applications. Section 4 presents the implementation details. Finally, Section 5 concludes the paper.

2   Application Scenario

The current networked environment is characterised by different types of security attacks and the attacks dynamically changing to avoid detection and prevention. Given the heterogeneous nature of the technology spectrum with different operating system platforms, fixed and mobile, with different networks and numerous different applications, the range of attacks possible is wide ranging. Hence it is complex and difficult to detect and prevent these different types of attacks using single security technologies such as access control or intrusion detection and prevention. There is a need to develop integrated security architecture combining different security functionalities as well as deploy a range of security tools such as access control mechanisms and intrusion detection systems. Such an integrated architecture is necessary to deal with emerging attacks. Let us consider an example scenario which illustrates the need for integrated security architecture.

Consider the scenario in Figure 1, where we have distributed system architecture with applications running on virtual machines (VMs) on top of a Virtual Machine Monitors (VMMs) [7]. Let us assume that a customer requests to host virtual machines in this distributed datacentre architecture. Consider the case where the VMMs have security tools such as access control and intrusion detection to protect their resources from security attacks. Each VMM may have its own access control policies for hosting virtual machines. For instance, assume that Chinese wall access policy [8] is being enforced by the access control system as shown in Figure 1. Assume that there are VMs hosting requests from banks and oil companies. With the Chinese wall policy, if Bank A's VM is hosted on VMM1, then say Bank B's VM cannot be hosted on the same VMM1. However it can be deployed on VMM2. Now consider a Bank C's VM which cannot be hosted on any of the VMMs. If Bank C's VM is hosted on VMM1, then there is a possibility for information leakage between Bank A's VM and Bank C's VM. Similarly if Bank C's VM is instantiated on VMM2, then there could be information leakage between Bank B's VM and Bank C's

VM. Hence the security architecture should not allow Bank C's VM to be deployed on any of the VMMs. However, it will allow virtual machines belonging to an oil company to be hosted on the VMM. Either the datacentre administrator has to deploy a new physical server to host the Bank C's VM or host the Bank C's VM only when one of the other Banks' VM terminates or shuts down.

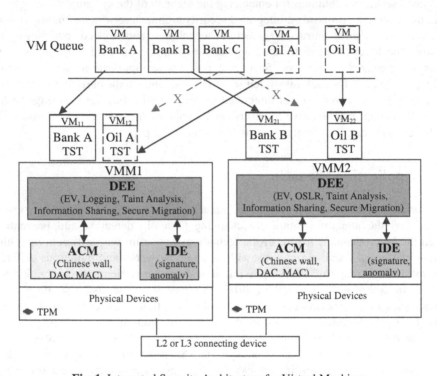

Fig. 1. Integrated Security Architecture for Virtual Machines

In addition, there is also a need to ensure secure operation of the virtual machines. Note that the intrusion detection tools have been deployed at the VMM instead of the VMs to ensure that they themselves do not succumb to attacks at the VMs (which are the ones that are being monitored). Hence the intrusion detection security tool at the VMM should detect if an attacker exploits some known vulnerabilities in the VM (or any traditional security tools (TST) such as [6] that are present at the VM) to generate attacks. Furthermore, in the distributed environment, there may be a need for migration of virtual machines to different physical machines. That is, a VM1 running on top of VMM1 may migrate to a VMM2. Hence the security architecture needs to ensure that the virtual machine can be migrated in a secure manner. Hence we can see the need for a security architecture that brings together access control policies and mechanisms with the intrusion detection and prevention mechanisms in a trusted manner to respond to dynamic changes in attacks.

2.1   Integrated Security Approach

Let us now consider logical security functionalities that need to be combined in the integrated security architecture.

There have been numerous security models that focus on access controls. We mentioned the Chinese wall policy in the previous section above when describing the application scenario. The traditional access control models include discretionary access control models such as those based on access control lists, mandatory access control models such as those based on security labels, type enforcement models, information flow models as well as role based access control models. In principle, each of these can be applied in a virtual machine based distributed systems context. For instance, sHype architecture [9] addressed the enforcement of mandatory access control for virtual machine based systems. It provides a reference monitor interface inside the hypervisor (VMM) to enforce information flow constraints between virtual machine partitions. When a virtual machine partition makes a request to access a shared virtual resource, an access control module in the VMM acting as the reference monitor enforces the mandatory access control policy. Extending this to a distributed system, a distributed application can be represented as a collection of virtual machines that execute across different physical machines. Using such a system, we can achieve a range of access policies such as type enforcement, Bell-LaPadula [10], Chinese wall as well as information flow type security policies.

Access control systems are concerned about preventing access to the resources by the unauthorised users. However if a user (attacker) is successful in obtaining high level privileges through any means such as exploiting a vulnerability such as buffer overflow or by using stolen credentials, access control systems will not be able to differentiate these (malicious) users and are not able to enforce any restrictions on the actions performed by them. Hence by gaining unlawfully the higher level privileges, the attackers are successful in performing malicious activities such as installing malicious software or altering the legitimate applications and using these compromised systems to generate attacks. Such attacks are often detected by the intrusion detection systems in the traditional environment since they have signatures or baseline behaviour for the normal use of the systems or entities. In this case, although the attacker has obtained higher privileges, the actions performed by the malicious users (such as installing root kits and altering ls code to hide the malicious process) either match with the signatures stored in the attack signature database or deviate from the normal behaviour of the system. Hence the intrusion detection system raises an alarm when suspicious activity is detected.

Integrating the intrusion detection mechanisms in the VMM gives rise to several advantages. It provides isolation as the VMM itself is protected from the vulnerabilities in the applications and operating system in the guest virtual machines. Also as the VMM has control on the resources of the system such as memory and I/O devices, it is able to inspect the resources allocated to virtual machines. Hence the intrusion detection mechanisms if they are placed in the VMM can take advantage of this capability in their evaluations. Furthermore, as the intrusion detection code is interposed between a malicious virtual machine and the attacked resource, this interposition enables efficient detection of attacks. For instance, Dunlap et al [11] proposed ReVirt architecture for secure logging by placing the logging tool inside the VMM. Garfinkel [12] proposed a Livewire intrusion detection system which makes use of the VMM to achieve introspection and obtain the state of the virtual machines. However in a distributed environment, we need to be able to detect attacks not only from a single VMM but from distributed VMMs by sharing information about intrusions between them in a secure manner. Lycosid [13] detects hidden process in the virtual machines by comparing the implicit guest view with the VMM image. If the number of processes reported by the guest VM does not match with the number of processes identified by the VMM then there is a hidden process. It does not address attacks generated by visible process.

However there are also some additional challenges with the intrusion detection systems. For example, signature based systems cannot deal with the zero day attacks and anomaly based tools have higher false alarms. Our observations confirm that many attacks first exploit one or more weaknesses in access control followed by the malicious activity. However since the access control and intrusion are often implemented separately, they are not efficient in detecting and preventing sophisticated attacks. Furthermore, traditionally access control systems have been implemented in the operating system or at the applications by the respective vendors, and intrusion detection systems are installed and configured by the end users. Hence there is a need for integrating the access control and intrusion detection tools in a virtualised environment for greater efficient detection of attacks. Such an integrated security architecture should also address additional challenges that arise in a virtual environment such as dynamic hosting of virtual machines on the VMM, dynamic varying of the allocated resources and migration of the virtual machines between different physical servers. Hence the architecture should support techniques that can ensure secure hosting, secure operation, and secure migration of the virtual machines.

Finally let us consider the integrity and trustworthiness of the VMM platform itself. The third logical functionality that we would like to consider in the integrated security approach is that of trust management, which helps to establish the trust on the VMM platform. The notion of trust is the expectation that an entity will behave in a particular manner for a specific purpose. A trusted platform is a platform that contains hardware based subsystem and special processes (Trusted Platform Module (TPM) [14]), which dynamically collect and provide evidence of behaviour. These special processes themselves are "trusted" to collect evidence properly. There are also third parties endorsing platforms which underlie the confidence that the platform can be "trusted". The basic idea is if the physical machine has the TPM, then using its mechanisms, one can measure the state of the VMM on boot and confirm that the VMM is brought into a trustworthy state, if it matches with some reference state. Once the VMM with its access control and intrusion detection functionalities are in a trustworthy state, then the guest virtual machines can be loaded onto the secure VMM.

This completes our integrated security architecture which brings together the access control, intrusion detection and trust management functionalities into the virtual machine based distributed system environment.

3   Security Architecture Overview

Consider the secure and trusted VMM based architecture diagram shown in Figure 1, where each physical server is equipped with a hardware trusted platform module (TPM) chip. Within the VMM, security functionalities of access control, intrusion detection and security decision evaluation have been implemented using the modules Access Control Module (ACM), Intrusion Detection Engine (IDE) and Decision Evaluation Engine (DEE) respectively. This architecture is used to manage the security life cycle of a virtual machine such as secure hosting of a virtual machine, its secure operation as well as secure migration of virtual machines.

There are several components to the DEE module that perform entity validation, logging, taint analysis, information sharing, and secure migration. The entity validation in the DEE is responsible for determining the entity at fine granular level. Note that the entity can vary depending on the action associated with the virtual machine. For example, before hosting a VM on the VMM, the VM is considered as an entity. After the VM is hosted, the processes running in the VM can be considered as entities. After the entity is determined by the entity validation component, the DEE makes a decision on the entity by considering the security policies in the ACM and the IDE components. The ACM module is used for enforcing different access control policies such as Chinese wall to prevent conflicting virtual machines being hosted on the same server; e.g. virtual machines from Bank A and Bank B. Furthermore, it also has techniques to detect privilege escalation attacks performed by the users in the virtual machines. The IDE module is used for detection of both known attacks as well as suspicious behavior by monitoring the interactions of virtual machines. Some components such as entity validation and logging are active for all events on the virtual machines whereas other components such as taint analysis [15] are invoked for specific actions on virtual machines. Taint analysis is invoked only when the ACM or IDE detects some suspicious activity in the virtual machine. Information sharing component is only used for sharing attack information between different secure VMM based physical servers in the distributed environment. Secure migration component is used to validate the capability of the remote physical server to which the virtual machine will be migrated.

Now let us consider how these modules in our secure and trusted VMM based architecture can be used for securing the life cycle of the virtual machines.

3.1   Secure Hosting

Most of the current virtualisation systems support dynamic hosting of virtual machines. However there is a need to ensure secure hosting of the virtual machines. The DEE module in our model is concerned with ensuring secure hosting of virtual machines on the VMM. Before hosting a virtual machine on the VMM, the entity validation component in the DEE module determines whether the virtual machine conflicts with any of the access control policies enforced in the ACM module. If any of the conflicting virtual machines are already running on the VMM, then the DEE module prevents hosting of the virtual machine on the VMM. If hosting of the virtual machine does not conflict with any of the running virtual machines, then the DEE evaluates other factors such as the available resources. If the DEE then decides to host the virtual machine, then the TPM based system is used to measure the state of the virtual machine and ensures it is trustworthy at boot time.

Now let us consider briefly how TPM based system can be used to ensure that VM boots into secure state for completeness. A Trusted Platform includes a Trusted Platform Module (TPM) chip, a Core Root of Trust for Measurement (CRTM), TCG Software Stack (TSS) and the related certification. The TPM is a hardware chip that performs cryptographic functions and is separate from the main CPU. The CRTM is the first piece of software to run as the platform is booted. The TSS is the software code that is needed to perform various functions of the Trusted Platform. There are also a number of Certification Authorities that issue a certificate vouching that various features of the Trusted Platform are genuine. Once the platform is booted, the CRTM measures itself to ensure that it has not been compromised and stores the measured value in the Platform Configuration Register (PCR) of the Trusted Platform Module. For this reason, the TPM is also called as the Root of Trust for Storage (RTS). Then, the CRTM passes control to the first measurement agent (MA). A bootstrapping process follows where all agents measure the software modules they are responsible for and store the measured values inside the PCRs. The process continues until the last measurement agent has recorded the value inside the TPM. This way, at every boot, the TPM stores the measurement values of all the software components of the Trusted Platform. This ensures that the VMM, the VM operating system and its applications are in secure state during boot time.

3.2   Secure Operation

Now let us consider how the DEE ensures secure operation of the virtual machines.

The entity validation and the logging in the DEE are invoked for all the actions on the virtual machines. The entity validation component identifies the entities at fine granular level and determines which security policies in the ACM or IDE component need to be enforced on the interactions of the entity. Logging is used for capturing the specific features of the virtual machine and the entity interactions. In addition to the security policies in the ACM and the IDE which are able to detect the attacks, the DEE determines whether additional policies need to be enforced on the VM entities. Whenever suspicious behaviour is identified by the ACM or the IDE components, the DEE can decide to perform taint analysis to determine if the suspicious behaviour is actually malicious. The DEE can also be used for sharing of information between the different secure VMM physical servers. For instance, this can happen when new attacks are discovered by one physical server and shared with others.

Now let us consider a common attack scenario involving privilege escalation during the operation of the system and see how this attack can be detected with the proposed integrated security architecture. For example, consider a user who has logged on with limited privileges exploits some vulnerability to obtain higher privileges and performs malicious activities such as disabling security tools that have been installed in a virtual machine or installs some malicious programs in the virtual machine.

First let us consider the privilege escalation by exploiting vulnerabilities in the SQL server. In one of the attacks mentioned in [16], a user who has logged in with limited privileges obtains administrative privileges by changing three bytes in the memory by exploiting buffer overflow vulnerability. SQL server validates the user id before giving access to any of the objects. If the user id is set to 1, then the user is considered to have the administrative privileges. The user can alter the id in the memory in the vulnerable server after calling VirtualProtect(). The administrative privileges of such malicious users will be valid until the SQL server is restarted. Hence a malicious user can use such temporary higher privileges to perform malicious activity. Hence there is a need to detect such attacks during runtime by detecting the user privilege escalation.

Note initially when the user first logged in as a normal user, the ACM has details of the user and his/her privileges in its user_store. Let us now consider how the runtime privilege escalation by the user, by altering the bits in the memory, is detected by the ACM module in the secure VMM. Recall the VMM is used to access and monitor the runtime state information of guest virtual machine such as vCPU registers, process and applications running in the guest virtual machine. There are three different types of memory in the VMM which are known as machine, physical and virtual. Machine memory is the real memory which is controlled by the VMM. Physical memory is the memory assigned to the virtual machine and the virtual machine is under the illusion that the physical memory is the actual memory. The virtual memory is similar to the usage in traditional operating systems. The conversion between machine address to physical addresses is performed using a lookup table in the VMM. The ACM module makes use of the xc_map_foreign_range function in the VMM to access the memory contents of the guest virtual machine. Now the runtime privileges of the logged users are determined by analysing the memory allocated to the virtual machine and the actual privileges of the users are available in user_store. Hence in this case, the ACM module can detect the privilege escalation of the logged users.

Another example attack scenario is when a virtual machine is infected with malware such as conficker [17], torpig [18] or LOIC [19]. In such cases, the IDE module comes into play in the detection of such attacks. This happens when the interactions in the virtual machines are found to be suspicious. For example, the LOIC attack floods the victim machines with TCP, UDP and HTTP messages. Such flooding attacks are detected by the signature or anomaly detection component in the IDE module. For example, such attacks are detected when the traffic from the VM matches with the known attack signatures or exceeds a predefined threshold. The virtual machine is then suspended and taint analysis is performed in an isolated environment.

Secure operation also should consider techniques for secure update of the virtual machines. One approach is to apply the updates to the snapshot image and then validate the image in an isolated environment before applying the updates to the virtual machine in the production environment.

3.3   Secure Migration

Let us now consider the situation when a virtual machine which is running on a one VMM based physical server has to be migrated to another one. It is role of the DEE to ensure that the virtual machine is migrated to a secure platform. If the remote physical server does not have the capabilities to enforce the current virtual machine specific policies, then the virtual machine should not be migrated to the remote location. For example, the DEE needs to ensure that the remote server which needs to host the migrated VM does not have any conflicting VMs already running on it. Similarly, in some cases the remote server may not have hardware support for virtualisation. In such cases, the capabilities of the VMM based security modules may not be capable of enforcing the security policies which require hardware support for virtualisation.

When there is virtual machine migration, the DEE determines whether the set of security policies from the ACM and IDE that are specific to the virtual machine are satisfied. Then the information sharing component in the DEE contacts the remote server to check whether it has the required resources to host the virtual machine to be migrated. Then the capabilities of remote server are checked to ensure that the current level of VM security policies can be enforced at the remote server. Our architecture makes use of TPM based validation to ensure that the remote server is capable of achieving a similar level of security for the virtual machine. An additional challenge arises in the migration of virtual machines between physical servers, when different representations for specification of security policies have been used by the different servers. We have assumed that the specification of security policies have been done using the same language. In our case, we use XML based specification of the security policies for virtual machines.

4   Implementation

In this section we consider a malicious user, with limited privileges, exploiting vulnerability in a virtual machine by performing privilege escalation and then compromising the anti-virus software running in the virtual machine. Then the attacker uses compromised system to generate further attacks. Let us consider how our security architecture is able to deal with such an attack scenario.

In our attack scenario, we have used the anti-virus software Avira [20]. Note that Avira is one of the major anti-virus software providers and is an excellent security product. We have just used this as an example to illustrate how a malicious user to exploit current security measures to conduct attacks. Our research confirms similar attacks are also possible with other anti-virus software.

4.1 Anti-Virus Software Overview

Now let us consider a simplified description of Avira Antivirus Free Software and its security features that is relevant for our illustration purposes. It consists of several Windows services, user-level processes, and kernel-mode drivers. Among these modules, Realtime Protection service is crucial in Avira's protection mechanism, as it provides realtime protection not only to the system (e.g. on-access detection of malware), but also to itself (self-protection such as prevention of unauthorised alteration on Avira-related files). In particular, unloading the kernel-mode drivers and the filter driver is blocked by Realtime Protection service as shown in Figure 2. Also, a user cannot stop, pause, or restart the service, as the service ignores such requests. Also one cannot terminate or kill the processes associated with the service (blocked by the driver).

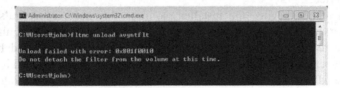

Fig. 2. Driver Protection in Antivirus Tool

Kernel-mode drivers further strengthen Avira's self-protection. One of them locks Avira-related registry keys so that they cannot be modified by the system users. Avira's program folder is protected by the filter driver so that even the user with administrator privilege cannot add any file and delete or modify its files. Furthermore, the processes of Avira are protected by the kernel-driver in a way that even the user cannot kill them. Last but not least, Avira uses files in FAILSAFE folder if some its files in its installation folder are corrupted. To sum up, the protection architecture of Avira has security enforcements to defend it from the malicious users.

Avira also checks for updates regularly and downloads the latest signatures and engines to deal with new types of attacks. There are three ways for carrying out the updates. First, the update of the definitions occurs automatically on a daily basis. Next, a user can trigger an automatic update via a menu or a command-line. Thirdly, a user can download the latest definitions from the Internet, and manually update Avira antivirus with the downloaded definitions. Once an automatic update is started, Avira first checks the current definition and engine versions to determine whether an update is indeed required or not. If so, it downloads the latest definition and engine files from a few dedicated servers, and then checks and installs them. While updating, Avira keeps logging all relevant events so that a user or an administrator can infer possible reasons if the update fails.

4.2 Attack Scenario

In this section, we describe an attack on the file replacement to compromise the anti-virus software and the operating system. Once this can be achieved, the attacker has complete control of the virtual machine and hence can use the system to generate different types of attacks. We will present an attack scenario where the attacker uses a compromised virtual machine to flood the network with malicious traffic and describe how our architecture can prevent such attacks. Our experiment environment was a virtual machine with Windows 7 Ultimate with Avira Free Antivirus 2012 which was running on Xen VMM

We have used a staged malware in this scenario: First the malicious user runs a malware installer (first stage); the malware installer performs only the actions that are permitted under any anti-virus software's realtime protection. In this particular example, it checks the following: OS version, privilege of current user, anti-virus solution installed on the system, and version of currently active signatures and engines. If Avira is installed on the target system, then the installer triggers an update; alternatively, s/he may just wait for an update to be started by the Avira's scheduler service.

When an update begins, the installer monitors the status of Avira's Realtime Protection service. Once the service is deactivated during the update, the installer performs the required actions that are normally blocked or prevented by Avira's Realtime Protection service. In this example, the installer's ultimate goal is to replace Avira's sqlite3.dll with a malicious one (second stage) so as to subvert both Avira and the system.

Fig. 3. Real-time Protection Service Process after update

It performed the following tasks:

- For privilege escalation, it dropped and executed any known or zero-day exploit that is normally detected by Avira. Notice that this local privilege escalation (e.g. from admin to SYSTEM) is required only once. After this file replacement process, the malware obtains SYSTEM privilege on the target machine.
- Unloads Avira's filter driver that is normally protected by the service.
- Dropped the real payload (fabricated sqlite3.dll) and replaced the original file in Avira's installation folder with the malicious one. This file operation is shown in Figure 3.
- The installer deletes itself as a clean-up process to erase its existence; alternatively, the payload may delete the installer.

As the filter driver has been unloaded, it should be restored, even though Realtime Protection service automatically loads and attaches the filter driver when it restarts. The reason for the restoration is that the service's restart triggered by Avira after an update proceeds to some extent and fails if the driver remains unloaded; of course, the installer can manually restart the service after the first restart by Avira fails. But still the best solution is to restore the driver, because the service restart by Avira succeeds if the filter driver is restored. Interestingly enough, even if the start of the service was triggered and failed, it is logged as successfully started in the Avira's update log file, which is good from the attacker's point of view.

Fig. 4. Successful Attack

On restarting, Realtime Protection service loads the malicious sqlite3.dll which provides full SQLite functionalities, and becomes active without any problem. However, once loaded by the service, the malicious sqlite3.dll obtains SYSTEM privilege on the target machine. In other words, this attack allows the malware to escalate its privilege from a user to SYSTEM, which means UAC (User Access Control) on Windows becomes ineffective. Also, almost any malicious activity becomes possible, as it is loaded and executed in the context of Avira's Realtime Protection service. Furthermore, the DLL can perform file operations on the installation folder, even while the filter driver is loaded; this allows the attacker to update the malicious DLL. The result of this file replacement and loading operations is shown in Figure 4. The original sqlite3.dll (sqlite3_ori.dll, 389KB) has been replaced with the malicious version (sqlite3.dll, 612KB), and the fabricated DLL has been loaded by the service (window on the left side). Here, the original DLL was not removed to show its replacement. After becoming a part of Avira, the malware might be able to modify Avira's memory area. If so, it is possible to make Avira to look normal (with the tray icon's umbrella open), but totally ineffective.

In the above scenario, the TPM prevents such unauthorised services during restart of the service. However it is important to note that the attacker can also generate attacks by compromising his virtual machine during runtime and generate attacks without restating the service. In our architecture, such runtime attacks are prevented by the secure VMM when the ACM module detects the privilege escalation of the logged user to system level or when the IDE module detects malicious traffic originating from the compromised virtual machine. Although the attacker is successful in compromising the virtual machine, s/he does not have access to the security components in VMM. Hence such attacks will not be successful with our integrated security architecture.

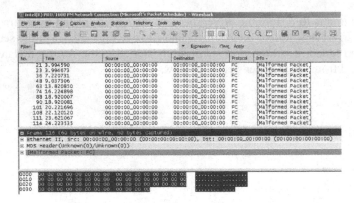

Fig. 5. Flooding with Malicious Traffic

Now let us consider an attack scenario. Figure 5 shows the case where an attacker has compromised a virtual machine during runtime and generates malicious traffic without restarting the virtual machine. Such an attack will be successful and the attacking source can remain anonymous in a traditional datacenter. Since the attacker has obtained complete control of the virtual machine and the traditional security tools in the virtual machine, s/he can alter the logs in the compromised system. Hence it is extremely difficult for the datacenter administrator to determine the attacking source for such attacks since the attack traffic does not have any valid MAC or IP address.

With our architecture, the attacks shown in Figure 5 are not possible in the first place. Since the traffic does not have valid MAC or IP address it will be blocked by the IDE module and an alert will be raised to the administrator. Hence our architecture can detect and prevent such an attack even before the attack traffic is placed on the network.

5   Concluding Remarks

We have proposed integrated security architecture which combines trusted computing, access control and intrusion detection techniques for securing the life cycle of the virtual machines. We have also shown how our architecture can prevent attacks from malicious users exploiting vulnerabilities to achieve privilege escalation and then using the compromised machines to generate further attacks.

References

1. Ferraiolo, D., Kuhn, R.: Role-based access control. In: Proceedings of the 15th NIST-NCSC National Computer Security Conference, pp. 554–563 (1992)
2. Jajodia, S., Samarati, P., Subrahmanian, V.S.: A logical language for expressing authorizations. In: Proceedings of the 1997 IEEE Symposium on Security and Privacy. IEEE Computer Society, Washington, DC (1997)

3. DeTreville, J.: Binder: A logic-based security language. In: SP 2002: Proceedings of the 2002 IEEE Symposium on Security and Privacy, p. 105. IEEE Computer Society, Washington, DC (2002)
4. Li, N., Mitchell, J.C.: Rt: A role-based trust-management framework. In: Proceedings of the Third DARPA Information Survivability Conference and Exposition, pp. 201–212. IEEE Computer Society (2003)
5. Herzberg, A., Mass, Y., Michaeli, J., Ravid, Y., Naor, D.: Access control meets public key infrastructure, or: Assigning roles to strangers. In: SP 2000: Proceedings of the IEEE Symposium on Security and Privacy. IEEE Computer Society, Washington, DC (2000)
6. The Open Source Network Intrusion Detection System: Snort, http://www.snort.org/docs/iss-placement.pdf
7. Smith, J.E., Nair, R.: The Architecture of Virtual Machines. IEEE Internet Computing (May 2005)
8. Brewer, D.F.C., Nash, M.J.: The Chinese Wall security policy. In: Proc. of IEEE Sympoisum on Security and Privacy, pp. 206–214 (1989)
9. Sailer, R., Jaeger, T., Valdez, E., Caceres, R., Perez, R., Berger, S., Griffin, J.L., van Doorn, L.: Building a MAC-based security architecture for the Xen open-source hypervisor. In: Proceedings of the 21st IEEE Annual Computer Security Applications Conference, Washington, DC, USA (2005)
10. Bell, D.E., La Padula, L.J.: Secure Computer Systems: Unified Exposition and Multics Interpretation. ESD-TR-75-306, MTR 2997 Rev. 1, The MITRE Corporation (March 1976)
11. Dunlap, G.W., King, S.T., Cinar, S., Basrai, M.A., Chen, P.M.: ReVirt: Enabling Intrusion Analysis through Virtual-Machine Logging and Replay. In: Proceedings of OSDI (2002)
12. Garfinkel, T., Rosenblum, M.: A virtual machine introspection based architecture for intrusion detection. In: Proceedings of NDSS (February 2003)
13. Jones, S.T., Arpaci-Dusseau, A.C., Arpaci-Dusseau, R.H.: VMM-based hidden process detection and identification using Lycosid. In: Proc. of ACM VEE (March 2008)
14. Trusted Computing Group, TCG Specification, Architecture Overview, Specification Revision 1.2 (April 2004), http://www.trustedcomputinggroup.org
15. Newsome, J., Song, D.: Dynamic taint analysis: Automatic detection and generation of software exploit attacks. In: Proceedings of NDSS (February 2005)
16. Litchfield, D.: Threat Profiling Microsoft SQL Server, http://www.cgisecurity.com/lib/tp-SQL2000.pdf (last viewed: July 31, 2013)
17. Seungwon, S., Guofei, G.: Conficker and Beyond: A Large-Scale Empirical Study. In: Proceedings of the 26th Annual Computer Security Applications Conference, Austin, Texas, USA, December 6-10, pp. 151–160. ACM Press, New York (2010)
18. Stone-Gross, B., Cova, M., Gilbert, B., Kemmerer, R., Kruegel, C., Vigna, G.: Analysis of a Botnet Takeover. In: Proc. of IEEE Symposium on Security & Privacy, vol. 9(1), pp. 64–72 (2011)
19. LOIC, http://sourceforge.net/projects/loic/
20. Avira Antivirus Software for home and business, http://www.avira.com

Generic Mediated Encryption

Ibrahim Elashry, Yi Mu, and Willy Susilo

Centre for Computer and Information Security Research
School of Computer Science and Software Engineering
University of Wollongong, Wollongong NSW2522, Australia
ifeae231@uowmail.edu.au, {ymu,wsusilo}@uow.edu.au

Abstract. We propose a generic mediated encryption (GME) system that converts any identity based encryption (IBE) to a mediated IBE. This system is based on enveloping an IBE encrypted message using a user's identity into another IBE envelope, using the identity of a security mediator (SEM) responsible for checking users for revocation. We present two security models based on the role of the adversary whether it is a revoked user or a hacked SEM. We prove that GME is as secure as the SEM's IBE (the envelope) against a revoked user and as secure as the user's IBE (the letter) against a hacked SEM. We also present two instantiations of GME. The first instantiation is based on the Boneh-Franklin (BF) FullIBE system, which is a pairing-based encryption system. The second instantiation is based on the Boneh, Gentry and Hamburg (BGH) system, which is a non pairing-based encryption system.

Keywords: Key Revocation Problem, Identity-based Encryption, Double Encryption.

1 Introduction

The key revocation problem has received the attention of the cryptography community because the user's public key cannot be used if the corresponding private key is compromised. This problem occurs in public key cryptography because it depends on digital certificates. Digital certificates are signatures issued by a trusted certificate authority (CA) that securely ties together a number of quantities. Typically, these quantities contain at least the ID of a user (U) and its public key (PK). Frequently, the CA comprises a serial number (SN) for the purpose of managing the certificates. The CA also binds the certificates to an issue date D_1 and an expiration date D_2. By issuing the signature of $SigCA(U, PK, SN, D_1, D_2)$, the CA provides PK, which is the user's public key, between the current date D_1 and the future date D_2.

A user's public key may have to be revoked before its expiration date D_2. For Instance, if a user's secret key is accidentally leaked or an attacker is successful in compromising it, the user's public key and private key should be revoked; a new key pair should be generated and the corresponding certificate should be issued.

T. Zia et al. (Eds.): SecureComm 2013, LNICST 127, pp. 154–168, 2013.
© Institute for Computer Sciences, Social Informatics and Telecommunications Engineering 2013

If the CA can revoke a certificate, then third parties cannot depend on this certificate unless the CA shares certificate status information indicating whether this certificate is still valid. This certificate status information has to be recently generated. In addition, it must be widely distributed. Sharing a great deal of fresh certification information periodically leads to the key revocation problem. which consumes large amount of computation power and bandwidth. This is considered a hindrance to global application of public-key cryptography.

1.1 Some Previous Solutions to the Key Revocation Problem

The most widely-known and a very ineffective way to solve the key revocation problem is the certificate revocation list (CRL)[17,7]. A CRL is a list that contains certificates revoked before their due date. The CA produces this list periodically, with its signature. Since the CA will probably revoke many of its certificates -say 10 %- if they are produced for a validity time of one year[15,11], the CRL will be too lengthy if the CA has many clients. Despite this, the complete CRL must be sent to any party that needs to carry out a certificate status check. There are improvements to this approach, such as delta CRLs[2] which list only those certificates revoked since the CA's last update, but the consumed transmission bandwidth costs, and the computation costs required to enable the transmission of these lists are still very high. Another method of solving the key revocation problem is the online certificate status protocol (OCSP)[13].

Micali [15,11,14] proposed a promising way to solve this problem. (See also [16,9,10].) Similar to previous PKI proposals, Micali's Novomodo system includes a CA, one or more directories (to distribute the certification information) and the users. Despite this similarity, however, it is more efficient than CRLs and OCSP, without sacrificing security.

The advantage of Novomodo over a CRL-based system is that a directory's reply to a certificate status query is brief, only 160 bits per query (if T has cached $SigCA(U, PK, SN, D_1, D_2, X_n)$). On the other hand, the length of a CRL, increases with the number of certificates that have been revoked (i.e. number of clients). Novomodo has several advantages over OCSP. First, Novomodo depends on hashing while OCSP depends on signing. Because hashing has lower computation costs than signing, the CA's computational costs in Novomodo is typically much lower. Second, the directories in Novomodo do not have to be trusted, unlike the distributed components of an OCSP CA. Instead of issuing signatures depended on third parties, the directories only publish hash pre-images sent by the CA (which cannot be produced by Novomodo directories). Third, the directories do not perform any online computation and make Novomodo less vulnerable to DoS attacks. Finally, although OCSP does not consume too much bandwidth because it only generates one signature per query, Novomodo's bandwidth consumption is typically even lower, since public-key signatures are typically longer than 160 bits (length of X_{n-i} sent per query).

A disadvantage of all the above techniques for solving the key revocation problem is relaying on third-party queries[11]. It is preferable to eliminate third-party queries for several reasons. First, since anyone can ask for third-party queries, each certificate server in the system must be able to get the certificate status of every client in the system. The situation is much simpler if third-party queries are eliminated. Each server is only required to have certification proofs for the clients that it works for. In addition, multi-cast can be used to push certificate proofs to clines and consequently, the transmission costs are reduced. Second, third-party queries multiply the query computation costs of the CA and/or its servers. For example, if each client queries the certification status of X other clients per day, then the system must process XN queries (where N is the number of clients). Third, from a business model perspective, non-client queries are not recommended because if T is not a client of the user's CA, what motivation does the CA have to deliver T fresh certificate status information? Finally, since the CA must reply to queries from non-clients, it becomes more vulnerable to DoS attacks, and this is a security concern. In summary, removing third-party queries leads to a reduction in infrastructure costs, simplifies the business model and increases security. We can completely remove third-party queries by using an implicit certification where T, without acquiring any information other than the user's public key and the parameters of the user's CA, can encrypt its message to the user so that he can decrypt only if the key is currently certified. This allows us to enjoy the infrastructure benefits of eliminating third-party queries. This can be achieved by identity-based encryption (IBE).

The notion of identity-based cryptography was put forth by Shamir [19]. In the same paper, Shamir also proposed a concrete construction of an identity-based signature system. Identity-based cryptography offers the advantage of simplifying public key management, as it eliminates the need for public key certificates. In Shamir's seminal paper, he successfully achieved this goal by designing an identity-based signature based on RSA, but the construction for identity-based encryption can not be achieved using a similar approach since sharing a common modulus between different users make RSA insecure. Examples of cryptanalysis RSA with the same modulus used for different encryption/decryption pairs are [20,1]. Sixteen years later, Sakai, Ohgishi and Kasahara [18] proposed the first identity-based cryptography and independently, Boneh and Franklin [4] proposed the first reliable and provable identity-based cryptography, which is based on Weil pairings over elliptic curves. Cocks [6] presented a system that is based on factorisation of a composite integer. These cryptosystems opened a new era in cryptography.

Gentry presented the notion of certificate-based encryption (CBE)[11]. This system combines public-key encryption (PKE) and IBE while keeping most of the advantages of each. Using PKE, each client creates its own public-key/secret-key pair and asks for a certificate from the CA. The CA uses an IBE system to create the certificate. This certificate has all of the functionality of a conventional PKI certificate as well as also being able to be used as a decryption key. This double encryption gives us implicit certification. If T wants to encrypt a message to the user, it double encrypts the message using PKI and IBE, and then the user uses both his secret key and an up-to-date certificate from his CA to decrypt the message. CBE has no escrow (since the CA does not know the user's secret key), and it does not a have secret key distribution problem since the CA's certificate needs not be kept secret. Although CBE consumes less computation and transmission costs than Novomodo, it is preferable to completely eliminate the use of certificates to preserve the infrastructure costs.

Boneh, Ding, Tsudik and Wong were the first to introduce the notion of mediated cryptosystems in [3]. They designed a variant of RSA that allows an immediate revocation of, for instance, an employee's key by an employer for any reason. Their system is based on the so-called security mediator (SEM) architecture, in which SEM is a semi-trusted server. If an employee wants to decrypt/sign a message, he must co-operate with the SEM to do so. The idea behind their system is based on splitting the secret key of an employee between the employee himself and the SEM. Hence, without the SEM cooperation, the employee cannot sign or encrypt the message. This is also helpful to monitor the security of sent/received secure messages in the company. This SEM architecture was proven useful [3] to simplify signature validation and enable key revocation in legacy systems. Although this system does not require a CA to create a certificate or send certificate status information and hence, the computation and transmission costs are kept to minimum, it has two major security concerns. First, There is a security flaw in [8,12]. Second, since SEM is centralised, it represents a single point of failure for the system and hence the system is vulnerable to DOS attacks. Moreover, because SEM is a semi-trusted server, a hacked SEM can be a major threat to the system security.

1.2   Our Contribution

Assume that there is a company, XYZ, and the security manager of this company wants to upgrade the currently-used IBE system to one that supports key revocation. The security manager has two options. He can install a CBE system [11], but he has to uninstall the currently used IBE and install a PKE. PKE certificates will lead to more computation and transmission costs. The other option is using SEM structure as presented in [3,12]. The security manager also has to uninstall the current IBE system and install a new one that supports key revocation. The system will be more vulnerable to DoS attacks. The process of uninstalling the currently used IBE and install a new encryption system is time-consuming and expensive. It is like having a safe with a one-key lock and you want to replace it with a two-key lock, you will have to completely remove the old lock and install the new one. The question we address in this paper is "Is there a way to make any IBE support key revocation without having to uninstall it?".

In this paper, we present a technique that is capable of making any IBE system support key revocation. This idea is based on a letter-envelope technique. If T wants to encrypt a message to U, he first encrypts it, normally using U's identity (letter), then he encrypts the letter again using SEM identity (envelope). After that, the message is sent back to SEM. If U is revoked, SEM will not open the envelope for him. If U is not revoked, the SEM will open the envelope and send the letter to U who decrypts the message using his private key. This is like installing a new lock beside the old one. The original key is with the user and the other key is with the SEM.

The structure of our system combines the advantages of both Gentry[11] and Boneh *et al.* [3]. It eliminates completely the use of certificates. In addition, the SEM in our system is not a single point of failure. If the SEM is compromised, the system can continue working using the IBE system. In addition, the SEM does not have to be trusted or semi-trusted. If the SEM is compromised, all the messages sent to the SEM, before or after an attack, are safe and secure.

Paper Organization. The rest of the paper is organized as follows: Section 2 presents the generic mediated encryption (GME) and its security proof. Section 3 presents two implementations of GME, the first one based on the BF IBE system[4], which is based on pairings, and the second one based on the BGH system[5], which is not based on pairing. The last section presents the conclusions of the paper.

2   Generic Mediated Encryption

In the following section, we explain the security model and security proof of GME. Table 1 presents the definitions of the symbols used.

Table 1. Symbols

Symbol	Definition
U	User
S	SEM
P	System Parameters
Gen	IBE Setup Algorithm
KG	IBE Key Generation Algoritm
Enc	Encryption Algorithm
Dec	Decryption Algorithm
r	The private Key

2.1   The Model

Definition 1. *A Generic Mediated Encryption system is a 6- tuple of algorithms. These algorithms are $(Gen_S, KG_S, Gen_U, KG_U, Enc, Dec_S, Dec_U)$ such that:*

- $Gen_U(1^{k_1})$: *The private key generator (PKG) runs the probabilistic IBE key generation algorithm Gen_S, which takes as input a security parameter 1^{k_1}. It returns MSK_S (first PKG master secret) and public parameters P_S.*
- $Gen_U(1^{k_2})$:*PKG runs the probabilistic IBE key generation algorithm Gen_U, which takes as input a security parameter 1^{k_2}. It returns MSK_U (second PKG master secret) and public parameters P_U.*
- $KG_S(MSK_S, P_S, ID_S)$: *This algorithm generates the secret key r_S for SEM with identity ID_S using P_S and MSK_S.*

- $KG_U(MSK_U, P_U, ID_U)$: This algorithm generates the secret key r_U for user with identity ID_U using P_U and MSK_U.
- $Enc(P_S, P_U, ID_U, ID_S, m)$: The probabilistic encryption algorithm Enc takes P_S, P_U, ID_U, ID_S, m. It returns a ciphertext C on message m.
- $Dec_S(P_S, r_S, C)$: The deterministic decryption algorithm Dec_S takes (P_S, r_S, C) as input along with the user revocation status. If the user is revoked, Dec_S returns $\perp$. Otherwise it returns C_U.
- $Dec_U(P_U, r_U, C_U)$: The deterministic decryption algorithm Dec_U takes (P_U, r_U, C_U) as input. It returns m.

2.2   Security

Our main concern is the GME security against two different types of attacks: 1) by a revoked user and 2) by a compromised SEM. GME must be secure against each of these individuals, considering that each obtains 'half' of the information needed to decrypt. Correspondingly, we define IND-CCA security using two different games. The adversary selects the game to play. In the first game, Type 1, the adversary plays the role of a revoked user. After demonstrating knowledge of the private key related to his identity, the revoked user can make Dec_S queries. In the second game, Type 2, the adversary plays the role of a compromised SEM. After demonstrating knowledge of the private key related to his identity, a compromised SEM can make Dec_U queries. We can say that our system is secure if no adversary can win either game.

Type 1: The challenger runs $Gen_S(1^{k_1}, t_1)$ and $Gen_U(1^{k_2}, t_2)$, and gives P_S and P_U to the adversary. The adversary then interleaves key extraction quires and decryption queries with a single challenge query. These queries are answered as follows:

- On key extraction queries (MSK_U, P_U, ID_U), the challenger outputs r_U corresponding to the identity ID_U, otherwise it returns $\perp$.
- On decryption queries $(P_S, P_U, ID_U, ID_S, r_U, C)$, the challenger checks that r_U is the private key related to ID_U. If so, it generates r_S and outputs $Dec_U(Dec_S(C))$, otherwise it returns $\perp$.
- On challenge query $(P_S, P_U, ID'_U, r'_U, M_0, M_1)$ the challenger checks that r_U is the private key related to ID_U. If so, it chooses random bit b and returns $Enc(m)$, otherwise it returns $\perp$.

In the end, the adversary outputs a guess $b' \in \{0, 1\}$. The adversary wins the game if $b' = b$ and ID'_U, r'_U was not a subject of a valid decryption query after the challenge. The adversary's advantage is defined to be the absolute value of the difference between $1/2$ and its probability of winning.

Type 2: The challenger runs $Gen_S(1^{k_1}, t_1)$ and $Gen_U(1^{k_2}, t_2)$, and gives P_S and P_U to the adversary. The adversary then interleaves key extraction quires and decryption queries with a single challenge query. These queries are answered as follows:

- On key extraction queries (MSK_S, P_S, ID_S), the challenger outputs r_S corresponding to the identity ID_S, otherwise it returns $\perp$.
- On decryption queries $(P_S, P_U, ID_U, ID_S, r_S, C)$, the challenger checks that r_S is the private key related to ID_S. If so, it generates r_U and outputs $Dec_U(Dec_S(C))$, otherwise it returns $\perp$.
- On challenge query $(P_S, P_U, ID'_S, r'_S, M_0, M_1)$ the challenger checks that r_S is the private key related to ID_S. If so, it chooses random bit b and returns $Enc(m)$, otherwise it returns $\perp$.

In the end, the adversary outputs a guess $b' \in \{0, 1\}$. The adversary wins the game if $b' = b$ and $(ID'_S, r'_S$ was not a subject of a valid decryption query after the challenge. The adversary's advantage is defined to be the absolute value of the difference between $1/2$ and its probability of winning.

Definition 2. *A generic mediated encryption system is secure against adaptive chosen ciphertext attack (IND-GME-CCA) if no PPT adversary has non-negligible advantage in either Type 1 or Type 2.*

Remark: Type 1 and Type 2 are IND-GME-CCA secure if both IBE_S and IBE_U are IND-ID-CCA secure. If IBE_S and IBE_U are IND-ID-CPA secure, then Type 1 and Type 2 are modified by eliminating the decryption queries to get IND-GME-CPA security.

2.3   Security Proof

The security proof of GME is defined by the following two theorems.

Theorem 1. *If an adversary A, who plays the role of a revoked user, has an advantage ϵ against GME, then this adversary has the same advantage against IBE_S.*

Theorem 2. *If an adversary A, who plays the role of a compromised SEM, has an advantage ϵ against GME, then this adversary has the same advantage against IBE_U.*

Proof: Theorem 1 means that the game between adversary A, who plays the role of a revoked user, and challenger B against GME (Type 1) is identical to the game between the same adversary A and the challenger B against IBE_S. To prove that, we rewrite Type 1 as follows:

Type 1'

- The Setup phase is the same as Type 1.
- Key extraction queries are the same as Type 1.
- Decryption queries are the same as Type 1.
- On challenge query $(P_S, P_U, ID'_U, r'_U, M_0, M_1)$ the challenger checks that r_U is the private key related to ID_U. If so, it chooses random bit b and returns $C = Enc(m)$, otherwise it returns $\perp$. Since the revoked user has r_U, then he can partially decrypt the message to get $C_S = Enc_S(m)$, where Enc_S is the the SEMs IBE encryption algorithm.

In the end, the adversary outputs a guess $b' \in \{0, 1\}$. The adversary wins the game if $b' = b$ and $(ID'_S, r'_S$ was not a subject of a valid decryption query after the challenge. The adversary's advantage is defined to be the absolute value of the difference between $1/2$ and its probability of winning. This concludes Type 1'.

From Type 1', we can see that:

- Type 1' represents a game against IBE_S, because in the challenge phase, the adversary A has to attack $C_S = Enc_S(m)$ to get the message m.
- The only difference between a game against GME (in the case of a revoked user) and IBE_S is the excess information of P_U which does not give the adversary any information to identify m.

This concludes the proof of Theorem 1. The proof of Theorem 2 is similar.

3 Implementation of GME

Generally speaking, a GME system is produced by the combination of two IBE systems. To prove that GME is generic, we present GME in two different instantiations. The first one is based on the BF FullIBE [4] which is based on pairings. The other instantiation is based on BGH IBE system[5], which is not based on pairings . We first briefly review bilinear pairings, and the bilinear Diffi-Helman assumption, which is the base of the BF FullIBE security. Then we present GME using BF FullIBE. After that, we briefly review some of the security topics related to the BGH IBE system, then we represent GME using BGH IBE system.

3.1 Review on Pairings

BF IBE [4] is based on bilinear map called a 'pairing'. The pairing which is often used to construct BF IBE is a modified Weil or Tate pairing on a supersingular elliptic curve or Abelian variety. However, we review pairings and the related mathematics in a more general form here.

Let $\mathbb{G}_1$ and $\mathbb{G}_2$ be two cyclic groups of a large prime order q. $\mathbb{G}_1$ is an additive group and $\mathbb{G}_2$ is a multiplicative group.

Admissible Pairings: $\hat{e}$ is called an admissible pairing if $\hat{e} : \mathbb{G}_1 \times \mathbb{G}_1 \to \mathbb{G}_2$ is a map with the following properties:

- Bilinear: $\hat{e}(aQ, bR) = \hat{e}(Q, R)^{ab}$ for all $Q, R \in \mathbb{G}_1$ and all $a, b \in \mathbb{Z}$.
- Non-degenerate: $\hat{e}(Q, R) \neq 1$ for all $Q, R \in \mathbb{G}_1$.
- Computable: There is an efficient algorithm to compute $\hat{e}(Q, R)$ for any $Q, R \in \mathbb{G}_1$.
- Symmetric: $\hat{e}(Q, R) = \hat{e}(R, Q)$ for any $Q, R \in \mathbb{G}_1$.

Bilinear Diffie-Hellman (BDH) Parameter Generator: As in [4], we say that a randomized algorithm $\mathcal{IG}$ is a BDH parameter generator if $\mathcal{IG}$ takes a security parameter $k > 0$, runs in time polynomial in k, and outputs the description of two groups $\mathbb{G}_1$ and $\mathbb{G}_2$ of the same prime order q and the description of an admissible pairing $\hat{e} : \mathbb{G}_1 \times \mathbb{G}_1 \to \mathbb{G}_2$.

BDH Problem: Given a randomly chosen $P \in \mathbb{G}_1$, as well as aP, bP and cP (for unknown randomly chosen $a, b, c \in \mathbb{Z}_q$), compute $\hat{e}(P, P)^{abc}$.

For the BDH problem to be hard, $\mathbb{G}_1$ and $\mathbb{G}_2$ must be chosen so that there is no known algorithm for efficiently solving the Diffie-Hellman problem in either $\mathbb{G}_1$ or $\mathbb{G}_2$.

BDH Assumption: As in [6], if $\mathcal{IG}$ is a BDH parameter generator, the advantage $Adv_{\mathcal{IG}}(B)$ that an algorithm B has in solving the BDH problem is defined to be the probability that the algorithm B outputs $\hat{e}(P, P)^{abc}$ when the inputs to the algorithm are $\mathbb{G}_1$, $\mathbb{G}_2, \hat{e}, aP, bP$ and cP where $(\mathbb{G}_1, \mathbb{G}_2, \hat{e})$ is $\mathcal{IG}$'s output for large enough security parameter k, P is a random generator of $\mathbb{G}_1$, and a, b, c are random elements of $\mathbb{Z}_q$. The BDH assumption is that $Adv_{\mathcal{IG}}(B)$ is negligible for all efficient algorithms B.

3.2 GME_{BF}

Let k be the security parameter given to the setup algorithm, and let $\mathcal{IG}$ be a BDH parameter generator.

- **Setup**: The algorithm works as follows:
- Public key generator (PKG) runs $\mathcal{IG}$ on input k to generate groups $\mathbb{G}_1$, $\mathbb{G}_2$ of some prime order q and an admissible pairing $\hat{e} : \mathbb{G}_1 \times \mathbb{G}_1 \to \mathbb{G}_2$.
- Picks an arbitrary generator $P \in \mathbb{G}_1$.
- Picks a master secret $s \in \mathbb{Z}_q$ and sets $P_{pup} = sP$.
- Chooses cryptographic hash functions $H_1\{0,1\}^* \to \mathbb{G}_1$, $H_2 : \mathbb{G}_1 \to \{0,1\}^n$, $H_3 : \{0,1\}^n \times \{0,1\}^n \to \mathbb{Z}_q$ and a hash function $H_4 : \{0,1\}^n \to \{0,1\}^n$ for some n.

The system parameters are $P = (\mathbb{G}_1, \mathbb{G}_2, \hat{e}, P, Q, H_1, H_2, H_3, H_4)$. The message space is $\mathcal{M} = \{0,1\}^n$. The master secret is $s \in \mathbb{Z}_q$.

- **Extract**: For given strings $ID_U, ID_S \in \{0,1\}^*$, the algorithm do the following:
- Computes $Q_S = H_1(ID_S)$ and $Q_U = H_1(ID_U)$.
- Sets the private key $r_S = sQ_S$ and $r_U = sQ_U$.

- **Encrypt**: To encrypt $M \in \mathcal{M}$ for a user with public key ID_U, do the following:
- Compute $Q_S = H_1(ID_S)$ and $Q_U = H_1(ID_U)$.
- Chooses a random $\sigma \in \{0,1\}^n$.
- Sets $r = H_3(\sigma, M)$.
- Sets the ciphertext C as:

$$C = \langle rp, \sigma \oplus H_2(g_U^r) \oplus H_2(g_S^r), M \oplus H_4(\sigma) \rangle$$

where $g_U = \hat{e}(Q_U, P_{pub})$ and $g_S = \hat{e}(Q_S, P_{pub})$.

- **Decrypt**: To decrypt $C = \langle U, V, W \rangle \in \mathcal{C}$ for a user with public key ID_U, the user sends C to the SEM. The SEM does the following:
- if user is revoked, the SEM returns $\perp$.
- if user is not revoked, the SEM returns

$$C_U = \langle U, V \oplus H_2(\hat{e}(d_S, U)), W \rangle$$

- The SEM sends C_U to user.
- After receiving $C_U = \langle U, V_U, W \rangle$, the user calculates M as follows:
- Computes $V_U \oplus H_2(\hat{e}(d_U, U)) = \sigma$.
- Computes $W \oplus H_4(\sigma) = M$.
- Sets $r = H_3(\sigma, M)$. Test that $U = rp$. If not, reject the ciphertext, otherwise the user outputs M as a decryption of C.

This concludes GME_{BF}.
Remark : As in [4], a symmetric encryption E can be used instead of Xor to encrypt the message m.

3.3   Security Proof

Lemma 1. *Let A be a IND-CCA adversary that has advantage ϵ against GME_{BF}. This adversary A can be a revoked client or a hacked SEM. Then, there is an IND-CCA adversary B with the same probability ϵ against the BF FullIBE.*

Proof. If an adversary A simulates the role of a revoked user, then he plays Type 1 with the challenger. The ciphertext sent to the adversary is $C = \langle rp, M \oplus H_2(g_U^r) \oplus H_2(g_S^r) \rangle$. The adversary then partially decrypts it using his secret key r_U to get $C_S = \langle rp, M \oplus H_2(g_S^r) \rangle$, which is the message m encrypted by FullIBE using the SEM's ID. This also can be applied for a hacked SEM.

3.4   Boneh-Gentry-Hanburg (BGH) Scheme

Boneh, Gentry and Hamburg presented an Anon-IND-ID-CPA scheme [5]. Unlike the Boneh-Franklin scheme, this scheme is secure based on the quadratic residuosity (QR) assumption. In the following, we present the QR assumption and Jacobi symbols, then we present GME based on the BGH scheme.

3.5   QR Assumption and Jacobi Symbols

For a positive integer N, define the following set:

$$J(N) = [a \in \mathbb{Z}_N : \tfrac{a}{N} = 1]$$

where $\tfrac{a}{N}$ is the Jacobi symbol of a w.r.t N. The quadratic residue set $QR(N)$ is defined as follows

$$QR(N) = [a \in \mathbb{Z}_N : gcd(a, N) \wedge x^2 \equiv a \bmod N \text{ has a solution}].$$

Definition 1. *Quadratic Residuosity Assumption: Let $RSAgen(1^k)$ be a probabilistic polynomial time (PPT) algorithm. This algorithm generates two equal size primes p, q. The QR assumption holds for RSAgen if it cannot distinguish between the following two distributions for all PPT algorithms A.*

$$P_{QR}(1^k) : (N, V)(p, q) \leftarrow RSAgen(1^k), N = pq, V \in_R QR(N)$$
$$P_{NQR}(1^k) : (N, V)(p, q) \leftarrow RSAgen(1^k), N = pq, V \in_R J(N) \setminus QR(N)$$

i.e. adversary A cannot distinguish between elements in $J(N) \setminus QR(N)$ and elements in $QR(N)$.

Definition 2. *Interactive Quadratic Residuosity Assumption: Let H be a collision free hash function such that $H : [0, 1]^* \rightarrow J(N)$. Let $\mathcal{O}$ be a square root oracle that picks $u_N \leftarrow J(N) \setminus QR(N)$ and maps input pair (N, x) to one of $H_N(x)^{\frac{1}{2}}$ or $u_N H_N(x)^{\frac{1}{2}}$ in $\mathbb{Z}_N$ based on which value is quadratic residue. The Interactive Quadratic residue assumption holds for the pair $(RSAgen, H)$ if for all PPT algorithms A, the function $IQRAdv_{A,(RSAgen(1^k), H)} =$*

$$| \Pr[(N, V) \leftarrow P_{QR}(1^k) : A^{\mathcal{O}}(N, V) = 1] - | \Pr[(N, V) \leftarrow P_{NQR}(1^k) : A^{\mathcal{O}}(N, V) = 1]|$$

is negligible. $IQRAdv_{A,(RSAgen(1^k), H)}$ is the IQR advantage of A against $(RSAgen, H)$.

3.6 $\overline{Q}$ Algorithm

$\overline{Q}$ is a deterministic algorithm with inputs (N, u, R, I), where $N \in \mathbb{Z}^+$ and $R, u, I \in \mathbb{Z}_N$. This algorithm outputs four polynomial functions $f, \overline{f}, g, \tau \in Z[x]_N$. This Algorithm must satisfy the following conditions to be Enhanced IBE compatible:

- If R and I are quadratic residues, then $f(r)g(i)$ is also quadratic residue for all values of $r \leftarrow R^{\frac{1}{2}}$ and $i \leftarrow I^{\frac{1}{2}}$.
- If uR and I are quadratic residues, then $\overline{f}(\overline{r})g(i)\tau(i)$ is also quadratic residue for all values of $\overline{r} \leftarrow uR^{\frac{1}{2}}$ and $i \leftarrow I^{\frac{1}{2}}$.
- If R is quadratic residue, then $f(r)f(-r)I$ is quadratic residue for every $r \leftarrow R^{\frac{1}{2}}$.
- If uR is quadratic residue, then $\overline{f}(\overline{r})\overline{f}(-\overline{r})I$ is quadratic residue for every $\overline{r} \leftarrow uR^{\frac{1}{2}}$.
- If I is quadratic residues, then $\tau(i)\tau(-i)u$ is also quadratic residue for all values of $i \leftarrow I^{\frac{1}{2}}$.
- τ is independent of R, that is $\overline{Q}(N, u, R_1, I)$ and $\overline{Q}(N, u, R_2, I)$ produces the same value of τ for any value of N, u, R_1, R_2, I.

An example of $\overline{Q}$ is explained in [5] as follows:

- Find a solution $(x, y) \in \mathbb{Z}_N^2$ to the equation $Rx^2 + Sy^2 = 1 \bmod N$.

- Find a solution $(\alpha, \beta) \in \mathbb{Z}_N^2$ to the equation $u\alpha^2 + I\beta^2 = 1 \bmod N$.
- Calculate the polynomials $f(r) \leftarrow xr + 1$, $\overline{f}(\overline{r}) \leftarrow 1 + Sy\beta + \alpha x\overline{r}$, $g(i) \leftarrow 2ys + 2$, $\tau(i) = 1 + \beta i$.

The proof that $\overline{Q}$ Algorithm is Enhanced IBE Compatible can be found in [5].

3.7 GME_{BGH}

- Setup(1^k): Using RSAgen(1^k), generate (p,q). Calculate the modulus $N \leftarrow pq$. Choose $u \in j(N) \setminus QR(N)$, and choose a hash function $H : ID \times [1,l] \rightarrow j(N)$. The public parameters P are $[N, u, H]$. The master secret MSK parameters are p, q and a secret key K for a pseudorandom function $F_K : ID \times [1,l] \rightarrow [0,1,2,3]$.
- KG(MSK, ID_U, ID_S, l): Using the master secret MSK, ID, and the message length l, the private key for decryption (r_j) is generated using the following algorithm:

> **foreach** $j \in [1, l]$ **do**
> $\quad$ $R_{U,j} \leftarrow H(ID_U, j) \in j(N)$
> $\quad$ $R_{S,j} \leftarrow H(ID_S, j) \in j(N)$
> $\quad$ $w \leftarrow F_K(ID, j) \in [0,1,2,3]$
> $\quad$ choose $a_U \in [0,1]$ such that $u^{a_U} R_{U,j} \in QR(N)$
> $\quad$ choose $a_S \in [0,1]$ such that $u^{a_S} R_{S,j} \in QR(N)$
> $\quad$ let$[z_{U,0}, z_{U,1}, z_{U,2}, z_{U,3}]$ be the four square roots of $u^{a_U} R_{U,j} \in \mathbb{Z}_N$
> $\quad$ let$[z_{S,0}, z_{S,1}, z_{S,2}, z_{S,3}]$ be the four square roots of $u^{a_S} R_{S,j} \in \mathbb{Z}_N$
> $\quad$ $r_{U,j} \leftarrow z_{U,w}$
> $\quad$ $r_{S,j} \leftarrow z_{S,w}$
> **end**

The decryption key for User is $d_{U,ID} \leftarrow (P, r_{U,1}, ..., r_{U,L})$ and the decryption key for the SEM is $d_{S,ID} \leftarrow (P, r_{S,1}, ..., r_{S,L})$.
- Enc(P, ID_U, ID_S, m): Generate a random value $i \leftarrow \mathbb{Z}_N$ and calculate $I \leftarrow i^2$ and then encrypt $m \in [-1,1]^L$ using P as follows:

> $\tau(i) \leftarrow \overline{Q}(N, u, 1, I)$
> $k \leftarrow (\frac{\tau(i)}{N})$
> **foreach** $j \in [1, L]$ **do**
> $\quad$ $R_{U,j} \leftarrow H(ID_U, j) \in j(N)$
> $\quad$ $R_{S,j} \leftarrow H(ID_S, j) \in j(N)$
> $\quad$ $[x_{U,j}, y_{U,j}] \leftarrow \overline{Q}(N, u, R_{U,j}, I)$
> $\quad$ $[x_{S,j}, y_{S,j}] \leftarrow \overline{Q}(N, u, R_{S,j}, I)$
> $\quad$ $g_{U,j}(i) \leftarrow 2y_{U,j}i + 2$
> $\quad$ $g_{S,j}(i) \leftarrow 2y_{S,j}i + 2$
> $\quad$ $c_j \leftarrow m_j.(\frac{g_{U,j}(i)}{N}).(\frac{g_{S,j}(i)}{N})$
> $\quad$ $c \leftarrow c_1 ...... c_L$
> **end**

The ciphertext is (I, k, c).

- Decrypt(C, d_{ID}): To decrypt a ciphertext $C = (I, K, c)$ for User with public key ID_U, User sends C to the SEM. The SEM then does the following:
- if User is revoked, the SEM returns $\perp$.
- if User is not revoked, the SEM Calculates c_U as follows:

> **foreach** $j \in [1, L]$ **do**
> $\quad R_{S,j} \leftarrow H(ID_S, j) \in j(N)$
> $\quad$ **if** $r_{S,j}^2 = R_{S,j}$ **then**
> $\quad\quad [x_{S,j}, y_{S,j}] \leftarrow \overline{Q}(N, u, R_{S,j}, I)$
> $\quad\quad f_j \leftarrow x_{S,j} r_{S,j} + 1$
> $\quad\quad c_{U,j} \leftarrow c_j . (\frac{f_j}{N})$
> $\quad$ **end**
> $\quad$ **if** $\overline{r}_{S,j}^2 = u R_{S,j}$ **then**
> $\quad\quad [x_{S,j}, y_{S,j}, \alpha, \beta] \leftarrow \overline{Q}(N, u, R_{S,j}, I)$
> $\quad\quad \overline{f}_j \leftarrow 1 + I^{2j-1} y_{S,j} \beta + \alpha x_j \overline{r}_{S,j}$
> $\quad\quad c_{U,j} \leftarrow c_j . (\frac{\overline{f}_j}{N})$
> $\quad$ **end**
> **end**

and returns $C_U = (I, K, c_U)$ to User. Then User decrypts C_U as follows:

> **foreach** $j \in [1, L]$ **do**
> $\quad R_{U,j} \leftarrow H(ID_U, j) \in j(N)$
> $\quad$ **if** $r_{U,j}^2 = R_{U,j}$ **then**
> $\quad\quad [x_{U,j}, y_{U,j}] \leftarrow \overline{Q}(N, u, R_{U,j}, I)$
> $\quad\quad f_j \leftarrow x_{U,j} r_{U,j} + 1$
> $\quad\quad m_j \leftarrow c_j . (\frac{f_j}{N})$
> $\quad$ **end**
> $\quad$ **if** $\overline{r}_{U,j}^2 = u R_{U,j}$ **then**
> $\quad\quad [x_{U,j}, y_{U,j}, \alpha, \beta] \leftarrow \overline{Q}(N, u, R_{U,j}, I)$
> $\quad\quad \overline{f}_j \leftarrow 1 + I^{2j-1} y_{U,j} \beta + \alpha x_j \overline{r}_{U,j}$
> $\quad\quad m_j \leftarrow c_j . k . (\frac{\overline{f}_j}{N})$
> $\quad$ **end**
> **end**

This concludes BGH_{BGH}.

3.8   Security Proof

Lemma 2. *Let A be an Anon-IND-CPA adversary that has advantage ϵ against GME_{BGH}. This adversary A can be a revoked client or hacked SEM. Then, there is an Anon-IND-CPA adversary B with the same probability ϵ against the BGH system.*

Proof. If an adversary A simulates the role of a revoked user, then he plays Type 1 with the challenger. The ciphertext sent to the adversary is $c_j \leftarrow m_j . (\frac{g_{U,j}(i)}{N}) . (\frac{g_{S,j}(i)}{N})$. The adversary then partially decrypts it using his secret key r_U to get $c_{S,j} \leftarrow m_j.(\frac{gs,j(i)}{N})$, which is the message m encrypted by BGH using SEM's ID. This also can be applied for a hacked SEM.

Remark: Using the same encryption system for both the SEM and the users has a unique advantage. If roles of the SEM and a user are exchanged, the system will not be effected. For example, if the employee responsible for the SEM is promoted or fired and another employee becomes the one responsible for the SEM, all we have to do is assign the ID for the SEM to the the the new employee's ID. On the other hand, the system will be vulnerable to escrow. This implementation is more suitable for closed environments, such as a company. If escrow is really a serious security concern, however, the public parameters can be generated using two PKGs, one for the users and the other for the SEMs.

4   Conclusion

In this paper, we present a generic mediated encryption (GME) system that converts any IBE system to a mediated system. Although it is based on double encryption, our system is efficient. The ciphertext size is the same as a single IBE. It combines the advantage of CBE and SEM structures. Our system is more efficient than CBE because it does not depend on certificates, and it is more secure than [3] and [12] because the SEM in GME is not a single point of failure and can be untrusted. We prove that GME is as secure as the IBE system used in the case of a revoked user or a hacked SEM.

References

1. Boneh, D., Boyen, X.: Efficient selective-ID secure identity-based encryption without random oracles. In: Cachin, C., Camenisch, J.L. (eds.) EURO-CRYPT 2004. LNCS, vol. 3027, pp. 223–238. Springer, Heidelberg (2004), http://www.cs.stanford.edu/~xb/eurocrypt04b/
2. Boneh, D., Ding, X., Tsudik, G.: Fine-grained control of security capabilities. ACM Trans. Internet Technol. 4(1), 60–82 (2004)
3. Boneh, D., Ding, X., Tsudik, G., Wong, C.M.: A method for fast revocation of public key certificates and security capabilities. In: Proceedings of the 10th Conference on USENIX Security Symposium, SSYM 2001, vol. 10, p. 22. USENIX Association, Berkeley (2001)
4. Boneh, D., Franklin, M.: Identity-based encryption from the weil pairing. In: Kilian, J. (ed.) CRYPTO 2001. LNCS, vol. 2139, pp. 213–229. Springer, Heidelberg (2001)
5. Boneh, D., Gentry, C., Hamburg, M.: Space-efficient identity based encryption without pairings. In: Proceedings of the 48th Annual IEEE Symposium on Foundations of Computer Science, FOCS 2007, pp. 647–657. IEEE Computer Society, Washington, DC (2007)
6. Cocks, C.: An identity based encryption scheme based on quadratic residues. In: Honary, B. (ed.) Cryptography and Coding 2001. LNCS, vol. 2260, pp. 360–363. Springer, Heidelberg (2001)
7. Cooper, D., Santesson, S., Farrell, S., Boeyen, S., Housley, R., Polk, W.: Rfc5280: Internet x.509 public key infrastructure certificate and certificate revocation list (crl) profile (May 2008)

8. Ding, X., Tsudik, G.: Simple identity-based cryptography with mediated RSA. In: Joye, M. (ed.) CT-RSA 2003. LNCS, vol. 2612, pp. 193–210. Springer, Heidelberg (2003)

9. Aiello, W., Lodha, S., Ostrovsky, R.: Fast digital identity revocation. In: Krawczyk, H. (ed.) CRYPTO 1998. LNCS, vol. 1462, pp. 137–152. Springer, Heidelberg (1998)

10. Gassko, I., Gemmell, P.S., MacKenzie, P.: Efficient and fresh certification. In: Imai, H., Zheng, Y. (eds.) PKC 2000. LNCS, vol. 1751, pp. 342–353. Springer, Heidelberg (2000)

11. Gentry, C.: Certificate-based encryption and the certificate revocation problem. In: Biham, E. (ed.) EUROCRYPT 2003. LNCS, vol. 2656, pp. 272–293. Springer, Heidelberg (2003)

12. Gentry, C.: Practical identity-based encryption without random oracles. In: Vaudenay, S. (ed.) EUROCRYPT 2006. LNCS, vol. 4004, pp. 445–464. Springer, Heidelberg (2006)

13. Myers, M., Ankney, R., Malpani, A., Galperin, S., Adams, C.: Rfc 2560: Internet public key infrastructure online certificate status protocol - ocsp

14. Micali, S.: Efficient certificate revocation (1996)

15. Micali, S.: Novomodo: Scalable certificate validation and simplified pki management. In: 1st Annual PKI Research Workshop (2002)

16. Naor, M., Nissim, K.: Certificate revocation and certificate update. IEEE Journal on Selected Areas in Communications 18(4), 561–570 (2000)

17. Housley, R., Polk, W., Ford, W., Solo, D.: Rfc3280: Internet x.509 public key infrastructure certificate and certificate revocation list (crl) profile (April 2002)

18. Sakai, K.O.R., Kasahara, M.: Cryptosystems based on pairing. In: Symposium on Cryptography and Information Security (SCIS 2000), Japan (2000)

19. Shamir, A.: Identity-based cryptosystems and signature schemes. In: Blakely, G.R., Chaum, D. (eds.) CRYPTO 1984. LNCS, vol. 196, pp. 47–53. Springer, Heidelberg (1985)

20. Waters, B.: Efficient identity-based encryption without random oracles. In: Cramer, R. (ed.) EUROCRYPT 2005. LNCS, vol. 3494, pp. 114–127. Springer, Heidelberg (2005)

An Efficient Reconfigurable II-ONB
Modular Multiplier

Li Miao[1,2], He Liangsheng[1], Yang Tongjie[1,*] Gao Neng[2],
Liu Zongbin[2], and Zhang Qinglong[2]

[1] Zhengzhou Information Science and Technology Institute, Zhengzhou, 450004, China
[2] SKLOIS, Institute of Information Engineering,
Chinese Academy of Sciences, Beijing, 100093, China
{limiao12,lshhe,tjyang,gaoneng,zbliu,qlzhang}@is.ac.cn

Abstract. In Elliptic Curve Cryptography(ECC), due to the characteristic of high efficiency, the modular multiplication operation in type II optimal normal basis(II-ONB) over binary field has become a key research trend. Based on B. Sunar's basis conversion theory, in this paper, an improved II-ONB modular multiplication algorithm has been proposed and an efficient reconfigurable modular multiplier, which can support different lengths has been implemented. This work has been simulated using ModelSim and synthesized under 0.18µm CMOS technology. Then, complexity comparison has also been accomplished. The results prove that our proposed reconfigurable II-ONB modular multiplier can not only guarantee high flexibility for arbitrary modular multiplication, but also have area advantage in resource-constrained ECC applications.

Keywords: Elliptic Curve Cryptography; Type II Optimal Normal Basis; Reconfigurable Modular Multiplier; Basis Conversion.

1 Introduction

In modern age, along with flourishing development of E-Commerce, E-Administration and military communications, information security has been more and more widely focused by people. The public-key cryptography system can effectively solve problems like anti-repudiation, authentication and key distribution on public channels. Based on the elliptic curve discrete logarithm problem(ECDLP), Elliptic Curve Cryptography(ECC)[1-2] has already been proved to be more secure and more efficient than RSA. Therefore, ECC has gradually replaced RSA as the next generation of public-key cryptography standard[3]. Modern cryptanalysis indicates that ECC provides high security strength per bit[4], so at the same security level, it can offer the fastest computation, the least storage requirement and the lowest communication bandwidth, which is very suitable for resource restriction devices[5-6] like mobile telephones, PDA, wireless network and smart cards. In fields of high-end applications, such as network server and certificate authority, due to large secure connection number and certain real-time requirement, ECC can provide signature authentication service with higher throughput, too.

---

* Corresponding author.

T. Zia et al. (Eds.): SecureComm 2013, LNICST 127, pp. 169–181, 2013.
© Institute for Computer Sciences, Social Informatics and Telecommunications Engineering 2013

Finite field multiplication is a critical operation for ECC implementation performance, and how to design an efficient and flexible finite field multiplier has also become a focus in cryptographic applications[7-11]. At present, these are two main implementation methods for large integer multiplication: the software and the hardware. The software method is highly flexible and convenient to use, but restricted by the general purpose microprocessor instruction system, the operation efficiency is so low that it can't meet the need for high speed applications. Therefore, it's necessary to design application specific integrated circuit(ASIC). This hardware method can reach high speed and low power consumption, but the specific property in structure is too inflexible to further development. ECC usually chooses keys with different lengths for information graded protection. When key length changes, the hardware circuit must be redesigned that results in a waste of manpower and material resources. In the meanwhile, it increases ECC chip types and managing difficulty. One efficient solution is to design a kind of parameter reconfigurable hardware circuit to improve ECC chips flexibility, in which the reconfigurable design of finite field multiplier is the kernel[12-14].

Normal basis[15] is one of the most important representation over binary field. Currently, there is no flexible and reconfigurable design scheme for normal basis multiplier at all times. In order to simplify extremely complicated multiplication operation in normal basis, researchers have found a special class of normal basis called optimal normal basis(short for ONB)[16]. The ONB has the lowest computational complexity, whose exponentiation and multiplication operations are very simple. Type I ONB and type II ONB(short for II-ONB) are two kinds of most commonly used ONB[17], while with the highest efficiency, II-ONB multiplication operation has been widely used. For $GF(2^m)$, there are 174 m values in the range $m \in [2,1000]$, for which a II-ONB exists. And multiplication matrix M of II-ONB has the minimum number of "1", which is equal to $2m-1$. Except the first column, every other column has only two "1", which greatly reduces space complexity and computational complexity of modular multiplication operation. Consequently, designs for II-ONB multiplier have become hot.

In 2001, B.Sunar proposed an idea and concrete method of basis conversion[18], which provided a new thinking for II-ONB multiplier. In 2008, A. H. Namin of Canada Windsor University brought forward a word-level multiplier for II-ONB[19]. This multiplier had advantage in computation speed, but disadvantage in circuit area. Moreover, it could not support modular multiplication operation with variable lengths. In 2009, T. F. Al-Somani of Saudi Umm Kula University presented an improved Massey-Omura normal basis multiplier using three-stage pipelines[20]. It had been advanced significantly in performance, but could not support modular multiplication operation with diverse lengths, too.

Up to now, almost all II-ONB multipliers were designed fixed in structure and only achieved a sort of specific ECC operation over binary field. The bad flexibility was difficult to meet the need for ECC flexible processing. Therefore, this paper aims to do some research and design an efficient reconfigurable II-ONB multiplier to meet the needs of II-ONB multiplication operation with different lengths, and provide a new design method and technology for solving problems of II-ONB multiplier in multiplication operation with single length and poor flexibility.

2   Type II Optimal Normal Basis and Multiplication Operation

For element $\beta \subset GF(2^m)$, a normal basis can be expressed as $\{\beta, \beta^2, \cdots, \beta^{2^{m-1}}\}$ and the corresponding normal polynomial is defined as $F(t)=t^m + c_{m-1}t^{m-1} + \cdots + c_1t + c_0$. II-ONB can be constructed[17] if $2m+1$ is a prime and if either 2 is a primitive root modulo $2m+1$ or $2m+1=3 \pmod 4$ and the multiplicative order of 2 modulo $2m+1$ is m holds. Then, $\alpha = r+r^{-1}$ generates an optimal normal basis for $GF(2^m)$, where r is a primitive $(2m+1)^{th}$ root of unity, i.e., $r^{2m+1}=1$ and $r^i \neq 1$ for any $1 \leq i < 2m+1$.

In normal basis, the square operation of A is just simple cyclic shift operation, namely $A^2=(a_m\ a_1\ a_2\ \cdots\ a_{m-1})$. However, the multiplication operation is relatively complex. Firstly, a multiplication matrix M should be computed, whose calculation steps are as follows[21]:

1. Calculate the convert matrix E from $(1, t, \cdots, t^{m-1})$ to $(t, t^2, \cdots, t^{2^{m-1}})$:

$$t = e_{0,0} + e_{0,1} \cdot t + e_{0,2} \cdot t^2 + \cdots + e_{0,m-1} \cdot t^{m-1} \bmod F(t)$$

$$t^2 = e_{1,0} + e_{1,1} \cdot t + e_{1,2} \cdot t^2 + \cdots + e_{1,m-1} \cdot t^{m-1} \bmod F(t)$$

$$t^4 = e_{2,0} + e_{2,1} \cdot t + e_{2,2} \cdot t^2 + \cdots + e_{2,m-1} \cdot t^{m-1} \bmod F(t)$$

$$\cdots$$

$$t^{2^{m-1}} = e_{m-1,0} + e_{m-1,1} \cdot t + e_{m-1,2} \cdot t^2 + \cdots + e_{m-1,m-1} \cdot t^{m-1} \bmod F(t)$$

The coefficients meeting all above equations form convert matrix E:

$$E = \begin{bmatrix} e_{0,0} & e_{0,1} & \cdots & e_{0,m-1} \\ e_{1,0} & e_{1,1} & \cdots & e_{1,m-1} \\ \vdots & \vdots & \ddots & \vdots \\ e_{m-1,0} & e_{m-1,1} & \cdots & e_{m-1,m-1} \end{bmatrix}$$

2. Calculate the inverse matrix of E: $G=E^{-1}$.
3. Suppose matrix Q is expressed as:

$$Q = \begin{bmatrix} 0 & 1 & 0 & \cdots & 0 \\ 0 & 0 & 1 & \cdots & 0 \\ \vdots & \vdots & \vdots & \ddots & \vdots \\ 0 & 0 & 0 & \cdots & 1 \\ q_0 & q_1 & q_2 & \cdots & q_{m-1} \end{bmatrix}$$

Calculate matrix $D = EQG$.
4. Suppose $\mu_{i,j}=d_{j-i,-i}(i, j=0, 1, \cdots, m-1)$ and subscripts of d get the least non-negative integer values of modulo m. The multiplication matrix M is obtained:

$$M = \begin{bmatrix} \mu_{0,0} & \mu_{0,1} & \cdots & \mu_{0,m-1} \\ \mu_{1,0} & \mu_{1,1} & \cdots & \mu_{1,m-1} \\ \vdots & \vdots & \ddots & \vdots \\ \mu_{m-1,0} & \mu_{m-1,1} & \cdots & \mu_{m-1,m-1} \end{bmatrix}$$

The product of $A \cdot B$ in normal basis can be expressed as $C = AMB^T$, where B^T denotes the transpose of B.

The modular multiplication algorithm in normal basis is shown as Algorithm 1. The core operation is the matrix multiplication (step 3), which calculates 1 bit product in every cycle.

Algorithm 1. Modular multiplication algorithm in normal basis[21]

Input: $A = (a_1, a_2, \cdots, a_m)$, $B = (b_1, b_2, \cdots, b_m)$,

$\qquad$ multiplication matrix M for $GF(2^m)$

Output: Product $C = (c_1, c_2, \cdots, c_m)$

1. $x = A$, $y = B$

2. for $i = 1$ to m do

3. $\qquad c_i = f(x, y) = xMy^T$

4. $\qquad x <<< 1$ $\quad$ (1 bit cyclic left shift of x)

5. $\qquad y <<< 1$ $\quad$ (1 bit cyclic left shift of y)

$\qquad$ end for

6. $C = (c_1, c_2, \cdots, c_m)$

3   II-ONB Modular Multiplication Algorithm

There are two important steps during the design of II-ONB modular multiplier: the first step is converting elements represented in II-ONB to a specific basis $\underline{N}'$, which makes multiplication operation in basis $\underline{N}'$ have a regular representation; the second step is multiplying the elements in basis $\underline{N}'$.

3.1   Basis Conversion Theory

According to II-ONB construction method, for $GF(2^m)$, normal element $\beta = r + r^{-1}$, where r is a primitive $(2m + 1)^{th}$ root of unity, i.e., $r^{2m+1} = 1$ and $r^i \neq 1$ for any $i \in [1, 2m+1)$, the normal basis is given as $\underline{N} = \{\beta, \beta^2, \cdots, \beta^{2^{m-1}}\}$. If 2 is a primitive root modulo $2m+1$, then the set of powers of 2 modulo $2m + 1$ is:

$$P_1 = \{2, 2^2, \cdots, 2^{2m}\} \bmod (2m+1) \tag{1}$$

Equation (1) is equivalent to $Q_1 = \{1, 2, \cdots, 2m\}$. Therefore, a basis element $r^{2^i} + r^{-2^i}$ can be written as $r^i + r^{-j}$ for $j \in [1, 2m]$. Furthermore, it is always possible to rewrite $r^i + r^{-j}$ as $r^{(2m+1)-j} + r^{-(2m+1)+j}$. If $j \geq m+1$, then this has the benefit of bringing the power of r to the range $[1, m]$. If the multiplicative order of 2 modulo $2m+1$ is equal to m, then the set of powers of 2 modulo $2m + 1$ is:

$$P_2 = \{2, 2^2, \cdots, 2^m\} \bmod (2m+1) \tag{2}$$

Equation (2) is equivalent to $Q_2 = \{1, 2, \cdots, m\}$. As a result, a basis element $r^{2^i} + r^{-2^i}$ can be written uniquely as $r^j + r^{-j}$ with $j \in [1, m]$. The basis whose element is $r^j + r^{-j}$ is defined as $\underline{N}' = \{\beta_1, \beta_2, \cdots, \beta_m\}$, where $\beta_j = r^j + r^{-j}$ and $j \in [1, m]$.

Let A be expressed in the basis $\underline{N}$ as $A = a_1'\beta + a_2'\beta^2 + a_3'\beta^4 + \cdots + a_m'\beta^{2^{m-1}}$ where $\beta = r + r^{-1}$. The representation of A in the basis $\underline{N}'$ is given as $A = a_1\beta_1 + a_2\beta_2 + a_3\beta_3 + \cdots + a_m\beta_m$ where $\beta_i = r^i + r^{-i}$. We can express the permutation between the coefficients $a_j = a_i'$ as [18,22]:

$$j = \begin{cases} k & \text{if } k \in [1, m] \\ (2m+1) - k & \text{if } k \in [m+1, 2m] \end{cases} \tag{3}$$

Where $k = 2^{i-1} (\bmod\ 2m + 1)$ for $i = 1, 2, \cdots, m$. Not a normal basis, basis $\underline{N}'$ is just a shifted form of canonical basis[16].

3.2 II-ONB Modular Multiplication Algorithm Based on Basis Conversion

Adopt Equation (3) for basis conversion. $A, B \in GF(2^m)$, can be represented in basis $\underline{N}'$ as $A = \sum_{i=1}^{m} a_i \beta_i = \sum_{i=1}^{m} a_i (r^i + r^{-i})$ and $B = \sum_{i=1}^{m} b_i \beta_i = \sum_{i=1}^{m} b_i (r^i + r^{-i})$. Then product $C = A \cdot B$ can be written as:

$$\begin{aligned}
C = A \cdot B &= \left(\sum_{i=1}^{m} a_i (r^i + r^{-i}) \right) \left(\sum_{j=1}^{m} b_j (r^j + r^{-j}) \right) \\
&= \sum_{i=1}^{m} \sum_{j=1}^{m} a_i b_j (r^{i-j} + r^{-(i-j)}) + \sum_{i=1}^{m} \sum_{j=1}^{m} a_i b_j (r^{i+j} + r^{-(i+j)}) \\
&= C_1 + C_2
\end{aligned} \tag{4}$$

If $i = j$, then $r^{i-j} + r^{-(i-j)} = r^0 + r^0 = 0$, so the coefficients of β_k in C_1 are the sum of all $a_i b_j$ for which $k = |i - j| \in [1, m]$. In C_2, $|i + j| \in [1, 2m]$ can be divided into $|i + j| \in [1, m]$ and $|i + j| \in [m+1, 2m]$, while the latter case can be replaced by $2m + 1 - |i + j|$. So C_2 can be transformed into the following:

$$\begin{aligned}
C_2 &= \sum_{i=1}^{m} \sum_{j=1}^{m} a_i b_j (r^{i+j} + r^{-(i+j)}) \\
&= \sum_{i=1}^{m} \sum_{j=1}^{m-i} a_i b_j (r^{i+j} + r^{-(i+j)}) + \sum_{i=1}^{m} \sum_{j=m-i+1}^{m} a_i b_j (r^{i+j} + r^{-(i+j)}) \\
&= D_1 + D_2
\end{aligned} \tag{5}$$

In Equation (5), the coefficients of β_k in D_1 are the sum of all $a_i b_j$ for which $k=|i + j|\in[1, m]$ where $i\in[1, m]$ and $j\in[1, m-i]$. And D_2 can be represented as:

$$D_2 = \sum_{i=1}^{m} \sum_{j=m-i+1}^{m} a_i b_j (r^{i+j} + r^{-(i+j)})$$

$$= \sum_{i=1}^{m} \sum_{j=m-i+1}^{m} a_i b_j (r^{2m+1-(i+j)} + r^{-(2m+1-(i+j))})$$

$$(6)$$

In Equation (6), the coefficients of β_k in D_2 are the sum of $a_i b_j$ for which $k = 2m + 1 - |i + j|\in[1, m]$ where $i\in[1, m]$ and $j\in[m-i+1, 2m]$.

Suppose $k(i) = \begin{cases} i & \mod 2m+1 \quad (0 \le i \mod 2m+1 \le m) \\ 2m+1-i & \mod 2m+1 \quad (others) \end{cases}$. According to above

deduce, it is easy to prove that $\beta_j A = \beta_j \sum_{i=1}^{m} a_i \beta_i = \sum_{i=1}^{m} a_i (\beta_{k(i+j)} + \beta_{k(i-j)}) = \sum_{i=1}^{m} (a_{k(i+j)} + a_{k(i-j)})\beta_i$ [19].

Thus, product C also can be represented as:

$$C = A\sum_{j=1}^{m} b_j \beta_j = \sum_{j=1}^{m} b_j (\beta_j A)$$

$$= \sum_{j=1}^{m} b_j \sum_{i=1}^{m} a_i (\beta_{k(i+j)} + \beta_{k(i-j)})$$

$$= \sum_{j=1}^{m} b_j \sum_{i=1}^{m} (a_{k(i+j)} + a_{k(i-j)})\beta_i$$

$$= \sum_{i=1}^{m} \sum_{j=1}^{m} b_j (a_{k(i+j)} + a_{k(i-j)})\beta_i$$

$$(7)$$

The single bit c_i can be written as:

$$c_i = \sum_{j=1}^{m} b_j (a_{k(i+j)} + a_{k(i-j)}) = \sum_{j=1}^{m} a_j (b_{k(i+j)} + b_{k(i-j)})$$

$$(8)$$

From above analysis, II-ONB modular multiplication algorithm based on basis conversion is brought forward, as shown in Algorithm 2. This is a serial algorithm, composed by outer and inner loops. Operations of AND (&), XOR ($\oplus$) and cyclic shift (>>>) can be directly mapped to hardware implementation.

Algorithm 2. II-ONB modular multiplication algorithm based on basis conversion

Input: $A = (a_1', a_2' \cdots, a_m'), B = (b_1', b_2', \cdots, b_m')$ *in normal basis* $\underline{N}$

Output: Product $C = (c_1', c_2', \cdots, c_m')$ *in normal basis* $\underline{N}$

1. *Basis conversion* : $A = (a_1, a_2 \cdots, a_m), B = (b_1, b_2, \cdots, b_m)$ *in basis* $\underline{N}'$

2. $C = 0, b_0 = 0$

3. $D[1 : 2m + 1] = \{b_0, b_1, b_2, \cdots, b_m, b_m, \cdots, b_2, b_1\}$

4. for $i = 1$ to m do

5.   for $j = 1$ to m do

6. $c_i = c_i \oplus (a_j \ \& \ (D[j] \oplus D[2m + 1 - j]))$

      end for

7. $D \ggg 1$ (1*bit cyclic right shift of D*)

   end for

8. *Basis conversion* : $C = (c_1', c_2', \cdots, c_m')$ *in normal basis* N

In Algorithm 2, input data $A = (a_1', a_2' \cdots, a_m')$ and $B = (b_1', b_2', \cdots, b_m')$ are in normal basis $\underline{N}$. Firstly, convert operands A and B from normal basis $\underline{N}$ to basis $\underline{N}'$. Then, calculate 1 bit c_i after m inner loops and product C after m outer loops. Finally, convert product C from basis $\underline{N}'$ back to normal basis $\underline{N}$ after the operation is completed. From analysis we can learn that the computational complexity of Algorithm 2 is $O(m^2)$, which can be further improved adopting parallel computation. Therefore, this paper proposes an improved II-ONB modular multiplication algorithm based on basis conversion, as shown in Algorithm 3.

Algorithm 3. An improved II-ONB modular multiplication algorithm based on basis conversion

Input: $A = (a_1', a_2' \cdots, a_m'), B = (b_1', b_2', \cdots, b_m')$ *in normal basis* $\underline{N}$

Output: Product $C = (c_1', c_2', \cdots, c_m')$ *in normal basis* $\underline{N}$

1. *Basis conversion* : $A = (a_1, a_2 \cdots, a_m)$, $B = (b_1, b_2, \cdots, b_m)$ *in basis* $\underline{N}'$

2. $C = 0, b_0 = 0$

3. $D[1 : 2m + 1] = \{b_0, b_1, b_2, \cdots, b_m, b_m, \cdots, b_2, b_1\}$

4. for $i = 1$ to m do

5. $C = C \oplus a_i \ \& \ (D[1 : m] \oplus D[2m : m + 1])$

6. $D \ggg 1$ (1*bit cyclic right shift of D*)

   end for

7. *Basis conversion* : $C = (c_1', c_2', \cdots, c_m')$ *in normal basis* $\underline{N}$

In Algorithm 3, there exists only one layer loop that can generate product C in basis $\underline{N}'$ after m loops. So, the computational complexity reduces to $O(m)$. In public-key cryptography, it usually performs continuous modular multiplication operations, so basis conversion is only needed before the first modular multiplication operation and after the last modular multiplication operation. Consequently, the implementing time of basis conversion can be ignored.

4   Design of Reconfigurable II-ONB Modular Multiplier

4.1   Reconfigurable Basis Conversion Circuit

According to above analysis, based on B. Sunar's basis conversion theory, the basis conversion circuit is designed adopting reconfiguration method in this paper. The implementation of basis conversion circuit is closely related to the finite field length m. Basis conversion of fixed length can be accomplished by simple connections, but for different lengths, it requires very complex computing circuit. In ECC algorithms, basis conversion is only demanded before and after continuous modular multiplication operations respectively and the implementing time of basis conversion can be ignored, hence it can be realized by SW/HW method. From basis conversion theory we can see the corresponding relationship between j and i is fixed when m is determinate. So in this paper, we calculate corresponding position information in advance by software, then write them into configuration registers. In this way, when performing basis conversion by hardware, choosing values through configuration registers is enough.

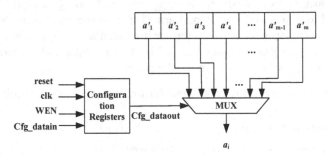

Fig. 1. Reconfigurable basis conversion circuit

The reconfigurable basis conversion circuit is shown in Fig. 1. It requires m clock cycles to complete once basis conversion. If hardware resources are adequate, it can use multiple MUXs in parallel to increase basis conversion implementing efficiency. In the best situation, it can complete basis conversion in only one clock cycle.

4.2   Reconfigurable Modular Multiplier Design

In order to support modular multiplication in II-ONB with different lengths, according to Algorithm 3, this paper designs an efficient reconfigurable II-ONB modular multiplier based on basis conversion, as shown in Fig. 2. In the right part, there are two 385-bit registers R1 and R2, both of which are used to store B values and b_0 is constant "0". In every one clock cycle, these two registers carry out 1-bit joint shift operation: for R1, $b_i=b_{i+1}$; for R2, $b_i=b_{i-1} \oplus (b_j$ & Datapath_ctl[i-1]). Register C is used to store product C. Datapath_ctl[0:383] is the control signal of the data path, whose value is also associated with the finite field length $\text{Datapath\_ctl} = \{\underbrace{00\cdots0}_{384-\text{length}},1,\underbrace{0\cdots00}_{\text{length}-1}\}$. In the left part, there are two shift registers, which are used to store A and B separately. Their control signals RegA_ctl[7:0] and RegB_ctl[7:0] are given by the control unit. In all the clock cycles, RegA_ctl=RegB_ctl=1.

When signal start is valid, the multiplier begins initialization. The controlled registers R1 and R2 jointly shift 1 bit. At the same time, in order to make the MSB of operation data and registers align right, two barrel shift registers shift (384-length) bits. After length clock cycles, the multiplier generates product C in basis $\underline{N}'$. The maximum length of the multiplier is set 384. When operands are less than 384 bits, all data in registers align right and high bits are filled up zero. According to different length ranges, registers in our design also can be extended to support modular multiplication operation of larger length.

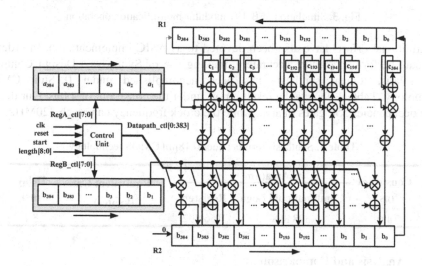

Fig. 2. Reconfigurable II-ONB modular multiplier structure

5 Implementation and Performance Analysis

5.1 Simulation and Synthesis

In order to validate our design, the proposed reconfigurable II-ONB modular multiplier has been modeled in Verilog HDL and simulated functionally with ModelSim SE 6.1f. The implementation has verified our design's function correctly [21]. Fig. 3 depicts simulation results of B-191.

The operation data are:

A= 7a12de5c_d5e55e5a_d587dc51_a51c551a_de1b2151_b11a21de
B= 64545d85_5da54d5e_c4b545a5_d45e4456_7aadcccd_dbeebdad

The modular multiplication product is:

C=18db1d7c_d6274cb7_d760e71a_35ae72e5_6de25e4a_73e6fac9

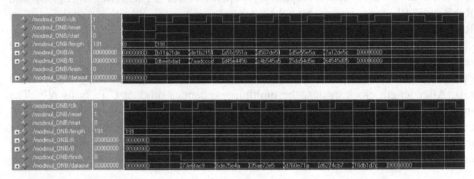

Fig. 3. Simulation of B-191 modular multiplication operation

Additional efforts have also been devoted to as ASIC implementation. In order to evaluate performance more accurately, making use of Synopsys's Design Complier for Solaris, logical synthesis has been accomplished under 0.18μm CMOS technology. Table 1 depicts the result report under the constraint of 4.0ns. Our design only occupancies 55k gates in area, while the clock frequency can reach 320MHz.

Table 1. Synthesis results under 0.18μm CMOS technology

Constraint	Area(μm²)		Equivalent Gates	Delay
(ns)	Combinational Logic	Registers	(kgates)	(ns)
4.0	398 868	156 892	55	3.1

5.2   Analysis and Comparison

Area-Timing complexity comparison of different II-ONB modular multipliers are shown in Table 2. The delays of a two-input AND gate and an n-input XOR gate have been approximated by T_A and $\lceil \log_2 n \rceil T_X$ separately. In [19] and [23], multipliers were both designed on word-level, where m denotes the finite field length, k denotes the number of parallel modules and w denotes the word length. Because the hardware structure of our design is fixed, the area and delay of circuit are finalized. The space complexity of this work is 768#AND+1152#XOR and the computational complexity is $2T_A+3T_X$. In order to compare our design with others, we have chosen the practical finite field size of m=233 that is a recommended NIST(National Institute of Standards and Technology) binary field degree with k=8 and w=32 which are practical for VLSI implementation. The complexity comparison of different II-ONB modular multipliers in F_2233 with $k=8$ and $w=32$ are shown in Table 3.

Table 2. Area-Timing complexity comparison of different II-ONB modular multipliers

Designs	# AND	# XOR	Multiplication Delay
Namin[19]	$2km$	$(4k-1)m$	$wT_A+(w+\lceil \log_2 2k \rceil)T_X$
Massey[23]	$k(2m-1)$	$k(2m-2)$	$w(T_A+(1+\lceil \log_2 m \rceil)T_X)$
This work	768	1152	$2T_A+3T_X$

Table 3. Complexity comparison of different II-ONB modular multipliers in F_2233 with $k=8$ and $w=32$

Designs	# of AND	# of XOR	Multiplication Delay
Namin[19]	3728	7223	$32T_A+36T_X$
Massey[23]	3720	3712	$32T_A+288T_X$
This work	768	1152	$64T_A+96T_X$

It can be seen from Table 3 that, due to the word-level structure, compared to our design, in spite of owning shorter multiplication delays, Namin's and Massey-Omura's multipliers occupied much more hardware resources. In addition, both of these two multipliers couldn't support modular multiplication operation with scalable lengths, and it required to re-design the hardware circuit when parameters changed. However, our proposed reconfigure multiplier is one efficient solution for modular multiplications with variable parameters. When parameters changed, only reconfiguring the structural parameters is enough, and the hardware structure doesn't need to change. So, among above designs, our reconfigurable multiplier is the most flexible in structure.

6   Conclusions

In this paper, some researches on reconfiguration design of II-ONB modular multiplier over binary field in ECC have been done. According to B. Sunar's basis conversion theory, operation data in normal basis have been converted to a new defined basis. On this condition, an improved II-ONB modular multiplication algorithm has been proposed, and an efficient reconfigurable modular multiplier supporting different lengths has been implemented. Finally, this work has been simulated and synthesized. Besides, performance analysis has also been accomplished. The experimental results prove that our design has higher flexibility and smaller area, which is the most suitable to resource-constrained ECC applications.

Acknowledgments. This work is partially supported by National Natural Science Foundation of China grant 70890084/G021102 and 61003274, Strategy Pilot Project of Chinese Academy of Sciences sub-project XDA06010702, and National High

Technology Research and Development Program of China (863 Program, No. 2013AA01A214 and 2012AA013104).

References

1. Kammler, D., Zhang, D., Schwabe, P., Scharwaechter, H., Langenberg, M., Auras, D., Ascheid, G., Mathar, R.: Designing an ASIP for Cryptographic Pairings over Barreto-Naehrig Curves. In: Clavier, C., Gaj, K. (eds.) CHES 2009. LNCS, vol. 5747, pp. 254–271. Springer, Heidelberg (2009)
2. Gura, N., Shantz, S.C., Eberle, H., Gupta, S., Gupta, V., Finchelstein, D., Goupy, E., Stebila, D.: An End-to-End Systems Approach to Elliptic Curve Cryptography. In: Kaliski Jr., B.S., Koç, Ç.K., Paar, C. (eds.) CHES 2002. LNCS, vol. 2523, pp. 349–365. Springer, Heidelberg (2003)
3. Chen, H.: Research on Elliptic Curve Cryptography Algorithm and Chip Implementation Method, pp. 56-60. Zhengjia University, Hangzhou (2008)
4. Certicom White Papers, The Elliptic Curve Cryptosystem (1997-1998), http://www.certicom.com
5. Okada, S., Torii, N., Itoh, K., Takenaka, M.: Implementation of Elliptic Curve Cryptographic Coprocessor over GF(2m) on an FPGA. In: Paar, C., Koç, Ç.K. (eds.) CHES 2000. LNCS, vol. 1965, pp. 25–40. Springer, Heidelberg (2000)
6. Potgieter, M.J., van Dyk, B.J.: Two Hardware Implementations of the Group operations Necessary for Implementing an Elliptic Curve Cryptosystem over a Characteristic Two Finite Field. In: IEEE Africon 2002, pp. 187–192 (2002)
7. Kitsos, P., Theodoridis, G., Koufopavlou, O.: An Efficient Reconfigurable Multiplier Architecture for Galois Field GF(2m). Microelectronic Journal 34, 975–980 (2003)
8. Amanor, D.N.: Efficient Hardware Architecture for Modular Multiplication. Master. Thesis, The University of Applied Science Offenburg, Germany (2005)
9. Kaihara, M.E., Takagi, N.: Bipartite Modular Multiplication Method. IEEE Transactions on Computers 57(2), 157–164 (2008)
10. Chu, J., Benaissa, M.: Polynomial Residue Number System GF(2m) Multiplier Using Trinomials. In: 17th European Signal Processing Conference (EUSIPCO 2009), pp. 958–962 (2009)
11. Knežević, M., Vercauteren, F., Verbauwhede, I.: Speeding Up Bipartite Modular Multiplication. In: Hasan, M.A., Helleseth, T. (eds.) WAIFI 2010. LNCS, vol. 6087, pp. 166–179. Springer, Heidelberg (2010)
12. Estrin, G., et al.: Parallel Processing in a Restructurable Computer System. IEEE Trans. on Electronic Computers, 747–755 (December 1963)
13. Sigh, H., Lee, M.H., Lu, G., et al.: An Integerated Reconfigurable System for Data-Parallel and Computation-Intensive Applications. IEEE Transcations on Computer 49(5), 465–481 (2000)
14. Bouma, H.: Design and Implementation of an FPGA. University of Twente, Twente (2001)
15. Masoleh, A.R., Hasan, M.A.: Efficient Multiplication beyond Optimal Normal Bases. IEEE Trans. Computers 52(4), 428–439 (2003)
16. Koc, C.K., Sunar, B.: Low-Complexity Bit-Parallel Canonical and Normal Basis Multipliers for a Class of Finite Fields. IEEE Trans. Computers 47(3), 353–356 (1998)
17. Liao, Q.: On Multiplication Tables of Optimal Normal Bases over Finite Fields. Acta Mathematica Sinica 45(5), 947–954 (2005)

18. Sunar, B., Koc, C.K.: An Efficient Optimal Normal Basis Type II Multiplier. IEEE Transactions on Computers 50(1), 83–87 (2001)
19. Namin, A.H., Wu, H., Ahmadi, M.: A High Speed Word Level Finite Field Multiplier Using Reordered Normal Basis. In: IEEE International Symposium on Circuits and Systems, pp. 3278–3281 (2008)
20. Al-Somani, T.F., Amin, A.: High performance Elliptic Curve Point Operations with Pipelined GF(2m) Field Multiplier. Journal of Communication and Computer 6(10), 62–69 (2009)
21. IEEE STD 1363-2000. IEEE Standard Specifications for Public-Key Cryptography (2000)
22. Fang, B., Fan, H., Dai, Y.: An Optimal Normal Basis Type II Multiplier over GF(2n) for FPGAs. Chinese Journal of Electronics 30(12A), 2045–2048 (2002)
23. Massey, J.L., Omura, J.K.: Computational Method and Apparatus for Finite Arithmetic. US: Patent No.4587627 (1986)

Public-Key Encryption Resilient to Linear Related-Key Attacks

Hui Cui, Yi Mu, and Man Ho Au

School of Computer Science and Software Engineering,
University of Wollongong, Wollongong, NSW 2522, Australia
hc892@uowmail.edu.au, {ymu,aau}@uow.edu.au

Abstract. In this paper, we consider the security of public-key encryption schemes under linear related-key attacks, where an adversary is allowed to tamper the private key stored in a hardware device, and subsequently observe the outcome of a public-key encryption system under this modified private key. Following the existing work done in recent years, we define the security model for related-key attack (RKA) secure public-key encryption schemes as chosen-ciphertext and related-key attack (CC-RKA) security, in which we allow an adversary to issue queries to the decryption oracle on the linear shifts of the private keys. On the basis of the adaptive trapdoor relations via the one-time signature schemes, Wee (PKC'12) proposed a generic construction of public-key encryption schemes in the setting of related-key attacks, and some instantiations from Factoring, BDDH with CC-RKA security, and DDH but with a weaker CC-RKA security. These schemes are efficient, but one-time signatures still have their price such that in some cases they are not very efficient compared to those without one-time signatures. Bellare, Paterson and Thomson (ASIACRYPT'12) put forward a generic method to build RKA secure public-key encryption schemes, which is transformed from the identity-based encryption schemes. However, so far, the efficient identity-based encryption schemes are generally based on parings. To generate a specific construction of public-key encryption schemes against related-key attacks without pairings, after analyzing the related-key attack on the Cramer-Shoup basic public-key encryption scheme, we present an efficient public-key encryption scheme resilient against related-key attacks without using one-time signature schemes from DDH. Finally, we prove the CC-RKA security of our scheme without random oracles.

Keywords: Public-key encryption, Related-key attack, CC-RKA security.

1 Introduction

In the traditional security model, it is assumed that the adversary is isolated from the internal states of the honest communication parties. However, with the development of information technologies, the security of cryptographic algorithms in modern cryptography is analyzed in the black-box model, where an adversary may view the algorithm's inputs and outputs, but the private key as

T. Zia et al. (Eds.): SecureComm 2013, LNICST 127, pp. 182–196, 2013.
© Institute for Computer Sciences, Social Informatics and Telecommunications Engineering 2013

well as all the internal computation remains perfectly hidden. Unfortunately, this idealized assumption is often hard to satisfy in real systems. In many situations, the adversary might get some partial information about private keys through methods which were not anticipated by the designer of the system and, correspondingly, not taken into account when arguing its security. Such attacks, referred to as key-leakage attacks, come in a large variety. An important example is side-channel [18] attacks that exploit information leakage from the implementation of an algorithm, where an adversary observes some "physical output" of a computation (such as radiation, power, temperature, running time), in addition to the "logical output" of the computation.

In recent two decades, this requirement has been relaxed to capture security under the scenarios where some information of the keys is leaked to the adversary. When an adversary tampers the private key stored in a cryptographic hardware device, and observes the result of the cryptographic primitive under this modified private key, there is a related-key attack (RKA) [4,11]. The key here could be a signing key of a certificate authority or a decryption key of an encryption scheme. In related-key attacks, the adversary attempts to break an encryption scheme by invoking it with several private keys satisfying some known relations.

Wee [20] proposed a generic construction of public-key encryption schemes in the setting of linear related-key attacks. In [20], the constructions exploit certain existing public-key encryption schemes that are susceptible to linear related-key attacks, to obtain public-key encryption schemes that are secure against linear related-key attacks from adaptive trapdoor relations via strong one-time signatures, which generates a *tag* in the ciphertext of the concrete scheme. The security of this realization is analogous to those for obtaining chosen-ciphertext attack (CCA) security from extractable hash proofs [19], and trapdoor functions [15], which implies a trick that the RKA decryption oracle will return $\perp$ for *tag* $= tag^*$ generated from an one-time signature scheme, whenever the ciphertext with *tag* given by the adversary matches the challenge ciphertext with tag^* or not. Briefly, RKA.Decrypt oracle outputs $\perp$ when given a ciphertext with *tag* $= tag^*$ even $\phi(sk) \neq sk$, where ϕ denotes a linear shift. That is to say, the RKA decryption query will not help the adversary to obtain more information if $tag = tag^*$. Besides, Wee [20] designed some efficient strong one-time signatures to reduce the total overhead of the specific schemes. However, though one-time signatures are easy to construct in theory, and are more efficient than full-fledged signatures, they still have their price. Particularly,

- Known one-time signature schemes based on general one-way functions [10] allow very efficient signing, key generation and signature verification, but they require the expensive valuations of the one-way function. More problematic, such schemes usually have long public keys and signatures, resulting in long ciphertexts.
- Although one-time signature schemes constructed based on number-theoretic assumptions by adapting full-fledged signature schemes have the advantage of shorter public keys and signatures, but this yields schemes of which computational cost for key generation, signing, and verifying is more expensive.

Bellare, Paterson and Thomson [6] provided a framework to enable the construction of identity-based encryption schemes that are secure under related-key attacks. In [6], a very particular type of framework, which allows to reduce RKA security of a modified identity-based encryption scheme directly to the normal identity-based encryption security of a base identity-based encryption scheme, is used. Because of this framework, exploiting known results on identity-based encryption in a black-box way is allowed and re-entering the often complex security proofs of the base identity-based encryption schemes is avoided. Based on this, they constructed the RKA secure schemes for public-key encryption. Their schemes are achieved in the standard model and hold under reasonable hardness assumptions in the standard model, but they are transformed from the identity-based encryption schemes. Anyway, most of the current identity-based encryption schemes based on bilinear pairings, which are not very efficient.

Our Contributions. Inspired by the above, in this paper, we attempt to bridge this gap in Wee's public-key encryption schemes resilient against related-key attacks from DDH [20] without using any one-time signature schemes. First of all, we review the definition of linear related-key attacks introduced by Wee [20] in the setting of public-key encryption, and describe how to attack the public-key encryption system of Cramer and Shoup [9] in our RKA security model, which is a bit different from that described in [20]. In Wee's attack [20], a related-key deriving function only changes one part of the secret keys, while our attack changes all parts of the secret keys with the same linear shift function ϕ. In the second place, on the practical side, with some trivial modifications to the basic cryptosystem of Cramer and Shoup [9], we obtain an efficient scheme that is RKA secure based on the decisional Diffie-Hellman assumption. Our technique is to hide the functions related to the randomness that appear in the Cramer-Shoup scheme, such that even given the private keys used in the encryption function of the message, the adversary still has no idea to output the message under the modified secret keys without the hiding information. Our scheme is very efficient, as we do not need any pairing computation to implement encryption and decryption. Finally, we prove the CC-RKA security of our scheme under the DDH assumption. Interestingly, regarding the CC-RKA security proof, [20] simulates the RKA decryption queries via key homomorphism and make the adversary fail through key fingerprint, and [6] uses key malleability to simulate the RKA decryption queries and collision-resistant identity renaming to make the proof goes; however, in our specific construction, we avoid to make use of such techniques to claim the security.

To begin with, we briefly describe the framework introduced in [4]. Informally, a public-key encryption scheme is resilient to related-key attacks, then it is chosen-ciphertext attack secure even when the adversary obtains partial information of the message in the scheme under the modified private keys of the adversary. This is modeled by providing the adversary with access to a related-key attack decryption oracle: the adversary can query the decryption oracle with any function (ϕ, C), and then receive $(\phi(sk), C)$, where sk is the secret key (we note that the related-key deriving functions can be chosen depending on the public key, which is known to the adversary). The adversary can query the related-key attack decryption oracle adaptively, with only one restriction that the decryption of a ciphertext C with the private key $\phi(sk)$ cannot equal the decryption of the challenge ciphertext C^* with the original private key sk.

1.1 Related Works

Micali and Reyzin [17] put forward a comprehensive framework for modeling security against side-channel attacks in 2004, which relies on the assumption that there is no leakage of information in the absence of computation. Later in 2008, Halderman et al. [14] described a set of attacks violating the assumption of the framework of Micali and Reyzin. Specially speaking, their "cold boot" attacks showed that a significant fraction of the bits of a cryptographic key can be recovered if the key is ever stored in memory, of which the framework was modeled by Akavia, Goldwasser and Vaikuntanathan [1]. Similarly, fault injection techniques can be used to falsify, inducing the internal state of the devices being modified, if given physical access to the hardware devices [7].

Bellare and Kohno [5] investigated related-key attacks from a theoretical point of view and presented an approach to formally handle the notion of related-key attacks. Followed the approach in [5], Lucks [16] presented some constructions for block ciphers and pseudorandom function generators. To solve the open problem in related-secret security whether or not related-key secure blockciphers exist, Bellare and Cash [3] provided the first constructions to create related-secret pseudorandom bits. Based on the work in [3], Applebaum, Harnik, and Ishai [2] gave RKA secure symmetric encryption schemes, which can be used in garbled circuits in secure computation. Later, Bellare, Cash and Miller [4] proposed approaches to build high-level primitives secure against related-key attacks like signatures, CCA secure public-key encryption, identity-based encryption, based on RKA secure pseudorandom functions. Also, there are a lot of other works about cryptographic systems with RKA security such as signatures [6,13], CCA secure public-key encryption [6,20], identity-based encryption [6].

The remainder of this paper is organized as follows. In Section 2, we briefly present the basic definitions, and the security assumptions that are used in our construction. In Section 3, we review the concepts associated to this work and the security model of RKA secure public-key key encryption systems. In Section 4, we propose an efficient public-key encryption scheme resilient against related-key attacks, after the analysis of a linear attack on the Cramer-Shoup cryptosystem [9], and prove its security under the hardness of the DDH problem. Finally, we conclude this paper in Section 5.

2 Preliminaries

In this section, we look back some basic notions, definitions, and tools that are used in our construction. We formally state the decisional Diffie-Hellman assumptions, and present the technical definitions that will be used repeatedly in our analysis.

2.1   Complexity Assumptions

Suppose that Groupgen is a probabilistic polynomial-time algorithm that inputs a security parameter 1^λ, and outputs a triplet (G, p, g) where G is a group of order p that is generated from g, and p is a prime number.

The Decisional Diffie-Hellman Assumption. The decisional Diffie-Hellman (DH) assumption is that the ensembles $\{G, g, f, g^r, f^r\}$ and $\{G, g, f, g^{r_1}, f^{r_2}\}$ are computationally indistinguishable, where $(G, p, g) \leftarrow$ Groupgen(1^λ), and the elements $g, f \in G$, $r, r_1, r_2 \in Z_p$ are chosen independently and uniformly at random.

A Basic Scheme Based on DDH. Since the introduction of DDH assumption [8], it has already found several interesting applications. Note that the DDH assumption readily gives a chosen-plaintext attack (CPA) secure public-key encryption scheme. Let the public key consist of random elements $g, f, g^{x_1}, f^{x_2} \in G$, and the secret key consist of random element $x_1, x_2 \in Z_p$. The encryption of a message $M \in G$ is given by $(C_1, C_2, C_3) = (g^r, f^r, (g^{x_1} f^{x_2})^r \cdot M)$, where $r \in Z_p$ is a random element. The message M can be recovered with the secret key x_1, x_2 by computing $M = C_3 \cdot (C_1)^{-x_1} \cdot (C_2)^{-x_2}$.

2.2   Public-Key Encryption

A public-key encryption scheme is composed of the following four randomized algorithms [12]: Keygen, Encrypt, and Decrypt.

- Keygen$(1^\lambda) \rightarrow (sk, pk)$: Taking a security parameter λ as input, this algorithm outputs a private key and a public key pair (sk, pk).
- Encrypt$_{pk}(m) \rightarrow C$: Taking a plaintext m (in some implicit message space), and a public key pk as input, this algorithm outputs a ciphertext C.
- Decrypt$_{sk}(C) \rightarrow m$: Taking a plaintext m, a ciphertext C, and a private key sk as input, this algorithm outputs m for a valid ciphertext or $\perp$ for an invalid ciphertext.

We require that a public-key encryption system is correct, meaning that if $(sk, pk) \leftarrow$ Keygen(1^λ), and $C \leftarrow$ Encrypt$_{pk}(m)$, then Decrypt$_{sk}(C) \rightarrow m$.

3   Modeling Related-Key Attacks

In this section, we define the notion of a chosen-ciphertext attack; in addition, we present a natural extension of this notion to the setting of related-key attacks, as introduced by Bellare, Cash and Miller [4]. Also, we introduce some notions about related-key attacks, as proposed in [2].

3.1 Chosen-Ciphertext Attacks

A public-key encryption scheme (Keygen, Encrypt, Decrypt) is secure against chosen-ciphertext attacks (CCA security) if for a stateful adversary algorithm $\mathcal{A}$, the advantage in the following game is negligible in the security parameter λ.

1. $(sk, pk) \leftarrow \text{Keygen}(1^\lambda)$.
2. $(m_0, m_1) \leftarrow \mathcal{A}^{\text{Decrypt}_{sk}(\cdot)}(pk)$ such that $|m_0| = |m_1|$.
3. $C^* \leftarrow \text{Encrypt}_{pk}(m_d)$ where $d \in \{0, 1\}$.
4. $d' \leftarrow \mathcal{A}^{\text{Decrypt}_{sk}(\cdot)}(C^*)$.
5. Output d'.

Here $\text{Decrypt}_{sk}(\cdot)$ is an oracle that on an input C, it returns $\text{Decrypt}_{sk}(C)$.

The weaker security notion of CPA security (i.e. secure against CPAs) is obtained in the above security game when depriving adversary $\mathcal{A}$ of the the access to the decryption oracle.

3.2 RKA Security

Related-Key Deriving Functions. Our definition follows the notion of related-key deriving functions given in [5]. Briefly speaking, a class Φ of related-key deriving functions $\phi\colon sk \to sk$ is a finite set of functions with the same domain and range, which map a key to a related key. Additionally, Φ should allow an efficient membership test, and ϕ should be efficiently computable. Note that in our concrete constructions, we only consider the class Φ^+ as linear shifts.

The family Φ^+. Any function $\phi : Z_p \to Z_p$ in this class is indexed by $\triangle \in Z_p$, where $\phi_\triangle(sk) := sk + \triangle$.

We constraint that if sk is composed of several elements as $(sk_1, \ldots, sk_n)$ with $n \in Z^+$, for any sk_i where $i \in \{1, \ldots, n\}$, $\phi_\triangle(sk_i) := sk_i + \triangle$ with $\triangle \in Z_p^n$.

CC-RKA Security. A public-key encryption scheme (Keygen, Encrypt, Decrypt) is Φ-CC-RKA secure if for a stateful adversary algorithm $\mathcal{A}$, the advantage in the following game is negligible in the security parameter λ.

1. $(sk, pk) \leftarrow \text{Keygen}(1^\lambda)$.
2. $(m_0, m_1) \leftarrow \mathcal{A}^{\text{RKA.Decrypt}_{sk}(\cdot, \cdot)}(pk)$ such that $|m_0| = |m_1|$.
3. $C^* \leftarrow \text{Encrypt}_{pk}(m_d)$ where $d \in \{0, 1\}$.
4. $d' \leftarrow \mathcal{A}^{\text{RKA.Decrypt}_{sk}(\cdot, \cdot)}(C^*)$.
5. Output d'.

Here $\text{RKA.Decrypt}_{sk}(\cdot, \cdot)$ is an oracle that on an input (ϕ, C), it returns $\text{Decrypt}_{\phi(sk)}(C)$. We constraint that algorithm $\mathcal{A}$ can only make queries (ϕ, C) such that $\phi \in \Phi$ and $(\phi(sk), C) \neq (sk, C^*)$.

We say that algorithm $\mathcal{A}$ succeeds if $d' = d$, and algorithm $\mathcal{A}$'s advantage can be defined as

$$\text{Adv}_{\Phi, \mathcal{A}}^{\text{CCRKA}}(\lambda) \overset{\text{def}}{=} |\text{Pr}_{\Phi, \mathcal{A}}^{\text{CCRKA}}[\text{Succ}] - 1/2|,$$

where $\mathrm{Pr}_{\Phi,\mathcal{A}}^{\mathrm{CCRKA}}[\mathrm{Succ}]$ denotes the event that algorithm $\mathcal{A}$ outputs the bit $d' = d$.

Briefly speaking, key fingerprint means that any attempt to forge sk induces a random output of $\mathrm{Decrypt}_{sk}(c')$.

4   An Efficient Construction without Pairings

In this section, we put forward our construction based on the Cramer-Shoup cryptosystem [9], and present its security proof under the DDH assumption. To begin with, we describe a simple linear related-key attack on the Cramer-Shoup public-key encryption scheme, which to some extent illustrate some technical obstacles in achieving RKA security.

4.1   Related-Key Attacks on Cramer-Shoup Cryptosystem

We point out a linear related-key attack on the CCA secure encryption scheme based on the DDH assumption proposed by Cramer and Shoup [9]. The details of the Cramer-Shoup public-key encryption scheme is given as follows.

- Key generation. Choose random $g,\ f \in G,\ x,\ y,\ a,\ b,\ \alpha,\ \beta \in Z_p$, a collision resistant hash function $H\colon G^3 \to Z_p$, and sets $u_1 = g^x f^y$, $u_2 = g^a f^b$, $u_3 = g^\alpha f^\beta$.
  The public key is $PK = (g,\ f,\ u_1,\ u_2,\ u_3,\ H)$, and the secret key is $SK = (x,\ y,\ a,\ b,\ \alpha,\ \beta)$.
- Encryption. To encrypt message $M \in G$,
  1. choose random $r \in Z_p$, and set $C_1 = g^r$, $C_2 = f^r$, $C_3 = u_1{}^r \cdot M$.
  2. compute $t = H(C_1, C_2, C_3)$, $C_4 = (u_2 u_3{}^t)^r$.
  3. output ciphertext $C = (C_1,\ C_2,\ C_3,\ C_4)$.
- Decryption. To decrypt ciphertext $C = (C_1,\ C_2,\ C_3,\ C_4)$,
  1. compute $t = H(C_1, C_2, C_3)$, and output $\perp$ if $C_4 \neq C_1{}^{a+t\alpha} C_2{}^{b+t\beta}$.
  2. otherwise, output $M = C_3 \cdot C_1{}^{-x} \cdot C_2{}^{-y}$.

Suppose we are given a valid ciphertext (C_1, C_2, C_3, C_4) of some message M. We can recover M by making decryption queries to RKA.Decrypt oracle on related secret keys via the following attack. For any $\triangle \in Z_p$, we change the secret key $(x, y, a, b, \alpha, \beta)$ to $(x+\triangle, y+\triangle, a+\triangle, b+\triangle, \alpha+\triangle, \beta+\triangle)$, then $(C_1, C_2, C_3, C_4 \cdot (C_1 \cdot C_2)^{\triangle+t\cdot\triangle})$ can be decrypted to $M \cdot (C_1 \cdot C_2)^{-\triangle}$ under the modified secret keys. As C_1, C_2 and $\triangle$ are known to us, we can obtain M easily by computing $M \cdot (C_1 \cdot C_2)^{-\triangle} \cdot (C_1 \cdot C_2)^{\triangle}$.

Obviously in the above cases, message M can be easily recovered given the output of the decryption algorithm on the modified secret keys.

4.2   Our Construction

Let G be a group of prime order p. We present a public-key encryption scheme which is CCA secure under the linear related-key attacks as follows.

- Key generation. Choose random elements g, f, $h \in G$, x, y, a, b, α, β, γ $\in Z_p$, a collision resistant hash function $H: G^4 \to Z_p$, and sets $u_1 = g^x f^y$, $u_2 = g^a f^b$, $u_3 = g^\alpha f^\beta$, $v = h^\gamma$.
  The public key is $PK = (g, h, f, u_1, u_2, u_3, v)$, and the secret key is $SK = (x, y, a, b, \alpha, \beta, \gamma)$.
- Encryption. To encrypt message $M \in G$,
  1. choose random elements $r, r' \in Z_p$, and set

$$C_1 = g^r v^{r'}, \quad C_2 = f^r v^{r'}, \quad C_3 = h^{r'}, \quad C_4 = u_1{}^r \cdot M.$$

  2. compute $t = H(C_1, C_2, C_3, C_4)$, $C_5 = (u_2 u_3{}^t)^r$.
  3. output ciphertext $C = (C_1, C_2, C_3, C_4, C_5)$.
- Decryption. To decrypt ciphertext $C = (C_1, C_2, C_3, C_4, C_5)$,
  1. compute $t = H(C_1, C_2, C_3, C_4)$, and output $\bot$ if the following equation holds.

$$C_5 \neq (C_1 \cdot C_3{}^{-\gamma})^{a+t\alpha}(C_2 \cdot C_3{}^{-\gamma})^{b+t\beta}.$$

  2. otherwise, output M as $M = C_4 \cdot (C_1 \cdot C_3{}^{-\gamma})^{-x} \cdot (C_2 \cdot C_3{}^{-\gamma})^{-y}$.

Correctness. For any sequence of the key generation and encryption algorithms, it holds that

$$
\begin{aligned}
(u_2 u_3{}^t)^r &= (C_1 \cdot C_3{}^{-\gamma})^{a+t\alpha}(C_2 \cdot C_3{}^{-\gamma})^{b+t\beta} \\
&= (g^a f^b (g^\alpha f^\beta)^t)^r, \\
M = C_4 \cdot (C_1 \cdot C_3{}^{-\gamma})^{-x} &\cdot (C_2 \cdot C_3{}^{-\gamma})^{-y} \\
&= C_4 \cdot (g^x f^y)^{-r},
\end{aligned}
$$

and therefore the decryption algorithm is always correct.

Remarks. Note that compared to the scheme proposed in [20], our construction is more efficient. The CCA-RKA secure public-key encryption schemes in [20] are built from adaptive trapdoor relations [15] to generate a *tag* for every ciphertext via a strong one-time signature scheme, which implies a trick in it such that the adversary cannot obtain more information if *tag* of a ciphertext C equals *tag** of the challenge ciphertext C^*, not to mention $C = C^*$; while in our construction, we use the Cramer-Shoup public-key encryption scheme [9] as the basis, and the strong one-time signature schemes are replaced by the ciphertext to generate *tag*, such that RKA.Decrypt oracle will still not facilitate the adversary when a given ciphertext C matches the challenge one C^*, as long as SK does not equal to $\phi(SK)$ for any $\phi \in \Phi$.

4.3   Security

Theorem 1. *Assume the hardness of decisional DH problem, the above public-key encryption scheme is secure in the CC-RKA security game regarding linear related-key deriving function ϕ^+.*

Proof. The proof of security is based on augmenting the proof of Cramer and Shoup with the ideas of generating a generic construction. Specifically, we show that any algorithm $\mathcal{A}$ that breaks the security of the scheme, we can build an algorithm $\mathcal{B}$ that can distinguish between a DH instance and a non-DH instance, which is given a random tuple $(g, f, Z_1 = g^r, Z_2 = f^r) \in G^4$ as input.

Setup. Algorithm $\mathcal{B}$ chooses random elements $h \in G$, $x, y, a, b, \alpha, \beta, \gamma \in Z_p$, and a collision resistant hash function $H: G^4 \rightarrow Z_p$, and then sets $u_1 = g^x f^y$, $u_2 = g^a f^b$, $u_3 = g^\alpha f^\beta$, $v = h^\gamma$.

Algorithm $\mathcal{B}$ sends the public key $PK = (g, h, f, u_1, u_2, u_3, v)$ to algorithm $\mathcal{A}$, and keeps the private key $SK = (x, y, a, b, \alpha, \beta, \gamma)$.

Phase 1. Algorithm $\mathcal{A}$ queries (ϕ, C) to RKA.Decrypt oracle. Algorithm $\mathcal{B}$ responds using the private key $\phi(SK)$.

Challenge. Algorithm $\mathcal{A}$ outputs two messages M_0, M_1 on which it wishes to be challenged. Algorithm $\mathcal{B}$ chooses a random bit $d \in \{0,1\}$, and a random element $r' \in Z_p$, and then responds with the ciphertext $C^* = (C_1^*, C_2^*, C_3^*, C_4^*, C_5^*)$, where

$$C_1^* = Z_1 v^{r'}, \quad C_2^* = Z_2 v^{r'}, \quad C_3^* = h^{r'},$$
$$C_4^* = Z_1{}^x Z_2{}^y \cdot M_d, \quad C_5^* = Z_1{}^{a+\alpha t^*} Z_2{}^{b+\beta t^*}.$$

Here $t^* = H(C_1^*, C_2^*, C_3^*, C_4^*)$.

Phase 2. Algorithm $\mathcal{A}$ continues to adaptively issue queries (ϕ, C) to RKA.Decrypt oracle.

- If $\phi(SK) = SK$ and $C = C^*$, such queries are ruled out by the definition of CC-RKA security game, so algorithm $\mathcal{B}$ responds with $\bot$.
- Otherwise, algorithm $\mathcal{B}$ responds as in Phase 1.

Output. Algorithm $\mathcal{A}$ output a guess $d' \in \{0,1\}$. If $d' = d$, algorithm $\mathcal{B}$ output 1; otherwise, algorithm $\mathcal{B}$ outputs 0.

Obviously, if (g, f, Z_1, Z_2) is a DH instance, then the simulation will be identical to the actual attack, such that algorithm $\mathcal{A}$ has a non-negligible advantage in outputting the bit $d' = d$.

Lemma 1. *If (g, f, Z_1, Z_2) is a DH instance then algorithm $\mathcal{A}$'s view is identical to the actual attack.*

Proof. The actual attack and simulated attack are identical except for the challenge ciphertext. It remains to prove that the challenge ciphertext has the correct distribution when (g, f, Z_1, Z_2) is a DH instance. Actually, in this case, for a random $r \in Z_p$, $Z_1 = g^r$ and $Z_2 = f^r$, the ciphertext $C^* = (C_1^*, C_2^*, C_3^*, C_4^*, C_5^*)$ as it should be. Assume that algorithm $\mathcal{A}$'s advantage in breaking the CC-RKA security of the above scheme is ϵ, then we can see that algorithm $\mathcal{A}$'s probability in outputting the bit $d = d'$ could be $1/2 + \epsilon$.

Next, we show that if (g, f, Z_1, Z_2) is a non-DH instance, then algorithm $\mathcal{A}$ has a negligible advantage in outputting the bit $d' = d$. We assume that (g, f, Z_1, Z_2) is a non-DH instance, where $\log_g Z_1 = r_1$, $\log_f Z_2 = r_2$, and $r_1 \neq r_2$.

Let $(C_1^*, C_2^*, C_3^*, C_4^*)$ be the challenge ciphertext given to algorithm $\mathcal{A}$ by algorithm $\mathcal{B}$. We use Failure to denote the event where for RKA decryption queries (ϕ, C) it holds that $(C_1, C_2, C_3, C_4) \neq (C_1^*, C_2^*, C_3^*, C_4^*)$, and $H(C_1, C_2, C_3, C_4) = H(C_1^*, C_2^*, C_3^*, C_4^*)$. Note that the event Failure has a negligible probability to occur because hash function H is collision resistant. We say that a ciphertext C is invalid if $\log_g \frac{C_1}{C_3^{\gamma + \triangle}} \neq \log_f \frac{C_2}{C_3^{\gamma + \triangle}}$ for any $\triangle \in Z_p^n$.

Below we prove that algorithm $\mathcal{A}$ has a negligible advantage in outputting the bit $d' = d$ if the event Failure does not happen. Specifically speaking, we perform it in two cases: (1) if the event Failure does not happen, then the RKA decryption oracle rejects all invalid ciphertexts except with a negligible probability; (2) if the RKA decryption oracle rejects all invalid ciphertexts, then algorithm $\mathcal{A}$ has a negligible advantage in outputting the bit $d' = d$. We conclude by the fact that the event Failure occurs with a negligible probability.

Lemma 2. *If (g, f, Z_1, Z_2) is a non-DH instance and the event Failure does not happen, then the RKA decryption algorithm rejects all invalid ciphertexts except with a negligible probability.*

Proof. The probability of the invalid ciphertexts happening in our security game is analogous to that in the Cramer-Shoup public-key encryption scheme [9] except that for the RKA decryption oracles, some invalid ciphertexts which will be rejected in the security game of the Cramer-Shoup scheme will be accepted in our security game. Suppose that algorithm $\mathcal{A}$ is given the public key $PK = (g, h, f, u_1, u_2, u_3, v)$, and the challenge ciphertext $C^* = (C_1^*, C_2^*, C_3^*, C_4^*, C_5^*)$. We prove this lemma via considering $(a, b, \alpha, \beta) \in Z_p$ from algorithm $\mathcal{A}$'s point of view, such that for $k = \log_g f$, (a, b, α, β) is uniformly random subject to

$$\begin{cases} \log_g u_2 = a + kb \\ \log_g u_3 = \alpha + k\beta \\ \log_g C_5^* = r_1 a + r_2 kb + t^* r_1 \alpha + t^* r_2 k\beta \end{cases}.$$

Note that algorithm $\mathcal{A}$ learns nothing on (a, b, α, β) by querying valid ciphertexts to the decryption oracle. Actually, from submitting a valid ciphertext, algorithm $\mathcal{A}$ only learns a linear combination of the constraint $\log_g u_1 = x + ky$ which is know from the public key.

We denote $(C_1, C_2, C_3, C_4, C_5) \neq (C_1^*, C_2^*, C_3^*, C_4^*, C_5^*)$ as the first invalid ciphertext queried by algorithm $\mathcal{A}$, where $C_1 = g^{r_1} v^r$, $C_2 = f^{r_2} v^r$, $r_1 \neq r_2$, and $t = H(C_1, C_2, C_3, C_4)$. In this case, there are three cases we need to take into consideration.

- $(C_1, C_2, C_3, C_4) \neq (C_1^*, C_2^*, C_3^*, C_4^*)$ and $t = t^*$. This is impossible since we assume that the event Failure does not happen.

Note that the event Failure will never happen because the hash function H in our construction is collision resistant.

- $(C_1, C_2, C_3, C_4) \neq (C_1^*, C_2^*, C_3^*, C_4^*)$ and $t \neq t^*$. In this case, if the RKA decryption algorithm accepts the invalid ciphertext, we obtain the following equations.

$$\begin{cases} \log_g u_2 = a + kb \\ \log_g u_3 = \alpha + k\beta \\ \log_g C_5^* = r_1 a + r_2 kb + t^* r_1 \alpha + t^* r_2 k\beta \\ \log_g C_5 = r_1'(a + \triangle) + r_2' k(b + \triangle) + t r_1'(\alpha + \triangle) + t r_2' k(\beta + \triangle) \end{cases}$$

where $w = \log_g h$.

These equations are linearly independent as long as $k^2(r_1 - r_2)(r_1' - r_2')(t - t^*) \neq 0$, so algorithm $\mathcal{A}$ can be used to guess (a, b, α, β). Therefore, the probability that the decryption algorithm accepts the first invalid ciphertexts is at most $1/p$.

- $(C_1, C_2, C_3, C_4) = (C_1^*, C_2^*, C_3^*, C_4^*)$, $t = t^*$ but $C_5 \neq C_5^*$, In this case, if the RKA decryption algorithm accepts the invalid ciphertext, we obtain the following equations.

$$\begin{cases} \log_g u_2 = a + kb \\ \log_g u_3 = \alpha + k\beta \\ \log_g C_5^* = r_1 a + r_2 kb + t^* r_1 \alpha + t^* r_2 k\beta \\ \log_g C_5 = r_1(a + \triangle) + r_2 k(b + \triangle) + t^* r_1(\alpha + \triangle) + t^* r_2 k(\beta + \triangle) \\ \qquad - r'w\triangle(a + \triangle + t^*(\alpha + \triangle) + b + \triangle + t^*(\beta + \triangle)) \end{cases}$$

where $w = \log_g h$.

These equations are linearly independent as long as $\triangle \neq 0$, which is ruled out by the definition of CC-RKA security, so algorithm $\mathcal{A}$ can be used to guess (a, b, α, β).

For all the subsequent invalid decryption queries, the above analysis holds except that each time the RKA decryption oracle rejects an invalid ciphertext algorithm $\mathcal{A}$ can rule out one more value of (a, b, α, β).

Lemma 3. *If (g, f, Z_1, Z_2) is a non-DH instance and the RKA decryption algorithm rejects all invalid ciphertexts, then algorithm $\mathcal{A}$ has a negligible advantage in outputting the bit $d' = d$.*

Proof. We prove this lemma by considering the distribution of $(x, y, \gamma) \in Z_p$ from the view of algorithm $\mathcal{A}$. Algorithm $\mathcal{A}$ is given the public key $PK = (g, h, f, u_1, u_2, u_3, v)$, such that algorithm $\mathcal{A}$'s point of view, (x, y, γ) is uniformly random subject to $\log_g u_1 = x + ky$ where $k = \log_g f$ and $\log_g v = k'\gamma$ where $k' = \log_g h$. We suppose that the RKA decryption algorithm rejects all invalid ciphertexts, and note that by querying valid ciphertexts to the RKA decryption oracle, algorithm $\mathcal{A}$ does not learn any more information about (x, y, γ) except the relations of the constraint $\log_g u_1 = x + ky$ and $\log_g v = k'\gamma$.

Hence, algorithm $\mathcal{A}$ cannot learn any information about (x, y, γ) through the RKA decryption queries.

Let $C_1 = Z_1 v^{r'}$, $C_2 = Z_2 v^{r'}$, $C_3 = h^{r'}$. Note that as long as $k'k(r_1 - r_2) \neq 0$,

$$
\begin{cases}
\log_g u_1 = x + ky \\
\log_g v = k'\gamma \\
\log_g Z_1{}^x Z_2{}^y = r_1 x + k r_2 y
\end{cases}
$$

are linearly independent. In the following, we consider two cases.

- $\phi(SK) = SK$ and $(C_1, C_2, C_3, C_4, C_5) = (C_1^*, C_2^*, C_3^*, C_4^*, C_5^*)$. In this case, from the definition of the CC-RKA security game, such queries will be ruled out, therefore the RKA decryption algorithm outputs $\perp$ with noticeable probability.
- $\phi(SK) \neq SK$ and $(C_1, C_2, C_3, C_4) = (C_1^*, C_2^*, C_3^*, C_4^*)$. If the verification of C_5 on (C_1, C_2, C_3, C_4) with $\phi(SK)$ fails, the RKA decryption algorithm outputs $\perp$. Otherwise, the RKA decryption algorithm responds as

$$
\begin{aligned}
M' &= C_4^* \cdot (C_1^* \cdot C_3^{*-\gamma-\Delta})^{-x-\Delta} \cdot (C_2^* \cdot C_3^{*-\gamma-\Delta})^{-y-\Delta} \\
&= M_d \cdot g^{-r \cdot \Delta} \cdot h^{r' \cdot \Delta \cdot (x+\Delta)} \cdot f^{-r \cdot \Delta} \cdot h^{r' \cdot \Delta \cdot (y+\Delta)} \\
&= M_d \cdot g^{-r \cdot \Delta} \cdot f^{-r \cdot \Delta} \cdot h^{r' \cdot \Delta \cdot (x+y+\Delta+\Delta)}.
\end{aligned}
$$

We can see that even the all the ciphertexts submitted to RKA.Decrypt oracle are exactly the same as the challenge ciphertext, algorithm $\mathcal{A}$ procures nothing about (x, y, γ) from the RKA decryption queries under $(x+\Delta, y+\Delta, \gamma+\Delta)$, as long as $(x+\Delta, y+\Delta, \gamma+\Delta) \neq (x, y, \gamma)$. On the one hand, without (x, y, γ), algorithm $\mathcal{A}$ fails to compute $d' = d$ under the modified secret keys $(x+\Delta, y+\Delta, \gamma+\Delta)$. Therefore algorithm $\mathcal{A}$'s probability in outputting the bit $d' = d$ is $1/2$.

Lemma 2 makes sure that as long as the event Failure does not happen, the RKA decryption algorithm rejects all invalid ciphertexts except with a negligible probability. Lemma 3 proves that as long as the RKA decryption algorithm rejects all the invalid ciphertexts, algorithm $\mathcal{A}$ has a negligible advantage in outputting the bit $d' = d$. Therefore, we can say that algorithm $\mathcal{A}$'s probability in outputting the bit $d' = d$ is $1/2$.

To sum up, we can see that if (g, f, Z_1, Z_2) is a DH tuple, algorithm $\mathcal{A}$ wins the CC-RKA game with the probability $1/2 + \epsilon$, such that algorithm $\mathcal{B}$'s probability in solving the decisional DH problem is $1/2 + \epsilon$; if (g, f, Z_1, Z_2) is a non-DH tuple, algorithm $\mathcal{A}$ wins the CC-RKA game with the probability $1/2$, such that algorithm $\mathcal{B}$'s probability in solving the decisional DH problem is $1/2$. Denote by $\mathcal{B}(g, f, Z_1, Z_2) = 1$ the event that algorithm $\mathcal{B}$ solves the decisional DH problem. Hence, algorithm $\mathcal{B}$ has a non-negligible probability

$$
\Pr[\mathcal{B}(g, f, Z_1, Z_2) = 1] = 1/2 \cdot (1/2 + \epsilon) + 1/2 \cdot 1/2 = 1/2 + \epsilon/2
$$

of solving the decisional DH problem.

This concludes the proof of Theorem 1.

4.4   Efficiency

We compare Wee's CC-RKA secure public-key encryption scheme from factoring, from BDH, from DDH with weaker security and ours from DDH in Table 1.

In this table, "Pairing-E" means the sum of paring computation executed during the encryption phase, and "Pairing-D" means the sum of paring computation executed during the decryption phase. "Ex-E" means the the sum of exponentiation computation executed during the encryption phase, "Ex-D" means the the sum of exponentiation computation executed during the decryption phase.

Table 1. Comparison between public-key encryption schemes with CC-RKA security

Scheme	Ciphertext Size	Pairing-E	Pairing-D	Ex-E	Ex-D
Factoring[20]	6	0	0	9	7
BDH[20]	6	1	3	7	5
DDH[20]	7	0	0	9	9
Ours	5	0	0	7	5

5   Conclusions

Followed the work in [4], Wee [20] proposed the first public-key encryption scheme against related-key attacks via adaptive trapdoor relations [19] while paying a small overhead in efficiency, of which the existing public-key set-ups can be maintained without changing. In the constructions of [20], to make sure the efficiency of the specific constructions, Wee [20] designed some efficient strong one-time signatures in their instantiations. However, though one-time signatures are easy to construct in theory, and are more efficient than full-fledged signatures, (i.e., those which are strongly unforgeable under adaptive chosen-message attack), they still have their price.

Based on a framework to enable the construction of identity-based encryption schemes that are secure under related-key attacks, Bellare, Paterson and Thomson [6] provided a framework to enable the construction of public-key encryption schemes that are secure under related-key attacks. Public-key encryption schemes in [6] are achieved in the standard model and hold CC-RKA under reasonable hardness assumptions in the standard model, but they are transformed from the identity-based encryption schemes such that pairing computation is inevitable in the efficient instantiations.

To construct an efficient public-key encryption scheme under the setting of CC-RKA security without pairings and any one-time signature schemes, in this paper, we focus on the achievement of a full fledged CCA secure public-key encryption scheme in the context of related-key attack security. After a succinct review of the security notions related to public-key encryption schemes with RKA security, we start with pointing out a simple linear related-key attack on the Cramer-Shoup basic CCA secure public-key encryption scheme [9]. Next, we propose an efficient public-key encryption scheme which is resilient against related-key attacks from DDH, which is in fact a variant of the Cramer-Shoup public-key encryption scheme [9]. Finally, we prove its CC-RKA security under the difficulty of solving the DDH problem.

References

1. Akavia, A., Goldwasser, S., Vaikuntanathan, V.: Simultaneous hardcore bits and cryptography against memory attacks. In: Reingold, O. (ed.) TCC 2009. LNCS, vol. 5444, pp. 474–495. Springer, Heidelberg (2009)
2. Applebaum, B., Harnik, D., Ishai, Y.: Semantic security under related-key attacks and applications. In: ICS. Tsinghua University Press (2011)
3. Bellare, M., Cash, D.: Pseudorandom functions and permutations provably secure against related-key attacks. In: Rabin, T. (ed.) CRYPTO 2010. LNCS, vol. 6223, pp. 666–684. Springer, Heidelberg (2010)
4. Bellare, M., Cash, D., Miller, R.: Cryptography secure against related-key attacks and tampering. In: Lee, D.H., Wang, X. (eds.) ASIACRYPT 2011. LNCS, vol. 7073, pp. 486–503. Springer, Heidelberg (2011)
5. Bellare, M., Kohno, T.: A theoretical treatment of related-key attacks: RKA-PRPs, RKA-PRFs, and applications. In: Biham, E. (ed.) EUROCRYPT 2003. LNCS, vol. 2656, pp. 491–506. Springer, Heidelberg (2003)
6. Bellare, M., Paterson, K.G., Thomson, S.: RKA security beyond the linear barrier: IBE, encryption and signatures. In: Wang, X., Sako, K. (eds.) ASIACRYPT 2012. LNCS, vol. 7658, pp. 331–348. Springer, Heidelberg (2012)
7. Biham, E.: New types of cryptanalytic attacks using related keys. In: Helleseth, T. (ed.) EUROCRYPT 1993. LNCS, vol. 765, pp. 398–409. Springer, Heidelberg (1994)
8. Boneh, D.: The decision diffie-hellman problem. In: Buhler, J.P. (ed.) ANTS 1998. LNCS, vol. 1423, pp. 48–63. Springer, Heidelberg (1998)
9. Cramer, R., Shoup, V.: Design and analysis of practical public-key encryption schemes secure against adaptive chosen ciphertext attack. IACR Cryptology ePrint Archive, 2001:108 (2001)
10. Even, S., Goldreich, O., Micali, S.: On-line/off-line digital signatures. J. Cryptology 9(1), 35–67 (1996)
11. Gennaro, R., Lysyanskaya, A., Malkin, T., Micali, S., Rabin, T.: Algorithmic tamper-proof (ATP) security: Theoretical foundations for security against hardware tampering. In: Naor, M. (ed.) TCC 2004. LNCS, vol. 2951, pp. 258–277. Springer, Heidelberg (2004)
12. Goldwasser, S., Micali, S., Rivest, R.L.: A digital signature scheme secure against adaptive chosen-message attacks. SIAM J. Comput. 17(2), 281–308 (1988)
13. Goyal, V., O'Neill, A., Rao, V.: Correlated-input secure hash functions. In: Ishai, Y. (ed.) TCC 2011. LNCS, vol. 6597, pp. 182–200. Springer, Heidelberg (2011)
14. Halderman, J.A., Schoen, S.D., Heninger, N., Clarkson, W., Paul, W., Calandrino, J.A., Feldman, A.J., Appelbaum, J., Felten, E.W.: Lest we remember: Cold boot attacks on encryption keys. In: USENIX Security Symposium, pp. 45–60. USENIX Association (2008)
15. Kiltz, E., Mohassel, P., O'Neill, A.: Adaptive trapdoor functions and chosen-ciphertext security. In: Gilbert, H. (ed.) EUROCRYPT 2010. LNCS, vol. 6110, pp. 673–692. Springer, Heidelberg (2010)

16. Lucks, S.: Ciphers secure against related-key attacks. In: Roy, B., Meier, W. (eds.) FSE 2004. LNCS, vol. 3017, pp. 359–370. Springer, Heidelberg (2004)

17. Micali, S., Reyzin, L.: Physically observable cryptography (extended abstract). In: Naor, M. (ed.) TCC 2004. LNCS, vol. 2951, pp. 278–296. Springer, Heidelberg (2004)

18. Quisquater, J.-J., Samyde, D.: ElectroMagnetic analysis (EMA): Measures and counter-measures for smart cards. In: Attali, S., Jensen, T. (eds.) E-smart 2001. LNCS, vol. 2140, pp. 200–210. Springer, Heidelberg (2001)

19. Wee, H.: Efficient chosen-ciphertext security via extractable hash proofs. In: Rabin, T. (ed.) CRYPTO 2010. LNCS, vol. 6223, pp. 314–332. Springer, Heidelberg (2010)

20. Wee, H.: Public key encryption against related key attacks. In: Fischlin, M., Buchmann, J., Manulis, M. (eds.) PKC 2012. LNCS, vol. 7293, pp. 262–279. Springer, Heidelberg (2012)

Clonewise – Detecting Package-Level Clones
Using Machine Learning

Silvio Cesare, Yang Xiang, and Jun Zhang

School of Information Technology
Deakin University
Burwood, Victoria 3125, Australia
{scesare,yang,jun.zhang}@deakin.edu.au

Abstract. Developers sometimes maintain an internal copy of another software or fork development of an existing project. This practice can lead to software vulnerabilities when the embedded code is not kept up to date with upstream sources. We propose an automated solution to identify clones of packages without any prior knowledge of these relationships. We then correlate clones with vulnerability information to identify outstanding security problems. This approach motivates software maintainers to avoid using cloned packages and link against system wide libraries. We propose over 30 novel features that enable us to use to use pattern classification to accurately identify package-level clones. To our knowledge, we are the first to consider clone detection as a classification problem. Our results show our system, Clonewise, compares well to manually tracked databases. Based on our work, over 30 unknown package clones and vulnerabilities have been identified and patched.

Keywords: Vulnerability detection, code clone, Linux.

1 Introduction

Developers of software sometimes embed code from other projects. They statically link against an external library, maintain an internal copy of an external library's source code, or fork the development of an external library. A canonical example is the zlib compression library which is embedded in much software due to its functionality and permissive software license. In general, embedding software is considered as a bad development practice, but the reasons for doing so include reducing external dependencies for installation, or the need to modify functionality of an external library. The practice of embedding code is generally ill advised because it has implications on software maintenance and software security. It is a security problem because at least two versions of the same software exist when it is embedded in another package. Therefore, bug fixes and security patches must be integrated for each specific instance instead of being applied once to a system wide library. Because of these issues, for most Linux vendors, package policies exist that oppose the embedding of code, unless specific exceptions are required.

In the example of zlib, each time a vulnerability was discovered in the original upstream source, all embedded copies required patching. However, in the past, uncertainty existed in Linux distributions of which packages were embedding zlib and

T. Zia et al. (Eds.): SecureComm 2013, LNICST 127, pp. 197–215, 2013.

which packages required patching. In 2005, after a zlib [1] vulnerability was reported, Debian Linux [2] made a specific project to perform binary signature scans against packages in the repository to find vulnerable versions of the embedded library. To create a signature the source code of zlib was manually inspected to find a version string that uniquely identified it. This manual and time consuming approach still finds vulnerable embedded versions of software today. We constructed signatures for vulnerable versions of compression and image processing libraries including bzip2, libtiff, and libpng. We performed a scan of the Debian and Fedora Linux [3] package repository and found 5 packages with previously unknown vulnerabilities. Even for actively developed projects such as the Mozilla Firefox web browser, we saw windows of exploitability between upstream security fixes and the correction of embedded copies of the image processing libraries. Even in mainstream applications such as Firefox, these windows of opportunity sometimes extended for periods of over 3 months.

The traditional approach for discovering duplicated fragments of insecure code has been through the use of code clone detection. Code clone detection applies pattern recognition on the syntactic or structural nature using the insecure code fragment as a template. Then a search is performed over other code to identify duplication or near identical duplication.

1.1 Motivation for Package-Level Clone Detection

Clone detection theoretically solves the problem of insecure code fragments propagating to other locations. However, in practice the number of code clones is significantly high. For developers of individual projects, clone information may be useful. Yet, package maintainers and operating system distributions have no realistic actions to take with such clone information since they are not the primary developers of the software they release. What package maintainers and operating system vendors want is the ability to repackage or build the software in such a way that improves security and eliminates clones. If vendors know that an entire package is cloned in another, then they can modify the build process to use the operating system's system wide library package. This is an achievable goal and improves the security and stability of the system. This is our motivation and the reason we see package-level clone detection as an important addition to software engineering that traditional clone detection does not address.

1.2 Motivation for Automated Approaches

The approach of manually searching for embedded copies of specific libraries deals poorly with the scale of the problem. According to the list of tracked embedded packages in Debian Linux, there are over 420 packages which are embedded in other software in the repository. This list was created manually and our results show that it is incomplete. Other Linux vendors were not even tracking embedded copies before our research supplied them with relevant data. It is evident from this that an automated approach is needed for identifying embedded packages without prior knowledge of which packages to search for. This would aid security teams in performing audits on new vulnerabilities in upstream sources. This identifies the motivation for our system named Clonewise to identify package-level clones.

Previous systems that automate and address part of the problem are software provenance systems. Our system extends such works by recognising more features in software that can be used to fingerprint pacakges. Our system also addresses the problem of software being implemented in multiple languages, even within the same package. Our work is language agnostic. We also address the problem of requiring every version of a software to match it against a query. Our system can determine if a package is embedded, irrespective of which version number is used. This has advantages, but also makes identifying security problems in specific versions harder. We overcome this by using side-information that tracks the necessary information and that is maintained by operating system vendors.

Our work is also similar to the concept of structural or higher-level clones as proposed in [4]. We are much more specific in the type of structure we are searching for. That is, package-level clones. The structural clones in [4] use directory-level clones to simulate module-level clones which is not as accurate.

1.3   Generality

At first glance, package-level clone detection may appear to be a Linux distribution specific problem. However, this problem applies to any vendor who maintains a repository of software packages and shares common code amongst packages. This problem also applies to any vendor which for legal reasons needs to know the provenance of embedded packages such as open source libraries. Finally, the problem applies to any vendor who needs to know what open source libraries have been embedded so as to keep up-to-date with upstream releases. It is quite conceivable that any large software project may incorporate some permissively licensed open source software as an embedded library or package. For all of these reasons, software engineering needs to incorporate automated means to provide assurance that the state of software and the existence of package-level clones is known.

1.4   Innovation

Our approach is to consider code reuse detection as a binary classification problem between two packages. The classification problem is 'do these two packages share code?' We achieve this by performing feature extraction from the two packages and then performing statistical classification using a vector space model. The features we use are based on the filenames, hashes, and fuzzy content of files within the source packages

To identify security vulnerabilities we associate vulnerability information from public advisories to vulnerable packages and vulnerable source files. We then discover all clones of these packages in a Linux distribution. Finally, we check the manually tracked vulnerable packages that Debian Linux maintain for each vulnerability and report if any of our discovered clones are not identified as being vulnerable.

In this paper we make the following contributions:

- We define the problem of package clone detection, and the sub-categories of shared and embedded package clone detection.
- We are the first ones to formulate code reuse detection as a pattern classification problem. Then, it is feasible to apply traditional pattern

classification algorithms to achieve accurate clone detection. We employ a novel asymmetric bagging based classifier combination method to address the specific classification problem.

- We propose over 30 new features for the purpose of clone detection, which are fundamental to solve the specific pattern classification problem. In particular, the proposed features are basis to the accuracy of clone detection.
- We propose applications of package clone detection. We present algorithms to identify outstanding security vulnerabilities based on out-of-date clones.
- We implement a complete system, Clonewise, which demonstrates our system effectively identifies package clones, finds vulnerabilities and is useful to vendors. For example, Debian Linux is planning infrastructure integration of Clonewise.

The structure of this chapter is as follows: Section 2 defines the problem of package clone detection and outlines our approach. Section 3 describes how Clonewise detects shared and embedded package clones using machine learning. Section 4 describes the algorithms we use to identify vulnerabilities based on clone information. Section 5 evaluates our system. Section 6 examines related work. Section 7 outlines future work. Finally we present our conclusions in Section 8.

2   Problem Definition and Our Approach

2.1   Problem Definition

A package clone is the duplication of one package's code in another package. It is the presence of code reuse between packages. How do we find these package clones?

A package can be embedded in another package. How do we determine this knowing that a package clone exists?

A package clone may contain vulnerabilities or other security problems because the clone is out of date. How do we find these?

2.2   Our Approach

Our approach for detecting clones is based on binary classification and shown in Fig. 1 and described below. A key point is that if two packages share code, one is not necessarily embedded in the other. We therefore detect code reuse and embedding as related but distinct problems.

Our approach is to consider code reuse detection as a binary classification problem between two packages. The classification problem is 'do these two packages share code?' We achieve this by performing feature extraction from the two packages and then perform statistical classification using a vector space model. The features we use are based on the filenames, hashes, and fuzzy content of files within the source packages.

A package clone consisting of two packages can be analysed to determine if one package is embedded in the other. We use a binary classification problem to answer this. The features we use are based on the size of the cloned code relative to the size of each package, and other features such has how many packages are dependent on the packages we are analysing.

We determine vulnerable packages by correlating security tracking information with our package clone detection analysis.

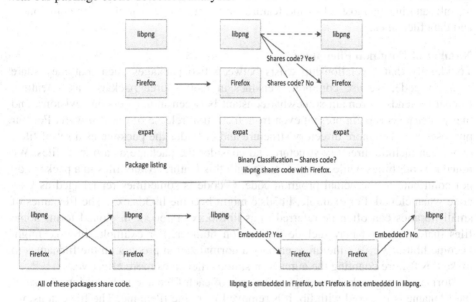

Fig. 1. Shared package clone detection (above) and embedded package clone detection (below)

3   Package Clone Detection

Clonewise is currently based on machine learning and we have found this approach to be most versatile and successful. We employ statistical classification to learn and then classify two packages as sharing or not sharing code.

Classification is a well-studied problem in machine learning and software is available to make analyses easy. Weka [5] is a popular data mining toolkit using machine learning that Clonewise uses to perform machine learning.

3.1   Shared Package Clone Detection

Feature extraction is necessary to perform shared package clone classification. We need to select features that reflect if two packages share or do not share code. The feature vector we extract is obtained from a pair of packages that we are testing for sharing of code. The 26 features we use are discussed in the following subsections.

Number of Filenames
Our first set of features is simply the number of filenames in the source trees of the two packages being compared.

Source Filenames and Data Filenames
In Clonewise, we distinguish between two types of filename features. Filenames that represent program source code and programs that represent non program source code.

We distinguish these two types of filenames by their file extension. The list of extensions used to identify source code are c, cpp, cxx, cc, php, inc, java, py, rb, js, pl, m, mli, and lua. Almost all of the features in Clonewise are applied for both source and data filenames.

Number of Common Filenames

To identify that a relationship exists between two packages such that they share common code, we use common filenames in their source packages as a feature. Filenames tends to remain somewhat constant between minor version revisions, and many filenames remain present even from the initial release of that software. For our purposes we can ignore directory structure and consider the package as a set of files, or we can include directory structure and consider the package as a tree of files. We noted several things while experimenting with this feature: Many files in a package do not contribute to the actual program code. C code is sometimes repackaged as C++ code when cloned. For example, lib3ds.c might become lib3ds.cxx. The filenames of small libraries can often be referred to as libfoo.xx or foo.xx in cloned form. Some files that are cloned may include the version number. For example, libfoo.c might become libfoo43.c. We therefore employ a normalization process on the filenames to make this feature counting the number of similar filenames more effective.

Normalization works by changing the case of each filename to be all lower case. If the filename is prefixed with lib, it is removed from the filename. The file extensions .cxx, .cpp, .cc are replaced with the extension .c. Any hyphens, underscores, numbers, or dots excluding the file extension component are removed.

Number of Similar Filenames

It is useful to identify similar filenames since they may refer to nearly identical source code. A fuzzy string similarity function is used that matches if the two filenames are 85% or more similar in relation to their edit distance.

Our similarity measure is defined as:

$$similarity(s,t) = 1 - \frac{edit\_dist(s,t)}{\max(len(s), len(t))}$$

We chose the edit distance as our string metric after experimenting with other metrics including the smith-waterman local sequence alignment algorithm and the longest common subsequence string metric.

Number of Files with Identical Content

We perform hashing of file content using the ssdeep software and do a comparison of hashes between packages to identify identical content without respect to the filenames used. Like the previous class of feature, we have a feature for the number of files having identical content that are all program source code, and a feature for the number of files having identical content that are non-program source code.

Number of Files with Common Filenames and Similar Content

To increase the precision of file matching from the previous feature, we employ a fuzzy hash of the file contents and then perform an approximate comparison of those hashes for files with similar filenames. While the previous approach is based on file names alone, the new approach is a combination of file names and content. Fuzzy hashing can be used to identify near identical data based on sequences within the data that remain constant using context triggered piecewise hashing [6]. The result of fuzzy hashing file content is a string signature known as its fuzzy hash. Approximate matching between hashes is performed using the string edit distance known as the Levenshtein distance. The distance is then transformed to a similarity measure. The similarity measured is a number between 0 and 100. Zero indicates that the hashes are not at all similar, and 100 indicates that the hashes are equal.

We have features for the number of files of similar content with a similarity greater than 0 of program source code and non-program source code. We also count the number of similar files having a similarity greater than 80.

Scoring Filenames

Not all filenames should be considered equal. Filenames, such as README or Makefile that frequently occur in different packages should have a lower importance than those filenames which are very specific to a package such as libpng.h. We account for this by assigning a weight for each filename based on its inverse document frequency [7]. The inverse document frequency lowers the weight of a term the more times it appears in a corpus and is often used in the field of information retrieval.

The inverse document frequency is defined as:

$$idf(t, D) = \log \frac{|D|}{|\{d \in D : t \in d\}|}$$

where D is the set of packages, d is a package, and t is a filename in a package.

We use features scoring the sum of matching filename weights to the number of similar files, the number of similar files and similar content with similarity greater than 0 and 80, for both program source code and non-program source code.

Matching Filenames between Packages

If filename matching between two packages was performed as an exact match, then the number of filenames shared would be the cardinality of the intersection between the two sets of filenames. However, in Clonewise the filename matching is approximate based on the string edit distance. This means that some filenames such as Makefile.ca could potentially match the filenames Makefile.cba and Makefile.cb. Moreover, the scores for each filename as discussed in the previous section can be different depending on which filename is deemed to be a match. We solve this problem by employing an algorithm from combinatorial optimization known as the assignment problem.

The assignment problem is to construct a bijective mapping between two sets, where each possible mapping has a cost associated with it, such that the mappings are chosen so that the sum of costs is optimal. Formally, the assignment problem is defined as:

Given two sets, A and T, of equal size, together with a weight function C: A × T →
R. Find a bijection f: A →T such that the cost function:

$$\sum_{a \in A} C(a, f(a))$$

is optimal.

In our work the sets are the two packages and the elements of each set are the
filenames in that package. The cost of the mapping between sets is the score of the
matching filename in the second set according to its inverse document frequency. Our
use of the assignment problem seeks to maximize the sum of costs.

The assignment problem can be solved in cubic time in relation to the cardinality
of the sets using the Hungarian or Munkres [8] algorithm.

The Munkres algorithm is effective, however for large N, a cubic running time is
not practical. We employ a greedy solution that is not optimal but is more efficient
when N is large.

3.2   Shared Package Clone Classification

The output of Clonewise is the set of packages where the classification determines the
package pairs share code. Clonewise also reports the filenames between the packages
and the weights of those filenames.

Clonewise uses supervised learning to build a classification model. We use the
manually created Debian embedded-code-copies database that tracks package clones
to train and evaluate our system. We employ a number of classifiers to evaluate our
system as described in Section 7.

3.3   Embedded Package Clone Detection

To detect embedded package clones we use the results of shared package clone
detection and apply a filtering stage to exclude packages where the first package is
not embedded in the second package. We solve this problem by considering the
problem as a binary classification problem.

Similar to the shared package clone detection approach, we perform feature
extraction before using statistical classification. The 18 features we use are
summarized in the following:

Number of Filenames
As in shared package clone detection, the number of filenames that are source and
data are used.

Percent of X Embedded in Y
These features say how much of one package is embedded in the other package.

Package X has Lib in Name
These features are useful in identifying if a package is a library, which increases its
likelihood that it is an embedding. If the package name is prefixed with 'lib', then the

feature is assigned a value of 1. If the prefix is not that, then the value is 0. The prefix is compared without regard to case.

A to B Ratio
These features inform us on how big the packages are relative to each other. It is typical that an embedded library is smaller than the software it is embedded in.

Package Dependents
These features inform us on how many other packages depend on the package in question. Libraries are typically used by many other packages and so the value for this feature will also be high. As explained earlier, that the package is library indicates that the package is more likely to be embedded.

3.4   Classification Using Asymmetric Bagging

For training our classifier, we have a finite set of labelled positive cases as obtained from vendor generated databases and we are able to arbitrarily generate labelled negative cases. We have many more negative cases than we have positive cases, wherein a positive case indicates an embedded package clone. This scenario represents the imbalanced class problem [9] where many classifiers favour the majority class. We decided to improve our detection rate of the positive class by addressing the imbalanced class problem by performing asymmetric bagging [10].

Asymmetric bagging uses all the labelled positive cases and use an equivalent number of negative cases obtained from a random sampling. This extends traditional bagging which uses a random and equal sampling from both classes. The asymmetric bagging approach described generates a single bag upon which a classification model is built from training. Many bags are created and classification models are built for each bag. When performing classification of an unlabelled instance, each bag makes a prediction and the results are aggregated using a majority vote. This has the effect or improving the accuracy when detecting positive cases. We implemented the asymmetric bagging algorithms by extending the bagging meta-classifier in the Weka machine learning toolkit.

4   Inferring Security Problems

In this section, we examine algorithms and approaches to detect software vulnerabilities. Package-level clone detection is not strictly the best method to discover security problems through code cloning. However, it is almost impossible in practice to apply code-level clone detection across tens of thousands of packages with potentially hundreds of thousands of clones and expect developers to integrate fixes. The reality is, a vendor's security team can fix high impact bugs and push for package maintainers to build their software using system wide package-level libraries. In effect, the only practically used system of bug fixing on a large scale in regards to clones, is by fixing package-level clones. Yet the problem still exists of how to motivate package maintainers or security teams to apply these fixes. The current practice is to highlight that the cloned package contains known security problems and pointing out that there is less cost in rebuilding the software to eliminate the higher-level clone than it is to apply individual patches. Therefore, we see value in Clonewise as being a tool that can bring about good practices of eliminating package clones by highlighting vulnerabilities. To achieve the task of vulnerability detection, we propose use-cases for clone detection by Linux security teams. We also propose a completely automated solution to find out-of-date clones that have outstanding security vulnerabilities.

4.1   Use-Case of Clone Detection to Detect Vulnerabilities

One method which we initially tried, for the purpose of vulnerability detection, was to look at packages that had reported vulnerabilities against them. We considered this a list of security sensitive packages. We used this list of packages as input to our clone detection analysis. Anytime a security sensitive package was cloned, we verified that the clone was not out of date. This is an effective method to detect vulnerabilities, but it requires manual analysis. Even though the technique we described is manual, it still has benefits today and can be used in an on-going basis to detect new vulnerabilities.

If a new vulnerability is found in a package, then clone detection should be performed on the Linux distributions because it is likely the same vulnerability is present in the cloned software. For example, if a vulnerability is reported for libpng, then clone detection should be performed and each libpng clone checked to see if the vulnerability is present. This method can be used by Linux security teams, but for old vulnerabilities it is not advisable since many clones would be patched but not reported by a Linux vendor. Therefore, we looked at other automated methods to detect out-of-date clones which we describe in the following sub-sections.

4.2   Automated Vulnerability Inference

In Clonewise, we can use clone detection in addition to Debian Linux's security tracking information to identify untracked vulnerabilities.

Clonewise takes a vulnerability report given as a CVE (Common Vulnerabilities and Exposures) number as input and extracts the vulnerable package from the data. The standardized package name associated with the vulnerability, given as a CPE (Common Platform Enumeration) package name, is translated to a native Debian package name.

Clonewise then parses the summary of the CVE report to find the vulnerable source files. It is possible to extract theses vulnerable source files from the summary by tokenizing the summary into words and extracting words that have a file extension of known programming languages.

Clonewise then looks at all the clones of the vulnerable package and trims the list by ensuring one of the vulnerable source files is present in the clone and that the fuzzy hash between the vulnerable package's source is similar to the clone's.

We also trim the list by ignoring clones that we believe have been patched to use the system wide dynamic library. We did this by checking if in the binary version of the package the embedded package was a package dependency. If the embedded package is a dependency, then the main package almost certainly uses it for dynamic linking. Dynamic linking is the normal approach vendors use to address the security implications of package clones.

Finally, Clonewise checks to see if Debian Linux is tracking this package clone as being affected by that particular CVE. If it is not being tracked, then Clonewise will report the package as being potentially vulnerable.

This process of finding outstanding vulnerabilities is applied to every CVE of interest in the database, and a final report is generated. The normal process is that a security analyst then verifies each reported vulnerability and eliminates any false positives.

5   Results and Evaluation

In this section, we discuss how we use an Amazon EC2 cluster to generate our results. We then discuss how our system performs against a labelled dataset of package clones and the security vulnerabilities our system has discovered. Finally, we discuss a web service to perform online scanning of software using our EC2 generated database.

5.1   Clonewise Compute Cluster

Our system employs multicore and clustering. We analysed our Linux distribution using a high performance compute cluster. We purchased 4 hours of cluster computing time from the Amazon EC2 cloud computing service. We built a 4 node cluster with dual CPUs per node, Intel Xeon E5-2670, eight-core "Sandy Bridge" architecture), 60.5G of memory per node, and CPU performance identified as 88 EC2 compute units. We then performed package-level clone detection on this infrastructure.

5.2   Establishing the Ground Truth for Training and Evaluation

Debian Linux maintain a manually created database of packages that are cloned in their security tracker database. We use this list of entries to establish the ground truth for our labelled data in an evaluation.

The Debian database was not originally created to be processed by a machine, so some of the data is not consistent in referencing packages with their correct machine readable names. Instead, shorthand or common names for packages and libraries are sometimes used. We cull all those entries which do not reference package sources and are therefore not suitable for our system.

Table 1. Accuracy of Shared Package Clone Detection

CLASSIFIER	PRECISION	RECALL	ACCURACY	F-MEASURE
Naïve Bayes	0.47562	0.57687	0.98599	0.52137
Multi. Perceptron	0.80555	0.26806	0.98948	0.40225
C4.5	0.85878	0.68725	0.99436	0.76349
Random Forest	0.89881	0.70039	0.99499	0.78728
Rand. Forest (0.8)	0.96746	0.58607	0.99426	0.72994

Table 2. Accuracy of Shared Package Clone Detection

CLASSIFIER	TP/FN	FP/TN	TP RATE	FP RATE
Naïve Bayes	439/322	484/56296	57.69%	0.85%
Multilayer Perceptron	204/557	48/56732	26.81%	0.08%
C4.5	523/238	86/56694	68.73%	0.15%
Random Forest	533/228	60/56720	70.04%	0.11%
Random Forest (0.8)	446/315	15/56765	58.61%	0.03%

Table 3. Accuracy of Embedded Package Clone Detection

CLASSIFIER	PRECISION	RECALL	ACCURACY	F-MEASURE
Naïve Bayes	0.10171	0.94349	0.35580	0.18362
Multi. Perceptron	0.75229	0.43101	0.94540	0.54802
C4.5	0.89235	0.75164	0.97396	0.81597
Random Forest	0.89067	0.72798	0.97225	0.80114
Asym. Bagging	0.53196	0.91852	0.93168	0.67372

Table 4. Accuracy of Embedded Package Clone Detection

CLASSIFIER	TP/FN	FP/TN	TP RATE	FP RATE
Naïve Bayes	718/43	6341/2808	94.35%	69.31%
Multilayer Perceptron	328/433	108/9041	43.10%	1.18%
C4.5	572/189	69/9080	75.16%	0.75%
Random Forest	554/207	68/9081	72.80%	0.74%
Asymmetric Bagging	699/62	615/8534	91.86%	6.72%

We had two types of negative labeled entries where two packages are said not to be cloned with each other. One case was for shared package clone detection, and the other was for embedded package clone detection. To establish true negatives for shared package clone detection, we randomly selected pairs of packages not in our true positive list. We label these package pairs as negatives. This data can be unclean since we observe the labeled true positives are incomplete, but even so, the true negatives we label are still useful for training our statistical model. In total, we obtained 761 labelled positives and 56780 negatives.

Table 5. Adhoc Detection of fedora Linux vulnerabilities

Package	Embedded Package
OpenSceneGraph	lib3ds
mrpt-opengl	lib3ds
mingw32-OpenSceneGraph	lib3ds
libtlen	expat
centerim	expat
mcabber	expat
udunits2	expat
libnodeupdown-backend-ganglia	expat
libwmf	gd
Kadu	mimetex
cgit	git
tkimg	libpng
tkimg	libtiff
ser	php-Smarty
pgpoolAdmin	php-Smarty
sepostgresql	postgresql

To generate true negatives for the embedded package clone detection, we paired up all packages that were reported as being embedded in X, ignoring those cases where

X was the embedded code. This is what we expect our system to report – that X is embedded in Y and Z, but Y is not embedded in Z, and Z is not embedded in Y. In total, we were able to label 9149 negative cases.

5.3   Accuracy of Shared Package Clone Detection

We employed 10-fold validation from our labeled dataset to evaluate the accuracy of our system and experimented with a number of classifiers including Naïve Bayes [11], Multilayer Perceptron, C4.5 [12], and Random Forest [13]. Our results are shown in Table 1 and Table 2. The data is very imbalanced and this skews the accuracy, which easily achieves better than 99%, because we can identify negative cases more easily than positive cases. We obtained the best result using the Random Forest classification algorithm. This classification algorithm performed significantly better than all other algorithms we evaluated. The true positive rate is 70.04%, the precision is 89.88%, the recall is 70.05%, and the f-measure is 78.73%, which we think is quite reasonable for the first implementation of an automated system for package clone detection. The false positive rate must be very low for our system to be used by Linux security teams. Our initial false positive rate is 0.11%. We then modified the decision threshold of the random forest algorithm to consider false positives as more significant than false negatives. Our false negative rate is 0.03% with a decision threshold of 0.8 which represents that 3 in every 10,000 package pairs is mislabeled as a positive. The true positive rate is lower with a higher decision threshold and is 58.61%. This is the trade-off we accept for a low false positive rate. There are about 18,000 source packages, so there are 18,000 package pairs that are classified when performing clone detection on an individual package. Therefore, if our training data were not noisy, we would predict 4 to 5 false positive per complete clone detection on an individual package. However, our labelled negatives are noisy, and some negatives are actually positives. Therefore, we think between 4 to 5 false positives is closer to an upper limit. This is reasonable for a manual analyst to verify and we think it will not cause significant burden on Linux security teams.

Table 6. Adhoc Detection of Debian Linux vulnerabilities

Package	Embedded Package
boson	lib3ds
libopenscenegraph7	lib3ds
libfreeimage	libpng
libfreeimage	libtiff
libfreeimage	openexr
r-base-core	libbz2
r-base-core-ra	libbz2
lsb-rpm	libbz2
criticalmass	libcurl
albert	expat
mcabber	expat
centerim	expat
wengophone	gaim
libpam-opie	libopie
pysol-sound-server	libmikod
gnome-xcf-thumnailer	xcftool
plt-scheme	libgd

Table 7. Automated Vulnerability Inference

TP + FP (Packages)	19
TP (Packages)	10
FP (Packages)	9
TP + FP (CVEs)	132
TP (CVEs)	81
FP (CVEs)	51

Table 8. Automated Detection of Potential Vulnerabilities

Package	Embedded Package
freevo	feedparser
hedgewars	freetype
ia32-libs	* (see text)
libtk-img	tiff
likewise-open	curl
luatex	poppler
planet-venus	feedparser
syslinux	libpng
vnc4	freetype
vtk	tiff

5.4   Accuracy of Embedded Package Clone Detection

We evaluated the embedded package clone detection using a number of classifiers including Naïve Bayes, Multilayer Perceptron, C4.5, and Random Forest. Our results are shown in Table 3 and Table 4. We obtained the best result using the C4.5 classification algorithm. The true positive rate was 75.16%, the false positive rate was 0.75%, the precision was 89.24%, the recall was 75.16%, and the f-measure was 81.60%. We then used this algorithm as a base classifier for our asymmetric bagging meta-classifier with 50 bags. This improved the true positive rate to 91.86% but also increased the false positive rate to 6.72%. We see this as an acceptable trade-off to improve the true positive rate.

5.5   Practical Package Clone Detection

As part of the practical results from our system we contributed 34 previously untracked package clones to Debian Linux's embedded code copies database. Thus, we feel that the package clone detection provides tangible benefit to the Linux community. We also verified if the embedded packages we detected were not in fact patched by the Linux vendors to link dynamically against a system wide library.

5.6   Vulnerability Detection

A consequence of package clone detection is determining if a clone is out of date and if it has any outstanding and unpatched vulnerabilities. As part of our work we detected over 30 vulnerabilities in Debian and Fedora Linux because of package clone issues by checking security sensitive packages manually, or using adhoc identification of out-of-date clones. The vulnerabilities in each package we found using clone detection are shown in Table 5 and 6.

5.7   Automated Vulnerability Detection

We performed a more recent evaluation of completely automated vulnerability inference over the years of 2010, 2011, and 2012. Clonewise reported 132 vulnerabilities across 19 packages. We submitted bug reports against each package to Debian Linux. Not all our submitted bug reports were actual vulnerabilities. Some reports were erroneous because Clonewise falsely identified a package clone when one did not exist. Another source of errors was that some bugs we reported as vulnerabilities could not be triggered, even though the clone was correctly identified and had unpatched CVEs. This was true of libpng image processing library being embedded in the syslinux boot loader package. Boot loading displays an image, but does not allow an attacker to control that image to trigger the vulnerability. A high number (64) of vulnerabilities were found in the ia32-libs package. This package contains a list of embedded libraries and is only updated by Debian on point releases. Debian informed us that this package would invariably contain vulnerabilities, but in the unstable release of Debian an alternative approach will be employed which resolves these issues by not embedding libraries.

Debian have not yet confirmed all our bug reports so we investigated each package manually to check that a package clone existed, and that the internal version number of the library was a version vulnerable to the CVE Clonewise reports. The results are shown in Table 7. It should be noted that the high number of true positives is largely accounted for by the 64 vulnerabilities we marked as such once Debian informed us that ia32-libs was by nature collecting vulnerabilities until point releases. Nonetheless, we detected unverified vulnerabilities in more than 50% of the packages Clonewise reported. We performed this manual analysis stage of all vulnerabilities, except for those in ia32-libs, in less than 2 hours. Our results are shown in Table 6. In the case that these potential vulnerabilities are not confirmed by Debian, then Debian will still need to update their internal CVE database to report that those packages are unaffected. Therefore, our work still remains beneficial.

The results of our system demonstrate that we effectively identify vulnerabilities with a false positive rate that is practical for manual verification in a feasible amount of time.

5.8   Clonewise as a Web Service

We have made available some functionality that Clonewise implements at http://www.codeclones.com. The web service takes a tarball of source code and reports if any of around 420 common open source libraries are embedded in it. The web service frontend is implemented in PHP, shell scripts, and Python. The frontend passes the request to HTTP-based load balancer located on another server. The load balancer then passes the request to a backend cluster. We can scale our system by running a script to add more nodes to the backend cluster as necessary. The web service uses Amazon EC2 to provide the virtual private servers.

6   Related Work

Large scale manual attempts at auditing specific Linux distributions for embedded packages have occasionally occurred in the past. In 2005, the Debian package repository was scanned for vulnerable zlib fingerprints based on version strings [14]. Antivirus signatures were generated and ClamAV performed the scanning. Our system improves practice by automating the discovery of embedded packages without prior knowledge of which packages are embedded. Additionally, our system automatically constructs the signatures to detect embedded packages.

Related works to ours is that of software clone detection [15]. Clone detection identifies duplicated copies of code fragments. This can be used to identify duplication of effort in source code which can be a source of software bugs or confusion. Work has been done on detecting higher-level clones, including file-level clones [4]. Our work extends higher-level clones by being more accurate for package-level duplication. Additionally, clone detection has been used on industrial sources like the Linux kernel [16] or as used by Microsoft engineers [17]. Our system is not as fine grained as traditional code clone detection and detects code similarity at the source file and package level. This allows us to integrate our system into existing practice as can be used by Linux vendors, and allows us to use vulnerability information which is provided at the package level. We believe that while our approach is simplistic, this method offers practical and immediately useful benefits to practitioners.

Software plagiarism is another software similarity problem and detection systems for this often make the distinction between attribute counting and structure based techniques. Attribute counting is based on software metrics, or the frequencies of particular features occurring, as in [18]. Structure based techniques rely on using program structure which typically include the use of dependency graphs or parse trees, as in [19] and [20]. Tree and graph edit distances show similarity. [21] and [22] use greedy string tiling. Another approach [23] considers tokenization of source code adaptive sequence alignment.

Clone detection can be performed on the textual stream in a source file once whitespace and comments are removed [24]. The key concept is that a fingerprint of a code fragment is obtained and then the remainder of the source scanned for possible matching duplicates. More recently [25, 26] has used the token approach with good success in large scale evaluations. Large scale copy and paste clones using a data mining approach was investigated in [27, 28].

An alternative approach is to use the abstract syntax tree of the source to generate a fingerprint [29]. Tree matching can subsequently be used to discover software clones. Abstract syntax trees are more impervious to superficial changes to the textual stream and textual organization of the code.

Other program abstractions can be used to fingerprint code fragments such as the program dependency graph which is a graph combining control and data dependencies [30]. An interesting semantic approach to clone detection is to use the memory states of a program [31].

In non-exact matching of code fragments, similarity searches can be used using appropriate distance metrics such as the Euclidean distance, given an appropriate threshold for similarity. In [32], trees were used to represent source code, and subtrees transformed to a vector representation. This allowed for the Euclidean distance and clustering to identify clones. Using non exact matching of code fragments allows detection of duplicated code that has been revised or that subjected to an evolutionary process. Our system allows for evolution and revision of code by using fuzzy hashing over the source. This has advantages in detecting package-level clones without storing all versions of a particular software package.

7   Future Work

Using our classification approach to clone detection, there are several ways we could see it applied to improve current practice. We could apply our system to more source code, including other Linux distributions, BSD vendors and also online source code repositories such as Sourceforge [33]. It is conceivable that source code repositories could offer services to find package clones. Our system could be integrated into a package build system to automatically update the embedded database information or ask for validation from a package maintainer. Debian Linux would like our Clonewise tool to run constantly in the background and scan the source code repository to update a live database of clones. If we did this, we could enforce build recommendations that aim for avoidance of embedded code. The Debian Linux security team has asked us to perform this integration into their distribution as part of a standard operating procedure for when a vulnerability is found in a package and this is a focus of our current work.

8   Conclusion

In addition to the number of reported vulnerabilities and subsequent patching and resolution of vulnerabilities, we believe our research has much value in the practical approach of coping with embedded code and packages that may or may not be known about. We believe all vendors benefit in creating and maintain databases of embedded code in their package repository and our research fills a gap when the manual task of auditing in excess of 10,000 packages per distribution is too time consuming to be practical. There is much work as a consequence that could be applied to current practice to aid operating system security and we feel our work is a good step towards this goal.

References

[1] Gailly, J.-L., Adler, M.: zlib (2011), http://zlib.net

[2] Debian Linux (2011), http://www.debian.org

[3] Red_Hat, Fedora Linux (2001), http://fedoraproject.org

[4] Basit, H.A., Jarzabek, S.: A Data Mining Approach for Detecting Higher-Level Clones in Software. IEEE Trans. Softw. Eng. 35, 497–514 (2009)

[5] Hall, M., Frank, E., Holmes, G., Pfahringer, B., Reutemann, P., Witten, I.H.: The WEKA data mining software: an update. SIGKDD Explor. Newsl. 11, 10–18 (2009)

[6] Kornblum, J.: Identifying almost identical files using context triggered piecewise hashing. Digital Investigation 3, 91–97 (2006)

[7] Salton, G., Buckley, C.: Term-weighting approaches in automatic text retrieval. Information Processing & Management 24, 513–523 (1988)

[8] Kuhn, H.W.: The hungarian method for the assignment problem. Naval Research Logistics Quarterly (1955)

[9] Japkowicz, N., Stephen, S.: The class imbalance problem: A systematic study. Intell. Data Anal. 6, 429–449 (2002)

[10] Dacheng, T., Xiaoou, T., Xuelong, L., Xindong, W.: Asymmetric bagging and random subspace for support vector machines-based relevance feedback in image retrieval. IEEE Transactions on Pattern Analysis and Machine Intelligence 28, 1088–1099 (2006)

[11] John, G.H., Langley, P.: Estimating continuous distributions in Bayesian classifiers. Presented at the Proceedings of the Eleventh Conference on Uncertainty in Artificial Intelligence, Montreal, Quebec, Canada (1995)

[12] Quinlan, J.R.: C4.5: programs for machine learning. Morgan Kaufmann Publishers Inc. (1993)

[13] Breiman, L.: Random Forests. Machine Learning 45, 5–32 (2001)

[14] Biedl, C., Adler, M., Weimer, F.: Discovering copies of zlib (2011), http://www.enyo.de/fw/security/zlib-fingerprint/

[15] Roy, C.K., Cordy, J.R.: A survey on software clone detection research. Queen's School of Computing TR 541, 115 (2007)

[16] Jiang, L., Su, Z., Chiu, E.: Context-based detection of clone-related bugs. Presented at the Proceedings of the the the 6th Joint Meeting of the European Software Engineering Conference and the ACM SIGSOFT Symposium on the Foundations of Software Engineering, Dubrovnik, Croatia (2007)

[17] Dang, Y., Ge, S., Huang, R., Zhang, D.: Code Clone Detection Experience at Microsoft. In: Proceedings of the 5th International Workshop on Software Clones (2011)

[18] Jones, E.L.: Metrics based plagarism monitoring. Journal of Computing Sciences in Colleges 16, 253–261 (2001)

[19] Son, J.-W., Park, S.-B., Park, S.-Y.: Program Plagiarism Detection Using Parse Tree Kernels. In: Yang, Q., Webb, G. (eds.) PRICAI 2006. LNCS (LNAI), vol. 4099, pp. 1000–1004. Springer, Heidelberg (2006)

[20] Liu, C., Chen, C., Han, J., Yu, P.S.: GPLAG: detection of software plagiarism by program dependence graph analysis. Presented at the Proceedings of the 12th ACM SIGKDD International Conference on Knowledge Discovery and Data Mining, Philadelphia, PA, USA (2006)

[21] Prechelt, L., Malpohl, G., Philippsen, M.: Finding plagiarisms among a set of programs with JPlag. Journal of Universal Computer Science 8, 1016–1038 (2002)

[22] Wise, M.J.: YAP3: improved detection of similarities in computer program and other texts. SIGCSE Bull. 28, 130–134 (1996)

[23] Ji, J.-H., Woo, G., Cho, H.-G.: A source code linearization technique for detecting plagiarized programs. SIGCSE Bull. 39, 73–77 (2007)

[24] Ducasse, S., Rieger, M., Demeyer, S.: A language independent approach for detecting duplicated code, p. 109 (1999)

[25] Kamiya, T., Kusumoto, S., Inoue, K.: CCFinder: a multilinguistic token-based code clone detection system for large scale source code. IEEE Transactions on Software Engineering, 654–670 (2002)

[26] Livieri, S., Higo, Y., Matushita, M., Inoue, K.: Very-large scale code clone analysis and visualization of open source programs using distributed CCFinder: D-CCFinder. In: Proceedings of the 29th International Conference on Software Engineering (ICSE 2007), pp. 106–115 (2007)

[27] Li, Z., Lu, S., Myagmar, S., Zhou, Y.: CP-Miner: A tool for finding copy-paste and related bugs in operating system code. In: Proceedings of the 6th Conference on Symposium on Opearting Systems Design & Implementation (OSDI 2004), p. 20 (2004)

[28] Li, Z., Lu, S., Myagmar, S., Zhou, Y.: CP-Miner: Finding copy-paste and related bugs in large-scale software code. IEEE Transactions on Software Engineering, 176–192 (2006)

[29] Baxter, I.D., Yahin, A., Moura, L., Sant'Anna, M., Bier, L.: Clone detection using abstract syntax trees, p. 368 (1998)

[30] Krinke, J.: Identifying similar code with program dependence graphs, p. 301 (2001)

[31] Kim, H., Jung, Y., Kim, S., Yi, K.: MeCC: memory comparison-based clone detector. Presented at the Proceedings of the 33rd International Conference on Software Engineering, Waikiki, Honolulu, HI, USA (2011)

[32] Jiang, L., Misherghi, G., Su, Z., Glondu, S.: DECKARD: Scalable and Accurate Tree-Based Detection of Code Clones. Presented at the Proceedings of the 29th International Conference on Software Engineering (2007)

[33] Geeknet, Sourceforge (2011), http://sourceforge.net/

Automatic Polymorphic Exploit Generation
for Software Vulnerabilities

Minghua Wang[1], Purui Su[1,*], Qi Li[2], Lingyun Ying[1],
Yi Yang[1], and Dengguo Feng[1]

[1] Trusted Computing and Information Assurance Laboratory,
Institute of Software, Chinese Academy of Sciences, Beijing 100190, China
{wangminghua,supurui,yly,yangyi,feng}@is.iscas.ac.cn
[2] Institute of Information Security, ETH Zurich, Switzerland
qi.li@inf.ethz.ch

Abstract. Generating exploits from the perspective of attackers is an effective approach towards severity analysis of known vulnerabilities. However, it remains an open problem to generate even one exploit using a program binary and a known abnormal input that crashes the program, not to mention multiple exploits. To address this issue, in this paper, we propose PolyAEG, a system that automatically generates multiple exploits for a vulnerable program using one corresponding abnormal input. To generate polymorphic exploits, we fully leverage different trampoline instructions to hijack control flow and redirect it to malicious code in the execution context. We demonstrate that, given a vulnerable program and one of its abnormal inputs, our system can generate polymorphic exploits for the program. We have successfully generated control flow hijacking exploits for 8 programs in our experiment. Particularly, we have generated 4,724 exploits using only one abnormal input for IrfanView, a widely used picture viewer.

Keywords: software vulnerability, dynamic taint analysis, exploit generation.

1 Introduction

Software vulnerability is one of the major threats to the computer system. Exploit generation from the perspective of attackers is one of the most effective approaches for vulnerability assessment. Traditionally, exploit generation is performed manually and requires prior knowledge of the vulnerabilities. However, manually generating exploits is time-consuming and highly dependent on the experience of the analysts, and cannot satisfy the demand for vulnerability assessment and defense.

To address this issue, many exploit generation schemes have been proposed. Brumley *et al.* [8] proposed an approach to automatically generate exploits for the potential vulnerabilities by comparing victim applications with their patched

---

* Corresponding author.

T. Zia et al. (Eds.): SecureComm 2013, LNICST 127, pp. 216–233, 2013.

versions. Lin *et al.* [14] presented a dynamic exploit generation method by mutating a set of input values relevant to the execution of a vulnerable code location. The exploits they generated can only crash the programs so that their approaches are not able to verify whether the vulnerability is used to execute malicious code. Avgerinos *et al.* [2] proposed the first system to generate exploits containing malicious code by source code analysis and preconditioned symbolic execution. However, such approach cannot be used for the closed source software.

In this paper, we propose an automatic polymorphic exploit generation (PolyAEG) system that aims to generate polymorphic exploits containing malicious code by given program binary and an abnormal input causing it to crash. To achieve PolyAEG, the following questions need to be answered.

In order to hijack the control flow and make sure malicious code execution, (i)which input bytes should be modified? and (ii)what values should be assigned to them? (iii)Based on the abnormal input, how can we diversify the exploit generation for a vulnerable program?

To answer these questions, PolyAEG traces program execution and performs dynamic taint analysis. During the taint analysis, PolyAEG detects all possible hijacking points, generalizes the constraints for the current execution path and identifies all user-controlled memory regions. When a hijacking point is detected, PolyAEG leverages trampoline instructions and one shellcode under the current runtime context, and accommodates them into the appropriate user-controlled memory regions to ensure that the hijacked execution flow reaches the shellcode. The data dependencies between the program input and the accommodated elements can be clearly identified by PolyAEG, so PolyAEG can find all relevant input bytes. They should be modified for exploit generation.(answer i)

In addition, as for an effective exploit, the values of the bytes to be modified should satisfy both data dependencies mentioned above and the path constraints. PolyAEG solves all the values for these bytes respectively, and use them to construct the new input, i.e., the exploit. When the program runs with this exploit, the control flow can be hijacked from the hijacking point and the trampoline instructions together with the shellcode can appear at expected memory locations.(answer ii)

PolyAEG can diversify combinations of different trampoline instructions and shellcode to generate polymorphic exploits. Moreover, PolyAEG is able to identify all possible hijacking points. For each hijacking point, PolyAEG performs the same exploit generation procedure as above, which contributes to more exploits.(answer iii). The generated exploits can be used to systematically evaluate the severity of the program vulnerability.

This paper makes the following contributions:

- We propose an PolyAEG architecture that can automatically generate polymorphic exploits by given program binaries and abnormal inputs. PolyAEG performs dynamic taint analysis to extract the execution information, analyzes the layout of the memory to accommodate the shellcode and trampoline instructions, and eventually constructs exploits by modifying relevant input bytes.

– We propose a novel approach to produce exploits by diversifying combinations of trampoline instructions and shellcode. It is not only increase the chance for generating one effective exploit, but also contribute to polymorphic exploit generation, which is important for a systematic evaluation of a found vulnerability.
– We implement PolyAEG and verify it by generating exploits for several real-world program vulnerabilities. PolyAEG successfully generated control flow hijacking exploits for each program. Especially, it generates 4,724 exploits for IrfanView, a widely used picture viewer, using one abnormal input.

   The remainder of paper is organized as follows: Section 2 introduces PolyAEG's overview. We present different phases for exploit generation in Section 3 to 5. PolyAEG was evaluated with different vulnerable programs in Section 6. We discuss limitations and future work in Section 7. Related work is presented in Section 8 and conclusions are in Section 9.

2   Overview of PolyAEG

PolyAEG takes in one vulnerable program and one abnormal input, and generates polymorphic exploits. Figure 1 shows the architecture of PolyAEG. Basically, PolyAEG is performed in the following three phases: *Dynamic Information Extraction*, *Constraint Generation*, and *Exploit Generation*.

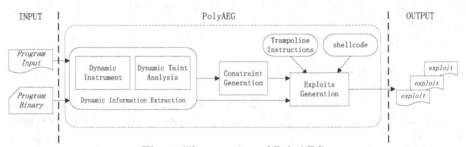

Fig. 1. The overview of PolyAEG

– *Phase 1: Dynamic Information Extraction.* In this phase, we dynamically run the vulnerable program with the given abnormal input that can crash the program, trace each instruction and perform dynamic taint analysis to collect execution information. We analyze the taint propagation procedure to detect hijacking points of the control flow and extract tainted memory regions for storing utilized trampoline instructions and shellcode.
– *Phase 2: Constraint Generation.* The goal of this phase is to generate the path constraints which ensure that the hijacking point is reachable when the program runs with the exploit as input. The path constraints are generated based on the tainted execution information from Phase 1. They are represented by a set of constraint formulas with the input data as variables to check.

– *Phase 3: Exploit Generation.* In Phase 3, we leverage trampoline instructions to construct a trampoline instruction chain which redirects the program's execution to the shellcode. We accommodate the chain and the shellcode into tainted memory regions. We eventually generate one exploit by modifying the relevant input bytes according to specified data dependencies and path constraints identified in previous phases. Diverse patterns of trampoline instruction chains and multiple alternatives for shellcode location contribute to polymorphic exploit generation.

We will further discuss the details in the following sections.

3   Dynamic Information Extraction

An effective exploit must ensure the program's execution could be hijacked and the trampoline instructions and shellcode should be located at the appropriate places in the memory when the program runs with it as input. Therefore, we need to detect hijacking points, identify the path constraints restricting the execution to the hijacking point, and extract the layout of user-controlled memory regions that could be applied to accommodate trampoline instructions and the shellcode.

To achieve this, we trace the vulnerable program running with the abnormal input and perform fine-grained dynamic taint analysis at byte level. We enhance existing taint analysis approaches [10,15] especially by constructing *iTPG*(*instruction-level Taint Propagation Graph*) and *GTSR*(*Global Taint State Record*), which not only records taint propagation but supports backtracking analysis.

iTPG records the taint propagation information during the vulnerable program running at instruction level. As is shown in Figure 2, a grey node represents a memory taint source corresponding to the data coming from the program input(e.g., files or network); a white node represents a tainted instruction. The edges linking nodes represents the data flow dependency among tainted data.

GTSR records taint states of memory bytes, general registers and bit flags in EFLAGS. Each item is represented by a 3-tuple < *TaintId*, *TaintStat*, *iTNode*>, where *TaintId* denotes the identifier of each byte or bit, *TaintStat* denotes whether it is tainted or not, and *iTNode* denotes a pointer which points to the tainted instruction last modifying the byte indicated by *TaintId*. Note that, a 32 bit register is specified by four bytes in *GTSR*.

iTPG and *GTSR* reflect the runtime context about taint propagation. The relationship between them is illustrated by Figure 2. When one tainted instruction *ti* modifies tainted bytes recorded in *GTSR*, a new *iTPG* node representing *ti* will be added into *iTPG*. We find the last tainted instruction *ti'* that modified those tainted bytes, and then link *ti* to *ti'*. Meanwhile, we update the corresponding *iTNode* pointing *ti'* before to point to *ti*. If executing *ti* also influences some bit flags in EFLAGS, we handle it similarly.

From *iTPG* and *GTSR*, we can idenfity the relevant input bytes of a tainted byte and the data dependencies between them. As is shown in Figure 2, a tainted

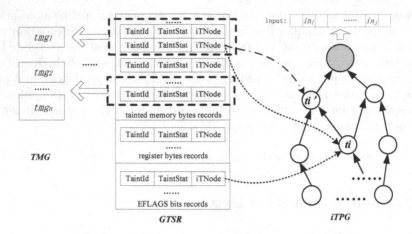

Fig. 2. *iTPG*, *GTSR* and *TMG*

byte *tb* corresponds to one item in *GTSR*. The *iTNode* points to a node in *iTPG* which represents the tainted instruction last modifying *tb*. Backtracking along *iTPG* from this node to taint source nodes, we obtain a trace consisting of recorded tainted instructions. From that, we can identify the *tb*'s relevant input bytes $in_i, ..., in_j$ and their data dependencies $value(tb) = f(value(in_i), ..., value(in_j))$, where f can be educed by the semantics of the tainted instructions within the trace.

During dynamic taint analysis of the vulnerable program, we detect hijacking points by checking if tainted data are used in indirect control transfer(i.e., loaded on EIP) with *ret*, *jmp* and *call* instructions. When a hijacking point is detected, we identify the layout of tainted memory areas and path constraints. A tainted memory area consists of successive tainted bytes. We denote it as *tmg(tainted memory garget)*. It can be expressed as *<start, end>*, where *start* indicates the starting address of this area and *end* indicates the ending address. We extract all the *tmg*, denoted as *TMG*, from *GTSR*, and will utilize them to accommodate shellcode and trampoline instructions. Path constraints are identified by analyzing the executed path indicated by *iTPG*. We discuss it in the next section.

4   Constraint Generation

The exploits are generated by modifying relevant input bytes. The modifications should satisfy specified predicates that guarantee the program can execute to the hijacking point, especially when the input contains checksum fields. To ensure the hijacking point is reachable, we identify all "input-derived" branches within the path to the hijacking point, and generalize the constraints which reflect all the corresponding branch-taken results.

We denote "input-derived" branches as *tainted branches*. At each *tainted branch*, we identify the relevant input bytes that influence its branch-taken result, and generalize the corresponding constraints. A *tainted branch* instruction corresponds to an *iTPG* node in *iTPG*. Backtracking along *iTPG* from this node to taint source nodes, we can obtain the relevant input bytes and an *iTPG* nodes sequence which represents a trace of recorded tainted instructions. The trace can be used to symbolically generalize constraints for this *tainted branch*. In this paper, we utilize Z3 [11] which is a high-performance SMT solver to achieve this. First, we assign the relevant input bytes to different symbolic variables, and then perform concolic symbolic execution for each tainted instruction within the trace. At the branch instruction, since the corresponding bits in EFLAGS indicate the branch-taken result, we generate constraint formulas according to their values in SMT format [3].

Path constraints generated at *tainted branches* definitely guarantee that the hijacking point can be reached. However, it may have side effects, such as the following example.

```
    if(strcmp(taintstr,"http"))
        goto loc_1;
    else
        goto loc_2;
loc_1:
    //do sth causing the return address overwritten.
    // ...
    return; // hijacking point!
    // ...
loc_2:
    return;
```

If taintstr is "xttp", the hijacking point can be reached and the corresponding constraint will be generated as "$taintstr[0]! = h$" at one branch instruction in *strcmp*. However, according to the constraint, when taintstr is "hxtp", the hijacking point cannot be reached which is obviously incorrect. If we generalize constraints when *strcmp* returns instead of generalizing constraints at *tainted branches* within *strcmp*, we can obtain "$taintstr[0]! = h || taintstr[1]! = t || taintstr[2]! = t || taintstr[3]! = p$" which makes more sense.

To solve this problem, we perform constraint generation primarily at *tainted branches*, and secondarily at *tainted library calls*. When a tainted library function is called, we pause *tainted branches* constraint generation procedure, and identify the return address and the arguments of the function. When the function returns, we generate constraint formulas with the tainted arguments as symbolic variables according to the function's semantics and return result. After that, we resume *tainted branches* constraint generation. In our implementation, we handle comparison library functions for strings or memory such as *strcmp*, *strncmp*, *memcpy* etc. They are commonly used in vulnerable programs and influence whether hijacking points can be reached.

5   Exploit Generation

The exploit generation procedure is conducted when one hijacking point is detected. According to current execution context, we construct a trampoline instruction chain consisting of different trampoline instructions to redirect the control flow to the shellcode. Diverse patterns of trampoline instruction chains enable the variety of generated exploits. Together with the shellcode, the trampoline instructions within an adopted trampoline instruction chain should be accommodated into the tainted memory regions, since they must be contained within the exploit.

To construct the exploit, we find all relevant input bytes for the shellcode and the trampoline instructions within the chain. Then, we modify them to the appropriate values to ensure the expected exploiting procedure, i.e., when the vulnerable program runs with the generated exploit, 1)the utilized trampoline instructions and the shellcode can appear at the expected locations, 2)the control flow can be taken over at the hijacking point, and 3)the trampoline instructions are executed one by one until the execution of the shellcode eventually.

5.1   Trampoline Instruction Chain Construction

We mainly leverage three types of trampoline instructions to construct a trampoline instruction chain.

- {call/jmp register} For this type of trampoline instructions, the only operand is register. Normally, eight general registers can be used as the operands of the call/jmp instructions. Therefore, we can obtain 16 trampoline instructions.
- {call/jmp [register + offset]} The only indirect memory operand is decided by eight general registers and an offset. In this paper, the offset range is set between -256 and 256, and then we can construct 8192 trampoline instructions.
- {successive instructions sequence} Each trampoline of this type is a sequence of successive instructions in the code sections loaded into the process address space. They act as one instruction during executing, so we regard them as one trampoline instruction. We only consider one trampoline instruction of this type, i.e., *pop*, *pop*, *ret*, in this paper. It is commonly utilized for SEH exploits.

Given a trampoline instruction I, we can accurately compute its execution target address which is denoted as $I.target$ in the current runtime context. Only when $I.target$ is in one tmg, i.e., $tmg.start \leq I.target < tmg.end$, it is considered as a candidate for constructing a trampoline instruction chain. We denote this tmg as $I.tmg$. Therefore, we can obtain a set of candidate trampoline instructions $Cand = \{I | tmg.start \leq I.target < tmg.end, tmg \in TMG\}$.

We denote a trampoline instruction chain as $TrampChain = I_0, I_1 \cdots, I_n$, where $1 \leq n \leq |Cand|$, $I_0, I_1 \cdots, I_n \in Cand$ and different from one another. A successful execution redirection by them is illustrated with the dotted line in Figure 3, where $I.addr$ represents the I's memory address in the process address space and $I.code$ represents the opcode of I. We can obtain the following characteristics:

(i)$I_0.addr$ replaced the tainted data used in indirect control transfer(i.e., the tainted return address or function pointer).

(ii)$I_{j+1}.code$ is accommodated at $I_j.target$, where $0{\leq}j{<}n$;

(iii)shellcode s is accommodated at $I_n.target$.

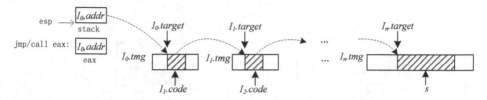

Fig. 3. The demonstration of a *TrampChain*

Inspired by the characteristics above, we construct *TrampChains* by analyzing all the possibilities of combining different candidate trampoline instructions in *Cand*. Then we select the *TrampChains* that meet the following three criteria.

(i) $I_0.addr$ can be found in the non-randomized modules loaded into the process address space;

(ii) $len(I_{j+1}.code) \leq I_j.tmg.end - I_j.target$, for $1{<}j{<}n$;

(iii) $I_n.tmg.end - I_n.tmg.start >= len(s)$;

There may be address conflicts in accommodating the trampoline instructions in a *TrampChain*. We mainly consider two cases of address conflicts:(i) I_j and I_k are accommodated in the same *tmg* and I_j is overlapped by I_k, where $0{<}j{<}k{\leq}n$, (ii)I_j is overlapped by the return address pushed when one *call* trampoline instruction I_m executes. We solve these conflicts as follows.

The address conflicts for case (i) contain two situations respectively shown in Figure 4(a),(b). For the former situation, i.e., $I_{k-1}.target < I_{j-1}.target < (I_{k-1}.target + len(I_k.code))$, we try to put $I_k.code$ into another memory area in this *tmg* which is long enough and not occupied by trampoline instructions, for instance, at $I_{k-1}.target'$. Meanwhile, we utilize an extra *jmp* instruction which is accommodated at $I_{k-1}.target$ to reach that position. For the latter situation, i.e., $I_{j-1}.target \leq I_{k-1}.target < (I_{j-1}.target + len(I_j.code))$, it cannot be solved and the corresponding trampoline instruction chain under construction cannot be used to generate a valid exploit.

For the case (ii), for any $0{<} j \leq n$, if $j{>}m{\geq}0$, the return address of I_m will corrupt I_j that has not executed, so the trampoline instruction chain will be destroyed. This address conflict cannot be solved and we discard the chain. However, if $j{<}m{\leq}n$, since I_j finishes executing before I_m, the execution flow to the shellcode will not be influenced. In this situation, we enlarge the length of I_j from $len(I_j)$ to $len(I_j)'$, as is shown in Figure 5. We then use $len(I_j)'$ to solve the following address conflicts related to I_j.

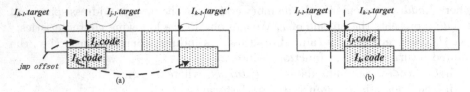

Fig. 4. Address conflicts for case(i) and the solutions

Fig. 5. Address conflicts for case(ii) and the solutions

Diverse trampoline instruction chains can contribute to polymorphic exploit generation for the vulnerable program. Meanwhile, we know that the size of $I_n.tmg$ may be larger than $len(s)$. Besides $I_n.target$, s has multiple alternatives to locate itself, i.e., the addresses before or after $I_n.target$, as is shown in Figure 6. We can enumerate all alternative positions for locating s in $I_n.tmg$ to enable more exploits by leveraging an extra jmp instruction at $I_n.target$ if needed. Address conflicts may happen in this situation as well. We use a similar approach to resolve them.

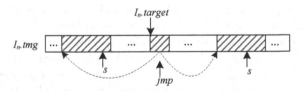

Fig. 6. Multiple alternatives for shellcode location in $I_n.tmg$

Although tmgs may be loaded at different places because of stack or heap randomization when the program runs again, the offset between $I.target$ and $I.tmg.start$ will keep the same. After I_0 seizes the program's execution, the other trampolines within the $TrampChain$ can be surely executed one after another as expected and the shellcode will get executed ultimately.

5.2   Exploit Construction

If the hijacking point is detected and we finish accommodating the trampoline instruction chain and the shellcode without address conflicts in the tainted memory regions, we can finally construct the exploit by modifying all relevant input bytes.

Figure 7 demonstrates the exploit construction. The hacked return address or function pointer is replaced by $I_0.addr$. The other instructions within the *TrampChain* and the shellcode are correspondingly accommodated at the previous instruction's target address. Any tainted byte *tb* is relevant to specific input bytes $in_i, ..., in_j$ and satisfy the formula $value(tb)=f(value(in_i), ..., value(in_j))$, as is discussed in Section 3. We collect all such formulas for all accommodated bytes and submit them to a SMT solver [11] together with the path constraints that guarantee the hijacking point can be reached. If we successfully obtain the satisfying answers to all relevant input bytes, the exploit can be constructed by only modifying these input bytes to such new values.

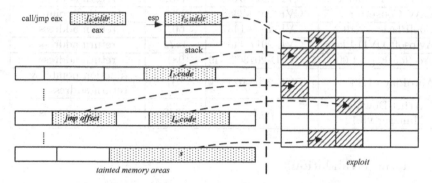

Fig. 7. The demonstration of exploit construction

Note our method can also be applied when only partial bytes(i.e., not 4-bytes) are controlled in the hacked return address or function pointer, which traditionally means insufficient control over the program's execution so that exploiting cannot be successful. We enumerate all possible values of the hacked return address or function pointer by altering the values of its controlled bytes. If there exists one alternative equivalent to one available trampoline's address, we are able to hijack the program's execution and conduct the following execution flow redirection. Our current approach for this case works well in the systems without module randomization. We leave that as our future work.

6   Evaluation

We developed PolyAEG based on QEMU [4]. We modified QEMU to support process identification, dynamic instrumentation, system call interception and dynamic taint analysis. We use Z3 [11] to generalize path constraints and query satisfying answers. We searched trampolines' addresses from the modules loaded into the vulnerable process. We generate trampolines' opcodes according to Intel assembly syntax. Shellcodes are selected from Metasploit [1]. We produce diverse exploit data containing trampolines and shellcode based on the program input, and eventually write them into files respectively as final multiple exploits. In all, PolyAEG consists of approximately 30,000 lines of C/C++ code. We evaluated PolyAEG on a Linux machine with a 3.2 GHz Intel(R) Core(TM) i5-3470 CPU, 500 GB hard disk and 4 GB RAM. We used 8 real world vulnerable programs. Their information are shown in Table 1. They all were performed in Windows XP SP2, QEMU's guest OS.

Table 1. List of programs that PolyAEG generated exploits for

Program	Advisory ID.	Input Size	Type of hijacking points
IrfanView v3.99	CVE-2007-2363	2648	return address
Mp3 CD Ripper v2.6	CVE-2011-5165	4432	return address
WAV Converter v1.5	CVE-2010-2348	8208	function pointer
CoolPlayer v2.19.2	CVE-2009-1437	601	return address
Aviosoft DVD Player	CVE-2011-4496	1472	return address
FreefloatFtp v1.00	CNNVD-201302-349	981	return address
AutoPlay v1.33	CVE-2009-0243	701	function pointer & return address
Internet Download Manager v6.12	N/A	2340	return address

6.1   Method Validation

We use a test case to illustrate the process of exploit generation for vulnerable programs. For convenience, we present it using the statistics collected from the runtime context. They might be different as the program runs again. However, the offset between a trampoline's target and the corresponding tmg's starting address would be unchanged, as mentioned in Section 5. It guarantees the correct execution flow redirection.

Freefloat Ftp will crash when it processes malformed remote user commands. In this experiment, we sent a user command(a string consisting of 1024 'A')that could crash it. PolyAEG performed dynamic taint analysis and showed that when "ret 0x8" at 0x00402ebb was executed, the taint data '0x41414141' would be loaded to EIP as a return address. Therefore, PolyAEG detected one hijacking point.

We used 338-bytes shellcode $BIND$ shown in Table 5 to produce exploits. Table 2 shows candidate trampoline instructions for the vulnerable program. We denote $Cand_L$ as the set of trampoline instructions whose corresponding tmg's size is larger than the shellcode, while $Cand_S$ is the ones whose corresponding tmg's size is smaller than that. We know that $call\ esp$ and $call\ [ebp+0x14]$ could be employed as I_n within $TrampChain$, since their corresponding tmgs were large enough to accommodate the shellcode. In addition, only the addresses of $call\ edi$ and $call\ esp$ were available in the code sections of the process address space, they could be employed as I_0 within $TrampChain$. After analyzing different possibilities to construct $TrampChain$s with these trampolines, we obtained four effective $TrampChain$s shown in Table 3, with $\#exploit$ representing the corresponding count of generated exploits.

Table 2. The *Cand* of Freefloat Ftp when using shellcode *BIND*

Cand	trampoline	target	tmg
$Cand_S$	call edi	0x911b24	<0x911b24,0x911c4d>
$Cand_L$	call esp	0xc0fc2c	<0xc0fb25,0xc0fef9>
	call [ebp+0x14]	0x911850	<0x911735,0x911b09>

We choose the fourth *TrampChain* shown in Table 3 to elaborate the execution flow redirection. The trampolines applied within the *TrampChain* were shown in Table 4. For *call esp*, as I_0, we used its address 0x7c934393 which was found in ntdll module and placed it at the stack space where stored the tainted return address, i.e., 0xc0fc20. As for *call edi* and *call [ebp+0x14]*, they were put at the previous instruction's target respectively. We used their opcodes. The execution flow was redirected as follows: *call esp* initially hijacked the program's execution when "ret 0x8" was called. The execution flow reached 0xc0fc2c where *call edi* was placed. Then *call [ebp+0x14]* at 0x911b24 gained the execution flow after executing *call edi*. Finally, the shellcode located at 0x911850, the target address of *call [ebp+0x14]*, got executed successfully.

Table 3. *TrampChain*s and the corresponding number of generated exploits

TrampChain	#exploit
call esp	128
call esp − > call [ebp+0x14]	37
call edi − > call [ebp+0x14]	102
call esp − > call edi − > call [ebp+0x14]	100

Multiple alternatives in *tmg*<0x911735,0x911b09> were available for accommodating the shellcode besides 0x911850. We put the shellcode at other places in this *tmg* and leveraged an extra *jmp* at 0x911850 to reach the shellcode. Thus, we obtained multiple exploits (i.e., 100) under this *TrampChain*.

The exploits were eventually constructed by modifying all relevant input bytes according to the path constraints and the data dependencies between accommodated bytes and the program input. We validate them by running the vulnerable program. They turned out to be effective and could be applied to exploit the program.

Table 4. The statistics of trampolines in the 4th *TrampChain*

I	trampoline	target	address	contents of I
I_0	call esp	0xc0fc2c	0xc0fc20	\x93\x43\x93\x7c
I_1	call edi	0x911b24	0xc0fc2c	\xff\xd7
I_2	call [ebp+0x14]	0x911850	0x911b24	\x33\xc0\xc6\xc0\x14\xff\x14\x28

Diverse patterns of *TrampChain*s and multiple choices for shellcode accommodations contribute to polymorphic exploit generation. Note that the length of the shellcode decides the last trampoline leveraged(i.e., I_n) to construct a *TrampChain*. Thus, if another shellcode with a different length is leveraged, we can obtain another set of different *TrampChain*s. Further, more exploits are available.

6.2 Polymorphic Exploit Generation

PolyAEG generated polymorphic exploits for 8 real world vulnerable programs. It identified 9 hijacking points. Of these, AutoPlay had two hijacking points. Both of them could be leveraged to generate exploits. In the experiments, we used AutoPlay$_1$ and AutoPlay$_2$ to denote the program with different hijacking points. Exploits were generated by hijacking function pointers in WAV Converter and AutoPlay$_2$. In other programs, PolyAEG generated exploits by hijacking return addresses.

PolyAEG could generate exploits containing various shellcode. We selected one shellcode for each vulnerable program randomly. Their properties are shown in Table 5. Table 6 illustrates the statistics about polymorphic exploit generation. $|Patrn|$ is the number of effective *TrampChain*s and $\#exploit$ is the number of generated exploits. Among these vulnerable programs, PolyAEG generated the most exploits for IrfanView. The main reason is that IrfanView had a broad memory area to accommodate the shellcode. CoolPlayer had the second quantity of exploits with the most patterns of trampoline instruction chains. The produced exploits with various attacking patterns are beneficial for systematically evaluating the vulnerability in CoolPlayer.

Table 5. The properties of shellcodes

ID	Functionality	Length	ID	Functionality	Length
CMD	spawn a shell	21	CALC	pop up a calculator	226
MSG	pop up a message box	45	RVSE	bind reverse tcp	366
ADD	add a new local account	233	NTPD	popup a notepad	86
DWN	download and execute	297	BIND	listen at port 4444	338

As GS security cookie protection has been imported, the successful rate to exploit by hijacking an overflowed return address has reduced. Exploiting SEH(Structured Exception Handler) is a more effective and practical exploiting method. However, safeseh mechanism was introduced to prevent such exploits in Windows operating systems. Despite all this, SEH exploits can successfully be produced by our approach. Since not all modules loaded by a process arm with safeseh, we choose trampoline instructions in non-safeseh modules to bypass this protection mechanism. AutoPlay$_2$ and WAV Converter are such samples that we handled in this way.

Table 6. The statistics of polymorphic exploit generation for all programs

Program	shellcode	$|Patrn|$	#exploit	Program	shellcode	$|Patrn|$	#exploit
IrfanView	DWN	3	4724	Mp3CDRipper	ADD	1	3399
FreefloatFtp	BIND	4	367	WAVConverter	CALC	4	180
CoolPlayer	CMD	29	3750	Internet DMgr	NTPD	3	112
AutoPlay$_1$	MSG	3	282	Aviosoft DTV Player	RVSE	1	126
AutoPlay$_2$	MSG	1	64				

Address conflicts could be well addressed. For instance, in an exploit of WAV Converter, *pop,pop,ret* was used as the trampoline instruction to hijack the program's execution and it would be overwritten if shellcode were located at its target address. To solve this problem, the shellcode was stored at a address before *pop,pop,ret* and *jmp* was used to redirect the execution flow to the shellcode.

In conclusion, PolyAEG is capable of generating exploits automatically and polymorphically for vulnerable programs. The polymorphic exploits generated with various attacking patterns will be conductive to systematically assess the severity of the vulnerabilities.

6.3 Performance Overhead

The overhead is dominated by the cost on dynamic taint analysis and exploit generation. The former is basically decided by recording taint propagation, and the latter is mainly decided by solving constraints. Figure 8 shows the quantities of tainted instructions(*#tainted inst*), and the average counts of constraint formulas(*#constraints*) and symbolic variables(*#variables*) for one exploit generation. *#tainted insts* could reflect the overhead of taint propagation for the program. Both *#constraints* and *#variables* indicated the overhead of solving constraints to construct exploits.

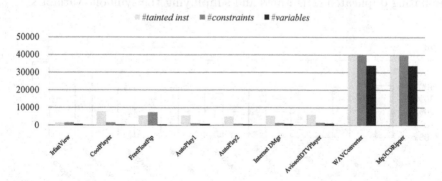

Fig. 8. The statistics about tainted instructions, constraint formulas and symbolic variables for all programs

Figure 9 presents the time overhead of generating one exploit for each program. Mp3 CD Ripper and WAV Converter cost far more time than the others because they cost the most both on dynamic taint analysis and constraint solving. Freefloat Ftp ranked third since it had to solve the most constraints amongst all the programs except for Mp3 CD Ripper and WAV Converter.

We evaluated memory overhead of polymorphic exploit generation for each program. We used %MEM, i.e., the program's share of the physical memory, to present memory cost. It was mainly dominated by the quantity of all produced exploits and the expense for each exploit generation. From Figure 10, we know that both of these factors contributed to the highest cost of Mp3 CD Ripper amongst these programs. In addition, AutoPlay2 not only cost the least memory on generating one exploit, which was indicated as Figure 8, but also had the least exploits. It thus consumed the lowest memory resource.

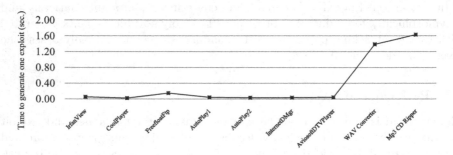

Fig. 9. The time overhead on one exploit generation

In summary, as an off-line exploits generation system, PolyAEG has reasonable overhead on both time and memory consuming. We currently have little consideration on optimization of constraint solving. We will further handle it by eliminating duplicated constraints and simplifying the symbolic variables.

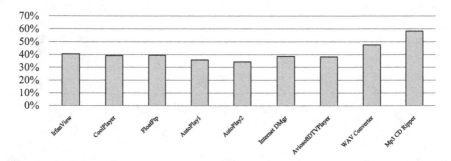

Fig. 10. The memory overhead on polymorphic exploit generation

7   Limitations and Future Work

Our approach has some limitations. First, PolyAEG generates control flow hijacking exploits. It makes limited effort to bypass ASLR and DEP. Second, partially controlling to a hacked return address or function pointer is an obstacle to exploiting. PolyAEG can produce exploits only under specified conditions. Third, shellcode is wholly stored. We do not consider the situation when shellcode is split into several units and placed into different tainted areas. In addition, PolyAEG does not identify all possible paths to a hijacking point due to high expense on whole-system symbolic execution [2,9]. But it generalizes path constraints that guarantee a reliable path to hijack program's execution.

We plan to extend PolyAEG to overcome those limitations in future work. We will also enhance PolyAEG to deal with more advanced exploitable situations about heap corruptions, use-after-free, and so on. Moveover, it is still an open problem to exploit non-control flow hijacked vulnerabilities, and we will do further research on it.

8   Related Work

Dynamic Taint Analysis. Dynamic taint analysis [16] can be used to tackle problems such as protocol reverse engineering, vulnerability detection, exploit generation, signature generation and so on. A few of general frameworks are available, such as [15,10,5,17,18]. TaintCheck [15] is one of the first dynamic taint analysis tools for protecting binary program from memory corruption attacks. TaintEraser [18] applies taint analysis for binaries to identify information leaks. Dytan [10] is flexible for taint analysis, allowing users to customize taint sources, sinks and propagation policy. Minemu [5] provides fastest taint analysis despite the limited functionally.

libdft [13] is a fast and reusable data flow tracking framework. It provides API for building dynamic taint analysis tools, e.g., libdft-DTA, and can be tailored to implement problem-specific instances.

Our enhanced taint analysis techniques with supporting backtracking analysis can be applied to support various analysis situations. Specifically for exploit generation, it enable us to accurately identify control flow hijacking, path constraints and data flow dependency.

Automatic Exploit Generation. Avgerios et al. [2] proposed AEG for potential buggy programs. They used preconditioned symbolic execution to find exploitable paths and generated exploits by solving path predicate and exploit predicate. AEG worked solely on close source programs, and used hardened memory address of shellcode instead of trampolines, which would failed to exploit under address randomization. By contrast, PolyAEG aimed to generate exploits for vulnerable binary programs, and leveraged trampolines to redirect the execution flow to shellcode. Thus the generated exploits turned out to be more effective and practical to exploit a vulnerable program.

Heelan *et al.* [12] described a technique to automatically generate an exploit by given a crashing input for a vulnerable program by employing jump-to-register trampolines. However, few candidates for trampolines limited the ability of polymorphic exploit generation. PolyAEG provided multiple alternatives for trampolines, and leveraged them to construct diverse trampoline instruction chains. It not only increased the successful rate to generate one effective exploit, but enabled to generate multiple exploits which contributed to systematical evaluation of the severity of the vulnerability.

Cha *et al.* implemented MAYHEM [9] for finding exploitable bugs in binary programs and proving with working shell-spawning exploits. They proposed hybrid symbolic execution and index-based memory modeling that made exploitable bugs discovered efficiently. However, the exploit generation policy was similar to related works above. Thus, polymorphic exploit generation was not addressed in their system.

Brumley *et al.* [8,7,6]and Lin *et al.* [14] also gave solutions to automatic exploit generation problems. However, the exploits they generated in their works were not the same with ours. Their exploits were simply aimed to make the program run in an unsafe state, such as crashing or consuming 100% CPU, instead of executing a injecting shellcode.

9   Conclusions

We propose PolyAEG, a system that automatically generates multiple exploits for a vulnerable program using one corresponding abnormal input. To generate different polymorphic exploits, we fully leverage trampolines to construct diverse trampoline instruction chains in order to hijack execution flow and redirect it to shellcode within the runtime context. We used PolyAEG to successfully generate exploits for 8 vulnerable binary programs. In particular, we have generated 4,724 exploits using only one abnormal input for IrfanView, a widely used picture viewer.

Acknowledgments. This research was supported by the National Program on Key Basic Research Project (Grant No. 2012CB315804), the Major Research Plan of the National Natural Science Foundation of China (Grant No. 91118006), the National Natural Science Foundation of China (Grant No. 61073179), and the Beijing Municipal Natural Science Foundation (Grant No. 4122086).

References

1. Metasploit, http://www.metasploit.com/
2. Avgerinos, T., Cha, S., Hao, B., Brumley, D.: Aeg: Automatic exploit generation. In: Proc. of Network and Distributed System Security Symposium, NDSS (2011)
3. Barrett, C., Stump, A., Tinelli, C.: The smt-lib standard: Version 2.0. In: Proceedings of the 8th International Workshop on Satisfiability Modulo Theories, vol. 13 (2010)

4. Bellard, F.: Qemu, a fast and portable dynamic translator. USENIX (2005)
5. Bosman, E., Slowinska, A., Bos, H.: Minemu: The world's fastest taint tracker. In: Sommer, R., Balzarotti, D., Maier, G. (eds.) RAID 2011. LNCS, vol. 6961, pp. 1–20. Springer, Heidelberg (2011)
6. Brumley, D., Newsome, J., Song, D., Wang, H., Jha, S.: Towards automatic generation of vulnerability-based signatures. In: 2006 IEEE Symposium on Security and Privacy, pp. 15–16 (May 2006)
7. Brumley, D., Newsome, J., Song, D., Wang, H., Jha, S.: Theory and techniques for automatic generation of vulnerability-based signatures. IEEE Transactions on Dependable and Secure Computing 5(4), 224–241 (2008)
8. Brumley, D., Poosankam, P., Song, D., Zheng, J.: Automatic patch-based exploit generation is possible: Techniques and implications. In: IEEE Symposium on Security and Privacy, SP 2008, pp. 143–157 (May 2008)
9. Cha, S.K., Avgerinos, T., Rebert, A., Brumley, D.: Unleashing mayhem on binary code. In: 2012 IEEE Symposium on Security and Privacy (SP), pp. 380–394. IEEE (2012)
10. Clause, J., Li, W., Orso, A.: Dytan: a generic dynamic taint analysis framework. In: Proceedings of the 2007 International Symposium on Software Testing and Analysis, pp. 196–206. ACM (2007)
11. de Moura, L., Bjørner, N.: Z3: An efficient SMT solver. In: Ramakrishnan, C.R., Rehof, J. (eds.) TACAS 2008. LNCS, vol. 4963, pp. 337–340. Springer, Heidelberg (2008)
12. Heelan, S.: Automatic generation of control flow hijacking exploits for software vulnerabilities. PhD thesis, University of Oxford (2009)
13. Kemerlis, V.P., Portokalidis, G., Jee, K., Keromytis, A.D.: libdft: Practical dynamic data flow tracking for commodity systems. In: Proceedings of the 8th ACM SIGPLAN/SIGOPS Conference on Virtual Execution Environments, pp. 121–132. ACM (2012)
14. Lin, Z., Zhang, X., Xu, D.: Convicting exploitable software vulnerabilities: An efficient input provenance based approach. In: IEEE International Conference on Dependable Systems and Networks With FTCS and DCC, DSN 2008, pp. 247–256 (June 2008)
15. Newsome, J., Song, D.: Dynamic taint analysis for automatic detection, analysis, and signature generation of exploits on commodity software. In: Network and Distributed System Security Symposium (NDSS 2005). Internet Society (2005)
16. Schwartz, E.J., Avgerinos, T., Brumley, D.: All you ever wanted to know about dynamic taint analysis and forward symbolic execution (but might have been afraid to ask). In: 2010 IEEE Symposium on Security and Privacy (SP), pp. 317–331 (May 2010)
17. Zavou, A., Portokalidis, G., Keromytis, A.D.: Taint-exchange: A generic system for cross-process and cross-host taint tracking. In: Iwata, T., Nishigaki, M. (eds.) IWSEC 2011. LNCS, vol. 7038, pp. 113–128. Springer, Heidelberg (2011)
18. Zhu, D.Y., Jung, J., Song, D., Kohno, T., Wetherall, D.: Tainteraser: protecting sensitive data leaks using application-level taint tracking. ACM SIGOPS Operating Systems Review 45(1), 142–154 (2011)

A Novel Web Tunnel Detection Method Based on Protocol Behaviors

Fei Wang[*], Liusheng Huang, Zhili Chen, Haibo Miao, and Wei Yang

National High Performance Computing Center at Hefei,
Department of Computer Science and Technology,
University of Science and Technology of China,
Hefei, Anhui, 230027, P.R. China
wf616528291@gmail.com

Abstract. The web tunnel is a common attack technique in the Internet and it is very easy to be implemented but extremely difficult to be detected. In this paper, we propose a novel web tunnel detection method which focuses on protocol behaviors. By analyzing the interaction processes in web communications, we give a scientific definition to web sessions that are our detection objects. Under the help of the definition, we extract four first-order statistical features which are widely used in previous research of web sessions. Utilizing the packet lengths and inter-arrival times in the transport layer, we divide TCP packets into different classes and discover some statistical correlations of them in order to extract another three second-order statistical features of web sessions. Further, the seven features are regarded as a 7-dimentional feature vector. Exploiting the vector, we adopt a support vector machine classifier to distinguish tunnel sessions from legitimate web sessions. In the experiment, our method performs very well and the detection accuracies of HTTP tunnels and HTTPS tunnels are 82.5% and 91.8% respectively when the communication traffic is above 500 TCP packets.

Keywords: web tunnel detection, protocol behaviors, packet analysis, feature vector, support vector machine.

1 Introduction

In contemporary, people rely more and more on computers and the Internet. Network applications such as webpage browsing, business e-mail exchanging, microblog posting and online shopping become indispensable elements in people's jobs and daily lives. The accelerating rise in the demand for those techniques motivates diverse attacks from malicious users. The attackers utilize the legitimate-looking traffic generated by application-layer protocols (ALP) widely used in the Internet to launch imperceptible intrusions like implanting computer viruses, exposing sensitive information and filching confidential files.

At present, firewalls and application level gateways (ALG) configured to secure network boundaries can frustrate most bare attacks, for example downloading Trojans

---

[*] Corresponding author.

T. Zia et al. (Eds.): SecureComm 2013, LNICST 127, pp. 234–251, 2013.
© Institute for Computer Sciences, Social Informatics and Telecommunications Engineering 2013

from offensive websites and access violations from the extranet to the intranet. In their existing incarnations, they usually protect local networks from damages by concentrating on controlling which websites local hosts are allowed to visit and which ALPs are permitted for communications. In order to achieve this goal, security policies of firewalls and ALGs are commonly implemented as filter criteria intercepting packets containing prohibited IP addresses or typical features of unapproved ALPs. In general, the two categories of devices operate cooperatively to enforce the criteria: the firewall checks IP addresses and port numbers while the ALG judges whether the traffic of a certain protocol conforms to the corresponding rules. For instance, in the case of a network only approving the non-encrypted Internet browsing, the firewall is the first defensive line which merely hands outgoing (ingoing) TCP packets, to (from) port 80 or 8080 at IP addresses not in the forbidden set, over to the ALG. The ALG then scrutinizes the format of the HTTP content in order to ensure that the peers are really "speaking" HTTP. Additionally, the ALG can also rule out potential malicious behaviors by denying particular strings in some vulnerable fields such as URLs, Hosts, User-Agents and values of different keys.

Upon most occasions, firewalls and ALGs can deal with bare intrusions with ease. However, some artful covered attacks have been devised in the past decade. Those techniques can successfully bypass the filter criteria utilized in firewalls and ALGs as legitimate applications and the application-layer tunnel (ALT) is a celebrated one among them. Nowadays, the ALT has become a threat which can't be overlooked to the Internet. The ALT is easy to be implemented but extremely difficult to be detected. The main idea of the ALT is disguising an ALP as another. The technique carries out the tunneling process by encapsulating the traffic of prohibited ALPs inside the payload of allowed ALPs. What's more, the formats of the embedded traffic can be various so that the ALT can perform obfuscation of original data to thwart pattern-matching classifiers based on the formats of ALPs employed by ALGs. The ALT can be implemented in two ways: one is in clear-text ALPs (CALT) and the other is in encrypted ALPs (EALT). As Fig. 1 shows, the CALT has a transport-layer shell and an unsuspicious header of a permitted clear-text ALP and the forbidden traffic is camouflaged in the body of entity data. Illustrated in Fig. 1, the EALT only has a transport-layer shell of an allowed encrypted ALP while the encrypted payload

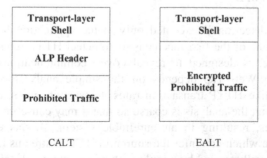

Fig. 1. The message structure of the two kinds of ALTs

is actually the encrypted prohibited traffic. In practice, because of the ubiquity of the web usage, the HTTP tunnel and the HTTPS tunnel are prevalent implementations for the CALT and the EALT respectively. As a result, the detection method we propose in this paper is aimed at the two ALT implementations.

1.1   Outline of Our Contributions

We propose a novel detection method to thwart web tunnels. Our technique is designed based on the protocol behaviors of HTTP and HTTPS. By analyzing the interaction processes in web communications, we give a scientific definition to web sessions which are our detection objects. Under the help of the definition, we firstly extract four first-order statistical features which are widely used in previous research of web sessions. Further, we concentrate on the TCP packets in the transport layer. Utilizing the packet lengths and inter-arrival times, we divide TCP packets into different classes and dig out the statistical correlations of them. With these correlations, we extract another three second-order statistical features of web sessions. Then, the seven features we have obtained can compose a 7-dimentional feature vector and we believe that the vector can fully reflect the statistical characteristics of web traffic. Exploiting the vector, we adopt a support vector machine classifier to distinguish tunnel sessions from legitimate web sessions. In our method, the detection rates of HTTP tunnels and HTTPS tunnels can reach above 80% and 90% respectively when the communication traffic is above 500 TCP packets.

1.2   Paper Organization

The rest of this paper is organized as follows. Section 2 summarizes the related work. Section 3 introduces some important notions and techniques used in this paper. Section 4 describes the work flow of our detection method. Section 5 discusses the process of the protocol feature extraction. Section 6 shows the detection results of our method. Section 7 is the conclusion.

2   Related Work

Early web tunnel detection is executed only at the application layer. Borders and Prakash proposed one of the first mechanisms to detect HTTP tunnels, named "Web Tap" [1]. The filter is designed to reveal covert communications tunneled in the HTTP traffic. The Web Tap depends on the simple analysis of features at the application layer, like HTTP transaction rates, transaction times, access frequency, etc. Strictly speaking, the analysis is coarse so that it may cause many false positives and false negatives, resulting in an unreliable system. Bissias et al. invented a statistical technique which can infer the source in HTTPS streams [2]. The technique shapes a website usually visited by a tuple with two elements: the size profile and the time profile. Given a website, the authors collect the HTTP packet sequences composing each HTTP request for the website. Then the mean value sequence of the lengths of these packets is the size profile and the mean value sequence of the inter-arrival times between the same packets is the time profile. HTTPS traces to be tested will be compared to the shapes of websites with the similarity computed from the cross-correlation between the sequences, making it possible to discover the destination. Subsequently, Liberatore et al. improved the technique and they extended the work to each URL to assign a given trace to a gathered profile, the Jaccard and the naïve Bayes similarity metrics [3]. Campos et al. exploited a clustering scheme to recognize different traffic patterns by a sequence of application-layer triples containing interactive features between peers: the length of data from the client, the length of data from the server and the time interval between data pairs [4].

Recently, researchers turned to the transport layer in order to devise advanced detection techniques and many methods based on both application-layer features and transport-layer features were worked out. McGregor et al. used many features of TCP packets to cluster the traffic so as to identify different ALPs [5]. The features include packet length, length percentile, etc. Moore and Zuev proposed a naive Bayes classifier to recognize ALPs and the results of classification were excellent [6]. The method firstly deploys some deep inspection in the TCP packets to dig out almost all the available features in TCP flows. Then it utilizes statistical approaches to kick out irrelevant factors in the feature vector, which can significantly improve the performance. Wright et al. adopted a similar technique to propose a k-nearest-neighbors classifier according to the K-L distance between feature vectors form different ALPs and the technique performed well in the identification of HTTP and HTTPS [7].

Most of the techniques listed above are utilized for traffic classification. They operate on the features collected from massive packets generated by ALPs and the experimental results are considerable. Nevertheless, the effects on the ALT of these classifiers have not been demonstrated. The ALT has the same transport-layer shell as that of normal ALPs, which may disable the classifiers. The detection method which is really effective on the HTTP tunnels was proposed by Crotti et al [8]. The technique runs on the fingerprint of ALPs and has a high detection rate against the HTTP tunnel. The fingerprint is trained from single TCP flows and it consists of two elements: TCP packet length sequence and TCP packet inter-arrival time sequence. Although the method can find out most HTTP tunnels, it still has some flaws in the fingerprint measurement which is its core concept. The packet classification in the fingerprint evaluation is coarse and the technique ignores many remarkable protocol behaviors in HTTP, so the fingerprint detection is inefficient and it is vulnerable in theory.

3   Preliminaries

In this section, we will introduce some important notions and useful techniques which can help us expose protocol behaviors in HTTP utilized in our detection method.

3.1   HTTP Flow and HTTP Session

In the fingerprint detection technique, the authors define an HTTP flow by a pair of reversed TCP flows: the client to the server and the server to the client. In computer networks, a TCP flow can be defined as a tetrad: source IP address, destination IP address, source port number and destination port number, while absolutely an HTTP flow can't be defined in the same way. When browsing a website, the requests for associated objects of an HTML file can be sent on other ports different from the original one which sends the request for the text webpage. Especially, in the keep-alive visiting method, requests for different HTML files may be sent on the same port. In addition, the HTTP server can also be a set of hosts. As we know, the associated objects of HTML files can be stored in different servers (it is extremely popular for large websites). As a result, the requests for an HTML file can refer to more than one server and we can't define the HTTP server as a single host. From the above, the definition of HTTP flows in the fingerprint detection technique is obviously unreasonable and it will doubtlessly lose many crucial characteristics of HTTP flows.

The scenario in Fig. 2 shows the amounts of HTTP requests at different times when a client is browsing a website. In this figure, we can see that the request distribution has crests and troughs. Each crest is a busy time interval with the outburst in requests and every trough is a silent period containing no requests. In terms of the behaviors of HTTP, a crest represents the requests for an integrated HTML file including the text webpage and its associated objects, while a trough between two consecutive crests is the time for visitors to handle the documents, such as reading news, thinking over a problem and saving elements. According to this, an HTTP flow can be defined as a pair of crests: a request crest in the client and the corresponding response crest in the server. The definition is not limited to a tetrad and it can scientifically describe the features in HTTP. The trough is called "Think Time" [4] and it is a significant factor in the analysis of HTTP flows. In practice, the length of the silent period is flexible and it differs from user to user. Therefore, the "Think Time" is not a main object in the study of HTTP, but it is only used to separate different HTTP flows. HTTP flows will be cut into pieces if the "Think Time" is too short. Considering the response time of the human body and the network delay, we hold the view that a reasonable "Think Time" should be longer than 5 seconds, which means that any two consecutive crests, with a trough less than or equal to 5 seconds between them, should belong to the same HTTP flow.

With the concepts discussed above, we can obtain the complete definition of HTTP flows. An HTTP flow consists of a series of requests from a client to a server and the corresponding responses from the server to the client. The interval between adjacent requests should not be more than 5 seconds. The client is a single host defined as an IP address. The server is a set of hosts with similar IP addresses. In general, the different servers in a large website are deployed in the same subnet. Hence, we can define the similar IP addresses as follows. If we have two IP addresses denoted by two 32-bit (IPV4) unsigned integers ipa and ipb, we will say they are similar when:

$$\begin{cases} ipa \oplus ipb \leq 255 & \text{if } ipa \text{ and } ipb \text{ both belong to Class C} \\ ipa \oplus ipb \leq 65535 & \text{if } ipa \text{ and } ipb \text{ both belong to Class B} \\ ipa \oplus ipb \leq 16777215 & \text{if } ipa \text{ and } ipb \text{ both belong to Class A} \end{cases} \quad (1)$$

Where $\oplus$ is the operator of the binary "XOR". Owning the definition of HTTP flows, an HTTP session can be easily defined as a set of HTTP flows with the same client and server in a certain period (the interval between any adjacent flows in a session should be less than or equal to this period). In this paper, we set this period to half an hour. Since HTTPS is the encrypted version of HTTP and there is no essential discrepancy in them, HTTPS flows and sessions can be defined in the same way.

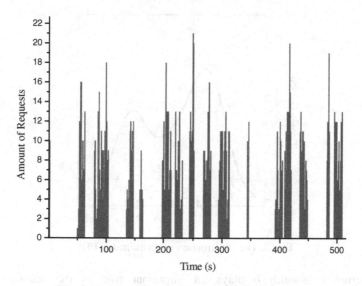

Fig. 2. The distribution of requests in the browsing

3.2   Kernel Density Estimation

The Kernel Density Estimation (KDE) is a practical method to approximate the distribution of a random variable [9]. Here, we can utilize the technique to estimate the probability density functions (PDF) of some crucial parameters in our detection method. For a random variable X, if we have n samples $\{x_1, x_2, \ldots, x_n\}$, then we can approximate the distribution of X by the KDE:

$$\widehat{f}(x) = \frac{1}{nh} \sum_{i=1}^{n} K(\frac{x - x_i}{h}) \tag{2}$$

Where $\widehat{f}(x)$ is the estimated PDF of X, h is called the kernel bandwidth, and $K(\cdot)$ is the kernel which can be any non-negative function satisfying:

$$\int_{-\infty}^{+\infty} K(g)\, dg = 1 \tag{3}$$

In general, the kernel is assumed as a Gaussian distribution whose standard deviation is 1, because Gaussian distribution has desirable smoothness properties:

$$K(g) = \frac{1}{\sqrt{2\pi}} e^{\frac{-g^2}{2}} \tag{4}$$

Figure 3 [9] illustrates how an estimate of the PDF is constructed. For each data point, a Gaussian distribution centered on the very point is fitted. The summation of those functions gives an estimate of the real PDF.

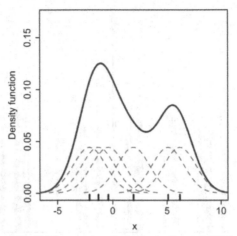

Fig. 3. The construction of an estimated PDF

The kernel bandwidth h plays an important role in the accuracy of the approximation. In practical estimation of the bandwidth, if the kernel is a Gaussian distribution, h can be optimized as [9]:

$$\hat{h} = (\frac{4\sigma^5}{3n})^{\frac{1}{5}} \approx 1.06\sigma n^{-\frac{1}{5}} \tag{5}$$

Where σ is the standard deviation of the samples.

4   Our Tunnel Detection Method

As mentioned before, our detection concentrates on the web tunnels (HTTP and HTTPS tunnels). If the length of a flow is short, the limited quantity of information in it will not sufficiently support us to judge whether it is a tunnel correctly. For this reason, our detection objects are HTTP and HTTPS sessions but not flows. Different from previous techniques, in our detection method, we discover some novel statistical features from protocol behaviors based on TCP packets in HTTP and HTTPS sessions. With these features, we can successfully identify the tunneled traffic in suspicious sessions. In the analysis of the TCP packets in sessions, we only focus on their lengths and inter-arrival times.

The work flow of our detection method is illustrated in Fig. 4. First, we collect plentiful legitimate sessions to obtain some significant statistical characteristics of

TCP packets in normal HTTP and HTTPS. Then, with the help of those characteristics, we extract seven features of suspicious sessions to be tested and those features are denoted by a 7-dimentional vector **FV**. Last, the vector **FV** is submitted to a classifier and the classifier identifies the types of the sessions. The classifier exploited here is a two-class Support Vector Machine (SVM) and we utilize the LIBSVM [10] as our tool. The SVM only identifies the suspicious sessions as two categories: normal HTTP (HTTPS) sessions and tunnel sessions, and the SVM is trained by feature vectors from the two categories of sessions in advance. We select the SVM as the classifier for our detection method due to its outstanding performance. Actually, if we collect tunnel sessions to compute the characteristics, the method can also operate well. But, after all, tunnel sessions are a tiny minority and to get massive normal HTTP and HTTPS sessions is much easier for us.

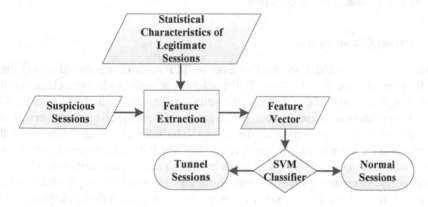

Fig. 4. The diagram of the work flow

5   Feature Extraction

In this section, we will discuss the seven features we collect from suspicious sessions. Four of the features are first-order statistics and the other three are second-order which can reveal the correlations between packets in sessions. The seven features are all extracted according to protocol behaviors. Hereafter, we use "HTTP" to represent both "HTTP" and "HTTPS".

5.1   First-Order Features

As Section 3 explains, HTTP requests can be sent in different ports and each port can send more than one request. In the observation of HTTP flows, we can find out that in a single TCP connection the next request will not be sent until the response from the server to the former one arrives. Specifically, if we denote a request by *req* and a response by *res*, in a TCP connection, we can only get the sequence (*req, res, req, res, req, res*), but can't get the sequence (*req, req, req, res, res, res*). Hence, we can easily calculate the sizes (Bytes) of requests and the sizes of their corresponding responses. Further, we can discover the following four first-order features in sessions.

Feature 1: Average Request Size (Req_{avg}). Req_{avg} is the arithmetic average of the sizes of HTTP requests in a session.

Feature 2: Request Size Variance (Req_{var}). Req_{var} is the variance of the sizes of HTTP requests in a session.

Feature 3: Average Response Size (Res_{avg}). Res_{avg} is the arithmetic average of the sizes of HTTP responses in a session.

Feature 4: Response Size Variance (Res_{var}). Res_{var} is the variance of the sizes of HTTP responses in a session.

The four simple features are widely used in previous work by other forms [1, 2, 3, 4, 5, 6]. The features are useful but obviously not enough because they don't have absolute exclusiveness in the detection.

5.2   Packet Classification

As what previous work did, in order to analyze TCP packets, we should divide them into different classes. We denote a TCP packet by a tuple with three elements: the packet length (exclude TCP header), the inter-arrival time and the direction. The direction here has two optional values: 0 (the packet is from the client to the server) and 1 (the packet is from the server to the client). The inter-arrival time represents the interval between the packet and the former one which has the same direction. We assume that there are no direct correlations between packets from different flows in a session, so the inter-arrival times are only computed in each flow respectively and the inter-arrival time of the first packet with either direction in each flow is regarded as 0. Flows are independent packet sequences in a session and flows are separated by the "Think Time". The TCP packets mentioned here do not contain the TCP control packets whose lengths are zero, such as SYN, FIN, RST and pure ACK, because they are irrelevant to HTTP behaviors. The coming problem is how to divide packet lengths and inter-arrival times into different bins. We utilize the KDE technique mentioned in Section 3. In the Ethernet, the maximum segment size (MSS) of TCP packet is 1460 bytes, so the packet lengths are between 1 and 1460. Owing to the "Think Time", the inter-arrival times are between 0 and 5000 (the unit is millisecond). The situation may happen that because of the network delay, the inter-arrival times of some packets from the server to the client in a flow may be a little longer than 5000ms, and we regard these times just as 5000ms. We select all the packets in the collected legitimate sessions as samples to estimate the PDF. We denote the counts of occurrences of the 1460 lengths and 5001 times by $\{CL_1, CL_2, ..., CL_{1460}\}$ and $\{CT_0, CT_2, ..., CT_{5000}\}$. Then, the PDF of the length $\widehat{f}(l)$ and the inter-arrival time $\widehat{f}(t)$ can be estimated by the KDE technique with the Gaussian kernel as the following formulas.

$$\widehat{f}(l) = \frac{1}{\sqrt{2\pi}\,\widehat{h}_l \sum\limits_{j=1}^{1460} CL_j} \sum_{i=1}^{1460} CL_i \times e^{\frac{-(l-i)^2}{2\widehat{h}_l^2}} \tag{6}$$

$$\widehat{f}(t) = \frac{1}{\sqrt{2\pi}\,\widehat{h}_t \sum_{j=0}^{5000} CT_j} \sum_{i=0}^{5000} CT_i \times e^{\frac{-(t-i)^2}{2\widehat{h}_t^2}} \tag{7}$$

The outline of the packet length division is as follows and the inter-arrival time division can be done by the same method.

Step 1. Calculate cumulative probability CP between 1 and 1460:

$$CP = \int_1^{1460} \widehat{f}(l)\, dl \tag{8}$$

Step 2. If we want to divide the lengths into b bins, we can split the interval [1, 1460] into b segments by $b-1$ cut points in ascending order $\{L_1, L_2, \ldots, L_{b-1}\}$. We can denote 1 and 1460 by L_0 and L_b, and then we can compute the cut points by:

$$\int_{L_i}^{L_{i+1}} \widehat{f}(l)\, dl = \frac{CP}{b} \quad (0 \le i \le b-1) \tag{9}$$

This division scheme is closely related to the real distribution of the two elements, which will help improve the detection performance remarkably. If we have BL bins of the packet lengths and BT bins of the inter-arrival times, we can obtain $2 \times BL \times BT$ classes of TCP packets. In the KDE of packet length, we rule out the packets from the servers because the overwhelming majority of them are in the size of 1460, which can cause the classification useless. It should be noted that $\widehat{f}(l)$ and $\widehat{f}(t)$ are non-integrable functions, so we adopt the infinitesimal method to compute the integral and the infinitesimal is 0.05. Then, in the collected legitimate sessions, we can count the packets and compute the occurrence probability of each class by the maximum likelihood estimation. In the estimation, we adopt the Good-Turing smoothing technique to handle the packet classes which are not observed [11].

5.3   Second-Order Features

The packet distribution is a typical feature in sessions. By the packet classification, we can get the occurrence probabilities of the $2 \times BL \times BT$ packets in legitimate sessions. Then we can utilize the K-L divergence to measure the difference between the packet distribution in suspicious sessions and that of legitimate sessions.

Feature 5: Packet Distribution Difference (D_{KL}). D_{KL} is the K-L divergence of legitimate packet distribution from suspicious packet distribution:

$$D_{KL} = \sum_{i=1}^{2 \times BL \times BT} P(i) \ln \frac{P(i)}{Q(i)} \tag{10}$$

Where $P(i)$ is the discrete probability density function of the packets in suspicious sessions and $Q(i)$ is the function for the normal ones. In the computation, we needn't take special handling on the situation $0 \ln 0$ because we have the equation:

$$\lim_{x \to 0^+} x \ln x = 0 \tag{11}$$

So, we can just interpret $P(i)\ln\dfrac{P(i)}{Q(i)}$ as zero when $P(i)$ is zero ($1 \le i \le 2 \times BL \times BT$).

Because we implement the Good-Turing smoothing technique in the maximum likelihood estimation, we can ensure that $Q(i) > 0$.

Flows in sessions can be expressed as different TCP packet sequences. HTTP has some particular interactive behaviors which can hardly be found in other ALPs. For example, when a packet from the server arrives at the client, the client will scan the data in the packet immediately. If some object links are in this packet or can be computed from the data in this packet, the client will send the requests on other ports dynamically regardless of whether the current response has been received integrally. In practice, these behaviors can be fully reflected by the packet sequences. So, we consider that the ordered packets in a flow are closely related and a packet is related to the ones nearby. In terms of protocol behaviors, correlations in packets are not merely restricted in the adjacent packets, but they are usually regarded as the collocations in some consecutive packets. In our detection method, we investigate pairs of packets within a certain range N (N is an integer greater than 1) in order to find out packet collocations in HTTP. For the analysis of collocations, we can adopt some techniques widely used in the statistical natural language processing [12].We define that any two packets in the same flow with a distance less than N is a packet pair and we denote a packet pair "xy" by an ordered pair $<x,y>$. These packet pairs are called N-Range Packet Pairs (N-RPP) [12]. Figure 5 illustrates an example for 3-RPPs, and in the dashed box we can observe three 3-RPPs: $<2,5>$, $<2,4>$ and $<5,4>$. The numbers in packet pairs here are labels of packet classes.

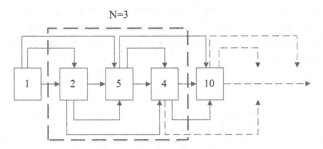

Fig. 5. An example for 3-RPPs

Because we have $2 \times BL \times BT$ packets, we can obtain $(2 \times BL \times BT)^2$ N-RPP theoretically. The occurrences of N-RPPs are prominent features in HTTP sessions. The entropy is usually utilized to evaluate the uncertainty and the potential regularity in random variables. For different protocols, the regularities of behaviors have significant difference, so we can also use the entropy to extract a feature of N-RPPs in sessions.

Feature 6: N-RPP Entropy ($E_{N\text{-}RPP}$). We regard the N-RPP as a random variable and $E_{N\text{-}RPP}$ is its entropy:

$$E_{N\text{-}RPP} = -\sum_{i=1}^{(2\times BL\times BT)^2} F(i)\log_2 F(i) \tag{12}$$

Where $F(i)$ is the occurrence probability of the ith N-RPP ($1\leq i \leq (2\times BL\times BT)^2$). Similar to Equation (11), when $F(i)$ is zero, we can treat $F(i)\log_2 F(i)$ as zero.

In the information theory, another measurement for discovering interesting collocations is the mutual information (MI). For two discrete random variables X and Y, the MI can be defined as:

$$MI(X;Y) = \sum_{y\in Y}\sum_{x\in X} p(x,y)\log_2 \frac{p(x,y)}{p(x)p(y)} \tag{13}$$

Where x and y represent all the possible values of X and Y. Here, $p(x,y)$, $p(x)$ and $p(y)$ are the occurrence probabilities of "xy", "x" and "y". However, the packets in a sequence are usually treated as different points. So, we utilize the pointwise mutual information (PMI) which is more suitable than the MI to evaluate the correlations of packets. The PMI between two particular points x and y can be defined as:

$$PMI(x;y) = \log_2 \frac{p(x,y)}{p(x)p(y)} \tag{14}$$

Here, in our case, we regard $p(x,y)$, $p(x)$ and $p(y)$ as the occurrence probabilities of the packet pairs "xy", "$x?$" and "$?y$", where the symbol "?" represents any packet.

Now we can obtain the definition of the N-Range Mutual Information (N-RMI). The N-RMI can be defined as the PMI of an N-RPP [12]. The N-RMI can measure the collocation degree of an N-RPP and the larger the N-RMI is, the more reasonable the occurrence of the corresponding N-RPP is. With the definition of the N-RMI, we can use Equation (14) to evaluate the N-RMI of a certain N-RPP $<x,y>$. Given an HTTP flow, we denote the counts of occurrences of any N-RPP, the N-RPPs $<x,y>$, $<x,?>$ and $<?,y>$ by C_{tot}, C_{xy}, $C_{x?}$ and $C_{?y}$ severally. Then, the N-RMI of the N-RPP $<x,y>$ can be calculated by [12]:

$$N\text{-}RMI_{<x,y>} = \log_2 \frac{p(x,y)}{p(x)p(y)} = \log_2 \frac{C_{xy}/C_{tot}}{(C_{x?}/C_{tot})(C_{?y}/C_{tot})} = \log_2 \frac{C_{xy}C_{tot}}{C_{x?}C_{?y}} \tag{15}$$

Here, we give an example to explain the computation of the N-RMI further. Given a packet sequence "2,5,1,3,4,15,103,19,2,3,3", we can evaluate the 4-RMI of the 4-RPP $<2,3>$. All the 4-RPPs in this flow are: $<2,5>$, $<2,1>$, $<2,3>$, $<5,1>$, $<5,3>$, $<5,4>$, $<1,3>$, $<1,4>$, $<1,15>$, $<3,4>$, $<3,15>$, $<3,103>$, $<4,15>$, $<4,103>$, $<4,19>$, $<15,103>$, $<15,19>$, $<15,2>$, $<103,19>$, $<103,2>$, $<103,3>$, $<19,2>$, $<19,3>$, $<19,3>$, $<2,3>$, $<2,3>$, $<3,3>$. Then, $C_{23}=3$, $C_{2?}=5$, $C_{?3}=8$ and $C_{tot}=27$, so we have:

$$4\text{-}RMI_{<2,3>} = \log_2 \frac{C_{tot}C_{23}}{C_{2?}C_{?3}} = \log_2 \frac{3\times 27}{5\times 8} = 1.0179 \tag{16}$$

If an N-RPP doesn't emerge in the legitimate sessions observed, we can infer that the appearance of the N-RPP is impossible and its occurrence is extremely anomalous. Therefore, instead of executing the smoothing technique in the computation of the packet distribution, we give a custom infinitesimal value INFS to the N-RPPs not observed as their N-RMIs. We can utilize the N-RMI to extract another feature of HTTP sessions.

Feature 7: N-RMI Distance ($D_{N\text{-}RMI}$). In a session, we may have many different N-RPPs. We select M N-RPPs which have the first M greatest N-RMIs in a suspicious session because we believe these N-RPPs can well present statistical correlations of this session. If a session only has S N-RPPs, where $S < M$, we'll regard the N-RPP with the smallest N-RMI in this session as the surplus $M - S$ N-RPPs. Then, $D_{N\text{-}RMI}$ can be defined as [12]:

$$D_{N\text{-}RMI} = \sum_{i=1}^{2\times BL\times BT} \sum_{j=1}^{2\times BL\times BT} | N\text{-}RMI_{<i,j>} - \overline{N\text{-}RMI_{<i,j>}} | \times \sigma(i,j) \qquad (17)$$

Where $N\text{-}RMI_{<i,j>}$ is the N-RMI of the N-RPP $<i,j>$ in the suspicious session and $\overline{N\text{-}RMI_{<i,j>}}$ is the N-RMI in legitimate sessions. The expression $\sigma(i,j)$ is evaluated as:

$$\sigma(i,j) = \begin{cases} 1 & \text{if } <i,j> \text{ is one of the } M \text{ selected N-RPPs} \\ 0 & \text{else} \end{cases} \qquad (18)$$

6   Experiment

6.1   Data Collection

The data collection is a crucial factor for our detection results, so it will be discussed with detail in this section. We deploy our packet sniffer on the gateway of our department which owns about 350 personal computers to collect legitimate HTTP and HTTPS sessions. Within a month, we collect 14462 HTTP and 9154 HTTPS legitimate sessions. Additionally, we generate some tunnel sessions: 200 HTTP (HTTPS) sessions with FTP encapsulated, 200 HTTP (HTTPS) sessions with SMTP encapsulated and 200 HTTP (HTTPS) sessions with POP3 encapsulated. The usage of those sessions is listed in Table 1, where "PD&N-RMI" is the amount of sessions used to compute the packet distribution and N-RMIs in legitimate sessions, "Train" is the amount of session samples used to train our classifier and "Test" is the amount of session samples to be tested.

In an SVM classifier, if the data sets used for training the classification model are not balanced, the classification accuracy may not be a good criterion for evaluating the effect of classifying, which will invalidate the detection results in our experiments. Therefore, in order to balance the scales of data sets for higher detection reliability, we set the amount of legitimate HTTP (HTTPS) sessions for training to 300, which is just the sum of all the tunnel sessions for training.

Table 1. The usage of collceted sessions

	PD&N-RMI	Train	Test
HTTP	14062	300	100
HTTPS	8754	300	100
FTP over HTTP (HTTPS)		100	100
SMTP over HTTP (HTTPS)		100	100
POP3 over HTTP (HTTPS)		100	100

In the data collection, we should bring out some processing details. The inter-arrival times may be distorted by network jitters. So, in order to reduce the impact of network noises as far as possible, all the data are collected in a certain time period on weekdays (14:00-17:30) and all the tunnel sessions are also generated in the same period. To simulate normal communication scenarios, when generating tunnel sessions, we deploy one host in our department LAN and the other in the WAN outside. We utilize the HTTPTunnel [13] to generate HTTP tunnel sessions and the Barracuda HTTPS Tunnel [14] to generate HTTPS tunnel sessions. There are two modes of the tunnel traffic generation, with a proxy (intermediary forwarding) and without proxies (direct connection). Since the proxy can visibly slow down the protocol interaction, which can be easily caught, we utilize the mode for direct connection. As explained in Section 4, we can't judge a session with few packets, so the sessions used for training and testing in our detection method all have more than 500 packets. In Section 6.2, we will use some or all of those packets for experiments.

6.2 Results

To implement our detection method, we should set the parameters firstly. In the packet classification, BL and BT can't be too large, which may ruin the similarities of packets. So, in our detection method, BL is 20 and BT is 15. We set N and M to 3 and 25 respectively, so we focus on the 3-RPP and the 3-RMI. The custom infinitesimal INFS we utilize to evaluate the 3-RMIs of unobserved 3-RPPs is set to -50. Figure 6 shows the results of the KDE and we can see that the estimated PDF can approximate the real density well. In the experiments, we use both our detection method and the fingerprint detection technique to detect the tunnel sessions to make a comparison. In our detection, in both training and testing, each session is denoted by its feature vector **FV** consisting of Req_{avg}, Req_{var}, Res_{avg}, Res_{var}, D_{KL}, E_{3-RPP}, D_{3-RMI}. In the fingerprint detection, the fingerprint is trained from all the legitimate sessions collected by us. The results for HTTP and HTTPS tunnel detection are shown in Table 2 and Table 3, where "Packet" is the amount of packets in training and testing session samples, "Legitimate" is the amount of sessions identified as the legitimate sessions, "Tunnel" is the amount of sessions identified as the tunnel sessions, "HTTP (HTTPS)" represents the legitimate HTTP (HTTPS) sessions, "FTP" represents HTTP (HTTPS) sessions tunneled with FTP, "SMTP" represents sessions tunneled with SMTP and "POP3" represents sessions tunneled with POP3.

Table 2. Detection results of HTTP tunnels

Packet	Type	Our Detection Method			Fingerprint Detection Technique		
		Legitimate	Tunnel	Accuracy	Legitimate	Tunnel	Accuracy
100	HTTP	62	38	62%	44	56	44%
	FTP	31	69	69%	42	58	58%
	SMTP	37	63	63%	33	67	67%
	POP3	46	54	54%	48	52	52%
				62.0%			55.3%
300	HTTP	75	25	75%	65	35	65%
	FTP	22	78	78%	38	62	62%
	SMTP	29	71	71%	39	61	61%
	POP3	39	61	61%	43	57	57%
				71.3%			61.3%
500 or more	HTTP	81	19	81%	63	37	63%
	FTP	8	92	92%	29	71	71%
	SMTP	17	83	83%	45	55	55%
	POP3	26	74	74%	39	61	61%
				82.5%			62.5%

Table 3. Detection results of HTTPS tunnels

Packet	Type	Our Detection Method			Fingerprint Detection Technique		
		Legitimate	Tunnel	Accuracy	Legitimate	Tunnel	Accuracy
100	HTTPS	69	31	69%	52	48	52%
	FTP	28	72	72%	40	60	60%
	SMTP	26	74	74%	32	68	68%
	POP3	45	55	55%	47	53	53%
				67.5%			58.3%
300	HTTPS	73	27	73%	70	30	70%
	FTP	15	85	85%	35	65	65%
	SMTP	25	75	75%	36	64	64%
	POP3	20	80	80%	49	51	51%
				78.3%			62.5%
500 or more	HTTPS	87	13	87%	57	43	57%
	FTP	2	98	98%	32	68	68%
	SMTP	7	93	93%	21	79	79%
	POP3	11	89	89%	42	58	58%
				91.8%			65.5%

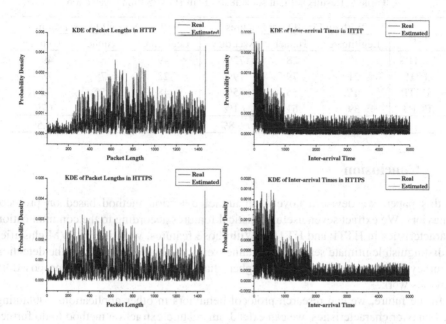

Fig. 6. Results of the KDE: up-left is the KDE of packet lengths in HTTP sessions, up-right is the KDE of inter-arrival times in HTTP sessions, down-left is the KDE of packet lengths in HTTPS sessions and down-right is the KDE of inter-arrival times in HTTPS sessions

As the results show, with the data collected, our detection method performs obviously better than the fingerprint detection technique does. Because we concentrate on protocol behaviors to extract useful features, our detection method is more effective. To improve the detection accuracy, the fingerprint detection technique needs many more sessions to train the fingerprint. With the amount of packets in sessions increasing, the detection rate rises significantly. Additionally, we can see that in our detection method the detection rate against HTTPS tunnels is higher. So, we can infer that protocol behaviors in HTTPS are more distinctive and pronounced than that in HTTP. Further, Table 4 and Table 5 show the detection results when we kick out partial features from the feature vector (the amount of packets in sessions is above 500). We can see that detection accuracies decrease significantly when we abandon the first-order features or the second-order features. Hence, we can conclude that the two categories of features both play important roles in our detection method.

Table 4. Results without some features in HTTP tunnel detection

Type	Without First-Order Features			Without Second-Order Features		
	Legitimate	Tunnel	Accuracy	Legitimate	Tunnel	Accuracy
HTTP	60	40	60%	53	47	53%
FTP	31	69	69%	30	70	70%
SMTP	53	47	47%	42	58	58%
POP3	46	54	54%	59	41	41%
			57.5%			55.5%

Table 5. Results without some features in HTTPS tunnel detection

Type	Without First-Order Features			Without Second-Order Features		
	Legitimate	Tunnel	Accuracy	Legitimate	Tunnel	Accuracy
HTTPS	72	28	72%	49	51	49%
FTP	21	79	79%	22	78	78%
SMTP	45	55	55%	48	52	52%
POP3	39	61	61%	33	67	67%
			66.8%			61.5%

7   Conclusion

In this paper, we devise a novel web tunnel detection method based on protocol behaviors. We extract seven useful statistical features according to the communication characteristics in HTTP and HTTPS. With those features, we utilize a SVM classifier to distinguish legitimate sessions and tunnel sessions. In the experiment, the detection accuracy of our method is much higher than that of the technique proposed in previous work.

In the future, we can research protocol behaviors in other applications. Obtaining the behavior characteristics, we can extend our feature extraction method to do further classification of network traffic.

Acknowledgement. This paper was supported by the National Natural Science Foundation of China (Nos.60903217 & 61202407), the Fundamental Research Funds for the Central Universities (Nos.WK0110000027 & WK0110000033), the Natural Science Foundation of Jiangsu Province of China (No.BK2011357), the Guangdong Province Strategic Cooperation Project with the Chinese Academy of Sciences (No.2012B090400013), and the Scientific and Technical Plan of Suzhou (No. SYG201010).

References

1. Borders, K., Prakash, A.: Web Tap: Detecting Covert Web Traffic. In: Proceedings of the 11th ACM Conference on Computer and Communication Security, pp. 110–120 (October 2004)
2. Bissias, G.D., Liberatore, M., Jensen, D., Levine, B.N.: Privacy Vulnerabilities in Encrypted HTTP Streams. In: Danezis, G., Martin, D. (eds.) PET 2005. LNCS, vol. 3856, pp. 1–11. Springer, Heidelberg (2006)
3. Liberatore, M., Levine, B.N.: Inferring the source of encrypted http connections. In: Proceedings of the 13th ACM Conference on Computer and Communications Security, Alexandria, Virginia, USA, pp. 255–263 (2006)
4. Hernández-Campos, F., Smith, F.D., Jeffay, K., Nobel, A.B.: Statistical Clustering of Internet Communications Patterns. Computing Science and Statistics 35 (2003)

5. McGregor, A., Hall, M., Lorier, P., Brunskill, J.: Flow Clustering Using Machine Learning Techniques. In: Barakat, C., Pratt, I. (eds.) PAM 2004. LNCS, vol. 3015, pp. 205–214. Springer, Heidelberg (2004)
6. Moore, A.W., Zuev, D.: Internet traffic classification using bayesian analysis techniques. In: SIGMETRICS 2005: Proceedings of the 2005 ACM SIGMETRICS International Conference on Measurement and Modeling of Computer Systems, Banff, Alberta, Canada, pp. 50–60 (2005)
7. Wright, C.V., Monrose, F., Masson, G.M.: On Inferring Application Protocol Behaviors in Encrypted Network Traffic. Journal of Machine Learning Research 7, 2745–2769 (2006)
8. Dusi, M., Crotti, M., Gringoli, F., Salgarelli, L.: Detecting Application-Layer Tunnels with Statistical Fingerprinting. Journal of Computer Networks 53(1), 81–97 (2009)
9. Wiki: Kernel Density Estimation (2013), http://en.wikipedia.org/wiki/Kernel_density_estimation
10. Chang, C., Lin, C.: LIBSVM: a library for support vector machines (2013), http://www.csie.ntu.edu.tw/~cjlin/libsvm/
11. Chen, S., Goodman, J.: An empirical study of smoothing techniques for language modeling. In: Proceedings of the 34th Annual Meeting on Association for Computational Linguistics (ACL 1996), NJ, USA, pp. 310–318 (June 1996)
12. Chen, Z., Huang, L., Yu, Z., Yang, W., Li, L., Zheng, X., Zhao, X.: Linguistic Steganography Detection Using Statistical Characteristics of Correlations between Words. In: Solanki, K., Sullivan, K., Madhow, U. (eds.) IH 2008. LNCS, vol. 5284, pp. 224–235. Springer, Heidelberg (2008)
13. HTTPTunnel v1.2.1 (2013), http://sourceforge.net/projects/http-tunnel/files/http-tunnel/HTTPTunnel%20v1.2.1
14. Barracuda HTTPS Tunnel (2013), http://barracudadrive.com/HttpsTunnel.lsp

Salus: Non-hierarchical Memory Access Rights to Enforce the Principle of Least Privilege

Niels Avonds, Raoul Strackx, Pieter Agten, and Frank Piessens

iMinds-DistriNet - KU Leuven,
Celestijnenlaan 200A, 3001 Heverlee, Belgium
niels.avonds@student.kuleuven.be,
firstname.lastname@cs.kuleuven.be

Abstract. Consumer devices are increasingly being used to perform security and privacy critical tasks. The software used to perform these tasks is often vulnerable to attacks, due to bugs in the application itself or in included software libraries. Recent work proposes the isolation of security-sensitive parts of applications into protected modules, each of which can only be accessed through a predefined public interface. But most parts of an application can be considered security-sensitive at some level, and an attacker that is able to gain in-application level access may be able to abuse services from protected modules.

We propose Salus, a Linux kernel modification that provides a novel approach for partitioning processes into isolated compartments. By enabling compartments to restrict the system calls they are allowed to perform and to authenticate their callers and callees, the impact of unsafe interfaces and vulnerable compartments is significantly reduced. We describe the design of Salus, report on a prototype implementation and evaluate it in terms of security and performance. We show that Salus provides a significant security improvement with a low performance overhead, without relying on any non-standard hardware support.

Keywords: Privilege separation, principle of least privilege, modularization.

1 Introduction

Both desktop and mobile devices are increasingly being used to perform security and privacy critical tasks, such as online banking, online tax declarations and e-commerce in general. The software to perform these tasks either runs inside a web browser, or is written as a standalone application. In both cases, the software is often vulnerable to attacks, either due to bugs in the application itself or due to bugs in included software libraries or in the runtime environment used to execute the application (e.g. the browser).

Because of their widespread use and potentially high-impact nature, such applications form an interesting target for cybercriminals. A lot of research has focused on defending against specific attack vectors such as buffer overflows[1,2,3,4], format string vulnerabilities[5] and non-control-data attacks[6]. Even though

T. Zia et al. (Eds.): SecureComm 2013, LNICST 127, pp. 252–269, 2013.

many of these defense mechanisms are applied in practice, successful attacks against high-value applications are still common.

To provide stronger security guarantees, research efforts have shifted to the isolation of small, security-sensitive parts of applications such as cryptographic libraries. By relying on hardware support for trusted computing, state-of-the-art research prototypes are able to achieve such isolation with a very small trusted computing base, in some cases even excluding the running kernel[7,8,9,10] or even having a zero-software TCB[11]. Recent work[12] has proven that such platforms can effectively isolate sensitive information in protected modules from the rest of the system; an in-process or in-kernel attacker is only able to interact with a module through its predefined interface. Hence, an attacker that has compromised a non-security-sensitive part of the application can still only perform the actions explicitly allowed by the interface of a security-sensitive part of the application.

In practice however, isolating security-sensitive parts of an application is difficult as most program logic can be considered security-sensitive at some level[13]. A too coarse-grained approach will result in bloated modules that may contain vulnerabilities and that are too big to be formally verified[14]. Minimum-sized modules on the other hand, can provide strong and easily verifiable guarantees, but may need to expose insecure interfaces to interact with other modules. This is a common problem of module-isolating security platforms, both in software as in hardware. For instance, in the recent DigiNotar attack, the root CA's private cryptographic key was safely stored in a hardware security module (HSM), but its insecure interface enabled attackers to sign arbitrary certificates.

In order to improve upon these shortcomings, we acknowledge that almost every part of an application performs security-sensitive operations. To reduce chances of a successful attack, we propose to partition the *entire* application into compartments and implement a non-hierarchical access control mechanism between compartments. Compartments not only provide provable secure isolation of stored private data (as modules in related work do), but are also able to confine software vulnerabilities to the compartments they occur in by restricting the types of system calls that they are allowed to perform. In addition, caller/callee authentication is able to reduce the impact of insecure interfaces. By separating likely attack vectors from attack targets and placing them into different compartments, an attacker has to find a vulnerability in multiple compartments to reach her goal.

Consider, as an example, a certificate signing application consisting of a parser, a validator, a signer and a logging component (Figure 1). When run as a single monolithic application, a vulnerability in any one of these components can lead to the compromise of the entire application. When placing each of these components in a separate compartment under Salus, components can only call each other through their well-defined interfaces and each component can authenticate both its callers and its callees. This restricts the flow of data and control between compartments to predefined patterns, which significantly raises the bar for an attacker, since she would need to exploit multiple vulnerabilities in different

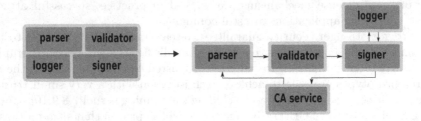

Fig. 1. Salus' compartmentalization enables strong isolation of security-sensitive data *and* contains possibly vulnerable code. Multiple vulnerable compartments need to be exploited to attack the system successfully.

components of the system in order to perform a successful attack. Furthermore, by restricting the types of system calls that can be made from each compartment, the impact of a successful attack is reduced.

Concretely, we make the following contributions in this paper:

- We present a novel approach for partitioning processes into compartments with support for strong isolation of sensitive data *and* containment of vulnerabilities. To the best of our knowledge, Salus is the first solution that simultaneously (1) reduces the impact of insecure compartment interfaces, (2) enables compartments to restrict the types of system calls they are allowed to perform and (3) executes compartments in same address space.
- We report on a prototype implementation of Salus in the Linux kernel.
- We evaluate the security of our approach and the performance of our prototype.

The remainder of this paper is structured as follows: in Section 2 we define our attacker model and describe our desired security properties. In Section 3 we provide a high-level overview of Salus, before presenting our prototype implementation in Section 4. Finally we evaluate our approach in Section 5, discuss related work in Section 6 and conclude in Section 7.

2   Attacker Model and Security Properties

We consider an attacker with the ability to inject and execute arbitrary code in a process, for instance by exploiting a buffer-overflow vulnerability. We assume the application under attack takes advantage of Salus' protection mechanism by authenticating caller and callee on each intercompartmental call and by restricting the possible system calls to those strictly required. Salus must protect against such an attacker in the following way:

- The exploitation of a compartment must not affect the security of compartments other than those that explicitly trust the compromised compartment, in the sense that an attacker should be able to interact with those trusted compartments only through their public interface. A compartment trusts another compartment when it is a caller or callee. Although this objective does not protect against abuse of poorly designed interfaces, Salus provides application developers with the primitives required to create secure compartment interfaces.

- Attackers are explicitly allowed to create new compartments. There is thus no guarantee that compartments requesting protection can be trusted. Hence, Salus must isolate compartments from one stakeholder from those of another, possibly malicious, stakeholder.
- An attacker should not be able to execute system calls that have been revoked.

Kernel-level and physical attacks are considered out of scope. Regarding the cryptographic primitives used, we assume the standard Dolev-Yao model[15]: An attacker can observe, intercept and adapt any message. Moreover, an attacker can create messages, for example by duplicating observed data. However, the cryptographic primitives used cannot be broken.

3   Overview of the Approach

This section presents a high-level overview to Salus. Section 3.1 describes the memory access control mechanisms on which Salus is based. Section 3.2 presents the services Salus provides to protected applications. Section 3.3 shows how these services are used in a typical life cycle of a compartmentalized application. Finally, section 3.4 describes how two compartments can securely communicate with each other.

3.1   Compartments of Least Privilege

Structure of a Compartment The basic layout of a compartment, shown in Figure 2, is a virtual memory region divided into two sections: a public section and a private section. The *public* section contains the compartment's code and any data that should be read accessible by other compartments of the same application. This section can never be modified after initialization, which enables other compartments to authenticate the compartment based on a cryptographic hash of the public section (see Section 3.4). The start of the functions that make up the compartment's public interface are marked as entry points. Execution of the compartment can only be entered through these memory locations (see Table 1).

The *private* section contains the compartment's private data, which consists of application-specific security-sensitive data (e.g. cryptographic keys) as well as data relevant to the correct execution of the compartment, such as the runtime call stack. The data in the private section is read and write accessible from within the compartment, but completely inaccessible for code executing outside of the compartment. Note that since each compartment has its own private call

Fig. 2. Salus' memory access control model enables the creation of compartments that provide strong isolation guarantees to sensitive data. Secure communication primitives reduce the impact of an insecure interface.

Table 1. The enforced memory access control model enforces, for example, that a compartment's private section (4th column) can only be read-write accessed from the public section of the same compartment (3rd row)

from\to	Entry pnt.	Public section	Private section	Unprot. mem.
Entry pnt.	---	--x	---	---
Public section	r-x	r-x	r-w	rwx
Private section	---	---	---	---
Unprot. mem/ other compartment	r-x	r--	---	rwx

stack, intercompartmental function call arguments and return addresses must be passed via CPU registers (as opposed to passing them using the runtime stack).

Applications can still have a memory region that is not part of any compartment. This region is termed *unprotected memory* and is read/write accessible from any compartment. All compartments of the same application run in the same address space, which facilitates the compartmentalization of legacy applications. Nonetheless, fine-grained compartmentalization of a large code base can still require significant developer effort. Therefore, Salus enables applications to be compartmentalized incrementally by storing code and/or data in unprotected memory. While unprotected memory does not provide any of the security guarantees of compartments, it does provide an incremental upgrade path for legacy applications.

As an example of a compartment, consider a single compartment providing a certificate signing service (see Figure 2). The compartment provides two functions as part of its public interface. The first function, set_key, allows setting the cryptographic key used to sign certificates. This key is stored as the m_key variable in the private section. The second function, sign_cert, handles the actual signing requests. Salus' memory access control model ensures that only these two functions are executable; any attempt to jump to another memory location in the compartment will fail. Similarly, any attempt to directly read or write the cryptographic key in the private section from unprotected code or from another compartment will be prevented. Only after calling a valid entry point will read and write access to the private section be enabled, making the cryptographic key only accessible while the compartment is being executed. When the function is terminated, execution returns to the caller and read/write access to the compartment's private section will again be disabled.

Special care is required when execution returns to a compartment after a call to another compartment. Execution must resume at the return location, which is the instruction right after the call instruction in the caller compartment. This location however does not typically correspond to an entry point and hence would cause a memory access violation according to Salus' memory access control model (see Table 1). Compartments can implement a *return entry point* to avoid this access violation. Right before calling another compartment, the return location is placed on the top of the calling compartment's private stack. When the intercompartmental call has finished, execution flow jumps to the return entry point where the return location is retrieved from the stack and jumped to. Note that a return entry point is a software implementation and follows the same access rights as any other entry points.

Restriction of Privileges. Salus provides two important primitives to limit the impact of a compromised compartment. The first primitive is caller and callee authentication. By authenticating callers and callees, a compartment can limit its interaction to trusted compartments only. Although this does not protect against trusted compartments that have been compromised, it does significantly limit the capabilities of an attacker after a successful exploit. Moreover, compartments can dynamically adjust their trust relations to other compartments. For instance, the certificate signing compartment introduced in the previous section (Figure 2) could restrict communication to the compartment that last set its cryptographic key. Secure communication between compartments is discussed in more detail in Section 3.4.

The second primitive allows compartments to disable specific system calls for any code executed from within their public section. Once a system call is disabled, it cannot be re-enabled. By carefully partitioning an application into compartments, each of which should disable any system call it doesn't need, the impact of the exploitation of a vulnerable compartment is minimized. Note that much more fine-grained solutions exist than restricting complete system calls[16]. However, we focus on providing strong compartmentalization primitives that can be used as a building blocks for finer-grained privilege restriction mechanisms.

3.2   Provided Services

To enable compartmentalization of applications, Salus provides runtime support of the following services:

Create. After code is loaded into memory, this service can be used to create a new compartment. Given a memory location and size for the compartment to create, Salus will enable memory protection for this region and will return a system-wide unique ID for the new compartment.

Destroy. A compartment can only be destroyed by the compartment itself. After destruction, the memory access protection is disabled. Hence, a compartment should overwrite any private data before destruction.

Request compartment ID. To support secure communication, Salus provides a service to request the ID and layout (i.e. the size and locations of the public and private sections and the available entry points) of a compartment covering a given memory location. If there is no compartment at the specified location, the service returns an error code. This service is used as a primitive in compartment authentication.

Request caller ID. To support caller authentication, Salus provides a service to request the ID and layout of the compartment that called an entry point of the current compartment.

Disable system call. To limit the impact of the exploitation of a compartment, unused system calls can be disabled. Once a system call is disabled, it cannot be re-enabled. To prevent an attacker from gaining system call privileges by creating a new compartment, compartments inherit system call privileges from their parent.

3.3   Life Cycle of a Compartmentalized Application

Compartmentalized applications can be started as any other application. After the (trusted) operating system or loader loads the application into memory and starts its execution, the application can create the required compartments. Finally, execution can jump to the compartment containing the application's main function. Compartments can be created at any point during the applications' execution, for example, at the time a new (compartmentalized) plugin is loaded.

Creation of Compartments. As the first step of setting up a new compartment, the application allocates (unprotected) memory and loads the compartment's code. Next, the application enables protection of this memory region, by calling Salus' creation service. Note that there is no guarantee that the new compartment's code has been loaded correctly into memory, since the creator might have been compromised already. However, any tampering with the code will be detected when the compartment tries to communicate with another compartment, as will be explained in Section 3.4.

When a new compartment is created, Salus clears the first byte of the private section. This serves as a flag to indicate to the compartment that it should initialize itself when its service is first requested. As part of its initialization, a compartment should clear the private memory locations it will use. This prevents an attacker from crafting a private section by setting it up in unprotected memory locations where a new compartment will later be created. Initialization code typically also disables the system calls that will not be used during further execution of the compartment.

Destruction of Compartments. A compartment can *only* be destructed by the compartment itself. This ensures that compartments can clear their private section (which may contain sensitive data), before the memory protection is lifted. In addition, trusted communication endpoints could be notified of the compartments' imminent destruction. After destruction, the unprotected memory area of the destructed compartment can be freed.

3.4 Secure Communication

Salus' memory isolation mechanism provides strong guarantees that sensitive data in the private section can only be accessed by code in the public section[12]. Reconsidering our certificate signing as an example (see Figure 1), we can prove that the signing key will never leave its compartment. But an attacker with access to the compartment's interface is still able to sign arbitrary certificates. Salus limits the feasibility of such attacks by enforcing both caller as callee authentication. The signing compartment, for example, may enforce that it can only be accessed by the validator compartment. Likewise, the validator authenticates the signing compartment to verify that it hasn't been tampered with before its memory protection was enabled.

Security Report. Authenticating a compartment consists of verifying whether that compartment adheres to a trusted *security report* of that compartment. A security report of a compartment consists of:

The cryptographic hash of its public section This allows any code to verify that the public section of the compartment has not been tampered with: the cryptographic hash should be recalculated at runtime and be compared to the known-good value stored in the security report. This protects against an attacker who is able to modify the public section of a compartment during its creation, before memory protection is enabled (see Section 3.3).

The layout of the compartment When a creation request originates from unprotected memory, the request itself may have been tampered with. An attacker could, for instance, specify an incorrect layout for the compartment to create. This may result in the use of unprotected memory that should be under Salus' protection. By storing the known-good layout of the compartment in the security report, any code can verify that the layout was not tampered with during creation of the compartment.

A cryptographic signature In order to have integrity protection and authentication of the security report, it is digitally signed by its issuer. Each compartment can decide independently whether or not to trust a certain issuer, which opens up the opportunity to integrate compartments from different parties into a single application. Since the cryptographic signature provides integrity protection, security reports can be placed in unprotected memory.

Authentication of Called Compartments. When exchanging sensitive information between compartments, caller and callee must authenticate each other *before* sensitive data is exchanged.

To authenticate a compartment to be called, its ID must first be obtained using Salus' 'request compartment ID' service. Next, the callee's security report must be acquired. For this a central service where each compartment registers to on initialization, can be used. Given the callee's ID, the service should return the (location of the) corresponding security report. Note that this service need not be trusted, as any tampering with the information returned will be detected during the next steps. Once the security report has been obtained, it should be validated by checking the cryptographic signature and by checking that the issuer is trusted. Each compartment should contain a private list of trusted security report issuers. Next, the callee compartment's layout should be requested from Salus and a hash of the Public section should be calculated. The layout and the hash must be compared to the values listed in the security report. This completes the authentication and allows the caller to securely call one of the callee's public functions.

When calling a compartment that has already been authenticated in the past, a re-validation must occur because the callee may have been destroyed since the last interaction. A full authentication using the security report on every call would be very time consuming, so to reduce the performance impact, Salus allows compartments to be re-authenticated quickly based on their ID. Salus ensures each compartment has an ID that is unique on the system until the next reboot. Hence, a re-authentication can simply consist of requesting the ID of the compartment to be called (using the 'request compartment ID' service) and checking that it is the same as during the initial authentication. Using unique identifiers has the added benefit that code can distinguish between different instances of the same compartment.

Authentication of Calling Compartments. To enable compartments to limit use of their (possibly insecure) interface to trusted caller compartments, Salus provides primitives for caller authentication. For a compartment to authenticate its caller, it can first request the caller's ID and memory location (using the 'request caller ID' service) and proceed to authenticate the caller similarly as described above.

4   Implementation

Access rights to compartment sections depend on the value of the program counter. For instance, only if execution is in the public section of a compartment, will the private section of that compartment be read/write accessible. This program counter-based memory access scheme is at the core of Salus' protection mechanism. Enforcing this scheme purely in software would have a huge performance impact as every memory access has to be checked. A pure hardware implementation of the scheme is possible[11], but prohibits its use on commodity, off-the-shelf PC platforms. The approach taken for Salus combines the best of both alternatives, by using the key insight that memory access rights for compartments only need to change when execution crosses a compartment border.

This allows Salus to use the standard memory management unit (MMU) to enforce the memory protection scheme.

A prototype for Salus has been implemented as a Linux kernel modification. Section 4.1 describes how the program counter-based access control mechanism is implemented in this prototype. Section 4.2 describes the API Salus provides to processes and finally Section 4.3 lists the Linux system calls that had to be modified in order to provide a secure implementation of the protection mechanism.

4.1   Program Counter-Based Access Control

By aligning compartment sections to pages, the standard MMU found on any recent commodity computer can be applied to enforce the required memory protection scheme. After a compartment is created (e.g. from unprotected memory), the MMU access rights for the pages of the new compartment are set up according to Table 1: the public section is world-readable while the private section is isolated completely.

When execution tries to enter a compartment (e.g. because of a call instruction), a page fault is generated by the MMU. Based on the memory location addressed and the access type (read, write or execute), Salus determines whether a valid entry point was called and, if necessary, modifies the access rights of only the public and private sections, according to Table 1. This minimizes the number of page faults and access right modifications, thereby reducing the overall performance impact.

Because unprotected memory is always readable, writable and executable, no page fault is generated when execution returns from a compartment to unprotected memory. To restore the access rights of the exited compartment, the compartment itself must issue a system call to Salus.

The Linux page fault handler was modified to implement these access right modifications. To keep track of a process' compartments, the Linux process descriptor data structure was extended with a list of `comp_struct` structures. Each `comp_struct` describes a single compartment and contains:

- The (virtual) start address and length of the public and private sections
- The compartment's unique ID
- The compartment's saved stack pointer
- A list of the compartment's remaining system call privileges

4.2   System Call API

The following new system calls were implemented in the Linux kernel. These system calls represent the API Salus provides to processes.

`void salus_create(void* start, uint len_pub, uint len_priv)` Before a new compartment is created, the list of existing compartments is checked to ensure that the new compartment will not overlap with any existing ones.

New compartments must also not overlap with the kernel or have their memory pages mapped to files. When these checks succeed, a new compartment is created and added to the current process' compartment list. It receives the same system call privileges as its parent.

void salus_destroy(void) Since compartments can only be destroyed from within their own public section, this system call does not require any arguments. This system call restores the original memory access rights on memory region occupied by the executing compartment and then removes the compartment from the current process' compartment list.

struct comp_layout* salus_layout(void* addr) This system call returns the ID and memory layout of the compartment covering a given memory location. It can be implemented by simply iterating over the current process' compartment list until a matching compartment is found. A null pointer is returned when there is no compartment covering the given address.

struct comp_layout* salus_caller(void) This system call returns the ID and memory layout of the compartment that last called an entry point of the current compartment. A null pointer is returned when the current compartment was last called from unprotected memory.

void salus_syscall_disable(uint syscall_id) This system call disables further use of the specified system call, by removing it from the list of system call privileges in the comp_struct of the current compartment. Once a system call is revoked, it cannot be re-acquired.

void salus_return(void* addr) Before execution returns from a called compartment back to its caller (i.e. unprotected memory or another compartment), the access rights of the called compartment's pages need to be restored. This system call performs this access rights modification and then continues execution at the specified address.

4.3   Conflicting System Calls

Some existing system calls in the Linux kernel conflict with Salus' compartmentalization. Additional security checks had to be inserted for these conflicting system calls.

mprotect. The mprotect system call can be used to change the access rights of pages in memory. Additional checks were added to prevent this system call from modifying the access rights of compartments.

mmap. Existing system calls such as mmap or mremap modify the virtual address space of a process. An attacker could abuse these system calls to map a compartment's private section to a file, for instance. Additional checks were added to prevent this type of abuse.

personality. In Linux, each process has a *personality*, which defines the process' execution domain. The personality includes, among other settings, a READ_IMPLIES_EXEC bit, which indicates whether read rights to a memory region should automatically imply executable rights as well. For compartments this would result in world-executable public sections, nullifying the use of designated compartment entry points. Therefore, Salus enforces that this bit is disabled for compartmentalized processes.

fork. The fork, vfork and clone system calls can be used to create a new process or thread. As these processes or threads share parts of their page tables, the elevated access rights of the private section of a called compartment, affects all processes/threads and enable its access from unprotected memory. While these system calls could be modified to create copies of the page tables, our prototype currently uses Linux' existing CLONE_VM and VM_DONTCOPY flags to prevent compartments being mapped in the new process or thread. Checks were also added to the madvice system call, since it can be used to modify the VM_DONTCOPY flag.

5   Evaluation

The effectiveness of Salus' protection mechanisms is evaluated in Section 5.1 and its performance impact is discussed in Section 5.2.

5.1   Security Evaluation

To evaluate Salus' security, we make a distinction between memory-safe and memory-unsafe compartments. A memory-unsafe compartment can be exploited by an attacker using low-level attack vectors such as buffer overflows[1,2,3,4], format string vulnerabilities[5] or non-control data attacks[6]. A memory-safe compartment does not contain such vulnerabilities, for instance because it was written in a memory-safe language or simply because the compartment doesn't contain any memory-safety bugs.

Since memory-safe compartments cannot be exploited directly, the only attack vector against them is through exploitation of another compartment in the same address space. However, recent research[12] has shown that memory protection mechanisms such as those offered by Salus, are able to provide full source code abstraction. This means that, even when other compartments have been successfully exploited, an attackers' capabilities are limited to interacting with the memory-safe compartment through its public interface. A carefully constructed interface can thus effectively limit the attack surface of a compartment. But in many cases, creating a secure interface is still a challenging problem[17]. Recall the example of a certificate signing compartment introduced in Section 3.1: even if the private cryptographic key is never exposed, an attacker could potentially still use the compartment's interface to sign arbitrary certificates[18]. By taking advantage of Salus' support for caller/callee authentication however, the risk of such an attack can be minimized by only servicing requests from compartments that would issue them as part of the normal operation of the application (e.g. in Figure 1, the signer compartment should only accept requests from the validator compartment).

Memory-unsafe compartments may still contain vulnerabilities that can be exploited by attackers. Even though Salus does not prevent such attacks, compartmentalization can still provide significant security benefits. Firstly, high-risk components can be identified and be placed in separate compartments. Effective but high-overhead countermeasures[19,20] can be used to harden such compartments. By only applying these countermeasures to likely vulnerable compartments, their performance impact remains limited.

Secondly, compartmentalization can automatically thwart certain types of attacks. For instance, limiting entrance of compartments to valid entry points significantly reduces the chance of an attacker finding enough gadgets to successfully execute a return-oriented-programming (ROP) attack[21,22].

Thirdly, compartmentalization can be used as a building block for new countermeasures. For instance, a custom loader could be implemented that loads compartments at different locations in memory for every program execution. This is similar to address space layout randomization (ASLR)[23], but can be applied at a much finer-grained level.

Finally, even when a compartment has been successfully exploited, Salus can still limit the impact of the attack. Because Salus provides entry point enforcement, caller/callee authentication and system call privilege containment, an attacker will likely have to compromise multiple vulnerable compartments before reaching her intended target. This significantly increases the effort an attacker must take to successfully exploit the application. The ability to confine attackers to the exploited compartment even allows implementing a tightly controlled sandbox where user-provided machine code can be executed safely.

5.2   Performance Evaluation

To evaluate the performance of Salus, we performed micro- and macrobenchmarks. All tests were run on a Dell Latitude E6510. This laptop is equipped with an Intel Core i5 560M processor running at 2.67 GHz and contains 4 GiB of RAM. A Ubuntu Server 12.04 distribution with (modified) Linux 3.6.0-rc5 x86_64 kernel was used as the operating system.

System-Wide Impact. To show that legacy applications not using the modularization technique are not impacted by our changes to the Linux kernel, we ran the SPECint 2006 benchmark. All tests finished within ±0.4% compared to the vanilla kernel.

Microbenchmarks. To measure the overhead caused by switching the access rights, we created a microbenchmark that measures the cost of a call to a secure compartment and compare it to the cost of calling a regular function and calling a system call. The compartment used in the benchmark immediately returns to the caller. The system call and function behave similarly.

Table 2 displays the results of this microbenchmark. Calling a compartment is about 677 times slower compared to calling a regular function. This overhead is attributed to the need to modify the access rights of pages. Compared to calling a system call, the compartment is only 20 times slower. Due to these high costs, there is a trade-off to be made between a low number of compartment transitions and small compartments with additional security guarantees.

Table 2. Compartment access overhead

Type	CPU cycles	Relative
Function Call	5,944	1
System Call	193,970	32.63
Compartment Call	4,024,227	677.02

Secure Web Server. As a macrobenchmark, we compartmentalized an SSL-enabled web server. For every new connection a new compartment is created, securing session keys even in the event that an attacker is able to inject shellcode in the compartment providing its own SSL session.

The secure compartment was built using the PolarSSL cryptographic library and a subset of the diet libc library. A simple static 74-byte page is returned to the clients over an SSL-connection protected by a 1024-bit RSA encryption key.

Table 3. Requests per second of an SSL-enabled webserver where every SSL session is protected in its own compartment, for an increasing number of clients

Concurrency	Vanilla kernel	Salus kernel	Relative perf.
1	109.11	96.54	-11.52%
2	165.56	153.62	-7.21%
4	184.31	164.78	-10.60%
8	199.98	175.35	-12.32%
16	206.82	181.00	-12.48%
32	207.78	181.50	-12.65%
64	206.64	180.35	-12.72%
128	206.49	180.97	-12.36%

We used the Apache Benchmark to benchmark this web server for an increasing number of clients that are concurrently requesting pages. The results are shown in Table 3. The performance overhead tops at 12.72% and is mainly attributed to the many compartment boundaries crosses during the SSL negotiation phase.

Compartmentalized Parser. As input files are often under the control of an attacker and sanitation of their content can be difficult, parsers are a likely attack vector for many applications. As a second benchmark, we isolated the decompressing function of gzip (GNU zip). While disabling unused system calls for the entire process would result in similar security guarantees, we are interested in the impact of repeated compartment crossings in a parser setting. Applications that place their parser and the rest of the application in different compartments, would incur a similar overhead as only one additional compartment boundary needs to be crossed.

To benchmark the application, we created input files with randomized content, ranging from 16 KiB to 64 MiB in size, compressed them and measured the time taken to decompress the files with the hardened application. The application was run 100 times on each file. File I/O used a buffer of 32 KiB and the output was redirected to the null device. Figure 3 displays the results.

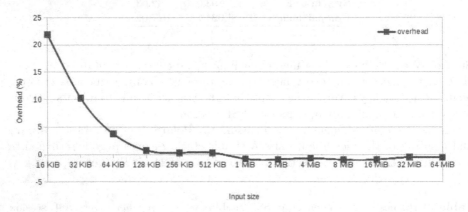

Fig. 3. Salus' performance overhead on the gzip macro benchmark drops significantly as the input file size increases

Given the relatively high overhead of a call to a compartment and the low computation cost of the decompressing function, it is unsurprising that for small input files the overhead can be as high as 21.9%. When the input size is increased however, the overhead drops steadily to -0.5% for 64 MiB input files, even though also the number of compartment-border crossings increases from 8 to 8200. We attribute this significant drop in overhead to the increased amount of slow disk I/O that needs to be performed as the input file size gets bigger, an effect that we predict to see in most parser-like compartments. The small performance gain of 0.5% can be attributed to cache effects.

The way an application is partitioned will have a significant impact on performance. Applications should be compartmentalized in logical blocks where each compartment has direct access to most of its required data. Once a logical block has finished, control and all data should be passed to the next compartment, reducing the number of inter-compartment calls. Smaller, heavily protected compartments such as an SSL compartment, provide strong security but may impact performance more significantly when called repeatedly. This makes the performance impact of compartmentalization difficult to predict. Therefore we advocate for automatic partitioning tools that reduce the number of compartment crosses and help the programmer decide which compartments should be hardened most thoroughly.

6   Related Work

Various security measures have been proposed to harden applications. Many of them aim to protect against very specific vulnerabilities such as buffer overflows

[1,2,3,4], format string vulnerabilities[5] or non-control data attacks[6]. While these countermeasures make it significantly more difficult for an attacker to compromise software applications, they cannot offer complete protection. Static verification of source code[24], in contrast, is able to provide such hard security guarantees, but typically comes at a significant economic cost in terms of programming and verification effort.

Singaravelu et al.[13] proposed to isolate security-sensitive parts of applications in complete isolation from the rest of the system. Many research proposals have since been filed based on this principle. Each of them provides some way of executing modules in isolation, relying on a trusted code base ranging from only a few thousands of lines of code[8,10] to only the protected modules themselves and a small runtime library[7,9]. While these research prototypes offer provable security to the sensitive data that they protect[12], they do not attempt to reduce the impact of a vulnerability elsewhere in the code by executing modules with the least amount of privileges possible[25]. An attacker who successfully gains control over the platform is still able to interact with protected modules unrestrictedly.

Other work focuses on confining possible software vulnerabilities. Early work focused on reducing the size of the kernel itself[26], where process privileges are managed by capabilities. Recently Watson et al.[16] proposed applying a similar idea to partition applications themselves, where capabilities can be granted to each created partition. As partitions live in their own process, interaction takes place through remote procedure calls and pointers cannot to passed directly. Salus avoids these drawbacks by executing compartments in the same address space and unprotected memory can be used to gradually partition legacy applications. While fine-grained privilege containment is out of scope for this paper, Salus can easily be extended with a capability mechanism.

Native Client (NaCl)[27,28], which builds upon the concepts of software fault isolation[29], takes another approach and attempts to completely sandbox x86 code. Accesses to the environment from within a sandbox are tightly controlled by runtime facilities. While NaCl focuses on downloaded, untrusted binary code, it could be used to partition entire applications. Interaction between two NaCl partitions is provided through a service similar to Unix domain sockets, making porting existing legacy applications a challenging undertaking. Salus on the other hand can provide a similar tightly controlled sandbox by placing such partitions in one compartment while the remaining legacy application is placed in another. A specially created wrapper can ensure that all system call privileges are revoked before execution control is given to the sandboxed code. There are however two major differences compared to NaCl. First, Salus only impacts performance when compartment boundaries are crossed. NaCl on the other hand places constraints on the binary code itself, resulting in a varying performance impact. Second, Salus employs a non-hierarchical separation of privilege, allowing compartments to be completely isolated from other compartments (possibly provided by other vendors) while compartments of the same vendor can co-operate easily.

Finally, our earlier work[30,10] is the most related to Salus. It also employs a program-counter based access control mechanism, but assumes a safe interface. Therefore it has the same limitation as other research prototypes[9,7,8] that provide strong isolation of sensitive data: it does not reduce the possible impact of exploited vulnerabilities.

7   Conclusion

Recent module-isolation security architectures provide strong security guarantees of sensitive data stored in small pieces of applications. In practice, however, it is hard to isolate such security-sensitive parts, as most code in an application is sensitive up to some level. As a result, modules of such platforms may need to provide unsafe interfaces. We presented Salus, a new security architecture that can not only provide strong isolation guarantees of sensitive data, but its mutual authentication support also reduces the impact of insecure interfaces. By placing likely attack vectors and targets into different compartments, multiple compartments need to be attacked successfully before an attack target is reached.

Acknowledgement. This work has been supported in part by the Intel Lab's University Research Office. This research is also partially funded by the Research Fund KU Leuven, and by the EU FP7 project NESSoS. With the financial support from the Prevention of and Fight against Crime Programme of the European Union (B-CCENTRE). Raoul Strackx holds a PhD grant from the Agency for Innovation by Science and Technology in Flanders (IWT). Pieter Agten holds a PhD fellowship of the Research Foundation - Flanders (FWO).

References

1. One, A.: Smashing the stack for fun and profit. Phrack Magazine 7(49) (1996)
2. Erlingsson, Ú.: Low-level software security: Attacks and defenses. In: Aldini, A., Gorrieri, R. (eds.) FOSAD 2006/2007. LNCS, vol. 4677, pp. 92–134. Springer, Heidelberg (2007)
3. Strackx, R., Younan, Y., Philippaerts, P., Piessens, F., Lachmund, S., Walter, T.: Breaking the memory secrecy assumption. In: EuroSec 2009, pp. 1–8. ACM (2009)
4. Younan, Y., Joosen, W., Piessens, F.: Code injection in c and c++: A survey of vulnerabilities and countermeasures. Technical report, KULeuven (2004)
5. Cowan, C., Barringer, M., Beattie, S., Kroah-Hartman, G., Frantzen, M., Lokier, J.: Formatguard: automatic protection from printf format string vulnerabilities. In: SSYM 2001, p. 15. USENIX Association, Berkeley (2001)
6. Chen, S., Xu, J., Sezer, E.C., Gauriar, P., Iyer, R.K.: Non-control-data attacks are realistic threats. In: USENIX 2005, vol. 14, p. 12 (2005)
7. McCune, J.M., Parno, B., Perrig, A., Reiter, M.K., Isozaki, H.: Flicker: An execution infrastructure for TCB minimization. In: EuroSys 2008. ACM (April 2008)
8. McCune, J.M., Li, Y., Qu, N., Zhou, Z., Datta, A., Gligor, V., Perrig, A.: TrustVisor: Efficient TCB reduction and attestation. In: SP 2010 (May 2010)

9. Azab, A., Ning, P., Zhang, X.: Sice: a hardware-level strongly isolated computing environment for x86 multi-core platforms. In: CCS 2011, pp. 375–388. ACM (2011)
10. Strackx, R., Piessens, F.: Fides: Selectively hardening software application components against kernel-level or process-level malware. In: CCS 2012 (October 2012)
11. Noorman, J., Agten, P., Daniels, W., Strackx, R., Herrewege, A.V., Huygens, C., Preneel, B., Verbauwhede, I., Piessens, F.: Sancus: Low-cost trustworthy extensible networked devices with a zero-software trusted computing base. In: Proceedings of the 22nd USENIX Security Symposium (2013)
12. Agten, P., Strackx, R., Jacobs, B., Piessens, F.: Secure compilation to modern processors. In: CSF 2012, pp. 171–185. IEEE Computer Society (2012)
13. Singaravelu, L., Pu, C., Härtig, H., Helmuth, C.: Reducing tcb complexity for security-sensitive applications: three case studies. In: EuroSys 2006 (2006)
14. Garfinkel, T., Pfaff, B., Chow, J., Rosenblum, M., Boneh, D.: Terra: A virtual machine-based platform for trusted computing. ACM SIGOPS 37(5) (2003)
15. Dolev, D., Yao, A.C.: On the security of public key protocols. IEEE Transactions on Information Theory 29(2), 198–208 (1983)
16. Watson, R.N., Anderson, J., Laurie, B., Kennaway, K.: Capsicum: practical capabilities for unix. In: USENIX Security (2010)
17. Longley, D., Rigby, S.: An automatic search for security flaws in key management schemes. Computers & Security 11(1), 75–89 (1992)
18. Hoogstraten, H., Prins, R., Niggebrugge, D., Heppener, D., Groenewegen, F., Wettinck, J., Strooy, K., Arends, P., Pols, P., Kouprie, R., Moorrees, S., van Pelt, X., Hu, Y.Z.: Black tulip - report of the investigation into the diginotar certificate authority breach. Technical report, FoxIT (2012)
19. Younan, Y., Philippaerts, P., Cavallaro, L., Sekar, R., Piessens, F., Joosen, W.: Paricheck: an efficient pointer arithmetic checker for c programs. In: ASIACCS 2010, pp. 145–156. ACM, New York (2010)
20. Akritidis, P., Costa, M., Castro, M., Hand, S.: Baggy bounds checking: An efficient and backwards-compatible defense against out-of-bounds errors. In: USENIX 2009 (2009)
21. Shacham, H.: The geometry of innocent flesh on the bone: Return-into-libc without function calls (on the x86). In: CCS 2007, pp. 552–561. ACM (2007)
22. Checkoway, S., Davi, L., Dmitrienko, A., Sadeghi, A.R., Shacham, H., Winandy, M.: Return-oriented programming without returns. In: CCS 2010, pp. 559–572. ACM, New York (2010)
23. Bhatkar, S., DuVarney, D.C., Sekar, R.: Address obfuscation: An efficient approach to combat a broad range of memory error exploits. In: USENIX 2003 (2003)
24. Jacobs, B., Piessens, F.: The VeriFast program verifier (2008)
25. Saltzer, J., Schroeder, M.: The protection of information in computer systems. Proceedings of the IEEE 63(9), 1278–1308 (1975)
26. Liedtke, J.: Toward Real Microkernels. Communications of the ACM 39(9) (1996)
27. Yee, B., et al.: Native client: A sandbox for portable, untrusted x86 native code. In: SP 2009, pp. 79–93. IEEE (2009)
28. Sehr, D., et al.: Adapting software fault isolation to contemporary cpu architectures. In: USENIX Security Symposium (2010)
29. Wahbe, R., Lucco, S., Anderson, T.E., Graham, S.L.: Efficient software-based fault isolation. In: Proceedings of the Fourteenth ACM Symposium on Operating Systems Principles, SOSP 1993, pp. 203–216. ACM, New York (1993)
30. Strackx, R., Piessens, F., Preneel, B.: Efficient Isolation of Trusted Subsystems in Embedded Systems. In: Jajodia, S., Zhou, J. (eds.) SecureComm 2010. LNICST, vol. 50, pp. 344–361. Springer, Heidelberg (2010)

Scalable Security Model Generation and Analysis Using k-importance Measures

Jin B. Hong and Dong Seong Kim

Computer Science and Software Engineering,
University of Canterbury,
Christchurch,
New Zealand
jho102@uclive.ac.nz, dongseong.kim@canterbury.ac.nz

Abstract. Attack representation models (ARMs) (such as attack graphs, attack trees) can be used to model and assess security of a networked system. To do this, one must generate an ARM. However, generation and evaluation of the ARM suffer from a scalability problem when the size of the networked system is very large (e.g., 10,000 computer hosts in the network with a complex network topology). The main reason is that computing all possible attack scenarios to cover all aspects of an attack results in a state space explosion. One idea is to use only important hosts and vulnerabilities in the networked system to generate and evaluate security. We propose to use k-importance measures to generate a two-layer hierarchical ARM that will improve the scalability of model generation and security evaluation computational complexities. We use k_1 number of important hosts based on network centrality measures and k_2 number of significant vulnerabilities of hosts using host security metrics. We show that an equivalent security analysis can be achieved using our approach (using k-importance measures), compared to an exhaustive search.

Keywords: Attack Models, Network Centrality, Security Analysis, Security Metrics.

1 Introduction

Attack representation models (ARMs) (e.g., Attack Graphs (AGs) [1] and Attack Trees (ATs) [2]) are widely used for computer and network security analysis. One main usage of ARMs is to formulate security solutions to enhance the network security while minimising the cost [3, 4]. One of limitations using ARMs is a scalability problem [5], because computing all possible attack scenarios has s state space explosion problem. There are two main types of ARMs; Graph-based and Tree-based. Graph-based (e.g., logical attack graphs [6], multiple prerequisite graphs [7]) and tree-based (e.g., protection trees [8], attack countermeasure trees [9]) ARMs are non-state space models, but graph-based ARMs have an exponential number of possible attack paths in security evaluation. Hierarchical attack representation models (HARMs) [10, 11] have been proposed to improve the scalability of non-state space models, but the scalability problem still remains when evaluating network security of a very large sized network system.

T. Zia et al. (Eds.): SecureComm 2013, LNICST 127, pp. 270–287, 2013.
ⓒ Institute for Computer Sciences, Social Informatics and Telecommunications Engineering 2013

ARMs have different phases in its lifecycle. The preprocessing phase collects network information (e.g., network reachability, vulnerabilities), and the generation (or construction) phase combines these information to build an ARM. The representation phase stores and visualises the ARM, and the evaluation phase analyses the network security via the ARM. The modification phase updates the ARM when the network changes. Generation of graph-based ARMs is scalable, but the evaluation has a scalability problem. In contrast, the evaluation of tree-based ARMs is scalable only if the size of the ARM has a polynomial size complexity.

Model simplifications (e.g., graph aggregation [12], adjacency matrix clustering [13], graph simplification via collapsing similar nodes [7]) and heuristic methods (e.g., Particle Swarm [14], new heuristic algorithms [15]) are used to improve the scalability, but these methods require an ARM generated specific to their evaluation method using all network information. We propose to use k-importance measure to rank hosts in the network and vulnerabilities of the hosts, and generate ARMs only using those selected hosts and vulnerabilities to improve the scalability of generation and evaluation of ARMs. We use network centrality measures (NCMs) (e.g., degree, closeness, and betweenness [16, 17]) to rank k_1 number of hosts in the network, and security metrics (e.g., Common Vulnerability Scoring System (CVSS) [18], risk [9]) to rank k_2 number of important vulnerabilities of the hosts.

NCMs identify characteristics of network components based on the structure. The structure of the network is important in a cyber attack, as some attacks (e.g., sequential attacks) progress based on how network components are connected. The reachability information is based on the network structure. As a result, NCMs can distinguish attack paths that are most likely be used in an attack than others. Security metrics reflect characteristics of vulnerabilities in hosts. Security metrics can be measured from real systems [19], cloud systems [20], emulations [21], and honey pots [22].

We propose to use a two-layer HARM to analyse network security [11], to capture network information (e.g., network reachability) in the upper layer and vulnerability information (e.g., CVSS) in the lower layer. NCMs are used on the upper layer to rank important hosts in the network, and security metrics on the lower layer to rank important vulnerabilities in the hosts.

The contributions of this paper are summarised as follows:

- To propose an efficient ARM generation method based on k-importance measures;
- To generate HARMs using k-importance measures and show that nearly equivalent security analysis can be achieved;
- To simulate scalability and accuracy of the HARMs (or ARMs) using k-importance measures against the exhaustive search method when analysing the network security.

The rest of the paper is as organised as follows. In Section 2, related work is given. In Section 3, an example network and HARMs are described in the phases of generation and evaluation, with an evaluation example based on risk analysis. Simulation results are shown in Section 4. Discussion is given in Section 5, and Section 6 concludes this paper.

2 Related Work

Security analysis using all possible attack scenarios can cover all set of known attacks. Various modelling techniques are proposed to improve the scalability of ARMs [6, 7, 10, 11], but computing all possible attack scenarios (e.g., full AG [1], attack response trees [23]) for a large sized network still suffers from a scalability problem [5]. Model simplifications and heuristic methods are widely used to improve scalability in the evaluation phase, but not in the generation phase.

Attack scenarios are often used to generate ARMs [23]. Chen *et al.* [24] used *compact* AG, similar to a logical AG in [6], to find *n*-valid paths that has less than *n* steps to reach the target, where *n* denotes the number of stepping stone hosts in the network. Further, they defined a *weighted-greedy* algorithm to find the optimal security solution in the evaluation phase. Their experiment results clearly showed that covering a larger set of attack scenarios is computationally expensive. Mehta *et al.* [25] ranked AG components based on attack probabilities. A full AG is constructed (i.e., capturing all possible attack scenarios [1]), which requires computing exponential number of attack paths in a large sized network. AG components cannot be ranked until full AG is generated. Sawilla *et al.* [26] used partial cuts in evaluation of AGs. Partial cuts divide network components by their importance, such that the relevance between a network component and the attack is decided based on the generated AG. However, the structure of the AG is heavily dependent on network reachability. That is, network structure affects how important network components are chosen in the AG. Various techniques (e.g., model simplification and heuristic methods) are proposed to improve scalability in the evaluation phase, but they did not consider reducing the computation complexity in the generation phase.

Importance measures are used in some application domains. Cadini *et al.* [17] used NCMs to capture strengths and weaknesses of network safety. Georgiadis *et al.* [16] described network security using NCMs, but only implications of NCMs are described. Gallon *et al.* [18] integrated CVSS framework with AGs to construct an AG, but the structure of the ARM is the same with other AGs. Previous works using NCMs and security metrics to assess the performance network security were applied only in the evaluation phase of ARMs.

We propose *k*-importance measures in the generation phase of ARMs using important hosts and vulnerabilities. To the best of our knowledge, no other work considered this approach to improve scalability. We show that our approach can provide nearly equivalent security analysis of a large sized networked system in a scalable manner. That is, by using only a subset of network components, it reduces the computational complexity in all phases of ARMs lifecycle. Important hosts are chosen based on NCMs (e.g., degree, closeness, betweenness [16, 17]), and important vulnerabilities are chosen based on security metrics (e.g., CVSS [18], structural importance [9]). Generation and evaluation of ARMs using *k*-importance measures and their computation methods are presented in Section 3.

3 A Network and Attack Models

Analysing network security follows procedural steps; (i) gather information from the network (e.g., reachability, vulnerabilities), (ii) generate an ARM using given network information, (iii) analyse network security via ARM using security metrics, and (iv) update the ARM if there is any change in the network. Figure 1 shows the steps taken to analyse the network security, with additional feature to use k-importance measures. Computations of k-importance measures are processed at the beginning of the generation phase.

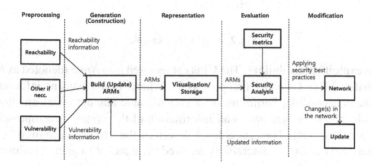

Fig. 1. Lifecycle of an ARM

3.1 Network Settings and the Attack Scenario

We use a network example as shown in Figure 2. We assume all host connections have the same cost (e.g., same throughput and attack probabilities), and the probability of attacks are the same for all hosts. However, different edge costs can be modelled with different edge weights, and also the probability of attacks can hold different values. H_1, H_2, H_3 and H_4 (intermediate host machines) are identical hosts with same vulnerabilities, and H_5 (a target machine) is running a virtual machine. We define an attack scenario with the location of an attacker outside the network (i.e., attack from Internet), and the goal is to compromise the target host (i.e., obtaining the administrator privilege of H_5).

Vulnerability information is collected from a real system using vulnerability scanners (e.g., $NESSUS$ [27]). On the intermediate host machines (based on Windows XP SP1), about 60 known vulnerabilities are found. Some vulnerability information is not given (e.g., $NESSUS$ plugin name, port number, CVSS BS, and Common Vulnerabilities and Exposures (CVE) ID). For automated generation of ARMs, it is difficult to interpret vulnerability description to model vulnerability interactions (e.g., difficulties in processing manual input of vulnerability information due to various language formats, such as grammar and choice of words). Therefore, we scope the list of known vulnerabilities only with identifications (e.g., CVE ID is given). Total 11 vulnerabilities are identified as shown in Table 1 with details including CVE ID, CVSS BS, impact, exploitability, confidentiality impact (CI) and access level. All vulnerabilities are accessible via the network (i.e., no local access is required) and no authentications are

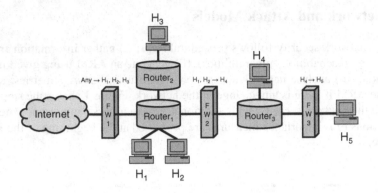

Fig. 2. A network example

required to exploit vulnerabilities. The CI is categorised into *None* (denoted as *N*), *Partial* (denoted as *P*), or *Complete* (denoted as *C*), where *None* means no information on the machine is accessible, *Partial* means a considerable amount of information could be accessible, and *Complete* means all information of the system is compromised, by the attacker respectively. The access level describes the privilege acquired by the attacker, where only a single vulnerability allowed the attacker to gain the administrator privilege.

Table 1. List of vulnerabilities in H_1-H_4

ID	CVE ID	CVSS BS	Impact	Exploitability	CI	Access Level	Authentication
v_1	CVE-2005-1794	6.4	4.9	10.0	P	None	None
v_2	CVE-2011-0661	10.0	10.0	10.0	C	None	None
v_3	CVE-2010-0231	10.0	10.0	10.0	C	None	None
v_4	CVE-2011-2552	7.8	6.9	10.0	N	None	None
v_5	CVE-1999-0520	6.4	4.9	10.0	P	None	None
v_6	CVE-2010-2729	9.3	10.0	8.6	C	None	None
v_7	CVE-1999-0505	7.2	10.0	3.9	C	Admin	None
v_8	CVE-2002-1117	5.0	2.9	10.0	P	None	None
v_9	CVE-2003-0386	4.3	2.9	8.6	P	None	None
v_{10}	CVE-2010-0025	5.0	2.9	10.0	P	None	None
v_{11}	CVE-1999-0497	0.0	0.0	10.0	N	None	None

A total of 23 vulnerabilities are found on the target machine (i.e., H_5 running a VMware ESXi). We assume that the attacker can only access network hosts via remote access (i.e., no physical access), then there are 11 vulnerabilities accessible via remote connections. The list of vulnerabilities of H_5 is shown in Table 2. In the authentication field, some vulnerabilities (CVE-2010-1142, CVE-2010-1141 and CVE-2008-2097) require a *SingleSystem* condition satisfied. These vulnerabilities require the attacker to have an access, such as command line, desktop session or web interface on the machine. Any vulnerability with disclosure of machine information (i.e., CI is either P or C) allows the attacker to gain an access to the machine (i.e., *SingleSystem* authentication is satisfied). There are vulnerabilities without any CI (i.e., CI is N), but they allow the attacker to distribute softwares (e.g., Trojan horse) that could be used to gain access of network hosts. However, we do not consider these cases.

Table 2. List of vulnerabilities in H_5

ID	CVE ID	CVSS BS	Impact	Exploitability	CI	Access Level	Authentication
v_{12}	CVE-2011-1789	5.0	2.9	10.0	N	None	None
v_{13}	CVE-2011-1786	5.0	2.9	10.0	N	None	None
v_{14}	CVE-2011-1785	7.8	6.9	10.0	N	None	None
v_{15}	CVE-2011-0355	7.8	6.9	10.0	N	None	None
v_{16}	CVE-2010-4573	9.3	10.0	8.6	C	None	None
v_{17}	CVE-2010-3609	5.0	2.9	10.0	N	None	None
v_{18}	CVE-2010-1142	8.5	10.0	6.8	C	None	Single System
v_{19}	CVE-2010-1141	8.5	10.0	6.8	C	None	Single System
v_{20}	CVE-2009-3733	5.0	2.9	10.0	P	None	None
v_{21}	CVE-2008-4281	9.3	10.0	8.6	C	None	None
v_{22}	CVE-2008-2097	9.0	10.0	8.0	C	Admin	Single System

3.2 Computing k-importance Measures

In this subsection, we describe how to rank and select important hosts and vulnerabilities based on k-importance measures. k_1 denotes the number of important hosts and k_2 denotes the number of important vulnerabilities used to generate ARMs, respectively.

Ranking k_1 Number of Important Hosts. We use network reachability information in conjunction with NCMs to rank important hosts. Among many NCMs, we use only basic NCMs (e.g., degree, closeness and betweenness centrality measures) [17]. The degree centrality computes the popularity of a node (e.g., a host in a network graph) based on number of direct connections with other nodes (e.g., single-hop neighbour hosts), with its computational complexity of $O(n)$ where n is the number of nodes in the graph. The closeness centrality computes the distance of a node to all other nodes, with its computational complexity of $O(n^3)$ using Floyd algorithm [28]. The betweenness centrality computes the significance of a node between all node pairs, with its computational complexity of $O(n^3)$ using Floyd algorithm. A problem using NCMs is when two or more nodes have the same rank. In this work, nodes with the same rank will be assigned with the same rank, and we will consider other approaches in future work. The normalised NCMs of the example network is shown in Table 3, where high values represent higher importance. Each NCM ranks are combined to give the overall rankings of the hosts. The final rank is determined by taking into account their ranks from each NCMs. A node with high scores in all three NCMs will have a higher rank (e.g., H_4 has highest score in all NCMs) than other nodes. *RankSum* values are calculated by adding up their ranks from each NCM (e.g., *RankSum* of H_1 is calculated by adding values of 1 (first equally important based on degree centrality), 1 (first equally important based on closeness centrality), and 2 (second equally important based on betweenness centrality) resulting in value of 4). Then, the *RankSum* values are used to give the final rank of each host in an ascending order. Since H_1 and H_2 have the same value of *RankSum*, they are equally ranked overall.

Table 3. Network Centrality Measurements

	Degree	Closeness	Betweenness	*RankSum*	Final Rank
H_1	3/4	4/5	8/12	4	2
H_2	3/4	4/5	8/12	4	2
H_3	2/4	4/7	4/12	12	4
H_4	3/4	4/5	10/12	3	1
H_5	1/4	4/12	4/12	14	5

Another importance of using NCMs is to compute the proportion of important hosts (i.e., the value of k_1). The density of the network (i.e., the proportion of host interconnections in respect to the number of hosts) is one of the important factors because the number of available attack paths are proportional to the network density (i.e., there are more available attack paths in a dense network (e.g., fully connected or mesh topologies) than a sparse network (e.g., star or tree topologies)). We use closeness centrality to compute the value for k_1, because the closeness centrality directly measures the amount of host connections in the network. In a fully connected network, the sum of normalised degree centrality measure is equal to the number of hosts in the network (i.e., all network components are used in at least one attack path). The sum of degree centrality is three (out of five), which we will assign as the value of k_1 (i.e., $k_1 = 3$).

3.3 Ranking k_2 important Number of Vulnerabilities in Hosts

Various security metrics evaluate different aspects of vulnerabilities. Values are assigned to security metrics (e.g., CVSS base score (BS) [18]) and these values are relative to each other. For our example, we use CVSS BS to rank vulnerabilities. The rank based on CVSS BS is shown in Table 4 and Table 5 for intermediate hosts and target host vulnerabilities, respectively. The proportion of important vulnerabilities is chosen by their CVSS BSs. The average CVSS BS is calculated, and vulnerabilities with CVSS BS higher than the average are selected. We determine the k_2 values with threshold values set to the average CVSS BSs. The average CVSS BSs are 6.5 and 7.3 for intermediate hosts and the target host, respectively. Therefore, in this example, the value of $k_2^{host} = 5$, and the value of $k_2^{target} = 7$.

3.4 Generation of HARMs

Generation of HARM Using All Network Information. We use a two-layer HARM to analyse security of the system. We generate the HARM in which an AG in the upper layer (e.g., using ARM generating tools, such as MulVAL [29]), and an AT in the lower

Table 4. Intermediate host vulnerability rankings

	v_1	v_2	v_3	v_4	v_5	v_6	v_7	v_8	v_9	v_{10}	v_{11}
CVSS BS	6.4	10.0	10.0	7.8	6.4	9.3	7.2	5.0	4.3	5.0	0.0
Rank	6	1	1	4	6	3	5	8	10	8	11

Table 5. target host vulnerability rankings

	v_{12}	v_{13}	v_{14}	v_{15}	v_{16}	v_{17}	v_{18}	v_{19}	v_{20}	v_{21}	v_{22}
CVSS BS	5.0	5.0	7.8	7.8	9.3	5.0	8.5	8.5	5.0	9.3	9.0
Rank	8	8	6	6	1	8	4	4	8	1	3

layer are used. The HARM of the example network is shown in Figure 3, where the attacker is denoted as A. H_1, H_2, H_3 and H_4 have identical lower layer ATs (i.e., the AT goal is defined as *Compromise Host*). We assume only one prerequisite condition is required when exploiting vulnerabilities with prerequisites (i.e., one vulnerability is chosen from a set of vulnerabilities satisfying the same condition).

Generation of a Reduced HARM Using k-importance Measures We generate a reduced HARM based on k-importance measures, denoted as ReHARM as shown in Figure 4. The size difference is significantly reduced in comparison to the HARM shown in Figure 3, even with the small network example. The selected important hosts with $k_1 = 3$ are H_1, H_2, H_4. Since H_5 is designated as the target, it must be included in the upper layer. If we want to assess security of the network system, only selected hosts are included in the AG model. The number of selected important vulnerabilities is $k_2^{*Host} = 5$ and $k_2^{*Target} = 7$ for intermediate hosts and the target host, respectively. It is also possible to generate a full HARM, then take into account important hosts and vulnerabilities to derive a ReHARM, which could be regarded as an abstract interpretation. However, it is an unnecessary step to generate the ReHARM because it can be derived directly from the preprocessing phase (i.e., with given network and vulnerability information).

3.5 Security Evaluation

We analyse the risk associated with each attack path using the HARM with all details (e.g., a full HARM), denoted by R_{ap}. The computation of the risk is shown in equation (1) [9], where P_{goal} is the probability of an attack, and I_{goal} is the impact value. Note that it is possible to apply different security analysis by adopting different methods or even different ARM in the lower level of the ReHARM. To compute the risk, we use impact values directly from Table 1 and Table 2, and the exploitability is scaled by a factor of 10, to represent the probability of an attack. The exploitability value is computed by taking into account access vector, access complexity and authentication of vulnerability, which reflect characteristics of attack probabilities.

$$R_{ap} = P_{goal} \times I_{goal} \qquad (1)$$

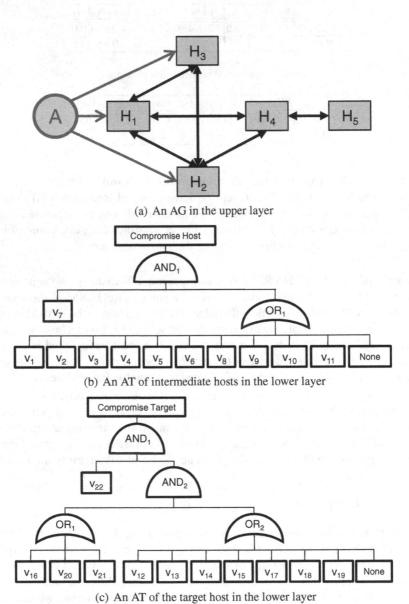

(a) An AG in the upper layer

(b) An AT of intermediate hosts in the lower layer

(c) An AT of the target host in the lower layer

Fig. 3. The HARM of the example network

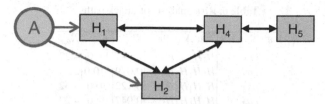

(a) A reduced AG in the upper layer

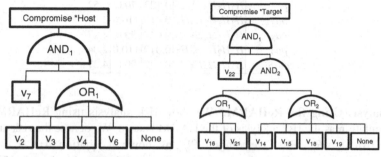

(b) A reduced AT of intermediate (c) A reduced AT of the target host in the
hosts in the lower layer   lower layer

Fig. 4. The ReHARM of the example network

Risk Computation Using the HARM. First, we compute P_{host} (i.e., probability of an
attack on intermediate hosts), as shown in equation (2). Note that $P_{None} = 1$ (i.e., not
choosing to exploit a vulnerability from the list has a probability of one).

$$
\begin{aligned}
P_{host} &= P_{v_7} \times P_{host_{OR_1}} \\
&= 0.39 \times [1 - ((1 - P_{v_1}) \times (1 - P_{v_2}) \times (1 - P_{v_3}) \times (1 - P_{v_4}) \times (1 - P_{v_5}) \\
&\quad \times (1 - P_{v_6}) \times (1 - P_{v_8}) \times (1 - P_{v_9}) \times (1 - P_{v_{10}}) \times (1 - P_{v_{11}}) \times (1 - P_{None}))] \\
&= 0.39
\end{aligned} \tag{2}
$$

Now we compute I_{host} as shown in equation (3). Note that $I_{None} = 0$ (i.e., not exploit
a vulnerability has no impact).

$$
\begin{aligned}
I_{host} &= I_{v_7} + I_{host_{OR_1}} \\
&= 10.0 + max(I_{v_1}, I_{v_2}, I_{v_3}, I_{v_4}, I_{v_5}, I_{v_6}, I_{v_8}, I_{v_9}, I_{v_{10}}, I_{v_{11}}, I_{None}) \\
&= 10.0 + 10.0 \\
&= 20.0
\end{aligned} \tag{3}
$$

Similarly, we can compute $P_{target} = 0.8$ and $I_{target} = 30.0$.

Now, we compute all possible attack paths, based on the HARM shown in Figure 3
using exhaustive search. The list of all possible attack paths and their risk analysis are
summarised in Table 6. Each attack path is presented with sequences of the hosts. We
observe the highest risk value is 8.52 (from paths pa_3 and pa_6).

Table 6. Risk analysis of attack paths

Path Number	Attack path	P_{goal}	I_{goal}	R_{ap}
pa_1	$H_1H_2H_4H_5$	0.047	90.0	4.27
pa_2	$H_1H_3H_2H_4H_5$	0.019	110.0	2.04
pa_3	$H_1H_4H_5$	0.122	70.0	8.52
pa_4	$H_2H_1H_4H_5$	0.047	90.0	4.27
pa_5	$H_2H_3H_1H_4H_5$	0.019	110.0	2.04
pa_6	$H_2H_4H_5$	0.122	70.0	8.52
pa_7	$H_3H_1H_2H_4H_5$	0.019	110.0	2.04
pa_8	$H_3H_1H_4H_5$	0.047	90.0	4.27
pa_9	$H_3H_2H_1H_4H_5$	0.019	110.0	2.04
pa_{10}	$H_3H_2H_4H_5$	0.047	90.0	4.27

Risk Analysis Using the ReHARM. We show risk analysis using ReHARM. The same calculation as the risk analysis of the HARM is used. We denote the risk analysis using ReHARM as R_{ap}^*. First, we compute P_{host}^* as shown in equation (4).

$$
\begin{aligned}
P_{host}^* &= P_{v_7} \times P_{host_{OR_1}}^* \\
&= 0.39 \times [1 - ((1 - P_{v_2}) \times (1 - P_{v_3}) \times (1 - P_{v_4}) \times (1 - P_{v_6}) \times (1 - P_{None}))] \\
&= 0.39 \times [1 - 0] \\
&= 0.39
\end{aligned} \tag{4}
$$

Now we compute I_{host}^*, as shown in equation (5).

$$
\begin{aligned}
I_{host}^* &= I_{v_7} + I_{host_{OR_1}}^* \\
&= 10.0 + max(I_{v_2}, I_{v_3}, I_{v_4}, I_{v_6}, I_{None}) \\
&= 10.0 + 10.0 \\
&= 20.0
\end{aligned} \tag{5}
$$

Similarly, we can compute $P_{target}^* = 0.7776$ and $I_{target}^* = 30.0$.

Based on the ReHARM as shown in Figure 4, we compute all possible attack paths using exhaustive search. Table 7 shows the risk analysis based on ReHARM. The highest risk value is 8.28 (from paths pa_2^* and pa_4^*), which is nearly equivalent to the risk analysis using the HARM shown in Table 6.

4   Simulation Results

We conduct simulations to investigate the effectiveness of security analysis using k-importance measures. Figure 5 shows the example network used for simulations. We were not able to use a real system with a large number of hosts to show the scalability of our proposed approach. The network consisted of 1000 hosts. 500 hosts were assigned in the DMZ network, 500 hosts were assigned in the Internal network, and one

Table 7. Risk analysis of attack paths using ReHARM

Path Number	Attack path	P^*_{goal}	I^*_{goal}	R^*_{ap}
pa^*_1	$H_1 H_2 H_4 H_5$	0.046	90.0	4.15
pa^*_2	$H_1 H_4 H_5$	0.118	70.0	8.28
pa^*_3	$H_2 H_1 H_4 H_5$	0.046	90.0	4.15
pa^*_4	$H_2 H_4 H_5$	0.118	70.0	8.28

target host was assigned in the Database network. Firewalls, denoted as FW_1 and FW_2, controls the data flow in the network, restricting access to the Internal and Database networks from outside. The attack scenario is for an attacker located outside the network to compromise the target host. All hosts were assigned with 10 vulnerabilities, where a single vulnerability (v_{root}) granted the admin privilege when exploited, two vulnerabilities (v^1_{user} and v^2_{user}) granted the user privilege, and the rest does not change the privilege status. To exploit v_{root}, the attacker must exploit either v^1_{user} or v^2_{user}. There is no restriction to exploit all other vulnerabilities. We use Intel(R) Core(TM)2 Quad CPU @ 2.66GHz with 3.24 GB of RAM on a Windows XP SP3 machine, and the simulation was coded in Python.

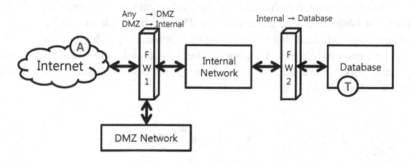

Fig. 5. An example network for simulation

4.1 Security Analysis Based on Host Importance

Risk of the network system is analysed, where different vulnerabilities are assigned with difference impact values chosen reasonably and randomly (v_{root} with 10, v^1_{user} and v^2_{user} with 5, and the rest with 1). We assume that the probability of an attack success on all vulnerabilities is one, but we can assign real probability values as in Section 3. We compare security analysis using exhaustive search and k-importance measures. We use degree centrality measures to rank k_1 important hosts. First, we consider all network hosts to compute the risk of the example network in Figure 5. Then, we continuously compute the risk value by generating the ReHARM by varying values of k_1. As the number of hosts modelled reduces, generation and evaluation times reduces although equivalent risk analysis is kept. The simulation result when $k_2 = 10$ is shown in Table 8. Generation and evaluation times are shown in Figure 6.

Table 8. Security analysis using k_1 values ($k_2 = 10$)

No. of hosts	Generation time (s)	Evaluation time (s)	Risk value	No. of attack paths
1000	0.725	113.515	348	55942475
900	0.603	108.358	348	55942475
800	0.528	104.626	348	55942475
700	0.456	102.873	348	55942475
600	0.372	101.780	348	55942475
500	0.309	96.998	348	5699925
400	0.241	42.796	348	3274425
300	0.181	8.172	348	848925
200	0.103	0.250	0	0
100	0.047	0.172	0	0
0	0.0	0.0	0	0

The density of simulation network is 0.006 (i.e., each host on average has a direct connection to six other hosts). The simulation result shows that the risk value is still equivalent when the network size has reduced by 70% (i.e., $k_1 = 300$). The generation time consistently reduces as the number of hosts modelled decreases as shown in Figure 6(a). The evaluation time decreases steadily down to 50% of hosts modelled. When the number of attack paths reduced, the evaluation time decreases rapidly. When the number of hosts modelled are reduced to 250, the hosts directly affecting the risk analysis are removed, such that the risk output is misleading. This is shown in Figure 6(b). Also, we can observe that changing number of vulnerabilities (i.e., k_2) does not affect the scalability of the evaluation phase. The optimal solution using degree centrality measures was found at $k_1 = 266$.

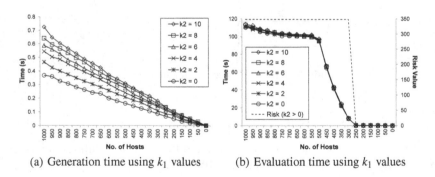

(a) Generation time using k_1 values   (b) Evaluation time using k_1 values

Fig. 6. Performance of security analysis using k_1 values

4.2   Security Analysis Based on Vulnerability Importance

We rank vulnerabilities with given impact value information. All network hosts are modelled to investigate the performance of risk analysis when k_2 number of important vulnerabilities are considered in the risk analysis. The simulation result is shown in Table 9. Generation and evaluation times are shown in Figure 7.

Table 9. Security analysis using k_2 values ($k_1 = 1000$)

No. of Vulnerabilities	Generation time (s)	Evaluation time (s)	Risk value
10	0.725	113.515	348
9	0.650	110.796	348
8	0.634	110.576	348
7	0.609	111.343	348
6	0.587	111.608	348
5	0.572	111.858	348
4	0.544	111.108	348
3	0.519	111.920	348
2	0.466	111.218	348
1	0.381	110.264	3
0	0.369	110.233	3

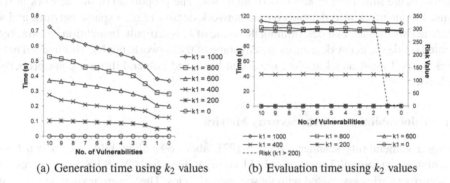

(a) Generation time using k_2 values   (b) Evaluation time using k_2 values

Fig. 7. Performance of security analysis using k_2 values

Table 10. Naive and optimal solution comparison

	Generation time (s)	Evaluation time (s)	Risk value	No. of attack paths
Naive	0.725	113.515	348	5942475
Optimal	0.097	0.578	348	24255

The generation time shows constant improvement, because there are a few numbers of components to generate in the lower layer. However, there are no improvements shown in the evaluation time for all k_1 values. It shows that k_2 values do not affect the performance of evaluation. If vulnerability models become more complex (i.e., multiple paths in exploiting vulnerabilities), the computational complexity of lower layer will also increase. The optimal solution is found when $k_2 = 2$. The naive solution compared to the optimal solution is shown in Table 10. The optimal solution shows approximately 87% generation time improvement and 99.5% evaluation time improvement respectively. We will investigate to find optimal k_1 and k_2 values in our future work.

5   Discussion

We used k-importance measures to generate a ReHARM. A risk analysis showed that an equivalent security solution can be achieved, while the size of the HARM is significantly reduced. Accuracy and performances of security analysis using k-importance measures are investigated through simulation. The NCM (e.g., closeness centrality) effectively ranked important hosts based on the network topology, and nearly equivalent risk value is computed. Moreover, the time performance was also improved for generating and evaluating the HARM.

However, the security analysis of the example system showed that not all vulnerabilities associated security metrics. Also, a single security metric often does not capture various effects of vulnerabilities (e.g., high CVSS BS, but low structural importance), and other requirements to satisfy the success of an attack are not well defined (e.g., privilege requirements). Network topologies and attack goals determine which hosts in a network are important in an event of an attack. The proportion of the network hosts unused in an attack also depends on the network density (e.g., a sparse network and a dense network), such that determining the value of k_1 is difficult. In addition, an attacker located inside the network reduces the coverage of the network, but NCMs cover all network hosts. Lastly, attack on less important hosts and vulnerabilities are not properly addressed.

5.1   Vulnerabilities without Security Metrics

Using a vulnerability scanner $NESSUS$ [27], about 60 vulnerabilities of a real host machine were reported. However, only 11 vulnerabilities had CVSS BS, which gives set of security metrics associated with these vulnerabilities. There were textual description of vulnerabilities (e.g., Vulnerability Synopsis and Vulnerability Description), but this is difficult to process automatically. Moreover, 10 vulnerabilities are scanned without any descriptions. Incomplete security data makes difficult to automate and analyse the network security. Other sources of vulnerability scanners and security metrics will be investigated in our future work.

5.2   Categorised Vulnerability Ranking

A single security metric cannot capture all aspects of vulnerabilities. The attack goal changes how vulnerabilities will be exploited by an attacker. For example, an attack goal of gaining the admin privilege defines a subset of vulnerabilities that must be exploited to achieve this, but an attack goal to hijack a communication of a host defines a different subset of vulnerabilities to achieve this goal. So, there needs a definition of vulnerability categories that satisfy different attack goals. Then vulnerabilities can be ranked within each subset. In addition, the ranking of vulnerabilities can be combined from vulnerability rankings based on various security metrics, such as CVSS BS rankings and structural importance rankings [9]. Improvements and effectiveness of categorising and combining vulnerability rankings should be further investigated.

5.3 Network Features for k_1 Selection

The network topology defines possible attack scenarios. A dense network (e.g., fully connected or mesh network topologies) allows the attacker to take many different attack paths to reach the target, so that a large proportion of network hosts will be used in at least one attack path. In contrast, a sparse network (e.g., star or tree network topologies) limits the number of attack paths, and the number of unused hosts (i.e., hosts that does not benefit the attacker in any attack scenario) increases. Therefore, the value of k_1 will depend on the attack scenario and the network topology. The effect of different network topologies for determining the value of k_1 importance measures needs to be studied, and the relationship between the number of hosts and the value of k_1 for the same network topology needs to be taken into account.

5.4 Modelling Attackers Located Inside the Network

Ranking important hosts using NCMs incorporates only the reachability of network hosts. However, an attacker located inside the network allows the attacker to bypass some of the network security (e.g., firewalls). Compared with an attack from outside the network, the scope of an attack is much smaller (i.e., only a subset of network hosts are considered) because the distance to the target is much closer. In such case, the ranking of important hosts using NCMs is inaccurate, because all network hosts are considered in NCMs. Therefore, one needs to consider an effective method to rank important hosts accurately for such attack scenarios.

5.5 Attack on Less Important Hosts and Vulnerabilities

By enforcing security only on important hosts and vulnerabilities allow attackers to exploit less important hosts and vulnerabilities, and security analysis based on important hosts and vulnerabilities cannot capture such attacks. One solution is that if all attack paths are covered with selected set of hosts and vulnerabilities, then any attack scenarios, regardless of using important or less important hosts and vulnerabilities, are covered. However, a naive approach to check the coverage of attack paths is computationally expensive (i.e., exponential number of attack paths need to be checked). More efficient method to cover all attack paths with a set of hosts and vulnerabilities will be studied in our future work.

6 Conclusion

Security analysis using the ARMs allows users and system administrators to become aware of vulnerable network components and configurations, and security solutions can be enforced or suggested to enhance the network security. However, existing ARMs have a scalability problem when the network size becomes large. Generating an ARM requires all the network information, and simplifications and heuristic methods are used in evaluation to improve the scalability. That is, not all network information is required for security analysis. Therefore, we proposed to use k-importance measures to improve generation and evaluation of ARMs. k_1 number of important hosts and k_2 number of important vulnerabilities are ranked and selected to generate an ARM (e.g., a two-layer HARM) and to evaluate the network security. We described methods to rank important hosts using NCMs and vulnerabilities using security metrics. We showed equivalent security solutions can be achieved using k-importance measures, while the performances improved in both generation and evaluation in terms of time and computation requirements. We also showed that time and computation requirements can be optimised by selecting appropriate number of important hosts and vulnerabilities, which showed a significant improvement compared to the exhaustive search method.

References

1. Sheyner, O., Haines, J., Jha, S., Lippmann, R., Wing, J.: Automated generation and analysis of attack graphs. Technical report, CMU (May 2002)
2. Schneier, B.: Secrets and Lies: Digital Security in a Networked World. John Wiley and Sons Inc. (2000)
3. Albanese, M., Jajodia, S., Noel, S.: Time-efficient and cost-effective network hardening using attack graphs. In: Proc. of Dependable Systems and Networks (DSN 2012). IEEE Computer Society, Los Alamitos (2012)
4. Roy, A., Kim, D., Trivedi, K.: Scalable optimal countermeasure selection using implicit enumeration on Attack Countermeasure Trees. In: Proc. of Dependable Systems and Networks (DSN 2012). IEEE Computer Society, Los Alamitos (2012)
5. Lippmann, R., Ingols, K.: An Annotated Review of Past Papers on Attack Graphs. ESC-TR-2005-054 (2005)
6. Ou, X., Boyer, W., McQueen, M.: A scalable approach to attack graph generation. In: Proc. of ACM Conference on Computer and Communications Security (CCS 2006). ACM (2006)
7. Ingols, K., Lippmann, R., Piwowarski, K.: Practical attack graph generation for network defense. In: Proc. of Computer Security Applications Conference, ACSAC 2006 (2006)
8. Edge, K.: A Framework for Analyzing and Mitigating the Vulnerabilities of Complex Systems via Attack and Protection Trees. PhD thesis, Air Force Institute of Technology (2007)
9. Roy, A., Kim, D., Trivedi, K.: Attack Countermeasure Trees (ACT): towards unifying the constructs of attack and defense trees. Security and Communication Networks 5(8) (2012)
10. Xie, A., Cai, Z., Tang, C., Hu, J., Chen, Z.: Evaluating network security with two-layer attack graphs. In: Proc. of Computer Security Applications Conference, ACSAC 2009 (2009)
11. Hong, J., Kim, D.: HARMs: Hierarchical Attack Representation Models for Network Security Analysis. In: Proc. of the 10th Australian Information Security Management Conference on SECAU Security Congress, SECAU 2012 (2012)
12. Noel, S., Jajodia, S.: Managing attack graph complexity through visual hierarchical aggregation. In: Proc. of the 2004 ACM Workshop on Visualization and Data Mining for Computer Security (VizSec 2004), pp. 109–118. ACM (2004)
13. Noel, S., Jajodia, S.: Understanding complex network attack graphs through clustered adjacency matrices. In: Proc. of the 21st Annual Computer Security Applications Conference (ACSAC 2005), pp. 160–169 (2005)
14. Abadi, M., Jalili, S.: A particle swarm optimization algorithm for minimization analysis of cost-sensitive attack graphs. The ISC International Journal of Information Security (ISeCure 2010) 2(1), 13–32 (2010)
15. Islam, T., Wang, L.: A Heuristic Approach to Minimum-Cost Network Hardening Using Attack Graph. In: Proc. of New Technologies, Mobility and Security, NTMS 2008 (2008)

16. Georgiadis, G., Kirousis, L.: Lightweight centrality measures in networks under attack. Complexus 3(1), 147–157 (2006)
17. Cadini, F., Zio, E., Petrescu, C.-A.: Using centrality measures to rank the importance of the components of a complex network infrastructure. In: Setola, R., Geretshuber, S. (eds.) CRITIS 2008. LNCS, vol. 5508, pp. 155–167. Springer, Heidelberg (2009)
18. Gallon, L., Bascou, J.: Using CVSS in Attack Graphs. In: Proc. of the Sixth International Conference on Availability, Reliability and Security (ARES 2011), pp. 59–66 (2011)
19. Sharma, A., Kalbarczyk, Z., Barlow, J., Iyer, R.: Analysis of security data from a large computing organization. In: Proc. of Dependable Systems Networks, DSN 2011 (2011)
20. Zhu, Y., Hu, H., Ahn, G., Huang, D., Wang, S.: Towards temporal access control in cloud computing. In: Proc. of Annual IEEE International Conference on Computer Communications (INFOCOM 2012), pp. 2576–2580 (2012)
21. Mirkovic, J., Benzel, T., Faber, T., Braden, R., Wroclawski, J., Schwab, S.: The DETER project: Advancing the science of cyber security experimentation and test. In: Proc. of IEEE International Conference on Technologies for Homeland Security (HST 2010), pp. 1–7 (2010)
22. Alata, E., Nicomette, V., Kaaniche, M., Dacier, M., Herrb, M.: Lessons learned from the deployment of a high-interaction honeypot. In: Proc. of Sixth European Dependable Computing Conference (EDCC 2006), pp. 39–46 (October 2006)
23. Zonouz, S., Khurana, H., Sanders, W., Yardley, T.: RRE: A game-theoretic intrusion Response and Recovery Engine. In: Proc. of IEEE/IFIP International Conference on Dependable Systems Networks (DSN 2009), pp. 439–448 (2009)
24. Chen, F., Liu, D., Zhang, Y., Su, J.: A scalable approach to analyzing network security using compact attack graphs. Journal of Networks 5(5) (2010)
25. Mehta, V., Bartzis, C., Zhu, H., Clarke, E., Wing, J.: Ranking attack graphs. In: Zamboni, D., Kruegel, C. (eds.) RAID 2006. LNCS, vol. 4219, pp. 127–144. Springer, Heidelberg (2006)
26. Sawilla, R., Skillicorn, D.: Partial cuts in attack graphs for cost effective network defence. In: Proc. of IEEE Conference on Technologies for Homeland Security, HST 2012 (2012)
27. Beale, J., Deraison, R., Meer, H., Temmingh, R., Walt, C.: The NESSUS project. Syngress Publishing (2002)
28. Floyd, R.: Algorithm 97: Shortest path. Commun. ACM 5(6), 345 (1962)
29. Ou, X., Govindavajhala, S.: Mulval: A logic-based network security analyzer. In: Proc. of the 14th USENIX Security Symposium (USENIX Security 2005), pp. 113–128 (2005)

The B-Side of Side Channel Leakage: Control Flow Security in Embedded Systems

Mehari Msgna, Konstantinos Markantonakis, and Keith Mayes

Smart Card Centre, Information Security Group,
Royal Holloway, University of London,
Egham, TW20 0EX, UK
{mehari.msgna.2011,k.markantonakis,k.mayes}@rhul.ac.uk

Abstract. The security of an embedded system is often compromised when a "trusted" program is subverted to behave differently. Such as executing maliciously crafted code and/or skipping legitimate parts of a "trusted" program. Several countermeasures have been proposed in the literature to counteract these behavioural changes of a program. A common underlying theme in most of them is to define security policies at the lower level of the system in an independent manner and then check for security violations either statically or dynamically at runtime. In this paper we propose a novel method that verifies a program's behaviour, such as the control flow, by using the device's side channel leakage.

Keywords: Side Channel Leakage, Power Consumption, Program's Control Flow, Hidden Markov Model, Principal Components Analysis, Linear Discriminant Analysis.

1   Introduction

In recent years, embedded systems have been proliferated into wide range of modern life applications. One of the main application vector of embedded systems is communication [1,2,3]. A typical embedded system application contains hardware and software components. The hardware component includes storage area, execution engine and other peripherals required to successfully execute instructions. The software component is a written procedures or rules stored in a memory pertaining to the operation of a computer system or part of the system itself.

The execution of a software program always involves incrementing the program counter (a special register which stores the address of the next instruction). Normally the program counter is incremented by "1"; however, certain instructions change its value by more than one in both directions. This kind of change is known as *Control Flow Change* and can be caused by both conditional and unconditional branching instructions. According to [4], program control flow is the most attacked target in software and such attacks are called *Control Flow Attacks*. A *Control Flow Attack* is one of the main threats for embedded systems [5,6,7]. *Control Flow Attacks* can be performed on embedded systems for

T. Zia et al. (Eds.): SecureComm 2013, LNICST 127, pp. 288–304, 2013.
© Institute for Computer Sciences, Social Informatics and Telecommunications Engineering 2013

two reasons. Firstly, the attacker installs his code segment on the target device. Later on when the device executes a genuine program, the attacker targets saved function return addresses to divert the control flow into his previously installed code. Secondly, the attacker does not install any code but instead when the program is executed the attacker changes the saved return addresses just in order to skip the execution of certain parts of the program.

In the literature, several countermeasures have been proposed to counteract these kinds of intrusions. To explain some of them; in [8], the authors discuss a technique that employs a dedicated hardware module to detect and prevent unintended program behaviors. In this method the program's properties are extracted through a static code analysis and the hardware module uses them to enforce a permissible program behavior at runtime. Another countermeasure, described in [9] introduces *Control-Flow Integrity (CFI)* enforcement. The CFI dictates that software execution must follow the path of a *Control-Flow Graph (CFG)* determined ahead of time. The work of Michael Frantzen and Michael Shuey [10], presents a buffer overflow prevention method. This is acheived via a kernel modification that performs transparent, automatic and atomic operations on the function return addresses before they are written into the stack and before the program transfers execution back to the saved return addresses. In [11], Aurélien et al. discussed a control flow enforcement technique based on Instruction Based Memory Access Control (IBMAC). This is done by using a simple hardware modification to divide the stack into a data and a control flow stack (or return stack). Moreover, access to the control flow stack is restricted only to return and call instructions, which prevents control flow manipulation. More countermeasures can be found in [12,13,14]. Most of the proposed countermeasures are demanding in terms of computational capability, memory usage and often rely on a hardware module that is not present on simple devices.

In this paper we present a novel approach to verify a program's control flow by using the device's side channel leakage. In our proposal we modelled the device as a *Markov Process* with hidden states, each state belonging to a part of the program. Then a verifying device extracts the control flow transition that the device had followed when executing the program from its side channel leakage (power consumption). This extracted control flow (state sequence) is then verified against a list of valid state transitions of the application which was calculated ahead of time.

The rest of the paper is structured as follows. Section 2 briefly provides background information on side channel leakage. Section 3 discusses the proposed control flow verification methodology. Section 4 discusses our experimental results. Finally, section 5 concludes the paper.

2   Side Channel Leakage

Side channel leakage is information revealed by a device about its internal state while processing a certain procedure. Smart cards and other embedded devices use electric current to turn transistors on and off. The instantaneous electric current that the device consumes depends on how many transistors that the executed instructions and data turn on and off. This difference in the electric current is then reflected in the power consumption and electromagnetic emission of the device. The power consumption and/or electromagnetic emission can then be recorded and analysed to extract secret information from the target device.

In the context of cryptology, side channel leakage can be employed in retrieving cryptographic secret keys from target devices, such as smart cards. Side channel information such as timing [15,16,17], power consumption [18,19,20] and electromagnetic emission [21,22,23] have been used in attacking implementations of cryptographic algorithms including AES [24], DES [25] and RSA [26].

Besides extracting cryptographic keys, side channel information has also been used to reverse engineer embedded device applications [27,28,29]. This is done by constructing a power consumption template of the target device using an identical reference device. Then use the templates to recognise executed instructions from the target device's power consumption waveform. In addition, side channel information can also be used by device manufacturers and application developers to detect cloned devices and design advanced applications. Instruction-level power consumption model of an embedded device has been used to design a low-power consuming applications for mobile embedded devices where batteries are the main power source [30,31]. In [32], the authors discuss, theoretically, how side channel leakage can be used to fingerprint a smart card platform and then use it later to detect cloned cards.

3   Control Flow Verification

An application is a combination of basic blocks. A basic block is a linear sequence of executable instructions with only one entry point (the first instruction executed) and one exit point (the last instruction executed) [33]. After executing one basic block the processor jumps into another basic block based on the branching instruction executed at the end of the current basic block. This branching instruction can be conditional or unconditional. A basic block may have many predecessors and many successors. It might also be its own successor. Program entry basic blocks might not have predecessors that are within the program and program ending basic blocks never have successors within the program itself.

An embedded device, with one or two programs installed in its non-volatile memory, can be modelled as a state machine with each state corresponding to a basic block of the program(s). When the program is being executed we can not directly observe the states that the processor is going through but we can observe the side channel information emitted by the device. Such information can be the power consumption [18,34] or the electro-magnetic emission [22,21,23] of the device. The side channel information emitted by the device is directly dependent on the states executed by the processor.

The questions here are, by only using this observable physical emission can we reconstruct the state sequence that the processor went through when executing the program? Furthermore, once the sequence is reconstructed can we verify it?

3.1   Control Flow Reconstruction

To reconstruct the state sequence that a device followed during the execution of a program from its side channel leakage we modelled the device as a *Hidden Markov Model (HMM)* [35,36]. A *Markov Model* is a memoryless system with a finite number of hidden states. It is called memoryless because the next state depends only on the current state.

In such a model the states are not directly observable. However, there has to be (at least) one observable output of the process that reveals partial information about the state sequence that the device has followed. Fig. 1, illustrates a *Markov Process* with five hidden states (i.e A to E).

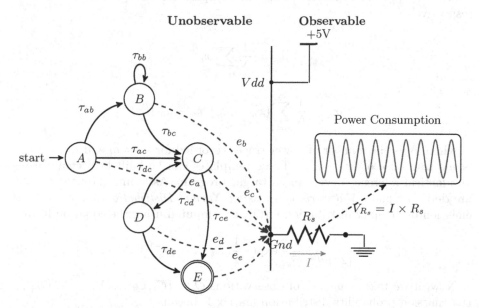

Fig. 1. A Markov model representing a device executing a program with five states (A, B, C, D and E). The power consumption is the observable output that reveals partial information about the state sequence of the device.

In case of the *Markov Process* illustrated in Fig. 1, the hidden states are the program's basic blocks and the observable output is the power consumption of the device. This observable output is measured via a resistor (R_s) connecting the ground pin of the device and ground pin of the voltage source.

Building the Hidden Markov Model. Building a *Hidden Markov Model (HMM)* requires a set of finite states q_i's, a transition probability distribution matrix $\mathbf{T} = \{\tau_{ij}\}$, emission probability distribution matrix $\mathbf{E} = \{e_i\}$ and initial state distribution π. Given these probability distribution matrices, the HMM is defined as $\lambda = (\mathbf{T}, \mathbf{E}, \pi)$.

The transition probability distribution τ_{ij}, is the probability that the next state is q_j if the current state is q_i, for $1 \leq i, j \leq S$ where S is the number of states. If we denote s_t the current state of the system at a time t, $\tau_{ij} = \mathcal{P}(s_{t+1} = q_j \mid s_t = q_i)$ is the probability of transitioning from state q_i to state q_j. Given an observation (power consumption) $\mathcal{O}_t$ at a time t, the emission probability distribution $e_i(\mathcal{O}_t) = \mathcal{P}(\mathcal{O}_t \mid s_t = q_i)$ is the probability that $\mathcal{O}_t$ was emitted by the state q_i. To compute $e_i(\mathcal{O}_t)$ first we need to build a power consumption template for each state. The template of each state is generated by computing the mean, μ_{q_i}, and the covariance, σ_{q_i} of the state's power consumption traces.

Let us consider N L-dimensional power consumption traces $\{x_n\}$ generated by the device while executing the state q_i were recorded. The mean, μ_{q_i}, and covariance, σ_{q_i}, are calculated using the computation in equations (1) and (2) respectively.

$$\mu_{q_i} = \frac{1}{N} \sum_{n=1}^{N} x_n \tag{1}$$

$$\sigma_{q_i} = \frac{1}{N} \sum_{n=1}^{N} (x_n - \mu_{q_i})(x_n - \mu_{q_i})^T \tag{2}$$

where N is the number of power traces recorded for state q_i and $(x_n - \mu_{q_i})^T$ is the transpose of $(x_n - \mu_{q_i})$. These templates can be built beforehand using an identical reference device and a target program. Assuming the power traces are derived from a *Multivariate Gaussian Normal Distribution Model* [37], the emission probability distribution $e_i(\mathcal{O}_t)$ is computed using the equation in (3).

$$e_i(\mathcal{O}_t) = \frac{1}{(2\pi)^{L/2}\sqrt{\sigma_{q_i}}} \exp(-\frac{1}{2}(\mathcal{O}_t - \mu_{q_i})\sigma_{q_i}^{-1}(\mathcal{O}_t - \mu_{q_i})^T) \tag{3}$$

Now, if we take a number of observations $\mathcal{O} = \{\mathcal{O}_t, \mathcal{O}_{t+1}, \mathcal{O}_{t+2}, \cdots, \mathcal{O}_{t+n}\}$, the emission probability distribution matrix $\mathbf{E}$ becomes:

$$\mathbf{E} = \begin{bmatrix} e_1(\mathcal{O}_t) & e_1(\mathcal{O}_{t+1}) & e_1(\mathcal{O}_{t+2}) & \cdots & e_1(\mathcal{O}_{t+n}) \\ e_2(\mathcal{O}_t) & e_2(\mathcal{O}_{t+1}) & e_2(\mathcal{O}_{t+2}) & \cdots & e_2(\mathcal{O}_{t+n}) \\ \vdots & \vdots & \vdots & \ddots & \vdots \\ e_S(\mathcal{O}_t) & e_S(\mathcal{O}_{t+1}) & e_S(\mathcal{O}_{t+2}) & \cdots & e_S(\mathcal{O}_{t+n}) \end{bmatrix} \tag{4}$$

Normally when an application is invoked, the execution always starts at the program entry point (*main()*). Therefore, the initial state distribution for the first basic block is always 1 and 0 for the other basic blocks. For example, for the system depicted in Fig. 1 the execution of the application always starts at A. So, the initial state distribution becomes $\pi_A = 1$ and $\{\pi_B, \pi_C, \pi_D, \pi_E\} = 0$.

To successfully compute $\mathbf{E}$ using equation (3), all observations $\{\mathcal{O}_t, \cdots, \mathcal{O}_{t+n}\}$ must have equal dimensionality. In other words, the power consumption traces generated by all states must have the same number of sample points. However, in reality this may not always be true. In addition, the dimension of the emissions (power traces) may be too large for a robust and fast classification. A common way to attempt to resolve this problem is to use a dimensionality reduction technique. In doing this we have to maintain as much information about the original emission (power consumption) as possible. Two of the most popular techniques for this purpose are: *Principal Components Analysis (PCA)* and *Fisher's Linear Discriminant Analysis (F-LDA)*.

Principal Components Analysis (PCA) is a technique used to reduce the dimension of an observation while keeping as much of its variance as possible [38]. This is achieved by orthogonally projecting the observation onto a lower dimensional subspace vector.

Let us consider an N L-dimensional observations of emissions $\{x_n\}$, where $n = 1, ..., N$ and their covariance matrix σ. A lower dimensional subspace in this Euclidean space can be defined by a D-dimensional unit vector $\vec{u_1}$, where $D < L$. The projection of each observation, x_n, onto that subspace is given by $\vec{u_1}^T x_n$. Now if we stack up all the emissions into a matrix of $N \times L$ matrix, where L is the number of samples of each observation, the projection of each row of the matrix is represented as $U^T X$, where U is a matrix of *eigenvectors* of the covariance matrix σ. The projection of the observations onto a D-dimensional subspace that maximizes the projected variance is given by D *eigenvectors* [39] $\vec{u_1}, ..., \vec{u_d}$ with the D largest *eigenvalues* $\lambda_1, ..., \lambda_d$.

Fisher's Linear Discriminant Analysis (F-LDA) is a method used in statistics, pattern recognition and machine learning to find a linear combination of features which characterises two or more class observations [40,41,42]. The resulting combination may be used as a linear classifier for dimensionality reduction before classification. However, instead of maximising the variance of the original data like PCA, information regarding the covariance of different classes is taken into consideration. These are the "between-class" and "within-class" covariance matrices.

Now, let us consider again the N L-dimensional observations for each class. Then the "within-class" covariance σ_W is computed as,

$$\sigma_W = \sum_{i=1}^{S} \sum_{w \in x_i} (w - \mu_{q_i})(w - \mu_{q_i})^T = \sum_{i=1}^{S} N_{q_i} \sigma_{q_i} \tag{5}$$

In the above equation, N_{q_i}, σ_{q_i} and w are the number of observations, the covariance and the power traces of class q_i. The "between-class" covariance σ_B is computed as

$$\sigma_B = \sum_{i=1}^{S} (\mu_{q_i} - \mu)(\mu_{q_i} - \mu)^T \tag{6}$$

where μ_{q_i} is the individual class's mean as defined in equation (1) and μ is the mean of the entire observation which is computed as shown in equation (7).

$$\mu = \frac{1}{N} \sum_{\forall x} x = \frac{1}{N} \sum_{i=1}^{S} N_{q_i} \mu_{q_i} \tag{7}$$

Now, let us consider a D-dimensional unit vector $\vec{u_1}$ onto which the data is projected. This time the objective is to maximise both the projected "between-class" and the projected "within-class" covariance:

$$\mathcal{J}(\vec{u_1}) = \frac{\vec{u_1}^T \sigma_B \vec{u_1}}{\vec{u_1}^T \sigma_W \vec{u_1}} \tag{8}$$

The projected $\mathcal{J}$ is maximised if $\vec{u_1}$ is the *eigenvector* of $\sigma_W^{-1} \sigma_B$. The D-dimensional subspace is created by the first D orthogonal directions that maximise the projected $\mathcal{J}$. These are given by the D *eigenvectors* $\vec{u_1}, \cdots, \vec{u_D}$ of $\sigma_W^{-1} \sigma_B$ with the largest *eigenvalues* $\lambda_1, \cdots, \lambda_D$.

Calculating the Most Probable State Sequence. The probability distribution matrices $\mathbf{E}$, $\mathbf{T}$ and π can be constructed ahead of time using an identical reference device and the target application. Now let us consider we observe emissions (power consumption traces) $\mathcal{O} = \{\mathcal{O}_t, \mathcal{O}_{t+1}, \mathcal{O}_{t+2}, \cdots, \mathcal{O}_{t+n}\}$, where n is the length of the state sequence. These emissions were recorded while the device was executing the target application. The most likely sequence of states that produces the observations $\mathcal{O}$ is calculated using the *Viterbi Algorithm* [43] as shown in equations (9) and (10). This state sequence is regarded as the control flow that the device has followed when executing the program.

$$\mathcal{V}_{1,j} = \mathcal{P}(\mathcal{O}_1 \mid s_1 = q_j) \cdot \pi_j \tag{9}$$

$$\mathcal{V}_{t,j} = \mathcal{P}(\mathcal{O}_t \mid s_t = q_j) \cdot max_{i \in S}(\tau_{ij} \cdot \mathcal{V}_{t-1,j}) \tag{10}$$

In equation (10), S is the state space of the *Markov Process*, π_j the probability of state q_j being the initial state and τ_{ij} probability of transitioning from state q_i to state q_j. The $\mathcal{V}_{t,j}$ is the probability of the most probable state sequence responsible for the first t emissions that has q_j as its final state. The state sequence that resulted in highest probability, according to equation (10), from all possible state sequences of the same length as the emission is regarded as the most probable state sequence that generated the emissions.

3.2   Verifying the Reconstructed State Sequence

As described in section 3, a program is a combination of basic blocks. Before loading the program into the target device, a list of valid transitions between the states (basic blocks) are extracted using a code analysis tool. This list of valid transitions is known as the *Control Flow Graph (CFG)*. A CFG, $G = (I, P)$, is represented by the program's states identity, I, and control flow path, P. For instance, for the program illustrated in Fig. 1, the CFG is given as $G = (I, P)$,

where $I = \{A, B, C, D, E\}$ and $P = \{(A, B), (A, C), (B, B), (B, C), (C, D),$
$(C, E), (D, C), (D, E)\}$. The CFG is then installed into the verifying device (i.e
the terminal in the case of a smart card application).

Now the task is verifying if the reconstructed state sequence is among the
valid transitions in the CFG. However, since the reconstruction of the state
sequence (explained in section 3.1) from the power consumption is a probabilistic
process, we have to first confirm that the reconstructed state sequence is the
actual state sequence that the device followed when executing the program.
This can be acheived by comparing a hash value generated over the identity of
actually executed states (H^*) with a hash value generated over the identity of
reconstructed states from the power trace (H'). In equation (11), H^* is generated
by the device that executes the program and sent to the verifying device that
generates H'.

$$f(H^*, H') = \begin{cases} 1, & \text{if } H^* = H' \\ 0, & \text{otherwise} \end{cases} \tag{11}$$

If it is a match, the reconstructed sequence is what the processor went through
when executing the program. Otherwise, the reconstructed sequence is not the
path that was followed by the device. Equation (11) can only verify that the
execute state sequence and the extracted state sequence are the same. Unfortunately, this does not verify if the executed state sequence (control flow) is valid.
Therefore, the validity of the control flow is verified by comparing it against
the pre-calculated paths, P, in CFG. If the reconstructed state sequence is not
among the valid paths in CFG, the device/program is regarded as compromised.

4   Experimental Results

To implement the techniques discussed above we chose *ATMega163 + 24C256*
based smart card. ATMega163 is an 8-bit microcontroller based on AVR architecture. Note that this smart card does not have any countermeasure against
power analysis attacks. To construct a more reliable template for the states of the
test program (see Fig (3)), we removed all other factors that influence the power
consumption of the device. Such factors can be the intrinsic and ambient noise
introduced by the measurement setup. To minimise the influence of the ambient
noise, we have properly warmed up the measurement equipment beforehand so
that it is all running at a uniform temperature during the power trace collection phase. This requires running few test measurements to be discarded before
the actual power trace collection starts. The intrinsic noise introduced into the
measurement can be minimised by collecting several traces for each state and
calculating the mean. This reduces the standard deviation of the noise by a factor of $\sqrt{n}$, given that n is the number of power traces involved in calculating the
mean.

The power consumption is measured as a voltage drop across a resistor connecting the ground pin of the smart card and the ground pin of the voltage

source. The smart card is running at a 4 MHz clock cycle and is powered up by a +5V supply from the reader. The measurements are performed using a *LeCroy WaveRunner 6100A* [44] oscilloscope capable of measuring traces at a rate of 5 billion samples per second (5GS/s). The shunt resistor is connected with the oscilloscope using a *Pomona 6069A* [45] *probe*, a 1.2m co-axial cable with a 250MHz bandwidth, 10MΩ input resistance and 10pf input capacitance. All measurements are sampled at a rate of 500 MS/s and the same setup is used throughout the experiment.

4.1   Control Flow Reconstruction

For our experiment we implemented a test application with five basic blocks (states). Each state accomplishes certain task within the program. The processor follows different control flow paths to execute the application depending on a value "V_{reader}" sent from a terminal. The state machine diagram of the test application is presented in the Fig. 2.

Fig. 2. Test program's control flow diagram

Fig. 3. High-level description of the test program

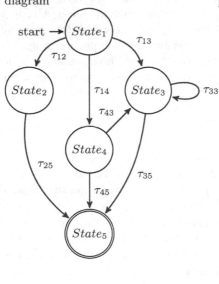

```
State1:  Par = receive()
         Vreader = receive()
         Vnvm = read(nvm)
         if(Vreader == Vnvm)
State2:      par = (par)^2
             goto State5
         end
         else if(Vreader > Vnvm)
State4:      par = par + 216
             par = par/5
             Vreader = Vreader - 2
             if(Vreader < Vnvm)
                 goto State3
             end
             else
                 goto State5
             end
         end
         else if(Vreader < Vnvm)
State3:      par = par * 2
             par = par - 129
             Vreader = Vreader + 1
             if (Vreader < Vnvm)
                 goto State3
             end
             else
                 goto State5
             end
         end
State5:  clear_registers
         clear_memory
```

Invoking the test program requires passing two arguments: "V_{reader}" ($0 \leq V_{reader} \leq 9$) and "Par" ($0 \leq Par \leq 255$). The "V_{reader}" is compared with a reference value "V_{nvm}" ($0 \leq V_{nvm} \leq 9$) (stored in the non-volatile memory of the smart card) before changing a state. For our experiment the V_{nvm} is initialised to "4" and the arguments Par and V_{reader} are randomly generated and passed to the program through the smart card reader.

Building the Hidden Markov Model. As discussed in Section 3.1, building a *Hidden Markov Model* requires the initial probability distribution π, transition probability distribution $\mathbf{T}$ and the emission probability distribution $\mathbf{E}$. As illustrated in Fig. 2, the execution of the test program always starts at $State_1$. Therefore, the probability of $State_1$ being the initial state is "1", and "0" for all other states. If π_i is the probability of $State_i$ being the initial state in the execution of the program, the initial probability distribution vector of our test program is given as:

$$\pi = \{\pi_1 = 1, \pi_2 = 0, \pi_3 = 0, \pi_4 = 0, \pi_5 = 0\} \tag{12}$$

To compute the transition probability distribution matrix, $\mathbf{T}$, we invoked the program with a randomly generated "Par" and all possible values (i.e. 0 to 9) of "V_{reader}" and record the control-flow transition of the program. Note that for each different value of "V_{nvm}" the matrix $\mathbf{T}$ is different.

Table 1. Transition probability distribution of the program illustrated in Fig. 2 and 3. The columns represent next states and the rows represent current states.

Transition from	Transition to [%]				
	$State_1$	$State_2$	$State_3$	$State_4$	$State_5$
$State_1$	$\tau_{11}=0$	$\tau_{12}=0.1$	$\tau_{13}=0.4$	$\tau_{14}=0.5$	$\tau_{15}=0$
$State_2$	$\tau_{21}=0$	$\tau_{22}=0$	$\tau_{23}=0$	$\tau_{24}=0$	$\tau_{25}=1$
$State_3$	$\tau_{31}=0$	$\tau_{32}=0$	$\tau_{33}=0.55$	$\tau_{34}=0$	$\tau_{35}=0.45$
$State_4$	$\tau_{41}=0$	$\tau_{42}=0$	$\tau_{43}=0.2$	$\tau_{44}=0$	$\tau_{45}=0.8$
$State_5$	$\tau_{51}=0$	$\tau_{52}=0$	$\tau_{53}=0$	$\tau_{54}=0$	$\tau_{55}=0$

To compute the emission probability distribution matrix $\mathbf{E}$, we collected 1000 traces for each state. Using these traces we computed the mean μ_{q_i}, and covariance, σ_{q_i}, for each state as a template.

As shown in figure 4, the states of the test application generate power consumption traces of different dimension. In our experiment $\mathbf{E}$ is computed over the first 250 sample points of the traces. However, a covariance matrix of 250×250 is still too large to compute its inverse. For this purpose we applied the techniques discussed in Section 3.1 (PCA and F-LDA) on the first 250 sample points of the state emission (power consumption) before computing $\mathbf{E}$.

Principal Components Analysis (PCA) is used to find a subspace whose basis vectors corresponding to the maximum variance directions in the original data. In other words PCA searches for those vectors in the underlying data that best describes the data. When applying *PCA* the dimensionality of the

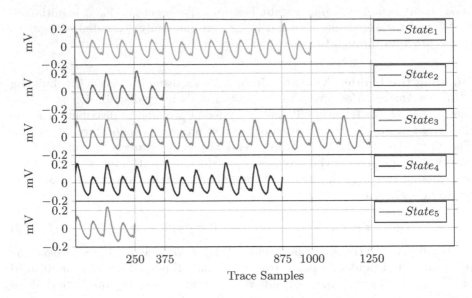

Fig. 4. Mean of the power traces of the states illustrated in Fig. 2

projected data has to be selected carefully. On the one hand, if it is too small, too much of variance of the original data may get lost and with it important information about the state emissions. On the other hand, if it is too large, the state classification becomes less reliable again. This might be because of the bad conditioning of large covariance matrix. Another reason can be, as the dimension increase the class emission cross-correlation increases. Therefore, when choosing the dimensionality for the projected data we have to decide how much of variance of the original data that we can afford to lose.

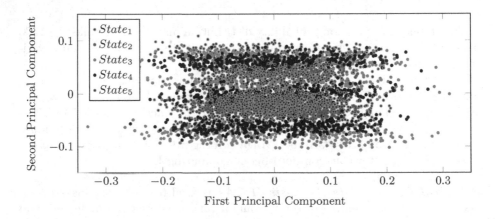

Fig. 5. Original data after PCA

For example, in our experiment the first 100 principal components were accounted for 54.76% of the variance of the original emission. the first 250 principal components are accounted for 80.74% of the variance of the original emission. In Fig.5 we show plots of the first two principal components after PCA.

Fisher's Linear Discriminant Analysis (F-LDA) is a technique used to classify between classes by finding discriminant features of the class data and projecting them onto these discriminant vectors. In other words, F-LDA searches for those vectors in the underlying data that best separates among the classes.

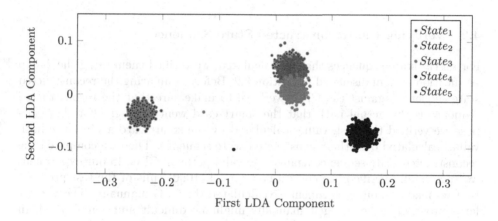

Fig. 6. Original data after F-LDA

In Fig. 6 we present the first two components of the state emissions after F-LDA. As discussed earlier PCA searches for vectors that best describes the original data. However, it does not take the other classes into consideration. For this reason PCA may not produce a satisfactory result when classifying different classes. We can see that in Fig. 5 the principal components of classes emissions overlap. However, as shown in Fig. 6 the classes are better separated after F-LDA.

Calculating the Most Probable State Sequence. To calculate the most probable state sequence, first we have to implement the *Viterbi Algorithm* discussed in Section 3.1. To do this we have two options: use the MATLAB [46] Statistics Toolbox implementation *hmmviterbi*[47] or create our own implementation of the equations (9) and (10). Although, the MATLAB Statistics Toolbox implementation of *Viterbi Algorithm* might be useful for some statistical calculations we could not use it in our experiment. This was because firstly it does not utilise the initial probability distribution (π) and secondly the output is not in the format that we want it to be. Therefore, we created our own MATLAB implementation and the source code is available at the end of the paper in Appendix A. As you can see it from the source code, our implementation takes all three matrices (π, $\mathbf{E}$ and $\mathbf{T}$) that we discussed in Section 3 and gives us the most likely state sequence as a vector.

Our test program has six valid control-flow paths from the initial state, $state_1$, to the final state, $state_5$. Our implementation of the *Viterbi algorithm* calculates a sequence of states with the highest probability of generating the emission $\mathcal{O}$. We ran the test program for all possible valid paths by varying the argument "V_{reader}" and calculated the most probable state sequence from the smart cards power consumption trace. We ran the test program 1000 times by varying "V_{Reader}", recorded the power trace and calculated the most likely sequence of states for each run.

4.2   Verifying the Reconstructed State Sequence

For all the state sequences that we calculated, we verified them using the 2-step verification system discussed in Section 3.2. Before comparing the reconstructed state sequence against the CFG, we have to make sure that the reconstructed sequence is the actual path that the smart card went through. For that purpose we verified the hash values calculated by the smart card against the hash values calculated over the reconstructed state sequence. Then we compared the reconstructed state sequence against the valid paths in CFG. In our experiment we successfully verified the control flow for all (1000) runs of the test program that we made. In our experiment we calculated the CFG manually; however, for large programs calculating it manually might be difficult and complicated. In such a case the CFG may be extracted using a source code analysis tools, such as MALPAS [48].

5   Conclusion

In the literature several methods have been proposed to counteract a program's control flow violation. In most of them the proposed solutions require either a dedicated hardware module or the main processor to perform extra computations to check the control flow security of the program(s) at runtime. Usually this computation utilises the program's properties which are extracted ahead of time, such as CFG. These properties are then used to check the program's behaviour dynamically. However, these kind of solutions may not be suitable for low-end devices deployed as coprocessors in bigger systems, such as hardware security modules in communication devices.

In this paper we proposed a novel approach into checking a program's control flow integrity by using the side channel leakage of the target device. In our method the device is not required to perform extra computation. However, it requires another device to check for its program's control flow integrity as it executes the program. This method can be used in smart card (or any other embedded device that need to connect to an external device to execute the application) where the terminal (external device) acts as the verifying device.

References

1. Feng, A., Knieser, M., Rizkalla, M.E., King, B., Salama, P., Bowen, F.: Embedded system for sensor communication and security. IET Information Security 6(2), 111–121 (2012)
2. Shoufan, A.: A hardware security module for quadrotor communication. In: International Conference on Field-Programmable Technology (FPT), December 10-12, 2012, pp. 253–256. IEEE (2012)
3. Jaeger, A., Stuebing, H., Huss, S.: A dedicated hardware security module for field operational tests of Car-to-X communication. In: 4th ACM Conference on Wireless Network Security (WiSec 2011) (June 2011)
4. Parameswaran, S., Wolf, T.: Embedded systems security - an overview. Design Autom. for Emb. Sys. 12(3), 173–183 (2008)
5. Bouffard, G., Iguchi-Cartigny, J., Lanet, J.-L.: Combined software and hardware attacks on the Java Card control flow. In: Prouff, E. (ed.) CARDIS 2011. LNCS, vol. 7079, pp. 283–296. Springer, Heidelberg (2011)
6. Francillon, A., Castelluccia, C.: Code injection attacks on Harvard-architecture devices. In: ACM Conference on Computer and Communications Security, October 27-31, pp. 15–26. ACM (2008)
7. Delalleau, G.: Large memory management vulnerabilities: System, compiler and application issues, http://cansecwest.com/core05/memory_vulns_delalleau.pdf (visited April 2013)
8. Arora, D., Ravi, S., Raghunathan, A., Jha, N.K.: Hardware-assisted run-time monitoring for secure program execution on embedded processors. IEEE Trans. VLSI Syst. 14(12), 1295–1308 (2006)
9. Abadi, M., Budiu, M., Erlingsson, Ú., Ligatti, J.: Control-flow integrity principles, implementations, and applications. ACM Trans. Inf. Syst. Secur. 13(1) (2009)
10. Frantzen, M., Shuey, M.: StackGhost: Hardware facilitated stack protection. In: Wallach, D.S. (ed.) 10th USENIX Security Symposium, August 13-17. USENIX (2001)
11. Francillon, A., Perito, D., Castelluccia, C.: Defending embedded systems against control flow attacks. In: Proceedings of the First ACM Workshop on Secure Execution of Untrusted Code, SecuCode 2009, pp. 19–26. ACM, New York (2009)
12. Kil, C., Jun, J., Bookholt, C., Xu, J., Ning, P.: Address space layout permutation (aslp): Towards fine-grained randomization of commodity software. In: Annual Computer Security Applications Conference (ACSAC), December 11-15, pp. 339–348. IEEE Computer Society (2006)
13. Cowan, C., Pu, C., Maier, D., Hinton, H., Walpole, J., Bakke, P., Beattie, S., Grier, A., Wagle, P., Zhang, Q.: Stackguard: Automatic adaptive detection and prevention of buffer-overflow attacks. In: Proceedings of the 7th USENIX Security Symposium, vol. 81, pp. 346–355 (1998)
14. Edward Suh, G., Lee, J.W., Zhang, D., Devadas, S.: Secure program execution via dynamic information flow tracking. In: International Conference on Architectural Support for Programming Languages and Operating Systems (ASPLOS), October 7-13, pp. 85–96. ACM (2004)
15. Kocher, P.C.: Timing attacks on implementations of Diffie-Hellman, RSA, DSS, and other systems. In: Koblitz, N. (ed.) CRYPTO 1996. LNCS, vol. 1109, pp. 104–113. Springer, Heidelberg (1996)
16. Dhem, J.-F., Koeune, F., Leroux, P.-A., Mestré, P., Quisquater, J.-J., Willems, J.-L.: A practical implementation of the timing attack. In: Quisquater, J.-J., Schneier, B. (eds.) CARDIS 1998. LNCS, vol. 1820, pp. 167–182. Springer, Heidelberg (2000)

17. Arnaud, C., Fouque, P.-A.: Timing attack against protected RSA-CRT implementation used in PolarSSL. In: Dawson, E. (ed.) CT-RSA 2013. LNCS, vol. 7779, pp. 18–33. Springer, Heidelberg (2013)
18. Kocher, P.C., Jaffe, J., Jun, B.: Differential power analysis. In: Wiener, M. (ed.) CRYPTO 1999. LNCS, vol. 1666, pp. 388–397. Springer, Heidelberg (1999)
19. Popp, T., Mangard, S., Oswald, E.: Power analysis attacks and countermeasures. IEEE Design & Test of Computers 24(6), 535–543 (2007)
20. Oswald, D., Paar, C.: Breaking Mifare DESFire MF3ICD40: Power analysis and templates in the real world. In: Preneel, B., Takagi, T. (eds.) CHES 2011. LNCS, vol. 6917, pp. 207–222. Springer, Heidelberg (2011)
21. Heyszl, J., Mangard, S., Heinz, B., Stumpf, F., Sigl, G.: Localized electromagnetic analysis of cryptographic implementations. In: Dunkelman, O. (ed.) CT-RSA 2012. LNCS, vol. 7178, pp. 231–244. Springer, Heidelberg (2012)
22. Gu, K., Wu, L., Li, X., Zhang, X.: Design and implementation of an electromagnetic analysis system for smart cards. In: Wang, Y., Cheung, Y.M., Guo, P., Wei, Y. (eds.) CIS, Sanya, Hainan, China, December 3-4, pp. 653–656. IEEE (2011)
23. Van Eck, W., Laborato, N.: Electromagnetic radiation from video display units: An eavesdropping risk? Computers & Security 4, 269–286 (1985)
24. Daemen, J., Rijmen, V.: The Design of Rijndael: AES - The Advanced Encryption Standard. Information Security and Cryptography. Springer (2002)
25. Tuchman, W.: A brief history of the data encryption standard. In: Denning, D., Denning, P. (eds.) Internet Besieged, pp. 275–280. ACM Press/Addison-Wesley Publishing Co., New York (1998)
26. Rivest, R.L., Shamir, A., Adleman, L.M.: A method for obtaining digital signatures and public-key cryptosystems. Commun. ACM 21(2), 120–126 (1978)
27. Vermoen, D., Witteman, M., Gaydadjiev, G.N.: Reverse engineering Java Card applets using power analysis. In: Sauveron, D., Markantonakis, K., Bilas, A., Quisquater, J.-J. (eds.) WISTP 2007. LNCS, vol. 4462, pp. 138–149. Springer, Heidelberg (2007)
28. Eisenbarth, T., Paar, C., Weghenkel, B.: Building a side channel based disassembler. In: Gavrilova, M.L., Tan, C.J.K., Moreno, E.D. (eds.) Transactions on Computational Science X. LNCS, vol. 6340, pp. 78–99. Springer, Heidelberg (2010)
29. Clavier, C.: Side channel analysis for reverse engineering (SCARE) - an improved attack against a secret A3/A8 GSM algorithm. IACR Cryptology ePrint Archive 2004, 49 (2004)
30. Lee, S., Ermedahl, A., Min, S.L., Chang, N.: An accurate instruction-level energy consumption model for embedded RISC processors. In: Hong, S., Pande, S. (eds.) LCTES/OM, Snowbird, Utah, USA, June 22-23, pp. 1–10. ACM (2001)
31. Kavvadias, N., Neofotistos, P., Nikolaidis, S., Kosmatopoulos, C.A., Laopoulos, T.: Measurements analysis of the software-related power consumption in microprocessors. IEEE T. Instrumentation and Measurement 53(4), 1106–1112 (2004)
32. Mayes, K., Markantonakis, K., Chen, C.: Smart card platform-fingerprinting. In: Advanced Card Technology, pp. 78–82 (October 2006)
33. Allen, F.: Control flow analysis. In: Proceedings of a Symposium on Compiler Optimization, pp. 1–19. ACM, New York (1970)
34. Popp, T., Mangard, S., Oswald, E.: Power analysis attacks and countermeasures. IEEE Design & Test of Computers 24(6), 535–543 (2007)
35. Fink, A.: Markov Models for Pattern Recognition. Springer (2008)
36. Rabiner, L.: A tutorial on Hidden Markov Models and selected applications in speech recognition. Proceedings of the IEEE 77(2), 257–286 (1989)

37. Gut, A.: An Intermediate Course In Probability, 2nd edn. Springer, Department of Mathematics, Uppsala University, Sweden (2009)
38. Berrendero, J.R., Justel, A., Svarc, M.: Principal components for multivariate functional data. Computational Statistics & Data Analysis 55(9), 2619–2634 (2011)
39. Strang, G.: Introduction to Linear Algebra, 3rd edn. Wellesley-Cambridge Press, MA (2003)
40. Fisher, R.A.: The use of multiple measurements in taxonomic problems. Annals of Eugenics 7, 179–188 (1936)
41. Fukumi, M., Mitsukura, Y.: Feature generation by simple-FLDA for pattern recognition. In: CIMCA/IAWTIC, November 28-30, pp. 730–734. IEEE Computer Society (2005)
42. Zhang, L., Wang, D., Gao, S.: Application of improved Fisher Linear Discriminant Analysis approaches. In: International Conference on Management Science and Industrial Engineering (MSIE), pp. 1311–1314 (2011)
43. Forney Jr., D.: The Viterbi Algorithm: A personal history. CoRR, abs/cs/0504020 (2005)
44. Teledyne LeCroy. Teledyne LeCroy website, http://www.teledynelecroy.com (visited February 2013)
45. Pomona Electronics. 6069A Scope Probe, http://www.pomonaelectronics.com/pdf/d4550b-sp150b_6_01.pdf (visited October 2012)
46. MATLAB. Version 7.10.0.499 (R2010a). The MathWorks, Inc., Natick, Massachusetts (2013), http://www.mathworks.co.uk/index.html
47. MATLAB. Hidden Markov Model most probable state path, http://www.mathworks.co.uk/help/stats/hmmviterbi.html (visited March 2013)
48. Atkins Limited. MALPAS, http://www.malpas-global.com/ (visited April 2013)

Appendix

A   Viterbi MATLAB Implementation

Listing 1.1. MATLAB implementation of the Viterbi algorithm described in section 3.1

```
% [state_sequence] = viterbi_sequence(initial_probability,
%                                      transition_probability,
%                                      emission_probability)
% initial_probability = initial probability (\pi_{i})
% transition_probability = transition probatility (T)
% emission_probability = emission probability (E)
% state_sequence = most probable state sequence that would
%     have resulted to the emission of (O)
% Author: Mehari G. Msgna
% Date: 16 April, 2013

function [state_sequence] = viterbi_sequence(
    initial_probability, transition_probability,
    emission_probability)
    number_of_states = length(initial_probability(1,:));
    number_of_observations = length(emission_probability(1,:)
        );
    state_sequence = zeros(1,number_of_observations);
    sequence_probability = zeros(number_of_observations,
        number_of_states);

    for c = 1:number_of_states
        sequence_probability(1,c) = emission_probability(c,1)
            * initial_probability(1,c);
    end
    for r = 2:number_of_observations
        temp = zeros(1,number_of_states);
        for c = 1:number_of_states
            for c1 = 1:number_of_states
                temp(1,c1) = transition_probability(c1,c) *
                    sequence_probability(r-1,c1);
            end
            mx = max(temp(1,:));
            sequence_probability(r,c) = emission_probability(
                c,r) * mx;
        end
    end
    for j = 1:number_of_observations
        [value, index] = max(sequence_probability(j,:));
        state_sequence(1,j) = index;
    end
end
```

An e-payment Architecture Ensuring a High Level of Privacy Protection

Aude Plateaux[1,2], Patrick Lacharme[1], Vincent Coquet[2], Sylvain Vernois[1], Kumar Murty[3], and Christophe Rosenberger[1]

[1] ENSICAEN, 17 rue Claude Bloch, 14000 Caen, France
{aude.plateaux,patrick.lacharme,sylvain.vernois,
christophe.rosenberger}@ensicaen.fr
[2] BULL SAS, Avenue Jean Jaurès, 78340 Les Clayes-sous-Bois, France
vincent.coquet@bull.net
[3] Department of Mathematics, 40 St. George Street, Toronto, Canada
murty@math.toronto.edu

Abstract. Online shopping is becoming more and more interesting for clients because of the ease of use and the large choice of products. As a consequence, 2.3 billion online clients have been identified in 2011. This rapid increase was accompagnied by various frauds, including stolen smart cards or fraudulent repudiation. Several e-payment systems have been proposed to reduce these security threats and the 3D-Secure protocol is becoming a standard for the payment on the Internet. Nevertheless, this protocol has not been studied in-depth, particularly in terms of privacy. This paper proposes a detailed description and an analysis of the 3D-Secure protocol, through a new privacy-orienting model for e-payment architectures. Some improvements of 3D-Secure protocol, concerning the protection of banking information, are also presented. Then, this article presents and analyses a new online payment architecture centered on the privacy of individuals.

Keywords: Electronic payment, privacy and security.

1   Introduction

In recent years, e-commerce has considerably grown with the democratization of the Internet. Thus, online payments were adopted by 69% of Internet users in 2011. Fraud amount in e-payment has increased with the same regularity and become now a major concern for financial institutions and web clients [20]. Indeed, although the online payment only represents a small percentage of transactions, it concentrates, for instance, 40% of the amount of fraud in France and 54% in United Kingdom [23]. Clients and merchant websites are not always the only actors in the electronic payment architecture. In addition to the two banks, the security problem is sometimes modified by the introduction of another actor, the third-party cashiers, as Paypal or Amazon payment (called Cashier as a Service in [35]), but it is not the scope of this paper.

T. Zia et al. (Eds.): SecureComm 2013, LNICST 127, pp. 305–322, 2013.
© Institute for Computer Sciences, Social Informatics and Telecommunications Engineering 2013

Many directives are related to the security of online payments, as for instance, the European Directive 2000/31/EC on e-commerce security [13]. In the same way, the Directive on Payment Services, [14], provides an european wide single market for payments and a legal platform for SEPA (Single Euro Payment Area, [16]). The banking industry strategy is centered on identity spoofing and user authentication. The first protocol proposed to securize electronic transactions was SET (Secure Electronic Transactions, [32]). Standard e-payment protocols are later enhanced by an additional secret, sent by mobile phone, as for the 3D-Secure protocol [33] or an additional device as a CAP reader [25]. However, the results in terms of security of these responses are mitigated [28,18]. Moreover, if the SET protocol has been extensively studied by the academic literacy (for instance [27,8,9,10]), the 3D-Secure protocol is surprisingly overlooked, excepted in the security analysis of Murdoch and Anderson [28] and Pasupathinathan et al. [30] .

Security and authentication in e-business should not be strengthened to the detriment of users' privacy [26]. There are a lot of personal information involved in all steps of a payment on the Internet and these data should be protected. Principles of user centric architecture and *privacy by design* are more and more accepted by numerous organizations and actors of various areas. For example, the European Commision is more and more interested by the privacy protection. Thus, the principle of data minimization has been strengthened in 2010, requiring that the personal data disclosure should be limited to adequate, relevant and non-excessive data [15]. Another important aspect of user's privacy concerns the data sovereignty principle: the personal data belong to an individual, with a control and a consent on the use of data and their purposes. Finally, the data sensitivity principle applies personal data must be considered as sensitive and requires a decentralized structure for their storage. These principles should be applied to e-payment systems.

The e-payment development has strongly modified the traditional relationship between a bank and its clients. During these transactions, a large amount of user's personal information is requested and stored. It is therefore essential to focus on user privacy in online payments and services. Surprisingly, the e-payment industry does not seem concerned by privacy. PCI/DSS is a first step of payment industry into personal data protection [19]. However, this norm is mainly concerned by data security in payment systems. User's privacy protection has completely disappeared in e-payment protocols on the Internet by the transition from SET to 3D-Secure [28]. Some existing publications deal with e-payment protocol generally focused on the security of service providers and users without talking about the user's privacy. The aim of the proposed architecture is to meet all the requirements in terms of security and privacy protection.

Our Contribution. We propose a list of necessary requirements for security and privacy protection of users and merchants during online payments. Then, using these requirements, we analyze the level of privacy protection of the current 3D-Secure protocol and propose an improvement of the protocol in order to enhance some privacy criteria. Our main contribution is the proposition of an e-payment architecture providing security for the actors and more privacy protection for the users and the service providers. The presented solution allows the users to make a purchase on the Internet, with the generation of an electronic bank cheque. More precisely, the proposed solution ensures the data minimization, sensitivity and sovereignty principles without disclosing any user's banking information.

Organization. The reminder of this paper is organized as follows: Actors of the system and the security and privacy requirements are presented in Section 2. In Section 3, a description of existing e-payment solutions are presented, with a detailed focus on the 3D-Secure protocol, as well as an improvement of this latter. Finally, the context and the new solution are proposed and explained in Section 4, then analyzed in Section 5.

2   Security and Privacy Requirements of e-payment Systems

Four actors are present in electronic payments: The **client** C wants to purchase an online service with a credit card, through the website of a **service provider** SP. These two actors have one payment provider: the **debit account bank** and **credit account bank**, called respectively in this paper *client's bank* and *SP bank*. In most of e-payment architectures, a fifth actor is involved, the trusted party as a third-party cashier or the Directory used in 3D-Secure. The role of this fifth actor is consequenlty various. However, the security analysis of the payment scheme is generally similar and allows to authenticate the banks. The proposed architecture is concentrated on the payment phase. Thus, in the case where the authentication and/or the registration with the SP is required, we assume it is properly conducted. The protocol should securely ensure that the client is debited and the SP is paid, but the SP does not need to know inadequate client's information.

Several personal data are involved during an online payment. These data must be protected against numerous threats. A list of these potential threats has been presented by Antoniou and Batten in [5]. These threats notably concern the information revealed by a client to the SP. In order to ensure the minimization principle, the personal information must be divided in different parts. Indeed, depending on the data owner, the information will be differently protected. However, the data sovereignty and data sensitivity principles must also be applied to any e-payment architecture. In the proposed approach, the personal information is divided in three parts:

1. The identity information Id includes the information allowing to know the client's identity, for instance, his/her name.
2. The order information OI includes the detailed basket and other data linked to the expected service, as the SP name. These data are known by the SP.
3. The banking information BI is, for instance, composed of client's bank name, the personal account number (PAN) or the cryptogram $CVX2$. These data are known by the client's bank. As an indication, it is necessary to take note that the PAN can also allow to identify a client.

A list of fifteen requirements R_i including all privacy principles, as well as the risks raised in the literature, is established. These requirements should be taken into account by the e-payment architectures:

- R_1: The **confidentiality of transactions** requires that each exchanged data must be encrypted in order to protect these data against external entities.
- R_2: The **integrity of transmitted information** allows the accuracy of the content and so the non-alteration of data during transmission or storage.
- R_3: The **confidentiality of client's identity towards the SP** ensures that a client can access to a service without disclosing his/her identity to the SP. This requirement is waived if the customer wants a home delivery service.
- R_4: The **confidentiality of client's identity towards the SP bank** ensures that a client can access to a service without disclosing his/her identity to the SP bank.
- R_5: The **client's authentication** by a trusted party ensures the identity of the client. Depending on the situation, the trusted party can ideally be the client's bank or another trusted party *where the client is registered.*
- R_6: The **SP authentication** by the client or by a trusted party ensures the identity of the SP.
- R_7: The **banks authentication** by a trusted party ensures the identity of SP bank and client's bank.
- R_8: The **non-reusability** of transmitted information (banking or other) allows to have unique and non-reusable transactions.
- R_9: The **confidentiality of order information** OI ensures that only authorized persons have access to order information. This requirement includes that the client's basket is unknown to the client's bank.
- R_{10}: The **confidentiality of banking information** BI (or client's data minimization principle) ensures that only authorized persons have access to banking data. This requirement includes the fact that the SP does not know the client's banking information.
- R_{11}: The **client's anonymity** is ensured if the requirements R_3, R_4, R_9 and R_{10} are fulfilled. Indeed, OI or BI partially allows to identify the client.
- R_{12}: The **SP's data minimization** principle includes the fact that the client does not know the SP bank. This condition is very important when the SP is a very small organisation, for instance one person. Indeed, in this case, the SP bank is the same bank than the manager's personal bank. Moreover, the SP's data minimization principle includes the requirement R_4. The SP bank does not need to know the client.
- R_{13}: The **data sovereignty** principle involves the uses of personal data associated to the client with his/her control and consent.
- R_{14}: The **data sensitivity** principle involves that the personal data are considered as sensitive and requires a de-centralized structure for data storage.
- R_{15}: The **ownership of a certificate** for the client **should not be required** in order to facilitate the e-payment. This last requirement concerns the usability of payment systems.

3   Existing e-payment Architectures

3.1   Introduction and Related Works

An online service generally begins with an authentication and a secure connection between the client and the SP website, using a protocol such as SSL/TLS [22,17]. This protocol involves the client trusting in the SP to keep this payment information and is aware of known published browser attacks [34,24,3]. However, the client can use a trusted partyner, such as Paypal. This service implies the creation of a Paypal account for the client and, consequently, a large amount of personal data is registered: name, email, address, PAN, $CVX2$ and expiration date. Then, the client can send and receive online payments without providing new data, through the Paypal platform. Nevertheless, although Paypal specifies *not sell or rent this information*, its privacy policy [31] adds it can *share some of your personal information with third parties* in the world. If the client does not use a trusted partyner, he/she must supply the SP bank, through the SP website, his/her banking information: PAN, $CVX2$ and expiration date. Client's banking information is so directly sent to the SP.

Several payment schemes have been recently proposed. For instance, a secure payment protocol managing different aspects such as smart card with network capabilities or the multiplicity of entities is proposed in [11]. However, these scenarios do not manage user's privacy. Antoniou and Batten are interested in enforcing trust in e-commerce systems [5]. They propose four models with four levels of privacy protection. However, these protocols are centered around one deliverer which knows all stakeholders of the process. Another scheme is suggested by Ashrafi and Ng in [6], by using a non-reusable password based authentication. The process ensures the client's privacy and minimizes the SP business risks. This protocol uses the card company with an optional payment gateway and has the same complexity as the 3D-Secure protocol. However, all the security is based on the card company which stores all the client's payment details in a local centered database.

The SET protocol [32] was developed by a consortium of credit card companies, such as VISA [1] and MasterCard [2], and software corporations. It is a protocol for securing e-payment transactions by credit card which runs in two steps: registration and purchase. This protocol ensures the data confidentiality and integrity and provides a mutual authentication between the SP and the client, through a trusted third party, the SP bank. This secure protocol has many advantages considering client's and SP privacy. The SP does not know the client's banking information. The client bank does not see the contents of the order. And finally, the client does not know the identity of the SP bank. However, in terms of client's privacy, the client does not necessarily trust the SP bank which authenticates him/her. Therefore, the SP bank knows the client's identity. In addition, although the client's bank does not know the contents of the client's order, it knows the SP identity. SET has been extensively analyzed in the begining of the 2000s and improved [8,7,21]. Thus, the client's consent to send his/her credit card details cannot be proved [9]. Moreover, this protocol is complex from the client perspective and expensive for the SP. Indeed, a specific software must be installed by the client in order to prove card detention with an electronic signature. In addition, card readers and distribution of certificates by the SP are inevitable. Consequently, the successor of the SET protocol is the 3D-Secure protocol where the few parts concerning privacy of SET are simply deleted. The Fig.1 quickly analyses this protocol.

3.2   Description of the 3D-Secure Protocol

The 3D-Secure protocol [33] is the commonly used two-factors authentication system for e-payment, developed by VISA in 2001. Other financial organizations also developed their own implementations of VISA's 3D-Secure licensed architecture, such as MasterCard with its MasterCard SecureCode, American Express with SafeKey [30]. In order to use the 3D-Secure protocol, a dedicated module called MPI (Merchant Plug In) is implemented into the SP website. Moreover, a dedicated server (the Directory) is made available for this system. This scheme works as specified below (see Fig.4 in the Section Annexes):

A. The client sends to the SP his/her purchase intention, with his/her banking information: PAN, expiration date and $CVX2$.

B. MPI queries the Directory server with the VEReq (Verify Enrollment request) message.

C. The Directory server checks the SP identity, the card number and the client's bank. The Directory recovers the ACS (Access Control Server) managing the card and transfers the VEReq message. The PAN allows the Directory server to identify the ACS.

D. The ACS checks if the client's card is enrolled in the 3D-Secure program and sends the cardholder authentication URL to the MPI through the VERes (Verify Enrollment Result) message.

E. MPI sends the PAReq (Payer Authentication Request) message to the previous URL. This message contains the details of the authorized purchase and requests the ACS to authenticate the cardholder. The authentication protocol depends on the cardholder's bank.

F. The client provides the necessary information for authentication to the bank.

G. ACS sends to MPI a confirmation of client's authentication through PARes (Payer Authentication Responses) message.

H. MPI records PARes message as confirmation of client's authentication by ACS.

I. SP authenticates to the bank. The bank checks the nature of the transaction from the client's bank and confirms the payment authorization from the SP. The SP gets his/her payment and the client's bank stores payment information to ensure non-repudiation of the transaction.

The main security flaw of 3D-Secure implementations, underlined in [28], has been corrected by many banks. The client authentication with his/her date of birth or other trivial secrets is consequently replaced by an One Time Password sent to user's mobile phone. As an indication, the complete payment phase is not described. Thus, the entire payment system using 3D-Secure protocol contains more than nine steps.

3.3 Privacy Analysis and Improvements of 3D-Secure

In a first step (step A), the client sends his/her banking information to the SP bank. However, this information can identify him/her. Consequently, the requirements R_3 and R_{10} can not be guaranteed. The requirements R_4 and R_{12} are also not respected given that the client's bank knows the SP identity and the SP bank knows the client's identity. Then, even if the client's authentication is realized by his/her bank, this authentication is also realized by the Directory server (step C). Consequently, R_5 is partially ensured. Similarly, the SP authentication is not realized by the client or by a client's trusted party (step C. and I.), and R_6 is not respected. In addition, the order information is contained in the $PAReq$ message sent to ACS (step E.), these data are consequently not confidential (R_9). Thus, the requirements R_3, R_4, R_9 and R_{10} are not ensured, the requirement of anonymity R_{11} cannot be respected. Finally, R_{13} is only partially respected. Indeed, the client has not total control over these data which passes through many entities. In addition, in terms of privacy, the sensitivity of exchanged information is not enough taken into account. Therefore, R_{14} is not ensured. The 3D-Secure protocol ensures therefore only six of the fifteen requirements. However, the privacy protection of 3D-Secure can easily be improved by using the SP bank certificate. Indeed, in the 3D-Secure protocol, $CVX2$ and the expiration date are not necessary. These data are only used for the compatibility with classic existing payment systems. Thus, given that the client's authentication from his/her bank is strong, these two elements are unnecessary. The SP bank certificate contains the standard information, as well as the Directory public key. Only two steps must so be modified (the other seven steps are the same as above):

A. The SP **provides the SP bank certificate to the client**. Thus, the client sends to the SP his/her purchase intention, **with only his/her PAN encrypted by the Directory public key**. These data are intended for a dedicated module MPI implemented into the SP website.

C. The Directory server **decrypts the PAN with its private key** and checks the SP identity, the card number and the client's bank. The Directory recovers the ACS managing the card and transfers the VEReq message.

These small changes do not involve significant modifications in the 3D-Secure architecture. Moreover, these improvements involve none of the client's banking information is visible by the SP and thus ensure R_{10}. Indeed, through the SP bank certificate, the encryption of PAN is possible and use of $CVX2$ is avoided. In addition, only relevant data and useful data pass through the Directory server. The requirement R_{14} can be taken into account, as well as R_5. Indeed, the client is only authenticated by his/her bank. The Fig.1 shows the increase of the privacy protection level thanks to these modifications.

R_i	Properties	3D-Secure	3D-Secure Modified	SET
R_1	Confidentiality of transactions	Yes	Yes	Yes
R_2	Integrity	Yes	Yes	Yes
R_3	Confidentiality of client's identity for SP	No	No	No
R_4	Confidentiality of client's identity for SP bank	No	No	No
R_5	*Client*'s authentication	Partial	**Yes**	No
R_6	SP authentication	No	No	No
R_7	Banks authentication	Yes	Yes	Partial
R_8	Non-reusability	Yes	Yes	No
R_9	Confidentiality of OI	No	No	Partial
R_{10}	Confidentiality of BI	No	**Yes**	Yes
R_{11}	*Client*'s anonymity	No	No	No
R_{12}	SP data minimization	No	No	No
R_{13}	Data sovereignty	No	No	Partial
R_{14}	Data sensitivity	No	**Partial**	Partial
R_{15}	Ownership of certificate not necessary	Yes	Yes	No

Fig. 1. Properties of the 3D-Secure protocols and comparison with SET

Nevertheless, this improved protocol does not fulfill all requirements described in Section 2. The minimization principle, specially R_9, is not respected. For example, the client's bank knows the purchases of the client or at least the merchant category. The bank is so able to deduce the purchases type. Consequently, the anonymity principle is not respected. Moreover, as often in the existing e-payment architectures, the fifth actor always takes place in the middle of the transaction, for instance, the Directory server in 3D-Secure or the card company in the Ashrafi and Ng's model [6]. Thus, the privacy is always exposed to an impossibility of complete protection.

4   The New e-payment Architecture

The proposed architecture combines the advantages of electronic cheque systems and easy-of-use of online payment systems described in Section 3.1. However, the architecture is not considered as an electronic cheque scheme [4] which are often difficult to use for the average user. Indeed, these systems lead to the use of client's certificate and an electronic checkbook card. Many computations and storages by the client's bank are also required, even if [12] proposes a small improvement. Finally, these schemes do not generally take into account privacy protection, excepted in [29].

Thus, our new architecture involves five actors: the client, the merchant SP, both banks and an additional entity, the interbank system IS. The goal of this interbank trusted third party is detailed later. Each bank generates a key pair, where the public key is certified by the IS. This latter publishes these certificates which contain the following: its name; its public key; the hash function algorithm; the signature algorithm and the name of certification authority. Similarly, the SP has a key pair, where the public key is certified by the trusted third party contractualized with, for instance the interbank system. These certificates are composed by the following data: its name; its public key; the hash function algorithm; the signature algorithm; the name of certification authority and the parameters describing the payment scheme recognizing the SP and allowing to secure the future payment (American Express, VISA, MasterCard,..). In addition, as explained in the sequel, the new architecture allows the SP not to reveal the identity of its bank. Thus, in order to add privacy for the SP, the generation of the SP certificate by a trusted party different from the SP bank is preferable. For instance, the interbank trusted party could play this role.

Notations: The notations for the proposed e-payment protocol are:

- $Sign_X(m)$: Signature of message m by the actor X with message recovery;
- $[m]_{K_{PU_X}}$: Encryption of message m by the public key K_{PU} of the actors X;
- $[m]_{K_{S_X}}$: Encryption of message m by the session key K_S of the actors X;
- N_i: Random number i used to guarantee the freshness of messages;
- $H(m)$: Hashing of message m.

The online payment architecture respecting the users' privacy proposed in this article is based on the generation of two documents: a contract between the SP and the client, and another electronic bank document, called electronic bank cheque or cheque to simplify. As explained in the beginning of this section, this latter document is different from the cheque generated in the electronic cheque architecture. The interbank system IS plays the role of a trusted third party. It enables communication between banks without revealing information about the other actors. As explained in the following section, the fifth actor can not be excluded. However, IS has the smallest possible role for managing authentificaitons banks and prevent money laundering. The new solution is summarized in Fig.2. First, the client creates his/her basket and sends it to the SP with a random number N_1, as well as a session key K_{S_1} (Step 1). N_1 ensures the freshness of message and K_{S_1} encrypts data between the client and the SP. In the case where the client has a certificate, the session key is replaced by his/her public key.

$$Client \to SP : [Basket, N_1, K_{S_1}]_{K_{PU_{SP}}} \tag{1}$$

The SP then generates a contract with its client (Step 2), containing:

- The total amount $Amount$ of purchases;
- A random order number $Order$ generated by the SP. This number should not link to the SP identity;
- A symmetric random key K_{S_2} encrypted by the public key of the SP bank $K_{PU_{Bank_{SP}}}$;
- The beneficiary's name $Benef$ encrypted by the previous symmetric key K_{S_2};
- The URL of the SP in order to return to the payment page;
- The detailed shopping list $Basket$, such as quantity or unit price.

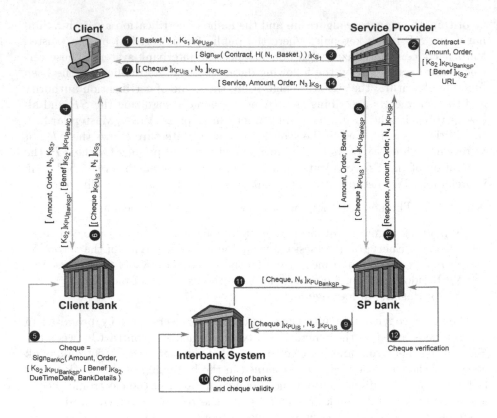

Fig. 2. The proposed e-payment architecture

$$SP : Contract = \{Amount, Order, [K_{S_2}]_{K_{PU_{BankSP}}}, [Benef]_{K_{S_2}}, \qquad (2)$$
$$URL, Basket\}$$

To avoid the non-repudiation and ensure the SP authenticity, the SP signs the contract. It is then sent to the client with the hash of $Basket$ and N_1 (Step 3).

$$Client \leftarrow SP : [Sign_{SP}(Contract, H(N_1, Basket))]_{K_{S_1}} \qquad (3)$$

Then, the client connects to his/her bank, using a macro of its Internet browser (Step 4). The macro establishes the HTTPS connection and sends a filtered contract. The authentication protocol depends on the client's bank. But, a strong authentication is recommended. The filtered contract only contains the necessary information of the contract for the client's bank: the whole amount, the currency, the encrypted symmetric key, the encrypted beneficiary's name and the random order number. Thus, the client's bank does not know the SP identity. Moreover, a random number N_2 ensures the freshness of messages. The client has no public key certificate, his/her bank will consequently use the session key K_{S_3} to encrypt the messages with his/her client. To encrypt the beneficiary's name, a session key is favoured in order to reduce the computation complexity.

$$Client \rightarrow Bank_C : [Amount, Order, [K_{S_2}]_{K_{PU_{Bank_{SP}}}}, [Benef]_{K_{S_2}}, \qquad (4)$$
$$N_2, K_{S_3}]_{K_{PU_{Bank_C}}}$$

Then, if the authentication is successful and the client is creditworthy, the bank positively responds to the client's request. The bank generates an electronic bank cheque to the SP (Step 5). This electronic cheque includes: the total; the currency; the random order number; the encrypted beneficiary's name; the encrypted symmetric key; the information of the client's bank and the signature of the client's bank. Thus, the cheque does not contain client's banking information.

$$Bank_C : Cheque = Sign_{Bank_C}(Amount, Order, [K_{S_2}]_{K_{PU_{Bank_{SP}}}}, \qquad (5)$$
$$[Benef]_{K_{S_2}}, DueTimeDate, BankDetails)$$

The client's bank signs the cheque and encrypts it with the interbank system public key. Thus, IS could check the banks identities and the cheque validity. The cheque is sent to the client (Step 6) who forwards it to SP (Step 7). N_2 and N_3 ensure the freshness of transactions. N_2 also gives the identity of the request. The result being encrypted, the SP cannot know client's banking information.

$$Client \leftarrow Bank_C : [[Cheque]_{K_{PU_{IS}}}, N_2]_{K_{S_3}} \qquad (6)$$
$$Client \rightarrow SP : [[Cheque]_{K_{PU_{IS}}}, N_3]_{K_{PU_{SP}}} \qquad (7)$$

Then, the SP obtains $[Cheque]_{K_{PU_{IS}}}$ and N_3 thanks to its private key. So, the SP authenticates to its bank (Step 8) and provides its filtered contract, the signed and encrypted electronic bank cheque. As previously, the authentication protocol depends of the SP bank. However, a strong authentication is recommended. The SP filtered contract contains: the whole amount, the currency, the beneficiary's name and the random number N_4.

$$SP \rightarrow Bank_{SP} : [Amount, Order, Benef, [Cheque]_{K_{PU_{IS}}}, N_4]_{K_{PU_{Bank_{SP}}}} \qquad (8)$$

In order to validate the banks identities and the cheque, the SP bank authenticates to the interbank system and transfers the cheque (Step 9), using N_5 for the freshness of the transaction.

$$Bank_{SP} \rightarrow IS : [[Cheque]_{K_{PU_{IS}}}, N_5]_{K_{PU_{IS}}} \qquad (9)$$

The interbank system checks the identity of the SP bank and decrypts the electronic cheque with its private key (Step 10). The validity of this cheque, its signature, and consequently the identity of the client's bank, are checked. Then, if the verifications are correct, the interbank system re-encrypts the cheque with the public key of the SP bank and the cheque is transferred to this bank (Step 11). N_5 is reused to identify the request.

$$Bank_{SP} \leftarrow IS : [Cheque, N_5]_{K_{PU_{Bank_{SP}}}} \tag{11}$$

The SP bank decrypts the cheque with its private key (Step 12). It firstly checks that the cheque amount and currency are similar to those provided by the SP in the filtered contract. Then, the bank decrypts the symmetric key with its private key. Thanks to this symmetric key, the SP bank decrypts the beneficiary's name. Afterwards, the bank compares the beneficiary's name of the filtered contract with the decrypted name of the electronic cheque. As indication, the verification of the client's bank signature by the SP bank is optionnal. Indeed, the interbank system has processed to this verification. The SP bank can use directly the client's bank information.

Finally, if one verification fails, the transaction is cancelled. However, if all verifications are correct, the SP bank contacts SP and validates the cheque as being authentic; that allows the SP to deliver service for its client (Step 13, 14). The random numbers N_3 and N_4 allow to identify the requests and to guarantee the freshness of transactions.

$$SP \leftarrow Bank_{SP} : [Response, Amount, Order, N_4]_{K_{PU_{SP}}} \tag{13}$$
$$Client \leftarrow SP : [Service, Amount, Order, N_3]_{K_{S_1}} \tag{14}$$

The SP bank also contacts the client's bank, located through the electronic cheque. The debit/credit process between banks completes this payment architecture in using the electronic cheque as payment proof.

5   Analysis of the Architecture

Most of security and privacy requirements are ensured by the first eight steps of the proposed architecture. Moreover, the proposed protocol has no more steps than 3D-Secure as the described steps of 3D-secure are not as detailed as our protocol. In addition, the last five steps allow to ensure the banks authentication by the interbank system (R_7) and so to avoid the money laundering.

5.1   Data Security and Authentication

The secure channel between actors and the encryption schemes ensure the confidentiality of exchanged data during the protocol. Consequently, the requirement R_1 is ensured. The use of random numbers garantees the freshness of messages, avoids the linkability and ensures the data integrity respecting R_2 and R_8. Entities authentication is realized through certificates, the first one for the SP and the second one for each bank. Thus, contrary to the SET protocol, the trusted third party is not one of banks. The banks own certificates issued by IS. The SP certificate is provided by IS or another trusted autority. These documents allow to sign, encrypt and decrypt information and to prove the validity of the SP and banks. The interbank system manages the bank certificates and authenticates the SP bank and the client's bank. Moreover, IS checks information contained in the signed electronic cheque and gives a validation of cheque for the SP bank. The contract signed by the SP then allows client to obtain his/her service with indicated conditions. Finally, validation of the client's bank identity by IS and verification of transaction information by the SP bank ensure the SP to be paid once the service provided. Thus, the requirement R_7 can be ensured. Moreover, these verifications by IS also allow to avoid money laundering by malicious SP and malicious SP bank.

5.2   Privacy Analysis

The proposed architecture is more respectful of the users' privacy than the SET protocol and 3D-Secure protocol. The SP authentication by the client and then the SP bank, ensures the SP validity and the client does not provide personal order data as long as he/she is not certain to use a service. The requirement R_6 is thus respected. Moreover, the client's identity is never disclosed and the SP bank does not know the client. This authentication is realized by the client's bank. Thus, R_3, R_4 and R_5 are respectively ensured. More precisely, in order to respect the client's privacy during the transfer of data to different banks, the order number, used in Step (3), should not contain SP information, such as the business number. Consequently, it must be random or unidentifiable. As an indication, in the case where the two banks would be the same, all requirements would be preserved except that the bank could know the SP and the client. Moreover, the client's bank knows neither contents of the basket, nor the SP with whom his/her client deals. The requirement R_9 is consequently ensured. This new proposition also solves the other privacy problems of 3D-Secure protocol. The client's banking information is preserved against the SP ensuring the requirement R_{10}. The encrypted cheque with IS public key allows the SP not to have knowledge of the client's bank. Moreover, contrary to all the existing e-payment architecture, the client's banking information is never disclosed to the SP. Thus, the requirements R_3, R_4, R_9 and R_{10} are respected. Consequently, the client can be anonymous and the requirement R_{11} can be ensured. Finally, the cheque encrypted with IS public key prevents the client to know the SP's bank. Consequently, the protection of some SP personal information, representing the requirement R_{12} is also ensured by this protocol. This requirement is important when the SP is a small organisation and consequently, when the SP bank is the same bank than the manager's personal bank.

The most sensitive data of client and SP are protected. The requirement R_{14} is ensured and the client only provides the necessary, appropriate and relevant information (minimization and sensitivity principles). In addition, contrary to the existing protocol, the fifth part performs at the end of the architecture. Thus, the privacy is not always exposed to an impossibility of complete protection. Once the SP has signed the contract, the client should click two times to accept it: one for the confirmation of his/her basket and one for the validation of the payment. Thus, the client has read two times the similar information. These two clicks are used to ensure the client's consent and, consequently R_{13}. These clicks could be replaced by a client's signature based on a certificate. In the future, the certificate will be possibly present in the client's identity card or his/her passport. Finally, the ownership of certificate by the client is not necessary (R_{15}), contrary to SET protocol. Figure 3 summarizes the analysis of the proposed architecture compared to the existing protocols 3D-Secure and SET protocol.

R_i	Properties	3DS	SET	Our protocol
R_1	Confidentiality of transactions	Yes	Yes	Yes
R_2	Integrity	Yes	Yes	Yes
R_3	Confidentiality of client's identity for SP	No	No	**Yes**
R_4	Confidentiality of client's identity for SP bank	No	No	**Yes**
R_5	C's authentication	Partial	No	**Yes**
R_6	SP authentication	No	No	**Yes**
R_7	Banks authentication	**Yes**	Partial	**Yes**
R_8	Non-reusability	**Yes**	No	**Yes**
R_9	Confidentiality of OI	No	Partial	**Yes**
R_{10}	Confidentiality of BI	No	**Yes**	**Yes**
R_{11}	C's anonymity	No	No	**Yes**
R_{12}	SP data minimization	No	No	**Yes**
R_{13}	Data sovereignty	No	Partial	**Yes**
R_{14}	Data sensitivity	No	Partial	**Yes**
R_{15}	Ownership of certificate not necessary	**Yes**	No	**Yes**

Fig. 3. Properties of the 3D-Secure, SET and the proposed protocols

6   Conclusion

A lot of sensitive information are transferred during current online payment transaction, introducing strong privacy problems. Current e-payment systems, such as 3D-Secure, are not designed to ensure user's privacy. Moreover, even if its proposed improvement is more respectful of the privacy, several underlined requirements are not ensured. The proposed architecture allows to overcome these weaknesses by respecting the client's privacy against the banks and the SP, as well as the SP privacy. This solution is mainly based on the generation of an electronic bank cheque associated with certificates.

This architecture is fully compliant with the data minimization, data sovereignty and data sensitivity principles. More particularly, the payment transaction never discloses any client's banking information. Moreover, the client does not need to have particular knowledge or cryptographic devices. The non-repudiation could be improved by supplying the client with a certificate.

Moreover, in order to prove the practicability of the proposed solution, a proof of concept and a statistical study are currently conducted (see Annexes).

Acknowledgment. The authors would like to thank Gabriel Frey and Arnaud Gouriou for their project concerning the implementation of our proof of concept, Roch Lescuyer for his proofreading, as well as the BULL company and the ANRT organization for their financial support.

References

1. Visa corporate (1958), http://corporate.visa.com/index.shtml
2. Mastercard worldwide (1966), http://www.mastercard.com/
3. Aciiçmez, O., Schindler, W., Koç, Ç.K.: Improving brumley and boneh timing attack on unprotected ssl implementations. In: Proceedings of the 12th ACM Conference on Computer and Communications Security, pp. 139–146. ACM (2005)
4. Anderson, M.: The electronic check architecture. In: Financial Services Technology Consortium (1998)
5. Antoniou, G., Batten, L.: E-commerce: protecting purchaser privacy to enforce trust. Electronic Commerce Research 11(4), 421–456 (2011)
6. Ashrafi, M.Z., Ng, S.K.: Enabling privacy-preserving e-payment processing. In: Haritsa, J.R., Kotagiri, R., Pudi, V. (eds.) DASFAA 2008. LNCS, vol. 4947, pp. 596–603. Springer, Heidelberg (2008)
7. Bella, G., Massacci, F., Paulson, L.: Verifying the SET purchase protocols. Journal of Automated Reasoning 36(1), 5–37 (2006)
8. Bella, G., Massacci, F., Paulson, L.C., Tramontano, P.: Formal verification of cardholder registration in SET. In: Cuppens, F., Deswarte, Y., Gollmann, D., Waidner, M. (eds.) ESORICS 2000. LNCS, vol. 1895, pp. 159–174. Springer, Heidelberg (2000)
9. Bella, G., Paulson, L., Massacci, F.: The verification of an industrial payment protocol: The set purchase phase. In: ACM CCS, pp. 12–20. ACM (2002)
10. Brlek, S., Hamadou, S., Mullins, J.: A flaw in the electronic commerce protocol set. Information Processing Letters 97(3), 104–108 (2006)
11. Carbonell, M., Torres, J., Izquierdo, A., Suarez, D.: New E-payment scenarios in an extended version of the traditional model. In: Gervasi, O., Murgante, B., Laganà, A., Taniar, D., Mun, Y., Gavrilova, M.L. (eds.) ICCSA 2008, Part II. LNCS, vol. 5073, pp. 514–525. Springer, Heidelberg (2008)
12. Chen, T.H., Yeh, S.C., Liao, K.C., Lee, W.B.: A practical and efficient electronic checkbook. Journal of Organizational Computing and Electronic Commerce 19(4), 285–293 (2009)
13. European Commission. Directive 2000/31/ec of the European parliament and of the council of 8 June 2000 on certain legal aspects of information society services, in particular electronic commerce, in the internal market ('directive on electronic commerce') (2000)
14. European Commission. Directive 2007/64/ec of the European parliament and of the council of 13 November 2007 on payment services in the internal market amending directives 97/7/ec, 2002/65/ec, 2005/60/ec and 2006/48/cc and repealing directive 97/5/ec (2007)
15. European Commission. Communication from the Commission to the Council, the European Parliament, the European Economic and Social Committee and the Committee of the Regions (2010)

16. European Payments Council. Sepa - single euro payment area (2007), http://www.sepafrance.fr/
17. Dierks, T.: Rfc 5246: The transport layer security (tls) protocol version 1.2 (2008)
18. Drimer, S., Murdoch, S.J., Anderson, R.: Optimised to fail: Card readers for online banking. In: Dingledine, R., Golle, P. (eds.) FC 2009. LNCS, vol. 5628, pp. 184–200. Springer, Heidelberg (2009)
19. PCI DSS. Payment card industry data security standard (2006), https://www.pcisecuritystandards.org/
20. Espelid, Y., Netland, L.-H., Klingsheim, A.N., Hole, K.J.: A proof of concept attack against norwegian internet banking systems. In: Tsudik, G. (ed.) FC 2008. LNCS, vol. 5143, pp. 197–201. Springer, Heidelberg (2008)
21. Fioravanti, A., Massacci, F.: How to model (and simplify) the set payment phase for automated verification (2001)
22. Freier, A., Kocher, P., Karlton, P.: Rfc 6101: The secure sockets layer (ssl) protocol version 3.0 (2011)
23. Frenkiel, M.: Cybercriminalité et crime organisé (2009), http://www.mag-securs.com/News/tabid/62/articleType/ArticleView/articleId/24583/Cybercriminalite-et-crime-organise.aspx
24. Gabrilovich, E., Gontmakher, A.: The homograph attack. Communications of the ACM 45(2), 128 (2002)
25. MasterCard International. Chip authentication program functional architecture (September 2004)
26. Katsikas, S.K., López, J., Pernul, G.: Trust, privacy and security in E-business: Requirements and solutions. In: Bozanis, P., Houstis, E.N. (eds.) PCI 2005. LNCS, vol. 3746, pp. 548–558. Springer, Heidelberg (2005)
27. Meadows, C., Syverson, P.: A formal specification of requirements for payment transactions in the SET protocol. In: Hirschfeld, R. (ed.) FC 1998. LNCS, vol. 1465, pp. 122–140. Springer, Heidelberg (1998)
28. Murdoch, S.J., Anderson, R.: Verified by visa and masterCard secureCode: Or, how not to design authentication. In: Sion, R. (ed.) FC 2010. LNCS, vol. 6052, pp. 336–342. Springer, Heidelberg (2010)
29. Pasupathinathan, V., Pieprzyk, J., Wang, H.: Privacy enhanced electronic cheque system. In: Seventh IEEE International Conference on E-Commerce Technology, CEC 2005, pp. 431–434. IEEE (2005)
30. Pasupathinathan, V., Pieprzyk, J., Wang, H., Cho, J.Y.: Formal analysis of card-based payment systems in mobile devices. In: The 2006 Australasian Workshops on Grid Computing and e-research, vol. 54, pp. 213–220. Australian Computer Society, Inc. (2006)
31. Paypal. Privacy policy for paypal services (2012)
32. S.E.T. Secure electronic transaction specification. Book 1: Business Description. Version, 1 (2002)
33. Visa. 3d secure protocol specification, core functions, July 16 (2002)
34. Wagner, D., Schneier, B.: Analysis of the ssl 3.0 protocol. In: The Second USENIX Workshop on Electronic Commerce Proceedings, pp. 29–40 (1996)
35. Wang, R., Chen, S., Wang, X.F., Qadeer, S.: How to shop for free online security analysis of cashier-as-a-service based web stores. In: IEEE Symposium on Security and Privacy (S&P 2011) (2011)

Annexes

3D-Secure Protocol

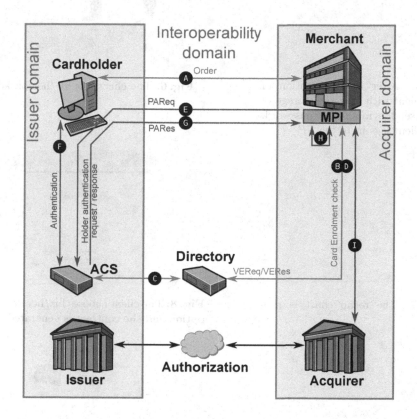

Fig. 4. The 3D-Secure protocol

Statistical Study

In order to justify the importance of the privacy protection issues during an on-line payment, a statistical study was conducted on a sample of 354 individuals. In particular, for the question "Are you concerned by the issues of privacy protection on the Internet?", 87% of responses are positive and 69% of individuals have apprehensions during this transaction.

Patent

There is a provisional application for patent cover sheet.
The docket number is 61/712616.
A U.S. patent deposit has been made with the patent number: US 04097.

Fig. 5. After the registration of the client with only the storage of one pseudonym and one password, the client logs in to the *SP*

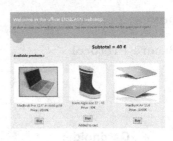

Fig. 6. The client fills his/her basket

Fig. 7. The recap chart is processed

Fig. 8. The client chooses his/her delivery option and the contract is generated

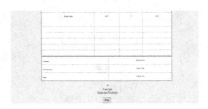

Fig. 9. After the contract uploaded and the cheque has been generated, the cheque is transmitted to the *SP* bank through the *SP*

Fig. 10. The transaction is concluded and the bill is sent to the client

Perspectives

A proof of concept has been developed to demonstrate the feasibility of the proposed protocol. The Figures 5, 6, 7, 8, 9 and 10 provide an overview of the current implementation.

Unveiling Privacy Setting Breaches
in Online Social Networks

Xin Ruan[1], Chuan Yue[2], and Haining Wang[1]

[1] The College of William and Mary, Williamsburg, VA 23187, USA
{xruan,hnw}@cs.wm.edu
[2] University of Colorado Colorado Springs, Colorado Springs, CO 80918, USA
cyue@uccs.edu

Abstract. Users of online social networks (OSNs) share personal information with their peers. To manage the access to one's personal information, each user is enabled to configure its privacy settings. However, even though users are able to customize the privacy of their homepages, their private information could still be compromised by an attacker by exploiting their own and their friends' public profiles. In this paper, we investigate the unintentional privacy disclosure of an OSN user even with the protection of privacy setting. We collect more than 300,000 Facebook users' public information and assess their measurable privacy settings. Given only a user's public information, we propose strategies to uncover the user's private basic profile or connection information, respectively, and then quantify the possible privacy leakage by applying the proposed schemes to the real user data. We observe that although the majority of users configure their basic profiles or friend lists as private, their basic profiles can be inferred with high accuracy, and a significant portion of their friends can also be uncovered via their public information.

1 Introduction

Online social network (OSN) websites have attracted a large number of users in the past few years. Facebook, the most popular OSN, was launched in 2004; by March 2013, the monthly active users exceeded 700 million [2]. Each user account typically includes the user's basic profile, such as gender, education, and friend list, and other personal data, such as photos and messages. Clearly not every user is willing to share all its information with peer users, either friends or strangers [18]. Accordingly, many social network sites allow a user to take control over its information visibility by configuring privacy settings. Thus, users are able to set their information visibility to different types, and the setting granularity varies from site to site. For instance, except for profile image and name, a Facebook user is capable of configuring its friend list, each piece of profile information, wall post and photo accessibility to strangers and specific friends.

However, some of an OSN user's private information that is protected by its privacy setting can be easily compromised. In other words, a privacy setting is

T. Zia et al. (Eds.): SecureComm 2013, LNICST 127, pp. 323–341, 2013.
© Institute for Computer Sciences, Social Informatics and Telecommunications Engineering 2013

not effective as what it claims to be. This is due to the intrinsic vulnerabilities inside the privacy setting policy. For instance, as shown in Figure 1, user A and user B are mutual friends; each configures its privacy independently such that their information visibility are as the figure shows. An attacker, who does not set up connections with user A or user B, has no access to user A's friend list, but can access some of its photos or posts; thus some of user A's friends, who responded to A's posts or left photo comments, are leaked. When the attacker also visits user B, who has a public friend list, the attacker can confirm the connection between A and B. Exploiting this kind of vulnerability, we wonder whether A's friends or B's basic information could be uncovered even with the protection of their personalized privacy settings. More generally, we attempt to measure, from an average attacker's perspective, with limited resources, how much of a user's privacy could possibly be compromised based on its plainly leaked information.

From the stance of a stranger to a target user, this paper strives to evaluate the user's privacy setting breaches on a large scale and attempts to answer the following questions:

- Can one's privacy setting be undermined by developing more sophisticated and practical schemes, which can infer more private profile information based on what has been directly published from the person's homepage?
- How accurate can users' privacy be inferred? While users can configure their privacy settings to different types, can the amount of inferred privacy be quantified given each privacy setting type?
- Is the amount of inferrable privacy mainly determined by the user's privacy setting? If so, can the number of affected users with a certain setting be estimated on a large scale?

Although previous research [16, 17] has investigated the gap between OSN users' privacy expectation and their actual privacy settings, the vulnerabilities in privacy settings themselves are not studied. Yet there are rare existing research that specifically examines whether a privacy setting can keep the privacy of user information as it is configured. While several efforts [8, 14, 29] have demonstrated the possibility to infer OSN users' one attribute value from another, or to infer the connections, they are based on (1) a large amount of training data [29] or (2) the assumption of the availability of specific kinds of information, such as group membership [14, 29] and music interests [8], which in reality may be set as private by users. The effects of users' privacy settings upon their profiles are not taken into account, let alone to measure the privacy setting breach. A large number of users, who share certain attribute values with the target users, are required as the training data to conduct the information inference. Thus, those strategies can only be taken by attackers with rich resources.

In this paper, we investigate whether certain privacy settings can effectively protect a user's private information as the user configured. We dwell on measuring and quantifying the unintentional leakage of a target user's basic profile information and friend list, which are the pivot of its social profile. For each target user with a certain privacy configuration, we propose the profile and connection inference

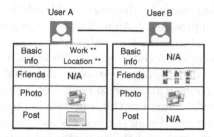

Fig. 1. An Attacker's View

schemes based on the user's publicly available information. In addition, instead of relying on a large amount of training data, our approach only needs a small number of users in the target user's neighborhood. The proposed schemes can be conducted by any average users without many resources. We crawl and collect about 300,000 Facebook users' publicly available information as our dataset. The status-quo of those users' privacy settings is measured. Then, we quantify the amount of inferrable private information by using our proposed schemes, and observe that a remarkable amount of privacy could be uncovered, indicating that privacy settings do not effectively guarantee users' information privacy.

The remainder of the paper is organized as follows. Section 2 surveys related work. Section 3 introduces the dataset we collected, and the privacy setting statistics. Section 4 illustrates the privacy breach of each primary setting case under different attack schemes. Section 5 quantifies the breach based on the Facebook dataset. Section 6 discusses the generality of privacy breach in other OSNs, and finally Section 7 concludes the paper.

2   Related Work

There are two major research directions on the privacy and security issues in OSNs: (1) to reveal the privacy threats in OSNs by conducting surveys [16, 17] and proposing attack models [26], information inference algorithms [6, 8, 9, 13, 14, 19, 28], de-anonymization algorithms [4, 21], and re-identification algorithms [27]; and (2) to reinforce users' privacy by redesigning the OSN system structure [5, 10, 20, 23] and conducting anonymization [22, 25]. This paper investigates the privacy setting breaches, which belongs to (1). We describe the related work as follows.

The disparity between users' actual privacy settings and their privacy expectation in Facebook has been studied by Madejski et al. [17] and Liu et al. [16]. They obtained users' expectations by conducting surveys and retrieved their factual privacy settings; and then detected the inconsistency between the two. Both found that there was a significant variance between users' privacy expectations and their privacy settings. But they assumed that the privacy setting can effectively protect the data that it is configured to protect. In contrast, this paper intends to challenge this assumption and unveils the privacy setting vulnerability in itself. In addition, we measure the privacy setting status-quo on a much larger scale.

Regarding information inference, there are profile mining [6, 8, 19, 29] and link mining [13–15, 24, 28] approaches, both of which this paper explores. Zheleva et al. [29] presented several classification models using links and group memberships to infer the target users' profiles. But in many OSNs such as Facebook, the group membership is covert by default. Moreover, it assumes that a specific percentage of attribute values are publicly available to perform the inference, and a user set that consists of thousands of users as training data is needed for classification.

Chaabane et al. [8] extracted semantic correlations among users' music interests, and computed each user's probability vector belonging to certain semantic topics. The users with similar vectors shared the same attribute value. However, this method is limited to those users who have published their music interests, and is not applicable to more general users who have not done so. A large dataset is also needed for classification.

Mislove et al. [19] assumed that users sharing the same attribute values were inclined to form dense communities. The traditional community detection algorithm is modified to take user's attribute values into consideration. The algorithm is applied to a school student dataset to infer their majors schools, and etc., but when it is applied to a larger user set from a broader geographical area, the accuracy is much lower than that using the student dataset.

Compared to these related works, this paper designs inference schemes from the stance of an individual user instead of a global view, thus it avoids the need of a large amount of training data and only demands the information of the target user's reachable neighbors. More importantly, our schemes take the actual availability of users' attribute values into consideration, instead of assuming specific attribute values to be in hand.

Another important privacy threat is the compromise of a user's connections, i.e., the friend list. Leroy et al. [14] uncovered the social graph given the user's group membership information. However, it is not easy to obtain these group-related data in most OSNs, in which group information is private. Staddon et al. [24] inferred a user's friend list based on the situation that most OSNs provide the shared friend function once a connection has been set up to the target user. However, the dilemma is if the attacker connects to the target user, likely the target user's friend list is already accessible to the attacker. Bonneau et al. [7] also aimed at uncovering a target user's friend list in Facebook by exploiting the public listing feature, but the feature has been disabled and is not available anymore.

3   The Facebook Dataset

Facebook was chosen as our research target because it is the world's most populous OSN providing many flexible features and diverse user resources. More importantly, its privacy setting policy is similar to the policies that most existing OSNs adopt, but in finer granularity. In Facebook, one can set each of its information item individually as "Public," which means to be visible to every user, or visible only to specific or all friends.

While collecting the dataset, the collector acts as a user who neither belongs to any specific group nor sets up connections with any of the sample users.

The retrieved data are all set as "Public," i.e., accessible to every normal user. Hence, the inference experiments can be reproduced by any other users. Moreover, since we only collected public information, none of Facebook's security policies were broken. For privacy concern, user names and IDs are anonymized.

The dataset is organized into a database, consisting of about 300,000 Facebook users. The crawling originated from 50 graduate students at the same institution and was conducted in a breadth-first manner. Out of the total users, about 120,000 users were crawled at the beginning phase, and all their main profile subpages were collected. The rest about 180,000 users were crawled thereafter, and all but their photo subpages were collected as photo pages are not used for evaluation. Out of the 300,000 users, there are 909 users all of whose friends' profiles are also in the dataset; for the rest of users, only some of their friends are in the dataset.

To quantify the information leakage, we emphasize the unintentional revelation of a user's $targetProfile$, including an attribute set: {location, institution} and the friend list. The attribute set is called the basic attribute set, and its element is basic attribute. While $targetProfile$ is the pivot of a user's social profile, other information items from wall like status, messages, to photos are not included in it because they are improvised and hard to infer.

We define the percentage of users that have certain information public as "public ratio." Based on our dataset, the public ratios of users' four main subpages are: 83.8% for profile page, 62.2% for friends page, 55.1% for wall page, and 45.6% for photo page. For a profile page, it is considered to be public when at least one value in the basic attribute set is visible. A photo or wall page is considered to be public if at least one album or post is visible. A friend list is considered public when it is visible.

As many as 37.8% of users conceal their friend lists from strangers. Compared to about 28% for the dataset in Gundecha's work [12], more users in our dataset are aware of connection privacy. Although about 83.8% of users publish one or more basic attribute values, a majority of them provide incomplete basic profiles. Based on the dataset, only 9.9% of users publish complete basic attribute values.

Those statistics demonstrate that a significant number of users customize their $targetProfiles$ as private or partially private. The inference of their $targetProfiles$ reflects the effectiveness of their privacy settings. Next, we present the schemes to infer each of the two $targetProfile$ items in detail.

4   Exploiting Privacy Setting Vulnerability

Targeting a user's $targetProfile$, we design different inference schemes for each possible privacy setting type on the four subpages, including profile, friends, wall, and photo. For easy presentation, the notations we used are listed as follows:

U : **user set.**

$PS(u)$: $u \in U$, user u's privacy setting on four subpages: profile, friends, wall, photo in sequence; denoted as a 4-tuple, and entry value 1 means all basic

Table 1. User Sets and ratio

User Set	$U1$	$U2$	$U3$		$U4$	
PS	0100 0101 0110 0111	0001 0010 0011	0001 0010 0011	1001 1010 1011	0000 1000	11xx
Ratio	54.0%	14.3%	15.4%		22.4%	8.2%

attributes are visible in the profile page, visible friend page, some visible posts on the wall or photos, respectively, while 0 represents the opposite.

$BA(u)$: $u \in U$, user u's basic attribute values.

$FL(u)$: $u \in U$, all users in u's friend list, denoted as a user set.

$targetProfile(u)$: $u \in U$, user u's $targetProfile$, that is $\{BA(u), FL(u)\}$.

$G = (V, E)$: the social graph formed by users in user set V, and E consists of the undirectional connections among users in V; $\forall u, v \in V$, if $v \in FL(u)$ and $u \in FL(v)$, $(u, v) \in E$. Most frequently it is used to denote a user's neighborhood graph.

$GC(k)$: $1 \leq k \leq n$, a set of members of a community structure detected in a user's neighborhood, and n communities detected in total.

The scenarios under which the $targetProfile$ has to be inferred include when $PS = (0, 1, x, x)$, $PS = (1, 0, x, x)$ and $PS = (0, 0, x, x)$, where x can be either 1 or 0. According to the inference objective and public information, we categorize users into four sets from $U1$ to $U4$ by their PS values. $U1$ and $U2$ consist of users whose BA values can be inferred while $U3$ consists of users whose FL can be inferred from their public information, and $U4$ consists of those whose BA or FL are hard to be directly inferred from their public information.

Table 1 shows the possible PS values in each user set and the ratio of users in it. About 8.2% of users display complete $targetProfiles$ to strangers, thus they are not the inference objects. The union of $U1$, $U2$ and $U3$ consists of 69.4% of users, those users' $targetProfiles$ are not complete with more or less additional information accessible. In the following subsections, we first illustrate BA inference followed by FL; in particular, we infer BA for users in $U1$ and $U2$, then we infer FL for users in $U3$, followed by the hardest case for users in $U4$.

4.1   Basic Attributes from Friends

The users in $U1$ display incomplete or no BA but their friend lists are visible, and their BAs should be inferred. Table 1 shows that 54% of users belong to $U1$, indicating that a large group of users' privacy are threatened if their BAs can be properly compromised. This scenario is formulated as:

$U1 = \{v | v \in U \ and \ PS(v) = (0, 1, x, x)\};$
Inference objective: $BA(v), v \in U1;$
Public information: $FL(v), v \in U1.$

Intuitively, a user's geographical location, occupation, and interests affect the formation of its social circle. Some connections are set up with colleagues or classmates, while others are from interest communities. Thus, its friends could be classified into different groups, each of which is distinguished by an attribute value shared by the group members and the user. Some of its friends may belong to multiple groups. For example, one author's Facebook friends can be classified into three main groups: one from college, one from graduate school, and one from the current city. Some friends from the graduate school are also in the current city, while no one from college is in the current city. The three groups are distinguished by attribute values at the city or institution level. The friends could be classified into smaller groups by using finer granularity attributes like class and department. The friends in the same group have a higher chance to connect to each other than those from different groups. In other words, community structure exists in the user's friend circle: the connections inside a community are denser than the connections among communities [11].

Therefore, for $v \in U1$, this feature can be exploited to infer $BA(v)$, i.e., to study the connections among v's neighbors and detect communities. We first obtain the social graph in v's neighborhood, $G = (V, E)$ and $V = FL(v)$, by traversing v's friends and retrieving their profile pages and friend lists, although some of them are private. Then, we conduct the community detection in the graph. After that, we identify the most widely shared basic attribute value within each community as the *community feature*, and assemble those features together to form $BA(v)$. During the neighborhood traversal, neither users who have private profiles nor those who have private friend lists are eliminated during the process. This is because their information could be leaked from their shared friends with v, who have looser privacy configurations. The steps to infer $BA(v)$ are detailed below as **Scheme 1:**

1. Traverse each user u for $u \in FL(v)$ and retrieve $BA(u)$ and $FL(u)$; then form v's neighborhood graph $G = (V, E)$, $V = FL(v)$, based on $FL(u)$ for each $u \in FL(v)$.
2. Detect the communities in v's neighborhood graph, $G = (V, E)$, $V = FL(v)$, using Girvan-Newman algorithm [11]; and the resulting communities are denoted as $GC(1), GC(2), \cdots, GC(n)$.
3. For each community $GC(k)$, $1 \leq k \leq n$, find the *community feature* $A(k)$ and its frequency such that $A(k) \in BA(u)$ for $u \in GC(k)$ and $A(k)$ is the most widely shared basic attribute value among the community members.
4. Merge $A(k)$s of the same value and sum up their frequencies for $1 \leq k \leq n$; then sort the merged $A(k)$s by institution and location separately in decreasing frequency order. The top-ranked values from the two sorted lists are taken as $BA(v)$.

The Girvan-Newman algorithm is chosen as our community detection algorithm because it does not hold bias against small-sized graphs. Since the detection algorithm is conducted on the v's neighborhood graph, which is on comparatively small scale, the algorithms that hold bias to sparsely connected or small graphs are excluded from our consideration. On the other hand, the

Girvan-Newman algorithm proceeds by removing the edges with the highest edge-betweenness [11] value iteratively, and the procedure is suitable to conduct on small-sized graphs.

As for the number of top values to take in step 4, it can be decided by the target user's number of friends and the frequency of sorted values. More friends indicate more experience, and more values should be taken. Meanwhile, the values whose frequency is comparable with that of the top one value could also be taken. Intuitively, the higher the frequency, the higher the probability the value is accurate.

4.2   Basic Attributes from Wall and Photos

The users in $U2$ display incomplete or no BA and conceal their friend lists from strangers, but some of their wall posts or photos are visible. We need to infer their BAs. Out of the dataset, 14.3% of the users belong to $U2$. It is formulated as:

$U2 = \{v \mid v \in U \text{ and } PS(v) = (0, 0, x_1, x_2), \ x_1, x_2 = 0, 1 \text{ and } x_1 + x_2 > 0\};$
Inference objective : $BA(v)$, $v \in U2$;
Public information : v's public wall posts or photos.

Although the target user v's friend list is private, a direct leakage of v's connections is in v's photos or wall posts where its friends leave comments or get tagged. Different numbers of connections are leaked for different users, depending on their activities and privacy settings on the wall and photo subpages. We randomly choose 330 users in the dataset seeds' neighborhood that belong to $U2$, and crawl their public photos and part of wall posts. The cumulative number of users having less than or equal to a certain number of leaked friends is depicted in Figure 2. While about 90 users have no friends leaked, over half of the users have more than five friends leaked and the maximum number of leaked friends is 295. If all the public wall posts are crawled, the number of leaked friends would increase.

Whereas v has some leaked friends, they may compose a small portion of v's total friends. Namely, the leaked friends can be too spare to form detectable communities in v's neighborhood. Therefore, Scheme 1 is not applicable to users in $U2$. We seek to uncover $BA(v)$ in v's leaked friends' neighborhood, instead of v's neighborhood. First we traverse the directly leaked friends to retrieve their public friend lists and verify their connections to v. For those verified friends, their own friends can be traversed to obtain their neighborhood graphs and then detect communities in their neighborhoods. As illustrated before, the *community feature* is supposed to be the most widely shared by community members. Here v is classified to a certain community in each of the verified friends' neighborhood, and it should have a high probability to share the *community feature*. Accordingly, the steps to reveal $BA(v)$ are detailed below as **Scheme 2**:

1. Look through v's wall and photos to retrieve leaked friends.
2. Traverse each leaked friend to retrieve its friend lists if public and verify its connection with v.

3. For each verified friend u, traverse its friends and detect communities in u's neighborhood using the Girvan-Newman algorithm, resulting in $GC(1)$, $GC(2), \cdots, GC(n)$; if $v \in GC(k)$, find the corresponding *community feature* $A(k)$ and its frequency.

4. Merge and sort $A(k)$s, found in v's leaked friends' neighborhoods, in decreasing frequency order and identify $BA(v)$ in the top values.

Intuitively, the more friends leaked, the more *community features* can be found to increase the inference accuracy. Figure 2 demonstrates the possibilities of conducting the scheme. However, some users may display their photo and wall subpages but no comments are there; hence no friends are leaked. These cases are treated the same as these users in $U4$.

Besides, Scheme 2 could also be improved by assigning weights to the leaked friends, under the observation that those friends who comment or leave messages to user v might be closer to v than other friends. Higher priority could be given to the *community feature* found in those closer friends.

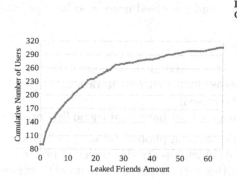

Fig. 2. Leaked Friends

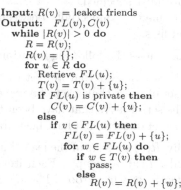

Algorithm 1. Traversal

4.3 Friends from Wall and Photos

Those users who conceal friend lists but display some wall posts or photos are categorized into $U3$. We need to infer their FLs. As Table 1 shows, 15.4% of users belong to $U3$. The scenario is formulated as:

$U3 = \{v \mid v \in U \text{ and } PS(v) = (x, 0, x_1, x_2), x, x_1, x_2 = 0, 1 \text{ and } x_1 + x_2 > 0\}$;
Inference objective : $FL(v)$, $v \in U3$;
Public information : v's public wall posts or photos.

We aim to uncover v's full friend list while there are some directly leaked friends from v's wall or photo subpages. Therefore, the inference task can be interpreted as traversing near v's neighborhood graph starting from the leaked friends and ascertaining whether those reachable users are v's friends. A few important issues must be considered to make the traversal practical. First, considering that the number of reachable users increases exponentially with the traversal depth, we should limit the depth so that the traversal is doable. Second, the v's neighborhood graph may be disconnected; thus, if there are components with no starting friends inside, it is arduous to measure the distance between disconnected components in hops by traversing beyond v's neighborhood. We use the word *component* to refer to a connected subgraph within v's neighborhood. Third, for traversed users having private friend lists, it is difficult to distinguish whether they are v's friends.

Taking these practical issues into account, we refrain the traversal from going beyond v's neighborhood graph. The traversal can be conducted in a breadth-first manner, starting from the leaked friends as roots. It proceeds only on those users whose friend lists include v, and stops on users whose friend lists exclude v. Those traversed users with private friend lists could be gathered together for further verification. Overall, the inference scheme consists of two steps and are detailed below as **Scheme 3:**

1. Traverse the v's neighborhood graph starting from the leaked friends as Algorithm 1 specified.
2. Determine the connectivity between v and traversed users who have private friend lists.

Algorithm 1 uses the following notations:

$R(v)$: the set of users that are yet to be traversed in the coming iteration;
R : the set of users that are to be traversed in the current iteration;
$T(v)$: the set of users that have been traversed;
$C(v)$: the set of users that have been traversed but have their friend lists private.

Initially, $R(v)$ consists of the leaked friends from photos and walls, while $T(v)$, $C(v)$, and $FL(v)$ are empty. Each iteration represents the traversal of users a certain depth away from roots. The algorithm terminates when no users traversed in the previous round are friends of v, that is $R(v)$ is empty. Furthermore, the algorithm could be adjusted to terminate in advance by confining the traversal depth. The depth can be recorded by counting the number of iterations, and the traversal terminates when the depth limit has been reached.

When the traversal algorithm terminates normally, all of v's friends who have public friend lists and are in the same components with the leaked friends should be included in the derived set $FL(v)$. On the other hand, users who are in different components from the leaked friends cannot be reached. This limitation is due to the feasibility concerns of Scheme 3. However, as the evaluation result in Section 5.2 indicates, on average the largest component in a user's neighborhood consists of over 75% of its friends. In other words, a leaked friend is likely to be included in the largest component; and thus the majority of v's friends are reachable from the leaked friends. Besides, as the component size and edge density vary in v's neighborhood, the traversal complexity differs.

Complexity of Algorithm 1. The complexity of algorithm 1 is analyzed in terms of the number of users whose information have to be retrieved. Assume that all users' numbers of friends are at the same magnitude, denoted as f. Algorithm 1 constrains the traversal to be within two hops away from the target user v; and thus all v's friends and its friends' friends are traversed in the worst case. We first take the v's f friends into count; and then we count its friends' friends as follows. In the algorithm, each user can only be traversed once. Thus, counting v's friends' friends should exclude v's friends. Let $G = (V, E), V = FL(v)$ denote v's neighborhood graph; and then for each $u \in V$, $f - degree(u)$ of its friends would be counted, which excludes v's friends. Thus, $\sum_{u \in V} f - degree(u)$ more users should be counted, that is, $f^2 - \sum_{u \in V} degree(u)$, in which $\sum_{u \in V} degree(u) = 2|E|$ according to graph theory. In total, the algorithm is in $\mathcal{O}(f + f^2 - 2|E|)$.

Therefore, the more densely v's friends connect to each other, the fewer users have to be traversed. The complexity varies between $\Theta(f^2)$ and $\Theta(f)$. The best case is when v's friends compose a complete graph, i.e. $|E| = \frac{f(f-1)}{2}$, then the complexity is $\mathcal{O}(f)$. When the algorithm terminates by limiting the traversal depth, the complexity would be lower.

As for the second step of Scheme 3, i.e., distinguishing the connectivity between v and traversed users who have private friend lists, the traditional link prediction algorithms such as common friends or Katz [15] can be employed.

4.4   No Leaked Friends

The users holding the strictest privacy settings are categorized into $U4$. These users set friends, wall and photo subpages as private and display some or no profile information. The users in this category constitute about 22.4% of the dataset. We need to infer both their FLs and BAs. While the inference schemes presented before start from some friend connections, the users in $U4$ display none of their friends.

Other means have to be sought to identify possible friends. One source to seek is the special friends or family member sections. Otherwise, the search people function could be exploited by using a user's location or institution, if provided, as keywords. Then, the search results can be traversed one by one to check whether the target user is included in their friend lists. As long as one of the target user's friends with public friend lists can be found, previous schemes can also be conducted to reveal its $targetProfile$. Otherwise, their privacy can not be inferred by our schemes.

In the next section, we apply these schemes to the dataset presented in Section 3 to quantify the privacy that can be compromised in each case.

5   Evaluation

The BA inference schemes are conducted on users who display their BA values, and the FL inference schemes are conducted on users who display their FL values; otherwise, the ground truth is not available for verification.

For the $targetProfile$ inference, evaluation bias may be induced in the results when a user's public profile is incomplete or fallacious. Considering the real name policy of Facebook [1], the problem of profile authenticity will not be as significant as incompleteness, which results in false positives. Especially for the location attribute values, only hometown and current city are available in the ground truth, while schemes 1 and 2 can also infer other cities where a user has ever stayed, such as those associated with the institutions where the user has ever been. Hence, the actual location inference accuracy should be higher than what the results illustrate.

5.1   Inferring Basic Attribute Values

Scheme 1 is evaluated first, which can be applied to the users with public friend lists. Out of the dataset,there are 909 users all of whose friends are in the dataset; thus, scheme 1 is applied to those users, referred to as evaluated users. Those who display nothing in their profiles are excluded due to the lack of ground truth for verification. Besides, users with more than 1,000 friends are excluded from the evaluation results. They consist of 5.17% of the total evaluated users, but less than three, if not zero, users fall into each user sample bin in this range; sparsity of user sample isn't likely to result in representative evaluation result.

We use the "igraph" [3] library to detect communities in each evaluated user's neighborhood with the Girvan-Newman algorithm [11]. In each community, the most frequently shared basic attribute value, the *community feature*, can be either a location or an institution value. We identify both the most-shared institution and location values when the community size is above average, and the one with lower frequency is called the *additional feature* of the community. Then we merge and sort those community features and additional features separately in decreasing frequency order by location and institution, respectively. The top ranked values are taken as the user's inferred basic attribute values.

We evaluate the basic attribute inference schemes from the following three aspects. (1) How many basic attribute values could be inferred? The number of public attribute values in evaluated users' homepages which are taken as ground truth, varies from user to user; thus, the number of basic attribute values that can be inferred for each user should be measured. (2) How accurate are inferred values? The number of top values from sorted community features, taken as inferred basic attribute values, can be adjusted; hence the accuracy of each value in the top rank should be be measured. (3) Whether the number of correctly inferred basic attribute values and the inference accuracy are affected by the number of the evaluated user's friends. Since the basic attribute values are inferred from the target user's friends' information, we want to know whether the number of friends affects the inference accuracy or number. Figures 3 to 6 give answers to those questions one by one. In all these figures except for Figure 6, the x-axis value is the number of users' friends and the y-axis value is the average value of users whose number of friends fall into the 20 user sample bin.

Figure 3 depicts the number of correctly inferred basic attribute values compared to the number of basic attribute values in ground truth. The figure shows that more attribute values could be inferred for users with more than 100 friends compared to those with less friends. It verifies the previous claim that the more friends a users has, the more attribute values could be derived; but the differences among users who have more than 120 friends are not significant. On average,

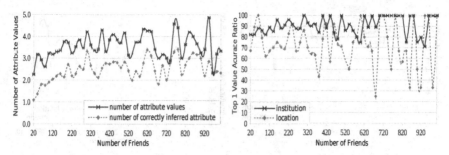

Fig. 3. Inferred Attribute Number   **Fig. 4.** Inference Accuracy

more than two attribute values could be correctly inferred. Attribute values that are not reflected in a user's community features cannot be inferred; one possible reason is that the user is not active in certain OSN communities, or its residence in a certain institution or city is too short to form a community.

The accuracy of the top values taken as inferred basic attribute values are shown in Figures 4 and 5. The accurate ratio is defined as the ratio between the number of verified inferred attribute values and the number of inferred values. In Figure 4 top 1 institution and location are taken as inferred values while in Figure 5 top 2 and top 3 institutions are taken as inferred values.

Figure 4 shows that the inference accurate ratio for institution is about 90% on average, and overall, the more friends the target user has, the higher the average accurate ratio is. Meanwhile the accurate ratio of location is not as good due to the false positives incurred by the incomplete ground truth of location values. As we mentioned at the beginning of this section, only hometown and current city are included in the ground truth for location while we infer all the places that the user has ever been. In addition, the accurate ratio of the top 1 location value for users with more than 500 friends fluctuates more strongly. One reason is that usually the larger the number of friends, the more experience a user has or the more locations a user has ever been, and in turn the less chance for the hometown or current city to be derived as the top 1 inferred location value. Another reason is that users with more than 500 friends are sparse at some point compared to users with fewer friends; thus the accurate ratio cannot be averaged and tends to go extremes due to the sparse user sample. This also explains the higher variance for those users in Figures 3 and 5.

Though the missing of ground truth for location leads to false positives, each institution is usually associated with a location; as long as institutions are correctly inferred, corresponding locations could also be derived. Hence, we further evaluate the accurate ratio of inferred institution information in Figure 5. Figure 5 depicts the accurate ratio of top 2 and top 3 ranked institution values. It shows the accuracy of top 2 institution values is over 80%, which on average is higher than that of top 3 institution values. It verifies our claim that higher-ranked community features hold higher probability to be shared by the target user. Besides, the accurate ratio is not largely affected by the number of users' friends.

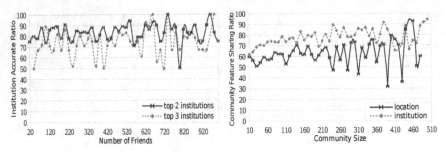

Fig. 5. Top Institutions Accuracy   **Fig. 6.** Community Feature Sharing

For users belonging to $U2$, we first measure the community feature sharing ratio to evaluate their basic attribute values inference accuracy, since their basic attributes are derived from the community feature in their leaked friends' neighborhood. Figure 6 depicts the community feature sharing ratio, and x-axis value is the community size. More than 8,500 communities are detected in the evaluated users' neighborhood. On average, the sharing ratio is higher when the community feature is an institution value compared to when it is a location value. This difference can also be explained by the ground truth incompleteness of location information. Though the community features are not 100% shared by all members, they will not be directly taken as the inferred basic attribute values and the wrong community features will be eliminated in the later steps of Scheme 2.

We further evaluate the inference accuracy of Scheme 2 on some of the dataset's seed users which belong to $U2$. Because seed users are from the same institution and location, the ground truth scraped from users' homepages are complemented by that fact. We detect those seed users' community memberships in their friends' neighborhood, and take the top ranked community features as their inferred attribute values. As a result, the inference accuracy of top 1 ranked feature is 100%.

In summary, for users who conceal their basic attribute values but have their friend list public or some friends leaked from other profile sections, those value could be uncovered with high accuracy by exploiting their friends' information.

5.2   Inferring Friend List

For a user v in $U3$, v's retrievable friends, according to Scheme 3, are confined to those who are in the same component with one of the leaked friends. As defined in Section 4.3, a component is a connected subgraph within v's neighborhood. We first measure the components in users' neighborhoods. Based on the evaluated users, most of their neighborhood graphs are disconnected, on average 20 components exist and the number of components increases with the number of a user's friends. While there are a noticeable number of components, most of them are small. Figure 7 illustrates the ratio of a user's friends that are in their largest neighborhood component, over 85% of friends on average are included in

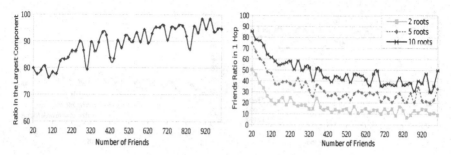

Fig. 7. Friends in the Largest Component   **Fig. 8.** Traversed Friends Ratio in 1 Hop

the largest component. The more friends a user has, the larger portion of friends are in the largest component. Thus, as the leaked friends are likely to be in the largest component, a majority of friends could be reached from them.

In Figure 8, the ratio of traversed friends in the evaluated users' neighborhoods is illustrated, and the traversal starts from different number of roots in one hop away. Each curve represents a different number of roots, which are randomly chosen from target user's friends. For users with fewer than 100 friends, a majority of friends could be traversed in one hop from five roots, while for users with more friends, about 10%, 25%, and 35% of friends could be traversed in one hop away from two, five, and ten roots, respectively. Over all, the more friends a user has, the more of its friends can be reached via traversal given the same number of roots and hops.

Figure 9 indicates the ratio of friends traversed in two hops away. About 70% of friends could be traversed from 5 roots, and 80% of friends could be traversed from 10 roots. The curve for two roots fluctuates more violently because the choice of roots affects the traversal path and a high-degree node results in more retrieved friends. When starting from 5 or 10 roots, the high-degree nodes stand a higher chance to be traversed as roots or within two hops. Still, on average about half of a user's friends could be retrieved from two randomly chosen roots in two hops. Interestingly, the ratio is not clearly affected by users' number of friends. It means that no matter how many friends a user has, most of its friends are closely connected while some are estranged from others.

To sum up, for users who conceal their friend lists but display other profile sections from which some of their friends could be leaked out, over half of their friends could be revealed using our traversal algorithm starting from the leaked friends in two hops. The complexity of the traversal algorithm ensures the traversal can be conducted in limited resource.

After that, we measure the second step of scheme 3, i.e., to distinguish the connections between user v and the traversed users who have private friend lists. Those users are those who connected to v's friends and have private friend lists. The number of common friends is taken as the metric to infer the connections. Those private-friend-listed users are sorted by their numbers of friends shared with v, which is leaked from v's public-friend-listed friends. The top quarter of users are taken as v's hidden friends. Figure 10 illustrates the inference accuracy,

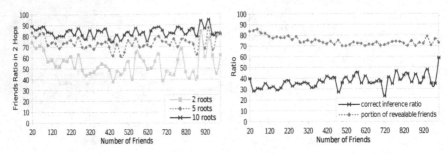

Fig. 9. Traversed Friends Ratio in 2 Hops   **Fig. 10.** Private-Friends Inference Ratio

and it also illustrates the total revealable friends ratio, which consists of both the public-listed friends and those hidden friends. Compared to the results of [15] which also used common neighbors as the metric to infer co-authorship, our accuracy is slightly higher. In total, for users belonging to $U3$, more than 70% of their friends could be correctly revealed on average by Scheme 3.

Users in $U4$ hide all connections, which is hardest to infer their $targetProfile$. However, if some of their friends are known beforehand or can be found by using the search people function mentioned in Section 4.4, their $targetProfile$ can be inferred and evaluated similar as stated above.

6   Discussion

While our approach explores a user's information visibility from the perspective of a stranger, it cannot know the privacy customization to the user's friends. However, the privacy setting for strangers can only be stricter than that for friends. In other words, friends must be able to access more information than strangers. Thus, if some private information could be correctly inferred by a stranger, the inference can also be reproduced by friends.

If a user does not post certain profile item on Facebook such as education, we cannot know whether the invisibility is due to privacy setting or vacancy. However, if the inferred information could be verified based on the ground truth retrieved from other sources, we still view such a case as privacy leakage.

Due to the lack of ground truth, the experiments are only conducted on users who display their $targetProfiles$ to strangers. However, we speculate that those users with stricter privacy are also inclined to be more prudent in setting up connections. Thus, their online friend circles are created in a more moderate manner, which does not increase the difficulty of community feature detection or neighborhood graph traversal. Therefore, our evaluation results reflect a possible privacy breach of average users.

The profile inference schemes proposed in this paper are not limited to Facebook. They could also be applied to other OSNs that enable privacy configuration and allow users to post a variety of data other than profile and connection. Those OSNs include MySpace, Google+, and Renren, in which users could also upload photos, leave messages or comments, and customize the visibility of different types of information. When the accessibility of a user's profile or connections is constrained, the information revelation could be initiated from public connections in the friend list or posts from friends by using our schemes 1, 2 or 3.

7   Conclusion

In this paper, we investigated the unintentional privacy disclosure of OSN users even with the protection of privacy settings. We first examined users' privacy settings on different information sections of a large dataset collected from Facebook. Then, for each possible privacy configuration, we proposed corresponding schemes to reveal basic profile and connection information starting from leaked public connections on the target user's OSN homepage. Finally, using our dataset, we quantified the achievable privacy exposure in each case, and measured the accuracy of our privacy inference schemes given a different amount of public information. The evaluation results indicate that a user's private basic profile could be inferred with high accuracy, while a user's covert connections could be uncovered in a significant portion based on even a small number of directly leaked connections.

Our privacy inference schemes can be conducted by attackers without much resources; and those schemes are applicable to users adopting specific privacy settings. The dataset statistics show that a majority of users are among that group. Therefore, the privacy of those users could be undermined facilely and the actual information privacy level of them may fail to meet what their privacy configuration specifies. We discussed that our privacy inference schemes could be applied to other OSNs that provide similar features as Facebook. We plan to analyze the privacy breach on those OSNs in the future.

Acknowledgement. We would like to thank the anonymous reviewers for their insightful feedback. This work was partially supported by ARO grant W911NF-11-1-0149.

References

[1] Facebook name policy, http://www.facebook.com/help/?page=258984010787183
[2] Facebook newsroom, http://newsroom.fb.com/
[3] IGRAPH, http://igraph.sourceforge.net/
[4] Backstrom, L., Dwork, C., Kleinberg, J.: Wherefore art thou r3579x?: anonymized social networks, hidden patterns, and structural steganography. In: Proceedings of the 16th WWW 2007 (2007)
[5] Baden, R., Bender, A., Spring, N., Bhattacharjee, B., Starin, D.: Persona: an online social network with user-defined privacy. In: Proceedings of the 2009 ACM SIGCOMM (2009)
[6] Balduzzi, M., Platzer, C., Holz, T., Kirda, E., Balzarotti, D., Kruegel, C.: Abusing social networks for automated user profiling. In: Jha, S., Sommer, R., Kreibich, C. (eds.) RAID 2010. LNCS, vol. 6307, pp. 422–441. Springer, Heidelberg (2010)

[7] Bonneau, J., Anderson, J., Anderson, R., Stajano, F.: Eight friends are enough: social graph approximation via public listings. In: Proceedings of the 2nd ACM EuroSys Workshop on SNS 2009 (2009)

[8] Chaabane, A., Acs, G., Kaafar, M.A.: You are what you like! information leakage through users' interests. In: Proceedings of the 19th NDSS 2012 (2012)

[9] Eyal, R., Kraus, S., Rosenfeld, A.: Identifying missing node information in social networks. Artificial Intelligence, 1166–1172 (2011)

[10] Feldman, A.J., Blankstein, A., Freedman, M.J., Felten, E.W.: Social networking with frientegrity: Privacy and integrity with an untrusted provider. In: The 21st USENIX Security 2012 (August 2012)

[11] Girvan, M., Newman, M.E.J.: Community structure in social and biological networks. Proceedings of the National Academy of Sciences 99(12), 7821–7826 (2002)

[12] Gundecha, P., Barbier, G., Liu, H.: Exploiting vulnerability to secure user privacy on a social networking site. In: Proceedings of the 17th ACM KDD 2011 (2011)

[13] Korolova, A., Motwani, R., Nabar, S.U., Xu, Y.: Link privacy in social networks. In: Proceedings of the 17th ACM CIKM 2008 (2008)

[14] Leroy, V., Cambazoglu, B.B., Bonchi, F.: Cold start link prediction. In: Proceedings of the 16th ACM KDD 2010 (2010)

[15] Liben-Nowell, D., Kleinberg, J.: The link prediction problem for social networks. In: Proceedings of the 12th CIKM 2003 (2003)

[16] Liu, Y., Gummadi, K.P., Krishnamurthy, B., Mislove, A.: Analyzing facebook privacy settings: user expectations vs. reality. In: Proceedings of the 2011 ACM SIGCOMM IMC 2011 (2011)

[17] Madejski, M., Johnson, M., Bellovin, S.M.: A study of privacy setting errors in an online social network. In: Proceedings of SESOC 2012 (2012)

[18] Mashima, D., Sarkar, P., Shi, E., Li, C., Chow, R., Song, D.: Privacy settings from contextual attributes: A case study using google buzz. In: PerCom Workshops, pp. 257–262. IEEE (2011)

[19] Mislove, A., Viswanath, B., Gummadi, K.P., Druschel, P.: You are who you know: inferring user profiles in online social networks. In: Proceedings of the 3rd ACM WSDM 2010 (2010)

[20] Mondal, M., Viswanath, B., Clement, A., Druschel, P., Gummadi, K.P., Mislove, A., Post, A.: Limiting large-scale crawls of social networking sites. SIGCOMM Computer Communication Review 41(4), 398–399 (2011)

[21] Narayanan, A., Shmatikov, V.: De-anonymizing social networks. In: Proceedings of 30th IEEE Symposium on Security and Privacy, S&P 2009 (May 2009)

[22] Pedarsani, P., Grossglauser, M.: On the privacy of anonymized networks. In: Proceedings of the 17th ACM KDD 2011 (2011)

[23] Singh, K., Bhola, S., Lee, W.: xbook: redesigning privacy control in social networking platforms. In: Proceedings of the 18th USENIX Security Symposium, SSYM 2009. USENIX Association, Berkeley (2009)

[24] Staddon, J.: Finding "hidden" connections on linkedin an argument for more pragmatic social network privacy. In: Proceedings of the 2nd ACM Workshop AISec 2009 (2009)

[25] Tai, C.-H., Yu, P.S., Yang, D.-N., Chen, M.-S.: Privacy-preserving social network publication against friendship attacks. In: Proceedings of the 17th ACM KDD 2011 (2011)

[26] Wondracek, G., Holz, T., Kirda, E., Kruegel, C.: A practical attack to de-anonymize social network users. In: Proceedings of the 2010 IEEE Symposium on Security and Privacy, S&P 2010 (2010)

[27] Yang, Y., Lutes, J., Li, F., Luo, B., Liu, P.: Stalking online: on user privacy in social networks. In: Proceedings of the Second ACM CODASPY 2012, New York, NY, USA (2012)

[28] Ying, X., Wu, X.: On link privacy in randomizing social networks. In: Theera-munkong, T., Kijsirikul, B., Cercone, N., Ho, T.-B. (eds.) PAKDD 2009. LNCS, vol. 5476, pp. 28–39. Springer, Heidelberg (2009)

[29] Zheleva, E., Getoor, L.: To join or not to join: the illusion of privacy in social networks with mixed public and private user profiles. In: Proceedings of the 18th WWW 2009 (2009)

Securing a Web-Based Anti-counterfeit RFID System

Belal Chowdhury[1], Morshed Chowdhury[2], and Jemal Abawajy[2]

[1] Melbourne Institute of Technology, Melbourne 3000, Australia
bchowdhury@mit.edu.au
[2] Deakin University, Melbourne 3125, Australia
{muc,Jemal}@deakin.edu.au

Abstract. The use of RFID (Radio Frequency Identification) technology can be employed for automating and streamlining safe and accurate brand identification (ID) uniquely in real-time to protect consumers from counterfeited products. By placing brand tags (RFID tags) on brands at the point of manufacture, vendors and retailers can trace products throughout the supply chain. We outline a Web-based Anti-counterfeit RFID System (WARS) to combat counterfeit branding. Despite these potential benefits, security, and privacy issues are the key factors in the deployment of a web-based RFID-enabled system in anti-counterfeiting schemes. This paper proposes an asymmetric cryptosystem to secure RFID transmission in retail supply chain using Elliptic Curve Cryptographic (ECC) techniques. The uses of ECC techniques provide greater strength than other current cryptosystems (such as RSA, and DSA) for any given key length, enables the use of smaller key size, resulting in significantly lower memory requirements, and faster computations, thus, making it suitable for wireless and mobile applications, including handheld devices.

Keywords: Asymmetric Cryptography, ECC, RFID, WARS and Counterfeit.

1 Introduction

Counterfeiting is a significant and growing problem worldwide, occurring both in less and well developed countries. Considering the countries worldwide, almost five percent of all products are counterfeited [1], [2]. Counterfeiting continues to increase globally because of the high margins achieved through counterfeiting by manufacturers and the demand for trade name goods at value prices by consumers [3]. The problem of counterfeiting is further magnified because of the opening of huge new economies in Eastern Europe and Asia [4]. In the past, counterfeit goods were easy to identify because these products typically represented luxury goods made with shoddy materials and sold in limited venues such as open-air markets in large, cosmopolitan cities as New York and Los Angeles. Today, however, counterfeiting impacts virtually every product category: from fake foods, beverages and everyday household products to pharmaceuticals, auto parts and consumer electronics [5]. Counterfeiting refers to the unauthorized production of goods protected by

T. Zia et al. (Eds.): SecureComm 2013, LNICST 127, pp. 342–355, 2013.

trademarks, copyrights, or patents. Due to the technological advancements in materials and processing techniques, many counterfeit goods have found their way to legitimate bricks-and-mortar retail stores, such as Walmart, and Target, in developed and developing countries. Many successful brands also become victims of the worldwide phenomenon of counterfeiting, where cheap impersonations of the brands are distributed by the counterfeiters. Nowadays, the brand counterfeiting context is increasingly dominated by the unconstrained presence of fake brands [6]. Therefore, this topic has generated a substantial body of scholarly discussion, research and thought [7].

The majority of the research on counterfeiting has focused attention on the demand side of counterfeiting [8], [9], [10] that is consumer accomplices who engage in aberrant consumer behaviour [11], [12] and deliberately purchase counterfeit goods with scant research addressing the supply side [13]. It can be argued that counterfeiters are good marketers because they have found a need and are finding a way to fulfill it [14]. To develop techniques that effectively combat the problem of counterfeiting, it is necessary to determine and identify the existence of the segment(s) of consumer accomplices who purchase counterfeit goods.

The economic and social consequences of counterfeiting are enormous. It is estimated that brand holders lose approximately $600 billion of revenue annually due to counterfeiting and make up approximately seven percent of world trade [15].In the USA economy, the cost of counterfeiting is estimated to be up to $200 billion per year [16]. A large majority of these products include clothing, luxury goods, entertainment equipment, medicines and pharmaceutical products, handbags, automotive parts and high tech products. Manufacturers of affected products have a direct loss in sale revenues; this is often directly related to losses in tax revenues, and may also result in job losses. Furthermore, counterfeit goods are everywhere on the Internet and if a brand has revenue generating capability or brand credibility, it will surely be counterfeited and sold online. Online auction sites and business-to-business websites also provide the ideal online medium for counterfeit sales that worth billions. Michael Danel, the secretary general of the World Customs Organization identified that if terrorism did not exist, counterfeiting would be the most important criminal act of the early 21st century.

The effect of counterfeiting is always greater than the value of the counterfeit product itself. By damaging consumers' perception of the performance, reliability, and safety of branded devices, counterfeiting tarnishes brand image, customer loyalty, and satisfaction. Actions to limit counterfeits can arise from both supply and demand side, considering the tactics companies employ to deter counterfeits [16] and the motivations that make a counterfeit an interesting option for some customers [17], [18]. Also, there is no single solution to this problem; anti-counterfeiting strategies should be multifaceted. The anti-counterfeiting strategies are possible by the use of mobile/wireless technology to combat counterfeiting. The application of these principles can be facilitated by the use of the wireless technology such as Radio Frequency Identification (RFID) [19]. Today's advanced technology is capable of uniting brand tags (RFID) and data processing into a single integrated system.

A Web-based Anti-counterfeit RFID System (WARS) can be used to automate and streamline safe and accurate brand identification (ID) uniquely in real-time by product marketing managers and to protect consumers from counterfeited products [20]. By placing brand tags (RFID tags) on brand items at the point of manufacture, manufacturers can trace products throughout the supply chain. The retail industry can use an online application, such as WARS at the point of sale to document the authenticity of their brand products at retail in real-time. The brand tags can store the unique product IDs and the product information can be stored in an associated (i.e., manufacturers) database. If the brand is not properly tagged or the brand tag is not associated (i.e., the product information is missing) with the database, then the retailers know the product is counterfeit. Additionally, by placing brand tags at the point of manufacture, not only can brands be traced throughout the supply chain, but it can also prevent counterfeit brands from entering into the supply chain.

These RFID-based systems can collect and organize data exponentially faster and more accurately. The unique ID number on standard RFID tags (e.g., passive) can be used to verify the authenticity of the products to which they are attached. As in the distribution chain, RFID-based systems in retail can greatly aid in reducing the cost of keeping accurate inventory data. With minimum staff and less time, retailers can keep accurate inventories. They can spend more time providing service to customers rather than counting product. In addition, the accuracy of the real time inventory data enables product marketing managers to ensure that hot selling items are properly stocked and to ensure replenishment order for these items are placed as quickly as possible. The RFID-based systems enable the product marketing managers to identify slow moving items quickly and to take corrective action to goose demand through promotional or advertising activity before a 'fire sale' is needed. Thus RFID systems help managers to maintain their margins. These systems are, also, a significant aid in deterring theft in retail environments. RFID enable brand tags to trigger alarms when they are removed from the store without a due process. In the past several decades, RFID-based systems have been successfully deployed for anti-theft purposes.

Despite these potential benefits, security, privacy and system deployment issues are the key factors in the deployment of a RFID-enabled system in anti-counterfeiting schemes and imposes significant threat on overall profitability [21]. Since a RFID-enabled web-based anti-counterfeiting systems use a wireless communication system, retailers or vendors and network servers need a strong security system (such as public-key cryptography) and mutual authentication protocol in their conversation [22]. Over the past three decades, public key cryptography such as RSA (Rivest, Shamir and Adelman) and DSA (Digital Signature Algorithm) has become a mainstay for secure communications. It provides the foundation for both key management and digital signatures. Public key cryptography is used to distribute the secret keys in key management and to authenticate the origin of data and protect the integrity of that data in digital signatures. However, over the past two decades, new techniques such as Elliptical Curve Cryptography (ECC) have been developed for better performance and higher security than these public key techniques [23].

One of the protocol proposed by Beller, Chang, and Yacobi [24], which provides mutual authentication and key agreement between users and servers with lower computational burden on the user side. This is important since the retailers usually communicate using a small, portable handset (e.g., smart phone) with limited power and processing capability. In this paper we will examine and propose a solution using ECC to address the security issues relating to RFID-enabled anti-counterfeiting systems.

The paper is structured as follows: Section 2 illustrates the application of a real-time Web-based Anti-counterfeit RFID System (WARS) to curb counterfeit branding. Section 3 discusses the Security issues and outlines the proposed solutions of WARS. Section 4 discusses the verification processes of counterfeit branding. Section 5 illustrates the practical implication of WARS and ECC. Section 6 concludes the paper.

2   Web-Based Anti-counterfeit RFID System

RFID is an advanced emerging technology that elegantly provides a solution to leading global brands in multiple industries including retail, pharmaceuticals, electronics, entertainment, aviation, IT and many more. WARS represent one of the most promising approaches to curb counterfeit branding. WARS mainly consist of smart brand tags, a RFID Reader and retailer's IT system. It can be embedded into the retailer's web portal (i.e., dashboard) to identify the authenticity of the brand tags. Each unique brand tag can be passive, semi-passive or active [25]. Passive tags can be used for both reading/writing capabilities by the RFID reader and do not need an internal power (i.e., battery). They get energized by the reader device and have a read range from 10 mm to almost 10 meters [26]. Passive tags are cheap, ranging from $0.25c to $0.40c each and life expectancy is unlimited. Thereby, we suggest the use of passive brand tags (13.56 MHz ISO 15693 tag) with the read range of one meter attached to each brand at the point of manufacture. The main components of the WARS are shown in Figure 1.

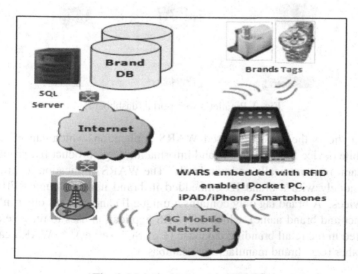

Fig. 1. Main components of WARS

The passive brand tag antenna picks up radio-waves or electromagnetic energy beamed at it from an RFID reader device attached to mobile devices (e.g., iPad, iPhone or smartphone) and enables the chip to transmit the brand's unique ID and other information to the reader device, allowing the product to be remotely identified [20]. A mobile device-based RFID reader will ensure that the identity of the brand product is passed to the device (e.g., iPhone) and automatically logged into an integrated database server (e.g., SQL server) using a wireless network. The RFID reader can also request any additional information from the brand tag that is encoded on it [26]. The reader converts the radio waves reflected back from the brand tag into digital information [27] then passed onto WARS (embedded in a smartphone/iPhone) for processing. The brand database can also link with other databases through Internet for retrieving specific brand information.

As the retail industry currently faces counterfeit branding issues, multi-layer RFID architecture can establish an infrastructure to address such a challenge, to automate and simplify the functionality for tracking and detecting brands wirelessly. Figure 2 shows a retailer's mobile-based web portal (i.e., dashboard) integrated with WARS. By clicking '**Brand Authenticity**' tab on the dashboard will enable WARS.

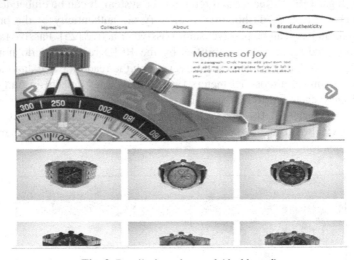

Fig. 2. Retailer's web portal (dashboard)

Figure 3 shows the windows based WARS application, which can be embedded with a mobile device for capturing brand information (e.g., product ID, product name, or brand name) automatically and wirelessly. The WARS application identifies every product uniquely with a brand ID embedded in brand items through RFID-enabled mobile devices. A brand tag only contains a unique ID and perhaps other information (e.g. product and brand name), which a WARS application uses to retrieve a product record stored in the retail branding database (e.g., SQL server). A WARS can also be linked to other (e.g., brand manufacturer) databases.

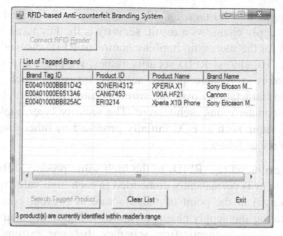

Fig. 3. WARS application for automatic brand detection

In case of counterfeit branding issues, a retailer or vendor can use WARS for detecting and determining the right brands. After running the WARS application, the retail staff needs to connect RFID reader first by clicking "Connect RFID Reader" button. Then detect brand product(s) by clicking "Search Tagged Product" button.

When the required brand items are in the mobile device-based RFID readers energizing field, the WARS application beeps, indicating that the identified brand is not counterfeited and displays the brand information (e.g., tag ID, product name, and brand name) in real-time in the list box as shown in Figure 3.

In case of counterfeit brand items, the WARS pop-up an error message, "Brand information is not found".

3   Security of WARS

Counterfeit branding has been an issue in many industries that affect only the bottom line and a company's reputation. High value luxury goods, such as handbags, wristwatches, and other products, are among the most susceptible to counterfeiting. The brand holders spend large amounts of money to trace and eliminate the counterfeit products and the people responsible to ensure that counterfeit products don't sully their brands.

Most of the security threats in retail supply chain are attributed to the security of the communication channel between authentic RFID-enable reader devices (e.g., smart phone) and the brand (RFID) tags through the air interface (i.e., wireless communication). A brand tag reading occurs when a reader device generates a radio frequency "interrogation" signal that communicates with the brand tag (e.g., a tagged camera), triggering a response from the brand tag [28]. Since RFID enabled anti-counterfeit systems uses open air space as a communication channel (wireless),   the content (such as brand name) of the communication may be exposed to an eavesdropper, or system services can be used fraudulently. Further with respect to

Read/Write (reprogrammable) tags, unauthorized alteration of brand data can be the possibility in the supply chain. As a result, security is the key issue which presents a host of challenges for the successful implementation of RFID-enabled anti-counterfeit branding systems. To address RFID security issues, we propose a separate security layer, which ensures a reliable proper security measures such as authenticity, confidentiality and intractability over the wireless communication channel [9] in the RFID-enable anti-counterfeiting architecture. The security layer implements a strong cryptographic algorithm such as ECC initially proposed by other researches [29].The security measures are as follows:

1) Attaching a brand tag (RFID) to the high value product – Brand tags can be attached to or is permanently embedded in each high value products (such as a wristwatch) at the point of manufacture to prevent counterfeit products from entering the supply chain. Including a digital signature in these brand tags can create authentication schemes that are extremely difficult for counterfeiters to circumvent. This will add an extra layer of security, which ensures that the counterfeiters cannot duplicate the signature as it is an effective measure to prevent a repudiation of service.

2) Strong cryptographic techniques and mutual authentication to protect high-value products - Cryptography is the science of keeping information secure. It provides confidentiality, authentication, integrity and non-repudiation. Cryptography can be classified into two categories: *symmetric* and *asymmetric*. In symmetric key cryptography, both parties share the same key for encryption as well as the corresponding decryption. Assymetric key cryptography uses pairs of keys – a public key, is used for encryption and its corresponding, intrinsically linked private/secret key is used for decryption. Both public and private keys can be used interchangeably.

   Asymmetric cryptography has proved to be so useful that it has become a common part of everyday life. Emerging technologies such as e-commerce web site uses a secure server employs asymmetric cryptography to secure online transactions. In this paper, we suggest an Asymmetric cryptography - the core technology behind digital signatures and authentication, offers the robust protection that can combat counterfeit branding.

3.1   Asymmetric Cryptography

Asymmetric cryptography uses a combined public and private key to encrypt messages and digital signatures. Although asymmetric cryptography offers superior security, it is by nature also demanding, complex, and costly to implement. Most of the public-key cryptosystems such as RSA and DSA are used for performing asymmetric authentication. The strength of technology provided by asymmetric cryptography is directly proportional to the key length used. As the key gets longer, the computational and software complexity also get longer. ECC can be an emerging alternative to public-key cryptosystems, and can be used to create faster, smaller, and more efficient cryptographic keys [30]. The countries like United States, United Kingdom, Canada and some NATO member countries have adopted some form of ECC for future systems to protect classified information between their governments. The United States Department of Defense aims at replacing almost 1.3 million existing equipment over the next 10 years that uses ECC for key management and digital signatures [23].

3.2   Elliptic Curve Cryptography

ECC is a public key encryption technique based on elliptic curve theory in cryptography was first proposed by Victor Miller and Neal Koblitz in 1985. ECC provides higher strength per bit than any other current cryptosystem (such as RSA, DSA, etc.), thus, making it suitable for wireless and mobile applications, including smartcards and handheld devices. The advantage of elliptic curve over the other public key systems such as RSA, DSA etc. is the key strength. The following table 1 summarizes the comparison of the key strengths ECC and other public key schemes [23].

Table 1. Comparison of the key strengths between RSA/DSA and ECC

RSA/DSA Key Size (bits)	ECC Key Size (bits)
1024	160
2048	224
3072	256
7680	384
15360	512

The above table shows that a 244-bit ECC key has the equivalent strength of a 2048-bit RSA key for security; a 384-bit ECC key matches a 7680-bit RSA key. So, it is clear that greater strength for any given key length enables the use of smaller key size, bandwidth savings, lower computational loads and memory requirements, and hence faster computations [23][30].

ECC generates keys through the properties of the elliptic curve equation instead of the traditional method of generation as the product of very large prime numbers. An elliptic curve E over a field R of real numbers, is defined by an equation, $E : y^2 + a_1xy + a_3y$ as shown in Figure 4. Where a_1, a_3 are real numbers belong to R, x and y take on values in the real numbers.

An elliptic curve represents a looping line intersecting two axes as shown in the following figure. ECC is based on properties of a mathematical equation derived from points where the line intersects the axes. Multiplying a point on the curve by a number will produce another point on the curve, but it is quite difficult to identify the number, even the original point and the result are known.

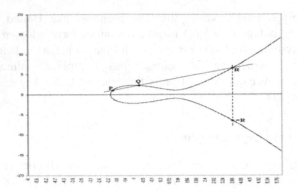

Fig. 4. Graph of the elliptic curve function

We propose an ECC public key [16] cryptosystem to communicate between two parties - sender and receiver. Both sender and receiver must agree to use an elliptic curve Ep (s,r) to communicate the messages, where p is a prime number. The sender (S) selects a large random number α, which is less than the order of Ep (s,r) and a random point A and C on the elliptic curve. The sender computes $S_1 = \alpha(C + A)$ and $S_2 = \alpha A$. S keeps the random number α, and the point A as his/her private keys and publishes S_1 and S_2 as a general public keys.

Similarly, the receiver (R) selects a large random number β and a point B on the elliptic curve. He/she computes $R_1 = \beta(C+B)$ and $R_2 = \beta B$. R keeps the random number β and the point B as his/her private keys and publishes R_1 and R_2 as general public keys. After publishing the public keys, the communicating parties again calculate the following quantities and publish them as their specific public keys of each other.

- The sender calculates $S_R = \alpha R_2$ and publishes it as his/her specific public key for receiver.
- The receiver calculates $R_S = \beta S_2$ and publishes it as his/her specific public key for sender.

The encryption and decryption processes are as follow:

Encryption: If R wants to communicate the message M then all the characters of the message are coded to the points on the elliptic curve using the code table, which is agreed upon by the both S and R. Then each message point is encrypted to a pair of cipher points E_1, E_2 . R uses a random number γ, which is different for the encryption of different message points.

$$E_1 = \gamma C$$
$$E_2 = M + (\beta + \gamma) S_1 - \gamma S_2 + S_R$$

After encrypting all the message character, the receiver converts the pair of points of each message point into the text characters using the code table. Then he/she sends the cipher text to S in the public channel (i.e., air).

Decryption: After receiving the cipher text, S converts the cipher text into the points on the elliptic curve and recognizes the points E_1 and E_2 of each character. Then he/she decrypts the message as follows.

$$M = E_2 - (\alpha E1 + \alpha R_1 + R_S)$$

An asymmetric scheme (using ECC) for security of WARS is shown in the following Figure 5.

Fig. 5. An asymmetric encryption (ECC) algorithm for secure communication

4   How Does WARS Work Using ECC?

The manufacturer embeds a brand tag (i.e., smart RFID tag) in each of its brand at the point of manufacture. Each brand tag contains a private key and a certificate that has the approval of luxury products (such as handbags, wristwatches, and other products) manufacturers, as well as identifying information about the brand, such as the name, description, etc. Retailers or vendors can use WARS at the point of purchase to verify the authenticity of high value products. The following steps are needed to verify counterfeit bands with retailers IT system using ECC:

a) A RFID-based smart phone (i.e., WARS) enables the brand tag to transmit brand's unique ID and pass it to the retailer's web-based IT (i.e., host) system.

b) The retailer's host system first requests a certificate (a random number along with a public key). The host then combines that number with the public key to create a challenge message, which the host sends back to the brand tag.

c) The brand tag uses its securely stored private key to compute the elliptic curve digital signature of the challenge message and sends this digital signature back to the host.

d) Using the corresponding public key, the host verifies the signature by decrypting random number is shown in the Figure 6.

Fig. 6. Verification processes of counterfeit branding

Only an authentic brand with knowledge of the private key can produce a correct digital signature. Using the verification result, the host decides whether to authenticate the brand to respond to RFID-enabled reader device. The host can also determine whether brand ID and other information are correct for use with the host and could also use the brand to track.

5   Practical Implication of WARS and ECC

A drawback of existing anti-counterfeiting measures (such as barcodes) is the low achievable degree of automation when checking the originality of a product. With existing schemes, large-scale checks, for example required in retail warehouses, are not feasible. RFID helps to address this problem, and provides the possibility to implement extensible, secure protection mechanisms in the retail supply chain. A RFID-based real-time automatic Anti-counterfeit RFID System (WARS) can be implemented in retail supply chain for combating counterfeit branding. Retailers or vendors would use WARS at the point of purchase to authenticate the brands [32].

As ECC employs both public and private key, a counterfeiter cannot derive one key based on knowledge of the other key. Thus, only brand tags that know the private key can respond correctly to a retailer's IT systems (i.e., host) challenge and the host system can determine this knowledge using only the corresponding public key. If a counterfeiter cannot obtain the private key, then the host can assume that any brand responding correctly is authentic.

In case of corrupt retailers or vendors, customer can verify the brand authenticity via SMS (Short Message Service), which is getting popular now-a-days and almost been used everywhere. Using SMS, consumers can send messages; make purchases and receive notification, all on a mobile device. For example, financial services institutions, such as banks, and credit card companies, are experiencing high rates of customer adoption and usage of SMS-based mobile banking services as the services become available on all mobile telephone technologies [33].

Upon purchasing a brand, customers can find an item specific code, such as brand serial number. Then, they text the code to manufacturer using their mobile phone and receive a reply confirming that the brand is genuine or warning that it may be counterfeited.

6   Conclusions and Future Work

In this paper we have outlined, and designed a Web-based Anti-counterfeit RFID System (WARS) to curb counterfeit branding. The authors have shown the application and practical implication of the above system. Efforts are being made to develop the complete system (i.e., WARS) for use in retail sectors to prevent counterfeiting. We also propose a separate security layer in WARS architecture to address RFID security issues and propose a reliable proper security measures such as authenticity, confidentiality and intractability using asymmetric cryptosystem (ECC) over the wireless communication. The advantage of elliptic curve over the other public key systems such as RSA, DSA etc, is the key strength, which provides greater security and more efficient performance.

The security and implementation properties of the ECC seem to be over the highest cryptographic strength per bit among all existing public-key systems. The RSA-based protocols have significant problems in terms of the bandwidth and storage requirements. For example, a 244-bit ECC key has the equivalent strength of a 2048-bit RSA key for security; a 384-bit ECC key matches a 7680-bit RSA key. So, it is clear that ECC is an emerging alternative to public-key cryptosystems, and has the smaller key sizes result in smaller system parameters, smaller public-key certificates, bandwidth savings, faster implementations, and lower power requirements. Thus, the use of the ECC in wireless communication system is highly recommended to combat counterfeit branding.

Nevertheless, implementation of such a security system requires specialized knowledge and a significant investment in hardware and software development, has prevented most manufacturers from employing it.

However, as the microprocessors available to counterfeiters wanting to hack these systems continue to become faster and cheaper, a key length that seemed adequate a few years ago may no longer offer adequate security. For this reason, effective asymmetric implementations have been too costly for all but the most high-end applications.

Finally the implementation of the proposed system could be an interesting area of future research.

References

1. International Anti-counterfeiting Coalition, IACC (2005)
2. International Intellectual Property Institute, IIPI (2003)
3. Amine, L.S., Magnusson, P.: Cost-benefit models of stakeholders in the global counterfeiting industry and marketing response strategies. Multinational Business Review, 1–23 (2007)

4. Organisation for Economic Co-operation and Development, The economic impact of counterfeiting. Organisation for Economic Co-operation and Development, Paris (1998)
5. WHO, The Need for Global Standards and Solutions to Combat Counterfeiting (2012), http://www.gs1.org/docs/GS1_Anti-Counterfeiting_White_Paper.pdf (accessed on July 05, 2013)
6. Phau, I., Teah, M., Lee, A.: Targeting buyers of counterfeits of luxury brands: A study on attitudes of Singaporean consumers. Journal of Targeting, Measurement & Analysis for Marketing 17(1), 3–15 (2009)
7. Staake, T., Thiesse, F., Fleisch, E.: The emergence of counterfeit trade: a literature review Export. European Journal of Marketing 43(3-4), 320–349 (2009)
8. Bloch, P.H., Bush, R.F., Campbell, L.: Consumer "accomplices" in product counterfeiting. Journal of Consumer Marketing 10(4), 27–36 (1993)
9. Cordell, V.V., Wongtada, N., Kieschnick, R.L.: Counterfeit purchase intentions: Role of lawfulness attitudes and product traits as determinants. Journal of Business Research 35(1), 41–53 (1996)
10. Wee, C.H., Ta, S.J., Cheok, K.H.: Non-price determinants of intention to purchase counterfeit goods: An exploratory study. International Marketing Revie 12(6), 19–46 (1995)
11. Bush, R.F., Bloch, P.H., Dawson, S.: Remedies for product counterfeiting. Business Horizons 32(1), 59–65 (1989)
12. Siponen, M.T., Vartiainen, T.: Unauthorized copying of software and levels of moral development: Implications for research and practice. Information Systems Journal 14(4), 387–407 (2004)
13. Cottman, L.: It's not the real thing. Security Management 36(12), 68–70 (1992); Cole, C.A.: Deterrence and consumer fraud. Journal of Retailing 65, 107–120 (1989)
14. Veloutsou, C., Bian, X.: A cross-national examination of consumer perceived risk in the context of non-deceptive counterfeit brands. Journal of Consumer Behavior 7(1), 3–20 (2008)
15. Richetto, D.: Advanced security prevents counterfeit products, Inside Secure - November 4 (2011)
16. Chaudhry, P.E., Cordell, V., Zimmerman, A.: Modeling anti-counterfeiting strategies in response to protecting intellectual property rights in a global environment (2005)
17. Phau, I., Prendergast, G.: 'Custom-made fakes: A mutant strain of counterfeit products'. In: Proceedings of Globalisation of Business Conference, Cyprus, November 16-18 (1998b)
18. International Trademark Association, Addressing the Sale of Counterfeits on the Internet (2009), http://www.inta.org/Advocacy/Documents/INTA%20Best%20Practices%20for%20Addressing%20the%20Sale%20of%20Counterfeits%20on%20the%20Internet.pdf (accessed on July 05, 2013)
19. Chowdhury, B., Khosla, R., Chowdhury, M.: Real-time Secured RFID-based Smart Healthcare Management System. International Journal of Computer & Information Science (IJCIS) 9(3) (2008)
20. Shepard, S.: RFID Radio Frequency Identification. The McGraw-Hall Companies, Inc., USA (2005)
21. Cottman, L.: It's not the real thing. Security Management 36(12), 68–70 (1992); Cole, C.A.: Deterrence and consumer fraud. Journal of Retailing 65, 107–120 (1989)
22. Die, W., van Oorschot, P.C., Wiener, M.J.: Authentication and authenticated key exchanges. Designs, Codes and Cryptography 2, 107–125 (1992)

23. National Security Agency, The Case for Elliptic Curve Cryptography (2009), http://www.nsa.gov/business/programs/elliptic_curve.shtml (accessed on July 09, 2013)
24. Beller, M.J., Chang, L.-F., Yacobi, J.: Privacy and authentication on a portable communications systems. IEEE Journal on Selected Areas in Communications 11(6), 821–829 (1993)
25. U.S. Government Accountability Office, "Radio Frequency Identification Technology in the Federal Government", 441 G Street NW, Room LM Washington, D.C. 20548 (2005)
26. Glover, B., Bhatt, H.: RFID Essentials. O'Reilly Media, Inc. 1005 Gravenstein Highway North, Sebastopol, CA 95472 (January 2006)
27. Denis, L.: What is WiFi? An Introduction to Wireless Networks for the Small/Medium Enterprise (SME), http://www.openxtra.co.uk/articles/wifiintroduction.php (accessed on February 10, 2007)
28. Bacheldor, B.: Strong sales growth expected for RFID tags, Manufacturers' Monthly (December 10, 2007), http://www.manmonthly.com.au/articles/Strong-salesgrowth-expected-for-RFID-tags_z138655.htm (accessed on February 11, 2011)
29. Enge, A.: Elliptic curves and their applications to cryptography. Kluwer Academic Publishers, Norwell (1999)
30. Menezes, J.: Elliptic Curve Public Key Cryptosystems. Kluwer Academic Publishers, Boston (1993)
31. Lopez, J., Dahab, R.: An overview of elliptic curve cryptography (May 2000)
32. Richetto, D.: Advanced security prevents counterfeit products, Inside Secure - November 4 (2011)
33. Riley, B., Schmidt, A., Tubin, G.: SMS in Financial Services: Accessing Your Customers on Their Terms, TowerGroup (2011), Research is available on the Internet at http://www.towergroup.com

Security Concerns and Remedy in a Cloud Based E-learning System

Md. Anwar Hossain Masud[1,*], Md. Rafiqul Islam[1], and Jemal Abawajy[2]

[1] School of Computing and Mathematics,
Charles Sturt University, Albury, Australia
{manwarhossain,mislam}@csu.edu.au
[2] School of Information Technology,
Deakin University, Australia
jemal.abawajy@deakin.edu.au

Abstract. Cloud computing is an emerging technology and it utilizes the cloud power to many technical solutions. The e-learning solution is one of those technologies where it implements the cloud power in its existing system to enhance the functionality providing to e-learners. Cloud technology has numerous advantages over the existing traditional e-learning systems. However security is a major concern in cloud based e-learning. Therefore security measures are unavoidable to prevent the loss of users' valuable data from the security vulnerabilities. This paper investigates various security issues involved in cloud based e-learning technology with an aim to suggest remedial in the form of security measures and security management standards. These will help to overcome the security threats in cloud based e-learning technology. Solving the key problems will also encourage the widespread adoption of cloud computing in educational institutes.

1   Introduction

E-learning is a form of learning created by combining digitally delivered content with learning support and services. E-learning systems usually require many hardware and software resources. Educational organizations cannot afford huge investments to obtain these resources. In past three decades, the computing world is based on the Internet, featured by the rapid development and application of computer technology. The cloud computing model is one of the very important shapes of a new era. This technology is based on the distributed computing, parallel computing, grid computing, Virtualization technologies; property- based remote attestation technologies, etc. Cloud computing is the best solution as it delivers the computing resources (hardware and software) as a service over the internet [1]. It provides resources and capabilities of information technology via services offered by CSP (cloud service provider). It is a way to increase the capacity or add capabilities dynamically without investing in new

---

* Corresponding author.

T. Zia et al. (Eds.): SecureComm 2013, LNICST 127, pp. 356–366, 2013.
© Institute for Computer Sciences, Social Informatics and Telecommunications Engineering 2013

infrastructure, training new personnel, or licensing new software. It extends Information Technology's (IT) existing capabilities. As cloud computing has become a research hotspot among modern technologies, researchers pay more attentions to its applications. When cloud computing is applied in the field of education, a lot of problems had been studied, such as the technology for future distance education cloud, teaching information system [2] [3] [4], the integration of teaching resources [5], and teaching systems development [6]. In integration of e-learning and network, emphasis is placed on building of software and hardware platform in e-learning system, functional structure, network security management and training, information technology integration to teaching [7], campus network environment [8], online education[9] and semantic web technologies-based multi-agent system [10] [12].

Cloud computing has grown from being a promising business concept to one of the fast growing segments of the IT industry. But as more and more information on individuals and companies are placed in the cloud, concerns are beginning to grow about just how safe an environment it is. Despite of all the hype surrounding the cloud, enterprise customers are still reluctant to deploy their business in the cloud. Security is one of the major issues which reduces the growth of cloud computing and complications with data privacy and data protection continue to plague the market. This paper examines security issues associated with e-learning. It investigates the more popular e-learning standards to determine their provisions and limitations for security. This paper also focuses on the basic way of cloud computing development in relation to e-learning, growths and common security issues arising from the usage of cloud services.

The rest of the paper is organized as follows. Section 2 describes traditional e-learning to cloud e-learning. Section 3 describes privacy and security in e-learning while section 4 explains the security concerns in cloud computing. Section 5 describes cloud based possible attacks, section 6 describes the proposed identity authentication in cloud based e-learning and section 7 is the conclusion.

2   From Traditional E-Learning Network to Cloud E-Learning

E-learning is an Internet-based learning process, using Internet technology to design, implement, select, manage, support and extend learning, which will not replace traditional education methods, but will greatly improve the efficiency of education. As e-learning has a lot of advantages like flexibility, diversity, measurement, opening and so on, it will become a primary way for learning in the new century as depicted in Fig. 1.[20]

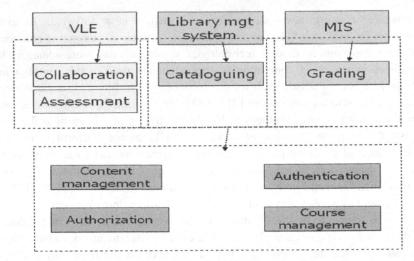

Fig. 1. Architecture of a simplified Learning System

Mendez [11] illustrates that in traditional web-based learning mode, system construction and maintenance are located inside the educational institutions or enterprises, which led to a lot of problems, such as significant investment needed but without capital gains for them, which leads to a lack of development potential. In contrast, cloud-based e-learning model introduces scale efficiency mechanism, i.e. construction of e-learning system is entrusted to cloud computing suppliers, which can make providers and users to achieve a win-win situation. The cloud-based environment supports the creation of new generation of e-learning systems, able to run on a wide range of hardware devices, while storing data inside the cloud. Ouf [19] has presented an innovative e-learning ecosystem based on cloud computing and Web 2.0 technologies. The article analyses the most important cloud-based services provided by public cloud computing environments such as Google App Engine, Amazon Elastic Compute Cloud (EC2) or Windows Azure, and highlights the advantages of deploying e-learning 2.0 applications for such an infrastructure. The authors also identified the benefits of cloud-based e-learning 2.0 applications (scalability, feasibility, or availability) and underlined the enhancements regarding the cost and risk management.

Chandran [17] focused on current e-learning architecture model and on issues in current e-learning applications. The article presents the Hybrid Instructional Model as the blend of the traditional classroom and online education and its customization for e-learning applications running on the cloud computing infrastructure. The authors underline the e-learning issues, especially the openness, scalability, and development/customization costs. The existing e-learning systems are not dynamically scalable and hard to extend integration with other e-learning systems is very expensive. The article proposed the hybrid cloud delivery model that can help in fixing the mentioned problems. In this article a new paradigm is highlighted in educational area by introducing the cloud computing in order to increase the scalability, flexibility and availability of e-learning systems. The authors have evaluated the traditional e-learning networking model, with its advances and issues, and the possibility to move the e-learning system out of schools or enterprises, inside a cloud computing infrastructure. The separation of entity roles and cost effectiveness can be considered important advantages. The institutions will be responsible for the education process, content management and delivery, and the vendor takes care of system construction, maintenance, development and management. The e-learning system can be scaled, both horizontally and vertically, and the educational organization is charged according to the number of used servers that depends on the number of students as shown in Fig.2.

The e-learning cannot completely replace teachers; it is only an updating for technology, concepts and tools, giving new content, concepts and methods for education, so the roles of teachers cannot be replaced [20]. The teachers will still play leading roles and participate in developing and making use of e-learning cloud. The blended learning strategy should improve the educational act. Moreover, the interactive content and virtual collaboration [13] guarantee a high retention factor. On the other hand, e-learning cloud is a migration of cloud computing technology in the field of e-learning, which is a future e-learning infrastructure, including all the necessary hardware and software computing resources engaging in e-learning. After these computing resources are virtualized, they can be afforded in the form of services for educational institutions, students and businesses to rent computing resources. The proposed e- learning cloud architecture can be divided into the following layers: Infrastructure layer as a dynamic and scalable physical host pool, software resource layer that offers a unified interface for e-learning developers, resource management layer that achieves loose coupling of software and hardware resources.

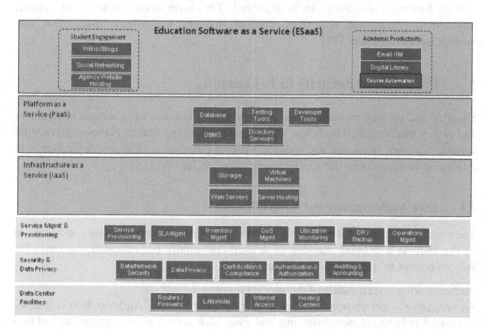

Fig. 2. Architecture for Cloud Based Higher Education System

Infrastructure layer is composed of information infrastructure and teaching resources. Information infrastructure contains Internet/Intranet, system software, information management system and some common software and hardware; teaching resources is accumulated mainly in traditional teaching model and distributed in different departments and domain. This layer is located in the lowest level of cloud service middleware, the basic computing power like physical memory, CPU, memory is provided by the layer. Through the use of virtualization technology, physical server, storage and network form virtualization group for being called by upper software platform. The physical host pool is dynamic and scalable, new physical host can be added in order to enhance physical computing power for cloud middleware services [14].

Software resource layer mainly is composed by operating system and middleware. Through middleware technology, a variety of software resources are integrated to provide a unified interface for software developers, so they can easily develop a lot of applications based on software resources and embed them in the cloud, making them available for cloud computing users. In ESaaS, cloud computing service is provided to customers. As is different from traditional software, users use software via the Internet, not need a one-time purchase for software and hardware, and not need to maintain and upgrade, simply paying a monthly fee.

Resource management layer is the key to achieve loose coupling of software resources and hardware resources. Through integration of virtualization and cloud computing scheduling strategy, on-demand free flow and distribution of software over various hardware resources can be achieved. This layer mainly consists of content production, educational objectives, content delivery technology, assessment and management component [15].

3   Privacy and Security in E-Learning

Security and privacy problems appear in e-learning because of operation mechanism and policy mechanism. The failure of security technology makes personal privacy be spread, diffused, aggrieved and scouted without permission. The primary concern in e-learning is the security that can be summarized as follows [18]:

3.1   User Authorization and Authentication

The elementary feature of e-learning system is the reliable identification – recognition of the user as a genuine member of a user community because it is the basis for Access control to the e-learning system.

Authentication – verification of the user's identity.
Authorization – permission to access specific resources. The Authorization is usually is granted only to registered students and even their access is generally restricted to a certain subset of the e-learning material based on the billing, if e-learning is offered on billing basis and on the level of learning of the registered student which will allow him/her to either to move to the next level or have a revision of the previous session.

3.2   Entry Points

There are many "entry points" in e learning system. A system can be attacked only through its "entry points". Designers can limit the security risks by reducing the number of entry points but E-Learning system cannot be implemented using this since there are a large number of multiple users from different geographic locations.

3.3   Dynamic Nature

The other challenge is the dynamic nature of these systems where any process may join or leave the group sessions at any time. Security is also concern with each particular member process, a strict session has to be maintained and the credentials are to be verified to control both at the session level and at the participant site.

3.4   Protection against Manipulation

One of the issues of e-learning is manipulation from the side of the students the system must be secured against manipulation. There are many possible solutions where any manipulations can be protected by using the techniques of encryption, digital signatures, firewalls, etc.

3.5   Confidentiality

Confidentiality refers to the assurance that information and data are kept secret and private and are not disclosed to unauthorized persons, processes or devices. In an e-learning perspective, students need the assurance that their assignments they submit online are kept private and only disclosed to the intended examiner.

3.6   Integrity

Integrity is that only authorized users are allowed to modify the contents which include creating, changing, appending and deleting data and metadata and the attacks on integrity are generally the attempts made to actively modify or destroy information in the e- learning site without proper authorization.

3.7   Availability

The e-learning material e-content, data (or metadata) are to be made available to the learner at the specified session when the user log on to the system for their session at the period of time, if the required material is not available the learner will lose interest and not get the at most use of e-learning system. Mainly there are two types of attacks, (i) blocking attack and (ii) flooding attack, e.g.: Denial of Service, Node attacks, Line attacks, Network infrastructure attacks[16].

3.8   Non-repudiation

Non-repudiation is another important step in information security where the learners have to be provided with E-Learning services without any possible fraud such as when computer systems are broken in to or infected with Trojan horses or viruses, to deny the works or changes done by them in the system elimination of a refuted activity performed by a user.

4   Security Concerns of Cloud Computing

Security is one of the people's peak concerns on all grounds. People are more concerned of the security especially when using the technologies that involve internet. Because the internet has many loopholes that can crash the application or hack the application to gain access to the users or company details by hackers worldwide. E-learning technology is now incorporated with many latest technologies to provide more provision and reduce the complexity from traditional e-learning methodology to their users. So there is a question raised on how the cloud provides security in e-learning technology and to the e-learners. So our research throws light to identify the security issues with cloud based e-learning and the countermeasures took recently on those problems.

The major security challenge with clouds is that the owner of the data may not have control of where the data is placed. Due to the extensive complexity of the cloud, we contend that it will be difficult to provide a holistic solution to securing the cloud, at present. Cloud system will: (i) support efficient storage of encrypted sensitive data. (ii) Store, manage and query massive amounts of data. (iii) Support fine-grained access control and (iv) support strong authentication. Security issues for many of these systems and technologies are applicable to cloud computing. For example, the network that interconnects the systems in a cloud has to be secure. Finally, data mining techniques may be applicable to malware detection in clouds.

5   Cloud Computing Based Possible Attacks

As more educational institutes move to cloud computing, more attack vectors criminals may attempt include:

Denial of Service (DoS) Attacks: Some security professionals have argued that the cloud is more vulnerable to DoS attacks, because it is shared by many users, which makes DoS attacks much more damaging. Twitter suffered a devastating DoS attack during 2009.

Cloud Malware Injection Attack: A first considerable attack attempt aims at injecting a malicious service implementation or virtual machine into the Cloud system [5]. Such kind of Cloud malware could serve any particular purpose the adversary is interested in, ranging from eavesdropping via subtle data modifications to full functionality changes or blockings. This attack requires the adversary to create its own malicious service implementation module (SaaS or PaaS) or virtual machine instance (IaaS), and add it to the Cloud system.

Side Channel Attacks: An attacker could attempt to compromise the cloud by placing a malicious virtual machine in close proximity to a target cloud server and then launching a side channel attack.

Authentication Attacks: Authentication is a weak point in hosted and virtual services and is frequently targeted. There are many different ways to authenticate users; for example, based on what a person knows, has, or is. The mechanisms used to secure the authentication process and the methods used are a frequent target of attackers. Currently, regarding the architecture of SaaS, IaaS, and Paas, there is only IaaS offering this kind of information protection and data encryption.

6   Proposed Identity Authentication in Cloud Based E-Learning

Traditionally, identity authentication is applied when an individual requests access to system. For this situation, the three elements or items used for identity authentication are what you have, what you know, and what you are. Cloud computing introduces a whole new challenge for identity authentication. For an identity authentication example, consider that when a program running within the cloud needs to access some data stored in the cloud, i.e., what you have and what you are criteria are irrelevant. However, the context of the access request is relevant and can be used [18]. Only some access key and the careful monitoring protects against unauthorized access. In cloud computing (as well as other systems), there are many possible layers of access control. For example, access to the cloud, access to servers, access to services, access to databases (direct and queries via web services), access to VMs, and access to objects within a VM. Depending on the deployment model used, some of these will be controlled by the provider and others by the consumer.

Google Apps, a representative SaaS Cloud controls authentication and access to its applications, but users themselves can control access to their documents through the provided interface to the access control mechanism. In IaaS type approaches, the user can create accounts on its virtual machines and create access control lists for these users for services located on the VM. Regardless of the deployment model, the provider needs to manage the user authentication and access control procedures (to the cloud). While some providers allow federated authentication – enabling the consumer-side to manage its users, the access control management burden still lies with the provider. This requires the user to place a large amount of trust on the provider in terms of security, management, and maintenance of access control policies. This can be burdensome when numerous users from different organizations with different access control policies, are involved. This proposal focuses on access control to the cloud. However, the concepts here could be applied to access control at any level, if deemed necessary. We propose a way for the consumer to manage the access control decision-making process to retain some control, requiring less trust of the provider as illustrated in Fig-3.

This approach requires the client and provider to have a pre-existing trust relationship, as well as a pre-negotiated standard way of describing resources, users, and access decisions between the cloud provider and consumer. It also needs to be able to guarantee that the provider will uphold the consumer-side's access decisions [20]. Furthermore, we need to show that this approach is at least as secure as the traditional access control model. This approach requires the data owner to be involved in all requests. Therefore, frequent access scenarios should not use this method if traffic is a concern. However, many secure data outsourcing schemes require the user to grant keys/certificates to the query side, so that every time the user queries a database, the owner needs to be involved.

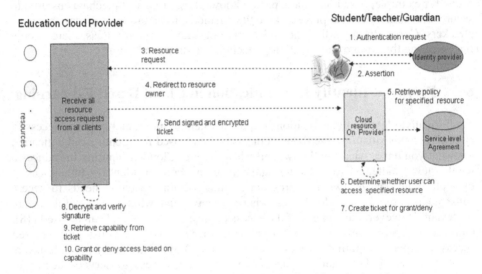

Fig. 3. Proposed Identity Authentication in cloud based e-learning

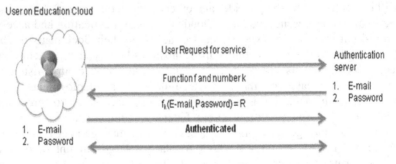

Fig. 4. Proposed Identity Authentication for proofing in details

The proposed method has the ability to use identity data on untrusted hosts i.e Self Integrity Check. It should be independent of third party. It establishes the trust of users through putting the user in control of who has his data. Identity is being used in the process of authentication, negotiation, and data exchange as in Fig. 4.

7   Conclusion

Computer security issues exacerbate with growth of Internet as more people and computers join the web, opening new ways to compromise an ever increasing amount of information and potential for damages. However, an even bigger challenge to information security has been created with the implementation of cloud computing. This paper gave a brief general description of cloud based e-learning security issues and possible directions of solutions. Some information security challenges that are specific to cloud computing have been described. Security solutions must make a trade-off between the amount of security and the level of performance cost.

Cloud computing has a dynamic nature that is flexible, scalable and multi-shared with high capacity that gives an innovative shape for e-learning systems. On the other hand, several deadly threats are affecting these benefits in cloud based e-learning systems. This research paper has discussed the influence of cloud computing in e-learning systems and the various security issues threatening the cloud based e-learning with the few guidelines to effectively handle these security issues.

The key thesis of this paper is that security solutions applied to cloud computing must span multiple levels and across functions. Our goal is spur further discussion on the evolving usage models for cloud computing and the increasing security cover these will need to address both the real and perceived issues, thus spurring new research in this area. Economic benefit of such research and resulting solutions will be increased trust in, and accelerated adoption of, cloud computing.

References

1. Masud, M. A.H., Huang, X.: ESaaS: A New Education Software Model in E-learning Systems. In: Zhu, M. (ed.) ICCIC 2011, Part V. CCIS, vol. 235, pp. 468–475. Springer, Heidelberg (2011)
2. Ahmed, S., Buragga, K., Ramani, A.K.: Security issues concern for E-Learning by Saudi universities, pp. 1579–1582. IEEE (2011)
3. Anwar, H.M., Huang, X.: Enhanced M-Learning with Cloud Computing: The Bangladesh Case. In: Proceedings of the 2011 15th International Conference on Computer Supported Cooperative Work in Design, IEEE CSCWD, Switzerland, pp. 735–741 (2011)
4. Armbrust, M., Fox, A., Griffith, R., Joseph, A.D., Katz, R., Konwinski, A., et al.: A View of Cloud Computing. ACM Communications 53, 50–58 (2010)
5. Viswanath, D.K., Kusuma, S., Gupta, S.K.: Cloud Computing Issues and Benefits Modern Education. Global Journal of Computer Science and Technology Cloud & Distributed, Version 1.0 12(10), 15–19 (2012)
6. Al-Rwais, S., Al-Muhtadi, J.: A Context-aware Access Control Model for Pervasive Environments. IETE Technical Review 27, 371–379 (2010)
7. Sehgal, N.K., Sohoni, S., Xiong, Y., Fritz, D., Mulia, W., Acken, J.M.: A Cross Section of the Issues and Research Activities Related to Both Information Security and Cloud Computing. IETE Tech. Rev. 28, 279–291 (2011)
8. Anwar, H.M., Huang, X.: An E-learning System Architecture based on Cloud Computing. World Academy of Science, Engineering and Technology 62 (2012), http://www.waset.org/journals/waset/v62/v62-15.pdf

9. Zhong-ping, Z., Hui-cheng, L.: The Development and Exploring of E-Learning System on Campus Network. Journal of Shanxi Teacher's University (Natural Science Edition) 18(1), 36–40 (2004)

10. Jian, T., Lijian, F., Tao, G.: Cloud computing-based Design of Network Teaching System. Journal of TaiYuan Urban Vocational College, 159–160 (March 2010)

11. Xin-ping, H., Zhi-mei, Z., Jian, D.: Medical Informatization Based on Cloud Computing Concepts and Techniques. Journal of Medical Informatics 31(3), 6–9 (2010)

12. Méndez, J.A., González, E.J.: Implementing Motivational Features in Reactive Blended Learning: Application to an Introductory Control Engineering Course. IEEE Transactions on Education PP(99) (2011)

13. Buyya, R., Yeo, C.S., Venugopal, S.: Market-oriented Cloud computing: Vision, hype, and reality of delivering IT services as computing utilities. In: 10th IEEE Int. Conf. High Performance Comput. Comm., pp. 5–13 (2009)

14. Lijun, M., Chan, W.K., Tse, T.H.: A tale of Clouds: Paradigm comparisons and some thoughts on research issues. In: IEEE Asia-pasific Services Comput. Conf., APSCCA 2008, pp. 464–469 (2008)

15. Praveena, K., Betsy, T.: Application of Cloud Computing in Academia. Iup J. Syst. Management 7(3), 50–54 (2009)

16. Delic, K.A., Riley, J.A.: Enterprise Knowledge Clouds, Next Generation Km Syst. In: Int. Conf. Inform. Process, Knowledge Management, Cancun, Mexico, pp. 49–53 (2009)

17. Chandran, D., Kempegowda, S.: Hybrid E-learning Platform based on Cloud Architecture Model: A Proposal. In: Proc. International Conference on Signal and Image Processing (ICSIP), pp. 534–537 (2010)

18. Méndez, J.A., González, E.J.: Implementing Motivational Features in Reactive Blended Learning: Application to an Introductory Control Engineering Course. IEEE Transactions on Education (99) (2011)

19. Ouf, S., Nasr, M., Helmy, Y.: An Enhanced E-Learning Ecosystem Based on an Integration between Cloud Computing and Web2.0. In: Proc. IEEE International Symposium on Signal Processing and Information Technology (ISSPIT), pp. 48–55 (2011)

20. Anwar, H.M., Huang, X.: A Novel Approach for Adopting Cloud-based E-learning System. In: IEEE/ACIS 11th International Conference on Computer and Information Science, China, pp. 37–42 (2012)

Ensuring Data Integrity by Anomaly Node Detection during Data Gathering in WSNs

Quazi Mamun, Rafiqul Islam, and Mohammed Kaosar

School of Computing and Mathematics, Charles Sturt University, NSW, Australia
{qmamun,mislam,mkaosar}@csu.edu.au

Abstract. This paper presents a model for ensuring data integrity using anomalous node identification in non-homogeneous wireless sensor networks (WSNs). We propose the anomaly detection technique while collecting data using mobile data collectors (MDCs), which detect the malicious activities before sending to the base station (BS). Our technique also protects the leader nodes (LNs) from malicious activities to ensure data integrity between the MDC and the LNs. The proposed approach learns the data characteristics from each sensor node and passes it to the MDC, where detection engine identifies the victim node and eventually alarm the LNs in order to keep the normal behaviour in the network. Our empirical evidence shows the effectiveness our approach.

Keywords: WSN, data integrity, mobile data collector, compromise, malicious, anomaly.

1 Introduction

The development of WSNs has attracted a lot of attentions due to the potentiality of broad applications in both military and civilian operations. Usually WSNs are deployed in unattended and often hostile environments such as military and homeland security operations [1, 2, 3, 6, 17, 18, 19, 22]. Recent advances in wireless sensor network research have shown that an attacker can exploit different mechanisms of sensor nodes spread malicious code through the whole network without physical contact [18, 19]. Therefore, it is imperative to adopt security mechanisms providing confidentiality, authentication, data integrity, and non-repudiation, among other security objectives, are vital to ensure accurate network operations.

A WSN may consist of hundreds or even thousands of sensor nodes. The sensor node consists of distributed autonomous devices using sensors to cooperatively monitor or collect sensing data at different locations. This renders it impractical to monitor and protect each individual node from a variety of malicious attacks. For instance, once a particular node is compromised, intruders can launch various malicious codes to launch attacks. They might spoof, alter or replay routing information to interrupt the network routing [1]. They may also launch the Sybil attack [2, 3], where a single node presents multiple identities to other nodes, or the

T. Zia et al. (Eds.): SecureComm 2013, LNICST 127, pp. 367–379, 2013.

identity replication attack, in which clones of a compromised node are put into multiple network places [3]. Moreover, adversaries may inject bogus data into the network to consume the scarce network resources [4, 5]. In addition, if the coordinators of the sensor networks are compromised, all members of the clusters become more vulnerable to different types of security attacks. This situation poses the demand for compromise-tolerant security design, especially for the coordinators.

A node can be captured by the intruder to find sensitive data or to compromise other nodes. In all of the WSN topologies, the sensor nodes send the sensed data to the coordinators. In a clustered based topology, the coordinators are called cluster heads, whereas in a chain oriented network the coordinators are called chain leaders. If the coordinator is compromised, these nodes can be used by the intruders to compromise other nodes. Thus coordinator compromise is a serious threat to wireless sensor networks deployed in unattended and hostile environments. To mitigate the impact of compromised nodes, we propose a model of compromise-tolerant security mechanism by adopting a detection engine within the MDC. This technique will enable to protect the BS as well as cluster coordinator and ensure the data integrity between MDC and BS.

The main contributions of this paper are three-folds:

- The design of deploying detection engine within the mobile data collectors to identify the malicious node of WSN cluster. As mobile data collection techniques are attracting attentions nowadays due to their energy-saving characteristics, the proposed idea is well fitted in this category of research.
- The proposed method prevents not only the members of a cluster or chain, but also the leader of the cluster/chain from malicious activities. Additionally, as the mobile data collectors are carrying messages to the BS, the BS can also be kept safe from the malicious activities.
- The proposed method reduces memory overhead. We adopt the mobility in collecting data by utilizing multiple mobile data collectors (MDCs) and enhanced the performance of data collection process by using the spatial division multiple access (SDMA) technique.

The rest of the paper is organized as follows. Section 2 presents the network architecture model of the proposed node anomaly detection technique. Section 3 describes details of our anomalous node detection method. In Section 4, we describe the experimental setup. Simulation results are presented in Section 5. Finally in Section 6, we draw the conclusion and describe the future work.

2   Network Architecture Model

The proposed anomaly node detection technique can be deployed over all hierarchical networks, either in cluster based or tree based or chain oriented network. In this paper, we consider the network topology is chain oriented topology. In a chain oriented sensor network, multiple chains can be constructed, where all the chains will be restricted to *Voronoi cell*s [22]. Furthermore, in these topological networks, mobile data collectors can be used to collect data from the deployed sensor nodes [8].

An overview of the architectural model is illustrated in Figure 1. The leader nodes are depicted using the blue coloured dots. All the sensor nodes deployed inside a

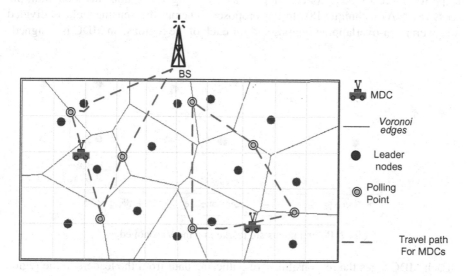

Fig. 1. The network architecture model for the proposed anomaly node detection technique

Voronoi cell send their data to the leader nodes. On the other hand, the mobile data collectors visits the polling points on a regular basis and collect data from the leader nodes. The data gathering scheme for large scaled wireless sensor networks can be extended by using multiple MDCs and the spatial division multiple access (SDMA) technique. This is described in details in [8]. For example, in Fig. 1, two MDCs travel within the network and collect data from the leaders. The two MDCs work at the same time, and when an MDC arrives at a polling point, leaders associated with this polling point are scheduled to communicate with the MDC. Two leaders in a compatible pair can upload data simultaneously in a time slot, while an isolated leader (i.e., a leader by itself or not in any compatible pair) sends data to the MDC separately.

The BS is usually situated outside the sensing field. Sending the data by the sensors to the remote BS may lead to non-uniform energy consumption among the sensors, because the sensor nodes (or leader nodes) that are responsible for sending data to the BS, need to cover long-range distances. As a result, they deplete energy much faster than other sensor nodes, and die quickly [9, 10, 11]. The consequence of this situation may result in partitioning the network and loss of robustness. However recent studies [12, 13, 14] have proposed sink mobility or collecting data using a mobile device as an efficient solution for data gathering problem. Employing mobile devices to collect data can reduce the effects of the hotspots problem, balance energy consumption among sensor nodes, and thereby prolong the network lifetime to a great extent [15, 16].

To solve the vital data gathering problem of large scaled WSNs, we adopt mobility in collecting data by utilizing multiple mobile data collectors (MDCs) and enhanced the performance of data collection process by using the spatial division multiple access (SDMA) technique [8]. In the proposed scheme, the sensing field is divided into several non-overlapping regions and for each of the regions, an MDC is assigned.

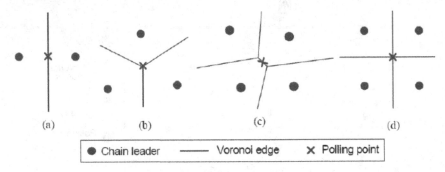

(a)   (b)   (c)   (d)

● Chain leader   ——— Voronoi edge   ✕ Polling point

Fig. 2. Polling points are marked on the Voronoi edges

Each MDC takes the responsibility of gathering data from the leaders in the region while traversing in their transmission ranges. The traversal paths of the MDCs are determined using the *Voronoi* diagram constructed with respect to the leader nodes. We also consider exploiting the SDMA technique by equipping each MDC with two antennas. With the support of SDMA, two distinct compatible leader nodes in the same region can successfully make concurrent data uploading to their associated MDC. Intuitively, if each MDC can simultaneously communicate with two compatible leader nodes, the data uploading time in each region can be cut in half in the ideal case.

We further focus on the problem of minimizing DGS time among different regions. Besides this, the data gathering problem using multiple MDCs and the SDMA technique requires optimal solutions, discussed in [8, 13]. These optimization problems can be formulated using an Integer Linear Programming (ILP) approach. However, the complexity of an ILP solution is generally high, which is not suitable for a large scaled WSN [11]. Therefore, a heuristic region-division and traversing algorithm was used in [8] to provide a feasible solution to the problem. One of the common challenges of the WSN is the conservation of power, thus elongating the life span of a sensor node. A lot of research is being carried out towards 'energy efficiency' of WSN. In this paper an attempt has been made to secure the WSNs with the help of 'Cross layer' approach. This is an extended and enhanced version of [8].

In our proposed model, an MDC travels within each region and stops at some locations to collect data from the leader nodes. These positions are called polling points. To take full advantage of the SDMA technique, polling points should be equidistant from the associated leader nodes. Figure 2 shows some positions of polling points in four different cases. If there are only two leader nodes, the position of the polling point can be found at the intersection between the *Voronoi* edge and the line joining the two leader nodes (Fig. 2(a)). For more than two leader nodes, the polling point can be found at the intersection of different *Voronoi* edges (Fig. 2(b-d)). Any two leader nodes associated with the same polling point are said to be compatible if an MDC arriving at this polling point can successfully decode the multiplexing signals concurrently transmitted from these two leader nodes. Detailed discussions on utilizing SDMA at physical layer for concurrent data uploading is provided in [8].

The following assumptions are made specific to our proposed DGS:

- It is assumed that MDCs have access to a continuous power supply. Usually the BS is equipped with the source of continuous power supply. Thus, when an MDC visits the base station, it can replace its battery.

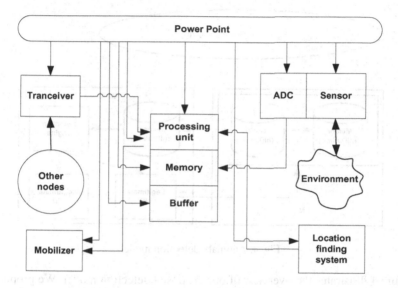

Fig. 3. Basic structure of a sensor node

- It is assumed that the MDCs are familiar with the target field. Location images of the target field can be stored in each MDC. Thus, an MDC is able to visit any point within the target field.
- It is also assumed that each MDC can forward the gathered data to one of the nearby MDCs when they are close enough, such that data can eventually be forwarded to the MDC that will visit the static data sink.

3   Anomaly Node Detection Method

In this section we present the scaffold of our anomaly detection technique. First we present the basic diagram of a sensor node which integrates hardware and software for sensing, data processing, and communications. They rely on wireless channels for transmitting data to and receiving data from other nodes. A sensor node is made up of a sensing unit, a processing unit and transceiver unit and a power unit, as illustrated in Figure34. They may also have additional application-dependent components such as a location finding system, power generator and mobilize. Sensors devices that can observe or control physical parameters of the environment is converted to digital signals by the ADC, and then fed into the processing unit. The processing unit which is generally associated with a small storage unit, manages the procedures that make the sensor node collaborate with the other nodes to carry out the assigned sensing tasks. A transceiver unit connects the node to the network. Power units may be supported by power scavenging units such as solar cells. Most of the sensor network routing techniques and sensing tasks require knowledge of location with high accuracy. Thus, it is common that a sensor node has a location finding system. A mobilize may sometimes be needed to move sensor nodes when it is required to carry out the assigned tasks.

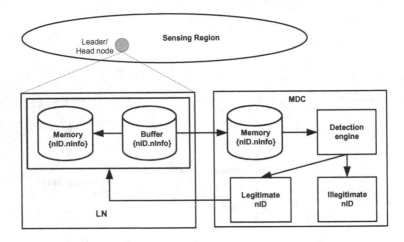

Fig. 4. Anomaly detection model

Figure 4 illustrates the overview of our proposed detection model. We propose two approaches for detecting the malicious node in our model. Firstly leader node, we called it LN, which will store the receiving data from all sensor nodes in the cluster into their buffer memory, as shown in Figure 4. Then the MDC node should use another buffer where the sensing data, from the LN, will be stored. In both cases every node ID (nID) will be considered as uniquely identifier of each node, so that after detection LN can identify the victim node. The detection engine will be deployed into the MDC node and the data will be passed to detection engine to identify the victim node. Finally the MDC will transfer the list of legitimate nID to the LN and then LN will transfer the data to its main memory based on the list of supplied nID. The MDC also send the information to BS based on the legitimate nID. If there is any malicious node identified, the MDC will immediately inform to the LN for taking protection measure.

4   Experimental Setup

The purpose of this experiment is to evaluate the effectiveness of anomaly detection of LN within WSN region. Our evaluation is based on a real-life dataset in which the modes or partitions in the data can be controlled.

We use a real-life dataset called the IBRL dataset in our evaluation [21]. The IBRL data set includes a log of about 2.3 million readings collected from 54 sensor nodes. The total log size is 150MB and the data were averages averaged over all time. The IBRL data is a publicly available set of sensor measurements gathered from a wireless sensor network deployed in the Intel Berkeley Research Laboratory [21]. In this data set the have used temperature and humidity data of 12 hour periods. In this period, as shown in Figure 5, one of the sensors started to report erroneous data or abnormal data. This can be seen as a dotted block in figure 5(a) and the elaboration in figure 5(b). Analysing the behaviour of the sensors showed that most had such behaviour toward the end of the experiment, but this particular sensor started its drift earlier than the others.

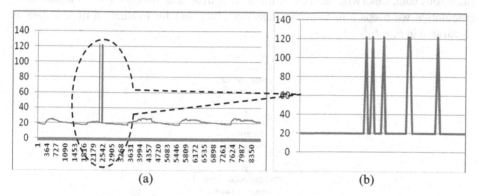

(a)   (b)

Fig. 5. Abnormal data reading from sensors

To investigate the effect of a non-homogeneous environment, a synthetic dataset, from real dataset, with five disjoint clusters was built. Data from each sensor was gathered randomly according to the distribution (cluster) assigned to that sensor. The data is generated so that it has the same range as the IBRL dataset. Since each sensor recorded multiple readings of the same temperature and humidity, we can compress the data. Instead of keeping all (temperature, humidity) attributers, only unique attributes have been kept with their relative frequency of occurrence. Also, temperature and humidity values have been rounded up to whole numbers. With this method, the volume of the data has been reduced significantly by over an order of magnitude.

Detection Engine: The first step of our detection engine is to select the parameters to monitor and group them in a pattern vector [x1] $x^\mu \in \mathfrak{R}$, $\mu = 1,..., N$, that is

$$x^\mu = \begin{bmatrix} x_1^\mu \\ x_2^\mu \\ \vdots \\ x_n^\mu \end{bmatrix} = \begin{bmatrix} KPI_1^\mu \\ KPI_2^\mu \\ \vdots \\ KPI_n^\mu \end{bmatrix}$$

where μ the observation index and n is the number of parameter types or key performance indices (KPI's) chosen to monitor the environmental condition. In our detection method we use the technique called discrete wavelet transform (DWT) method proposed in [19], which is a mathematical transform that separates the data signal into fine-scale information known as details coefficients, and rough-scale information known as approximate coefficients.

After selecting the data parameters from the data sets, we the produce our experimental databases and calculate the feature weights and averaged it to make a class value. In our technique we use two parameters; one is support thresholdθ, and other is correlation thresholdδ, in order to decide whether data is normal or abnormal. For instance the temperature is $> \theta$ and Humidity is $>\delta$ we called this data as malicious data, otherwise the rest of the data is treated as normal. After the threshold calculation we prepare to train the classifier algorithm for evaluation of test data as illustrated in Fig. 6.

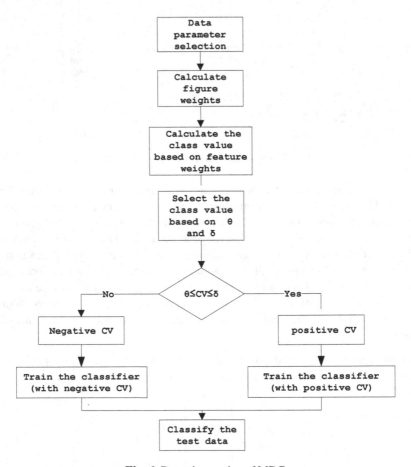

Fig. 6. Detection engine of MDC

5   Experimental Results

The effectiveness of our WSN malicious data detection technique can be measured by the number of FP (false positive) alarms and the TP (true positive) alarms. Since our dataset (IRBL), there are no predefined labels for malicious data, we assessed the data and labelled as malicious data that falls outside the expected value range. In our experiment, we have chosen two parameters, namely temperature and humidity.

Figure 7 shows the average performance of our experiment. In the graph it has been shown that the performance of detection ratio is approximately 95%. It is clear from the graph that the node n11 and n13~n19 shows abnormal behaviour which falls outside of our measured value. Also we can see some of nodes, n46~n51 shows the performance below the measured value. According to our estimation, those node will be identified as malicious node due to their abnormal behaviour of sending data.

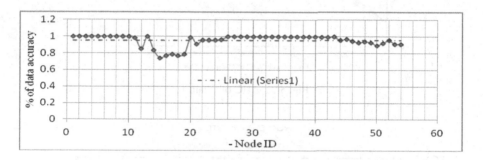

Fig. 7. The average performance of the experiment

The Fig. 8 shows the ROC (Receiver Operating Characteristic) report of our second data set, where we have used five different clusters. The AUC is a popular measure of the accuracy of an experiment. All things being equal, the larger the AUC, the better the experiment is at predicting by the existence of the classification. The possible values of AUC range from 0.5 (no diagnostic ability) to 1.0 (perfect diagnostic ability). The CI option specifies the value of alpha to be used in all CIs. The quantity (1-Alpha) is the confidence coefficient (or confidence level) of all CIs. The P-value represents the hypotheses tests for each of the criterion variables.

Obviously, a useful experiment should have a cut-off value at which the true positive rate is high and the false positive rate is low. In fact, a near-perfect classification would have an ROC curve that is almost vertical from (0, 0) to (0, 1) and then horizontal to (1, 1). The diagonal line serves as a reference line since it is the ROC curve of experiment that is useless in determining the classification. It has been shown from the figure that the abnormality of sensor node falls in second cluster (figure 8.b) and last cluster (figure 8.e). The best cluster is cluster 1 (figure 8.a) and cluster 4 (figure 8.d), which reflects the similar picture presented in figure 7.

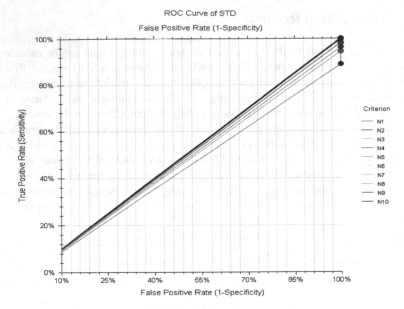

Fig. 8(a). AUC of Chain 1

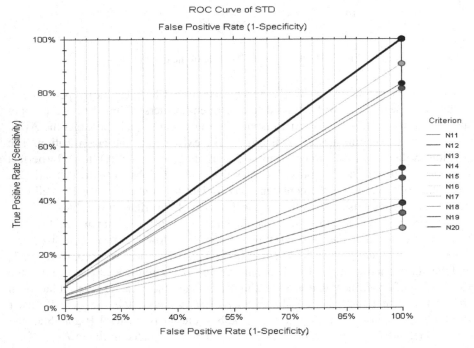

Fig. 8(b). AUC of Chain 2

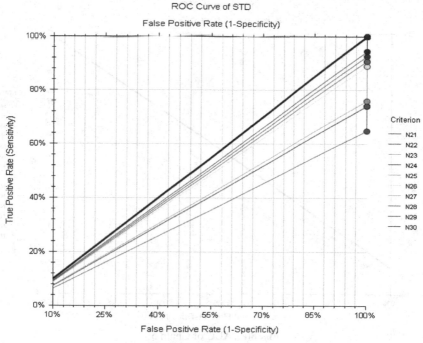

Fig. 8(c). AUC of Chain 3

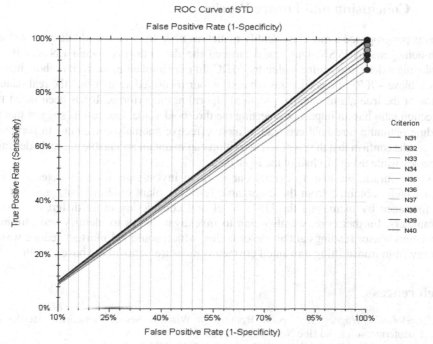

Fig. 8(d). AUC of Chain 4

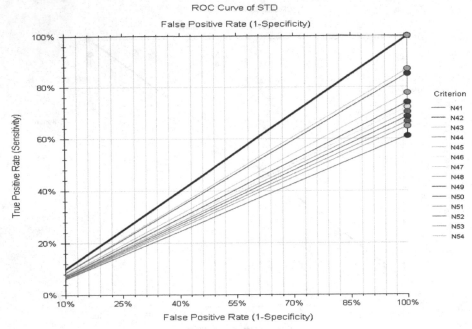

Fig. 8(e). AUC of Chain 5

6   Conclusion and Future Works

This paper proposed a model to identify malicious node from real-world datasets within a non-homogeneous WSN. Our model ensured the data integrity within LN and BS by deploying a detection engine within the MDC. In our simulation, the results show that we can achieve ~70% of detection rates based on our measured value using the real data. In terms of the true alarm rate, the proposed algorithm outperforms. It has been noted that detection ratio has an impact on selecting the threshold value. Our results suggest that the finding optimum threshold can lead to more effective anomaly detection. In particular, our results confirm that the proposed algorithm can maintain acceptable anomaly detection accuracy while using just half of the input data.

In the future, we plan to extend our work to investigate anomaly detection with actual faults obtained from the bioorganic fertilizer plant environment, and study its performance by increasing the DWT level and considering other different types of parameters. Furthermore, we also plan to investigate ways to identify and eliminate erroneous sensor readings at the sensor nodes, which could help further reduce wasted energy from transmitting unwanted erroneous measurements to the base station.

References

1. Karlof, C., Wagner, D.: Secure Routing in Wireless Sensor Networks: Attacks and Countermeasures. Ad Hoc Networks 1(1) (2003)
2. Douceur, J.R.: The Sybil Attack. In: Druschel, P., Kaashoek, M.F., Rowstron, A. (eds.) IPTPS 2002. LNCS, vol. 2429, pp. 251–260. Springer, Heidelberg (2002)

3. Newsome, J., Shi, E., Song, D., Perrig, A.: The Sybil Attack in Sensor Networks: Analysis & Defences. In: The Third International Symposium on Information Processing in Sensor Networks (IPSN 2004), Berkeley, CA (April 2004)
4. Ye, F., Luo, H., Lu, S., Zhang, L.: Statistical En-Route Filtering of Injected False Data in Sensor Networks. In: IEEE INFOCOM 2004, Hong Kong, China (March 2004)
5. Zhu, S., Setia, S., Jajodia, S., Ning, P.: An Interleaved Hop-By-Hop Authentication Scheme for Filtering of Injected False Data in Sensor Networks. In: IEEE Symp. Security Privacy, Oakland, CA (May 2004)
6. Ayman, K., Crussière, M., Hélard, J.-F.: Cross Layer Resource Allocation Scheme under Heterogeneous constraints for Next Generation High Rate WPAN. International Journal of Computer Networks and Communications (IJCNC) 2(3) (2010)
7. Xiao, M., Wang, X., Yang, G.: Cross-Layer Design for the Security of Wireless Sensor Networks. In: Proceedings of the 6th World Congress on Intelligent Control and Automation, Dalian, China (2006)
8. Mamun, Q.: Constraint-Minimizing Logical Topology for Wireless Sensor Networks, PhD Thesis. Faculty of IT, Monash University (2011)
9. Zhao, M., Yang, Y.: Bounded Relay Hop Mobile Data Gathering In Wireless Sensor Networks. IEEE Transactions on Computers 61(2), 265–277 (2012)
10. Chen, Y., Tang, Y., Xu, G., Qian, H., Xu, Y.: A Data Gathering Algorithm Based on Swarm Intelligence and Load Balancing Strategy for Mobile Sink. In: 9th World Congress on Intelligent Control and Automation (WCICA), pp. 1002–1007 (2011)
11. Zhao, M., Yang, Y.: Optimization-Based Distributed Algorithms for Mobile Data Gathering In Wireless Sensor Networks. IEEE Transactions on Mobile Computing 11(10), 1464–1477 (2012)
12. Liang, W., Schweitzer, P., Xu, Z.: Approximation algorithms for capacitated minimum forest problems in wireless sensor networks with a mobile sink. IEEE Transactions on Computers (2012)
13. Zhang, X., Chen, G.: Energy-efficient platform designed for SDMA applications in mobile wireless sensor networks. In: IEEE Wireless Communications and Networking Conference, pp. 2089–2094 (2011)
14. Fei, X., Boukerche, A., Yu, R.: An efficient markov decision process based mobile data gathering protocol for wireless sensor networks. In: IEEE Wireless Communications and Networking Conference (WCNC), pp. 1032–1037 (2011)
15. Zhi, Z., Dayong, L., Shaoqiang, L., Xiaoping, F., Zhihua, Q.: Data gathering strategies in wireless sensor networks using a mobile sink. In: 29th Chinese Control Conference (CCC), pp. 4826–4830 (2010)
16. Ma, M., Yang, Y.: Data Gathering In Wireless Sensor Networks With Mobile Collectors. In: IEEE International Symposium on Parallel and Distributed Processing, pp. 1–9 (2008)
17. Mamun, Q.: A Tessellation Based Localized Chain Construction Scheme for Chain Oriented Sensor Networks. IEEE Sensors Journal 13(7), 2648–2658 (2013)
18. Giannetsos, T., Dimitriou, T., Prasad, N.: Self-Propagating Worms in Wireless Sensor Networks. In: CoNEXT Student Workshop, Rome, Italy (2009)
19. Sharma, K., Ghose, M.: Cross Layer Security Framework for Wireless Sensor Networks. International Journal of Security and Its Applications 5(1), 39–52 (2011)
20. Siripanadorn, S., Hatagam, W., Teaumoroong, N.: Anomaly Detection in Wsns Using Self-Organizing Map and Wavelets. International Journal of Computing 4(3), 74–83 (2010)
21. IBRL-Web, http://db.lcs.mit.edu/labdata/labdata.html
22. Mamun, Q.: A tessellation based localized chain construction scheme for chain oriented sensor networks. IEEE Sensors Journal 13(7), 2648–2658 (2013)

$(k - n)$ Oblivious Transfer Using Fully Homomorphic Encryption System

Mohammed Kaosar[1], Quazi Mamun[1], Rafiqul Islam[1], and Xun Yi[2]

[1] School of Computing and Mathematics, Charles Sturt University, Australia
[2] School of Engineering and Science, Victoria University, Australia
{mkaosar,qmamun,mislam}@csu.edu.au, xun.yi@vu.edu.au

Abstract. Oblivious Transfer(OT) protocol allows a client retrieving one or multiple records from a server without letting the server know about the choice of the client. OT has been one of the emerging research areas for last several years. There exist many practical applications of OT, especially in digital media subscription. In this paper, we propose a fully homomorphic encryption based secure k out of n oblivious transfer protocol. This novel protocol, first ever to use fully homomorphic encryption mechanism for integers numbers, allows the client choosing its desired records by sending encrypted indexes to the server, server works on encrypted indexes and sends back encrypted result without knowing which records the client was interested in. From the encrypted response of the server, the client only can decrypt its desired records. The security analysis demonstrates that, the desired security and privacy requirement of OT is ensured by the proposed protocol. Some optimizations are also introduced in the proposed solution to reduce transmission overhead.

Keywords: Oblivious Transfer, Homomorphic Encryption, Private Information Retrieval, Data Outsourcing.

1 Introduction

In the current world, the use of information technology has increased tremendously. Consequently, secure storage, transmission and retrieval of information become one of the top concerns in the IT era. The diversity of devices, applications and infrastructures have increased this concern by another fold. The privacy of information in any transaction is no more a small issue. Private Information Retrieval (PIR) and Oblivious Transfer (OT) are some of the cryptographic protocols that ensures the privacy of the user in retrieving information from a storage or a server. Unlike PIR, OT ensures the server security too by not allowing the user retrieving unauthorised record(s). OT has been used in many applications including certifying email and coin flipping [1], simultaneous contract signing [2], digital right management [3], e-subscription to sell digital goods [4], privacy preserving data mining in distributed environment [5] etc.

To understand the basic principle of OT protocol, let us consider an example: let us say, a server stores n number of digital contents or records of information

T. Zia et al. (Eds.): SecureComm 2013, LNICST 127, pp. 380–392, 2013.

$x_1, x_2, ..., $ and x_n. Clients or users need to subscribe with the server to access an item. In such e-subscription, there will be two requirements to be fulfilled from the server's and the client's point of view respectively: (i) the client should not be able to retrieve any item(s) which it did not subscribe for and (ii) the server is not allowed to know which item(s) the client retrieved. That is, if the client wants to retrieve or access item x_i, OT protocol ensures that server cannot learn the value of i and the client cannot learn any x_j for all $j \neq i$.

In this paper our proposed solution uses a secure cryptographic protocol, particularly the fully homomorphic encryption over integer numbers proposed by Dijk and Gentry [6] in 2010, to ensure data privacy of the client. The server's security is ensured by encrypting all of its records using a symmetric key encryption system such as, AES [7] or DES [8]. k out-of n OT can be achieved by repeating 1 out-of n OT protocol k times. This approach incurs extremely high overhead. In this paper, we have proposed some optimizations in the $k - n$ OT protocol. It transmits the encrypted database only once at the beginning of the protocol. The server uses separate keys to encrypt each record using a symmetric key encryption technique. The protocol only allows the desired keys to be decrypted by the client. On the other hand, the client encrypts its choices using the homomorphic encryption technique and transmits to the server. The server encrypts and manipulates keys and indexes using the same technique without being able to decrypt any of the choices of the client. The fully homomorphic encryption of Dijk and Gentry is as strong as the approximate Greatest Common Divisor (GCD) problem (more detail of approximate GCD can be found in [9]). The security analysis shows that the proposed protocol ensures both the server's and the client's requirements.

The rest of the paper is organized as follows: Section 2 describes some background knowledge on the topic of the paper including the fully homomorphic encryption system which is used in the proposed protocol, Section 3 and 4 discuss our proposed model and the protocol, Section 5 discusses the security and performance analysis and finally, Section 6 concludes the paper with some hints towards the future research directions.

2   Background and Related Work

This section discusses about various OT protocols and existing solutions and the definition of homomorphic and fully homomorphic encryption system. This section also discusses how the fully homomorphic encryption for binary digits is extended to work for integer numbers.

2.1   Types of Oblivious Transfer Protocol

OT can be of three basic types:

- 1-*out-of*-2 *(1 − 2 OT)*:
  1 out-of 2 oblivious transfer protocol allows the client retrieving one item

out of 2 from the server. The server does not know which item was accessed by the client and the client does not know about any item it did not chose to retrieve. Rabin [10] first proposed $1-2$ OT protocol in 1981. In this RSA [11] based protocol, the server sends the message (an item) to the client with the probability of $1/2$ and hence, the server remain oblivious whether the message was received or not. Later on, $1-2$ OT was developed by Evan et al. [12] while applying it in randomized protocol for signing contracts, certifying mail and flipping coin.

- 1-*out-of-n (1-n OT):*
1 out-of- n oblivious transfer protocol allows the client retrieving one item out of n from the server. Often times 1-n OT is used as a generalization of 1-2 OT. 1-n OT is also similar to Private Information Retrieval (PIR), first proposed by Kushilevitz and Ostrovsky [13] in 1997, with an additional condition. In PIR the client can retrieve 1 item from n items without letting the server know its choice. The client may retrieve or access other items. Whereas, 1-n OT ensures the client won't be able to access anything other than what it retrieved. Some more about $1-n$ OT protocol can be found in [14,15].

- *k-out-of-n (k-n OT):*
k out-of- n oblivious transfer protocol allows the client retrieving k number of items out of n from the server. The client would send k number of indexes to the server. The server would return all those desired items without knowing client's choices. $k-n$ OT was first proposed by Ishai et al. in [16]. Additive homomorphic encryption based $k-n$ OT protocol is proposed in [17]. $k-n$ OT can also be achieved by repeated use of $1-n$ OT. However, this approach would be very inefficient due to huge amount of overhead transmitted from server to the client.

2.2   Fully Homomorphic Encryption System (FHES)

Homomorphic encryption is a special form of encryption where one can perform a specific algebraic operation on the plain-text by applying the same or different operation on the cipher-text. If X and Y are two numbers and E and D denote encryption and decryption function respectively, then homomorphic encryption holds following condition for an algebraic operation, such as $'+'$:

$$D[E(X) + E(Y)] = D[E(X + Y)] \tag{1}$$

Most homomorphic encryption system such as RSA [11], ElGamal [18], Benaloh [19], Paillier [20] etc. are capable to perform only one operation. But fully homomorphic encryption system can be used for many operations (such as, addition, multiplication, division etc.) at the same time. In the area of cryptography, fully homomorphic encryption system proposed by Dijk et al. in [6] is considered as a breakthrough work which can be used to solve many cryptographic problems [21]. We have used this fully homomorphic encryption technique with necessary improvements and variations in data mining [22,23] and in private information retrieval [24].

Fully Homomorphic Encryption for Binary Bits

Fully homomorphic encryption of [6] works both over binary and integer numbers. This scheme has the ability to perform both addition and multiplication over the cipher-text and these operations are represented in plain-text. Hence, a untrusted party is able to operate on private or confidential data, without the ability to know what data the untrusted party is manipulating.

The fully homomorphic scheme [6] is a simplification of an earlier work involving ideal lattices [25]. It encrypts a single bit (in the plain-text space) to an integer (in the cipher-text space). When these integers are added and multiplied, the hidden bits are added and multiplied (modulo 2). A simple encryption and decryption process of symmetric version of the scheme is as follows:

Encryption : Lets say, p is the private key, q and r are chosen random numbers, and m is a binary message *i.e.* $m \in \{0, 1\}$. Then the encryption of m would be $c = pq + 2r + m$.

Decryption : The message m is recovered simply by performing following operation: $m = (c \bmod p) \bmod 2$.

Thus, this encryption scheme works in the bit level and underlying bits are calculated accordingly if we add or multiply on cipher-text.

Using the symmetric version of the cryptosystem, it is possible to construct an asymmetric version. The asymmetric version is more useful especially when multiple parties are involved in the computation such as in data mining, data gathering, data outsourcing, OT, PIR etc. The asymmetric version of [6] would be as follows:

KeyGen(λ) : Choose a random n-bit odd integer p as the private key. Using the private key, generate the public key as $x_i = pq_i + 2r_i$ where q_i and r_i are chosen randomly, for $i = 0, 1, ..., \tau$. Rearrange $x - i$ such that, x_0 is the largest.

Encrypt$(pk, m \in \{0, 1\})$: Choose a random subset $S \subseteq \{1, 2, ..., \tau\}$ and a random integer r. m is encrypted to the cipher-text
$c = (m + 2r + 2 \sum_{i \in S} x_i)(\bmod x_0)$. Let us denote this operation as $E_{pk}(m)$.

Decrypt(sk, c): The message m is recovered simply by performing
$m = (c \bmod p) \bmod 2$. Let us denote this operation as $D_{sk}(c)$.

The asymmetric version works same way as the symmetric one with same correctness and security strength. We have discussed about this in [24] and [22]. The addition and the multiplication on cipher-texts are reflected as addition and multiplication being acted on the message bit respectively. This produces the correspondence between the cipher-text space and the plain-text space, as addition in the cipher-text space reduces to exclusive OR $(\oplus)$ in the plain-text space and multiplication in the cipher-text space reduces to AND $(\wedge)$. This correspondence (homomorphism) between these two operations, addition and multiplication, are shown in Equations 2 and 3, respectively.

$$E(m_1) + E(m_2) = E(m_1 \oplus m_2) \tag{2}$$

$$E(m_1) \cdot E(m_2) = E(m_1 \wedge m_2) \tag{3}$$

Hence, from this correspondence, it is possible to construct very complicated binary circuits to evaluate on the data, without exposing the actual data. More details regarding the implementation can be found in the original paper [6].

Fully Homomorphic Encryption for Integers

Oblivious transfer deals with the privacy and security of some numeric values being exchanged between the client and the server. Hence, we need to extend the underlying cryptosystem to accommodate integer numbers, so that integer numbers can be taken into consideration. This is achieved by representing the integer as a binary vector and encrypting each bit separately and maintaining their positions or orders. For instance, an 8-bit integer X can be encrypted and presented as cipher-text as shown in Equation 4, assuming the binary representation of X is $X_8 + X_7 + X_6 + X_5 + X_4 + X_3 + X_2 + X_1$.

$$
\begin{aligned}
E_{pk}(X) = \quad & \\
& E_{pk}(X_8) + E_{pk}(X_7) + E_{pk}(X_6) + E_{pk}(X_5) + E_{pk}(X_4) + \\
& E_{pk}(X_3) + E_{pk}(X_2) + E_{pk}(X_1) \\
& where + represents\ concatenation\ operation.
\end{aligned}
\tag{4}
$$

This representation of integer number allows encrypting and decrypting each bit using the fully homomorphic encryption and decryption for binary digits as discussed in section 2.2. Not only that, some binary operations such as XOR, OR, AND etc. can be performed on two encrypted integer numbers homomorphically. Let us consider two integers X and Y of ℓ-bit long each. That is, $X = \{X_\ell + ... + X_2 + X_1\}$ and $Y = \{Y_\ell + ... + Y_2 + Y_1\}$. Let us say we want to perform binary XOR operation on X and Y, i.e. $R = X\ XOR\ Y$, where $R = \{R_\ell + ... + R_2 + R_1\}$ and $R_i = X_i\ XOR\ Y_i$. Therefore, according to fully homomorphic encryption $R_i = D_{sk}(R_i\prime)$, where $R_i\prime = E_{pk}(X_i)\ XOR\ E_{pk}(Y_i)$. For all $i = 1\ to\ \ell$.

3　Model Definition

Let us consider a client C wants to access k number of records ($k \in \{1, 2, ..., n\}$) out of n records $\{R = R_1, R_2, ..., R_n\}$ stored in a database server S. Index of the interested records $\{I = I_1, I_2, ..., I_k\}$ are known to C only. C does not want S to discover which record(s) it is interested in. On the other hand, S wants to ensure only the desired record is received by C. Figure 1 illustrates the block diagram of the proposed model in brief.

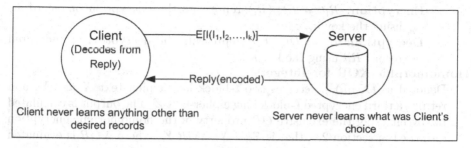

Fig. 1. Block diagram of the oblivious transfer protocol between the client and the server

The client C and the server S participates in the proposed OT protocol using the fully homomorphic encryption discussed in section 2.2. They also generate keys, encrypt, decrypt and transmit according to the protocol description discussed in following the section.

4 Proposed Solution

This section discusses our proposed OT protocol in the sequence of parameter setup, communication steps and algorithms.

4.1 Parameters and Initial Setup

Let us assume both the client C and the server S are capable to perform following operations to setup and carry on the proposed protocol:

Key generation

    Client: Client C generates its private key and public key sk and pk respectively using the key generation technique discussed in section 2.2.

    Server: Server S generates secret key sets $\chi = \{\kappa_1, \kappa_2, ..., \kappa_n\}$ using cryptographically secure pseudo-random number generator (CSPRNG). Standards of CSPRNG can be found in [26]. Each key is used to encrypt each record. That is, key κ_i is used to encrypt record R_i.

Encryption

    Two kind of cryptosystems will be used in the proposed protocol:

    FHES

        Fully homomorphic encryption system based encryption and decryption functions for integer numbers works as follows:

        Encryption: $E_{pk}(i)$ encrypts an ℓ-bit integer i using the public key pk, returning an encrypted ℓ-block long cipher-text c.

        Decryption: $D_{sk}(c)$ decrypts an ℓ-block long cipher-text c using the private key sk, returning a plain-text ℓ-bit integer i.

    Symmetric Key Cryptosystem

        A secured symmetric key cryptosystem (e.g. AES [7] or DES [8]) based encryption and decryption notations are as follows:

Encryption: $R_i\prime = E\prime_{\kappa_i}(R_i)$ represents the encryption of record R_i using the key κ_i.

Decryption: $R_i = D\prime_{\kappa_i}(R_i\prime)$ represents the decryption of encrypted record $R_i\prime$ using the key κ_i.

Homomorphic XOR for Integers

Denoted as $(X \boxplus Y)$, receives two ℓ-block long cipher-text X and Y, and returns a third encrypted ℓ-block long cipher-text Z. The output is calculated bit-by-bit using the exclusive OR property of the homomorphic encryption discussed in section 2.2, that is $Z_i = X_i\ XOR\ Y_i$, where XOR is evaluated using Equation 2.

Shuffle by random permutation

Denoted as $\zeta(B\prime)$, randomly rearranges all ℓ number of blocks of the cipher-text $B\prime$, where $B\prime = E_{pk}(B)$. That is, if $B\prime = \{E_{pk}(B_\ell) +\!+ ... +\!+ E_{pk}(B_2) + + E_{pk}(B_1)\}$, $\zeta(B\prime)$ will return $\{E_{pk}(B_i) +\!+ ... +\!+ E_{pk}(B_j) +\!+ E_{pk}(B_k)\}$ where values of i, j, k are non-repeating random numbers within the range of 1 to ℓ.

4.2   The Algorithm

Algorithm 1. Oblivious Transfer between C and S

---

input of C : pk, sk, k, n, I
input of S : pk, R, n
output to C : $R_{I_1}, R_{I_2}, ..., R_{I_k}$
Begin
Server S
Generate set of random keys $\chi = \{\kappa_1, \kappa_2, ..., \kappa_n\}$
Client C
for $All(i \in I)$ **do**
    $Q \leftarrow E_{pk}(I_i)$
  $SendToS(Q)$
  Server S
  $\Gamma \leftarrow \phi$ /* Initializes response string*/
  for $j = 1$ to n **do**
      $\alpha_j \leftarrow \zeta(Q \boxplus E_{pk}(j)) \boxplus E_{pk}(\kappa_j)$ /* ζ rearranges the order of the bits randomly*/
      $\beta_j \leftarrow E\prime_{k_j}(R_j)$
      $\Gamma_j \leftarrow \{\alpha_j \bigcup \beta_j\}$
      $\Gamma \leftarrow \Gamma \bigcup \Gamma_j$
  end for
  $SendToC(\Gamma)$
  Client C
      $\gamma \leftarrow \Gamma_{I_i}$ /* Extracts desired block from Γ. Components of γ are α and β*/
      $\alpha_i\prime \leftarrow \alpha$ /* Extracts encrypted keys*/
      $\beta_i\prime \leftarrow \beta$ /* Extracts encrypted record*/
      $\kappa_{I_i} \leftarrow D_{sk}(\alpha_i\prime)$ /* Decrypts the key to decrypt the desired record*/
      $R_{I_i} \leftarrow D\prime_{\kappa_{I_i}}(\beta_i\prime)$ /* This is the desired record of index I_i*/
  end for
End

4.3   Flow Diagram

The algorithmic flow diagram for one request is shown in Figure 2.

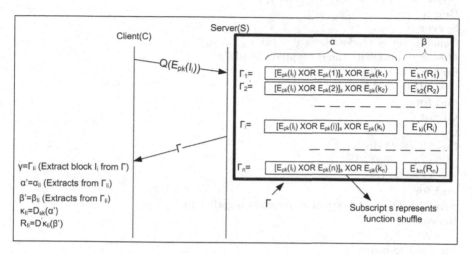

Fig. 2. Flow diagram of oblivious transfer protocol between C and S for one request

4.4   Further Optimization

In Algorithm 1, $k - n$ OT is implemented by repeated calling of $1 - n$ OT k times. The client C sends k encrypted requests separately to the server S. The server returns the encrypted records each time the client requests. In the case of big size of the records, this method will be very inefficient. Alternatively, the server can transmit the whole chunk of encrypted records once at the first time and later on can transmit only the encrypted keys (the key which is used to encrypt a particular record), every time the client sends a request. In summary, the part of β in Figure 2 can be transmitted once at the beginning of the protocol and α can be transmitted k times to the client. This would reduce the transmission overhead drastically. Moreover, the client also can send all the k number of requests at once. The optimized solution is described in Algorithm 2.

Algorithm 2. Efficient Oblivious Transfer between C and S

$input\ of\ C : pk,\ sk,\ k,\ n,\ I$
$input\ of\ S : pk,\ R,\ n$
$output\ to\ C : R_I = \{R_{I_1}, R_{I_2}, ..., R_{I_k}\}$
Begin
Server S
Generate set of random keys $\chi = \{\kappa_1, \kappa_2, ..., \kappa_n\}$
$\Omega \leftarrow \phi$ /* Initializes the encrypted records*/
for $i = 1\ to\ n$ **do**
     $\Omega \leftarrow \Omega \bigcup E\prime_{k_i}(R_i)$
end for
Client C
$Q \leftarrow \phi$
for $All(i \in I)$ **do**
     $Q_{I_i} \leftarrow E_{pk}(I_i)$
     $Q \leftarrow Q \bigcup Q_{I_i}$
end for
$SendToS(Q, k)$ /* C sends all requests together to S*/
Server S
$\beta \leftarrow \phi$
for $j = 1\ to\ n$ **do**
     $\beta_j \leftarrow E\prime_{k_j}(R_j)$
     $\beta \leftarrow \beta \bigcup \beta_j$
end for
$SendToC(\beta)$ /* Sends all the encrypted records together*/
for $i = 1\ to\ k$ **do**
   $\alpha_i \leftarrow \phi$
   for $j = 1\ to\ n$ **do**
         $\alpha_j \leftarrow \zeta(Q_{I_i} \boxplus E_{pk}(j)) \boxplus E_{pk}(\kappa_j)$ /* ζ rearranges the order of the bits randomly*/
         $\alpha_i \leftarrow \alpha_i \bigcup \alpha_j$
   end for
   $SendToC(\alpha_i)$
end for
Client C
for $i = 1\ to\ k$ **do**
   $\alpha_{I_i}\prime \leftarrow \alpha_i$ /* Extracts blocks from α that contain the key κ_{I_i}*/
   $\kappa_{I_i} \leftarrow D_{sk}(\alpha_{I_i})$
   $\gamma \leftarrow \beta_{I_i}$ /* Extracts desired block from β that contain R_{I_i}*/.
   $R_{I_i} \leftarrow D\prime_{\kappa_{I_i}}(\beta_i\prime)$ /* This is the desired record of index I_i*/
   $R_I \leftarrow R_I \bigcup R_{I_i}$
end for
return R_I

5   Analysis

The fully homomorphic encryption used in this protocol is as strong as approximate GCD problem, though its efficiency may not be very high. Some recent

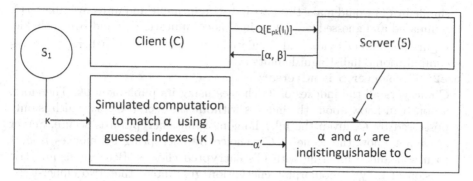

Fig. 3. C is adversary. S_1 guesses κ for C to compute a value to be equal to α.

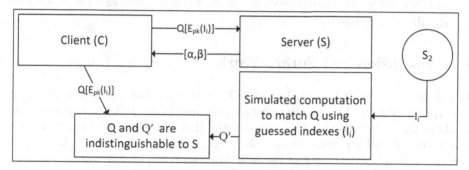

Fig. 4. S is adversary. S_2 guesses I_i for S to compute a value to be equal to $Q[E_{pk}(I_i)]$.

works and ongoing research on improving this protocol, such as [27,28,21], indicates its performance to be enhanced in near future.

In this protocol, C generates and stores its secret and public keys sk and pk respectively. C does not send any data to S without being encrypted by its public key pk. Therefore, C's data is secured by the security of the fully homomorphic encryption scheme of [6]. On the other hand, S encrypts its data using same public key pk and performs operations on its own ciphe-rtext and C's cipher-text. The cipher-text is again shuffled using the function $\zeta()$ which is XORed with secret key. S then discloses this cipher-text to C. Therefore, the privacy of S's data depends on whether C can learn anything from the result sent by S and vice-versa. Let us consider C and S being adversary in two different cases:

Case1: the client C is adversary

Let us say C wants to recover a key κ_j where $j \notin I$. That is C wants to recover a key of a record which it did not retrieve. For each item I_i the client request, it receives n blocks of cipher-text, which is $\alpha_j = \zeta(Q_{I_i} \boxplus E_{pk}(j)) \boxplus E_{pk}(\kappa_j)$ for all $j - 1, 2..., n$. Any block is only meaningful, in other word C can retrieve a key from, if $I_i = j$. This condition would make $Q_{I_i} \boxplus E_{pk}(j) = E_{pk}(I_i) \boxplus E_{pk}(j) = 0$ and hence, $\alpha_j = E_{pk}(\kappa_j)$ from which C can decrypt κ_j. For any other block where $I_i \neq j$, $Q_{I_i} \boxplus E_{pk}(j)$ would be non-zero and further shuffle by $\zeta()$ would make this part indistinguishable and unrecoverable to C. Simulated and guessed key values in C is computationally indistinguishable. Figure 3 shows C's view and simulated outcome $(\alpha \overset{c}{\equiv} \alpha\prime)$, where, $\overset{c}{\equiv}$ denotes computational indistinguishability..

Case2: The server S is adversary

C encrypts all the indexes of its choices using its public key pk. Therefore, no one can know about the indexes without the secret key sk which is only possessed by C, given the fully homomorphic encryption is secure. Server S cannot know the value of C's choice by encrypting all indexes from 1 to n and and comparing with C's encrypted choices. Because asymmetric version of fully homomorphic encryption guarantees that two cipher-texts of the same bits are always different. Moreover simulated or guessed index of C's choices are indistinguishable to S. Figure 4 illustrates S's view and simulated outcome $(Q \overset{c}{\equiv} Q\prime)$.

6   Conclusion and Future Work

In this paper, we have proposed a novel OT protocol using a fully homomorphic encryption system. The security of this protocol is as strong as approximate GCD problem. Security analysis also ensures that, the client C cannot discover any record it did not retrieve and the server S cannot learn the choice(s) of the client. The enhancement of the fully homomorphic encryption system used in this solution will influence the performance of the proposed protocol in great deal. Implementation and performance comparison with existing solution are left for the future research.

References

1. Blum, M.: Three application of oblivious transfer: Part i: Coin flipping by telephone; part ii: How to exchange secrets; part iii: How to send certified electronic mail (2001)
2. Líšková, L., Stanek, M.: Efficient Simultaneous Contract Signing. In: Deswarte, Y., Cuppens, F., Jajodia, S., Wang, L. (eds.) Security and Protection in Information Processing Systems. IFIP, vol. 147, pp. 440–455. Springer, Boston (2004)
3. Min Sun, H., Hang Wang, K., Fu Hung, C.: Towards privacy preserving digital rights management using oblivious transfer (2006)
4. Aiello, B., Ishai, Y., Reingold, O.: Priced oblivious transfer: How to sell digital goods. In: Pfitzmann, B. (ed.) EUROCRYPT 2001. LNCS, vol. 2045, pp. 119–135. Springer, Heidelberg (2001)
5. Wang, W., Deng, B., Li, Z.: Application of oblivious transfer protocol in distributed data mining with privacy-preserving. In: Proceedings of the First International Symposium on Data, Privacy, and E-Commerce, ISDPE 2007, pp. 283–285. IEEE Computer Society, Washington, DC (2007)
6. van Dijk, M., Gentry, C., Halevi, S., Vaikuntanathan, V.: Fully homomorphic encryption over the integers. In: Gilbert, H. (ed.) EUROCRYPT 2010. LNCS, vol. 6110, pp. 24–43. Springer, Heidelberg (2010)

7. FIPS-PUB.197: Advanced encryption standard. Federal Information Processing Standards Publications, US Department of Commerce/N.I.S.T., National Technical Information Service (2001)
8. FIPS-Pub.46: Data encryption standard. National Bureau of Standards, US Department of Commerce (1977)
9. Zeng, Z., Dayton, B.H.: The approximate gcd of inexact polynomials. In: Proceedings of the 2004 International Symposium on Symbolic and Algebraic Computation, ISSAC 2004, pp. 320–327. ACM, New York (2004)
10. Rabin, M.: How to Exchange Secrets by Oblivious Transfer. Technical Report TR-81, Harvard Aiken Computation Laboratory (1981)
11. Rivest, R.L., Shamir, A., Adleman, L.: A method for obtaining digital signatures and public-key cryptosystems. Commun. ACM 21, 120–126 (1978)
12. Even, S., Goldreich, O., Lempel, A.: A randomized protocol for signing contracts. Commun. ACM 28, 637–647 (1985)
13. Kushilevitz, E., Ostrovsky, R.: Replication is not needed: Single database, computationally-private information retrieval (extended abstract). In: Proc. of the 38th Annu. IEEE Symp. on Foundations of Computer Science, pp. 364–373 (1997)
14. Naor, M., Pinkas, B.: Oblivious transfer with adaptive queries. In: Wiener, M. (ed.) CRYPTO 1999. LNCS, vol. 1666, pp. 573–590. Springer, Heidelberg (1999)
15. Laur, S., Lipmaa, H.: A new protocol for conditional disclosure of secrets and its applications. In: Katz, J., Yung, M. (eds.) ACNS 2007. LNCS, vol. 4521, pp. 207–225. Springer, Heidelberg (2007)
16. Ishai, Y., Kushilevitz, E.: Private simultaneous messages protocols with applications. In: Proc. of 5th ISTCS, pp. 174–183 (1997)
17. Murugesan, M., Jiang, W., Nergiz, A.E., Uzunbaz, S.: k-out-of-n oblivious transfer based on homomorphic encryption and solvability of linear equations. In: CODASPY 2011, pp. 169–178 (2011)
18. El Gamal, T.: A public key cryptosystem and a signature scheme based on discrete logarithms. In: Blakely, G.R., Chaum, D. (eds.) CRYPTO 1984. LNCS, vol. 196, pp. 10–18. Springer, Heidelberg (1985)
19. Clarkson, J.B.: Dense probabilistic encryption. In: Proceedings of the Workshop on Selected Areas of Cryptography, pp. 120–128 (1994)
20. Paillier, P.: Public-key cryptosystems based on composite degree residuosity classes. In: Stern, J. (ed.) EUROCRYPT 1999. LNCS, vol. 1592, pp. 223–238. Springer, Heidelberg (1999)
21. Naehrig, M., Lauter, K., Vaikuntanathan, V.: Can homomorphic encryption be practical? In: Proceedings of the 3rd ACM Workshop on Cloud Computing Security Workshop, pp. 113–124. ACM, New York (2011)
22. Kaosar, M., Paulet, R., Yi, X.: Fully homomorphic encryption based two-party association rule mining. Data and Knowledge Engineering 76-78, 1–15 (2012)
23. Kaosar, M., Paulet, R., Yi, X.: Secure two-party association rule mining. In: Australasian Information Security Conference, AISC 2011 (2011)
24. Yi, X., Kaosar, M., Paulet, R., Bertino, E.: Single-database private information retrieval from fully homomorphic encryption. IEEE Transactions on Knowledge and Data Engineering 25, 1125–1134 (2013)
25. Gentry, C.: Fully homomorphic encryption using ideal lattices. In: STOC 2009: Proceedings of the 41st Annual ACM Symposium on Theory of Computing, pp. 169–178. ACM, New York (2009)

26. NIST: Recommendation for random number generation using deterministic random
    bit generators. U.S. Department of Commerce, National Institute of Standards and
    Technology (NIST) Special Publication 800-90A (January 2012)
27. Brakerski, Z., Gentry, C., Vaikuntanathan, V.: (leveled) fully homomorphic encryp-
    tion without bootstrapping. In: Proceedings of the 3rd Innovations in Theoretical
    Computer Science Conference, ITCS 2012, pp. 309–325. ACM, New York (2012)
28. Coron, J.-S., Mandal, A., Naccache, D., Tibouchi, M.: Fully Homomorphic Encryp-
    tion over the Integers with Shorter Public Keys. In: Rogaway, P. (ed.) CRYPTO
    2011. LNCS, vol. 6841, pp. 487–504. Springer, Heidelberg (2011)

Detection of Android API Call Using Logging Mechanism within Android Framework

Yuuki Nishimoto[1,*], Naoya Kajiwara[2,3], Shinichi Matsumoto[2,3],
Yoshiaki Hori[3,4], and Kouichi Sakurai[2,3]

[1] Department of EECS, Kyushu University, Fukuoka, Japan
[2] Department of Informatics, Kyushu University, Fukuoka, Japan
`kajiwara@itslab.inf.kyushu-u.ac.jp,`
`sakurai@csce.kyushu-u.ac.jp`
[3] Institute of Systems, Information Technologies and Nanotechnologies
`smatsumoto@isit.or.jp`
[4] Organization for General Education, Saga University, Saga, Japan
`horiyo@cc.saga-u.ac.jp`

Abstract. Android based smartphones have become popular. Accordingly, many malwares are developed. The malwares target information leaked from Android. However, it is difficult for users to judge the availability of application by understanding the potential threats in the application. In this paper, we focus on acquisition of information by using a remote procedure call when we invoke the API to acquire phone ID. We design a methodology to record invocation that are concerned the API by inserting Log.v methods. We examined our method, and confirm empirically the record of the call behavior of the API to acquire phone ID.

Keywords: Android, Malware, Privacy Protection, Dynamic Analysis.

1 Introduction

In recent years, Android phone is becoming popular. Simultaneously, many malicious applications called malware are developed for Android platform. Many malwares that target Android cause information leakages, and leakage of personal information is a big problem. However, it is difficult for a user to grasp threats of an application and judge the risk of it. Therefore, we focus on a measure method to prevent malwares from being distributed in the marketplace. In this method, an application developer and a marketplace operator can previously check the application on behalf of the user.

There are dynamic analysis and static analysis in approach of malware detection. However, in static analysis, there is a possibility that overlooking increases when the variants of the malware outbreak. In dynamic analysis, there are some problems too. With dynamic analysis, overhead of operation increases. Moreover,

---

* The first author currently works with Kyushu District Police Bureau. He contributed to this research when he was a undergraduate student of Kyushu University.

T. Zia et al. (Eds.): SecureComm 2013, LNICST 127, pp. 393–404, 2013.

there is a possibility that a malicious developer can make his application to circumvent the detection. In order to solve these problems, we focus on detection method using log output which is dynamic analysis. With marketplace operator using this method, detection which cannot be circumvented by malicious developer can be realized.

Linux debug utility named `strace` monitors system calls used by an application in Android. There is a method performing malware detection by analyzing system calls that are obtained using the `strace`. Behavior using services of the kernel can be detected by this method. However, there is a problem that system call is not issued in the behavior which doesn't use services of kernel, and it is impossible to detect such a behavior.

In this paper, we focus on the fact that when API that retrieve the phoneID is invoked, it is processed with remote procedure call. We propose a method recording the invocations in accordance with the API by inserting `Log.v` method. That is an output log API in remote procedure call by the Android Binder. The execution logging by this technique cannot be avoided even if modification of API is performed on the call side. Therefore, it is impossible to circumvent the detection even if a developer has malicious intention. Furthermore, we implemented proposal method tentatively and ran the application which acquires phoneID on the Android emulator. As a consequence, we confirm empirically record of invocation behavior of the phoneID acquisition API.

2   Android

Android is a platform that was developed targeting mobile information devices such as smart phones and tablet PCs. Android application is running on the Dalvik virtual machine(VM). When an Android application is launched, one Dalvik VM is dedicated to execute that application. When a user installs an application, by approving permissions, it becomes possible to take the cooperation with other applications or access files made by other applications deviating from the sandbox mechanism[1].

2.1   Android Application

Android consists of a Linux based OS kernel, a middleware and fundamental applications. The applications used by the user are on the top layer in AndroidOS. Developers can publish applications in the Android market.

In the application framework of Android, API is provided and Android application developer can use it freely. Application developers can use the result the API outputs by this mechanism, without knowing about the complicated procedures under the framework layer.

In AndroidOS, the independence of applications is maintained by the following mechanisms so that applications don't cause interference.

– Application execution and process

Android application is executed in an individual Linux process allocated to this sole application. Hence, a Linux process is started when an application is executed. However, this process is terminated when system resources are required from other applications, after this application is finished.

– Dalvik virtual machine allocation to every process

In Android, a Dalvik virtual machine is allocated to every process exclusively. In this way, one application is executed independently from other applications.

– Unique Linux user ID allocated to every application

During the installation, to every application is allocated unique ID. The assigned ID serves as an owner of the application, and manages the process. Files that the application creates are set up so that these files cannot be fundamentally read from applications which have other ID. For this reason, a file created by a certain application cannot be freely read from an application with another ID.

2.2   Binder

Binder is a driver which offers the functionality to communicate between processes. Even if some processes are in the same application, they run on separate area. Moreover, there is a possibility that activities and services respectively run on different processes in the application. Binder driver is used when exchanging information between these different processes. In this case, communications are controlled by the framework layer located above the kernel. Although a user doesn't use Binder directly, it plays an important role in interprocess communication.

2.3   AIDL

In Android, one process cannot usually access memory of other processes. Therefore, if a process wants to obtain data from other processes, interprocess communication is necessary. AIDL(Android Interface Definition Language) is an interface definition language used to generate some codes[2]. These codes undertake the communication between two processes possible using interprocess communication realized with Binder.

2.4   Android API

API, which means "Application Programming Interface", is an interface to access function from the library intended for the OS and for the programming language of the applications. Functions used in many applications are offered within the application framework of Android through API. Because it is unnecessary to develop functions offered by API, development of application becomes easy with API. Some of Android APIs also offer functions which serve as a base of the OS.

3 Existing Android Malware and Detection Method

There are static analysis and dynamic analysis among analysis methods of applications. Static analysis is a method that an application is decompiled and source code is examined, and dynamic analysis is a method that analyzes the behavior of an application by running it. There are both advantages and disadvantages for static analysis and dynamic analysis, and it is difficult to say which method is better than the other. In this section, we outline static analysis and dynamic analysis, as well as detection technique of malwares that both techniques use.

3.1 Android Malware

Malware is an application which performs a malicious action, such as causing a leakage of privacy information or making data destroyed. Malware is developed according to an environment with many targets. Therefore, malwares for Windows with many users have accounted for a large percentage of entire malwares until now. However, developers of malware also came to target AndroidOS. According to G Data Malware Report -Half yearly report January - June 2011 -[3], during the first half of 2011 from the second half of 2010, malwares that target smartphones with a focus on Android had increased from 55 to 803. Although this number is lower than the number of malwares which target Windows, considering the kind of information stored in Android devices is important personal information such as phone number or subscriber ID, it is thought that the risk from a security point of view becomes high compared with other OS. From these facts, despite enhancements of security including anti-malware in AndroidOS is in urgent, the present security is insufficient. Most threats caused by Android malwares are infection by installing the malwares that are obtained from a third party market that is not legitimate Android market of Google.

3.2 Static Analysis

Static analysis is a program analysis method which analyzes a program by decompiling the application without performing an executable file. Static analysis is mainly used when analyzing a source code.

Because analysis is performed without actually executing the application, the potential threat is detected before the damage of malware occurs. On the other hand, when the source code of the application is obfuscated or when the code for attack is placed outside the application code using a cooperation function with an external server, the possibility of being undetectable becomes high.

As static analysis method, there are many certification techniques and such techniques are served as service. Bouncer[4] is a service offered by Google. It prevents malware from spreading the market. However, malwares which have passed bouncer's certification had been reported[6].

3.3   Dynamic Analysis

Dynamic analysis is a program analysis method which checks what kind of action the application is carrying out by actually executing the application to be inspected. Because application is actually run unlike static analysis and it is inspected based on the action, malwares can be detected even when the source code is obfuscated, or when the code for an attack is placed outside the application code.

TaintDroid[5] and AppFence[7] are dynamic analysis methods using information flow tracking. TaintDroid monitors interprocess communications, and if information is sent out TaintDroid alerts that event. Appfense implements two information protections, replacing private data with shadow data and filtering to prevent information leakage by intercepting the network system call. Both researches modify Android kernel to conduct dynamic analysis for applications.

A logging system is used as a way of dynamic analysis. Isohara et al. proposed a logging system in Android[8]. System calls are collected as log data in the kernel level. These log data are analyzed with signature of threats to inspect the application's behavior. However, a problem is that action without system call is difficult to detect.

4   Design of Record Method of Process Operation Using Logcat

4.1   Record Method of Process Operation

strace is a debugging utility that supervises the system calls issued by a program. In the process action recording method using this strace, the system call about the API cannot be recorded if the API is belonged to TelephonyManager class, This is because the information is called without using a service of the kernel, when using API of a TelephonyManager class.

We insert a code that invokes Log.v method into the application framework of AndroidOS, and modify it so that event logs may be output. And when an application acquires the phoneID through API, the event log is recorded, and we use a method of performing detection of information retrieval based on that log. This method is also used in other OS. For example, in UNIX OS, a log is recorded using syslog, and in Windows, a log is recorded using the function named event log.

APIs which record logs are prepared within the application framework of AndroidOS. These logs can be viewed using the function called logcat. In this experiment, logs are collected and analyzed, which are output from a Log.v() method of the Log class. This method is implemented in the layer which uses Java language in application framework.

We examined interprocess communications which occur when using APIs of TelephonyManager class. As a result, it turned out that processes and methods communicate in the procedure as shown in a Figure 1.

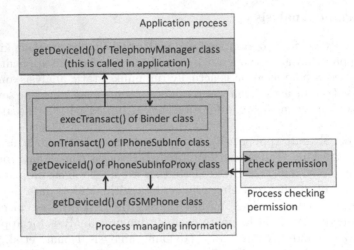

Fig. 1. Example of interprocess communication about getDeviceId()

The approach of checking which method is invoked by making log output is a general technique performed in other OS. When performing one application in Android, it is always run on independent Dalvik VM. Therefore, an application cannot communicate with other processes directly, and the application must use a driver called Binder. Then, we set a code that outputs a log in programs which perform this interprocess communication, and when an application invokes API, we detected and specified it based on the log information. This is the new point in this proposal method. With this method, retrieved information can be checked by seeing .aidl file without searching for the part which reads each information directly. In this experiment, after an application is executed, invoked API can be specified using the information acquired from the event log.

In this paper, the experiment was carried out for API contained in the `IPhoneSubInfo.aidl` file treating important information such as telephone number or subscriber ID. Concretely, at first the Log class of an `android.util` package is imported to `IPhoneSubInfo.java` file. Then, the code which outputs a log to an `onTransact` method is inserted. OS is recompiled after that. Application which invokes some APIs is installed to the emulator, and it is actually executed. From obtained event logs, we focus on the variable named `code` used in `onTransact`.

Table 1 shows the conversion table of the information about API contained in an `IPhoneSubInfo.aidl` file and each API. In this paper, experiments are not carried out for `getLine1AlphaTag()` and `getCompleteVoiceMailNumber()`. The reasons are the following two.

- In spite of being implemented in `TelephonyManager.java`, these two methods are undocumented as methods of the `TelephonyManager` class in the site of Android Developer.

Table 1. API defined in IPhoneSubInfo.aidl

API	Acquired Information
getDeviceId()	IMEI
getDeviceSvn() (Method within getDeviceSoftwareVersion())	Software version of device
getSubscriberId()	Subscriber ID
getIccSerialNumber() (Method within getSimSerialNumber())	Serial number of SIM card
getLine1Number()	Phone number
getLine1AlphaTag()	Alpha identifier
getVoiceMailNumber()	Voice mail number
getCompleteVoiceMailNumber()	Complete voice mail number
getVoiceMailAlphaTag()	Voice mail alpha identifier

- If we try to use these methods as methods of a TelephonyManager class in a application, the error message that it is undefined within TelephonyManager will come out.

From these reasons, experiments are carried out for seven APIs except the previously mentioned two.

4.2   Abstract of Experiment

The goal of these experiments is not the static analysis that decompiles application and analyzes a source code but the dynamic analysis that detects information leakages by actually running the application and taking event logs. In order to prevent from being detected by anti malware software, recent malwares obfuscate itself to make such an analysis difficult, or cause information leakages in cooperation with external server using webkit. The reason for using dynamic analysis in this paper is because it can deal with situations that static analysis cannot.

From the result of the record method using strace, it is predicted that personal information acquired by APIs of TelephonyManager is not retrieved by the kernel, but passed from other information managing processes. So, we focus on Binder driver which has an important role in interprocess communication. In this paper, we carried out the experiment which detects that event when APIs described in IPhoneSubInfor.aidl are invoked. We inserted a code that invokes Log.v methods which outputs a log message into onTransact method in IPhoneSubInfo class invoked only when these APIs are invoked. Then, we tried to specify the invoked API from the event logs. An argument called code exists in onTransact method of IPhoneSubInfo class. OnTransact method judges which API invoked information from this code value. Therefore, we think that we can specify which API is invoked from the event log of onTransact method and code variable.

```
@Override public boolean onTransact(int code, android.os.Parcel data, android.os.Parcel reply,
int flags) throws android.os.RemoteException
{
Log.v("EXTEST","IPhoneSubInfo.onTransact, code:" + code);
switch (code)
{
case INTERFACE_TRANSACTION:      code outputting log
{
reply.writeString(DESCRIPTOR);
return true;
}
case TRANSACTION_getDeviceId:
{
data.enforceInterface(DESCRIPTOR);
java.lang.String _result = this.getDeviceId();
reply.writeNoException();
reply.writeString(_result);
return true;
}
......
............
```

Fig. 2. Log outputting code inserted into IPhoneSubInfo.java

4.3   Proposal Method

Figure 2 shows a inserted code outputting a event log into IPhoneSubInfo.java. The place where a logging code is inserted was decided in consideration of the following conditions.

- It is not a method performed in the same process as an application.
  The getDeviceId() method of TelephonyManager class is run in the same process as the application. Such a method can be incorporated as a library in application by developer when application is developed. In the case of inserting the code which outputs the event log into getDeviceId() method, if a malware developer defines a method working similarly as getDeviceId() in that application and executes the method, information is retrieved without outputting the log. Therefore, it is very important to insert the code which outputs the log into a method running on a process which is not same as the application's process.
- API which invoked the method can be specified
  Even if a log is output from the code inserted into the program, this method is not realized if which API was invoked by the application cannot be checked from the log.
- Proposal method can be used to detect as many APIs as possible
  If the code which outputs a log is inserted into each API method (e.g. getDeviceId()), only that information can be monitored.

As a result of considering these three conditions, we concluded that a suitable inserted place should be onTransact method of IPhoneSubInfo class. There are some reasons for this decision. onTransact method doesn't run on the same process as application. Then, because the order of methods defined in

IPhoneSubInfo.aidl file and value of code variable are corresponded, it is possible to judge which API was invoked. This is because code variable is used within a switch statement in IPhoneSubInfo class. Furthermore, nine APIs defined in IPhoneSubInfo.aidl can be inspected with this method.

There is also an advantage that APIs which don't issue system call can be detected. In existing research, the detection of malware is performed by logging system call when using dynamic analysis[8]. However, in such a method, it is difficult to detect APIs which don't publish system call when running. On the other hand, because we focus on interprocess communication which occurs when the API is invoked, and insert a code which outputs the log when method is invoked, it becomes possible to realize detection of information retrieval without system call.

4.4 Experimental Procedure

1. Building of the source code
   The make command is used to build the source code. IPhoneSubInfo.java file is automatically generated from IPhoneSubInfo.aidl file at this time.
2. Insertion of a code which outputs a log
   Figure 2 shows modified IPhoneSubInfo.java to output the event log. This program outputs a log message which can be seen with Logcat view. Log.v is a method which outputs a log of a detailed message. There are other methods about log. Log.e outputs a log about error, Log.w outputs a log of warning, Log.i outputs a log about information, and Log.d outputs a log of the debug message. Fundamentally, usage of these methods is the same. String indicating tag is set as first argument and String which should be output as a log message is set as second argument. The differences among these five methods are found in use, and they are properly used so that acknowledgement of logs becomes convenient. In this experiment, a log message includes two contents. First content is a character string called IPhoneSubInfo.onTransact. And, second content is a value of code variable, which indicates a kind of privacy information acquired by an application.
3. Rebuild
   After rewriting and saving IPhoneSubInfo.java file, build is performed again.
4. Running application on the emulator
   This experiment is entirely conducted on the emulator.
5. Reference of logs
   Collected Logs are referred using Dalvik Debug Monitor Service tool. We describe and considerer the results from these collected logs.

4.5 Result

A kind of information acquired by API could be detected from output logs. Table 2 shows the correspondence of APIs used in experiment to code variables. This corresponds with the order of method defined in IPhoneSubInfo.aidl file.

Table 2. The correspondence table of API used in the experiment and code variable

code	API
1	getDeviceId()
2	getDeviceSvn() (Method within getDeviceSoftwareVersion())
3	getSubscriberId()
4	getIccSerialNumber() (Method within getSimSerialNumber())
5	getLine1Number()
6	getLine1AlphaTag()
7	getVoiceMailNumber()
8	getCompleteVoiceMailNumber()
9	getVoiceMailAlphaTag()

This shows that we can know `code` variables corresponding to each method from AndroidOS source code.

Figure 3 shows that logs output when `getDeviceId()` method is executed. The emphasized line in Figure 3 is a log message which outputs the necessary information in our proposal method.

4.6 Consideration

This experiment showed that detection and specification of API invoked from application can be possible. In this experiment, we inserted the code which outputs a log into `onTransact` method of `IPhoneSubInfo` class because we focus

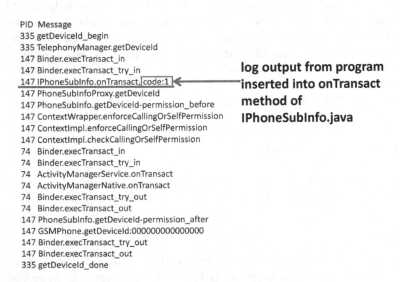

Fig. 3. Log output when executing getDeviceId() method

on APIs defined in `IPhoneSubInfo.aidl`. It is thought that APIs which are not mentioned in this paper are also defined in aidl file if they execute interprocess communication. Therefore, action of API is detectable by discovering the aidl file and conducting the same experiment as this one.

5   Conclusion

In this paper, a detection method of phoneID acquisition using `logcat` is proposed. With this method, it is possible to detect obfuscated applications which cannot be detected with static analysis, or phoneID acquisition of an application which sets attack code in an external server. The phoneID acquisition of API which cannot be detected with dynamic analysis using `strace` could be detected. Because we focus on the behavior of applications in our method, it is unnecessary to acquire signatures of malwares in advance. Therefore, unknown malwares can be detected with proposal method. Moreover, the system which outputs the log in the proposal method is completely independent of the structure of application thanks to the mechanism which retrieves phoneID as shown in Figure 1. For this reason, a malicious developer is unable to avoid the analysis by this technique.

In a practical use, the proposal method should be used by marketplace operator. One of the reasons is that the proposal method has no real-time properties. The proposal detection method needs to be performed before a user runs an application on his device because the method grasps the behavior of an application from the log output. Another reason is that the proposal method needs to rebuild AndroidOS and to prepare linux system for the analysis. From these reasons, the proposal method should be used in the marketplace operator's side.

As for future work, the distinction between malwares and legitimate applications is considered. This method detects all applications that acquire phoneID through API on the characteristics. When actually used, it is necessary to extract only malware from these applications and specify it. In this paper, we carried out experiments only about API defined in `IPhoneSubInfo.aidl`. However, we didn't carry out experiments about other APIs. As a future subject, we must confirm if proposal method can be applied to detection of other APIs.

Acknowledgments. We would like to thank Ayumu Kubota and Takamasa Isohara, KDDI R&D Labs for giving beneficial advices. This work was supported by Grants-in-Aid for Scientific Research (B)(23300027), Japan Society for the Promotion of Science (JSPS).

References

1. Permissions — Android Developers, `http://developer.android.com/guide/topics/security/permissions.html`
2. Android Interface Definition Language (AIDL) — Android Developers, `http://developer.android.com/guide/components/aidl.html`

3. Ralf Benzmüller, Sabrina Berkenkopf: G Data Malware Report Half-yearly report January [June 2011, http://www.gdatasoftware.co.uk/uploads/media/G_Data_MalwareReport_H1_2011_EN.pdf

4. Android and Security, http://googlemobile.blogspot.jp/2012/02/android-and-security.html

5. William Enck, Peter Gilbert, Byung-Gon Chun, Landon P. Cox, Jaeyeon Jung, Patrick McDaniel, and Anmol N. Sheth. , "TaintDroid: An Information-Flow Tracking System for Realtime Privacy Monitoring on Smartphones," In Proceedings of the 9th USENIX Symposium on Operating Systems Design and Implementation (OSDI), October, 2010. Vancouver, BC.

6. Dissecting Android's Bouncer, https://blog.duosecurity.com/2012/06/dissecting-androids-bouncer/

7. Peter Hornyack, Seungyeop Han, Jaeyeon Jung, Stuart Schechter, David Wetherall, "These Aren't the Droids You're Looking For: Retrofitting Android to Protect Data from Imperious Applications," In Proceedings of the 18th ACM Conference on Computer and Communications Security, October, 2011.

8. Takamasa Isohara, Keisuke Takemori, Ayumu Kubota, "Kernel-based Behavior Analysis for Android Malware Detection," In Proceedings of the 7th International Conference on Computational Intelligence and Security, December, 2011.

Reversible Data Hiding Scheme Based on 3-Least Significant Bits and Mix Column Transform

Wafaa Mustafa Abduallah[1], Abdul Monem S. Rahma[2], and Al-Sakib Khan Pathan[1]

[1] Department of Computer Science, International Islamic University Malaysia
Gombak, Kuala Lumpur, 53100, Malaysia
[2] Department of Computer Science, University of Technology, Baghdad, Iraq
{heevy9,monem.rahma}@yahoo.com, sakib@iium.edu.my

Abstract. Steganography is the science of hiding a message signal in a host signal, without any perceptual distortion of the host signal. Using steganography, information can be hidden in the carrier items such as images, videos, sounds files, text files, while performing data transmission. In image steganography field, it is a major concern of the researchers how to improve the capacity of hidden data into host image without causing any statistically significant modification. In this work, we propose a reversible steganography scheme which can hide large amount of information without affecting the imperceptibility aspect of the *stego-image* and at the same time, it increases the security level of the system through using different method for embedding based on distinct type of transform, called Mix Column Transform. Our experimental results prove the ability of our proposed scheme in balancing among the three critical properties: capacity, security, and imperceptibility.

Keywords: Data, Hiding, Mix Column Transform, Polynomial, Steganography.

1 Introduction

Steganography is considered a science or art of secret communication. In the recent years, digital steganography has become a hot research issue due to the wide use of the Internet as a popular communication medium. The goal of digital steganography is to conceal covert message in digital material in an imperceptible manner. Even though digital images, audio files, video data and all types of digital files can be considered as a cover item to conceal secret information, in this paper, we consider only digital images as cover item. After hiding a secret message into the *cover image*, we get an image with secret message; so-called *stego-image*, which is transmitted to a receptor via popular communication channels or put on some Internet website. To design useful steganography algorithm, it is very important that the *stego-image* does not have any visual artifact and it is statistically similar to natural images. If a third party or observer has some suspicion over the *stego-image*, steganography algorithm becomes useless [1]. Three common requirements can be used to rate the performance of steganographic techniques, which are: security, capacity, and imperceptibility [2].

T. Zia et al. (Eds.): SecureComm 2013, LNICST 127, pp. 405–417, 2013.

- *Security:* Many active or passive attacks could be launched against steganography. Hence, if the existence of the secret message can only be estimated with a probability not higher than *"random guessing"* when any steganalytic system is applied, then this steganography may be considered secure under such steganalytic system. Otherwise, we may claim it as insecure.
- *Capacity:* Capacity is a critical aspect of any steganography. The hiding capacity provided by any steganographic scheme should be as high as possible, which may be given with absolute measurement (e.g., the size of secret message), or with relative value (e.g., data embedding rate, such as bits per pixel, bits per non-zero discrete cosine transform coefficient, or the ratio of the secret message to the cover medium, etc.).
- *Imperceptibility:* *Stego images* should not have severe visual artifacts. Under the same level of security and capacity, the higher the fidelity of the *stego image* is, the better it is. If the resultant *stego image* appears innocuous enough, one can believe this requirement to be satisfied well for the possessor not having the original *cover image* to compare.

Steganography can be mainly classified into four categories: (1) Steganography in image, (2) Steganography in audio, (3) Steganography in video, and (4) Steganography in text. The image steganography algorithms can be divided into two categories, namely, spatial domain and frequency domain [3]. In this work, a distinct type of transform will be applied on the color image called "Mix Column Transform" (MCT) based on some different type of mathematics called irreducible polynomial mathematics, which can meet the requirements of good steganographic system (high capacity, good visual imperceptibility, and reasonable level of security).

After Section 1, in Section 2, we discuss the related works and our motivation for this work. The mathematical background of the proposed system is presented in Section 3. Then, in Section 4, the proposed algorithm is presented. Section 5 presents our results, analysis, and comparisons. Finally, Section 6 concludes the paper.

2   Related Works and Motivation

During the last decade, many steganography related works were proposed in both domains: spatial domain and transform domain. Many methods have been proposed so far for hiding secret information in spatial domain such as; LSB (Least Significant Bit) [4], [5], optimum pixel adjustment process [6], and so on.

The authors in [4] present a scheme which provides two levels of security. It uses RSA Algorithm for encrypting the secret message, then hides it in the four LSBs (Least Significant Bits) of one of the three channels that could be selected through calculating the sum of all pixels in each channel and the one having the maximum value would be the indicator to specify where to embed the secret bits in the other two channels. The experimental results showed that the largest capacity that could be used by the proposed method was 30,116 bytes (240,928 bits) with PSNR (Peak Signal-to-Noise Ratio) value 49.61 dB. However, adopting a combination of cryptography and steganography may increase the security of the system.

Various schemes also have been adopted by the researchers for embedding data in transform domain such as using wavelet transform [7], Discrete Cosine Transform (DCT) [8], Fourier Transform [9], and recently using contourlet transform [10]. The core idea of the last one is embedding the secret message in contourlet coefficients through an iterative embedding procedure to reduce the *stego-image* distortion. Hence, the embedding is done by changing the coefficient values proportional to the regions in which the coefficients reside and hidden data can be retrieved with zero bit error rate. The results showed that using cover selection can embed relatively more bits in a suitable *cover image*. The proposed method is robust against compression but the cost of embedding capacity has been decreased to only 10,000 bits.

After investigating various works, we have found that gaining capacity with visual imperceptibility should be the main objective of any good steganographic scheme. Consequently, we have come up with a reversible steganographic scheme based transform domain. Our adopted transform domain is distinguished from those mentioned in the previous works since it has not been used before in this way in steganographic technique as far as we have investigated in this area. In addition, it is provided with more than one *stego-key*, hence, the proposed method can achieve effective level of security with having reasonable imperceptibility at the same time.

3   Irreducible Polynomial Mathematics

The forward Mix Column Transformation, called Mix Columns, operates on each column individually. Each byte of a column is mapped into a new value that is a function of all four bytes in that column [11]. The results of the Mix Column operation are calculated using $GF(2^8)$ operations. Each element of $GF(2^8)$ is a polynomial of degree 7 with coefficients in $GF(2)$ (or, equivalently Z_2). Thus, the coefficients of each term of the polynomial can take the value 0 or 1. Given that there are 8 terms in an element of $GF(2^8)$, an element can be represented by bit string of length 8, where each bit represents a coefficient. The least significant bit is used to represent the constant of the polynomial, and going from right to left, represents the coefficient of x^i by the bit b_i where b_i is i bits to the left of the least significant bit. For example, the bit string (10101011) represents $(x^7 + x^5 + x^3 + x + 1)$. For convenience, a term x^i is found in the expression if the corresponding coefficient is 1. The term is omitted from the expression if the coefficient is 0. Addition of two elements in $GF(2^8)$ is simply accomplished using eight XOR gates to add corresponding bits. Multiplication of two elements in $GF(2^8)$ requires a bit more work. The multiplication of two elements of Z_2 is simulated with an AND gate. Multiplication in $GF(2^8)$ can then be accomplished by first multiplying each term of the second polynomial with all of the terms of the first polynomial. Each of these products should be added together. If the degree of the new polynomial is greater than 7, then it must be reduced modulo some irreducible polynomial using one of the polynomials which explained in Table 1. In the case of Advanced Encryption Standard (AES), the irreducible polynomial is $x^8 + x^4 + x^3 + x + 1$ [12]. Therefore, multiplication can be performed according to the following rule [11]:

$$x \times f(x) = \begin{cases} (b_6 b_5 b_4 b_3 b_2 b_1 b_0 0) & \text{if } b_7 = 0 \\ (b_6 b_5 b_4 b_3 b_2 b_1 b_0 0) \oplus (00011011) & \text{if } b_7 = 1 \end{cases}$$

In this work, the calculations of Mix Column Transform have been done using $GF(2^3)$ which has not been used before in the literature. Values in $GF(2^3)$ are 3-bits each, spanning the decimal range [0..7]. Multiplication takes place on 3-bit binary values (with modulo 2 addition) and then the result is computed modulo P(x) which can be $(1011) = 11$ (decimal) or $(1101) = 13$ (decimal). For example: $5 \times 6 = (101) \times (110) = (11110) = (011) \mod (1011) = 3$ (highlighted in Table 1) and $5 \times 3 = (101) \times (011) = (1111) = (010) \mod (1101) = 2$ (highlighted in Table 2). Hence, the specific polynomial P(x) provides the modulus for the multiplication results [13].

Table 1. Using Primitive Polynomial (11)

×	1	2	3	4	5	6	7
1	1	2	3	4	5	6	7
2	2	4	6	3	1	7	5
3	3	6	5	7	4	1	2
4	4	3	7	6	2	5	1
5	5	1	4	2	7	3	6
6	6	7	1	5	3	2	4
7	7	5	2	1	6	4	3

Table 2. Using Primitive Polynomial (13)

×	1	2	3	4	5	6	7
1	1	2	3	4	5	6	7
2	2	4	6	5	7	1	3
3	3	6	5	1	2	7	4
4	4	5	1	7	3	2	6
5	5	7	2	3	6	4	1
6	6	1	7	2	4	3	5
7	7	3	4	6	1	5	2

4   Our Proposed Approach

In our work, a distinct kind of transform will be applied on the color images to get new domain for embedding, which is sufficiently secure and can be applied for real-time applications. We present both the embedding and extraction algorithms here.

4.1   Embedding Algorithm

The procedure of embedding is described with the following steps:

Step 1. Dividing the *cover image* into blocks, each block of specified size which can be (3*3), (4*4), (5*5), etc.

Step 2. Selecting some of the blocks for embedding the secret message according to secure key.

Step 3. Pre-processing the specified blocks through taking out the 3 LSBs of from each value and storing it in a new matrix (block).

Step 4. Applying the proposed transform (Mix Column Transform) on each specified block individually.

Step 5. Hiding the secret bits within the matrix after transformation.

Step 6. Applying an inverse transform on the transformed blocks to get back the original blocks.

Step 7. Returning the resulted matrix of 3 LSBs and combing it with original one.

Step 8. Evaluating the proposed method through using the most common measurements that have been used in the literature such as Peak Signal Noise to Ratio (PSNR) and MSSIM for testing the invisibility and the quality of the *stego image.*

4.2   Extraction Algorithm

The proposed method is a blind algorithm so, there is no need for the original *cover image* during the process of extraction. Blind algorithm here refers to the ability of extracting the secret information from the *stego-image* without using the original cover. To recover the secret message, the following steps should be applied:

Step 1. Dividing the *stego-image* into blocks, each block of the same size that has been specified during the embedding.

Step 2. Determining the selected blocks that have been used for embedding the secret message through using the same secure key.

Step 3. Pre-processing the blocks through taking out the 3 LSB's and storing them in a new matrix (block).

Step 4. Applying the proposed transform on each block individually.

Step 5. Extracting the secret bits from the transformed blocks sequentially using secure key.

Step 6. Reconstructing the secret message from the extracted bits.

4.3   The Proposed Transform

In order to apply MCT, it is supposed to have a matrix called transformed matrix which can be generated randomly and should have an inverse. The size of this matrix is variable and can be any. An example could be (3*3) as shown below:

07	01	05
01	06	06
05	06	07

$\rightarrow$
$$\begin{bmatrix} 011 & 001 & 001 \\ 110 & 011 & 100 \\ 010 & 111 & 001 \end{bmatrix}$$

Transformed Matrix

In addition to this matrix, we should have a block matrix taken from a *cover image* with the same size (3*3) which can be referred to as block matrix. Before performing the proposed transform, the block matrix should be pre-processed, then taking the 3 least significant bits from the block matrix and placing in another matrix to get a new one as follows:

179	185	177
182	179	180
178	175	185

$$\begin{bmatrix} 10110011 & 10111001 & 10110001 \\ 10110110 & 10110011 & 10110100 \\ 10110010 & 10101111 & 10111001 \end{bmatrix} \rightarrow \begin{bmatrix} 011 & 001 & 001 \\ 110 & 011 & 100 \\ 010 & 111 & 001 \end{bmatrix}$$

Block Matrix

After that, both matrices have to be converted to polynomials as explained below:

$$\begin{bmatrix} x^2 + x + 1 & 1 & x^2 + 1 \\ 1 & x^2 + x & x^2 + x \\ x^2 + 1 & x^2 + x & x^2 + x + 1 \end{bmatrix} * \begin{bmatrix} x + 1 & 1 & 1 \\ x^2 + x & x + 1 & x^2 \\ x & x^2 + x + 1 & 1 \end{bmatrix}$$

Transformed Matrix   **Block Matrix**

The proposed transform can be performed via multiplying each row of the transformed matrix with each column of the original values of the block matrix:

$$x^2 + x + 1 \cdot (x + 1) + 1 \cdot (x^2 + x) + (x^2 + 1) \cdot x$$
$$= x^3 + x^2 + x + x^2 + x + 1 + x^2 + x + x^3 + x = x^2 + 1$$

The result is $= x^2 + 1 \rightarrow$ which represents $(101) = (5)$

The same operation can be done to get the whole values of the resultant matrix which is:

$$\begin{bmatrix} x^2 + 1 & x & x^2 + x \\ x^2 + x & x^2 & x \\ x + 1 & x^2 + x + 1 & x^2 + x + 1 \end{bmatrix} \rightarrow \begin{bmatrix} 101 & 010 & 110 \\ 110 & 100 & 010 \\ 011 & 111 & 111 \end{bmatrix}$$

The largest element appeared in this example is x^2 because the results of the Mix Columns operation are calculated using $GF(2^3)$ operations where, each element of $GF(2^3)$ is a polynomial of the 2nd degree with coefficients in $GF(2)$. Thus, if the result of multiplication leads to get a polynomial with degree larger than 2, then the resultant polynomial should be reduced through dividing it by the irreducible polynomial $(x^3 + x + 1)$ to get the remainder which will be used as a resulted polynomial. Next, the secret message for instance (111) can be embedded in the least significant bit (LSB) of the values of the middle column within the resultant matrix as follows:

$$\begin{bmatrix} 101 & 011 & 110 \\ 110 & 101 & 010 \\ 011 & 111 & 111 \end{bmatrix}$$

On the other hand, to get the original values of the block matrix, the resulting matrix from Mix Column Transform should be multiplied by the inverse matrix:

05	06	02
06	06	04
02	04	02

$$\rightarrow \begin{bmatrix} 101 & 110 & 010 \\ 110 & 110 & 100 \\ 010 & 100 & 010 \end{bmatrix} \rightarrow \begin{bmatrix} x^2 + 1 & x^2 + x & x \\ x^2 + x & x^2 + x & x^2 \\ x & x^2 & x \end{bmatrix}$$

Inverse Matrix

Again, each row of the inverse matrix will be multiplied by each column of the resulting matrix:

$$
\begin{bmatrix} x^2+1 & x^2+x & x \\ x^2+x & x^2+x & x^2 \\ x & x^2 & x \end{bmatrix} * \begin{bmatrix} x^2+1 & x+1 & x^2+x \\ x^2+x & x^2+1 & x \\ x+1 & x^2+x+1 & x^2+x+1 \end{bmatrix}
$$

Inverse Matrix   **Resulting Matrix**

To get back the first value (03), the first row of the inverse matrix should be multiplied by the first column of the resulted matrix (after transform):

$$
(x^2+1)\cdot(x^2+1)+(x^2+x)\cdot(x^2+x)+x\cdot(x+1)
$$
$$
= x^4+x^2+x^2+1+x^4+x^3+x^3+x^2+x^2+x = x+1
$$

The result is $= x+1 \rightarrow$ which represents $(011) = (03)$

To get back the second value (0), the first row of the inverse matrix should be multiplied by the second column of the resulted matrix (after transform):

$$
(x^2+1)\cdot(x+1)+(x^2+x)\cdot(x^2+1)+x\cdot(x^2+x+1)
$$
$$
= x^3+x^2+x+1+x^4+x^2+x^3+x+x^3+x^2+x
$$
$$
= x^4+x^3+x^2+x+1
$$

The result is $= x^4+x^3+x^2+x+1$ which has a degree $(4 > 3)$ so, it should be reduced through dividing it by (x^3+x+1). This polynomial can be considered as a secret key because it can be changed and it is possible to use either (x^3+x+1) or (x^3+x^2+1). Therefore, the attacker cannot guess the utilized polynomial in the proposed steganographic algorithm.

Consequently, all other values of the original matrix can be obtained through repeating the same operation.

$$
\begin{bmatrix} x+1 & x & 1 \\ x^2+x & x+1 & x^2 \\ x & 1 & 1 \end{bmatrix} \rightarrow \begin{bmatrix} 011 & 010 & 001 \\ 110 & 011 & 100 \\ 010 & 001 & 001 \end{bmatrix} \rightarrow \begin{bmatrix} 03 & 02 & 01 \\ 06 & 03 & 04 \\ 02 & 01 & 01 \end{bmatrix}
$$

The resulted matrix will again be combined with the block matrix:

$$
\begin{bmatrix} 10110011 & 10111010 & 10110001 \\ 10110110 & 10110011 & 10110100 \\ 10110010 & 10101001 & 10111001 \end{bmatrix} \rightarrow
$$

179	186	177
182	179	180
178	169	185

The Block Matrix after applying the transform and embedding the secret message.

Finally, the secret message can be retained through applying the Mix Column Transform on the final resulted matrix for instance:

$$
\begin{bmatrix} 07 & 01 & 05 \\ 01 & 06 & 06 \\ 05 & 06 & 07 \end{bmatrix} \quad * \quad \begin{bmatrix} 03 & 02 & 01 \\ 06 & 03 & 04 \\ 02 & 01 & 01 \end{bmatrix}
$$

The Transform Matrix   **Block Matrix (containing secret message)**

Converting again to polynomials:

$$
\begin{bmatrix} x^2 + x + 1 & 1 & x^2 + 1 \\ 1 & x^2 + x & x^2 + x \\ x^2 + 1 & x^2 + x & x^2 + x + 1 \end{bmatrix} \quad * \quad \begin{bmatrix} x + 1 & x & 1 \\ x^2 + x & x + 1 & x^2 \\ x & 1 & 1 \end{bmatrix}
$$

The first value can be got via multiplying the first row of the first matrix with the first column of the second matrix as explained below:

$$
(x^2 + x + 1) \cdot (x + 1) + 1 \cdot (x^2 + x) + (x^2 + 1) \cdot x
$$
$$
= x^3 + x^2 + x^2 + x + x + 1 + x^2 + x + x^3 + x = x^2 + 1
$$

The result is $= x^2 + 1 \rightarrow$ which represents $(101) = (5)$

The second value can be got via multiplying the first row of the first matrix with the second column of the second matrix as explained below:

$$
(x^2 + x + 1).x + 1.(x + 1) + (x^2 + 1).1 = x^3 + x^2 + x + x + 1 + x^2 + 1 = x^3
$$

$$
\begin{array}{r}
1 \hspace{3cm} \\
x^3 + x + 1 \overline{) \begin{array}{l} x^3 \\ x^3 + x + 1 \end{array}} \\
\overline{\hspace{2cm} x+1 \hspace{1cm}}
\end{array}
$$

The result is $= x + 1$ which is equivalent to $(011) = (03)$

So, taking the LSB from the resulting value which represents the value of the secret bit, the original value (02) can be obtained.

5   Experimental Results and Discussion

5.1   Experimental Setting

The proposed technique is tested by using sequence of color images of size (512*512) with JPEG formats as shown in Figure 1 (a, b, c, d). The experiments have been conducted using MATLAB [21]. The image quality of the proposed algorithm has been tested using PSNR, which is estimated in decibel (dB) and is defined as:

$$PSNR = 10 \log \frac{255^2}{MSE_{avg}}$$

$$MSE = \frac{1}{hw} \sum_{i=1}^{h} \sum_{j=1}^{w} (x_{ij} - y_{ij})^2$$

where (w and h) denote the width and height of the images respectively. x_{ij} and y_{ij} stand for the value of pixel [i,j] in the original and the processed images, respectively.

(a) image1.jpg   (b) image2.jpg

(c) image3.jpg   (d) image4.jpg

Fig. 1. Test images for the proposed technique

$$MSE_{avg} = \frac{MSE_R + MSE_G + MSE_B}{3}$$

where (MSE_R, MSE_G, and MSE_B) are mean square errors in the three channels; Red, Green, and Blue respectively. Table 3 shows the results of applying proposed technique using the mentioned test images [14]. Also Figure 2 and 3 show the output *stego-images*.

Table 3. Results of applying the proposed algorithm on the images of size (512*512)

Color Images of size (512*512)	Payload (Bits)	Block Size	PSNR (dB) of the Stego-image	MSSIM	Embedding Duration Time (seconds)
Image1.jpg	452925	4*4	40.3286	0.9522	100.5894
		8*8	40.3497	0.9529	88.5150
Image2.jpg	452925	4*4	41.2353	0.9515	101.0418
		8*8	40.3330	0.9433	88.2186
Image3.jpg	452925	4*4	40.7893	0.9677	100.6362
		8*8	40.3022	0.9644	88.2186
Image4.jpg	452925	4*4	40.7988	0.9733	99.6066
		8*8	40.3466	0.9714	88.3590

Table 4. Comparison between our proposed method and other related works

The Steganographic Schemes	The Cover Image	Capacity (Bits)	PSNR of the Stego-image in (dB)	Our Proposed Method		
				PSNR of the Stego-image in (dB)	MSSIM Index	Embedding Duration Time in Seconds
1	Reference [10]	Lena .jpg (512*512)	28,001	39.65	47.2571	0.9882	7.6440
2	Reference [19]	baboon .bmp (512*512)	162,775	30.02	40.0453	0.9841	36.4106

Another measure for understanding image quality is Mean Structural Similarity (MSSIM) [15] which seems to approximate the perceived visual quality of an image more than PSNR or various other measures. MSSIM index takes values in [0,1] and it increases as the quality increases. We calculate it based on the code in [16] using the default parameters. In case of color images, we extend MSSIM with the simplest way: calculating the MSSIM index of each RGB channel and then, taking the average [17].

5.2   Comparative Analysis

Comparing our proposed scheme with [18] and embedding the same secret message "AB1001CD" within the same *cover image* (baboon.jpg) of size (512*512), we got PSNR=77.3561 while [18] obtained PSNR=72.2156. So, our proposed method beats the scheme used by [18] significantly in terms of imperceptibility through getting higher PSNR. On the other hand, when comparing the proposed scheme with its alternative methods that used gray-scale images in their experiments as presented in [10] and [19], our proposed method exceeds those in terms of invisibility as shown in Table 4 (keeping the capacities same as were used in those schemes).

(a) image1_stego.jpg   (b) image2_stego.jpg

(c) image3_stego.jpg   (d) image4_stego.jpg

Fig. 2. Results of applying the proposed algorithm on the images of size (512*512) using block size (4*4)

(a) image1_stego.jpg   (b) image2_stego.jpg

(c) image3_stego.jpg   (d) image4_stego.jpg

Fig. 3. Results of applying the proposed algorithm on the images of size (512*512) using block size (8*8)

5.3   Security of the Proposed Transform

According to Kerckhoffs' principle [20], the security of a steganographic system is based on secret key shared between the sender and the receiver called the *stego-key* and, without this key; the attacker should not be able to extract the secret message. In our proposed method, the secret key was provided in more than one level; firstly the block size is variable and can be any size for instance (3*3), (4*4), etc. Secondly, the transformed matrix is generated randomly and it can be used in our transform if and only if it has inverse. Thirdly, not all the values of the specified block that have been selected for embedding will be used, instead, only 3 LSBs of each value will be taken out and saved separately in another block to be used in our proposed method which has not been used in the literature before. Finally, there is a secret key for selecting the blocks for embedding. That's why the security of our proposed scheme has been significantly increased.

6   Conclusion and Future Work

In this work, we have presented an efficient steganographic method which adopted different style for embedding to increase the security of the system. On the other hand, the capacity of embedding secret message has been maximized without affecting the quality of the *stego-image* as proved by the experiment results for MSSIM measurements which were close to 1. As future work, the robustness of the proposed scheme could be tested against different types of attacks such as the compression to test the efficiency of it and thus, a detailed understanding of the scheme's practicality could be realized.

Acknowledgments. The authors would like to heartily thank the reviewers for their valuable comments that helped improve the paper. This work was supported by NDC Lab, KICT, IIUM.

References

1. Hernandez-Chamorro, A., Espejel-Trujillo, A., Lopez-Hernandez, J., Nakano-Miyatake, M., Perez-Meana, H.: A Methodology of Steganalysis for Images. In: IEEE CONIELECOMP 2009, Cholula, Puebla, Mexico, pp. 102–106 (2009)
2. Li, B., He, J., Huang, J., Shi, Y.Q.: A Survey on Image Steganography and Steganalysis. Journal of Information Hiding and Multimedia Signal Processing 2(2), 142–172 (2011)
3. Lin, C.-C.: An information hiding scheme with minimal image distortion. Computer Standards & Interfaces 33(5), 477–484 (2011)
4. Swain, G., Lenka, S.K.: A Better RGB Channel Based Image Steganography Technique. In: Krishna, P.V., Babu, M.R., Ariwa, E. (eds.) ObCom 2011, Part II. CCIS, vol. 270, pp. 470–478. Springer, Heidelberg (2012)
5. Swain, G., Lenka, S.K.: LSB Array Based Image Steganography Technique by Exploring the Four Least Significant Bits. In: Krishna, P.V., Babu, M.R., Ariwa, E. (eds.) ObCom 2011, Part II. CCIS, vol. 270, pp. 479–488. Springer, Heidelberg (2012)
6. Pandian, N., Thangavel, R.: A Hybrid Embedded Steganography Technique: Optimum Pixel Method and Matrix Embedding. In: Proceedings of the International Conference on Advances in Computing, Communications and Informatics, pp. 1123–1130. ACM (2012)
7. Al-Hunaity, M.F., Najim, S.A., El-Emary, I.M.: Colored Digital Image Watermarking using the Wavelet Technique. American Journal of Applied Sciences 4(9), 658–662 (2007)

8. Liu, Q.: Steganalysis of DCT-Embedding Based Adaptive Steganography and YASS. In: The 13th ACM Multimedia Workshop on Multimedia and Security, pp. 77–85. ACM (2011)

9. Rabie, T.: Digital Image Steganography: An FFT Approach. In: Benlamri, R. (ed.) NDT 2012, Part II. CCIS, vol. 294, pp. 217–230. Springer, Heidelberg (2012)

10. Sajedi, H., Jamzad, M.: Using contourlet transform and cover selection for secure steganography. International Journal of Information Security 9(5), 337–352 (2010)

11. Stallings, W.: Cryptography and Network Security Principles and Practice. Prentice Hall, USA (2006)

12. Li, H., Friggstad, Z.: An Efficient Architecture for the AES Mix Columns Operation. In: Proceeding of ISCAS 2005, Kobe, Japan, pp. 4637–4640 (2005)

13. Addition and Multiplication Tables in Galois Fields GF(2^m), http://www.ee.unb.ca/cgi-bin/tervo/galois3.pl (last accessed May 30, 2013)

14. Yua, Y.-H., Chang, C.-C., Lin, I.-C.: A new steganographic method for color and grayscale image hiding. Computer Vision and Image Understanding 107(3), 183–194 (2007)

15. Wang, Z., Bovik, A.C., Sheikh, H.R., Simoncelli, E.P.: Image Quality Assessment: From Error Visibility to Structural Similarity. IEEE Transactions on Image Processing 13(4), 600–612 (2004)

16. Wang, Z., Bovik, A.C., Sheikh, H.R., Simoncelli, E.P.: The SSIM Index for Image Quality Assessment, http://www.cns.nyu.edu/~lcv/ssim/ (last accessed: May 19, 2013)

17. Roussos, A., Maragos, P.: Vector-Valued Image Interpolation by an Anisotropic Diffusion-Projection PDE. In: Sgallari, F., Murli, A., Paragios, N. (eds.) SSVM 2007. LNCS, vol. 4485, pp. 104–115. Springer, Heidelberg (2007)

18. Upreti, K., Verma, K., Sahoo, A.: Variable Bits Secure System for Color Images. In: Proceedings of the 2010 Second International Conference on Advances in Computing, Control, and Telecommunication Technologies, pp. 105–107. IEEE (2010)

19. Lee, C.-F., Chen, H.-L., Tso, H.-K.: Embedding capacity raising in reversible data hiding based on prediction of difference expansion. Journal of Systems and Software 83(10), 1864–1872 (2010)

20. Salomon, D.: Coding for Data and Computer Communications, p. 345. Springer (April 12, 2005) ISBN-13: 978-0387212456

21. MATLAB: The Language of Technical Computing, http://www.mathworks.com/products/matlab/ (last accessed May 30, 2013)

Author Index